PEARSON CRIMINAL JUSTICE

Criminal Justice
NHTI - Concord's Community College

PEARSON

Senior Vice President, Editorial: Patrick F. Boles
Senior Acquisitions Editor: Debbie Coniglio
Editorial Assistant: Jeanne Martin
Development Editor: Christina Martin
Operations Manager: Eric M. Kenney
Production Manager: Jennifer Berry
Art Director: Renée Sartell
Cover Designers: Josh Read and Kristen Kiley

Cover Art: Police Car: Courtesy of Veer/Alloy Photography. Gavel: Courtesy of iStockphoto/Christine Balderas. Behind the Bars: Courtesy of iStockphoto/Simon Podgorsek.

Printed in the United States of America.
V092
Please visit our website at *www.pearsonlearningsolutions.com.*

Attention bookstores: For permission to return any unsold stock, contact
us at *pe-uscustomreturns@pearson.com*.

Pearson Learning Solutions, 501 Boylston Street, Suite 900, Boston, MA 02116
A Pearson Education Company
www.pearsoned.com

PEARSON

ISBN 10: 1-256-54118-4
ISBN 13: 978-1-256-54118-9

Contents

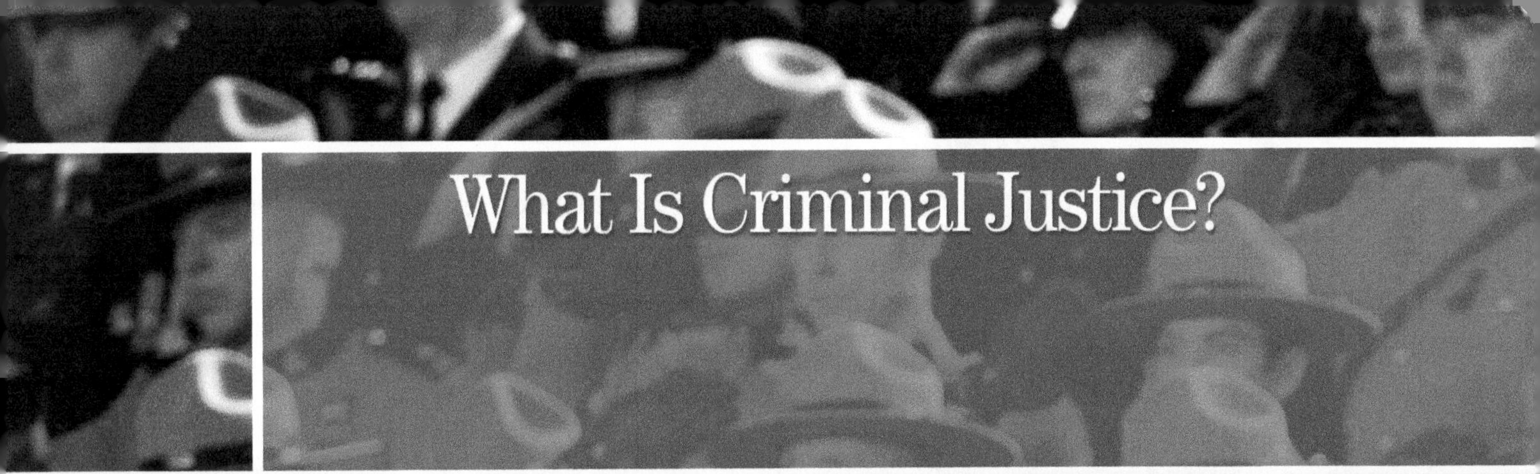

What Is Criminal Justice?

Ted S. Warren/Associated Press

Learning Objectives

After reading this chapter, you should be able to:

1. Provide a brief history of crime in America.
2. Identify the theme on which this textbook builds, and highlight the differences between the individual-rights and public-order perspectives.
3. Explain the relationship of criminal justice to fundamental notions of fairness and to other wider notions of equity and morality.
4. Explain the structure of the American criminal justice system in terms of its major components and the functions they serve.
5. Describe the stages typical of American criminal justice case processing.
6. Explain the meaning of due process of law, and identify where due process guarantees can be found in the American legal system.
7. Explain evidence-based practice, and describe the role of evidence-based research in contemporary criminal justice.
8. Explain how multiculturalism and diversity present special challenges to, and opportunities for, the American system of criminal justice.

"The rights guaranteed to criminal suspects . . . are fundamental political rights that protect all Americans from governmental abuse of power."

—American Civil Liberties Union[1]

"The Constitution is not a suicide pact."

—Former Secretary of State Warren Christopher, after terrorists destroyed the World Trade Center in New York City in 2001[2]

Introduction

Five days after Hurricane Katrina made landfall near New Orleans in 2005, the *Washington Post* described the devastated metropolitan area as "a city of despair and lawlessness."[3] The *Wall Street Journal* ran headlines proclaiming that the city had "plunged into anarchy."[4] As the winds relented, looters ravaged stores, gunshots rang out, and armed gangs could be seen roaming the streets that hadn't been flooded. Some looters used forklifts and construction equipment to bust through storm shutters and steel doors protecting gun shops, liquor stores, and pharmacies.[5] The New Orleans Police Department, hamstrung by the absence of one-third of its 1,600 officers and the loss of critical communications channels and emergency equipment, struggled to keep control over its facilities. In one unflooded precinct, officers used an armored personnel carrier to survey the chaos.[6] Officers from another precinct were forced to barricade themselves in their three-story administrative center, renaming it Fort Apache after a film in which a police station is attacked. "You have to understand," said Juan Lopez, one of the officers who took refuge in the precinct house, "New Orleans was a violent place before the hurricane. After the hurricane, the city just let loose."[7]

> You're looking now not only at a rescue operation but [at] a gigantic crime scene.
>
> —ABC newscaster, on the World Trade Center site a few days after the 9/11 attacks[i]

The storm set into motion a number of events that are still sending shock waves throughout American society. The physical damage done by the hurricane, estimated at billions of dollars, was made worse by the massive social disorder that followed. Thousands of displaced people left their homes—with many never expected to return. Law enforcement and assistance agencies throughout the region suffered serious disruptions in their ability to provide services. Some officers walked off the job, and citizens were left to fend for themselves until thousands of National Guard troops armed with automatic weapons arrived to restore order in the wind- and flood-ravaged area.

▲ New Orleans business owner Bob Rue standing in front of his rug store in the aftermath of Hurricane Katrina. His hastily created sign warns potential looters to stay away. Some say that the central purpose of the criminal justice system is the maintenance of social order. Others say that the justice system must respect the rights of those it processes. Are the two perspectives mutually exclusive?
Charlie Riedel/AP Wide World Photos

The Katrina disaster, which created opportunities for those bent on criminal activity, illustrated the tenuous nature of social order. The social disorganization that followed Katrina continued long after the storm and involved a myriad of criminal offenses—including thousands of people arrested for defrauding the Federal Emergency Management Agency (FEMA), the government agency responsible for helping out after a disaster. FEMA fraud was so widespread that reports showed the number of households receiving FEMA emergency checks in four Louisiana parishes exceeded the number of households that existed there before the storm hit.[8] Almost 360,000 households applied for FEMA's Expedited Assistance payments in Orleans Parish alone—although the area had only 182,000 homes before Katrina. In one case that drew the attention of federal prosecutors, 33-year-old Kenneth McClain was charged with 14 counts of fraud in an elaborate conspiracy that allegedly scammed more than $10,000 in federal relief checks. McClain, who had 27 aliases and a number of open arrest warrants when caught, lived in Texas, far from the storm's wrath. He is accused of using stolen identities, some belonging to dead people, to file for assistance and then waiting in a Texas motel room for the aid checks to arrive.[9]

A very different kind of criminal event thrust itself on American society and our justice system with the September 11, 2001, terrorist attacks that targeted New York City's World Trade Center and the Pentagon. Those attacks, including one on an airliner that crashed in the Pennsylvania countryside, left nearly 3,000 people dead and caused billions of dollars in property damage. They have since been classified as the most destructive criminal activity ever perpetrated on U.S. soil. The resulting "war on terrorism" changed the face of world politics and ushered in a new era in American society. Before the attacks, most Americans lived relatively secure lives, largely unfettered by fear of random personal attack. Following September 11, however, a heated debate has taken place between those wanting to enforce powerful crime-prevention and security measures and others seeking to preserve the individual rights and freedoms that have long been characteristic of American life. This issue, which has continued to feed TV talk shows and newspaper editorials nationwide, asks Americans to determine which rights, freedoms, and conveniences (if any) they are willing to sacrifice to increase personal and

An artist's rendition of the New York City skyline as it will look once buildings envisioned by renowned architect Daniel Libeskind are constructed on the 16-acre World Trade Center site. The plan includes a soaring Freedom Tower that will stand 1,776 feet tall, several other towers, and a memorial to the nearly 3,000 people who were killed in the terrorist attacks that demolished the twin towers in 2001. How did those attacks change the American justice system?
Skidmore, Owings & Merrill LLP/Getty Images—GINS/Entertainment News & Sports

crime
Conduct in violation of the criminal laws of a state, the federal government, or a local jurisdiction, for which there is no legally acceptable justification or excuse.[ii]

individual rights
The rights guaranteed to all members of American society by the U.S. Constitution (especially those rights found in the first ten amendments to the Constitution, known as the *Bill of Rights*). These rights are particularly important to criminal defendants facing formal processing by the criminal justice system.

public safety. It also anticipates the theme on which this text is based—and which is discussed at length later in this chapter.

Regardless of your personal position in the ongoing debate between freedom and safety, it is important to recognize that terrorism is a potentially horrendous **crime**. Many states and the federal government have statutes outlawing terrorism, although terrorism itself can involve many other kinds of crimes. In the case of the September 11 attacks, for example, the crimes committed included murder, kidnapping, hijacking, grand theft, felonious assault, battery, conspiracy, and arson.

A Brief History of Crime in America

1 Provide a brief history of crime in America.

What we call *criminal activity* has undoubtedly been with us since the dawn of history, and crime control has long been a primary concern of politicians and government leaders worldwide. Still, the American experience with crime during the last half century has been especially influential in shaping the criminal justice system of today (Figure 1). In this country, crime waves have come and gone, including an 1850–1880 crime epidemic that was apparently related to social upheaval caused by large-scale immigration and the Civil War.[10] A spurt of widespread organized criminal activity was associated with the Prohibition years of the early twentieth century. Following World War II, however, American crime rates remained relatively stable until the 1960s.

The 1960s and 1970s saw a burgeoning concern for the rights of ethnic and racial minorities, women, people with physical and mental challenges, and many other groups. The civil rights movement of the period emphasized equality of opportunity and respect for individuals, regardless of race, color, creed, gender, or personal attributes. As new laws were passed and suits filed, court involvement in the movement grew. Soon a plethora of hard-won individual rights and prerogatives, based on the U.S. Constitution, the Bill of Rights, and new federal and state legislation, were recognized and guaranteed. By the 1980s, the civil rights movement had profoundly affected all areas of social life—from education and employment to the activities of the criminal justice system.

This emphasis on **individual rights** was accompanied by a dramatic increase in reported criminal activity. While some researchers doubted the accuracy of official accounts, reports by the Federal Bureau of Investigation (FBI) of "traditional" crimes like murder, rape, and assault increased considerably during the 1970s and into the 1980s. Many theories were advanced to explain this leap in observed criminality. Some analysts of American culture, for example, suggested that the combination of newfound freedoms and long-pent-up hostilities

FIGURE 1
Milestones in Crime History

1850–1880 A crime epidemic spurred by social upheaval brought on by large-scale immigration and the Civil War.

1920–1933 Prohibition spurs the growth of organized crime.

Following World War II, American crime rates remained relatively stable until the 1960s.

1960–1970 The civil rights movement of the period emphasized equality of opportunity and respect for individuals regardless of race, color, creed, gender, or personal attributes. This period also saw a dramatic increase in reported criminal activity.

1970s Reports of crimes such as murder, rape, and assault increased considerably.

1980s By the mid-1980s the dramatic increase in sale and use of illicit drugs led to increased crime. Large cities became havens for drug gangs and cities experienced dramatic declines in property values and quality of life. President Reagan declared a "war on drugs."

1992 The videotaped beating of Rodney King, an African American, by Los Angeles–area police officers was seen as an example of the abuse of police power.

By the late **1990s** the public perception was that crime rates were growing and that many offenders went unpunished. This led to a growing emphasis on responsibility and punishment and the development of a "get tough on crime" era.

2001 A series of terrorist attacks on New York City, Washington, D.C., and elsewhere changed the focus of law enforcement to a proactive and more global approach.

2001 **USA PATRIOT Act** dramatically increases the investigatory authority of federal, state, and local police agencies.

The incidence of personal crime declined throughout the 1990s.

2009 Bernard Madoff plead guilty to the largest Ponzi scheme in history. The crimes of Madoff, and widespread suspicions about the activities of Wall Street financiers, led to a number of white-collar crime investigations. White-collar crime came into focus as a serious threat to the American way of life.

Photo sources (from top): Courtesy of the Library of Congress; Everett Collection/Sarryl Jacobson/Superstock; SuperStock Inc.; and Steven Hirsch/Splash News/NewsCom

of the socially and economically deprived worked to produce social disorganization, which in turn increased criminality.

By the mid-1980s, the dramatic increase in the sale and use of illicit drugs threatened the foundation of American society. Cocaine, and later laboratory-processed "crack," spread to every corner of America. Large cities became havens for drug gangs, and many inner-city areas were all but abandoned to highly armed and well-financed drug racketeers. Cities experienced dramatic declines in property values, and residents wrestled with an eroding quality of life.

A decade later, a few spectacular crimes that received widespread coverage in the news media fostered a sense among the American public that crime in the United States was out of hand and that strict new measures were needed to combat it. One such crime was the 1995 bombing of the Alfred P. Murrah Federal Building in Oklahoma City by antigovernment extremists. Another was the 1999 Columbine High School massacre in Colorado that left 12 students and one teacher dead.[11]

The public's perception that crime rates were growing, coupled with a belief that offenders frequently went unpunished or received only a judicial slap on the wrist, led to a burgeoning emphasis on responsibility and punishment. By the late 1990s, a newfound emphasis on individual accountability began to blossom among an American public fed up with crime and fearful of its own victimization. Growing calls for enhanced responsibility quickly began to replace the previous emphasis on individual rights. As a juggernaut of conservative opinion made itself felt on the political scene, Senator Phil Gramm of Texas observed that the public wants to "grab violent criminals by the throat, put them in prison [and] stop building prisons like Holiday Inns."[12]

Then, in an event that changed the course of our society, public tragedy became forever joined with private victimization in our collective consciousness after a series of highly destructive and well-coordinated terrorist attacks on New York City and Washington, D.C., on September 11, 2001. Those attacks resulted in the collapse and total destruction of the twin 110-story towers of the World Trade Center and a devastating explosion at the Pentagon. Thousands of people perished, and many were injured. Although law enforcement and security agencies were unable to prevent the September 11 attacks, many have since moved from a reactive to a proactive posture in the fight against terrorism.

The September 11 attacks also made clear that adequate law enforcement involves a global effort at controlling crime and reducing the risk of injury and loss to law-abiding people both at home and abroad. The attacks showed that criminal incidents that take place on the other side of the globe can impact those of us living in the United States, and they illustrated how the acquisition of skills needed to understand diverse cultures can help in the fight against crime and terrorism. Terrorism is a criminal act, and preventing terrorism and investigating terrorist incidents after they occur are highly important roles for local, state, and federal law enforcement agencies.

A different kind of offending, corporate and white-collar crime, took center stage in 2002 and 2003 as Congress stiffened penalties for unscrupulous business executives who knowingly falsify their company's financial reports.[13] The changes came amidst declining stock market values, shaken investor confidence, and threats to the viability of employee pension plans in the wake of a corporate crime wave involving criminal activities that had been planned and undertaken by executives at a number of leading corporations. In an effort to restore order to American financial markets, President George W. Bush signed the Sarbanes-Oxley Act on July 30, 2002.[14] The law, which has been called "the single most important piece of legislation affecting corporate governance, financial disclosure and the practice of public accounting since the US securities laws of the early 1930s,"[15] is intended to deter corporate fraud and to hold business executives accountable for their actions.

Today, white-collar crime continues to be a focus of federal prosecutors, and in 2009 investment fund manager Bernard Madoff pleaded guilty to operating a Ponzi scheme that defrauded investors out of as much as $50 billion.[16] Madoff pleaded guilty to 11 felony counts, including securities fraud, mail fraud, wire fraud, money laundering, and perjury. On June 29, 2009, Madoff was sentenced to serve 150 years in federal prison—three times as long as federal probation officers had recommended.[17]

For a detailed look at crimes that have shaped the past hundred years, see **Web Extra 1**. **Library Extra 1** also describes the changing nature of crime in America.

The Theme of This Text

This book examines the American system of criminal justice and the agencies and processes that constitute it. It builds on a theme that is especially valuable for studying criminal justice today: *individual rights versus public order.* This theme draws on historical developments that have shaped our legal system and our understandings of crime and justice. It is one of the primary determinants of the nature of contemporary criminal justice—including criminal law, police practice, sentencing, and corrections.

2 Identify the theme on which this text builds, and highlight the differences between the individual-rights and public-order perspectives.

Ponzi schemer Bernard Madoff being escorted by police and photographed by the media as he leaves U.S. Federal Court in New York after a hearing. Madoff, whose financial crimes may have cost investors as much as $50 billion, was sentenced to 150 years in prison in 2009. Should corporate criminals be treated differently from other offenders?
Lucas Jackson/Reuters/Landov Media

A strong emphasis on individual rights rose to the forefront of American social thought during the 1960s and 1970s, a period known as the *civil rights era.* The civil rights era led to the recognition of fundamental personal rights that had previously been denied illegally to many people on the basis of race, ethnicity, gender, sexual preference, or disability. The civil rights movement soon expanded to include the rights of many other groups, including criminal suspects, parolees and probationers, trial participants, prison and jail inmates, and victims. As the emphasis on civil rights grew, new laws and court decisions broadened the rights available to many.

The treatment of criminal suspects was afforded special attention by those who argued that the purpose of any civilized society should be to secure rights and freedoms for each of its citizens—including those suspected and convicted of crimes. Rights advocates feared unnecessarily restrictive government action and viewed it as an assault on basic human dignity and individual liberty. They believed that at times it was necessary to sacrifice some degree of public safety and predictability to guarantee basic freedoms. Hence criminal rights activists demanded a justice system that limits police powers and that holds justice agencies accountable to the highest procedural standards.

We must not defeat our liberties in trying to defend them.
—Anthony Lake, former national security adviser[iii]

During the 1960s and 1970s, the dominant philosophy in American criminal justice focused on guaranteeing the rights of criminal defendants while seeking to understand the root causes of crime and violence. The past 25 years, however, have witnessed increased interest in an ordered society, in public safety, and in the rights of crime victims. This change in attitudes was likely brought about by national frustration with the perceived inability of our society and its justice system to prevent crimes and to consistently hold offenders to heartfelt standards of right and wrong.Increased conservatism in the public-policy arena was given new life by the September 11, 2001, terrorist attacks and by widely publicized instances of sexual offenses targeting children. It continues to be sustained by the many stories of violent victimization that seem to be the current mainstay of the American media.

Today, public perspectives have largely shifted away from seeing the criminal as an unfortunate victim of poor social and personal circumstances who is inherently protected by fundamental human and constitutional rights to seeing him or her as a dangerous social predator who usurps the rights and privileges of law-abiding citizens. Reflecting the "get tough on crime" attitudes of today, many Americans demand to know how offenders can better be held accountable for violating the criminal law. In late 2010, for example, California state senators unanimously passed Chelsea's Law, a bill intended to increase prison sentences and extend parole terms for offenders who commit sex crimes against minors. The bill is named after 17-year-old Chelsea King who was raped and murdered by a convicted sex offender earlier in 2010.[18] The legislation is expected to be signed into law shortly after this text goes to press. Even in an era of difficult budgetary challenges, a number of states, like California, are continuing to extend prison sentences for sex offenders, restrict where released sex offenders can live, and improve public notification of their whereabouts.[19]

As state budgets constrict, the tension between individual rights and social responsibility still forms the basis for most policy-making activity in the criminal justice arena.

Freedom or Safety? You Decide.
Giuliani Says: "Freedom Is about Authority"

In 2009, U.S. Supreme Court Justice Clarence Thomas spoke to a group of high school essay contest winners in a Washington, D.C., hotel ballroom. Thomas used the occasion, which was dedicated to our nation's Bill of Rights, to point out the importance of obligations as well as rights. "Today there is much focus on our rights," said Thomas. "Indeed, I think there is a proliferation of rights." But then he went on to say, "I am often surprised by the virtual nobility that seems to be accorded those with grievances. Shouldn't there at least be equal time for our Bill of Obligations and our Bill of Responsibilities?"

The challenge for the criminal justice system today, it seems, is to balance individual rights and personal freedoms with social control and respect for legitimate authority. Years ago, during the height of what was then a powerful movement to win back control of our nation's cities and to rein in skyrocketing crime rates, the *New York Post* sponsored a conference on crime and civil rights. The keynote speaker at that conference was the mayor of New York, Rudolph W. Giuliani. In his speech, Giuliani, who sought the Republican nomination as a presidential candidate in 2008, identified the tension between personal freedoms and individual responsibilities as the crux of the crime problem then facing his city and the nation. We mistakenly look to government and elected officials, Giuliani said, to assume responsibility for solving the problem of crime when, instead, each individual citizen must become accountable for fixing what is wrong with our society. "We only see the oppressive side of authority. . . . What we don't see is that freedom is not a concept in which people can do anything they want, be anything they can be. Freedom is about authority. Freedom is about the willingness of every single human being to cede to lawful authority a great deal of discretion about what you do."

YOU DECIDE

How can we, as suggested by Justice Thomas, achieve a balance of rights and obligations in American society? What did Giuliani mean when he said, "What we don't see is that freedom is not a concept in which people can do anything they want, be anything they can be"? Is it possible to balance individual rights and personal freedoms with social control and respect for legitimate authority?

References: Adam Liptak, "Reticent Justice Opens Up to a Group of Students," *New York Times*, April 13, 2009, http://www.nytimes.com/2009/04/14/us/14bar.html (accessed June 2, 2010); and Philip Taylor, "Civil Libertarians: Giuliani's Efforts Threaten First Amendment," Freedom Forum Online, http://www.freedomforum.org.

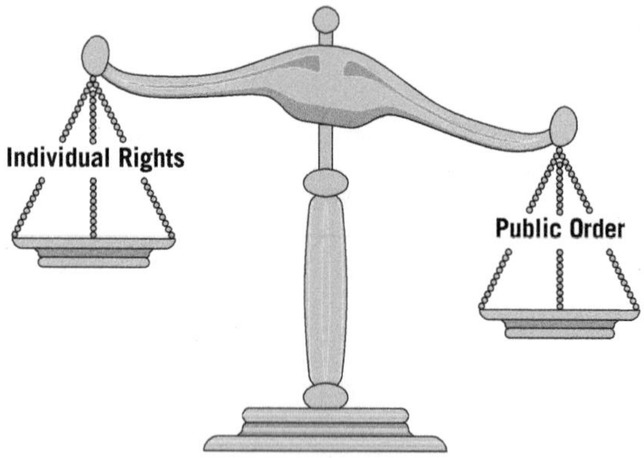

FIGURE 2
The Theme of This Text
Balancing the concern for individual rights with the need for public order through the administration of criminal justice is the theme of this book.

Those who fight for individual rights continue to carry the banner of civil and criminal rights for the accused and the convicted, while public-order activists proclaim the rights of the victimized and call for an increased emphasis on social responsibility and criminal punishment for convicted criminals. In keeping with these realizations, the theme of this book can be stated as follows:

> There is widespread recognition in contemporary society of the need to balance (1) the freedoms and privileges of our nation's citizens and the respect accorded the rights of individuals faced with criminal prosecution against (2) the valid interests that society has in preventing future crimes, in maintaining public safety, and in reducing the harm caused by criminal activity. While the personal freedoms guaranteed to law-abiding citizens as well as to criminal suspects by the Constitution, as interpreted by the U.S. Supreme Court, must be closely guarded, the urgent social needs of communities for controlling unacceptable behavior and protecting law-abiding citizens from harm must be recognized. Still to be adequately addressed are the needs and interests of victims and the fear of crime and personal victimization often prevalent in the minds of many law-abiding citizens.

individual-rights advocate
One who seeks to protect personal freedoms within the process of criminal justice.

public-order advocate
One who believes that under certain circumstances involving a criminal threat to public safety, the interests of society should take precedence over individual rights.

Figure 2 represents our theme and shows that most people today who intelligently consider the criminal justice system assume one of two viewpoints. We will refer to those who seek to protect personal freedoms and civil rights within society, and especially within the criminal justice process, as **individual-rights advocates**. Those who suggest that, under certain circumstances involving criminal threats to public safety, the interests of society (especially crime control and social order) should take precedence over individual rights will be called **public-order advocates**. Recently, retired U.S. Supreme Court Justice Sandra Day O'Connor summed up the differences between these two perspectives by asking, "At what point does the cost to civil liberties from legislation designed to prevent terrorism [and crime] outweigh the added security that that legislation provides?"[20] In this book, we seek to look at ways in which the individual-rights and public-order perspectives can be balanced to serve both sets of needs. Hence you will find our theme discussed throughout this text and within "Freedom or Safety?" boxes.

Michael Jackson fans gathering outside the courthouse where Jackson's physician, Conrad Murray, appeared on February 8, 2010. What does the word *justice* mean to you?
AP Photo/Jason Redmond

Criminal Justice and Basic Fairness

On Election Day in November 2008, as the final votes were being counted, President-Elect Barack H. Obama gave an inspiring victory speech addressed to the nation and the world. He said, "To all those who have wondered if America's beacon still burns as bright—tonight we proved once more that the true strength of our nation comes not from the might of our arms or the scale of our wealth, but from the enduring power of our ideals: democracy, liberty, opportunity, and unyielding hope." The president-elect concluded that night's remarks with an enduring phrase, telling listeners that "the arc of the moral universe is long, but it bends toward justice." The phrase, a favorite of Obama's, was adapted from remarks that Martin Luther King, Jr., made before the Southern Christian Leadership Conference in 1967.[21]

3 Explain the relationship of criminal justice to fundamental notions of fairness and to other wider notions of equity and morality.

There is no denying that the word *justice* is powerful, and—at the time—the president's choice of words spoke to all Americans. The reality, however, is that *justice* is an elusive term. Although most listeners came away inspired that night, few who heard the president's speech knew exactly what justice might mean and what form it might eventually take. Even to those living within the same society, *justice* means different things. And just as *justice* can be an ambiguous term for politicians, it is not always clear how justice can be achieved in the criminal justice system. For example, is "justice for all" a reasonable expectation of today's—or tomorrow's—system of criminal justice? The answer is unclear because individual interests and social needs often diverge. From the perspective of a society or an entire nation, justice can look very different than it does from the perspective of an individual or a small group of people. Because of this dilemma, we now turn our attention to the nature of justice.

British philosopher and statesman Benjamin Disraeli (1804–1881) defined **justice** as "truth in action." A popular dictionary defines it as "the principle of moral rightness, or conformity to truth."[22] **Social justice** is a concept that embraces all aspects of civilized life. It is linked to notions of fairness and to cultural beliefs about right and wrong. Questions of social justice can arise about relationships between individuals, between parties (such as corporations and agencies of government), between the rich and the poor, between the sexes, between ethnic groups and minorities—between social connections of all sorts. In the abstract, the concept of social justice embodies the highest personal and cultural ideals.

Civil justice, one component of social justice, concerns itself with fairness in relationships between citizens, government agencies, and businesses in private matters, such as those involving contractual obligations, business dealings, hiring, and equality of treatment. **Criminal justice**, on the other hand, refers to the aspects of social justice that concern violations of the criminal law. As mentioned earlier, community interests in the criminal justice sphere demand the apprehension and punishment of law violators. At the same time, criminal justice ideals extend to the protection of the innocent, the fair treatment of offenders, and fair play by the agencies of law enforcement, including courts and correctional institutions.

The arc of the moral universe is long, but it bends towards justice.
—Martin Luther King, Jr. (1929–1968)

justice
The principle of fairness; the ideal of moral equity.

social justice
An ideal that embraces all aspects of civilized life and that is linked to fundamental notions of fairness and to cultural beliefs about right and wrong.

civil justice
The civil law, the law of civil procedure, and the array of procedures and activities having to do with private rights and remedies sought by civil action. Civil justice cannot be separated from social justice because the justice enacted in our nation's civil courts reflects basic American understandings of right and wrong.

criminal justice
In the strictest sense, the criminal (penal) law, the law of criminal procedure, and the array of procedures and activities having to do with the enforcement of this body of law. Criminal justice cannot be separated from social justice because the justice enacted in our nation's criminal courts reflects basic American understandings of right and wrong.

administration of justice
The performance of any of the following activities: detection, apprehension, detention, pretrial release, post-trial release, prosecution, adjudication, correctional supervision, or rehabilitation of accused persons or criminal offenders.[iv]

Criminal justice, ideally speaking, is "truth in action" within the process that we call the **administration of justice**. It is therefore vital to remember that justice, in the truest and most satisfying sense of the word, is the ultimate goal of criminal justice—and of the day-to-day practices and challenges that characterize the American criminal justice system. Reality, unfortunately, typically falls short of the ideal and is severely complicated by the fact that justice seems to wear different guises when viewed from diverse vantage points. To some people, the criminal justice system and criminal justice agencies often seem biased in favor of the powerful. The laws they enforce seem to emanate more from well-financed, organized, and vocal interest groups than they do from any idealized sense of social justice. As a consequence, disenfranchised groups, those who do not feel as though they share in the political and economic power of society, are often wary of the agencies of justice, seeing them more as enemies than as benefactors.

On the other hand, justice practitioners, including police officers, prosecutors, judges, and corrections officials, frequently complain that their efforts to uphold the law garner unfair public criticism. The realities of law enforcement and of "doing justice," they say, are often overlooked by critics of the system who have little experience in dealing with offenders and victims. We must recognize, practitioners often tell us, that those accused of violating the criminal law face an elaborate process built around numerous legislative, administrative, and organizational concerns. Viewed realistically, although the criminal justice process can be fine-tuned to take into consideration the interests of ever-larger numbers of people, it rarely pleases everyone. The outcome of the criminal justice process in any particular case is a social product, and like any product that is the result of group effort, it must inevitably be a patchwork quilt of human emotions, reasoning, and concerns.

Whichever side we choose in the ongoing debate over the nature and quality of criminal justice in America, it is vital that we recognize the plethora of pragmatic issues involved in the administration of justice while also keeping a clear focus on the justice ideal.[23] Was justice done, for example, in the 2005 criminal trial of pop music superstar Michael Jackson on charges of child molestation or in the 1995 murder trial of former football great O. J. Simpson? After Jackson's death, was the investigation of his personal physician, Conrad Murray, just? Has justice been served in the case of Casey Anthony, whom authorities say killed her young daughter? Similarly, we might ask whether justice was done in the arrest and lengthy detention of hundreds of Muslims after September 11, 2001—even though most were later released when no evidence could be found linking them to any crime?[24] While answers to such questions may reveal a great deal about the American criminal justice system, they also have much to say about the perspectives of those who provide them.

criminal justice system
The aggregate of all operating and administrative or technical support agencies that perform criminal justice functions. The basic divisions of the operational aspects of criminal justice are law enforcement, courts, and corrections.

consensus model
A criminal justice perspective that assumes that the system's components work together harmoniously to achieve the social product we call *justice*.

> If we do not maintain Justice, Justice will not maintain us.
>
> —Francis Bacon (1561–1626)

American Criminal Justice: System and Functions

The Consensus Model

> 4 Explain the structure of the American criminal justice system in terms of its major components and the functions they serve.

We have been discussing a **criminal justice system**[25] consisting of the component agencies of police, courts, and corrections. Each of these components can, in turn, be described in terms of its functions and purpose (Figure 3).

The systems perspective on criminal justice is characterized primarily by its assumption that the various parts of the justice system work together by design to achieve the wider purpose we have been calling *justice*. Hence the systems perspective on criminal justice generally encompasses a point of view called the **consensus model**. The consensus model assumes that each of the component parts of the criminal justice system strives toward a common goal and that the movement of cases and people through the system is smooth due to cooperation between the various components of the system.

The systems model of criminal justice is more an analytic tool than a reality, however. An analytic model, whether in the hard sciences or in the social sciences, is simply a convention chosen for its explanatory power. By explaining the actions of criminal justice officials—such as arrest, prosecution, and sentencing—as though they were systematically related, we are able to envision a fairly smooth and predictable process.

The systems model has been criticized for implying a greater level of organization and cooperation among the various agencies of justice than actually exists. The word *system*

CJ News
Atlanta Seeks to Add 500 Surveillance Cameras

Atlanta's other reality show is taping today outside CNN Center, at Woodruff Park and in Midtown.

What you might call Real Pedestrians of Atlanta is a rather modest video surveillance: a few dozen cameras monitoring select locations in the city every second. But the city has applied for millions in federal stimulus funds so it can train about 500 more cameras on city streets. . . .

City officials are seeking $13.7 million in federal cash amid a series of high-profile crimes in recent months: a champion boxer shot dead in the street, a City Council member carjacked at gunpoint, a rash of armed robberies near Georgia Tech.

The system Atlanta plans to use could store images for up to 30 days and support software that reads license plate numbers and detects gunshots. Critics say the system conjures up images from George Orwell's "1984," a novel about a totalitarian state presided over by an all-seeing Big Brother. . . .

"It's kind of creepy," said Marc Rotenberg, executive director of the Washington-based Electronic Privacy Information Center. "Mass surveillance is essentially directed toward everyone, so it doesn't matter if you are someone planning a crime or if you are a resident or tourist or someone who is walking into an office building to go to work. Everyone gets swept into these big databases."

City police, however, point to the spread of such cameras across the country and around the world. Community improvement districts already operate dozens across downtown and Midtown Atlanta. . . .

"Times have changed," said Maj. Khirus Williams, commander [of] the city's downtown police zone. "We are no longer in the 1950s. The good of a camera certainly outweighs 'Is Big Brother watching me?' . . ."

POPULAR ELSEWHERE

Other cities have already installed thousands of these cameras. Baltimore has 480 and Chicago has 2,000, according to the Washington-based Urban Institute, which is studying their impact on crime.

Preliminary results from the study show crime has fallen in parts of both cities where the cameras are located. For example, violent crime and larcenies fell by 25 percent — or 30 incidents per month — in downtown Baltimore. . . .

The Urban Institute's study, meanwhile, has found the cameras are not without their problems. When they automatically pan areas, they may capture only portions of a sequence of events. At night and during bad weather, they might not capture images strong enough for evidence. They are sometimes targeted by vandals. And their maintenance costs can be high. Atlanta has estimated its annual personnel and maintenance cost at $3.2 million for its proposed network. . . .

▲ A Chicago police department surveillance camera system and microphone unit positioned high above the street. This surveillance system includes a camera, high-bandwidth wireless communication, a strobe light, and a gunshot-recognition system, all in a bulletproof enclosure. The city is installing the surveillance system to spot crimes or terrorist activity. Do such units infringe on the personal freedoms of city residents?
Safety Dynamics

"IT DOESN'T BOTHER ME"

. . . Just across the street from the CNN Center in downtown, where a sign declares "Area Under 24 Hours Video Surveillance," Cheryl Semands . . . wasn't troubled by the cameras perched around downtown.

"They do it in London all day long," she said of video surveillance. "It might bother the criminals. It doesn't bother me in the least bit to have security cameras. Of course, I'm not doing anything wrong."

A block away, Davis Petterson and his Zentropy band mates were packing up their instruments . . . in Centennial Olympic Park. Petterson said he would rather see the city hire more police officers instead of putting up cameras like the one that sat above him at Marietta Street and Andrew Young International Boulevard.

"It would get too Orwellian for me," the Little Five Points resident said of the city's plans to install hundreds of the cameras. "Cameras are weird."

Source: J. Redmon, "Atlanta Seeks to Add 500 Surveillance Cameras," *Atlanta Journal-Constitution*, www.ajc.com,

calls to mind a near-perfect form of social organization. The modern mind associates the idea of a system with machine-like precision in which the problems of wasted effort, redundancy, and conflicting actions are quickly corrected. In practice, the justice system has nowhere near this level of perfection, and the systems model is admittedly an oversimplification. Conflicts among and within agencies are rife; individual actors within the system often do not share immediate goals; and the system may move in different directions depending on political currents, informal arrangements, and personal discretion.

conflict model
A criminal justice perspective that assumes that the system's components function primarily to serve their own interests. According to this theoretical framework, justice is more a product of conflicts among agencies within the system than it is the result of cooperation among component agencies.

The Conflict Model

The **conflict model** provides another approach to the study of American criminal justice. The conflict model says that the interests of criminal justice agencies tend to make actors within the system self-serving. According to this model, the goals of individual agencies

FIGURE 3
The Core Components of the American Criminal Justice System and Their Functions

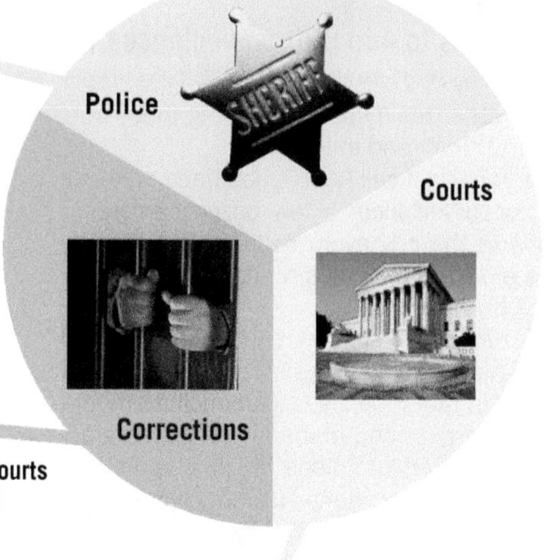

The Police

- Enforce the law
- Investigate crimes
- Apprehend offenders
- Reduce and prevent crime
- Maintain public order
- Ensure community safety
- Provide emergency and related community services
- Protect the fundamental rights and freedoms of individuals

Correctional Agencies

- Carry out sentences imposed by the courts
- Provide safe and humane custody and supervision of offenders
- Protect the community
- Rehabilitate, reform, and reintegrate convicted offenders back into the community
- Respect the legal and human rights of the convicted

Criminal Courts

- Conduct fair and impartial trials
- Decide criminal cases
- Ensure due process
- Determine guilt or innocence
- Impose sentences on the guilty
- Uphold the law
- Require fairness throughout the justice process
- Protect the rights and freedoms of anyone facing processing by the justice system
- Provide a check on the exercise of power by other justice system agencies*

*Fairness, professionalism, integrity, and impartiality are expected of all criminal justice personnel at every stage of criminal case processing, and it is a special duty of the courts to ensure that these expectations are met.

often conflict, and pressures for success, promotion, pay increases, and general accountability fragment the efforts of the system as a whole, leading to a criminal justice *non*system.[26]

A classic study of clearance rates by criminologist Jerome H. Skolnick provides support for the idea of a criminal justice nonsystem.[27] Clearance rates are a measure of crimes solved by the police. The more crimes the police can show they have solved, the better they look to the public they serve. Skolnick discovered an instance in which a burglar was caught red-handed during the commission of a burglary. After his arrest, the police suggested that he confess to many unsolved burglaries that they knew he had not committed. In effect they said, "Help us out, and we will try to help you out." The burglar did confess—to more than 400 other burglaries. Following the confession, the police were satisfied because they could say they had "solved" many burglaries, and the suspect was pleased as well because the police and the prosecutor agreed to speak on his behalf before the judge.

> Justice cannot be for one side alone, but must be for both.
>
> –Eleanor Roosevelt (1884–1962)

Both models have something to tell us. Agencies of justice with a diversity of functions (police, courts, and corrections) and at all levels (federal, state, and local) are linked closely enough for the term *system* to be meaningfully applied to them. On the other hand, the very size of the criminal justice undertaking makes effective cooperation between component agencies difficult. The police, for example, have an interest in seeing offenders put behind bars. Prison officials, on the other hand, are often working with extremely overcrowded facilities. They may favor early-release programs for certain categories of offenders, such as those judged to be nonviolent. Who wins out in the long run might just be a matter of internal politics and quasi-official wrangling. Everyone should be concerned,

FIGURE 4
The American Criminal Justice Process

Investigation ▶
After a crime has been discovered, evidence is gathered and follow-up investigations attempt to reconstruct the sequence of activities leading up to and including the criminal event. Efforts to identify suspects are initiated.

Warrant ▶
An arrest warrant issued by a judge provides the legal basis for an apprehension of suspects by police.

Arrest ▶
In an arrest, a person is taken into custody, limiting the arrestee's freedom. Arrest is a serious step in the process of justice. During arrest and before questioning, defendants are usually advised of their constitutional rights, or *Miranda* rights.

Booking ▶
Following arrest, suspects are booked. Booking is an administrative procedure where pictures, fingerprints, and personal information are obtained. A record of the events leading up to and including the arrest is created. In some jurisdictions, DNA evidence may be collected from arrestees.

however, when the goal of justice is affected, and sometimes even sacrificed, because of conflicts within the system.

American Criminal Justice: The Process

Whether part of a system or a nonsystem, the agencies of criminal justice must process the cases that come before them. An analysis of criminal justice case processing provides both a useful guide to this book and a "road map" to the criminal justice system itself. Figure 4 illustrates the processing of a criminal case through the federal justice system, beginning with the investigation of reported crimes. The process in most state systems is similar. See **Web Extra 2** for an expanded discussion of the process shown in the figure.

The stages illustrated in Figure 4 are discussed in detail at various places throughout this book. Chapter, "Policing: Legal Aspects," discusses investigation and arrest. All aspects of the first appearance and arraignment, including bail bonds and possible pretrial release, are discussed in Chapter, "The Courts." The criminal trial and its participants are described fully in Chapter, "The Courtroom Work Group and the Criminal Trial." Chapter, "Sentencing," outlines modern sentencing practices and describes the many modern alternatives to imprisonment. Chapter, "Probation, Parole, and Community Corrections," deals with the practice of probation and parole and with the issues surrounding it. Chapter, "Prisons and Jails," discusses the philosophy behind imprisonment, while Chapter, "Prison Life," portrays life on the inside and delineates the social structures that develop in response to the pains of imprisonment. Learn more about the criminal justice process at **Library Extra 2**. For a critical look at the justice system, visit **Web Extra 3**.

5 Describe the stages typical of American criminal justice case processing.

Due Process and Individual Rights

The U.S. Constitution requires that criminal justice case processing be conducted with fairness and equity; this requirement is referred to as **due process**, which, simply put, means procedural fairness.[28] It recognizes the individual rights of criminal defendants facing prosecution by a state or the federal government. Under the due process standard, rights violations may become the basis for the dismissal of evidence or of criminal charges, especially at the appellate level. Table 1 outlines the basic rights to which defendants in criminal proceedings are generally entitled.

6 Explain the meaning of due process of law, and identify where due process guarantees can be found in the American legal system.

Due process underlies the first ten amendments to the Constitution, which are collectively known as the *Bill of Rights.* It is specifically guaranteed by the Fifth, Sixth, and Fourteenth Amendments and is succinctly stated in the Fifth, which reads, "No person shall be . . . deprived of life, liberty, or property, without due process of law." The Fourteenth Amendment makes due process binding on the states, that is, it requires individual states to respect the due process rights of U.S. citizens who come under their jurisdiction.

due process
A right guaranteed by the Fifth, Sixth, and Fourteenth Amendments of the U.S. Constitution and generally understood, in legal contexts, to mean the due course of legal proceedings according to the rules and forms established for the protection of individual rights. In criminal proceedings, due process of law is generally understood to include the following basic elements: a law creating and defining the offense, an impartial tribunal having jurisdictional authority over the case, accusation in proper form, notice and opportunity to defend, trial according to established procedure, and discharge from all restraints or obligations unless convicted.

First Appearance

Within hours of arrest suspects must be brought before a magistrate (a judicial officer) for an initial appearance. The judge will tell them of the charges against them, advise them of their rights, and may provide the opportunity for bail.

Preliminary Hearing

The purpose of a preliminary hearing is to establish whether sufficient evidence exists against a person to continue the justice process. At the preliminary hearing, the hearing judge will seek to determine whether there is probable cause. The process provides the prosecutor with an opportunity to test the strength of the evidence.

Information or Indictment

In some states the prosecutor may seek to continue the case against a defendant by filing an information with the court. Other states require an indictment be returned by a grand jury. The grand jury hears evidence presented by the prosecutor and decides whether the case should go to trial.

Arraignment

At arraignment the accused stands before a judge and hears the information or indictment against him. Defendants are again notified of their rights and asked to enter a plea. Pleas include not guilty, guilty, and no contest. No contest may result in a conviction but cannot be used in trial as an admission of guilt.

TABLE 1
Individual Rights Guaranteed by the Bill of Rights[a]

- A right to be assumed innocent until proven guilty
- A right against unreasonable searches of person and place of residence
- A right against arrest without probable cause
- A right against unreasonable seizure of personal property
- A right against self-incrimination
- A right to fair questioning by the police
- A right to protection from physical harm throughout the justice process
- A right to an attorney
- A right to trial by jury
- A right to know the charges
- A right to cross-examine prosecution witnesses
- A right to speak and present witnesses
- A right not to be tried twice for the same crime
- A right against cruel or unusual punishment
- A right to due process
- A right to a speedy trial
- A right against excessive bail
- A right against excessive fines
- A right to be treated the same as others, regardless of race, sex, religious preference, and other personal attributes

[a]As interpreted by the U.S. Supreme Court.

The courts, and specifically the U.S. Supreme Court, have interpreted and clarified the guarantees of the Bill of Rights. The due process standard was set in the 1960s by the Warren Court (1953–1969), following a number of far-reaching Supreme Court decisions that affected criminal procedure. Led by Chief Justice Earl Warren, the Warren Court is remembered for its concern with protecting the innocent against the massive power of the state in criminal proceedings.[29] As a result of its tireless efforts to institutionalize the Bill of Rights, the daily practice of modern American criminal justice is now set squarely upon the due process standard.

The Role of the Courts in Defining Rights

Although the Constitution deals with many issues, what we have been calling *rights* are open to interpretation. Many modern rights, although written into the Constitution, would not exist in practice were it not for the fact that the U.S. Supreme Court decided, at some point in history, to recognize them in cases brought before it. In the well-known case of *Gideon* v. *Wainwright* (1963),[30] for example, the Supreme Court embraced the Sixth Amendment guarantee of a right to a lawyer for all criminal defendants and mandated that states provide lawyers for defendants who are unable to pay for them. Before *Gideon*, court-appointed attorneys for defendants unable to afford their own counsel were practically unknown, except in capital cases and in some federal courts. After the *Gideon* decision, court-appointed counsel became commonplace, and measures were instituted in jurisdictions across the nation to select attorneys fairly for indigent defendants. It is important to note, however, that while the Sixth Amendment specifically says, among other things, that "in all criminal prosecutions, the accused shall enjoy the right . . . to have the Assistance of Counsel for his defence," it does not say, in so many words, that the state is *required* to provide counsel. It is the U.S. Supreme Court interpreting the Constitution that has said that.

The U.S. Supreme Court is very powerful, and its decisions often have far-reaching consequences. The decisions rendered by the justices in cases like *Gideon* become, in effect,

Adjudication ▶

A criminal trial may be held, or the defendant may decide to enter a guilty plea. A criminal trial involves an adversarial process that pits the prosecution against the defense. In most trials, a jury hears the evidence and decides issues of guilt or innocence, while the judge ensures the fairness of the proceedings.

Sentencing ▶

After the person has been convicted it is up to the judge to determine the punishment. Prior to sentencing, a sentencing hearing is sometimes held in which attorneys for both sides can present information to influence the judge's decision.

Corrections ▶

The corrections period begins following sentencing. Corrections involves a variety of sentences that can be imposed on a defendant.

Probation and Parole

Not everyone who has been convicted of a crime goes to prison. Probation imposes requirements or restrictions upon offenders. Offenders are required to check in with a probation officer on a regular basis.

After the defendant has served a portion of his prison term he may be freed on parole. Like probation, parole may come with obligations and requires the offender to check in with a parole officer.

Photo sources (from left): Dave King © Dorling Kindersley; Gibson/Shutterstock; and Marc Dietrich/Shutterstock

the law of the land. For all practical purposes, such decisions often carry as much weight as legislative action. For this reason, we speak of "judge-made law" (rather than legislated law) in describing judicial precedents that affect the process of justice.

Rights that have been recognized by court decisions are subject to continual refinement, and although the process of change is usually very slow, new interpretations may broaden or narrow the scope of applicability accorded to constitutional guarantees.

▲ A criminal defendant at a preliminary hearing. Everyone facing criminal prosecution in the United States is guaranteed a constitutional right to due process, meaning that defendants must be afforded a fair opportunity to participate in every stage of criminal proceedings. Should due process rights extend to all offenders—even accused terrorists? *AP Wide World Photos*

The Ultimate Goal: Crime Control through Due Process

Two primary goals were identified in our discussion of this book's theme: (1) the need to enforce the law and to maintain public order and (2) the need to protect individuals from injustice, especially at the hands of the criminal justice system. The first of these principles values the efficient arrest and conviction of criminal offenders. It is often referred to as the **crime-control model** of justice. The crime-control model was first brought to the attention of the academic community in Stanford University law professor Herbert Packer's cogent analysis of the state of criminal justice in the late 1960s.[31] For that reason, it is sometimes referred to as *Packer's crime-control model*.

> Liberty is the perfection of civil society, but still authority must be acknowledged essential to its very existence.
>
> —David Hume (1711–1776)

The second principle is called the **due process model** because of its emphasis on individual rights. Due process is intended to ensure that innocent people are not convicted of crimes; it is a fundamental part of American criminal justice. It requires a careful and informed consideration of the facts of each individual case. Under the due process model, police are required to recognize the rights of suspects during arrest, questioning, and handling. Similarly, prosecutors and judges must recognize constitutional and other guarantees during trial and the presentation of evidence.

The dual goals of crime control and due process are often assumed to be opposing goals. Indeed, some critics of American criminal justice argue that the practice of justice is too often concerned with crime control at the expense of due process. Other analysts of the American scene maintain that our type of justice coddles offenders and does too little to protect the innocent. While it is impossible to avoid ideological conflicts like these, we can think of the American system of justice as representative of *crime control through due process*—that is, as a system of **social control** that is fair to those whom it processes. This model of *law enforcement infused with the recognition of individual rights* provides a workable conceptual framework for understanding the American system of criminal justice.

crime-control model
A criminal justice perspective that emphasizes the efficient arrest and conviction of criminal offenders.

due process model
A criminal justice perspective that emphasizes individual rights at all stages of justice system processing.

social control
The use of sanctions and rewards within a group to influence and shape the behavior of individual members of that group. Social control is a primary concern of social groups and communities, and it is their interest in the exercise of social control that leads to the creation of both criminal and civil statutes.

Evidence-Based Practice in Criminal Justice

In June 2010, Assistant Attorney General Laurie O. Robinson announced a new initiative at the Office of Justice Programs (OJP), an arm of the U.S. Department of Justice that funds implementation of state-of-the-art practices in criminal justice agencies across the country.[32] The initiative, which Robinson said was intended to help "criminal and juvenile justice professionals expand their base of scientific knowledge and transform research into practice," is known as the Evidence Integration Initiative (E2I). E2I is an ongoing OJP-wide effort to integrate science and research throughout the agency and the work it sponsors. "Most importantly," Robinson said, "we are working to move evidence into practice by funding evidence-based programs."

7 Explain evidence-based practice, and describe the role of evidence-based research in contemporary criminal justice.

As the word is used here, *evidence* does not refer to evidence of a crime but means, instead, findings that are supported by studies. Hence, **evidence-based practice** refers to crime-fighting strategies that have been scientifically tested and are based on social science research. Scientific research has become a major element in the increasing professionalization of criminal justice, both as a career field and as a field of study. As Robinson recognized, there is a strong call today within criminal justice policy-making circles for the application of evidence-based practices throughout the justice field.

evidence-based practice
Crime-fighting strategies that have been scientifically tested and are based on social science research.

In an initiative that strongly supports evidence-based practice, the National Criminal Justice Commission Act of 2010[33] passed the House of Representatives in July 2010 on a voice vote, and legislators were working to reconcile it with a Senate version of the bill. The goal of the proposed legislation is to create a blue-ribbon commission charged with conducting an 18-month top-to-bottom review of the nation's entire criminal justice system. In the words of the proposed legislation, the commission would "institute the use of policies and practices proven effective throughout the spectrum of criminal behavior." Evidence-based practices can be expected to play an expanded role in policy making and in the administration of criminal justice in the years to come.

▲ U.S. Senator Jim Webb, cosponsor of the National Criminal Justice Commission Act of 2010. What is the goal of the proposed legislation?
© Stefan Zaklin/zefa/CORBIS. All Rights Reserved.

The Start of Academic Criminal Justice

The study of criminal justice as an academic discipline began in this country in the late 1920s, when August Vollmer (1876–1955), the former police chief of the Los Angeles Police Department (LAPD), persuaded the University of California to offer courses on the subject.[34] Vollmer was joined by his former student Orlando W. Wilson (1900–1972) and by William H. Parker (who later served as chief of the LAPD from 1950 to 1966) in calling for increased professionalism in police work through better training.[35] Largely as a result of Vollmer's influence, early criminal justice education was practice oriented; it was a kind of extension of on-the-job training for working practitioners. Hence, in the early days of the discipline, criminal justice students were primarily focused on the application of general management principles to the administration of police agencies. Criminal justice came to be seen as a practical field of study concerned largely with issues of organizational effectiveness.

By the 1960s, however, police training came to be augmented by criminal justice education[36] as students of criminal justice began to apply the techniques of social scientific research—many of them borrowed from sister disciplines like **criminology**, sociology, psychology, and political science—to the study of all aspects of the justice system. Scientific research into the operation of the criminal justice system was encouraged by the 1967 President's Commission on Law Enforcement and Administration of Justice, which influenced passage of the Safe Streets and Crime Control Act of 1968. The Safe Streets Act led to the creation of the National Institute of Law Enforcement and Criminal Justice, which later became the National Institute of Justice (NIJ). As a central part of its mission, NIJ continues to support research in the criminal justice field through substantial funding for scientific explorations into all aspects of the discipline, and it funnels much of the

criminology
The scientific study of the causes and prevention of crime and the rehabilitation and punishment of offenders.

$3 billion spent annually by the U.S. Department of Justice to local communities to help fight crime. Now, almost 100 years after its beginnings as a field of study, criminal justice is being revitalized by an evidence-based approach to its subject matter. Assistant Attorney General Robinson puts it this way: "Justice professionals have been collecting, analyzing, and using evidence for centuries—in laboratories and courtrooms. As financial realities demand more innovative approaches, social science research is forming the basis for new programs in areas ranging from reentry to victim services. Evidence has found a new home: in the field."[37]

Multiculturalism and Diversity in Criminal Justice

8 Explain how multiculturalism and diversity present special challenges to, and opportunities for, the American system of criminal justice.

In 2007, polygamist Warren Steed Jeffs, a leader of the Fundamentalist Church of Jesus Christ of Latter Day Saints (FLDS), an offshoot of the mainstream Mormon church, was convicted of conspiring to rape a child and of being an accessory to child rape for performing a marriage involving a 14-year-old girl and her 19-year-old cousin. Jeffs, who was on the FBI's Ten Most Wanted list, was sentenced on November 20, 2007, to two consecutive sentences of five years to life in prison.[38]

The Church of Jesus Christ of Latter-day Saints brought plural marriage to Utah in the early nineteenth century, but the state legislature banned the practice more than 100 years ago. Today, the church officially excommunicates polygamists, although the FLDS practices polygamy as a central tenet. Some estimate the number of polygamists living in Utah and Arizona today at over 30,000.[39] The existence of such alternative family lifestyles is just one indicator that the United States is a multicultural and diverse society.

> Without security, government cannot deliver, nor can the people enjoy, the prosperity and opportunities that flow from freedom and democracy.
> —Alberto Gonzales, former U.S. attorney general[v]

Multiculturalism describes a society that is home to a multitude of different cultures, each with its own set of norms, values, and routine behaviors. While American society today is truly a multicultural society, composed of a wide variety of racial and ethnic heritages, diverse religions, incongruous values, disparate traditions, and distinct languages, multiculturalism in America is not new. For thousands of years before Europeans arrived in the Western Hemisphere, tribal nations of Native Americans each spoke their own language, were bound to customs that differed significantly from one another, and practiced a wide range of religions. European immigration, which began in earnest in the seventeenth century, led to greater diversity still. Successive waves of immigrants, along with the slave trade of the early and mid-nineteenth century,[40] brought a diversity of values, beliefs, and patterns of behavior to American shores that frequently conflicted with prevailing cultures. Differences in languages and traditions fed the American melting pot of the late nineteenth and early twentieth centuries and made effective communication between groups difficult.

multiculturalism
The existence within one society of diverse groups that maintain unique cultural identities while frequently accepting and participating in the larger society's legal and political systems.[vi] *Multiculturalism* is often used in conjunction with the term *diversity* to identify many distinctions of social significance.

The face of multiculturalism in America today is quite different than it was in the past, due largely to relatively high birthrates among some minority populations and the huge but relatively recent immigration of Spanish-speaking people from Mexico, Cuba, Central America, and South America. Part of that influx consists of substantial numbers of undocumented immigrants who have entered the country illegally and who, because of experiences in their home countries, may have a special fear of police authority and a general distrust for the law. Such fears make members of this group hesitant to report being victimized, and their undocumented status makes them easy prey for illegal scams like extortion, blackmail, and documentation crimes. Learn more about immigration and crime via **Library Extra 3**.

Diversity characterizes both immigrant and U.S.-born individuals. Census Bureau statistics show that people identifying themselves as white account for 71% of the U.S.

A group of immigrants taking the pledge of allegiance during a naturalization ceremony at the Miami Beach Convention Center in Florida. American society is multicultural, composed of a wide variety of racial and ethnic heritages, diverse religions, incongruous values, disparate traditions, and distinct languages. What impact does the multicultural nature of our society have on the justice system?
Jeff Greenberg/PhotoEdit Inc.

population—a percentage that has been dropping steadily for at least the past 40 years. People of Hispanic origin constitute approximately 12% of the population and are the fastest-growing group in the country. Individuals identifying themselves as African American make up another 12% of the population, and people of Asian and Pacific Island origin make up almost 4% of the total. Native Americans, including American Indians, Eskimos, and Aleuts, account for slightly less than 1% of all Americans.[41] Statistics like these, however, are only estimates, and their interpretation is complicated by the fact that surveyed individuals may be of mixed race. Nonetheless, it is clear that American society today is ethnically and racially quite diverse.

Race and *ethnicity* are only buzzwords that people use when they talk about multiculturalism. After all, neither race nor ethnicity determines a person's values, attitudes, or behavior. Just as there is no uniquely identifiable "white culture" in American society, it is a mistake to think that all African Americans share the same values or that everyone of Hispanic descent honors the same traditions or even speaks Spanish.

Multiculturalism, as the term is used today, is but one form of diversity. Taken together, these two concepts—multiculturalism and diversity—encompass many distinctions of social significance. The broad brush of contemporary multiculturalism and social diversity draws attention to variety along racial, ethnic, subcultural, generational, faith, economic, and gender lines. Lifestyle diversity is also important. The fact that influential elements of the wider society are less accepting of some lifestyles than others doesn't mean that such lifestyles aren't recognized from the viewpoint of multiculturalism. It simply means that, at least for now, some lifestyles are accorded less official acceptability than others. As a result, certain lifestyle choices, even within a multicultural society that generally respects and encourages diversity, may still be criminalized, as in the case of polygamy.

Multiculturalism and diversity will be discussed in various chapters throughout this textbook. For now, it is sufficient to recognize that the diverse values, perspectives, and behaviors characteristic of various groups within our society have a significant impact on the justice system. Whether it is the confusion that arises from a police officer's commands to a non-English-speaking suspect, the need for interpreters in the courtroom, a deep-seated distrust of the police in some minority communities, a lack of willingness among some immigrants to report crime, the underrepresentation of women in criminal justice agencies, or some people's irrational suspicions of Arab Americans following the September 11 terrorist attacks, diversity and multiculturalism present special challenges to the everyday practice of criminal justice in America. Finally, as we shall see, the demands and expectations placed on justice agencies in multicultural societies involve a dilemma that is closely associated with the theme of this text: how to protect the rights of individuals to self-expression while ensuring social control and the safety and security of the public.

Summary

WHAT IS CRIMINAL JUSTICE?

- The American experience with crime during the last half century has been especially influential in shaping the criminal justice system of today. Although crime waves have come and gone, some events during the past century stand out as especially significant, including a spurt of widespread organized criminal activity associated with the Prohibition years of the early twentieth century, the substantial increase in "traditional" crimes during the 1960s and 1970s, the threat to the American way of life represented by illicit drugs around the same time, and the terrorist attacks of September 11, 2001.
- The theme of this text is one of individual rights versus public order. As this chapter points out, the personal freedoms guaranteed to law-abiding citizens as well as to criminal suspects by the Constitution must be closely guarded. At the same time, the urgent social needs of communities for controlling unacceptable behavior and protecting law-abiding citizens from harm must be recognized. This theme is represented by two opposing groups: individual-rights advocates and public-order advocates. The fundamental challenge facing the practice of American criminal justice is in efficiently enforcing the laws while simultaneously recognizing and supporting the legal rights of suspects and the legitimate personal differences and prerogatives of individuals.
- Although justice may be an elusive concept, it is important to recognize that criminal justice is tied closely to notions of social justice, including personal and cultural beliefs about equity and fairness. As a goal to be achieved, criminal justice refers to those aspects of social justice that concern violations of the criminal law. While community interests in the administration of criminal justice demand the apprehension and punishment of law violators, criminal justice ideals extend to the protection of the innocent, the fair treatment of offenders, and fair play by justice administration agencies.
- In this chapter, we described the process of American criminal justice as a system with three major components—police, courts, and corrections—all of which can be described as working together toward a common goal. We warned, however, that a systems viewpoint is useful primarily for the simplification that it provides. A more realistic approach to understanding criminal justice may be the nonsystem approach. As a nonsystem, the criminal justice process is depicted as a fragmented activity in which individuals and agencies within the process have interests and goals that at times coincide but often conflict.
- The stages of criminal case processing include investigation, the issuance of a warrant, arrest, booking, first appearance in court, defendant's preliminary hearing, return of an indictment by the grand jury or filing of an information by the prosecutor, arraignment of the defendant before the court, adjudication or trial, sentencing, and corrections. As a field of study, corrections includes jails, probation, imprisonment, and parole.
- The principle of due process, which underlies the first ten amendments to the U.S. Constitution, is central to American criminal justice. Due process (also called *due process of law*) means procedural fairness and requires that criminal case processing be conducted with fairness and equity. The ultimate goal of the criminal justice system in America is achieving crime control through due process.
- The study of criminal justice as an academic discipline began in this country in the late 1920s and is well established today. Scientific research has become a major element in the increasing professionalization of criminal justice, and there is a strong call today for the application of evidence-based practices in the justice field. Evidence-based practices are crime-fighting strategies that have been scientifically tested and that are based on social science research.
- America today is a multicultural society, composed of a wide variety of racial and ethnic heritages, diverse religions, incongruous values, disparate traditions, and distinct languages. Multiculturalism complicates the practice of American criminal justice since there is rarely universal agreement in our society about what is right or wrong or about what constitutes justice. As such, multiculturalism presents both challenges and opportunities for today's justice practitioners.

QUESTIONS FOR REVIEW

1. Describe the American experience with crime during the last half century. What noteworthy criminal incidents or activities occurred during that time, and what social and economic conditions might have produced them?
2. What is the theme of this text? According to that theme, what are the differences between the individual-rights perspective and the public-order perspective?
3. What is justice? What aspects of justice does this chapter discuss? How does criminal justice relate to wider notions of equity and fairness?
4. What are the main components of the criminal justice system? How do they interrelate? How might they conflict?
5. List the stages of case processing that characterize the American system of criminal justice.
6. What is meant by the term *due process of law*? Where in the American legal system are guarantees of due process found?
7. What is meant by the term *evidence-based practice*, and what is the role of research in criminal justice? How can research influence crime-control policy?
8. What is multiculturalism? What is social diversity? What impact do multiculturalism and diversity have on the practice of criminal justice in contemporary American society?

Chapter Notes

i. ABC News, September 16, 2001.
ii. All boldfaced terms are explained whenever possible using definitions provided by the Bureau of Justice Statistics under a mandate of the Justice System Improvement Act of 1979. That mandate found its most complete expression in the *Dictionary of Criminal Justice Data Terminology* (Washington, DC: Bureau of Justice Statistics, 1982), the second edition of which provides the wording for many definitions in this text.
iii. ABC News, September 11, 2001.
iv. Adapted from U.S. Code, Title 28, Section 20.3 (2[d]). Title 28 of the U.S. Code defines the term *administration of criminal justice*.
v. Prepared remarks of U.S. Attorney General Alberto Gonzales, Address to the National Association of Counties Legislative Conference, Washington, DC, March 7, 2005.
vi. Adapted from Robert M. Shusta et al., *Multicultural Law Enforcement*, 2nd ed. (Upper Saddle River, NJ: Prentice Hall, 2002), p. 443.

---

1. American Civil Liberties Union website, http://www.aclu.org/issues/criminal/iscj.html (accessed January 22, 2010).
2. ABC News, September 11, 2001. Christopher was repeating a phrase generally attributed to former U.S. Supreme Court Justice Arthur Goldberg.
3. Sam Coates and Dan Eggen, "A City of Despair and Lawlessness," *Washington Post*, September 2, 2005, p. A1.
4. Mark Gongloff, "Anarchy in New Orleans," *Wall Street Journal*, September 1, 2005.
5. "Looters Ransack Stores in Downtown New Orleans," *Wall Street Journal*, August 31, 2005.
6. Ibid.
7. Kevin Johnson, "Officers at 'Fort Apache' Finally Get Breather," *USA Today*, September 7, 2005, p. 3A.
8. Kevin McCoy, "Fraud Mounts in Katrina Aid Program," *USA Today*, February 13, 2006, p. 1A.
9. Ibid.
10. For a thorough discussion of immigration as it relates to crime, see Ramiro Martinez, Jr., and Matthew T. Lee, "On Immigration and Crime," in National Institute of Justice, *Criminal Justice 2000, Vol. 1: The Nature of Crime—Continuity and Change* (Washington, DC: U.S. Department of Justice, Office of Justice Programs, 2000).
11. "Inside Columbine," *Rocky Mountain News*, http://www.rockymountainnews .com/drmn/columbine (accessed July 4, 2010).
12. "Cries of Relief," *Time*, April 26, 1993, p. 18.
13. Laurence McQuillan, "Bush to Urge Jail for Execs Who Lie," *USA Today*, July 9, 2002, http://www.usatoday.com/news/washdc/2002/07/09/bush-business.htm (accessed July 9, 2006).
14. Sarbanes-Oxley Act of 2002 (officially known as the Public Company Accounting Reform and Investor Protection Act), Public Law 107–204, 116 Stat. 745 (July 30, 2002).
15. PricewaterhouseCoopers, "The Sarbanes-Oxley Act," http://www.pwcglobal.com/Extweb/NewCoAtWork.nsf/docid/D0D7F79003C6D64485256CF30074D66C (accessed July 8, 2007).
16. Richard Esposito, Eloise Harper, and Maddy Sauer, "Bernie Madoff Pleads Guilty to Ponzi Scheme, Goes Straight to Jail, Says He's 'Deeply Sorry,'" ABC News, March 12, 2009, http://abcnews.go.com/Blotter/WallStreet/Story?id=7066715&page=1 (accessed July 4, 2010).
17. Robert Lenzner, "Bernie Madoff's $50 Billion Ponzi Scheme," Forbes.com, December 12, 2008, http://www.forbes.com/2008/12/12/madoff-ponzi-hedge-pf-ii-in_rl_1212croesus_inl.html (accessed September 28, 2010).
18. Emanuella Grinberg, "California Senate Passes Tougher Sentencing Laws for Sex Offenders," CNN Justice, August 24, 2010, http://www.cnn.com/2010/CRIME/08/24/california.chelseas.law/ (accessed September 4, 2010).
19. Wendy Koch, "States Get Tougher with Sex Offenders," *USA Today*, May 24, 2006, p. 1A.
20. Ibid.
21. Martin Luther King, in an address to the Tenth Anniversary Convention of the Southern Christian Leadership Conference in Atlanta, Georgia, on August 16, 1967. It was abolitionist and Unitarian minister Theodore Parker who first used a similar phrase in the mid-1800s, saying, "I do not pretend to understand the moral universe; the arc is a long one. . . . And from what I see I am sure it bends toward justice."
22. *The American Heritage Dictionary on CD-ROM* (Boston: Houghton Mifflin, 1991).
23. For a good overview of the issues involved, see Judge Harold J. Rothwax, *Guilty: The Collapse of Criminal Justice* (New York: Random House, 1996).
24. For one perspective on the detention of Muslims following September 11, 2001, see the plaintiff's motion to stay proceedings on defendant's summary judgment motion pending discovery, in *Center for National Security Studies* v. *U.S. Department of Justice*, U.S. District Court for the District of Columbia (Civil Action No. 01–2500; January 2002), http://www.aclu.org/court/cnssjan22.pdf (accessed September 24, 2007).
25. The systems model of criminal justice is often attributed to the frequent use of the term *system* by the 1967 Presidential Commission in its report *The Challenge of Crime in a Free Society* (Washington, DC: U.S. Government Printing Office, 1967).
26. One of the first published works to use the nonsystem approach to criminal justice was the American Bar Association's *New Perspective on Urban Crime* (Washington, DC: ABA Special Committee on Crime Prevention and Control, 1972).
27. Jerome H. Skolnick, *Justice without Trial* (New York: John Wiley, 1966), p. 179.
28. "The Defendants' Rights at a Criminal Trial," http://www.mycounsel.com/content/arrests/court/rights.html (accessed February 10, 2010).
29. For a complete and now-classic analysis of the impact of decisions made by the Warren Court, see Fred P. Graham, *The Due Process Revolution: The Warren Court's Impact on Criminal Law* (New York: Hayden Press, 1970).
30. *Gideon* v. *Wainwright*, 372 U.S. 353 (1963).

31. Herbert Packer, *The Limits of the Criminal Sanction* (Stanford, CA: Stanford University Press, 1968).
32. "Understanding and Using Evidence-Based Practices," Justice Resource Update, http://www.ojp.gov/justiceresourceupdate/june2010 (accessed June 3, 2010).
33. Senate Bill 714; H.R. 5143.
34. For an excellent history of policing in the United States, see Edward A. Farris, "Five Decades of American Policing, 1932–1982," *Police Chief* (November 1982), pp. 30–36.
35. Gene Edward Carte, "August Vollmer and the Origins of Police Professionalism," *Journal of Police Science and Administration*, Vol. 1, No. 1 (1973), pp. 274–281.
36. Chris Eskridge distinguishes between police *training*, which is "job-specific" and is intended to teach trainees *how* to do something (like fire a weapon), and *justice education*, whose purpose is to "develop a general spirit of inquiry." See C. W. Eskridge, "Criminal Justice Education and Its Potential Impact on the Sociopolitical-Economic Climate of Central European Nations," *Journal of Criminal Justice Education*, Vol. 14, No. 1 (spring 2003), pp. 105–118; and James O. Finckenauer, "The Quest for Quality in Criminal Justice Education," *Justice Quarterly*, Vol. 22, No. 4 (December 2005), pp. 413–426.
37. "Understanding and Using Evidence-Based Practices."
38. KVBC-TV (Las Vegas), "Warren Jeffs Sentenced," http://www.kvbc.com/Global/story.asp?S=7388968 (accessed May 1, 2010).
39. "Polygamist Wins Parole from Utah State Prison," Associated Press, August 27, 2007.
40. On March 22, 1794, the U.S. Congress barred American citizens from transporting slaves from the United States to another nation or between foreign nations. On January 1, 1808, the importation of slaves into the United States became illegal, and Congress charged the U.S. Revenue Cutter Service (now known as the U.S. Coast Guard) with enforcing the law on the high seas. Although some slave ships were seized, the importation of Africans for sale as slaves apparently continued in some southern states until the early 1860s. See U.S. Coast Guard, "U.S. Coast Guard in Illegal Immigration (1794–1971)," http://www.uscg.mil/hq/g-o/g-opl/mle/amiohist.htm (accessed October 13, 2009).
41. U.S. Census Bureau website, http://www.census.gov (accessed March 22, 2010). Population statistics are estimates because race is a difficult concept to define and Census Bureau interviewers allow individuals to choose more than one race when completing census forms.

The Crime Picture

Learning Objectives

After reading this chapter, you should be able to:

1. Describe the history and nature of the FBI's UCR/NIBRS Program, and explain what it can tell us about crime in the United States today.
2. Describe the history and nature of the National Crime Victimization Survey Program, and explain what it can tell us about crime in the United States today.
3. Point out significant differences between the UCR and the NCVS.
4. Identify the special categories of crime discussed in this chapter, and explain why they are of contemporary significance.

"No one way of describing crime describes it well enough."

—President's Commission on Law Enforcement and Administration of Justice

"It may turn out that a free society cannot really prevent crime. Perhaps . . . coping is the best that we can hope for."

—James Q. Wilson, Pepperdine University[1]

Monika Graff/The Image Works

Introduction

In 2010, the CBS-TV megahit series *NCIS: Naval Criminal Investigative Service* was recognized by the Paley Center for Media in Los Angeles as the most popular scripted TV show in the world.[2] With more than 20 million dedicated viewers in the United States alone, the show has achieved heights that most other shows can't even dream of. Another immensely popular series on the same network, *CSI: Miami*, has more than 50 million regular viewers in 55 countries. The *CSI* franchise, which follows teams of crime-scene investigators, now includes shows featuring New York City and other locales, and it is available to a global audience of nearly 2 billion viewers in 200 countries.[3]

▲ A scene from the CBS-TV show *NCIS*. The American public has long been enthralled with crime shows, and since the terrorist attacks of 2001, the public's concern with personal safety has surged. Why do so many people like to watch crime shows?
CBS/Cliff Lipson/Landov

The popularity of prime-time television crime shows is not limited to *NCIS* and *CSI*, as other widely followed series demonstrate: *Body of Proof, Castle*, and *Rookie Blue* on ABC; *Criminal Minds* on CBS; *The Good Guys* on Fox; *Law and Order* and its spin-offs on NBC; and *White Collar* on USA. Social commentators note that the plethora of crime shows bombarding the airwaves today reveals a penchant among American TV viewers for crime-related entertainment and a fascination with police work and the criminal justice system.

The public's interest in real-life stories of criminal victimization, revenge, and reformation has given birth to reality TV crime shows, including *America's Most Wanted* (which premiered on Fox in 1988) and *Cops* (also on Fox). Similarly, video magazine shows like *60 Minutes* (CBS), *20/20* (ABC), and *Nightline* (ABC) frequently focus on justice issues, and any number of movies play off the public's fascination with crime and the personal drama it fosters. Like this text, many of today's television shows deliver content across a variety of media. View the *CSI* show's website at **Web Extra 1**, or become a fan of *NCIS* on Facebook via **Web Extra 2**.

> We can have as much or as little crime as we please, depending on what we choose to count as criminal.
>
> —Herbert L. Packer (1925–1972)

This chapter has a dual purpose. First, it provides a statistical overview of crime in contemporary America by examining information on reported and discovered crimes. Second, it identifies special categories of crime that are of particular interest today, including crime against women, crime against the elderly, hate crime, corporate and white-collar crime, organized crime, gun crime, drug crime, cybercrime, and terrorism.

Although we will look at many crime statistics in this chapter, it is important to remember that statistical aggregates of reported crime, whatever their source, do not reveal the lost lives, human suffering, lessened productivity, and reduced quality of life that crime causes. Unlike the fictional characters on TV crime shows, real-life crime victims as well as real-life offenders lead intricate lives—they have families, hold jobs, and dream dreams. As we examine the crime statistics, we must not lose sight of the people behind the numbers.

Crime Data and Social Policy

Crime statistics provide an overview of criminal activity. If used properly, a statistical picture of crime can serve as a powerful tool for creating social policy. Decision makers at all levels, including legislators, other elected officials, and administrators throughout the criminal justice system, rely on crime data to analyze and evaluate existing programs, to fashion and design new crime-control initiatives, to develop funding requests, and to plan new laws and crime-control legislation. Many "get tough" policies, such as the three-strikes movement that swept the country during the 1990s, have been based in large part on the measured ineffectiveness of existing programs to reduce the incidence of repeat offending.

However, some people question just how objective—and therefore how useful—crime statistics are. Social events, including crime, are complex and difficult to quantify. Even the decision of which crimes should be included and which excluded in statistical reports is itself a judgment reflecting the interests and biases of policymakers. Moreover, public opinion about crime is not always realistic. As well-known criminologist Norval Morris points out, the news media do more to influence public perceptions of crime than any official data do.[4] During the four-year period (in the mid-1990s) covered by Morris's study, for example, the frequency of crime stories reported in the national media increased fourfold. During the same time period, crime was at the top of the list in subject matter covered in news stories at both the local and national levels. The irony, says Morris, is that "the grossly increasing preoccupation with crime stories came at a time of steadily declining crime and violence." However, as Morris adds, "aided and abetted by this flood of misinformation, the politicians, federal and state and local, fostered the view that the public demands our present 'get tough' policies."[5]

The Collection of Crime Data

Nationally, crime statistics come from two major sources: (1) the FBI's **Uniform Crime Reporting (UCR) Program** (also known today as the UCR/NIBRS Program), which produces an annual overview of major crime titled *Crime in the United States*; and (2) the **National Crime Victimization Survey (NCVS)** of the **Bureau of Justice Statistics (BJS)**. The most widely quoted numbers purporting to describe crime in America today probably come from the UCR/NIBRS Program, although the statistics it produces are based largely on *reports* to the police by victims of crime.

Another important source of crime data is offender self-reports based on surveys that ask respondents to reveal any illegal activity in which they have been involved. Offender self-reports are not discussed in detail in this chapter because surveys utilizing them are not national in scope and are not undertaken regularly. Moreover, offenders are often reluctant to accurately report ongoing or recent criminal involvement, making information derived from these surveys somewhat unreliable and less than current. However, the available information from offender self-reports reveals that serious criminal activity is considerably more widespread than most "official" surveys show (Figure 1).

Other regular publications also contribute to our knowledge of crime patterns throughout the nation. One such publication is the *Sourcebook of Criminal Justice Statistics*—an annual compilation of national information on crime and on the criminal justice system. The *Sourcebook* is produced by the BJS, and a Web-based version of the *Sourcebook* is continually updated as data become available. The National Institute of Justice (NIJ), the primary research arm of the U.S. Department of Justice; the Office of Juvenile Justice and Delinquency Prevention (OJJDP); the Federal Justice Statistics Resource Center; and the National Victims Resource Center provide still more information on crime patterns. Visit **Web Extra 3** for an overview of the many sources of crime data. The *Sourcebook* is available directly at **Library Extra 1**.

Uniform Crime Reporting (UCR) Program
A statistical reporting program run by the FBI's Criminal Justice Information Services (CJIS) division. The UCR Program publishes *Crime in the United States*, which provides an annual summation of the incidence and rate of reported crimes throughout the United States.

National Crime Victimization Survey (NCVS)
An annual survey of selected American households conducted by the Bureau of Justice Statistics to determine the extent of criminal victimization—especially unreported victimization—in the United States.

Bureau of Justice Statistics (BJS)
A U.S. Department of Justice agency responsible for the collection of criminal justice data, including the annual National Crime Victimization Survey.

The UCR/NIBRS Program

Development of the UCR Program

1 Describe the history and nature of the FBI's UCR/NIBRS Program, and explain what it can tell us about crime in the United States today.

In 1930, Congress authorized the U.S. attorney general to survey crime in America, and the Federal Bureau of Investigation (FBI) was designated to implement the program. In short order, the bureau built on earlier efforts by the International Association of Chiefs of Police (IACP) to create a national system of uniform crime statistics. As a practical measure, IACP had recommended the use of readily available information, and so it was that citizens' crime reports to the police became the basis of the FBI's plan.[6]

During its first year of operation, the FBI's UCR Program received reports from 400 cities in 43 states; 20 million people were covered by that first comprehensive survey. Today, approximately 18,000 law enforcement agencies provide crime information for the program, with data coming from city, county, university and college, tribal, and state departments. To ensure uniformity in reporting, the FBI has developed standardized definitions of offenses and terminologies used in the program. A number of publications, including the *Uniform Crime Reporting Handbook* and the *Manual of Law Enforcement Records*, are supplied to participating agencies, and training for effective reporting is available through FBI-sponsored seminars and instructional literature.

FIGURE 1
The Criminal Justice Funnel

Source: Derived from Thomas H. Cohen and Tracey Kyckelhahn, *Felony Defendants in Large Urban Counties, 2006* (Washington, DC: Bureau of Justice Statistics, 2010).

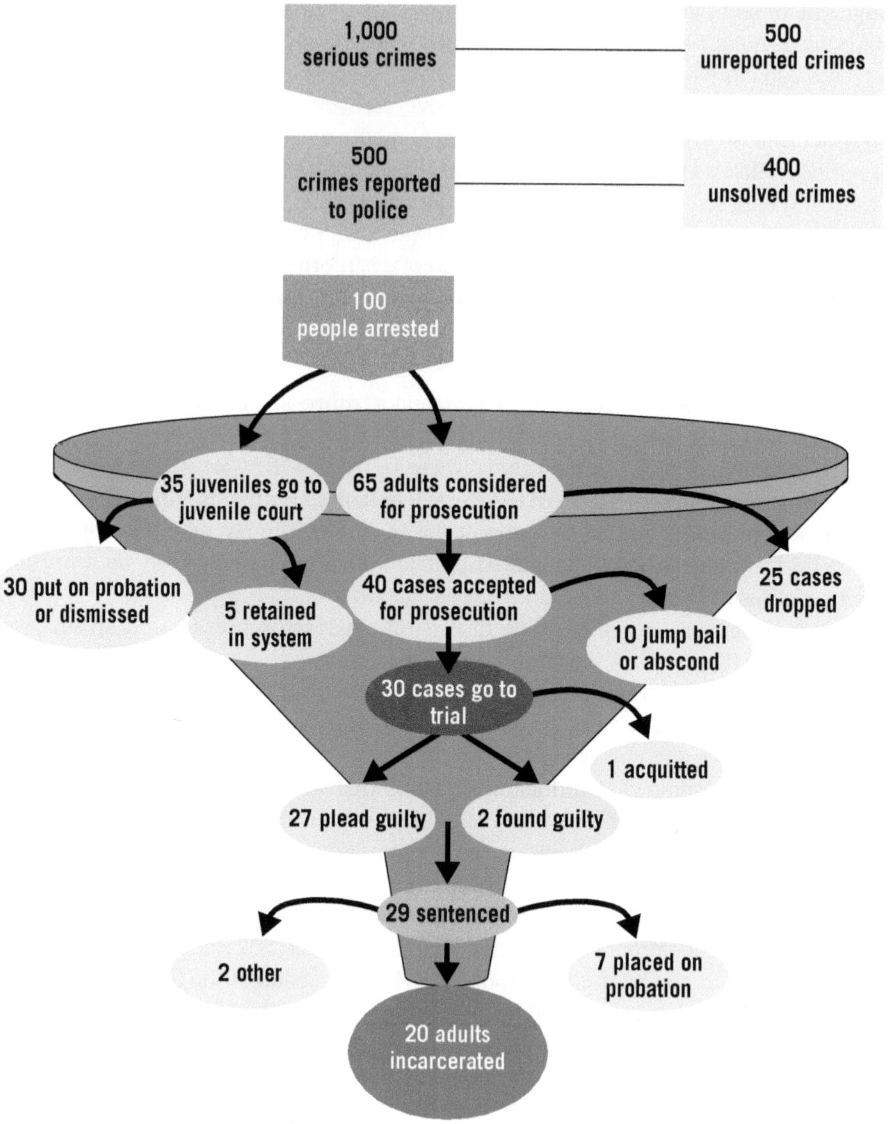

Crime Index
A now-defunct but once-inclusive measure of the UCR Program's violent and property crime categories, or what are called *Part I offenses*. The Crime Index, long featured in the FBI's publication *Crime in the United States*, was discontinued in 2004. The index had been intended as a tool for geographic (state-to-state) and historical (year-to-year) comparisons via the use of crime rates (the number of crimes per unit of population). However, criticism that the index was misleading arose after researchers found that the largest of the index's crime categories, larceny-theft, carried undue weight and led to an underappreciation of changes in the rates of more violent and serious crimes.

Following IACP recommendations, the original UCR Program was designed to permit comparisons over time through construction of a **Crime Index**, which was first published in *Crime in the United States* in 1960. The index summed the occurrences of seven major offenses—murder, forcible rape, robbery, aggravated assault, burglary, larceny-theft, and motor vehicle theft—and expressed the result as a crime rate based on population. In 1979, by congressional mandate, an eighth offense—arson—was added to the index. *Crime Index* was the title used for a simple aggregation of the seven main offense classifications (called Part I offenses).

Over the years, however, concern grew that the Crime Index did not provide a clear picture of criminality because it was skewed by the offense with the highest number of reports—typically larceny-theft. The sheer volume of larceny-theft offenses overshadowed more serious but less frequently committed offenses, skewing perceptions of crime rates for jurisdictions with high numbers of larceny-thefts but low numbers of serious crimes like murder and forcible rape. In June 2004, the FBI's Criminal Justice Information Services (CJIS) Advisory Policy Board officially discontinued the use of the Crime Index in the UCR/NIBRS Program and in its publications and directed the FBI to instead publish simple violent crime totals and property crime totals until a more viable index could be developed.[7]

Although work to develop such an index is still ongoing, UCR/NIBRS Program crime categories continue to provide useful comparisons of specific reported crimes over time and between jurisdictions. It is important to recognize, as you read through the next few pages, that today's UCR/NIBRS Program categories tend to parallel statutory definitions of criminal behavior, but they are not legal classifications—only conveniences created for statistical-reporting purposes. Because many of the definitions of crime used in this textbook are derived from official UCR/NIBRS Program terminology, these definitions may differ from statutory definitions of crime.

The National Incident-Based Reporting System

Beginning in 1988, the FBI's UCR Program initiated development of a new national crime-collection effort called the **National Incident-Based Reporting System (NIBRS)**. NIBRS represents a significant redesign of the original UCR Program. Whereas the original UCR system was summary based, the newly enhanced NIBRS is incident driven (Table 1). Under NIBRS, city, county, state, and federal law enforcement agencies throughout the country furnish detailed data on crime and arrest activities at the incident level either to the individual state incident-based reporting programs or directly to the federal NIBRS Program.

National Incident-Based Reporting System (NIBRS)
An incident-based reporting system that collects detailed data on every single crime occurrence. NIBRS data are replacing the kinds of summary data that have traditionally been provided by the FBI's Uniform Crime Reporting Program.

NIBRS is not a separate report; rather it is the new methodology underlying the contemporary UCR system—hence our use of the term *UCR/NIBRS* in describing today's Uniform Crime Reporting Program. Whereas the old UCR system depended on statistical tabulations of crime data, which were often little more than frequency counts, the new UCR/NIBRS system gathers many details about each criminal incident. Included among them is information on place of occurrence, weapon used, type and value of property damaged or stolen, personal characteristics of the offender and the victim, nature of any relationship between the two, and disposition of the complaint.

Under UCR/NIBRS, the traditional distinctions between Part I and Part II offenses are being replaced with 22 general offenses: arson, assault, bribery, burglary, counterfeiting, embezzlement, extortion, forcible sex offenses, fraud, gambling, homicide, kidnapping, larceny, motor vehicle theft, narcotics offenses, nonforcible sex offenses, pornography, prostitution, receiving stolen property, robbery, vandalism, and weapons violations. Other offenses on which UCR/NIBRS data are being gathered include bad checks, vagrancy, disorderly conduct, driving under the influence, drunkenness, nonviolent family offenses, liquor-law violations, Peeping Tom activity, runaways, trespassing, and a general category of all "other" criminal law violations. UCR/NIBRS also collects data on an expanded array of attributes involved in the commission of offenses, including whether the offender is suspected of using alcohol, drugs, or narcotics or may have used a computer in the commission of the offense.

TABLE 1
Differences between Traditional UCR and Enhanced UCR/NIBRS Reporting

Traditional UCR	Enhanced UCR/NIBRS
Consists of monthly aggregate crime counts	Consists of individual incident records for the eight major crimes and 38 other offenses, with details on offense, victim, offender, and property involved
Records one offense per incident, as determined by the hierarchy rule, which suppresses counts of lesser offenses in multiple-offense incidents	Records each offense occurring in an incident
Does not distinguish between attempted and completed crimes	Distinguishes between attempted and completed crimes
Records rape of females only	Records rape of males and females
Collects assault information in five categories	Restructures definition of *assault*
Collects weapon information for murder, robbery, and aggravated assault	Collects weapon information for all violent offenses
Provides counts on arrests for the eight major crimes and 21 other offenses	Provides details on arrests for the eight major crimes and 49 other offenses

Source: Adapted from *Effects of NIBRS on Crime Statistics*, BJS Special Report (Washington, DC: Bureau of Justice Statistics, 2000), p. 1.

The FBI began accepting crime data in NIBRS format in January 1989. Although the bureau intended to have NIBRS fully in place by 1999, delays have been routine, and the NIBRS format has not yet been fully adopted.[8] Because it is a flexible system, changes continue to be made in the data gathered under UCR/NIBRS. In 2003, for example, three new data elements were added to the survey to collect information on law enforcement officers killed and assaulted. Another new data element has been added to indicate the involvement of gang members in reported offenses.

The goals of the innovations introduced under NIBRS are to enhance the quantity, quality, and timeliness of crime-data collection by law enforcement agencies and to improve the methodology used for compiling, analyzing, auditing, and publishing the collected data. A major advantage of UCR/NIBRS, beyond the sheer increase in the volume of data collected, is the ability that NIBRS provides to break down and combine crime offense data into specific information.[9]

In keeping with the FBI's interest in technological improvements and in order to make reports of crime data more widely available, in 2006 the FBI moved all UCR/NIBRS data reporting to the Internet and stopped paper production of its annual publication, *Crime in the United States*. Efforts to improve the usefulness of electronic versions continue. The latest edition of *Crime in the United States* can be viewed at **Library Extra 2**. To learn more about the effects of NIBRS innovations on crime statistics, including comparisons of traditional UCR summary data with the newer, more detailed UCR/NIBRS data, see **Web Extra 4**. Finally, the BJS provides an NIBRS information website, which can be accessed via **Web Extra 5**.

Other changes in crime reporting were brought about by the 1990 Crime Awareness and Campus Security Act, which requires colleges to publish annual security reports.[10] Most campuses share crime data with the FBI, increasing the reported national incidence of a variety of offenses. The U.S. Department of Education reported that 55 murders and 3,287 forcible sex offenses occurred on and around college campuses in 2008. Also reported were 4,562 robberies, 5,026 aggravated assaults, 31,851 burglaries, and 7,465 motor vehicle thefts.[11] Although these numbers may seem high, it is important to realize that except for the crimes of rape and sexual assault, college students experience violence at average annual rates that are lower than those for nonstudents in the same age group.[12] Rates of rape and sexual assault do not differ statistically between students and nonstudents. For the latest campus crime statistics, see **Web Extra 6**. **Library Extra 3** provides statistical information on the sexual victimization of college women.

Historical Trends

Most UCR/NIBRS information is reported as a rate of crime. Rates are computed as the number of crimes per some unit of population. National reports generally make use of large units of population, such as 100,000 people. Hence, the rate of rape reported by the UCR/NIBRS Program for 2009 was 28.3 forcible rapes per every 100,000 inhabitants of the United States.[13] Rates allow for a meaningful comparison over areas and across time. The rate of reported rape for 1960, for example, was only about 10 per 100,000. We expect the number of crimes to increase as population grows, but rate increases are cause for concern because they indicate that reports of crime are increasing faster than the population is growing. Rates, however, require interpretation. Since the definition of rape that the FBI uses in reporting statistics on that crime includes only female victims, the rate of victimization might be more meaningfully expressed in terms of every 100,000 female inhabitants (56.6 in 2009). Similarly, although there is a tendency to judge an individual's risk of victimization based on rates, such judgments tend to be inaccurate since they are based purely on averages and do not take into consideration individual life circumstances, such as place of residence, wealth, and educational level. While rates may tell us about aggregate conditions and trends, we must be very careful when applying them to individual cases.

Since the FBI's UCR Program began, there have been three major shifts in crime rates—and we now seem to be witnessing the beginning of a fourth. The first occurred during the early 1940s, when crime decreased sharply due to the large number of young men who entered military service during World War II. Young males make up the most crime-prone segment of the population, and their deployment overseas did much to lower crime rates at home. From 1933 to 1941, the Crime Index declined from 770 to 508 offenses per every 100,000 members of the American population.[14]

The second noteworthy shift in offense statistics was a dramatic increase in most forms of crime between 1960 and the early 1990s. Several factors contributed to the increase in reported crime during this period. One was also linked to World War II. With the end of the war and the return of millions of young men to civilian life, birthrates skyrocketed between 1945 and 1955, creating a postwar baby boom. By 1960, the first baby boomers were teenagers—and had entered a crime-prone age. This disproportionate number of young people produced a dramatic increase in most major crimes.

Other factors contributed to the increase in reported crime during the same period. Modified reporting requirements made it less stressful for victims to file police reports, and the publicity associated with the rise in crime sensitized victims to the importance of reporting. Crimes that might have gone undetected in the past began to figure more prominently in official statistics. Similarly, the growing professionalization of some police departments resulted in greater and more accurate data collection, making some of the most progressive departments appear to be associated with the largest crime increases.[15]

The 1960s were tumultuous years. The Vietnam War, a vibrant civil rights struggle, the heady growth of secularism, a dramatic increase in the divorce rate, diverse forms of "liberation," and the influx of psychedelic and other drugs all combined to fragment existing institutions. Social norms were blurred, and group control over individual behavior declined substantially. The "normless" quality of American society in the 1960s contributed greatly to the rise in crime.

From 1960 to 1980, crime rates rose from 1,887 to 5,950 offenses per every 100,000 U.S. residents. In the early 1980s, when postwar boomers began to age out of the crime-prone years and American society emerged from the cultural drift that had characterized the previous 20 years, crime rates leveled out briefly. Soon, however, an increase in drug-related criminal activity led crime rates—especially violent crime rates—to soar once again. Crime rates peaked during the early 1990s (Figure 2).

> Crime is like cutting grass. Just because you cut it down doesn't mean it's going to stay there.
>
> —Joseph R. Biden, Jr., vice president of the United States[i]

A third major shift came with a significant decline in the rates of most major crimes being reported between 1991 and 2009. During these years, the crime rate dropped from 5,897 to 3,466 offenses per every 100,000 residents—sending it down to levels not seen since 1975. The U.S. Department of Justice suggests various reasons for the decline:[16]

- A coordinated, collaborative, and well-funded national effort to combat crime, beginning with the Safe Streets Act of 1968 and continuing through the USA PATRIOT Act of 2001
- Stronger, better-prepared criminal justice agencies, resulting from increased spending by federal and state governments on crime-control programs
- The growth in popularity of innovative police programs, such as community policing
- A strong victims' movement and enactment of the 1984 federal Victims of Crime Act and the 1994 Violence against Women Act (discussed later in this chapter), which established the Office for Victims of Crime in the U.S. Department of Justice
- Sentencing reform, including various "get tough on crime" initiatives
- A substantial growth in the use of incarceration due to changes in sentencing law practice
- The "war on drugs," begun in the 1970s,[17] which resulted in stiff penalties for drug dealers and repeat drug offenders
- Advances in forensic science and enforcement technology, including the increased use of real-time communications, the growth of the Internet, and the advent of DNA evidence

More important than new strict laws, an expanded justice system and police funding, or changes in crime-fighting technologies, however, may have been influential economic and demographic factors that were largely beyond the control of policymakers but that combined to produce substantial decreases in rates of crime—including economic expansion

FIGURE 2
American Crime Rates: Historical Trends

1933–1959

From 1933 to 1941, the crime rate declined from 770 to 508 offenses per every 100,000 Americans.

In 1941 crime decreased sharply based on the large numbers of young men entering the military during WWII.
Young men make up the most crime-prone segment of the population, and their removal to European and Pacific theaters of war reduced the incidence of offending throughout the country.

1960–1989

From 1960 to 1980, crime rates rose from 1,887 to 5,950 offenses per every 100,000 Americans.

Starting around 1960, crime rates began to increase based on several factors.
The end of the war brought many young men home to the U.S., and birthrates skyrocketed in the years between 1945 and 1955. By 1960 these baby boomers had become teenagers and had entered a crime-prone age.
Also, reporting procedures were simplified and publicity surrounding crime increased the number of reports. Police agencies were becoming more professional, resulting in increased data and more accurate data collection.
Moreover, the 1960s were tumultuous years. The Vietnam War, civil rights struggles, and an influx of drugs combined to create an imbalance in society that led to an increase in crime.

1933 1937 1941 1945 1949 1963 1967 1960 1963 1967 1975 1979 1983 1987

and a significant shift in demographics caused by the aging of the population. During the 1990s, unemployment decreased by 36% in the United States while the number of people ages 20 to 34 declined by 18%. Hence, it may have been the ready availability of jobs combined with demographic shifts in the population—not the official efforts of policymakers—that produced a noteworthy decrease in crime during the 1990s. Read noted criminologist Alfred Blumstein's analysis of crime's decline in **Library Extra 4** to learn more about why crime rates fell during the 1990s.

▲ Los Angeles emergency personnel working at the scene of an apparent gang-related shooting at Sunset Boulevard and Pacific Coast Highway. Some experts fear that violent crime may be starting to rise in big cities after two decades of decline. What would be the consequences for American cities if crime were to increase?
AP Photo/Andrew McKenzie

A fourth shift in crime trends seems to be starting now. Some think that recent economic uncertainty, an increased jobless rate among unskilled workers, the growing number of ex-convicts who are back on the streets, the recent growth in the teenage population in this country, the increasing influence of gangs, copycat crimes, and the lingering social disorganization brought on by natural disasters like Hurricane Katrina in 2005 may lead to sustained increases in crime.[18] "We're probably done seeing declines in crime rates for some time to come," says Jack Riley, director of the Public Safety and Justice Program at RAND Corporation in Santa Monica, California. "The question," says Riley, "is how strong and how fast will those rates [rise], and what tools do we have at our disposal to get ahead of the curve."[19]

In 2006, in an effort to draw attention to spiking rates of violent crime in a number of major cities, the Police Executive Research Forum (PERF) released a report titled *A Gathering Storm: Violent Crime in America.*[20] PERF was concerned that official FBI data would take too long to gather and might be released too late to effectively combat the growing trend in violence that PERF felt it had identified. The information used as the basis for the 2006 PERF report had been compiled from law enforcement executives at a "violent crime summit" held at the Mayflower Hotel in Washington, D.C. PERF said that its data show that there are a number of cities across the country reporting large changes in the extent and nature of violent crime.

A second PERF report, this one titled *Violent Crime in America: 24 Months of Alarming Trends*, was released in 2007 and found even more reason for concern.[21] The report noted that urban violent crime increased significantly in 2006 and that "many cities experienced double-digit or even triple-digit percentage increases in homicides and other violence."

1990–2009 ▶ **2010–present**

From 1991 to 2009, crime rates dropped from 5,897 to 3,466 offenses per every 100,000 Americans.

Strict laws, an expanded justice system, and increased police funding for personnel and for crime-fighting technologies are cited as reasons for the drop in crime. Other changes beyond the control of the police may have played a role as well and include economic expansion and an aging population. During the 1990s, unemployment decreased by 36% and likely contributed to the decline in crime rates.

In recent years, some cities have experienced double-digit and sometimes triple-digit increases in homicides and other violent crimes.

A fourth shift in crime trends may be about to begin. Economic uncertainty, increased jobless rates, a growing number of ex-convicts back on the streets as well as an increase in teen populations and gang activity may soon lead to sustained increases in crime.

1990 1994 1997 2001 2005 2009 2010 2011 2012

Photo sources (from left): Everett Collection/SuperStock, Inc.; Everett Collecti

PERF authors said that the most recent crime statistics showed a worsening of a trend first identified by PERF in mid-2005, "when PERF began to hear rumblings from its members that 'violent crime is making a comeback.' "[22]

Finally, in 2008, the Third Way Culture Program, a Washington, D.C.–based nonpartisan strategy center, released a report with conclusions similar to those reached by PERF. Titled *The Impending Crime Wave*,[23] the Third Way report identified what it called "four dangerous new trends" that it sees leading to heightened rates of serious crime in the near future. Those four trends are described as follows: (1) "the reentry explosion" (seen as "a massive and unprecedented population of prisoners reentering society and returning to their often troubled neighborhoods"); (2) "the lengthening shadow of illegal immigration" (said to attract a new kind of opportunistic criminal who serves members of a shadow economy); (3) "the sprawling parentless neighborhood of the Internet" (which puts children at risk of sexual predation and other crimes); and (4) "the surging youth population" (seen as "a demographic surge that is responsible for a million new teenagers and young adults, who are statistically far more prone to commit crimes than the general population"). The entire Third Way report is available online as **Library Extra 5**.

UCR/NIBRS in Transition

Reports of crime data available through the UCR/NIBRS Program are now going through a transitional phase as the FBI integrates more NIBRS-based data into its official summaries. The transition to NIBRS reporting is complicated by the fact that not only does NIBRS gather more kinds of data than the older summary UCR Program did but the definitions used for certain kinds of criminal activity under NIBRS are different than they were under the traditional UCR Program. The standard reference publication that the FBI designates for use by police departments in scoring and reporting crimes that occur within their jurisdiction is the *Uniform Crime Reporting Handbook*, and it is the most recent edition of that handbook that guides and informs the discussion of crime statistics that you will find in the next few pages. You can access the entire 164-page *Uniform Crime Reporting Handbook* at **Library Extra 6**. A thorough review of that document shows that much of the traditional UCR summary data-reporting terminology and structure remains in place. Learn more about the kinds of information recorded under NIBRS at **Library Extra 7**.

Figure 3 shows the FBI crime clock, which has long been calculated annually as a shorthand way of diagramming crime frequency in the United States. Note that crime clock data

Freedom or Safety? You Decide.
A Dress Code for Bank Customers?

Dark glasses, a hooded sweatshirt, and a hat have been called the "uniform of choice" for bank robbers. In an effort to thwart an increase in robberies, some banks have begun posting requests for customers to remove hats, hoods, and sunglasses before entering financial establishments. In 2009, for example, Houston-area banks began putting up signs requiring that customers remove even their cowboy hats—a request that some saw as going too far. Since Sterling Bank, with 60 branches across Texas, asked customers to follow such rules, none of its branches has been robbed. Graham Painter, a Sterling Bank spokesman, said, "We don't want our regular customers thinking that we're telling them how they ought to dress. But . . . it seems reasonable and not too much to ask to give us an advantage over the robber."

Not all banks, however, are following the trend. "I think what you have to weigh is convenience to customers versus the added benefits in terms of identifying suspects with a measure like this," said Melodie Jackson, spokeswoman for Citizens Bank of Massachusetts. "We're taking a very close look at things."

Nonetheless, dress code signs are becoming commonplace at banks throughout the country, and it is likely that this request will soon become the *de facto* standard at banking and other financial venues.

YOU DECIDE

Are bank "dress codes" asking too much of customers? How would you feel about doing business with a bank that posts requests like those described here?

References: Cindy Horswell, "Some Banks Strike Hats, Sunglasses from Dress Code," *Houston Chronicle*, April 23, 2009; Michael S. Rosenwald and Emily Ramshaw, "Banks Post Dress Code to Deter Robbers," *Boston Globe*, July 13, 2002; and "Missouri Banks Attempt Unmasking Robbers," *Police Magazine* Online, http://www.policemag.com/t_newspick.cfm?rank571952 (accessed October 25, 2009).

FIGURE 3
The FBI Crime Clock

Source: Adapted from Federal Bureau of Investigation, *Crime in the United States, 2009* (Washington, DC: U.S. Department of Justice, 2010).

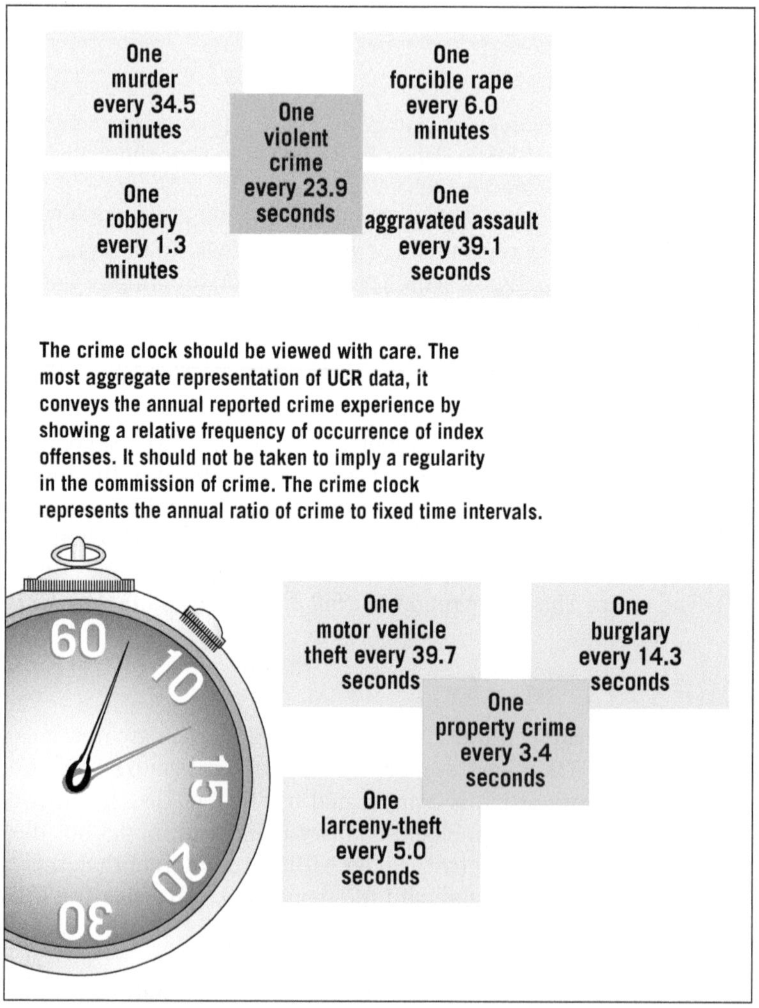

imply a regularity to crime that, in reality, does not exist.[24] Also, although the crime clock is a useful diagrammatic tool, it is not a rate-based measure of criminal activity and does not allow easy comparisons over time. Seven major crimes are included in the figure: murder, forcible rape, robbery, aggravated assault, motor vehicle theft, burglary, and larceny-theft.

The crime clock distinguishes between two categories of offenses: violent crimes and property crimes. The **violent crimes** (also called *personal crimes*) are murder, forcible rape, robbery, and aggravated assault. The **property crimes** are motor vehicle theft, burglary, and larceny-theft. Other than the use of this simple dichotomy, UCR/NIBRS data do not provide a clear measure of the severity of the crimes they cover.

violent crime
A UCR/NIBRS summary offense category that includes murder, rape, robbery, and aggravated assault.

property crime
A UCR/NIBRS summary offense category that includes burglary, larceny-theft, motor vehicle theft, and arson.

clearance rate
A traditional measure of investigative effectiveness that compares the number of crimes reported or discovered to the number of crimes solved through arrest or other means (such as the death of the suspect).

Like most UCR/NIBRS statistics, crime clock data are based on crimes reported to (or discovered by) the police. For a few offenses, the numbers reported are probably close to the numbers that actually occur. Murder, for example, is a crime that is difficult to conceal because of its seriousness. Even when the crime is not immediately discovered, the victim is often quickly missed by family members, friends, and associates, and someone files a "missing persons" report with the police. Auto theft is another crime that is reported in numbers similar to its actual rate of occurrence, probably because insurance companies require that the victim file a police report before they will pay the claim.

A commonly used term in today's UCR/NIBRS reports is **clearance rate**, which refers to the proportion of reported crimes that have been "solved." Clearances are judged primarily on the basis of arrests and do not involve judicial disposition. Once an arrest has been made, a crime is regarded as having been "cleared" for reporting purposes. Exceptional clearances (sometimes called *clearances by exceptional means*) can result when law enforcement authorities believe they know who committed a crime but cannot make an arrest. The perpetrator may, for example, have fled the country or died.

Table 2 summarizes UCR/NIBRS program statistics for 2009.

Part I Offenses

Murder

Murder is the unlawful killing of one human being by another.[25] UCR/NIBRS statistics on murder describe the yearly incidence of all willful and unlawful homicides within the United States. Included in the count are all cases of nonnegligent manslaughter that have been reported to or discovered by the police. Not included in the count are suicides, justifiable homicides (that is, those committed in self-defense), deaths caused by negligence or accident, and murder attempts. In 2009, some 15,241 murders came to the attention of police departments across the United States. First-degree murder is a criminal homicide that is planned; second-degree murder is an intentional and unlawful killing but one that is generally unplanned and that happens "in the heat of the moment."

murder
The unlawful killing of a human being. *Murder* is a generic term that in common usage may include first- and second-degree murder, manslaughter, involuntary manslaughter, and other similar offenses.

The typical mass murderer is extraordinarily ordinary.
—James Alan Fox, Northeastern University

TABLE 2
Major Crimes Known to the Police, 2009 (UCR/NIBRS Part I Offenses)

Offense	Number	Rate per 100,000	Clearance Rate
Personal/Violent Crimes			
Murder	15,241	5.0	66.6%
Forcible rape[a]	88,097	56.6	41.2
Robbery	408,217	133.0	28.2
Aggravated assault	806,843	262.8	56.8
Property Crimes			
Burglary	2,199,125	727.2	12.5
Larceny-theft	6,327,230	2,060.9	21.5
Motor vehicle theft	794,616	258.8	12.4
Arson[b]	58,871	21.3	34.7
U.S. Total	**10,698,240**	**3,465.5**	

[a]Rates of rape are shown per 100,000 females, but approximately half of that rate figures into the table's totals.
[b]Arson can be classified as either a property crime or a violent crime, depending on whether personal injury or loss of life results from its commission. It is generally classified as a property crime, however. Arson statistics are incomplete for 2009.

Source: Adapted from Federal Bureau of Investigation, *Crime in the United States, 2009* (Washington, DC: U.S. Department of Justice, 2010).

Part I offenses
A UCR/NIBRS offense group used to report murder, rape, robbery, aggravated assault, burglary, larceny-theft, motor vehicle theft, and arson, as defined under the FBI's UCR/NIBRS Program.

Murder is the smallest numerical category in the **Part I offenses**. The 2009 murder rate was 5 homicides for every 100,000 residents of the United States. Generally, murder rates peak in the warmest months; in 2009, the greatest number of murders occurred in August. Geographically, murder is most common in the southern states. However, because those states are also the most populous, a meaningful comparison across regions of the country is difficult.

Age is no barrier to murder. Statistics for 2009 reveal that 193 infants (children under the age of one) were victims of homicide, as were 296 people age 75 and over.[26] Young adults between ages 20 and 24 were the most likely to be murdered. Murder perpetrators were also most common in this age group.

The public is properly obsessed with safety. Of industrialized countries, the U.S. has the highest rate of violent crime.
—Bob Moffitt, Heritage Foundation

Firearms are the weapon used most often to commit murder. In 2009, guns were used in 67.1% of all killings. Handguns outnumbered shotguns almost 15 to one in the murder statistics, with rifles used almost as often as shotguns. Knives were used in approximately 13% of all murders. Other weapons included explosives, poison, narcotics overdose, blunt objects like clubs, and hands, feet, and fists.

Only 12.3% of all murders in 2009 were perpetrated by offenders classified as "strangers." In 43.9% of all killings, the relationship between the parties had not yet been determined. The largest category of killers was officially listed as "acquaintances," which probably includes a large number of former friends. Arguments cause most murders (41.2%), but murders also occur during the commission of other crimes, such as robbery, rape, and burglary. Homicides that follow from other crimes are more likely to be impulsive rather than planned.

Murders may occur in sprees, which "involve killings at two or more locations with almost no time break between murders."[27] One spree killer, John Allen Muhammad, 41, part of the "sniper team" that terrorized the Washington, D.C., area in 2002, was arrested along with 17-year-old Jamaican immigrant Lee Boyd Malvo in the random shootings of 13 people in Maryland, Virginia, and Washington, D.C., over a three-week period. Ten of the victims died.[28] In 2003, Muhammad and Malvo were convicted of capital murder; Muhammad was sentenced to die, and Malvo was given a second sentence of life without the possibility of parole in 2006 after he struck a deal with prosecutors in an effort to avoid the death penalty.[29]

▲ Self-confessed serial killer Gary L. Ridgway. The 54-year-old Ridgway, known as the Green River Strangler, is said to be the nation's worst captured serial killer. In 2003, Ridgway admitted to killing 48 women over a 20-year period in the Pacific Northwest. He is now serving life in prison without possibility of parole. What's the difference between serial killers and mass murderers?
Elaine Thompson/Reuters/Landov Media

In contrast to spree killing, mass murder entails "the killing of four or more victims at one location, within one event."[30] Recent mass murderers have included Seung-Hui Cho, who killed 33 people and wounded 20 on the campus of Virginia Polytechnic Institute and State University in Blacksburg, Virginia, in 2007; Timothy McVeigh, who was the antigovernment Oklahoma City bomber; Mohammed Atta and the terrorists he led, who carried out the September 11, 2001, attacks against American targets; and George Hennard, who killed 24 and wounded 20 at a Luby's Cafeteria in Killeen, Texas, in 1991.

Yet another kind of murder, serial murder, happens over time and officially "involves the killing of several victims in three or more separate events."[31] In cases of serial murder, days, months, or even years may elapse between killings.[32] Some of the more infamous serial killers of recent years are the confessed Wichita BTK murderer, Dennis Rader;[33] Jeffrey Dahmer, who received 936 years in prison for the murders of 15 young men (and who was himself later murdered in prison); Ted Bundy, who killed many college-age women; Henry Lee Lucas, now in a Texas prison, who confessed to 600 murders but later recanted (yet was convicted of 11 murders and linked to at least 140 others);[34] Ottis Toole, who was Lucas's partner in crime; cult leader Charles Manson, who is still serving time for ordering followers to kill seven Californians, including famed actress Sharon Tate; Andrei Chikatilo, the Russian "Hannibal Lecter," who killed 52 people, mostly schoolchildren;[35] David Berkowitz, also known as the "Son of Sam," who killed six people on lovers' lanes around New York City; Theodore Kaczynski, the Unabomber, who perpetrated a series of bomb attacks on "establishment" figures; and Seattle's Green River killer, Gary Leon Ridgway, a 54-year-old painter who in 2003 confessed to killing 48 women in the 1980s.

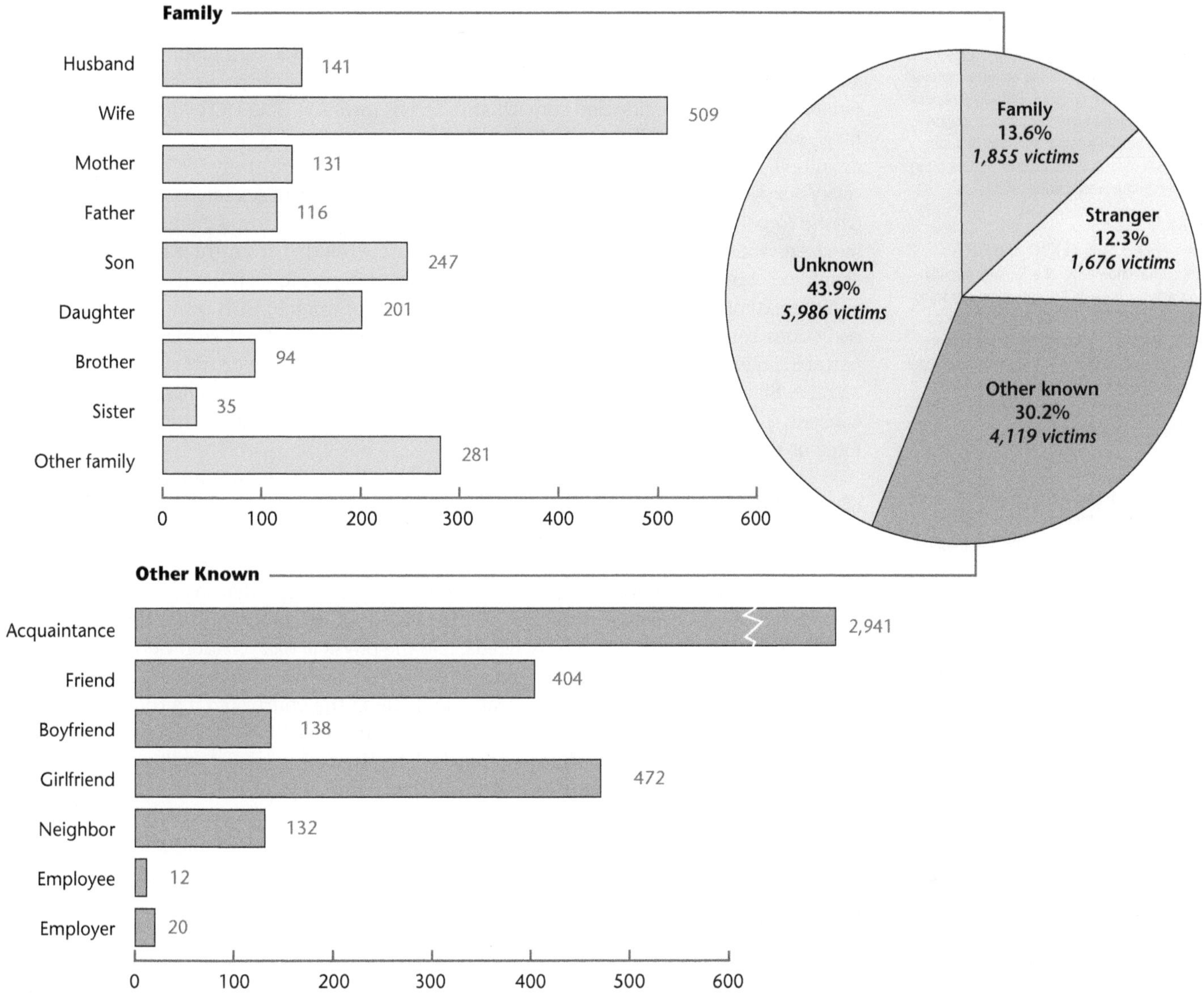

NOTE: Relationship is that of victim to offender. Percentages may not total 100 due to rounding.

FIGURE 4
Murder by Relationship, 2009
Source: Federal Bureau of Investigation, *Crime in the United States, 2009* (Washington, DC: U.S. Department of Justice, 2010).

Federal homicide laws changed in 2004 when President George Bush signed the Unborn Victims of Violence Act.[36] The act, which passed the Senate by only one vote, made it a separate federal crime to "kill or attempt to kill" a fetus "at any stage of development" during an assault on a pregnant woman. The fetal homicide statute, better known as Laci and Conner's Law, after homicide victims Laci Peterson and her unborn son (whom she had planned to name Conner), specifically prohibits the prosecution of "any person for conduct relating to an abortion for which the consent of the pregnant woman, or a person authorized by law to act on her behalf, has been obtained."

Because murder is such a serious crime, it consumes substantial police resources. Consequently, over the years the offense has shown the highest clearance rate of any major crime. Over 66.6% of all homicides were cleared in 2009. Figure 4 shows expanded homicide data from the FBI. Learn more about homicide trends in the United States at **Library Extra 8**.

Forcible Rape

rape
Unlawful sexual intercourse achieved through force and without consent. Broadly speaking, the term *rape* has been applied to a wide variety of sexual attacks and may include same-sex rape and the rape of a male by a female. Some jurisdictions refer to same-sex rape as *sexual battery*.

forcible rape (UCR/NIBRS)
The carnal knowledge of a female, forcibly and against her will. For statistical-reporting purposes, the FBI defines *forcible rape* as "unlawful sexual intercourse with a female, by force and against her will, or without legal or factual consent." Statutory rape differs from forcible rape in that it generally involves nonforcible sexual intercourse with a minor.

sexual battery
The intentional and wrongful physical contact with a person, without his or her consent, that entails a sexual component or purpose.

The term **rape** is often applied to a wide variety of sexual attacks, including same-sex rape and the rape of a male by a female. For statistical-reporting purposes, however, the term **forcible rape** has a specific and somewhat different meaning. The UCR/NIBRS Program defines *forcible rape* as "the carnal knowledge of a female forcibly and against her will."[37] By definition, rapes reported under the summary UCR Program are always of females. Although today our society acknowledges that males can be the victims of sexual assault, the *Uniform Crime Reporting Handbook*, which serves as a statistical-reporting guide for law enforcement agencies, says, "Sexual attacks on males are excluded from the rape category and should be classified as assaults or other sex offenses depending on the nature of the crime and the extent of the injury."[38] While it was not part of original UCR terminology, some jurisdictions refer to same-sex rape as **sexual battery**. Incidents of sexual battery are reportable under today's UCR/NIBRS Program as sexual offenses but do not enter the statistics on rape. Statutory rape, where no force is involved but the victim is younger than the age of consent, is not included in rape statistics, but attempts to commit the rape of a female by force or the threat of force are.

Forcible rape is the least reported of all violent crimes. Estimates are that only one out of every four forcible rapes is reported to the police. An even lower figure was reported by a 1992 government-sponsored study, which found that only 16% of rapes were reported.[39] The victim's fear of embarrassment was the most commonly cited reason for the failure to report. In the past, reports of rapes were often handled in ways that made victims feel further victimized. Information was usually taken by desk sergeants or male detectives who were typically insensitive to victims' needs, and the physical examination victims had to endure was often a traumatizing experience in itself. Also, many states routinely permitted the woman's past sexual history to be revealed in detail in the courtroom if a trial ensued. But the past few decades have seen many changes that have facilitated the accurate reporting of rape and other sex offenses. Trained female detectives often interview the victims, physicians have become better educated in handling the psychological needs of victims, and sexual histories are no longer regarded as relevant in most trials.

UCR/NIBRS statistics show 88,097 reported forcible rapes for 2009, a slight decrease over the number of offenses reported for the previous year. Rape reports, however, have sometimes increased, even in years when reports of other violent crimes have been on the decline. The offense of rape follows homicide in its seasonal variation. The greatest numbers of forcible rapes in 2009 were reported in the hot summer months, while the lowest numbers were recorded in January, February, November, and December.

date rape
The unlawful forced sexual intercourse with a female against her will that occurs within the context of a dating relationship. Date rape, or acquaintance rape, is a subcategory of rape that is of special concern today.

Rape is frequently committed by a man known to the victim, as in the case of **date rape**. Victims may be held captive and subjected to repeated assaults.[40] In the crime of heterosexual rape, any female—regardless of age, appearance, or occupation—is a potential victim. Through personal violation, humiliation, and physical battering, rapists seek a sense of personal aggrandizement and dominance. Victims of rape often experience a lessened sense of personal worth; feelings of despair, helplessness, and vulnerability; a misplaced sense of guilt; and a lack of control over their personal lives.

Contemporary wisdom holds that forcible rape is often a planned violent crime that serves the offender's need for power rather than sexual gratification.[41] The "power thesis" has its origins in the writings of feminist Susan Brownmiller, who argued in 1975 that the primary motivation leading to rape is the male desire to "keep women in their place" and to preserve gender inequality through violence.[42] Although many writers on the subject of forcible rape have generally accepted the power thesis, at least one study has caused some to rethink it. In a 1995 survey of imprisoned serial rapists, Dennis Stevens found that "lust" was reported most often (41%) as "the primary motive for predatory rape."[43]

Statistically speaking, most rapes are committed by acquaintances of the victims and often betray a trust or friendship. Date rape, which falls into this category, appears to be far more common than previously believed. Recently, the growing number of rapes perpetrated with the use of the "date rape drug" Rohypnol has alarmed law enforcement personnel. Rohypnol is an illegal pharmaceutical substance that is virtually tasteless. Available on the black market, it dissolves easily in drinks and can leave anyone who consumes it unconscious for hours, making them vulnerable to sexual assault.

Rape within marriage, which has not always been recognized as a crime, is a growing area of concern in American criminal justice, and many laws have been enacted during the past few decades to deter it. Similarly, even though UCR/NIBRS Program statistics officially report only the rape or attempted rape of females, some state statutes criminalize the rape of a male by a female. When it occurs, this offense is typically statutory rape. In 2009, for example, sixth-grade science teacher Rachel L. Holt, a 34-year-old divorcée from Wilmington, Delaware, was sentenced to ten years in prison after pleading guilty to second-degree rape. She had initially been charged with 28 counts of first-degree rape—which prosecutors said was based on the number of times she had had sex with a 13-year-old male student whom she had plied with alcohol and let drive her car. The intense affair took place over a one-week period.

Learn more about the crime of rape and what people can do to protect themselves at **Web Extra 7**. Read about statistical measures relating to the sexual victimization of women at **Library Extra 9**.

Robbery

Robbery is a personal crime involving a face-to-face confrontation between victim and perpetrator. It is often confused with burglary, which is primarily a property crime. (We'll examine burglary later.) Weapons may be used in robbery, or strong-arm robbery may occur through intimidation. Purse snatching and pocket picking are not classified as robbery by the UCR/NIBRS Program but are included under the category of larceny-theft.

robbery (UCR/NIBRS)
The unlawful taking or attempted taking of property that is in the immediate possession of another by force or violence and/or by putting the victim in fear. Armed robbery differs from unarmed, or strong-arm, robbery in that it involves a weapon. Contrary to popular conceptions, highway robbery does not necessarily occur on a street—and rarely in a vehicle. The term *highway robbery* applies to any form of robbery that occurs outdoors in a public place.

In 2009, individuals were the most common target of robbers. Banks, gas stations, convenience stores, and other businesses were the second most common target, with residential robberies accounting for only 15.2% of the total. In 2009, 408,217 robberies were reported to the police. Of that number, 42.8% were highway robberies, meaning that the crime occurred outdoors, most commonly as the victim was walking. Strong-arm robberies, in which the victim was intimidated but no weapon was used, accounted for 41.1% of the total robberies reported. Guns were used in 42.6% of all robberies, and knives were used in 7.7%. Armed robbers are dangerous; guns are actually discharged in 20% of all robberies.[44]

When a robbery occurs, the UCR/NIBRS Program scores the event as one robbery, even when a number of victims were robbed during the event. With the move toward incident-driven reporting, however, the revised UCR/NIBRS Program will soon make data available on the number of individuals robbed in each incident. Because statistics on crime follow what's known as the *hierarchy rule*, they show only the most serious offense that occurred during a particular episode. Hence, robberies are often hidden when they occur in conjunction with more serious crimes. For example, 3% of robbery victims are also raped, and a large number of homicide victims are robbed.[45]

Robbery is primarily an urban offense, and most arrestees are young male minorities. The robbery rate in cities in 2009 was 179 per every 100,000 inhabitants, whereas it was only 17.2 in rural areas. Eighty-eight percent of those arrested for robbery in 2009 were male, 65.2% were under the age of 25, and 56% were minorities.[46]

Aggravated Assault

In April 2006, Arthur J. McClure, 22, of Fort Myers, Florida, was arrested when he allegedly took the head off of an Easter Bunny costume that he was wearing and punched Erin Johansson of Cape Coral, Florida, after the young mother apparently became upset that a mall photo set was closing ten minutes early.[47] The incident was witnessed by dozens of people, including many children who had gathered to have their pictures taken with the rabbit. McClure, who denied he struck Johansson, was fired after the incident.

assault (UCR/NIBRS)
An unlawful attack by one person upon another. Historically, *assault* meant only the attempt to inflict injury on another person; a completed act constituted the separate offense of *battery*. Under modern statistical usage, however, attempted and completed acts are grouped together under the generic term *assault*.

Assaults are of two types: simple (misdemeanor) and aggravated (felonious). For statistical-reporting purposes, simple assaults typically involve pushing and shoving. While simple assault may also at times include fistfights, the correct legal term to describe such incidents is *battery*. **Aggravated assaults** are distinguished from simple assaults in that either a weapon is used or the assault victim requires medical assistance. When a deadly weapon is employed, an aggravated assault may be charged as attempted murder even if no injury results.[48] In some cases, the UCR/NIBRS Program scores these attempted assaults as aggravated assault because of the potential for serious consequences.

aggravated assault
The unlawful, intentional inflicting, or attempted or threatened inflicting, of serious injury upon the person of another. While *aggravated assault* and *simple assault* are standard terms for reporting purposes, most state penal codes use labels like *first-degree* and *second-degree* to make such distinctions.

A man threatening a police officer with a beer bottle in Sydney, Australia, in December 2005, after ethnic tensions erupted into running battles between police and a mob of thousands of youths. An assault is an unlawful attack upon one person by another. What is the difference between assault and aggravated assault?
Rob Griffith/AP Wide World Photos

In 2009, 806,843 cases of aggravated assault were reported to law enforcement agencies in the United States. Like reports of rape, assault reports were most frequent in the summer months and least frequent in January, February, November, and December. Most aggravated assaults were committed with blunt objects or objects near at hand (34%), while hands, feet, and fists were also commonly used (27%). Less frequently used were knives (19%) and firearms (21%). Because those who commit assaults are often known to their victims, aggravated assaults are relatively easy to solve. About 57% of all aggravated assaults reported to the police in 2009 were cleared by arrest.

Burglary

Although it may involve personal and even violent confrontation, **burglary** is primarily a property crime. Burglars are interested in financial gain and usually fence (that is, illegally sell) stolen items, recovering a fraction of their cash value. About 2.2 million burglaries were reported to the police in 2009. Dollar losses to burglary victims totaled $4.6 billion, with an average loss per offense of $2,096.

The UCR/NIBRS Program employs three classifications of burglary: (1) forcible entry, (2) unlawful entry where no force is used, and (3) attempted forcible entry. In most jurisdictions, force need not be employed for a crime to be classified as burglary. Unlocked doors and open windows are invitations to burglars, and the legal essence of burglary consists not so much of a forcible entry as it does of the intent to trespass and steal. In 2009, 61% of all burglaries were forcible entries, 32.6% were unlawful entries, and 6.5% were attempted forcible entries.[49] The most dangerous burglaries were those in which a household member was home (about 10% of all burglaries).[50] Residents who were home during a burglary suffered a greater than 30% chance of becoming the victim of a violent crime.[51] However, while burglary may evoke images of dark-clothed strangers breaking into houses in which families lie sleeping, burglaries more often are of unoccupied homes and take place during daylight hours.

> Those who insist that crime never pays have never met an identity thief. Identity theft not only pays, it pays extremely well.
> —Jonathan Turley[ii]

The clearance rate for burglary, as for other property crimes that we'll look at later, is generally low. In 2009, the clearance rate for burglary was only 12.5%. Burglars usually do not know their victims, and in cases where they do, burglars conceal their identity by committing their crime when the victim is not present.

burglary (UCR/NIBRS)
The unlawful entry of a structure to commit a felony or a theft (excludes tents, trailers, and other mobile units used for recreational purposes). Under the UCR/NIBRS Program, the crime of burglary can be reported if (1) an unlawful entry of an unlocked structure has occurred, (2) a breaking and entering (of a secured structure) has taken place, or (3) a burglary has been attempted.

identity theft
A crime in which an imposter obtains key pieces of information, such as Social Security and driver's license numbers, to obtain credit, merchandise, and services in the name of the victim. The victim is often left with a ruined credit history and the time-consuming and complicated task of repairing the financial damage.[iii]

larceny-theft (UCR/NIBRS)
The unlawful taking or attempted taking, carrying, leading, or riding away of property from the possession or constructive possession of another. Motor vehicles are excluded. Larceny is the most common of the eight major offenses, although probably only a small percentage of all larcenies is actually reported to the police because of the small dollar amounts involved.

Larceny-Theft

In 2002, 25-year-old Thad Roberts and 22-year-old Tiffany Fowler were arrested in Orlando, Florida, and charged with stealing moon rocks from the Johnson Space Center in Houston, Texas. Roberts had been working as a student intern at the center, and Fowler was a Space Center employee.[52] Officials realized that the lunar samples, along with a number of meteorites, were missing when they discovered that a 600-pound safe had disappeared from the Houston facility. They had been alerted to the loss by messages placed on a website run by a mineralogy club in Antwerp, Belgium, offering "priceless moon rocks collected by Apollo astronauts" for sale for up to $5,000 per gram. Roberts and Fowler were arrested by federal agents pretending to be potential purchasers.

Identity theft is a newer type of crime. See Exhibit 1 for more information on identity theft.

Larceny is another name for theft, and the UCR/NIBRS Program uses the term **larceny-theft** to describe theft offenses. Some states distinguish between simple larceny and grand larceny, categorizing the crime based on the dollar value of what is stolen. Larceny-theft, as defined by the UCR/NIBRS Program, includes the theft of valuables of any dollar amount.

Multiculturalism and Diversity
Race and the Criminal Justice System, Part I

Several years ago, Professor Lani Guinier of the University of Pennsylvania School of Law was interviewed on *Think Tank*, a public television show. Guinier was asked by Ben Wattenberg, the program's moderator, "When we talk about crime, crime, crime, are we really using a code for black, black, black?" Guinier responded this way: "To a great extent, yes, and I think that's a problem, not because we shouldn't deal with the disproportionate number of crimes that young black men may be committing, but because if we can't talk about race, then when we talk about crime, we're really talking about other things, and it means that we're not being honest in terms of acknowledging what the problem is and then trying to deal with it."[1]

Crimes, of course, are committed by individuals of all races. The link between crimes—especially violent, street, and predatory crimes—and race, however, shows a striking pattern. In most crime categories, arrests of black offenders equal or exceed arrests of whites. In any given year, arrests of blacks account for more than 50% of all arrests for violent crimes. Blacks, however, comprise only 12% of the U.S. population. When *rates* (which are based on the relative proportion of racial groups) are examined, the statistics are even more striking. The murder rate among blacks, for example, is ten times that of whites. Similar rate comparisons, when calculated for other violent crimes, show that far more blacks than whites are involved in other street crimes, such as assault, burglary, and robbery. Related studies show that 30% of all young black men in America are under correctional supervision on any given *day*—a far greater percentage than for members of any other ethnic group in the country.[2]

NAACP members protesting the police use of Tasers. Some claim that the justice system puts members of underrepresented groups at risk for unfair treatment. Others say the system is equitable. What do you think?
Rick Wood/Milwaukee Journal Sentinel/*NewsCom*

The real question for anyone interested in the justice system is how to explain such huge race-based disparities. Some authors maintain that racial differences in arrests and in rates of imprisonment are due to the differential treatment of African-Americans at the hands of a discriminatory criminal justice system. University of Wisconsin-Whitewater criminologist Marvin D. Free, Jr., for example, says that the fact that African Americans are underrepresented as criminal justice professionals results in their being overrepresented in arrest and confinement statistics.[3] Some police officers, says Free, are more prone to arrest blacks than whites, frequently arrest blacks without sufficient evidence to support criminal charges, and overcharge in criminal cases involving black defendants—resulting in misleading statistical tabulations that depict blacks as being responsible for a greater proportion of crime than is, in fact, the case.

Even if blacks do engage in more criminal activity than whites, says noted criminologist Thomas J. Bernard, higher rates of offending may be due, at least in part, to their perception that members of their group have historically been treated unfairly by agents of social control—resulting in anger and defiance, which express themselves in criminal activity.[4] Hence, says Bernard, crime—at least crime committed by minority group members—becomes a kind of protest against a system that is perceived as fundamentally unfair.

The question of *actual* fairness of the justice system can be quite different from one of *perceived* fairness. As Katheryn K. Russell of the University of Maryland points out, "Study after study has shown that blacks and whites hold contrary views on the fairness of the criminal justice system's operation; blacks tend to be more cautious in their praise and frequently view the system as unfair and racially biased; by contrast whites have a favorable impression of the justice system. . . . The point is not that whites are completely satisfied with the justice system, but rather that, relative to blacks, they have faith in the system."[5] One reason for such differences may be that blacks are more likely to be victims of police harassment and brutality or may know someone who has been.

According to Russell, inequities in the existing system may propel African Americans into crime and combine with stereotypical images in the popular media to perpetuate what she calls the *criminalblackman myth*. The criminalblackman myth, says Russell, is a stereotypical portrayal of black men as *inherently* more sinister, evil, and dangerous than their white counterparts. The myth of the criminalblackman, adds Russell, is self-perpetuating, resulting in continued frustration, more crime, and growing alienation among African Americans.

---

[1]Quoted in "For the Record," *Washington Post* wire service, March 3, 1994.
[2]Marvin D. Free, Jr., *African-Americans and the Criminal Justice System* (New York: Garland, 1996).
[3]Ibid.
[4]Thomas J. Bernard, "Angry Aggression among the 'Truly Disadvantaged,'" *Criminology*, Vol. 28, No. 1 (1990), pp. 73–96.
[5]Katheryn K. Russell, "The Racial Hoax as Crime: The Law as Affirmation," *Indiana Law Journal*, Vol. 71 (1996), pp. 593–621.

CJ Exhibit 1
Identity Theft: A New Kind of Larceny

In May 2010, 26-year-old Facebook founder and billionaire Mark Zuckerberg announced that his company would provide users with the ability to significantly upgrade personal security settings.[1] Facebook, said Zuckerberg, would enhance privacy choices in order to reduce the amount of personal information that is publicly available by default. Online settings, which Zuckerberg pledged would become easier to find and to change, would also allow users to opt out of third-party applications associated with Facebook.[2] The announcement came after users, privacy advocates, and lawmakers voiced their concerns over lax security features on the highly popular site. Many were concerned that criminals could use Facebook to acquire information about its users and steal their identities.[3]

Identity theft, which involves obtaining credit, merchandise, or services by fraudulent personal representation, is a special kind of larceny. According to a recent federal survey, 9.9 million Americans were victims of identity theft in 2007, although most did not report the crime.[4] Information from the Bureau of Justice Statistics shows that 6.6% of all households in the United States had at least one member who had been a victim of one or more types of identity theft in 2007.[5] BJS also says that identity theft is the fastest-growing type of crime in America.[6]

Identity theft became a federal crime in 1998 with the passage of the Identity Theft and Assumption Deterrence Act.[7] The law makes it a crime whenever anyone "knowingly transfers or uses, without lawful authority, a means of identification of another person with the intent to commit, or to aid or abet, any unlawful activity that constitutes a violation of federal law, or that constitutes a felony under any applicable state or local law."

The 2004 Identity Theft Penalty Enhancement Act[8] added two years to federal prison sentences for criminals convicted of using stolen credit card numbers and other personal data to commit crimes. It also prescribed prison sentences for those who use identity theft to commit other crimes, including terrorism, and it increased penalties for defendants who exceed or abuse the authority of their position in unlawfully obtaining or misusing means of personal identification.

According to the National White Collar Crime Center, identity thieves use several common techniques. Some engage in "Dumpster diving," going through trash bags, cans, or Dumpsters to get copies of checks, credit card and bank statements, credit card applications, or other records that typically bear identifying information. Others use a technique called "shoulder surfing," which involves looking over the victim's shoulder as he or she enters personal information into a computer or on a written form. Eavesdropping is another simple, yet effective, technique that identity thieves often use. Eavesdropping can occur when the victim is using an ATM machine, giving credit card or other personal information over the phone, or dialing the number for a telephone calling card. Criminals can also obtain personal identifying information from potential victims through the Internet. Some Internet users, for example, reply to "spam" (unsolicited e-mail) that promises them all sorts of attractive benefits while requesting identifying data, such as checking account or credit card numbers and expiration dates, along with their name and address.[9] Identity theft perpetrated through the use of high technology depends on the fact that a person's legal and economic identity in contemporary society is largely "virtual" and supported by technology.

▲ World-renowned film director, producer, and screenwriter Steven Spielberg arriving at the Los Angeles premiere of HBO's *The Pacific* in 2010. Spielberg has been a victim of identity theft at least twice. Why is identity theft so prevalent today? How can it be stopped?
AP Photo/Tammie Arroyo

Learn more about identity theft via **Library Extra 10**, and read the National Strategy to Combat Identity Theft at **Library Extra 11**. You can take the ID Theft Safety Quiz online at **Library Extra 12**.

[1]Jon Swartz, "Facebook Simplifies Its Privacy Controls," *USA Today*, May 27, 2010, p. 1B.
[2]David Gelles and Richard Waters, "Facebook Backtracks on Privacy Controls," *Financial Times*, May 27, 2010, 1A.
[3]"Facebook Warns of Gift Card Scam," *MSN Money*, April 13, 2010, http://articles.moneycentral.msn.com/Banking/FinancialPrivacy/facebook-warns-of-gift-card-scam.aspx (accessed May 27, 2010).
[4]United States Postal Service, Postal Inspectors, "Identity Theft Is America's Fastest-Growing Crime," http://www.usps.com/postalinspectors/idthft_ncpw.htm (accessed May 21, 2008).
[5]Lynn Langton and Katrina Baum, *Identity Theft Reported by Households, 2007—Statistical Tables* (Washington, DC: Bureau of Justice Statistics, 2010).
[6]Katrina Baum, *Identity Theft, 2005* (Washington, DC: Bureau of Justice Statistics, 2007).
[7]U.S. Code, Title 18, Section 1028.
[8]Public Law 108–275.
[9]Much of the information in this paragraph is adapted from National White Collar Crime Center, "WCC Issue: Identity Theft," http://www.nw3c.org/papers/Identity_Theft.pdf (accessed May 18, 2010).

The reports specifically list the following offenses as types of larceny (listed here in order of declining frequency):

- Thefts from motor vehicles
- Shoplifting
- Thefts from buildings
- Thefts of motor vehicle parts and accessories
- Thefts of bicycles
- Thefts from coin-operated machines
- Purse snatching
- Pocket picking

From a statistical standpoint, the most common form of larceny in recent years has been theft of motor vehicle parts, accessories, and contents. Tires, wheels, hubcaps, radar detectors, satellite radios, CD players, compact discs, and cellular phones account for many of the items reported stolen (Figure 5).

Thefts of farm animals (known as *rustling*) and thefts of most types of farm machinery also fall into the larceny category. In fact, larceny is such a broad category that it serves as a kind of catchall in the UCR/NIBRS Program. In 1995, for example, Yale University officials filed larceny charges against 25-year-old student Lon Grammer, claiming that he had fraudulently obtained university funds.[53] The university maintained that Grammer had stolen his education by forging college and high school transcripts and concocting letters of recommendation prior to admission. Grammer's alleged misdeeds, which Yale University officials said misled them into thinking that Grammer, a poor student before attending Yale, had an exceptional scholastic record, permitted him to receive $61,475 in grants and loans during the time he attended the school. Grammer was expelled.

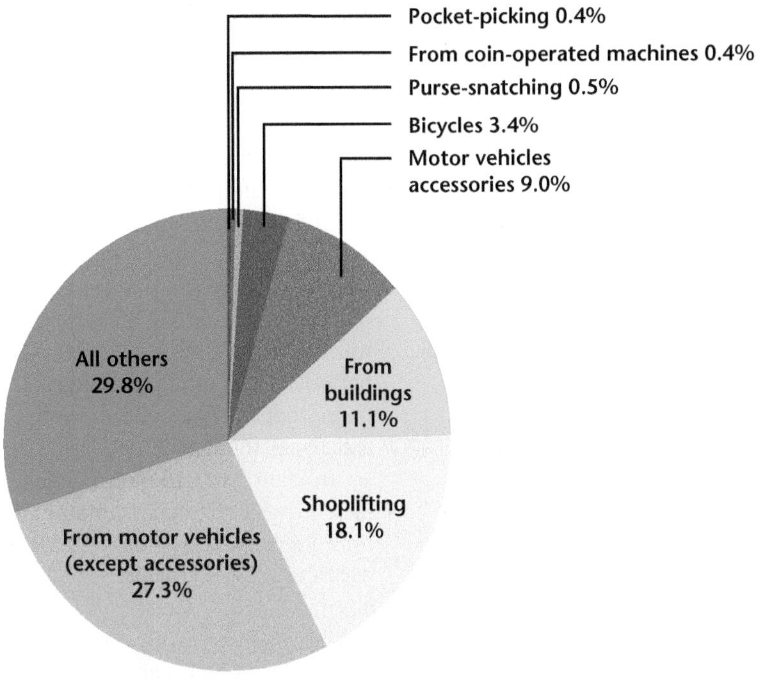

Due to rounding, the percentages may not total 100.

FIGURE 5
Larceny-Theft Distribution, 2009

Source: Federal Bureau of Investigation, *Crime in the United States, 2009* (Washington, DC: U.S. Department of Justice, 2010).

Reported thefts vary widely, in terms of both the objects stolen and their value. Stolen items range from pocket change to a $100 million aircraft. For reporting purposes, crimes entailing embezzlement, con games, forgery, and worthless checks are specifically excluded from the count of larceny. Because larceny has traditionally been considered a crime that requires physical possession of the item appropriated, some computer crimes, including thefts engineered through online access or thefts of software and information, have not been scored as larcenies unless computer equipment, electronic circuitry, or computer media were actually stolen. In 2004, however, the FBI confirmed that it was working with Cisco Systems, Inc., to investigate the possible theft of some of the company's intellectual property.[54] The theft involved approximately 800 megabytes of proprietary software code used to control the company's Internet routers. Since hardware manufactured by Cisco Systems accounts for more than 60% of all routers used on the Internet,[55] officials feared that the lost software could represent a major security threat for the entire Internet.

> In a field like criminal justice, where sensitive issues abound, none is more sensitive than the issue of race and gender bias.
> —Gary LaFree, University of New Mexico

Reports to the police in 2009 showed 6,327,230 larcenies nationwide, with the total value of property stolen placed at $5.5 billion. Larceny-theft is the most frequently reported major crime, according to the UCR/NIBRS Program. It may also be the program's most underreported crime category because small thefts rarely come to the attention of the police. The average value of items reported stolen in 2009 was about $864.

Motor Vehicle Theft

For record-keeping purposes, the UCR/NIBRS Program defines *motor vehicles* as self-propelled vehicles that run on the ground and not on rails. Included in the definition are automobiles, motorcycles, motor scooters, trucks, buses, and snowmobiles. Excluded are trains, airplanes, bulldozers, most farm and construction machinery, ships, boats, and spacecraft; the theft of these would be scored as larceny-theft.[56] Vehicles that are temporarily taken by individuals who have lawful access to them are not thefts. Hence, spouses who jointly own all property may drive the family car, even though one spouse may think of the vehicle as his or her exclusive personal property.

motor vehicle theft (UCR/NIBRS)
The theft or attempted theft of a motor vehicle. *Motor vehicle* is defined as a self-propelled road vehicle that runs on land surface and not on rails. The stealing of trains, planes, boats, construction equipment, and most farm machinery is classified as larceny under the UCR/NIBRS Program, not as motor vehicle theft.

As we said earlier, because most insurance companies require police reports before they will reimburse car owners for their losses, most occurrences of **motor vehicle theft** are reported to law enforcement agencies. Some reports of motor vehicle thefts, however, may be false. People who have damaged their own vehicles in solitary crashes or who have been unable to sell them may try to force insurance companies to "buy" them through reports of theft.

In 2009, 794,616 motor vehicles were reported stolen. The average value per stolen vehicle was $6,505, making motor vehicle theft a $5.2 billion crime. The clearance rate for motor vehicle theft was only 12.9% in 2009. Large city agencies reported the lowest rates of clearance (8.6%), while rural counties had the highest rate (23.6%). Many stolen vehicles are quickly disassembled and the parts resold, since auto parts are much more difficult to identify and trace than are intact vehicles. In some parts of the country, chop shops—which take stolen vehicles apart and sell their components—operate like big businesses, and one shop may strip a dozen or more cars per day.

Motor vehicle theft can turn violent, as in cases of carjacking—a crime in which offenders usually force the car's occupants onto the street before stealing the vehicle. For example, in February 2000, Christy Robel watched helplessly as her six-year-old son, Jake, was dragged to his death after a man jumped behind the wheel of her car and sped off.[57] Robel had left the car running with the boy inside as she made a brief stop at a Kansas City sandwich shop. The carjacker, 35-year-old Kim L. Davis, tried to push Jake from the car as he made his escape, but the boy became entangled in his seat belt and was dragged for five miles at speeds of more than 80 mph. In October 2001, Davis was convicted of murder and was sentenced to spend the rest of his life in prison without possibility of parole.[58] The BJS estimates that around 34,000 carjackings occur annually and account for slightly more than 1% of all motor vehicle thefts.[59] Arrest reports for motor vehicle theft show that the typical offender is a young male: 56% of all arrestees in 2009 were under the age of 25, and 82.2% were male.

Arson

arson (UCR/NIBRS)
Any willful or malicious burning or attempt to burn, with or without intent to defraud, a dwelling house, public building, motor vehicle or aircraft, personal property of another, and so on. Some instances of arson result from malicious mischief, some involve attempts to claim insurance money, and some are committed in an effort to disguise other crimes, such as murder, burglary, or larceny.

The UCR/NIBRS Program received crime reports from nearly 18,000 law enforcement agencies in 2009.[60] Of these, only 14,957 submitted data on **arson** (the intentional burning of property). Even fewer agencies provided complete data as to the type of property burned, the estimated monetary value of the property, the ownership, and so on. Arson data include only the fires that are determined through investigation to have been willfully or maliciously set. Fires of unknown or suspicious origin are excluded from arson statistics.[61]

The intentional and unlawful burning of structures (houses, storage buildings, manufacturing facilities, and so on) was the type of arson reported most often in 2009 (22,867 instances). The arson of vehicles was the second most common category, with 14,577 such burnings reported. The average dollar loss per instance of arson in 2009 was $17,411, and total nationwide property damage was placed at close to $1 billion.[62] As with most property crimes, the clearance rate for arson was relatively low—34.7% nationally. The crime of arson exists in a kind of statistical limbo. In 1979, Congress ordered that it be added as an eighth Part I offense. Today, however, many law enforcement agencies still have not begun making regular reports to the FBI on arson offenses in their jurisdictions.

Some of these difficulties have been resolved through the Special Arson Program, authorized by Congress in 1982. In conjunction with the National Fire Data Center, the FBI now operates a Special Arson Reporting System, which focuses on fire departments across the nation. The reporting system is designed to provide data to supplement yearly UCR arson tabulations.[63]

Career Profile
Instructor of Criminal Justice

Name: Amy Carrino

Position: Instructor of Criminal Justice, Gateway Community and Technical College, Park Hills, Kentucky

Colleges attended: Northern Kentucky University (BA, Political Science), Salmon P. Chase College of Law (JD)

What criminal justice-related jobs have you held? GED and life skills instructor at three correctional transitional facilities, 1993–2004. Adjunct instructor of Criminal Justice, Gateway Community and Technical College, spring 2009. Full-time instructor of Criminal Justice, Gateway Community and Technical College, fall 2009–present.

What position did you like most? My current position is by far my favorite. It is an honor to teach criminal justice classes to students who will influence our society's future.

What qualities or characteristics most helped you succeed in the field? Dedication to the students you teach and to the institution that employs you. Students must be your top priority in every decision you make. Continue to educate yourself in the best practices that are available, for criminal justice issues and laws are constantly changing and you must prepare your students to enter the workforce. You must make a huge investment in the institution for which you are working. Working as a team member with colleagues is an ongoing process that requires commitment. Hard work, organization, courage to do innovative programming, and passion for your students and your subject area will help you succeed.

What advice would you give students early in their college career to help them find a rewarding job in criminal justice? Be passionate about what you are doing. Become familiar with the idea that you will become a public servant in some form and that serving the public comes with heightened expectations. Take your studies seriously. Be ethical, organized, on time, and acquire all the knowledge you can while you are in school. Honesty, integrity, hard work, and dedication will take you far.

Source: Reprinted with permission of Amy Carrino, Ph.D. Photo courtesy of Amy Carrino. Logo courtesy of Gateway Community and Technical College.

Part II Offenses

The UCR Program also includes information on what the FBI calls **Part II offenses**. Part II offenses, which are generally less serious than those that make up the Part I offenses category, include a number of social-order, or so-called victimless, crimes. The statistics on Part II offenses are for recorded arrests, not for crimes reported to the police. The logic inherent in this form of scoring is that most Part II offenses would never come to the attention of the police were it not for arrests. Part II offenses are shown in Table 3, with the number of estimated arrests made in each category for 2009.

Part II offenses
A UCR/NIBRS offense group used to report arrests for less serious offenses. Agencies are limited to reporting only arrest information for Part II offenses, with the exception of simple assault.

TABLE 3
UCR/NIBRS Part II Offenses, 2009

Offense Category	Number of Arrests
Simple assaults	1,319,458
Forgery and counterfeiting	85,844
Fraud	210,255
Embezzlement	17,920
Stolen property (e.g., receiving)	105,303
Vandalism	270,439
Weapons (e.g., carrying)	166,334
Prostitution and related offenses	71,355
Sex offenses (e.g., statutory rape)	77,326
Drug-abuse violations	1,663,582
Gambling	10,360
Offenses against the family (e.g., nonsupport)	114,564
Driving under the influence	1,440,409
Liquor-law violations	570,333
Public drunkenness	594,300
Disorderly conduct	655,322
Vagrancy	33,388
Curfew violations/loitering	112,593
Runaways	93,434

Source: Adapted from Federal Bureau of Investigation, *Crime in the United States, 2009* (Washington, DC: U.S. Department of Justice, 2010).

A Part II offense arrest is counted each time a person is taken into custody. As a result, the statistics in Table 3 do not report the number of suspects arrested but rather the number of arrests made. Some suspects were arrested more than once.

The National Crime Victimization Survey

2 Describe the history and nature of the National Crime Victimization Survey Program, and explain what it can tell us about crime in the United States today.

dark figure of crime
Crime that is not reported to the police and that remains unknown to officials.

A second major source of statistical data about crime in the United States is the NCVS, which is based on victim self-reports rather than on police reports. The NCVS is designed to estimate the occurrence of all crimes, whether reported or not.[64] The NCVS was first conducted in 1972. It built on efforts in the late 1960s by both the National Opinion Research Center and the President's Commission on Law Enforcement and the Administration of Justice to uncover what some had been calling the **dark figure of crime**. This term refers to those crimes that are not reported to the police and that remain unknown to officials. Before the development of the NCVS, little was known about such unreported and undiscovered offenses.

Early data from the NCVS changed the way criminologists thought about crime in the United States. The use of victim self-reports led to the discovery that crimes of all types were more prevalent than UCR statistics indicated. Many cities were shown to have victimization rates that were more than twice the rate of reported offenses. Others, like Saint Louis, Missouri, and Newark, New Jersey, were found to have rates of victimization that very nearly approximated reported crime. New York, often thought of as a high-crime city, was discovered to have one of the lowest rates of self-reported victimization.

NCVS data are gathered by the BJS through a cooperative arrangement with the U.S. Census Bureau.[65] Twice each year, Census Bureau personnel interview household members in a nationally representative sample of approximately 43,000 households (about 76,000 people). Approximately 150,000 interviews of individuals age 12 or older are conducted annually. Households stay in the sample for three years, and new households rotate into the sample regularly.

The NCVS collects information on crimes suffered by individuals and households, whether or not those crimes were reported to law enforcement. It estimates the proportion of each crime type reported to law enforcement, and it summarizes the reasons that victims give for reporting or not reporting. BJS statistics are published in annual reports titled *Criminal Victimization* and *Crime and the Nation's Households.*

Using definitions similar to those employed by the UCR/NIBRS Program, the NCVS includes data on the national incidence of rape, sexual assault, robbery, assault, burglary, personal and household larceny, and motor vehicle theft. Not included are murder, kidnapping, and victimless crimes (crimes that, by their nature, tend to involve willing participants). Commercial robbery and the burglary of businesses were dropped from NCVS reports in 1977. The NCVS employs a hierarchical counting system similar to that of the pre-NIBRS system: It counts only the most "serious" incident in any series of criminal events perpetrated against the same individual. Both completed and attempted offenses are counted, although only people 12 years of age and older are included in household surveys.

NCVS statistics for recent years reveal the following:

- Approximately 15% of American households are touched by crime every year.
- About 20 million victimizations occur each year.
- City residents are almost twice as likely as rural residents to be victims of crime.
- About half of all violent crimes, and slightly more than one-third of all property crimes, are reported to police.[66]
- Victims of crime are more often men than women.
- Younger people are more likely than the elderly to be victims of crime.
- Blacks are more likely than members of other racial groups to be victims of violent crimes.
- Violent victimization rates are highest among people in lower-income families.

A report by the BJS found that in 2009, NCVS crime rates had reached their lowest level since the survey began.[67] Declines began in the mid-1990s, with violent crime rates dropping

TABLE 4
Comparison of UCR/NIBRS and NCVS Data, 2009

Offense	UCR/NIBRS	NCVS[a]
Personal/Violent Crimes		
Homicide	15,241	—
Forcible rape[b]	88,097	125,910
Robbery	408,217	533,790
Aggravated assault	806,843	823,340
Property Crimes		
Burglary[c]	2,199,125	3,134,920
Larceny	6,327,230	11,709,830
Motor vehicle theft	794,616	735,770
Arson[d]	58,871	—
Total Crimes	**10,698,240**	**20,057,180**

[a] NCVS data cover "households touched by crime," not absolute numbers of crime occurrences. More than one victimization may occur per household, but only the number of households in which victimizations occur enters the tabulations.

[b] NCVS statistics include both rape and sexual assault.

[c] NCVS statistics include only household burglary and attempts.

[d] Arson data are incomplete in the UCR/NIBRS and are not reported by the NCVS.

Source: Compiled from Federal Bureau of Investigation, *Crime in the United States, 2009* (Washington, DC: U.S. Department of Justice, 2010); and Jennifer L. Truman and Michael R. Rand, *Criminal Victimization, 2009* (Washington, DC: Bureau of Justice Statistics, 2010).

60% between 1993 and 2009.[68] While these statistics indicate that in recent years crime rates have declined, UCR statistics, which go back almost another 40 years, show that today's crime rate is still many times what it was in the early and middle years of the twentieth century.[69] A comparison of UCR/NIBRS and NCVS data can be found in Table 4. Explore the latest NCVS data at **Web Extra 8**. Like the UCR/NIBRS, the NCVS is also undergoing change. The Bureau of Justice Statistics says that an impending redesign of the NCVS will "improve its methodology, assure its sustainability, increase its value to national and local stakeholders, and better meet the challenges of measuring the extent, characteristics, and consequences of criminal victimization."[70] Learn more about the redesign of the NCVS at **Web Extra 9**.

Many researchers trust NCVS data more than UCR/NIBRS data because they believe that self-reports provide a more accurate gauge of criminal incidents than do police reports. Learn more about the use of self-report surveys in the measurement of crime and delinquency via **Library Extras 13** and **14**.

Comparisons of the UCR and the NCVS

3 Point out significant differences between the UCR and the NCVS.

As mentioned earlier in this chapter, crime statistics from the UCR/NIBRS and the NCVS reveal crime patterns that are often the bases for social policies created to deter or reduce crime. These policies also build on explanations for criminal behavior found in more elaborate interpretations of the statistical information. Unfortunately, however, researchers too often forget that statistics, which are merely descriptive, can be weak in explanatory power. For example, NCVS data show that "household crime rates" are highest for households (1) headed by blacks, (2) headed by younger people, (3) with six or more members, (4) headed by renters, and (5) located in central cities.[71] Such findings, combined with statistics that show that most crime occurs among members of the same race, have led some researchers to conclude that values among certain black subcultural group members both propel them into crime and make them targets of criminal victimization. The truth may be, however, that crime is more a function of inner-city location than of culture. From simple descriptive statistics, it is difficult to know which is the case. Learn more about the UCR/NIBRS Program and the NCVS, and see how they compare, by viewing **Web Extra 10**.

Like most statistical data-gathering programs in the social sciences, the UCR/NIBRS and the NCVS programs are not without problems. Because UCR/NIBRS data are based primarily on citizens' crime reports to the police, there are several inherent difficulties.

Multiculturalism and Diversity
Race and the Criminal Justice System, Part II

In *The Myth of a Racist Criminal Justice System*, William Wilbanks claims that while the practice of American criminal justice may have been significantly racist in the past and while some vestiges of racism may indeed remain, the system today is by and large objective in its processing of criminal defendants.[1] Using statistical data, Wilbanks shows that "at every point from arrest to parole there is little or no evidence of an overall racial effect, in that the percentage outcomes for blacks and whites are not very different."[2] Wilbanks claims to have reviewed "all the available studies that have examined the possible existence of racial discrimination from arrest to parole." In essence, he says, "this examination of the available evidence indicates that support for the 'discrimination thesis' is sparse, inconsistent, and frequently contradictory."

Wilbanks is careful to counter arguments advanced by those who continue to suggest that the system is racist. He writes, for example, "Perhaps the black/white gap at arrest is a product of racial bias by the police in that the police are more likely to select and arrest black than white offenders. The best evidence on this question comes from the National Crime Survey [that] interviews 130,000 Americans each year about crime victimization. . . . The percent of offenders described by victims as being black is generally consistent with the percent of offenders who are black according to arrest figures."

Other contemporary research also appears to discount claims that today's American justice system is racist. In 2006, for example, Pauline K. Brennan, a criminologist at the University of Nebraska at Omaha, examined the effects of race and ethnicity on the sentencing of female misdemeanants and found that "race/ethnicity did not directly affect sentencing."[3] Brennan discovered, however, that black and Hispanic females "were more likely to receive jail sentences than their White counterparts due to differences in things like prior record and charge severity."

Similarly, in 2008, a review of the impact of race on parole decision making found that "race did not have a significant impact on decisions at the preliminary screening stage or the parole release stage."[4]

A fundamental critique of statistical studies such as these, however, was offered by Coramae Richey Mann (1931–2002), professor emeritus of criminal justice at the University of Illinois at Chicago, who said that overreliance on quantitative or statistical data fails to capture the reality of racial discrimination within the justice system.[5] White victims, said Mann, tend to overreport being victimized by black offenders because they often misperceive Hispanic and other minority offenders as black. Similarly, she said, black victims are sometimes reluctant to report victimization—especially at the hands of whites.

Mann's arguments are discounted by those who point out that the statistics appear to be overwhelming. *If* they are accurate, then another question emerges: Why do blacks commit more crimes? Wilbanks says, "The assertion that the criminal justice system is not racist does not address the reasons why blacks appear to offend at higher rates than whites before coming into contact with the criminal justice system. . . . It may be that racial discrimination in American society has been responsible for conditions (for example, discrimination in employment, housing, and education) that lead to higher rates of offending by blacks."

Marvin Free, Jr., suggests that African Americans are still systematically denied equal access to societal resources that would allow for full participation in American society—resulting in a higher rate of law violation. In a work that considers such issues in great detail, John Hagan and Ruth D. Peterson acknowledge the reality of higher crime rates among some ethnic minorities and attribute them to (1) concentrated poverty, (2) joblessness, (3) family disruption, and (4) racial segregation.[6]

[1] William Wilbanks, *The Myth of a Racist Criminal Justice System* (Monterey, CA: Brooks/Cole, 1987).
[2] William Wilbanks, "The Myth of a Racist Criminal Justice System," *Criminal Justice Research Bulletin*, Vol. 3, No. 5 (Huntsville, TX: Sam Houston State University, 1987), p. 2.
[3] Pauline K. Brennan, "Sentencing Female Misdemeanants: An Examination of the Direct and Indirect Effects of Race/Ethnicity," *Justice Quarterly*, Vol. 23, No. 1 (March 2006), pp. 60–95.
[4] Kathryn D. Morgan and Brent Smith, "The Impact of Race on Parole Decision-Making," *Justice Quarterly*, Vol. 25, No. 2 (June 2008), pp. 411–412.
[5] Coramae Richey Mann, "The Reality of a Racist Criminal Justice System," in Barry W. Hancock and Paul M. Sharp, eds., *Criminal Justice in America: Theory, Practice, and Policy* (Upper Saddle River, NJ: Prentice Hall, 1996), pp. 51–59.
[6] John Hagan and Ruth D. Peterson, *Crime and Inequality* (Stanford, CA: Stanford University Press, 1995).

First, not all people report when they are victimized. Some victims are afraid to contact the police, while others may not believe that the police can do anything about the offense. Second, certain kinds of crimes are reported rarely, if at all. These include victimless crimes, also known as *social-order offenses*, such as drug use, prostitution, and gambling. Similarly, white-collar and high-technology offenses, such as embezzlement and computer crime—because they often go undiscovered—probably enter the official statistics only rarely. Third, victims' reports may not be entirely accurate. Victims' memories may be faulty, victims may feel the need to impress or please the police, or they may be under pressure from others to misrepresent the facts. Finally, all reports are filtered through a number of bureaucratic levels, which increases the likelihood that inaccuracies will enter the data. As noted methodologist Frank Hagan points out, "The government is very keen on amassing statistics. They collect them, add to them, raise them to the nth power, take the cube root, and prepare wonderful diagrams. But what you must never forget is that every one of these figures comes in the first instance from the *chowty dar* [village watchman], who puts down what he damn pleases."[72]

In contrast to the UCR/NIBRS dependence on crimes reported by victims who seek out the police, the NCVS relies on door-to-door surveys and personal interviews for its data. Survey results, however, may be skewed for several reasons. First, no matter how objective survey questions may appear to be, survey respondents inevitably provide their personal interpretations and descriptions of what may or may not have been a criminal event. Second, by its very nature, the survey includes information from those people who are most willing to talk to surveyors; more reclusive people are less likely to respond regardless of the level of victimization they may have suffered. Also, some victims are afraid to report crimes even to nonpolice interviewers, while others may invent victimizations for an interviewer's sake. As the first page of the NCVS report admits, "Details about the crimes come directly from the victims, and no attempt is made to validate the information against police records or any other source."[73]

Finally, because both the UCR/NIBRS and the NCVS are human artifacts, they contain only data that their creators think appropriate. UCR/NIBRS statistics for 2001, for example, do not include a tally of those who perished in the September 11, 2001, terrorist attacks because FBI officials concluded that the events were too "unusual" to count. Although the FBI's 2001 *Crime in the United States* acknowledges "the 2,830 homicides reported as a result of the events of September 11, 2001," it goes on to say that "these figures have been removed" from the reported data.[74] Crimes resulting from an anomalous event but excluded from reported data highlight the arbitrary nature of the data-collection process itself.

Special Categories of Crime

A **crime typology** is a classification scheme used in the study and description of criminal behavior. There are many typologies, all of which have an underlying logic. The system of classification that derives from any particular typology may be based on legal criteria, offender motivation, victim behavior, characteristics of individual offenders, or the like. Criminologists Terance D. Miethe and Richard C. McCorkle note that crime typologies "are designed primarily to simplify social reality by identifying homogeneous groups of crime behaviors that are different from other clusters of crime behaviors."[75] Hence one common but simple typology contains only two categories of crime: violent and property. In fact, many crime typologies contain overlapping or nonexclusive categories—just as violent crimes may involve property offenses, and property offenses may lead to violent crimes. Thus no one typology is likely to capture all of the nuances of criminal offending.

crime typology
A classification of crimes along a particular dimension, such as legal category, offender motivation, victim behavior, or characteristics of individual offenders.

Social relevance is a central distinguishing feature of any meaningful typology, and it is with that in mind that the remaining sections of this chapter briefly highlight crimes of special importance today. They are crime against women, crime against the elderly, hate crime, corporate and white-collar crime, organized crime, gun crime, drug crime, high-technology and computer crime, and terrorism.

4 Identify the special categories of crime discussed in this chapter, and explain why they are of contemporary significance.

Crime against Women

The victimization of women is a special area of concern, and both the UCR/NIBRS and the NCVS contain data on gender as it relates to victimization. Statistics show that women are victimized less frequently than men in every major personal crime category other than rape.[76] The overall U.S. rate of violent victimization is about 25 per 1,000 males age 12 or older, and 18 per 1,000 females.[77] When women become victims of violent crime, however, they are more likely than men to be injured (29% versus 22%, respectively).[78] Moreover, a larger proportion of women than men make modifications in the way they live because of the threat of crime.[79] Women, especially those living in cities, have become increasingly careful about where they travel and the time of day they leave their homes—particularly if they are unaccompanied—and in many settings are often wary of unfamiliar males.

Date rape, familial incest, spousal abuse, **stalking**, and the exploitation of women through social-order offenses like prostitution and pornography are major issues facing American society today. Testimony before Congress tagged domestic violence as the largest cause of injury to American women.[80] Former Surgeon General C. Everett Koop once identified

stalking
Repeated harassing and threatening behavior by one individual against another, aspects of which may be planned or carried out in secret. Stalking might involve following a person, appearing at a person's home or place of business, making harassing phone calls, leaving written messages or objects, or vandalizing a person's property. Most stalking laws require that the perpetrator make a credible threat of violence against the victim or members of the victim's immediate family.

> Cyberspace has become a fertile field for illegal activity.
> —Linda Fairstein, chief of the Sex Crimes Prosecution Unit, Manhattan District Attorney's Office[iv]

violence against women by their partners as the number one health problem facing women in America.[81] Findings from the National Violence against Women Survey (NVAWS) reveal the following:[82]

- Physical assault is widespread among American women. Fifty-two percent of surveyed women said that they had been physically assaulted as a child or as an adult.
- Approximately 1.9 million women are physically assaulted in the United States each year.
- Eighteen percent of women experienced a completed or attempted rape at some time in their lives.
- Of those reporting rape, 22% were under 12 years old, and 32% were between 12 and 17 years old, when they were first raped.
- Native American and Alaska Native women were most likely to report rape and physical assault, while Asian/Pacific Islander women were least likely to report such victimization. Hispanic women were less likely to report rape than non-Hispanic women.
- Women report significantly more partner violence than men. Twenty-five percent of surveyed women and only 8% of surveyed men said they had been raped or physically assaulted by a current or former spouse, cohabiting partner, or date.
- Violence against women is primarily partner violence. Seventy-six percent of the women who had been raped or physically assaulted since age 18 were assaulted by a current or former husband, cohabiting partner, or date, compared with 18% of the men.
- Women are significantly more likely than men to be injured during an assault. Thirty-two percent of the women and 16% of the men who had been raped since age 18 were injured during their most recent rape; 39% of the women and 25% of the men who were physically assaulted since age 18 were injured during their most recent physical assault.
- Eight percent of surveyed women and 2% of surveyed men said they had been stalked at some time in their lives. According to survey estimates, approximately 1 million women and 371,000 men are stalked annually in the United States.

Learn more about violence against women via **Library Extra 15**.

Survey findings like these show that more must be done to alleviate the social conditions that result in the victimization of women. Suggestions already under consideration call for expansion in the number of federal and state laws designed to control domestic violence, broadening of the federal Family Violence Prevention and Services Act, federal help in setting up state advocacy offices for battered women, increased funding for battered women's shelters, and additional funds for prosecutors and courts to develop spousal abuse units. The federal Violent Crime Control and Law Enforcement Act of 1994 was designed to meet many of these needs through a subsection titled the Violence against Women Act (VAWA). That act signified a major shift in our national response to domestic violence, stalking (which is often part of the domestic-violence continuum), and sexual assault crimes. For the first time in our nation's history, violent crimes against women were addressed in relation to the more general problem of gender inequality.

The VAWA seeks to eradicate violence against women at all levels, and the act allocated $1.6 billion to fight violence against women. Included are funds to (1) educate police, prosecutors, and judges about the special needs of female victims; (2) encourage pro-arrest policies in cases of domestic abuse; (3) provide specialized services for female victims of crime; (4) fund battered women's shelters across the country; and (5) support rape education in a variety of settings nationwide. The law also extends "rape shield law" protections to civil cases and to all criminal cases in order to bar irrelevant inquiries into a victim's sexual history. VAWA was reauthorized by Congress in 2000. Read the text of the original VAWA legislation at **Web Extra 11**.

Multiculturalism and Diversity
Gender Issues in Criminal Justice

The Violent Crime Control and Law Enforcement Act of 1994 included significant provisions intended to enhance gender equality throughout the criminal justice system. Title IV of the Violent Crime Control and Law Enforcement Act, known as the Violence against Women Act (VAWA) of 1994, contains the Safe Streets for Women Act. This act increased federal penalties for repeat sex offenders and requires mandatory restitution for sex crimes, including costs related to medical services (including physical, psychiatric, and psychological care); physical and occupational therapy or rehabilitation; necessary transportation, temporary housing, and child-care expenses; lost income; attorneys' fees, including any costs incurred in obtaining a civil protection order; and any other losses suffered by the victim as a result of the offense. The act also requires that compliance with a restitution order be made a condition of probation or supervised release (if such a sentence is imposed by the court) and provides that violation of the order will result in the offender's imprisonment.

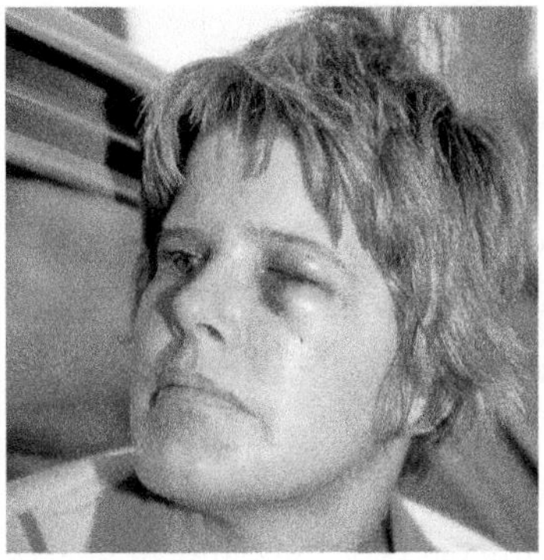

A battered woman posing for police photographers who are documenting her injuries. Intimate partner violence is a problem of special concern to the criminal justice system, and violence against women is an area that is receiving legislative attention, as evidenced by the federal Violence against Women Act. How might laws designed to protect women be improved?
Michael Newman/PhotoEdit Inc.

Chapter 2 of VAWA provided funds for grants to combat violent crimes against women. The purpose of funding was to assist states and local governments to "develop and strengthen effective law enforcement and prosecution strategies to combat violent crimes against women, and to develop and strengthen victim services in cases involving violent crimes against women."

The act also created the crime of crossing state lines in violation of a protection order and the crime of crossing state lines to commit assault on a domestic partner. It established federal penalties for the latter offense of up to life in prison in cases where death results.

Chapter 3 of the act provided funds to increase the "safety for women in public transit and public parks." It authorized up to $10 million in grants through the Department of Transportation to enhance lighting, camera surveillance, and security telephones in public transportation systems used by women.

Chapter 5 of VAWA funded the creation of hot lines, educational seminars, informational materials, and training programs for professionals who provide assistance to victims of sexual assault. Another portion of the law, titled the Safe Homes for Women Act, increased grants for battered women's shelters, encouraged arrest in cases of domestic violence, and provided for the creation of a national domestic-violence hot line to provide counseling, information, and assistance to victims of domestic-violence. The act also mandates that any protection order issued by a state court must be recognized by the other states and by the federal government and must be enforced "as if it were the order of the enforcing state."

VAWA was reauthorized by Congress in 2000 and again in 2005.[1] The 2000 reauthorization provided $3.3 billion in continuation funding and earmarked a portion of the money for programs that coordinate the work of victims' advocates, police, and prosecutors in the fight against domestic violence. The second reauthorization provided continuation monies for critical programs and funded the development of new services to respond to evolving community needs. In recognition of the fact that domestic violence sometimes leaves victims without homes, the 2006 legislation made funds available to expand services to the homeless, including the development of transitional housing options. VAWA will again be up for reauthorization in 2011, about the time that this book goes to press. Reauthorization is expected to pass Congress without difficulty.

[1] VAWA 2005 was signed into law by President George W. Bush on January 5, 2006. It is officially known as the Violence against Women and Department of Justice Reauthorization Act of 2005 (Public Law 109–162).

Finally, the passage of antistalking legislation by all 50 states and the District of Columbia provides some measure of additional protection to women, who comprise 80% of all stalking victims.[83] On the federal level, the seriousness of stalking was addressed when Congress passed the interstate stalking law in 1996.[84] The law[85] also addresses **cyberstalking**, or the use of the Internet by perpetrators seeking to exercise power and control over their victims by threatening them directly or by posting misleading and harassing information about them. Cyberstalking can be especially insidious because it does not require that the perpetrator and the victim be in the same geographic area. Similarly, electronic communication technologies lower the barriers to harassment and threats; a cyberstalker does not need to confront the victim physically.[86] Learn more about stalking and cyberstalking at **Library Extra 16**.

cyberstalking
The use of the Internet, e-mail, and other electronic communication technologies to stalk another person.[v]

Crime against the Elderly

Relative to other age groups, older victims rarely appear in the crime statistics. Criminal victimization seems to decline with age, suggesting that older people are only infrequently targeted by violent and property criminals. Moreover, older people are more likely than younger individuals to live in secure areas and to have the financial means to provide for their own personal security.

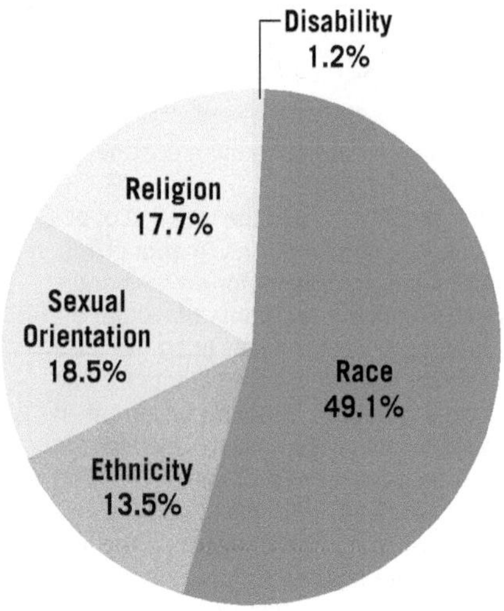

FIGURE 6
Motivation of Hate-Crime Offenders, 2009

Source: Total does not equal 100% due to rounding.
Federal Bureau of Investigation, *Crime in the United States, 2009* (Washington, DC: U.S. Department of Justice, 2010).

Victimization data pertaining to older people come mostly from the NCVS, which, for such purposes, looks at people age 65 and older. The elderly generally experience the lowest rate of victimization of any age group in both violent and property crime categories.[87] Some aspects of crime against older people are worth noting, however. In general, elderly crime victims are more likely than younger victims to

- Be victims of property crime (nine out of ten crimes committed against the elderly are property crimes, compared to fewer than four in ten crimes against people between ages 12 and 24)
- Face offenders who are armed with guns
- Be victimized by strangers
- Be victimized in or near their homes during daylight hours
- Report their victimization to the police, especially when they fall victim to violent crime
- Be physically injured

The elderly face special kinds of victimization that only rarely affect younger adults, such as physical abuse at the hands of caregivers. Criminal physical abuse of the elderly falls into two categories: domestic and institutional. Domestic abuse often occurs at the hands of caregivers who are related to their victims; institutional abuse occurs in residential settings like retirement centers, nursing homes, and hospitals. Both forms of elder abuse may also involve criminal sexual victimization. To learn more about domestic and institutional elder abuse, visit the National Center on Elder Abuse (NCEA) via **Web Extra 12**.

The elderly are also more often targeted by con artists. Confidence schemes center on commercial and financial fraud (including telemarketing fraud), charitable donation fraud, funeral and cemetery fraud, real estate fraud, caretaker fraud, automobile and home repair fraud, living trust fraud, health-care fraud (e.g., promises of "miracle cures"), and health-care-provider fraud (overbilling and unjustified repeat billing by otherwise legitimate health-care providers). False "friends" may intentionally isolate elderly targets from others in the hopes of misappropriating money through short-term secret loans or outright theft. Similarly, a younger person may feign romantic involvement with an elderly victim or pretend to be devoted to the senior in order to solicit money or receive an inappropriate gift or inheritance. The U.S. Senate's Special Committee on Aging provides additional information on such crimes at its Elder Justice Center website, which can be accessed via **Web Extra 13**.

Finally, crime against the elderly will likely undergo a significant increase as baby boomers enter their retirement years. Not only will the elderly comprise an increasingly larger segment of the population as boomers age, but it is anticipated that they will be wealthier than any preceding generation of retirees, making them attractive targets for scam artists and property criminals.[88]

Hate Crime

hate crime (UCR/NIBRS)
A criminal offense committed against a person, property, or society that is motivated, in whole or in part, by the offender's bias against a race, religion, disability, sexual orientation, or ethnicity/national origin.

A significant change in crime-reporting practices resulted from the Hate Crime Statistics Act,[89] signed into law by President George H. W. Bush in 1990. The act mandates a statistical tally of **hate crimes**; data collection under the law began in 1991. Congress defined *hate crime* as an offense "in which the defendant's conduct was motivated by hatred, bias, or prejudice, based on the actual or perceived race, color, religion, national origin, ethnicity, gender, or sexual orientation of another individual or group of individuals."[90] In 2009, police agencies reported a total of 6,604 hate-crime incidents, including three murders, across the country. As Figure 6 shows, 17.7% of the incidents were motivated by religious bias, 49.1% were caused by racial hatred, and 13.5% were driven by prejudice against ethnicity or national origin. Another 18.5% of all hate crimes were based on sexual orientation, most committed against males believed by their victimizers to be homosexuals.[91] A relatively small number of hate crimes targeted people with physical or mental disabilities.

▲ Evidence of a hate crime: Nazi symbols spray-painted on Arab graves. Why are hate crimes given special attention under the law?
Reuters/Vincent Kessler/Landov Media

Following the terrorist attacks of September 11, 2001, authorities in some jurisdictions reported a dramatic shift in the nature of hate crime, with race-motivated crimes declining and crimes motivated by religion or ethnicity increasing sharply.[92] Islamic individuals, in particular, became the target of many such crimes.

Most hate crimes consist of intimidation, although vandalism, simple assault, and aggravated assault also account for a number of hate-crime offenses. A few robberies and rapes were also classified as hate crimes in 2009.

Although hate crimes are popularly conceived of as crimes motivated by racial enmity, the Violent Crime Control and Law Enforcement Act of 1994 created a new category of "crimes of violence motivated by gender." Congress defined this crime as "a crime of violence committed because of gender or on the basis of gender, and due, at least in part, to an animus based on the victim's gender." The 1994 act did not establish separate penalties for gender-motivated crimes, anticipating that they would be prosecuted as felonies under existing laws. The 1994 act also mandated that crimes motivated by biases against people with disabilities be considered hate crimes.

Hate crimes are sometimes called *bias crimes.* One form of bias crime that bears special mention is *homophobic homicide*, a term that refers to the murder of a homosexual by those opposed to that lifestyle. The Southern Poverty Law Center, which tracks hate groups, identified 888 such groups operating in the United States in 2007.[93] The center, which is based in Montgomery, Alabama, says that the number of hate groups has jumped 48% since 2000, mostly because of the formation of new anti-immigrant organizations. Learn more about hate crime and what can be done to address it at **Library Extras 17** and **18**.

Corporate and White-Collar Crime

In 2009, investment fund manager Bernard ("Bernie") Madoff plead guilty to operating a Ponzi scheme that defrauded investors out of as much as $50 billion.[94] Called "Wall Street's biggest fraud" by some, Madoff's shenanigans purportedly cost investors $50 billion in money that seemed to simply disappear.[95] Madoff, a former chairman of the NASDAQ stock market, pleaded guilty to 11 felony counts, including securities fraud, mail fraud, wire fraud, money laundering, and perjury. He was sentenced to 150 years in prison.[96]

> With each arrest, indictment and prosecution, we sent this clear, unmistakable message: corrupt corporate executives are no better than common thieves.
>
> —John Ashcroft, former U.S. attorney general[vi]

The recent economic downturn, combined with the collapse of the housing market and the loss of jobs in many sectors of the economy, sparked a rapid growth in mortgage fraud scams. There are three types of mortgage fraud, which is a federal crime. The first, fraud for profit, involves a scheme by "ghost buyers" to collect cash; these buyers have no interest in owning the property against which money is being borrowed. The second type is fraud for housing, or application fraud, in which otherwise legitimate home buyers fake documents to make them appear eligible for a loan that they would not otherwise get. According to one report, 61% of all reported mortgage frauds in 2008 involved misrepresentations made on applications for a mortgage. The third type of mortgage fraud involves overestimating a property's valuation or submitting a false appraisal to defraud purchasers and lenders.

A study by the Mortgage Asset Research Institute concluded that mortgage fraud was more prevalent in 2009 than it had been at the height of the nation's building boom just a few years earlier.[97] Federal agencies say they're inundated with mortgage fraud cases but are also starting to look into a new breed of scams perpetrated by those who offer to refinance homes or save them from foreclosure. In one of the new scams, criminals offer to help people who are about to lose their homes, collecting several thousand dollars up front before disappearing.[98] In early 2009, the Federal Trade Commission announced a wave of law enforcement actions against businesses using deceptive tactics to market mortgage modification and home foreclosure relief services, including firms that gave the false impression they were affiliated with the federal government.[99]

Under the American system of criminal justice, corporations can be treated as separate legal entities and can be convicted of violations of the criminal law under a legal principle

corporate crime
A violation of a criminal statute by a corporate entity or by its executives, employees, or agents acting on behalf of and for the benefit of the corporation, partnership, or other form of business entity.[vii]

white-collar crime
Violations of the criminal law committed by a person of respectability and high social status in the course of his or her occupation. Also, nonviolent crime for financial gain utilizing deception and committed by anyone who has special technical or professional knowledge of business or government, irrespective of the person's occupation.

organized crime
The unlawful activities of the members of a highly organized, disciplined association engaged in supplying illegal goods or services, including gambling, prostitution, loan-sharking, narcotics, and labor racketeering, and in other unlawful activities.[viii]

transnational organized crime
Unlawful activity undertaken and supported by organized criminal groups operating across national boundaries.

known as the *identification doctrine.* In 2002, for example, a federal jury convicted global accounting firm Arthur Andersen of obstruction of justice after its employees shredded documents related to Enron's bankruptcy in an effort to impede an investigation by securities regulators. The conviction, which was overturned by a unanimous U.S. Supreme Court in 2005,[100] capped the firm's demise, and it ended U.S. operations in August 2002.[101]

Although corporations may be convicted of a crime, the human perpetrators of **corporate crime** are business executives known as *white-collar criminals.* **White-collar crime** was first defined in 1939 by Edwin H. Sutherland in his presidential address to the American Sociological Society.[102] Sutherland proposed that "crime in the suites" (a reference to corporate offices) rivaled the importance of street crime in its potential impact on American society.

In July 2002, President George W. Bush unveiled plans to create a new Corporate Fraud Task Force within the federal government and proposed a new law providing criminal penalties for corporate fraud. He told corporate leaders on Wall Street, "At this moment, America's greatest economic need is higher ethical standards—standards enforced by strict laws and upheld by responsible business leaders."[103] A few months later, the president signed into law the Sarbanes-Oxley Act.[104] The new law created tough provisions designed to deter and punish corporate and accounting fraud and corruption and to protect the interests of workers and shareholders. Under the Sarbanes-Oxley Act, corporate officials (chief executive officers and chief financial officers) must personally vouch for the truth and accuracy of their companies' financial statements, and federal penalties for obstructing justice and, specifically, for shredding or destroying documents that might aid in a criminal investigation of business practices are substantially increased. Learn more about corporate and white-collar crime at the National White Collar Crime Center (NW3C) via **Web Extra 14**. Established in 1992, the NW3C provides a national support system for the prevention, investigation, and prosecution of multijurisdictional economic crimes. Learn more about how corporations can be held accountable from CorpWatch via **Web Extra 15**.

Organized Crime

For many people, the term **organized crime** conjures up images of the Mafia (also called the *Cosa Nostra*) or the hit HBO TV series *The Sopranos.* Although organized criminal activity is decidedly a group phenomenon, the groups involved in such activity in the United States today display a great deal of variation. During the past few decades in the United States, the preeminence of traditional Sicilian American criminal organizations has fallen to such diverse criminal associations as the Black Mafia, the Cuban Mafia, the Haitian Mafia, the Colombian cartels, and Asian criminal groups like the Chinese Tongs and street gangs, Japanese yakuza, and Vietnamese gangs. Included here as well might be inner-city gangs, the best known of which are probably the Los Angeles Crips and Bloods and the Chicago Vice Lords, international drug rings, outlaw motorcycle gangs like the Hell's Angels and the Pagans, and other looser associations of small-time thugs, prison gangs, and drug dealers. Noteworthy among these groups—especially for their involvement in the lucrative drug trade—are the Latino organized bands, including the Dominican, Colombian, Mexican, and Cuban importers of cocaine, heroin, marijuana, and other controlled substances.

▲ Actor James Gandolfini (Tony Soprano) from HBO's hit series *The Sopranos*, on right. The popular show explored the life of fictionalized organized crime figures in New Jersey. Why was the show such a hit with viewers?
Globe Photos, Inc.

The unlawful activities of organized groups that operate across national boundaries are especially significant. Such activity is referred to as **transnational organized crime**. Transnational criminal associations worthy of special mention are the Hong Kong–based Triads, the South American cocaine cartels, the Italian Mafia, the Japanese yakuza, the Russian *Mafiya*, and the West African crime groups—each of which extends its reach well beyond its home country. In some parts of the world, close links between organized crime and terrorist groups involve money laundering, which provides cash to finance the activities of terrorist cells and to finance paramilitary efforts to overthrow established governments.

Former CIA Director R. James Woolsey points out that "while organized crime is not a new phenomenon today, some governments find their authority besieged at home and their foreign policy interests imperiled abroad. Drug trafficking, links between drug traffickers and terrorists, smuggling of illegal aliens, massive financial and bank fraud, arms smuggling, potential involvement in the theft and sale of nuclear material, political intimidation, and corruption all constitute a poisonous brew—a mixture potentially as deadly as what we faced during the cold war."[105] The challenge for today's criminal justice student is to recognize that crime does not respect national boundaries. Crime is global, and what happens in one part of the world could affect us all.[106]

Gun Crime

Guns and gun crime seem to pervade American culture. Constitutional guarantees of the right to bear arms have combined with historical circumstances to make ours a well-armed society. Guns are used in many types of crimes. Each year, approximately 1 million serious crimes—including homicide, rape, robbery, and assault—involve the use of a handgun. In a typical year, approximately 10,000 murders are committed in the United States with firearms. A recent report by the BJS found that 18% of state prison inmates and 15% of federal inmates were armed at the time they committed the crime for which they were imprisoned,[107] and 9% of those in state prisons said they fired a gun while committing the offense for which they were serving time.[108]

Both federal and state governments have responded to public concern over the ready availability of handguns with regulatory statutes. In 1994, Congress passed the Brady Handgun Violence Prevention Act,[109] which President Bill Clinton signed into law. The law was named for former Press Secretary James Brady, who was shot and severely wounded in an attempt on President Ronald Reagan's life on March 30, 1981. The law mandates a five-day waiting period before the purchase of a handgun, and it established a national instant criminal background check system that firearms dealers must use before selling a handgun.[110]

While the Brady law may limit retail purchases of handguns by felons, a BJS study found that most offenders obtain weapons from friends or family members or "on the street" rather than attempt to purchase them at retail establishments.[111] In 2001, undercover congressional investigators were able to show that applicants using fake forms of identification, such as counterfeit driver's licenses with fictitious names, could easily circumvent Brady law provisions.[112] Moreover, according to these studies, an ever-growing number of violent criminals are now carrying handguns. A 2006 study found no evidence that stringent gun-control laws have an impact on crime.[113] The study, which used data from all 50 states, found that gun-control laws do not have an impact on the crime rate or on the occurrence of any specific type of serious crime. Such laws are ineffective in reducing crime, the study authors said, because they do not substantially reduce the availability of firearms to criminal offenders.

▲ Los Angeles County Deputy Sheriff Jason Molina with a cache of guns turned in by citizens in South Central Los Angeles in exchange for $100 gift cards. The "Gun for Gift Card" exchange event is held twice yearly, on Mother's Day and Christmas. Do you think such programs help reduce gun violence in our society?
AFP Photo/Mark Ralston/NewsCom.com

Among other legislation, the Violent Crime Control and Law Enforcement Act of 1994[114] regulated the sale of firearms within the United States and banned the manufacture of 19 military-style assault weapons, including those with specific combat features such as high-capacity ammunition clips capable of holding more than ten rounds. The federal ban on assault weapons ended in 2004, however, when it was not renewed by Congress.

The 1996 Domestic Violence Offender Gun Ban[115] prohibited individuals convicted of misdemeanor domestic-violence offenses from owning or using firearms. Soon after the law was passed, however, it became embroiled in controversy when hundreds of police officers across the country who had been convicted of domestic-violence offenses were found to be in violation of the ban. A number of officers lost their jobs, while others were placed in positions that did not require them to carry firearms.[116]

Following the 1999 Columbine High School shooting, many states moved to tighten controls over handguns and assault weapons. The California legislature, for example, restricted gun purchases to one per month and tightened a ten-year-old ban on assault weapons. Similarly, Illinois passed a law requiring that gun owners lock their weapons away from anyone under age 14.

In 2005, in a move that some saw as promoting handgun sales, the federal Protection of Lawful Commerce in Firearms Act granted gunmakers and most gun dealers immunity from lawsuits brought by victims of gun crimes and their survivors. The law removed negligence as viable grounds for a civil suit against a gun dealer who carelessly sells a gun to someone who is at risk for using it in a crime. The law states that the dealer can be sued only if he or she knew of the gun buyer's criminal intent before the purchase. Gunmakers were also made immune from suits alleging product liability for having manufactured potentially lethal items.

In 2008, in the case of *District of Columbia* v. *Heller*,[117] the U.S. Supreme Court came down firmly in support of private gun ownership when it ruled that the Constitution's Second Amendment protects an individual's right to possess a firearm and to use that firearm for traditionally lawful purposes, such as self-defense within the home. The *Heller* case addressed three strict gun-control ordinances that the District of Columbia City Council had enacted in 1976 and that entirely banned anyone from carrying a handgun or other deadly or dangerous weapon without a license. The ordinances also required that any firearms, such as rifles and shotguns, be kept either disassembled or with a trigger lock in place. Prior to *Heller*, the Supreme Court had not squarely addressed a Second Amendment case since 1939 and had never previously decided whether the Second Amendment confers a right to bear arms upon individuals or only upon the militias it refers to in its opening clause. In the intervening 69 years, however, many federal and state governments had passed laws regulating and restricting the ownership and use of guns, making the *Heller* decision especially significant.

Because *Heller* concerned a District of Columbia law, gun-control advocates interpreted it as applicable only to federal enclaves and soon questioned the applicability of the Court's ruling to jurisdictions not under direct federal control. In 2010, in the important case of *McDonald* v. *City of Chicago*,[118] the Court established an individual's right to keep a gun for self-defense in the home as a "fundamental" constitutional right. Any right that the Court declares to be fundamental cannot be contravened by laws at any level unless the government can demonstrate a compelling need to do so and only if limits imposed take the narrowest possible approach to addressing the issue. Consequently, in the wake of *McDonald,* states and local jurisdictions may still place restrictions on gun ownership, such as registration requirements or prohibiting the possession of handguns by convicted felons, but those restrictions must be reasonable and cannot be extreme.

In Congress, debate continues about whether to require gun manufacturers to create and retain "ballistic fingerprints" (the marks left on a bullet by the barrel of the gun from which it was fired) of each weapon they produce. Although a national ballistics fingerprinting requirement may still be years away, three states—California, Maryland, and New York—and the District of Columbia already require that a record be kept of the "fingerprint" characteristics of each new handgun sold.[119] Microstamping uses laser engraving to encode a weapon's serial number on each cartridge that it fires, and California authorities believe that the technology will allow handguns to be traced to their manufacturer and then the first purchaser using only spent cartridges left at crime scenes.

For more about issues related to guns and crime, read the 2007 Report to the President on the Virginia Tech campus shooting at **Library Extra 19**, and learn more about promising strategies to reduce gun violence at **Library Extra 20**. For the latest information on gun violence and gun laws, visit the Brady Center to Prevent Gun Violence via **Web Extra 16**. The National Rifle Association (NRA) site at **Web Extra 17** provides arguments in support of responsible access to firearms.

Drug Crime

In 2008, 96 young men—including 75 San Diego State University (SDSU) students—were arrested on a variety of drug and weapons charges as a result of a joint Drug Enforcement Agency (DEA)/local police operation called Sudden Fall. During the operation, undercover officers infiltrated seven of the university's fraternity houses and seized four pounds of cocaine, 50 pounds of marijuana, 48 hydroponic marijuana plants, 350 Ecstasy pills, 30 vials of hash oil, methamphetamine, psilocybin (mushrooms), various illicit prescription drugs, a shotgun, three semiautomatic pistols, various sets of brass knuckles, and $60,000 in cash. The agents said that they also found evidence of widespread drug dealing at SDSU's fraternity houses. The investigation had begun a year earlier after a cocaine overdose caused the death of a

19-year-old female student on the SDSU campus. "This operation shows how accessible and pervasive illegal drugs continue to be on our college campuses and how common it is for students to be selling to other students," said San Diego County District Attorney Bonnie Dumanis.[120]

▲ San Diego County Deputy District Attorney Damon Mosler (at podium) pointing to drugs and firearms seized during the arrest of 96 people, including 75 students at San Diego State University, in 2008 after an extensive undercover investigation called Operation Sudden Fall. How common are illegal drugs on the nation's campuses?
Dennis Poroy/AP Wide World Photos

The White House Office of National Drug Control Policy (ONDCP) estimates annual illicit drug sales in the United States of around $65 billion, while the United Nations says that illegal drug revenue in the United States, Canada, and Mexico totals around $142 billion yearly.[121] Unlike most major crimes, drug-law violations continue to increase, lending support to those who feel that this country is experiencing more overall crime than traditional tabulations show. The relentless increase in drug violations largely accounts for the fact that America's prison populations have continued to grow, even when official crime rates are declining. Figure 7 shows the number of suspects arrested for drug-law violations in the United States between 1975 and 2009.

Alone, drug-law violations are themselves criminal, but more and more studies are linking drug abuse to other serious crimes. An early study by the RAND Corporation found that most of the "violent predators" among prisoners had extensive histories of heroin abuse, often in combination with alcohol and other drugs.[122] Some cities reported that a large percentage of their homicides were drug related.[123] More recent studies also link drug abuse to other serious crimes. Community leaders perceive, and data analyses confirm, that crack cocaine profoundly impacts violent crime, with homicide rates closely tracking cocaine-use levels among adult male arrestees.[124] Prisoner survey data show that 19% of state inmates and 16% of federal prisoners reported committing their most recent offense to obtain money for drugs.[125] A 2000 study found that 13.3% of convicted jail inmates said that they had committed their offense to get money for drugs.[126]

Criminal justice system costs associated with the handling of drug offenders have increased substantially in recent years. Between 1984 and 2002, for example, the annual number of defendants charged with a drug offense in federal courts increased from 11,854 to more than 30,000.[127] Similarly, between 1984 and 2002, drug offenses accounted for an increased proportion of the federal criminal caseload, even when charges weren't brought. During 1984, 18% of referrals to U.S. attorneys were drug related, compared to 31% during 2002.[128] Some of the increase stems from changes in federal drug laws. Whatever the cause, the drug–crime link is costly to society and shows few signs of abating. Learn more about drug crime and efforts being made to combat it at **Library Extra 21**.

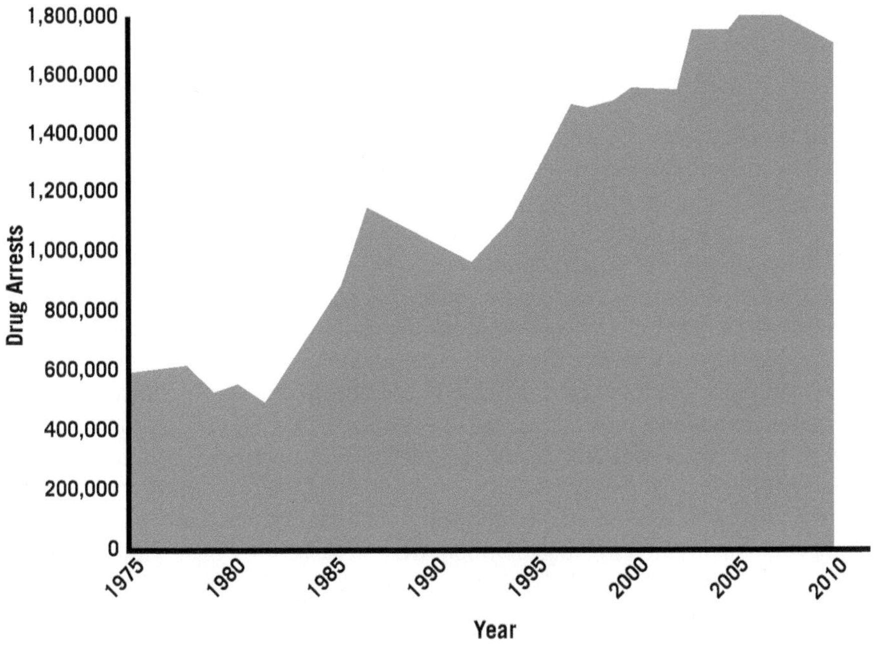

FIGURE 7
Drug Arrests in the United States, 1975–2009

Source: Federal Bureau of Investigation, *Crime in the United States* (Washington, DC: U.S. Department of Justice, various years).

malware
Malicious computer programs such as viruses, worms, and Trojan horses.

computer crime
Any crime perpetrated through the use of computer technology. Also, any violation of a federal or state computer-crime statute. Also called *cybercrime*.

High-Technology and Computer Crime

A few years ago, the Ziff Davis digital publication *eWeek* reported the release on the Internet of a **malware** software program that encrypts files on an infected computer and then demands a $300 ransom for e-mail delivery of a decryption password.[129] The malware, identified as Cryzip, makes data files on infected computers unavailable to legitimate users and displays step-by-step instructions on how to pay a ransom with a credit card for file retrieval. Cryzip is a type of software known as *ransomware*, and its release points to an increasing level of sophistication among online thieves practicing computer crime.

▲ Albert Gonzalez, a 28-year-old American believed to be one of the nation's cybercrime kingpins. Gonzales was indicted in 2009 along with two Russian accomplices on charges that they carried out the largest hacking and identity-theft caper in U.S. history. What is cybercrime, and why is it a threat? *Reuters/US Law Enforcement via Wired.com/Landov*

Computer crimes, also called *cybercrimes* or *information technology crimes*, use computers and computer technology as tools in crime commission. Thefts of computer equipment, although sometimes spectacular, are not computer crimes but are instead classified as larcenies. "True" computer criminals go beyond the theft of hardware, focusing instead on the information stored in computer systems and manipulating it in a way that violates the law.

While a generally accepted typology of computer-based crime has yet to be developed,[130] Peter Grabosky of the Australian Institute of Criminology suggests that most such crimes fall into one of the following broad categories:[131] (1) theft of services, such as telephone or long-distance access; (2) communications in furtherance of criminal conspiracies—for example, the e-mail communications said to have taken place between members of Osama bin Laden's al-Qaeda terrorist network;[132] (3) information piracy and forgery—that is, the stealing of trade secrets or copyrighted information; (4) dissemination of offensive materials, such as child pornography, and extortion threats, such as those made against financial institutions by hackers claiming the ability to destroy the institutions' electronic records; (5) electronic money laundering and tax evasion through electronic funds transfers that conceal the origin of financial proceeds; (6) electronic vandalism and terrorism, including computer viruses, worms, Trojan horses, and cyberterrorism—that is, cyberattacks on critical components of a nation's infrastructure, such as its banking system; (7) telemarketing fraud, including investment frauds and illegitimate electronic auctions; (8) illegal interception of telecommunications—that is, illegal eavesdropping; and (9) electronic funds transfer fraud—specifically, the illegal interception and diversion of legitimate transactions.

Many of the crimes committed via the Internet—like prostitution, drug sales, theft, and fraud—are not new forms of offending. They are, rather, traditional forms of offending that use new technology in their commission. In 2010, for example, more than 50 people were arrested in the United States and charged with distributing pornographic images of children following a two-year international law enforcement effort dubbed Operation Nest Egg.[133] The investigation freed 16 child victims, some of whom had been forced to perform sexual activities on adults while video cameras rolled. At one point, according to investigators, the group encompassed more than 1,000 paying members who traded millions of sexually explicit images of children.

U.S. Customs and Border Protection Senior Special Agent Donald Daufenbach, an international expert in child pornography and the Internet, points out that "the Internet is like anything else: It can be bent or perverted for nefarious purposes. . . . The Internet has absolutely changed the way people communicate with each other, changed the way people conduct commerce, changed the way people do research, changed the way people entertain themselves and changed the way people break the law."[134] Daufenbach added, "It's just a new version of what the mails or what the telephones used to be. . . . People are catching on pretty quick, but law enforcement is lagging behind miserably in this whole endeavor."

computer virus
A computer program designed to secretly invade systems and either modify the way in which they operate or alter the information they store. Viruses are destructive software programs that may effectively vandalize computers of all types and sizes.

Computer viruses have become a special concern of the general computer user during the past several years, especially as more people have connected to the Internet. Computer viruses were brought to public attention in 1988 when the Pakistani virus (or Pakistani brain virus) became widespread in personal and office computers across the United States.[135] The Pakistani virus was created by Amjad Farooq Alvi and his brother Basit Farooq Alvi, two cut-rate computer software dealers in Lahore, Pakistan. The Alvi brothers made copies of costly software products and sold them at low prices to mostly Western shoppers looking for a bargain. Motivated by convoluted logic, the brothers hid a virus on each disk they sold to punish buyers for seeking to evade copyright laws. Since then, many other virus attacks have made headlines, including the infamous Michelangelo virus in 1992; the intentional distribution of infected software on an AIDS-related research CD-ROM distributed about the same time; the Kournikova virus in 2000; and the Sircam, Nimda, W32, NastyBrew, Berbew, Mydoom, and Code Red worms, all of which made their appearance or were substantially modified by their creators between 2001 and 2006.

In 2003, federal legislators acted to criminalize the sending of unsolicited commercial e-mail, or **spam**. The federal CAN-SPAM Act (Controlling the Assault of Nonsolicited Pornography and Marketing), which took effect on January 1, 2004, regulates the sending of "commercial electronic mail messages."[136] The law, which applies equally to mass mailings and to individual e-mail messages, defines commercial electronic mail messages as electronic mail whose *primary purpose* is the "commercial advertisement or promotion of a commercial product or service." The CAN-SPAM law requires that a commercial e-mail message include the following three features: (1) a clear and conspicuous identification that the message is an advertisement or solicitation, (2) an opt-out feature allowing recipients to opt out of future mailings, and (3) a valid physical address identifying the sender. Some experts estimate that 80% of all e-mail today is spam,[137] and a number of states have enacted their own antispam laws.

spam
Unsolicited commercial bulk e-mail whose primary purpose is the advertisement or promotion of a commercial product or service.

Computer-related crimes can also involve copyright infringement. In 2005, for example, the U.S. Supreme Court agreed to hear an appeal from the music industry, and in the landmark case of *MGM* v. *Grokster*,[138] the Court found that online file-sharing services may be held liable for copyright infringement if they promote their services explicitly as a way for users to download copyrighted music and other content.

One form of cybercrime that relies primarily on social engineering to succeed is *phishing* (pronounced *fishing*). Phishing is a relatively new form of high-technology fraud that uses official-looking e-mail messages to elicit responses from victims, directing them to phony websites. Microsoft Corporation says that phishing is "the fastest-growing form of online fraud in the world today."[139] Phishing e-mails typically instruct recipients to validate or update account information before their accounts are canceled. Phishing schemes, which have targeted most major banks, the Federal Deposit Insurance Corporation, IBM, eBay, PayPal, and some major health-care providers, are designed to steal valuable information such as credit card numbers, Social Security numbers, user IDs, and passwords. Gartner Inc., a leading provider of research and analysis on the global information technology industry, released a report estimating that some 57 million adult Americans received phishing e-mails during the spring of 2004 and that 11 million recipients clicked on the link contained in the messages.[140] Gartner estimated that 1.78 million recipients actually provided personal information to the thieves behind the phishing schemes.

Symantec Corporation's 2010 Information Protection Survey determined that 73% of small and medium-sized businesses experienced cyberattacks in the previous 12 months.[141] Of those, 30% were said to be somewhat or extremely effective, and all attacks resulted in losses ranging from downtime to theft of corporate data. The average annual cost of cyberattacks to small and medium-sized businesses in the year preceding the Symantec survey was $188,242.

Other researchers have determined that some of the most serious corporate computer security threats come from employees, including 70% of all incidents involving unauthorized access to information systems and 95% of all network intrusions that result in significant financial loss.[142]

▲ A commuter being helped away from the Edgware Road Station following terrorist bombings in London's subway system in 2005. How might future acts of terrorism be prevented?
Jane Mingay/AP Wide World Photos

In 2004, the BJS released initial results from its 2001 National Computer Security Survey (NCSS), which was conducted in collaboration with the U.S. Census Bureau.[143] The 2004 report summarized findings from a pilot survey of 500 companies nationwide. Nearly three-fourths of businesses surveyed reported detecting at least one computer security incident during the previous 12-month period. Computer viruses were the most common type of incident reported (65%), followed by denial-of-service attacks (25%) and vandalism or

CJ Exhibit 2
What Is Terrorist Activity?

Federal law enforcement efforts directed against agents of foreign terrorist organizations derive their primary authority from the Immigration and Nationality Act, found in Chapter 12 of the U.S. Code. The act defines *terrorist activity* as follows:

(ii) "Terrorist activity" defined

As used in this chapter, the term "terrorist activity" means any activity which is unlawful under the laws of the place where it is committed (or which, if committed in the United States, would be unlawful under the laws of the United States or any State) and which involves any of the following:

I. The hijacking or sabotage of any conveyance (including an aircraft, vessel, or vehicle).
II. The seizing or detaining, and threatening to kill, injure, or continue to detain, another individual in order to compel a third person (including a governmental organization) to do or abstain from doing any act as an explicit or implicit condition for the release of the individual seized or detained.
III. A violent attack upon an internationally protected person (as defined in section 1116(b)(4) of title 18) or upon the liberty of such a person.
IV. An assassination.
V. The use of any—
   a. biological agent, chemical agent, or nuclear weapon or device, or
   b. explosive or firearm (other than for mere personal monetary gain), with intent to endanger, directly or indirectly, the safety of one or more individuals or to cause substantial damage to property.
VI. A threat, attempt, or conspiracy to do any of the foregoing.

(iii) "Engage in terrorist activity" defined

As used in this chapter, the term "engage in terrorist activity" means to commit, in an individual capacity or as a member of an organization, an act of terrorist activity or an act which the actor knows, or reasonably should know, affords material support to any individual, organization, or government in conducting a terrorist activity at any time, including any of the following acts:

I. The preparation or planning of a terrorist activity.
II. The gathering of information on potential targets for terrorist activity.
III. The providing of any type of material support, including a safe house, transportation, communications, funds, false documentation or identification, weapons, explosives, or training, to any individual the actor knows or has reason to believe has committed or plans to commit a terrorist activity.
IV. The soliciting of funds or other things of value for terrorist activity or for any terrorist organization.
V. The solicitation of any individual for membership in a terrorist organization, terrorist government, or to engage in a terrorist activity.

sabotage of computer equipment or computer networks (19%). Other crimes, such as fraud, theft of proprietary information, and embezzlement, were also reported. Not surprisingly, the largest companies experienced the greatest number of incidents. The NCSS was sponsored by the U.S. Department of Justice, Bureau of Justice Statistics and the U.S. Department of Homeland Security, National Cyber Security Division. This data-collection effort was part of the President's 2003 National Strategy to Secure Cyberspace. You may access the NCSS at **Library Extra 22**. The CSI/FBI Computer Crime and Security Survey can be found online at **Library Extra 23**.

Terrorism

Terrorism as a criminal activity and the prevention of further acts of terrorism became primary concerns of American justice system officials following the September 11, 2001, attacks on the World Trade Center and the Pentagon. Long before the September 11 attacks, however, terrorism was a concern of law enforcement and other government officials. In 2001, for example, international terrorist attacks totaled 864 worldwide—down from the 1,106 reported a year earlier.[144]

There is no single definition of terrorism that is applicable to all places and all circumstances. Some definitions are statutory in nature, while others were created for such practical purposes as gauging success in the fight against terrorism. The FBI, for example, defines **terrorism** as "a violent act or an act dangerous to human life in violation of the criminal laws of the United States or of any state to intimidate or coerce a government, the civilian population, or any segment thereof, in furtherance of political or social objectives."[145] One of the most comprehensive and widely used definitions of terrorist activity can be found in the federal Immigration and Nationality Act, an excerpt of which appears in CJ Exhibit 2.

terrorism
A violent act or an act dangerous to human life in violation of the criminal laws of the United States or of any state, committed to intimidate or coerce a government, the civilian population, or any segment thereof in furtherance of political or social objectives.[ix]

Types of Terrorism

It is important to distinguish between two major forms of terrorism: domestic and international. Such distinctions are generally made in terms of the origin, base of operations, and objectives of a terrorist organization. **Domestic terrorism** refers to the unlawful use of force or violence by a group or an individual who is based and operates entirely within the United States and its territories without foreign direction and whose acts are directed against elements of the U.S. government or population.[146] **International terrorism**, in contrast, is the unlawful use of force or violence by a group or an individual who has some connection to a foreign power or whose activities transcend national boundaries against people or property to intimidate or coerce a government, the civilian population, or any segment thereof in furtherance of political or social objectives.[147] International terrorism is sometimes mistakenly called *foreign terrorism*, a term that, strictly speaking, refers only to acts of terrorism that occur outside the United States.

domestic terrorism
The unlawful use of force or violence by a group or an individual who is based and operates entirely within the United States and its territories without foreign direction and whose acts are directed at elements of the U.S. government or population.[x]

international terrorism
The unlawful use of force or violence by a group or an individual who has some connection to a foreign power or whose activities transcend national boundaries against people or property in order to intimidate or coerce a government, the civilian population, or any segment thereof in furtherance of political or social objectives.[xi]

cyberterrorism
A form of terrorism that makes use of high technology, especially computers and the Internet, in the planning and carrying out of terrorist attacks.

Another new kind of terrorism, called **cyberterrorism**, is lurking on the horizon. Cyberterrorism makes use of high technology, especially computers and the Internet, in the planning and carrying out of terrorist attacks. The term was coined in the 1980s by Barry Collin, a senior research fellow at the Institute for Security and Intelligence in California, who used it to refer to the convergence of cyberspace and terrorism.[148] It was later popularized by a 1996 RAND report that warned of an emerging "new terrorism" distinguished by how terrorist groups organize and by how they use technology. The report warned of a coming "netwar" or "infowar" consisting of coordinated cyberattacks on our nation's economic, business, and military infrastructure.[149] A year later, FBI Agent Mark M. Pollitt offered a working definition of *cyberterrorism*, saying that it is "the premeditated, politically motivated attack against information, computer systems, computer programs, and data which results in violence against noncombatant targets by subnational groups or clandestine agents."[150]

Scenarios describing cyberterrorism possibilities are imaginative and diverse. Some have suggested that a successful cyberterrorist attack on the nation's air traffic control system might cause airplanes to collide in midair or that an attack on food- and cereal-processing plants that drastically altered the levels of certain nutritional supplements might sicken or kill a large number of our nation's young children. Other such attacks might cause the country's power grid to collapse or might muddle the records and transactions of banks and stock exchanges. Possible targets in such attacks are almost endless. A 2005 national survey of computer security experts found that almost half were expecting a "digital Pearl Harbor," in which American society would be plunged into chaos by malicious hackers, to occur within the next few years.[151]

Organization and Scope of Terrorist Groups

In 2008, FBI Director Robert S. Mueller III identified three organizational levels that characterize violent extremists seeking to damage the United States and its interests.[152] The top tier, Mueller said, "is the core al-Qaeda organization, which has established new sanctuaries in the ungoverned spaces, tribal areas, and frontier provinces of Pakistan." The middle tier Mueller called the most complex. "We are finding," he said, "small groups who have some ties to an established terrorist organization but are largely self-directed. Think of them as al-Qaeda franchises—hybrids of homegrown radicals and more sophisticated operatives." The bottom tier, Mueller noted, "is made up of homegrown extremists. They are self-radicalizing, self-financing, and self-executing. They meet up on the Internet instead of in foreign training camps. They have no formal affiliation with al-Qaeda, but they are inspired by its message of violence."

Terrorist groups are active throughout the world, and the United States is not their only target. Terrorist organizations operate in South America, Africa, the Middle East, Latin America, the Philippines, Japan, India, Ireland, England, Nepal, and some of the now independent states of the former Soviet Union. The Central Intelligence Agency (CIA) reports that "between now and 2015 terrorist tactics will become increasingly sophisticated and designed to achieve mass casualties."[153] The CIA also notes that nations "with poor governance; ethnic, cultural, or religious tensions; weak economies; and porous borders will be prime breeding grounds for terrorism."[154] Read the entire CIA report on global trends that may increase the risk of terrorism at **Library Extra 24**. The U.S. Department of State's annual report, *Patterns of Global Terrorism*, can be found at **Library Extra 25**, and the 2004 final report of the National Commission on Terrorist Attacks upon the United States (the 911 Commission) can be read at **Library Extra 26**.

CJ News
FBI Warns of Growing Threat from Islamic Extremists "Next Door"

Plots by American-based Islamic terrorists with no direct ties to international terror networks form a large and growing threat to the American homeland, FBI and other security officials say.

"The trend we're seeing is that we are uncovering more instances of people here who have been radicalized . . . where there is not a direct thumbprint of al-Qaeda," says John Miller, the FBI's assistant director for public affairs.

Justice Department records show that the FBI and other federal and local agencies have led prosecutions of a dozen such alleged plots since the Sept. 11 attacks on New York City and Washington. One such prosecution began in May 2007, when five New Jersey Muslim men were charged with plotting to kill soldiers at the Army's Fort Dix, N.J., compound. A sixth man was charged with helping the group obtain illegal firearms.

The government has won terrorism convictions in seven cases. Others are ongoing.

The focus on American-based terror cells is a shift from post 9/11 thinking, when intelligence and security officials expected attacks to come from "sleeper cells" of al-Qaeda agents who, like the Washington and New York City attackers, had filtered into the USA from abroad.

"That was my intuition at the time," says George Tenet in an interview. Tenet was CIA director from 1997 to 2004 and just released a book, *At the Center of the Storm*, about his tenure. Tenet says the lesson is "don't get fixed on a particular face [because] there may be multiple kinds of faces."

Pasquale D'Amuro, the FBI's counterterrorism chief in 2002 and 2003, says the alleged New Jersey plot appears to be such a case. The six men arrested, he notes, were born in the former Yugoslavia, Jordan and Turkey and had lived in the USA without incident. One was a citizen, two were legal residents and three were here illegally. They had lived here at least six years, neighbors told the Associated Press.

"If they look like the neighbors next door, it's because that's what they are," says D'Amuro, CEO of Giuliani Security and Safety in New York.

"That they would come here, be welcomed and then want to attack us—that's what people have a hard time understanding."

In some cases, such as that of six Yemeni-Americans in Lackawanna, N.Y., the accused plotters had undergone training at terrorist camps overseas but had not focused on an American target. In others, such as the New Jersey plot, the government alleges that plotters had identified targets and were trying to purchase arms.

▲ A mosque in Dearborn, Michigan. The greater Detroit area is thought to have about 200,000 Arab Americans—said to be the densest Arab population of any community outside the Middle East. While most American Muslims are peaceful, law-abiding citizens, the FBI has warned about a threat from homegrown radical Islamic fundamentalists. Do you think such a threat should be taken seriously?
Getty Images, Inc.

In six cases, accused plotters sought out undercover agents or informers posing as al-Qaeda representatives. In two cases, alleged plotters are accused of swearing allegiance to al-Qaeda in ceremonies staged by the phony Islamists. In eight cases, the accused plotters were native-born Americans, including about a dozen who were converts to Islam.

Intelligence analysts say the lack of an al-Qaeda-led terror strike here may signal that the group is waiting until it can mount an attack that will equal the 9/11 strikes in casualties and publicity value.

Source: Richard Willing, "FBI, Security Officials Warn of Growing Threat from Islamic Extremists 'Next Door,'" *USA Today*, May 13, 2007. Reprinted with permission.

Initial efforts to develop a comprehensive plan of protection for the nation's critical infrastructure began in 2001 when President George W. Bush created the Office of Homeland Security, making its director a cabinet member. It became a department of the federal government in 2002. Visit the Department of Homeland Security via **Web Extra 18**, and view **Library Extra 27** to learn more about ways of protecting the nation's critical information infrastructure from attacks by terrorists, criminals, and vandals. You can track national and international terror incidents as they occur through the National Counterterrorism Center's Worldwide Incidents Tracking Center, which is available via **Web Extra 19**.

Summary

THE CRIME PICTURE

- The FBI's Uniform Crime Reporting (UCR) Program began in the 1930s when Congress authorized the U.S. attorney general to survey crime in America. Today's UCR/NIBRS Program provides annual data on the number of reported Part I offenses, or major crimes, as well as information about arrests that have been made for less serious Part II offenses. The Part I offenses are murder, forcible rape, robbery, aggravated assault, burglary, larceny-theft, motor vehicle theft, and arson. The Part II offenses category covers many more crimes, including drug offenses, driving under the influence, and simple assault. Modifications to the UCR Program, which has traditionally provided only summary crime data, are occurring with the implementation of the National Incident-Based Reporting System (NIBRS). It represents a significant redesign of the original UCR Program and gathers many details about each criminal incident, such as place of occurrence, weapon used, type and value of property damaged or stolen, personal characteristics of the offender and the victim, nature of any relationship between the two, and disposition of the complaint.
- The National Crime Victimization Survey (NCVS) is the second major source of statistical data about crime in the United States. The NCVS, which was first conducted in 1972, is based on victim self-reports rather than on police reports. The NCVS originally built on efforts by both the National Opinion Research Center and the 1967 President's Commission on Law Enforcement and the Administration of Justice to uncover what some had been calling the *dark figure of crime*—that is, those crimes that are not reported to the police and that are relatively hidden from justice system officials. An analysis of victim self-report data led to the realization that crimes of all types were more prevalent than UCR statistics had previously indicated.
- The UCR/NIBRS and NCVS differ in a number of significant ways. First, while the UCR/NIBRS Program makes use of data gleaned from citizens' reports of crime made to enforcement agencies, the NCVS utilizes survey data in compiling its reports. Second, because both the UCR/NIBRS and the NCVS are human creations, they contain only data that their creators think appropriate, and the reports they generate are structured differently.
- This chapter discusses a number of special categories of crime, including crime against women, crime against the elderly, hate crime, corporate and white-collar crime, organized crime, gun crime, drug crime, high-technology and computer crime, and terrorism. Each of these categories is of special concern in contemporary society.

QUESTIONS FOR REVIEW

1. Describe the historical development of the FBI's Uniform Crime Reporting Program, and list the crimes on which it reports. How is the ongoing implementation of the National Incident-Based Reporting System changing the UCR Program? How will data reported under the new UCR/NIBRS differ from the crime statistics reported under the traditional UCR Program?
2. Describe the history of the National Crime Victimization Survey. What do data from the NCVS tell us about crime in the United States today?
3. What are the special categories of crime discussed in this chapter? Why are they important?

Chapter Notes

i. Dan Eggen, "Major Crimes in U.S. Increase: 2001 Rise Follows Nine Years of Decline," *Washington Post*, June 23, 2002, p. A1.
ii. Jonathan Turley, "Arrest Me . . . Before I Strike Again," *USA Today*, February 22, 2005, p. 13A.
iii. Identity Theft Resource Center website, http://www.idtheftcenter.org (accessed April 24, 2010).
iv. Violence against Women Office, *Stalking and Domestic Violence: Report to Congress* (Washington, DC: U.S. Department of Justice, 2001), p. 5.
v. Ibid.
vi. Andrew Backover, "Two Former WorldCom Execs Charged," *USA Today* Online, August 1, 2002, http://www.usatoday.com/money/industries/telecom/2002-08-01-worldcom-execs-surrender_x.htm (accessed August 2, 2006).
vii. Michael L. Benson, Francis T. Cullen, and William J. Maakestad, *Local Prosecutors and Corporate Crime* (Washington, DC: National Institute of Justice, 1992), p. 1.
viii. The Organized Crime Control Act of 1970.
ix. Federal Bureau of Investigation Counterterrorism Section, *Terrorism in the United States, 1987* (Washington, DC: FBI, December 1987).
x. Federal Bureau of Investigation, *FBI Policy and Guidelines: Counterterrorism*, http://www.fbi.gov/contact/fo/jackson/cntrterr.htm (accessed August 26, 2009).
xi. Ibid.

---

1. James Q. Wilson, "Point of View," *Chronicle of Higher Education*, June 10, 1992, p. A40.
2. Chris Balish, "NCIS Honored as Top Scripted TV Series," OnTheRedCarpet.com, March 23, 2010, http://ontheredcarpet.typepad.com/ontheredcarpet/2010/03/crime-drama-ncis-honored-as-top-scripted-tv-series.html (accessed September 1, 2010).
3. Gerard Gilbert, "*CSI*: The Cop Show That Conquered the World," *The (London) Independent*, December 19, 2006, http://www.findarticles.com/p/articles/mi_qn4158/is_20061219/ai_n17081057 (accessed March 10, 2010).
4. Norval Morris, "Crime, the Media, and Our Public Discourse," National Institute of Justice, Perspectives on Crime and Justice video series, recorded May 13, 1997.
5. Ibid.
6. Federal Bureau of Investigation, *Crime in the United States, 1987* (Washington, DC: U.S. Department of Justice, 1988), p. 1.
7. Federal Bureau of Investigation, "About the UCR Program," no date, http://www.fbi.gov/ucr/05cius/about/about_ucr.html (accessed May 29, 2009). The term *crime index* was originally recommended for reevaluation in 2004, but it wasn't until 2006 that use of the term was officially discontinued.
8. Statistics on state agency participation in NIBRS can be seen at Bureau of Justice Statistics, "UCR and NIBRS Participation," http://bjs.ojp.usdoj.gov/content/nibrsstatus.cfm (accessed September 4, 2010).
9. See the FBI's UCR/NIBRS website at http://www.fbi.gov/hq/cjisd/ucr.htm (accessed August 27, 2010).
10. The 1990 Crime Awareness and Campus Security Act (Public Law 101–542) required college campuses to commence publishing annual security reports beginning in September 1992.
11. U.S. Department of Education, *Summary Campus Crime and Security Statistics, 2006–2008: Criminal Offenses* (Washington, DC: U.S. Department of Education, 2010), http://www2.ed.gov/admins/lead/safety/criminal2006-08.xls (accessed September 4, 2010).
12. Katrina Baum and Patsy Klaus, *Violent Victimization of College Students, 1995–2002* (Washington, DC: Bureau of Justice Statistics, 2005).
13. Federal Bureau of Investigation, *Crime in the United States, 2009* (Washington, DC: U.S. Department of Justice, 2010).
14. President's Commission on Law Enforcement and Administration of Justice, *The Challenge of Crime in a Free Society* (Washington, DC: U.S. Government Printing Office, 1967). The commission relied on UCR data. The other crime statistics reported in this section come from Uniform Crime Reports for various years.
15. Frank Hagan, *Research Methods in Criminal Justice and Criminology* (New York: Macmillan, 1982).
16. U.S. Department of Justice, *Fiscal Years 2000–2005 Strategic Plan* (Washington, DC: U.S. Government Printing Office, 2000).
17. The war on drugs, and the use of that term, can be traced back to the Nixon administration. See Dan Baum, *Smoke and Mirrors: The War on Drugs and the Politics of Failure* (reprint, Boston: Little, Brown, 1997).
18. John J. DiIulio, Jr., "The Question of Black Crime," *Public Interest* (fall 1994), pp. 3–12.
19. Quoted in Eggen, "Major Crimes in U.S. Increase," p. A1.
20. Police Executive Research Forum, *A Gathering Storm* (Washington, DC: PERF, 2006).
21. Police Executive Research Forum, *Violent Crime in America: 24 Months of Alarming Trends* (Washington, DC: PERF, 2007).
22. Ibid., p. i.
23. Jim Kessler, Rachel Laser, Michael Earls, and Nikki Yamashiro, *The Impending Crime Wave: Four Dangerous New Trends and How to Stop Them* (Washington, DC: Third Way Foundation, February 2008).
24. For example, while crime clock data may imply that one murder occurs every half hour or so, most murders actually occur during the evening, and only a very few take place around sunrise.
25. Most offense definitions in this chapter are derived from those used by the UCR/NIBRS Program and are taken from the FBI's *Crime in the United States, 2009*, or from the Bureau of Justice Statistics, *Criminal Justice Data Terminology*, 2nd ed. (Washington, DC: BJS, 1981).
26. These and other statistics in this chapter are derived primarily from the FBI's *Crime in the United States, 2009.*
27. Bureau of Justice Statistics, *Report to the Nation on Crime and Justice*, 2nd ed. (Washington, DC: U.S. Government Printing Office, 1988), p. 4.
28. "Feds Deny Thwarting Sniper Suspect's Confession," CNN.com, October 31, 2002, http://www.cnn.com/2002/US/10/30/snipers.interrogation/index.html (accessed October 31, 2002).
29. "Sniper Malvo Given Second Life Sentence," *USA Today*, October 27, 2004, p. 3A.
30. BJS, *Report to the Nation on Crime and Justice*, p. 4.

31. Ibid.
32. For excellent coverage of serial killers, see Steven Egger, *The Killers among Us: An Examination of Serial Murder and Its Investigation* (Upper Saddle River, NJ: Prentice Hall, 1998); Steven A. Egger, *Serial Murder: An Elusive Phenomenon* (Westport, CT: Praeger, 1990); and Stephen J. Giannangelo, *The Psychopathology of Serial Murder: A Theory of Violence* (New York: Praeger, 1996).
33. *BTK* stands for "Bind, Torture, and Kill," an acronym that Rader applied to himself in letters he sent to the media during the 1970s.
34. Several years ago, Lucas recanted all of his confessions, saying that he had never killed anyone—except possibly his mother, a killing he said he didn't remember. See "Condemned Killer Admits Lying, Denies Slayings," *Washington Post*, October 1, 1995.
35. Chikatilo was executed in 1994.
36. Public Law 108–212.
37. FBI, *Crime in the United States, 2009.*
38. Federal Bureau of Investigation, *Uniform Crime Reporting Handbook, 2004* (Washington, DC: FBI, 2005), p. 19.
39. "Study: Rape Vastly Underreported," Associated Press, April 26, 1992.
40. Ronald Barri Flowers, *Women and Criminality: The Woman as Victim, Offender, and Practitioner* (Westport, CT: Greenwood Press, 1987), p. 36.
41. A. Nichols Groth, *Men Who Rape: The Psychology of the Offender* (New York: Plenum Press, 1979).
42. Susan Brownmiller, *Against Our Will: Men, Women, and Rape* (New York: Simon and Schuster, 1975).
43. Dennis J. Stevens, "Motives of Social Rapists," *Free Inquiry in Creative Sociology*, Vol. 23, No. 2 (November 1995), pp. 117–126.
44. BJS, *Report to the Nation on Crime and Justice*, p. 5.
45. Ibid.
46. FBI, *Crime in the United States, 2009.* For UCR Program reporting purposes, *minorities* are defined as African Americans, Native Americans, Asians, Pacific Islanders, and Alaskan Natives.
47. "Easter Bunny Charged with Battery for Mall Attack," Associated Press, April 18, 2006.
48. This offense is sometimes called *assault with a deadly weapon with intent to kill (AWDWWITK).*
49. FBI, *Crime in the United States, 2009.*
50. BJS, *Report to the Nation on Crime and Justice*, p. 6.
51. Ibid.
52. "Four Arrested for Stealing Moon Rocks," Associated Press, July 23, 2002; and Sheena McFarland, "U. Student Arrested for Moon Rock Theft," *Daily Utah Chronicle*, http://www.dailyutahchronicle.com/main.cfm/include/detail/storyid/259076.html (accessed August 22, 2005).
53. "Yale Says Student Stole His Education," *USA Today*, April 12, 1995.
54. Steven J. Vaughan-Nichols, "Cisco Source Code Reportedly Stolen," *eWeek*, May 18, 2004, http://www.eweek.com/article2/0,1759,1593862,00.asp (accessed May 17, 2009).
55. Ibid.
56. FBI, *Uniform Crime Reporting Handbook, 2004*, p. 28.
57. Matt Stearns and Donald Bradley, "Boy's Last Moments of Life Are Frozen in Mother's Memory," *Kansas City Star*, February 23, 2000.
58. "Jury Recommends Life Term in Dragging Death Wednesday," Associated Press, October 3, 2001.
59. Patsy Klaus, *Carjacking, 1993–2002* (Washington, DC: Bureau of Justice Statistics, July 2004).
60. FBI, *Crime in the United States, 2009.*
61. As indicated in the UCR definition of *arson*. See Federal Bureau of Investigation, *Crime in the United States, 1998* (Washington, DC: U.S. Department of Justice, 1999).
62. FBI, *Crime in the United States, 2009.*
63. Ibid.
64. "Trends in Crime and Victimization," *Criminal Justice Research Reports*, Vol. 2, No. 6 (July/August 2001), p. 83.
65. For additional information, see Michael Rand and Shannan M. Catalano, *Criminal Victimization, 2006* (Washington, DC: Bureau of Justice Statistics, 2007); and Patsy A. Klaus, *Crime and the Nation's Households, 2006* (Washington, DC: Bureau of Justice Statistics, 2007).
66. Klaus, *Crime and the Nation's Households, 2006.*
67. Rand and Catalano, *Criminal Victimization, 2006.*
68. Ibid., p. 1.
69. See, for example, President's Commission on Law Enforcement and Administration of Justice, *The Challenge of Crime in a Free Society*, pp. 22–23.
70. Bureau of Justice Statistics, *NCVS Redesign*, http://bjs.ojp.usdoj.gov/index.cfm?ty=tp&tid=91 (accessed September 13, 2010).
71. BJS, *Report to the Nation on Crime and Justice*, p. 27.
72. Hagan, *Research Methods in Criminal Justice and Criminology*, p. 89.
73. Bureau of Justice Statistics, *Criminal Victimization in the United States, 1985* (Washington, DC: U.S. Government Printing Office, 1987), p. 1.
74. FBI, *Crime in the United States, 2001*, preliminary data, http://www.fbi.gov./ucr/01prelim.pdf (accessed August 27, 2002).
75. Terance D. Miethe and Richard C. McCorkle, *Crime Profiles: The Anatomy of Dangerous Persons, Places, and Situations* (Los Angeles: Roxbury, 1998), p. 19.
76. The definition of *rape* employed by the UCR/NIBRS Program, however, automatically excludes crimes of homosexual rape such as might occur in prisons and jails. As a consequence, the rape of males is excluded from the official count for crimes of rape.
77. Rand and Catalano, *Criminal Victimization, 2006*, p. 4.
78. Thomas Simon et al., *Injuries from Violent Crime, 1992–98* (Washington, DC: Bureau of Justice Statistics, 2001), p. 5.
79. See, for example, Elizabeth Stanko, "When Precaution Is Normal: A Feminist Critique of Crime Prevention," in Loraine Gelsthorpe and Allison Morris, eds., *Feminist Perspectives in Criminology* (Philadelphia: Open University Press, 1990).
80. For more information, see Eve S. Buzawa and Carl G. Buzawa, *Domestic Violence: The Criminal Justice Response* (Thousand Oaks, CA: Sage, 1996).
81. "Battered Women Tell Their Stories to the Senate," *Charlotte (NC) Observer*, July 10, 1991.
82. Patricia Tjaden and Nancy Thoennes, *Full Report of the Prevalence, Incidence, and Consequences of Violence against Women: Findings from the National Violence against Women Survey* (Washington, DC: National Institute of Justice, 2000).
83. Violence against Women Office, *Stalking and Domestic Violence: Report to Congress* (Washington, DC: U.S. Department of Justice, 2001).
84. U.S. Code, Title 18, Section 2261A.
85. As modified through VAWA 2000.
86. Violence against Women Office, *Stalking and Domestic Violence.*
87. Many of the data in this section come from Bureau of Justice Statistics, *Crimes against Persons Age 65 or Older, 1993–2002* (Rockville, MD: BJS, 2005).
88. Lamar Jordan, "Law Enforcement and the Elderly: A Concern for the Twenty-First Century," *FBI Law Enforcement Bulletin*, May 2002, pp. 20–23.

89. Public Law 101–275.
90. H.R. 4797, 102d Cong. 2d Sess. (1992).
91. FBI, *Crime in the United States, 2007* (Washington, DC: U.S. Dept. of Justice, 2008).
92. "Sept. 11 Attacks Cited in Nearly 25 Percent Increase in Florida Hate Crimes," Associated Press, August 30, 2002.
93. "Number of Hate Groups Rises, Poverty Law Center Reports," *Criminal Justice Newsletter*, April 15, 2008, p. 7.
94. Richard Esposito, Eloise Harper, and Maddy Sauer, "Bernie Madoff Pleads Guilty to Ponzi Scheme, Goes Straight to Jail, Says He's 'Deeply Sorry,'" ABC News, March 12, 2009, http://abcnews.go.com/Blotter/WallStreet/Story?id=7066715&page=1 (accessed July 4, 2009).
95. Joanna Chung and Henny Sender, "Investors Fear $50bn Loss in Madoff's 'Big Lie,'" *Financial Times*, December 14, 2008.
96. Diana B. Henriques, "Madoff Is Sentenced to 150 Years for Ponzi Scheme," *New York Times*, June 29, 2009, http://www.nytimes.com/2009/06/30/business/30madoff.html (accessed September 28, 2010).
97. Dina ElBoghdady, "Mortgage Fraud Up as Credit Tightens," *Washington Post*, March 17, 2009, http://www.washingtonpost.com/wp-dyn/content/article/2009/03/16/AR2009031601612.html (accessed May 13, 2009).
98. Jennifer Liberto, "More Muscle Sought in Fraud Fight," CNNMoney.com, May 8, 2009, http://money.cnn.com/2009/05/08/news/economy/mortgage_fraud/index.htm (accessed May 13, 2009).
99. Federal Trade Commission, "Federal and State Agencies Crack Down on Mortgage Modification and Foreclosure Rescue Scams," http://www.ftc.gov/opa/2009/04/hud.shtm (accessed May 13, 2009).
100. *Andersen* v. *U.S.*, 544 U.S. 696 (2005).
101. Public Broadcasting System, "Enron: After the Collapse," http://www.pbs.org/newshour/bb/business/enron/player6.html (accessed August 27, 2005).
102. Edwin H. Sutherland, "White-Collar Criminality," *American Sociological Review* (February 1940), p. 12.
103. Scott Lindlaw, "Bush to Propose Crackdown on Corporate Abuses: President's Own Business Dealings Come under Scrutiny," Associated Press, July 9, 2002, http://www.washingtonpost.com/wp-dyn/articles/A43384-2002Jul9.html (accessed May 17, 2005).
104. Public Law 107–204.
105. Quoted on the Transnational Threats Initiative home page of the Center for Strategic and International Studies (CSIS), http://www.csis.org/tnt/index.htm (accessed August 22, 2007).
106. These ideas were originally expressed by Assistant U.S. Attorney General Laurie Robinson in an address given at the Twelfth International Congress on Criminology, Seoul, Korea, August 28, 1998.
107. Caroline Wolf Harlow, *Firearm Use by Offenders* (Washington, DC: Bureau of Justice Statistics, 2001).
108. Ibid., p. 1.
109. Public Law 103–159.
110. U.S. Code, Title 18, Section 922(q)(1)(A).
111. Harlow, *Firearm Use by Offenders*.
112. *Firearms Purchased from Federal Firearm Licensees Using Bogus Identification* (Washington, DC: General Accounting Office, 2001).
113. John C. Moorhouse and Brent Wanner, "Does Gun Control Reduce Crime or Does Crime Increase Gun Control?" *CATO Journal*, Vol. 103 (2006), pp. 103–124.
114. Public Law 103–322, 108, Stat. 1796 (codified as amended in scattered sections of 18, 21, 28, 42, etc., U.S. Code).
115. Public Law 104–208, an amendment to U.S. Code, Title 18, Section 921(a). Also known as the Lautenberg Amendment.
116. Jacob R. Clark, "Police Careers May Take a Beating from Fed Domestic-Violence Law," *Law Enforcement News*, Vol. 23, No. 461 (February 14, 1997), p. 1.
117. *District of Columbia* v. *Heller*, 554 U.S. ___ (2008).
118. *McDonald* v. *City of Chicago*, U.S. Supreme Court, No. 08-1521 (decided June 28, 2010).
119. Sarah Brady, "Statement on the Sniper Shootings," October 8, 2002, http://www.bradycampaign.org/press/release.asp?Record 5429 (accessed October 16, 2007); and Microstamping of Firearms Required by California Law," *Criminal Justice Newsletter*, October 2, 2007, p. 1.
120. Tony Perry, "96 Arrested in San Diego State Drug Bust," *Los Angeles Times*, May 7, 2008, http://www.latimes.com/news/local/la-me-drugbust7-2008may07,0,3741335.story?page=1 (accessed May 7, 2008).
121. As cited in Donna Leinwand, "Drug, Terror Rings Find New Ways to Launder Money," *USA Today*, January 12, 2006.
122. J. M. Chaiken and M. R. Chaiken, *Varieties of Criminal Behavior* (Santa Monica, CA: RAND Corporation, 1982).
123. D. McBride, "Trends in Drugs and Death," paper presented at the annual meeting of the American Society of Criminology, Denver, 1983.
124. National Criminal Justice Reference Service, *The Micro Domain: Behavior and Homicide*, http://www.ncjrs.org/pdffiles/167262-3.pdf (accessed February 23, 2002).
125. Bureau of Justice Statistics, *Substance Abuse and Treatment: State and Federal Prisoners* (Washington, DC: U.S. Department of Justice, January 1999).
126. Bureau of Justice Statistics, *Drug Use, Testing, and Treatment in Jails* (Washington, DC: U.S. Department of Justice, May 2000).
127. Information in this paragraph comes from John Scalia, *Federal Drug Offenders, 1999, with Trends, 1984–99* (Washington, DC: Bureau of Justice Statistics, 2001); and Bureau of Justice Statistics, *Federal Criminal Case Processing, 2002—With Trends, 1982–2002* (Washington, DC: BJS, 2005).
128. Ibid.
129. Ryan Naraine, "Cryzip Trojan Encrypts Files, Demands Ransom," eWeek.com, March 13, 2006, http://www.eweek.com/article2/0,1895,1937408,00.asp?kc=ewnws031406dtx1k0000599 (accessed January 5, 2007).
130. For suggested computer-crime categories, see Peter Grabosky, "Computer Crime: A Criminological Overview," paper presented at the Workshop on Crimes Related to the Computer Network, Tenth United Nations Congress on the Prevention of Crime and the Treatment of Offenders, Vienna, Austria, April 15, 2000, http://www.aic.gov.au/conferences/other/compcrime/computercrime.pdf (accessed January 12, 2002). Also see David L. Carter, "Computer Crime Categories: How Techno-Criminals Operate," *FBI Law Enforcement Journal* (July 1995), pp. 21–26.
131. Grabosky, "Computer Crime."
132. Kevin Johnson, "Hijackers' E-Mails Sifted for Clues," *USA Today*, October 11, 2001.
133. Wendy Koch, "Dozens Arrested in Online Child Porn Ring," *USA Today*, May 27, 2010.
134. Richard Zitrin, "Woman Charged with Online Prostitution," APB Online, June 10, 1999, http://www.apbonline.com/911/1999/06/10/hooker0610_01.html (accessed June 19, 1999).
135. "Invasion of the Data Snatchers!" *Time*, September 26, 1988, pp. 62–67.
136. Public Law 108–187.
137. Peter Firstbrook, "META Trend Update: The Changing Threat Landscape," Meta Group, March 24, 2005,

http://www.metagroup.com/us/displayArticle.do?oid551768 (accessed July 5, 2005).
138. *MGM* v. *Grokster*, 545 U.S. 913 (2005).
139. Gregg Keizer, "Microsoft Says Phishing Bad, Offers Little New for Defense," *TechWeb News*, March 15, 2005, http://www.techweb.com/wire/159900391 (accessed July 7, 2005).
140. Avivah Litan, "Phishing Victims Likely Will Suffer Identity Theft Fraud," Gartner, Inc., May 14, 2004, http://www.gartner.com/Display-Document?ref5g_search&id544811 (accessed July 6, 2005).
141. Symantec Corporation, *2010 SMB Information Protection Survey*, http://www.slideshare.net/symantec/2010-smb-information-protection-survey#text-version (accessed September 8, 2010).
142. "Focus on Physical Security, Too," *eWeek*, January 27, 2003, p. 6a.
143. Ramona R. Rantala, *Cybercrime against Businesses: Pilot Test Results, 2001 Computer Security Survey* (Washington, DC: Bureau of Justice Statistics, 2004).
144. Emergency Response and Research Institute, *Summary of Emergency Response and Research Institute Terrorism Statistics: 2000 and 2001*, http://www.emergency.com/2002/terroris00-01.pdf (accessed August 22, 2002).
145. Federal Bureau of Investigation, Counterterrorism Section, *Terrorism in the United States, 1987* (Washington, DC: FBI, 1987), in which the full version of the definition offered here can be found. See also *FBI Policy and Guidelines: Counterterrorism*, which offers a somewhat less formal definition of the term; http://www.fbi.gov/contact/fo/jackson/cntrterr.htm (accessed January 15, 2002).
146. Adapted from *FBI Policy and Guidelines*.
147. Ibid.
148. See Barry Collin, "The Future of Cyberterrorism," *Crime and Justice International* (March 1997), pp. 15–18.
149. John Arquilla and David Ronfeldt, *The Advent of Netwar* (Santa Monica, CA: RAND Corporation, 1996).
150. Mark M. Pollitt, "Cyberterrorism: Fact or Fancy?" in *Proceedings of the Twentieth National Information Systems Security Conference*, October 1997, pp. 285–289.
151. "Chief Security Officers Remind Citizens of the Dangers of Cyberattacks and Recommend Tips," *CSO Magazine*, http://www2.csoonline.html/info/release.html?CID=9065 (accessed August 28, 2006).
152. Robert S. Mueller III, executive speech at Chatham House, London, England, April 7, 2008, http://www.fbi.gov/pressrel/speeches/mueller040708.htm (accessed May 20, 2008).
153. Central Intelligence Agency, National Foreign Intelligence Council, *Global Trends, 2015: A Dialogue about the Future with Nongovernment Experts* (Washington, DC: U.S. Government Printing Office, 2000).
154. Ibid.

Criminal Law

Criminal Law

Learning Objectives

After reading this chapter, you should be able to:

1. Explain the nature and purpose of law.
2. Discuss the nature of the rule of law, and describe its importance in Western democratic societies.
3. Identify the various categories or types of law, and explain the purpose of each.
4. List and describe the five categories of crime.
5. List and describe the eight general features of crime.
6. Explain what is meant by the elements of a specific criminal offense.
7. Discuss the four broad categories of criminal defenses that our legal system recognizes.

JG Photography/Alamy

"Law is the art of the good and the fair."

—Ulpian, Roman judge (circa A.D. 200)

"Law should be like death, which spares no one."

—Montesquieu (1689–1755)

"Every law is an infraction of liberty."

—Jeremy Bentham (1748–1832)

Introduction

In 2003, after the American military had toppled the regime of Iraqi dictator Saddam Hussein but before the establishment of a new Iraqi government, soldiers of the U.S. Third Infantry Division had to release a man who had taken his beaten and bloodied wife to a Baghdad hospital for treatment and had continued to beat her while waiting for doctors to arrive.[1] When soldiers restrained the man, he exclaimed that he was exercising his marital rights under Islamic tradition and was beating his wife because she had interfered with his attempts to have intercourse with the couple's 14-year-old daughter. "The sad thing is there was nothing we could do," said Sergeant First Class Michael Shirley of Hinesville, Georgia, "apart from separate them and send her to her mother's house in a taxi, because there are no laws against domestic violence here. The women have to respect their husband's decisions. We can't get involved with religious or cultural beliefs."[2]

In contrast to prewar Iraq, modern postindustrial societies like the United States have developed highly formalized secular legal systems. Laws govern many aspects of our lives, and we are expected to know what the law *says* as it applies to our daily lives and to *follow* it. But do we really know what law is? The job of this chapter is to discuss the law both as a product of rule creation and as a guide for behavior. We will also examine criminal law in some detail, and we will discuss defenses commonly used by defendants charged with violations of the criminal law.

The Nature and Purpose of Law

Imagine a society without laws. A **law** mandates or proscribes a certain behavior and can be a product of rule creation, a guide for people's behavior, or both. Without civil law, people would not know what to expect from one another, nor would they be able to plan for the future with any degree of certainty. Without criminal law, people wouldn't feel safe because the more powerful could take what they wanted from the less powerful. Without constitutional law, people could not exercise the basic rights that are available to them as citizens of a free nation. A society needs laws to uphold fairness and to prevent the victimization of innocents.

1 Explain the nature and purpose of law.

law
A rule of conduct, generally found enacted in the form of a statute, that proscribes or mandates certain forms of behavior.

statutory law
The written or codified law; "the law on the books," as enacted by a government body or agency having the power to make laws.

penal code
The written, organized, and compiled form of the criminal laws of a jurisdiction.

case law
The body of judicial precedent, historically built on legal reasoning and past interpretations of statutory laws, that serves as a guide to decision making, especially in the courts.

Practically speaking, laws regulate relationships between people and also between parties, such as government agencies and individuals. They channel and simultaneously constrain human behavior, and they empower individuals while contributing to public order. Laws also serve other purposes. They ensure that the philosophical, moral, and economic perspectives of their creators are protected and made credible. They maintain values and uphold established patterns of social privilege. They sustain existing power relationships; finally, they support a system for the punishment and rehabilitation of offenders (Table 1). Modifications of the law, when gradually induced, promote orderly change in the rest of society.

Our laws are found in statutory provisions and constitutional enactments,[3] as well as in hundreds of years of rulings by courts at all levels. According to the authoritative *Black's Law Dictionary*, the word *law* "generally contemplates both statutory and case law."[4] **Statutory law** is "the law on the books." It results from legislative action and is often thought of as "the law of the land." Written laws exist in both criminal and civil areas and are called *codes.* Once laws have been written down in organized fashion, they are said to be *codified.* Federal statutes are compiled in the United States Code (U.S.C.), which is available online in its entirety at **Library Extra 1**. State codes and municipal ordinances are also readily available in written, or statutory, form. The written form of the criminal law is called the **penal code**. **Case law**, which we will discuss in detail a bit later, is the law that results from judicial decisions.

TABLE 1
What Do Laws Do?

- Laws maintain order in society.
- Laws regulate human interaction.
- Laws enforce moral beliefs.
- Laws define the economic environment.
- Laws enhance predictability.
- Laws support the powerful.
- Laws promote orderly social change.
- Laws sustain individual rights.
- Laws redress wrongs.
- Laws identify wrongdoers.
- Laws mandate punishment and retribution.

common law
The body of law originating from usage and custom rather than from written statutes. The term refers to an unwritten body of judicial opinion, originally developed by English courts, that is based on nonstatutory customs, traditions, and precedents that help guide judicial decision making.

rule of law
The maxim that an orderly society must be governed by established principles and known codes that are applied uniformly and fairly to all of its members.

But the laws of our country are not unambiguous. If all of "the law" could be found in written legal codes, it would be plain to nearly everyone, and we would need far fewer lawyers than are practicing today. But some laws—the precedents established by courts—do not exist "on the books," and even those that do are open to interpretation. This is where common law comes into play. **Common law** is the traditional body of unwritten historical precedents created from everyday social customs, rules, and practices, many of which were supported by judicial decisions during early times. Common law principles are still used to interpret many legal issues in quite a few states. Hence it is not uncommon to hear of jurisdictions within the United States referred to as "common law jurisdictions" or "common law states."

The Rule of Law

> 2 Discuss the nature of the rule of law, and describe its importance in Western democratic societies.

The social, economic, and political stability of any society depends largely on the development and institutionalization of a predictable system of laws. Western democratic societies adhere to the **rule of law**, which is sometimes also referred to as the *supremacy of law*. The rule of law centers on the belief that an orderly society must be governed by established principles and known codes that are applied uniformly and fairly to all of its members. Under this tenet, no one is above the law, and those who make or enforce the law must also abide by it. The principle was well illustrated when, in 2007, former Ohio Republican Congressman Robert W. Ney was sentenced to 30 months in prison for corrupt dealings with convicted congressional lobbyist Jack Abramoff.[5]

> The law isn't justice. It's a very imperfect mechanism. If you press exactly the right buttons and are also lucky, justice may show up in the answer.
> —Raymond Chandler (1888–1959)[i]

The rule of law has been called the greatest political achievement of our culture. Without it, few other human achievements—especially those that require the coordinated efforts of a large number of people—would be possible. President John F. Kennedy eloquently explained the rule of law, saying, "Americans are free to disagree with the law, but not to disobey it; for [in] a government of laws and not of men, no man, however prominent and powerful, no mob, however unruly or boisterous, is entitled to defy a court of law."[6]

The rule of law has also been called "the foundation of liberties in the Western world,"[7] for it means that due process has to be followed in any criminal prosecution, and it is due process that serves as a check on arbitrary state power.

The American Bar Association notes that the rule of law includes these elements:[8]

- Freedom from private lawlessness provided by the legal system of a politically organized society
- A relatively high degree of objectivity in the formulation of legal norms and a like degree of evenhandedness in their application
- Legal ideas and juristic devices for the attainment of individual and group objectives within the bounds of ordered liberty
- Substantive and procedural limitations on governmental power in the interest of the individual for the enforcement of which there are appropriate legal institutions and machinery

jurisprudence
The philosophy of law. Also, the science and study of the law.

criminal law
The body of rules and regulations that define and specify the nature of and punishments for offenses of a public nature or for wrongs committed against the state or society. Also called *penal law*.

Jurisprudence is the philosophy of law or the science and study of the law, including the rule of law. To learn more about the rule of law, including its historical development, visit **Web Extra 1**.

Types of Law

> 3 Identify the various categories or types of law, and explain the purpose of each.

Criminal and civil law are the best-known types of modern law. However, scholars and philosophers have drawn numerous distinctions between categories of law that rest on the source, intent, and application of the law (Figure 1).

Criminal law, also called *penal law*, refers to the body of rules and regulations that define and specify the nature of and punishments for offenses of a public nature or for

▲ Former Detroit Mayor Kwame Kilpatrick, former Illinois Governors George Ryan and Rod Blagojevich, and former U.S. Representative William Jefferson. As their cases demonstrate, the rule of law means that no one is above the law—not even those who make it. Kilpatrick (*top left*), charged with ten felony counts, pleaded guilty to reduced charges and served 99 days in jail before being released in February 2009; he reentered prison in 2010 for violating probation. Ryan (*bottom right*) was sentenced to six and a half years in federal prison for racketeering and fraud. He entered prison in November 2007. Blagojevich (*top right*) was tried in 2010 on federal criminal conspiracy charges and convicted on one count of making false statements to investigators. Jefferson (*bottom left*) served nine terms in the U.S. House of Representatives prior to being sentenced in 2009 to 13 years in prison for using his office to solicit bribes. How would you explain the rule of law to someone who is unfamiliar with it?

From left to right: Getty Images, Inc./Bill Pugliano; AP Photo/Seth Perlman; AP Photo/Kevin Wolf; and © Tanen Maury/epa/CORBIS All Rights Reserved

wrongs committed against the state or society. Public order is compromised whenever a criminal act occurs, and those found guilty of violating the criminal law are punished. Punishment for crime is philosophically justified by the fact that the offender *intended* the harm and is responsible for it. Criminal law, which is built on constitutional principles and which operates within an established set of procedures applicable to the criminal justice system, is composed of both statutory (written law) and case law.

Written law is of two types: substantive and procedural. **Substantive criminal law** describes what constitutes particular crimes, such as murder, rape, robbery, and assault, and specifies the appropriate punishment for each particular offense. **Procedural law** is a body of rules that determines the proceedings by which legal rights are enforced. The law of criminal procedure, for example, regulates the gathering of evidence and the processing of offenders by the criminal justice system. General rules of evidence, search and seizure, procedures to be followed in an arrest, trial procedures, and other specified processes by which

substantive criminal law
The part of the law that defines crimes and specifies punishments.

procedural law
The part of the law that specifies the methods to be used in enforcing substantive law.

FIGURE 1
Types of Law

CRIMINAL LAW

Criminal law is defined as the body of rules and regulations that define and specify the nature of and punishments for offenses of a public nature or for wrongs committed against the state or society. Fundamental to the concept of criminal law is the assumption that crimanal acts injure not just individuals but society as a whole. Criminal law is also called *penal law.*

These crimes not only offend their victims but also disrupt the peaceful order of society. It is for this reason that the state begins the official process of bringing the offender to justice. The state will be the plaintiff in the criminal proceeding. Those found guilty of violating a criminal law are punished.

EXAMPLES: Murder, rape, robbery, and assault are examples of criminal offenses against which there are laws.

ADMINISTRATIVE LAW

Administrative law is the body of regulations that governments create to control the activities of industries, businesses, and individuals. For the most part, a breach of administrative law is not a crime.

Administrative agencies will sometimes arrange settlements that fall short of court action but that are considered binding on individuals or groups that have not followed the rules of administrative law.

EXAMPLES: Tax laws, health codes, restrictions on pollution and waste disposal, vehicle regulation laws, and building codes are examples of administrative laws.

STATUTORY LAW

Refers to the law on the books; written, codified laws.

EXAMPLE: The acts of legislatures.

Substantive criminal law is a form of statutory law that describes what constitutes particular crimes and specifies the appropriate punishment for the offense.

Procedural law is a type of statutory law. It is a body of rules that determines the proceedings by which legal rights are enforced. These laws regulate the gathering of evidence and the processing of offenders by the criminal justice system.

CIVIL LAW

Civil law governs relationships between and among people, businesses and other organizations, and agencies of government. In contrast to the criminal law, whose violation is against the state or the nation, civil law governs relationships between parties.

Typically civil suits seek compensation (usually in the form of property or money). A violation of the civil law is not a crime. It may be a contract violation or a tort. A tort is a wrongful act, damage, or injury not involving a breach of contract. Because a tort is a personal wrong and not a crime, it is left to the aggrieved individual to bring the case to court. Civil law is more concerned with assessing liability than it is with intent. Civil suits can also be brought against a crime where the intent is clear. His or her victim may decide to seek monetary compensation.

EXAMPLES: Includes things such as rules for contracts, divorces, child support and custody, the creation of wills, property transfers, libel, and many other contractual and social obligations.

CASE LAW

Case law comes from judicial decisions and is also referred to as the law of precedent. It represents the accumulated wisdom of trial and appellate courts. Once a court decision is rendered, it is written down. At the appellate level, the reasoning behind the decision is recorded as well.

The Supreme Court is the highest-level appellete court. *Stare decisis* refers to the principle of recognizing previous decisions as precedents for guiding future deliberations.

A vertical rule requires that decisions made by a higher court be taken into consideration by lower courts.

The horizontal dimension refers to cases handled by the same court that should be decided in a similar way.

EXAMPLES: Under the law of precedent, the reasonings of previous courts should be taken into consideration by other courts in settling similar future cases.

COMMON LAW

Common law is that body of law originating from usage and custom rather than from written statutes.

EXAMPLE: English common law is the basis for much Armerican criminal law, although most states have codified common law principles in their written statutes.

the justice system operates are all contained in procedural law. Each state has its own set of criminal procedure laws, as does the federal government. Laws of criminal procedure balance a suspect's rights against the state's interests in the speedy and efficient processing of criminal defendants. View the Federal Rules of Criminal Procedure and the Federal Rules of Evidence at **Library Extras 2** and **3**.

civil law
The branch of modern law that governs relationships between parties.

Civil law, in contrast to criminal law, governs relationships between and among people, businesses and other organizations, and agencies of government. It contains rules for contracts, divorces, child support and custody, the creation of wills, property transfers, negligence, libel, unfair practices in hiring, the manufacture and sale of consumer goods with hidden hazards for the user, and many other contractual and social obligations. When the civil law is violated, a civil suit may follow. Typically, civil suits seek compensation (usually in the form of property or monetary damages), not punishment. A violation of the civil law is not a crime. It may be a contract violation or a **tort**—which is a wrongful act, damage, or injury not involving a breach of contract. Because a tort is a personal wrong and not a crime, it is left to the aggrieved individual to set the machinery of the court in motion—that is, to bring a suit. The parties to a civil suit are referred to as the *plaintiff*, who seeks relief, and the *defendant*, against whom relief is sought. Civil suits are also sometimes brought by crime victims against those whose criminal intent is clear. Once the perpetrator of a crime has been convicted, the victim may decide to seek monetary compensation from him or her through our system of civil laws.

tort
A wrongful act, damage, or injury not involving a breach of contract. Also, a private or civil wrong or injury.

Still another kind of law, *administrative law,* is the body of regulations that governments create to control the activities of industries, businesses, and individuals. Tax laws, health codes, restrictions on pollution and waste disposal, vehicle registration laws, and building codes are examples of administrative laws. Other administrative laws cover practices in the areas of customs (imports and exports), immigration, agriculture, product safety, and most areas of manufacturing. For the most part, a breach of administrative law is not a crime. However, criminal law and administrative regulations may overlap. For instance, organized criminal activity is prevelant in the area of toxic waste disposal—an area covered by many administrative regulations—which has led to criminal prosecutions in several states.

Legal experts also talk about case law, or the law of **precedent**. Case law comes from judicial decisions and represents the accumulated wisdom of trial and appellate courts (those that hear appeals) in criminal, civil, and administrative law cases over the years. Once a court decision is rendered, it is written down. At the appellate level, the reasoning behind the decision is recorded as well. Under the law of precedent, this reasoning is then taken into consideration by other courts in settling similar future cases. The principle of recognizing previous decisions as precedents to guide future deliberations, called ***stare decisis***, forms the basis for our modern law of precedent. *Stare decisis* makes for predictability in the law. The court with the greatest influence, of course, is the U.S. Supreme Court, and the precedents it establishes are used as guidelines in the process of legal reasoning by which lower courts reach conclusions.

precedent
A legal principle that ensures that previous judicial decisions are authoritatively considered and incorporated into future cases.

> The greatest happiness of the greatest number is the foundation of morals and legislation.
> —Jeremy Bentham (1748–1832)

stare decisis
A legal principle that requires that in subsequent cases on similar issues of law and fact, courts are bound by their own earlier decisions and by those of higher courts having jurisdiction over them. The term literally means "standing by decided matters."

Learn more about the evolution of American criminal law at **Library Extra 4**. Online criminal law journals may be accessed at **Library Extras 5** and **6**.

General Categories of Crime

Violations of the *criminal* law can be of many different types and can vary in severity. Five general categories of criminal law violations can be identified: (1) felonies, (2) misdemeanors, (3) offenses, (4) treason and espionage, and (5) inchoate offenses (Figure 2).

> 4 List and describe the five categories of crime.

Felonies are serious crimes; they include murder, rape, aggravated assault, robbery, burglary, and arson. Today, many felons receive prison sentences, although the range of potential penalties includes everything from probation and a fine to capital punishment. Under common law (which was discussed earlier in this chapter), felons could be sentenced to death, could have their property confiscated, or both. Following common law tradition, people who are convicted of felonies today usually lose certain privileges. Some states, for example, make a felony conviction and incarceration grounds for uncontested divorce. Others prohibit offenders from voting, running for public office, or owning a firearm and exclude them from some professions, such as medicine, law, and police work.

felony
A criminal offense punishable by death or by incarceration in a prison facility for at least one year.

Misdemeanors are relatively minor crimes, consisting of offenses such as petty theft, which is stealing items of little worth; simple assault, in which the victim suffers no serious injury and in which none was intended; breaking and entering; possessing burglary tools; being disorderly

misdemeanor
An offense punishable by incarceration, usually in a local confinement facility, for a period whose upper limit is prescribed by statute in a given jurisdiction, typically one year or less.

Freedom or Safety? You Decide.
Should Violent Speech Be Free Speech?

In 2005, a Virginia jury convicted 42-year-old Muslim scholar Ali al-Timimi of a number of offenses, including the crime of incitement, conspiring to carry firearms and explosives, and soliciting others to make war against the United States. The U.S.-born Islamic spiritual adviser had spoken frequently at the Center for Islamic Information and Education—also known as the Dar al Arqam Islamic Center—in Falls Church, Virginia. Prosecutors told jurors that al-Timimi had verbally encouraged his followers to train with terrorist organizations and to engage in violent Jihad, or holy war, against America and its allies. Al-Timimi lived much of his life in the Washington, D.C., area and had earned a doctorate in computational biology from George Mason University. As a teenager he spent two years in Saudi Arabia with his family, where he became interested in Islam.

Following conviction, al-Timimi was sentenced to life in prison without the possibility of parole, plus 70 years—a sentence meant to guarantee that he would never leave prison.

The al-Timimi case raises a number of interesting issues, among them the question of when violent speech crosses the line from free expression into criminal advocacy. The First Amendment to the U.S. Constitution guarantees the right to free speech. It is a fundamental guarantee of our democratic way of life. So, for example, the speech of those who advocate a new form of government in the United States is protected, even though their ideas may appear anti-American and ill considered. In the 1957 case of *Roth* v. *United States*, the U.S. Supreme Court held that "the protection given speech and press was fashioned to assure unfettered interchange of ideas for the bringing about of political and social changes desired by the people."

It is important to remember, however, that constitutional rights are not without limit—that is, they have varying applicability under differing conditions. Some forms of speech are too dangerous to be allowed, even under our liberal rules.

Freedom of speech does not mean, for example, that you have a protected right to stand up in a crowded theater and yell "Fire!" That's because the panic that would follow such an exclamation would likely cause injuries and would put members of the public at risk of harm. Hence the courts have held that although freedom of speech is guaranteed by the Constitution, there are limits to it. (Shouting "Fire!" in a public park would likely not be considered an actionable offense.)

Similarly, saying, "The president deserves to die," horrific as it may sound, may be merely a matter of personal opinion. Anyone who says "I'm going to kill the president," however, can wind up in jail because threatening the life of the president is a crime—as is the act of communicating threats of imminent violence in most jurisdictions.

Al-Timimi's mistake may have been the timing of his remarks, which were made to a public gathering in Virginia five days after the September 11, 2001, attacks. In his speech, al-Timimi called for a "holy war" and "violent Jihad" against the West. He was later quoted by converts with whom he met as referring to American forces in Afghanistan as "legitimate targets."

Critics of al-Timimi's conviction point to a seeming double standard under which people can be arrested for unpopular speech, but not for popular speech—regardless of the degree of violence it implies. They note, for example, that conservative columnist Ann Coulter has suggested in writing that "we should invade (Muslim) countries, kill their leaders and convert them to Christianity," but she was never arrested for what she wrote.

YOU DECIDE

Should al-Timimi's advocacy of violence be unlawful? Why or why not? Might we have more to fear from the suppression of speech (even speech like al-Timimi's) than from its free expression? If so, how?

References: "Virginia Man Convicted of Urging War on U.S.," *USA Today*, April 27, 2005; Jonathan Turley, "When Is Violent Speech Still Free Speech?" *USA Today*, May 3, 2005; and Eric Lichtblau, "Administration Continues Eavesdropping Defense," *New York Times*, January 24, 2006, http://www.nytimes.com/2006/01/24/politics/24cnd-wiretap.html (accessed August 28, 2008).

FIGURE 2
General Categories of Crime

FELONY
A criminal offense punishable by death or by incarceration in a prison facility for at least one year.

INCHOATE OFFENSE
An offense not yet completed. Also, an offense that consists of an action or conduct that is a step toward the intended commission of another offense.

OFFENSE
A violation of the criminal law. Also, in some jurisdictions, a minor crime, such as jaywalking, that is sometimes described as *ticketable*. Such minor offenses are also known as *infractions*.

MISDEMEANOR
An offense punishable by incarceration, usually in a local confinement facility, for a period whose upper limit is prescribed by statute in a given jurisdiction, typically one year or less.

TREASON
A U.S. citizen's actions to help a foreign government overthrow, make war against, or seriously injure the United States. Also, the attempt to overthrow the government of the society of which one is a member.

ESPIONAGE
The "gathering, transmitting, or losing" of information related to the national defense in such a manner that the information becomes available to enemies of the United States and may be used to their advantage.

in public; disturbing the peace; filing a false crime report; and writing bad checks, although the amount for which the check is written may determine the classification of this offense. In general, misdemeanors are any crime punishable by a year or less in prison. In fact, most misdemeanants receive suspended sentences involving a fine and supervised probation.

A third category of crime is the **offense**. Although, strictly speaking, all violations of the criminal law can be called *criminal offenses*, the term *offense* is used specifically to refer to minor violations of the law that are less serious than misdemeanors. When the term is used in that sense, it refers to such things as jaywalking, spitting on the sidewalk, littering, and committing certain traffic violations, including the failure to wear a seat belt. Another word used to describe such minor law violations is **infractions**. People committing infractions are typically ticketed and released, usually on a promise to appear later in court. Court appearances may often be waived through payment of a small fine that can be mailed to the court.

Felonies, misdemeanors, offenses, and the people who commit them constitute the daily work of the justice system. However, special categories of crime do exist and should be recognized. They include treason and espionage, two crimes that are often regarded as the most serious of felonies. **Treason** can be defined as "a U.S. citizen's actions to help a foreign government overthrow, make war against, or seriously injure the United States."[9] **Espionage**, an offense akin to treason but which can be committed by noncitizens, is the "gathering, transmitting, or losing" of information related to the national defense in such a manner that the information becomes available to enemies of the United States and may be used to their advantage.[10]

Justice is incidental to law and order.
—J. Edgar Hoover (1895–1972)[ii]

Another special category of crime is called *inchoate*. The word *inchoate* means "incomplete or partial," and **inchoate offenses** are those that have not been fully carried out. Conspiracies are an example. When a person conspires to commit a crime, any action undertaken in furtherance of the conspiracy is generally regarded as a sufficient basis for arrest and prosecution. For instance, a woman who intends to kill her husband may make a phone call or conduct an Internet search to find a hit man to carry out her plan. The call and search are themselves evidence of her intent and can result in her imprisonment for conspiracy to commit murder. Another type of inchoate offense is the attempt to commit a crime, which occurs when an offender is unable to complete the intended crime. For example, homeowners may arrive just as a burglar is beginning to enter their residence, causing the burglar to drop his tools and run. In most jurisdictions, this frustrated burglar can be arrested and charged with attempted burglary.

General Features of Crime

From the perspective of Western jurisprudence, all crimes can be said to share certain features (Figure 3), and the notion of crime itself can be said to rest on such general principles. Taken together, these features, which are described in this section, make up the legal essence of the concept of crime. Conventional legal wisdom holds that the essence of crime consists of three conjoined elements: (1) the criminal act, which in legal parlance is termed the *actus reus*; (2) a culpable mental state, or *mens rea*; and (3) a concurrence of the two. Hence, as we shall see in the following paragraphs, the essence of criminal conduct consists of a concurrence of a criminal act with a culpable mental state.

The Criminal Act (*Actus Reus*)

A necessary first feature of any crime is some act in violation of the law. Such an act is termed the ***actus reus*** of a crime. The term means "guilty act." Generally, a person must commit some voluntary act before he or she is subject to criminal sanctions. To *be something* is not a crime; to *do something* may be. For example, someone who is caught using drugs can be arrested, while someone who simply admits that he or she is a drug user (perhaps on a TV talk show or on a website) cannot be arrested on that basis. Police who hear the drug user's admission might begin gathering evidence to prove some specific law violation in that

▲ An artist's drawing of Chi Mak, a Chinese-born and naturalized U.S. citizen, listening to testimony from his 2007 trial in federal court in Santa Ana, California. Mak was convicted of espionage—specifically, conspiracy to export U.S. defense technology to China—and was sentenced in 2008 to 24 and a half years in federal prison. What's the difference between espionage and treason?
Bill Robles/AP Wide World Photos

offense
A violation of the criminal law. Also, in some jurisdictions, a minor crime, such as jaywalking, that is sometimes described as *ticketable*.

infraction
A minor violation of state statute or local ordinance punishable by a fine or other penalty or by a specified, usually limited, term of incarceration.

treason
A U.S. citizen's actions to help a foreign government overthrow, make war against, or seriously injure the United States.[iii] Also, the attempt to overthrow the government of the society of which one is a member.

espionage
The "gathering, transmitting, or losing"[iv] of information related to the national defense in such a manner that the information becomes available to enemies of the United States and may be used to their advantage.

inchoate offense
An offense not yet completed. Also, an offense that consists of an action or conduct that is a step toward the intended commission of another offense.

actus reus
An act in violation of the law. Also, a guilty act.

FIGURE 3
The Features of a Crime

By definition, a crime requires *actus reus*, *mens rea*, and the concurrence of the two:

Actus Reus

A necessary feature of any crime is some act in violation of the law. This violation is called the *actus reus* (guilty act). Generally a person must commit the act voluntarily for it to be considered a crime.

Mens Rea

A second component of crime is *mens rea*, or guilty mind. This refers to the person's state of mind when they commit the act. There are four types of *mens rea*:

Purposeful (intentional) is an act that is undertaken to achieve some goal.

Knowing behavior is undertaken with awareness. A person who acts purposefully always acts knowingly, but a person may act in a knowing way, but without criminal intent.

Reckless behavior is activity that increases the risk of harm. In this activity, the person may not have intended harm but should know that his behavior could endanger others.

Negligent behavior refers to a situation where the person should have known better and her act, or failure to act, endangers others.

Motive is not the same as *mens rea*. A motive refers to a person's reason for committing a crime. Motive is not an essential feature of a crime.

Concurrence

Concurrence requires that the act and the mental state occur together in order for a crime to have taken place.

Special Categories of Crime

Strict liability (or absolute liability) is a special category of crime that requires no culpable mental state and presents a significant exception to the principle that all crimes require *actus reus* and *mens rea*. These offenses make it a crime to simply do something without the intention of violating the law. Routine traffic offenses are considered an example of strict liability.

Source: Illustration from Frank J. Schmalleger, Daniel E. Hall, and John J. Dolatowski, *Criminal Law Today*, 4th Ed. (Upper Saddle River: NJ 2010), pg. 46. Reprinted by permission of Pearson Education, Inc., Upper Saddle River, NJ.

person's past, or perhaps they might watch that individual for future behavior in violation of the law. A subsequent arrest would then be based on a specific action in violation of the law pertaining to controlled substances.

Vagrancy laws, popular in the early part of the twentieth century, have generally been invalidated by the courts because they did not specify what act violated the law. In fact, the less a person did, the more vagrant he or she was. An omission to act, however, may be criminal where the person in question is required by law to do something. Child-neglect laws, for example, focus on parents and guardians who do not live up to their responsibility to care for their children.

Threatening to act can be a criminal offense. For example, threatening to kill someone can result in an arrest for the offense of communicating threats. Such threats against the president of the United States are taken seriously by the Secret Service, and individuals are arrested for boasting about planned violence directed at the president. Attempted criminal activity is also illegal. An attempt to murder or rape, for example, is a serious crime, even when the planned act is not accomplished.

Conspiracies (mentioned earlier in this chapter) are another criminal act. When a conspiracy unfolds, the ultimate act that it aims to bring about does not have to occur for the parties to the conspiracy to be arrested. When people plan to bomb a public building, for example, they can be legally stopped before the bombing. As soon as they take steps to "further" their plan, they have met the requirement for an act. Buying explosives, telephoning one another, and drawing plans of the building may all be actions in "furtherance of the conspiracy." But not all conspiracy statutes require actions in furtherance of the "target crime" before an arrest can be made. Technically speaking, crimes of conspiracy can be seen as entirely distinct from the target crimes that the conspirators are contemplating. For example, in 1994 the U.S. Supreme Court upheld the drug-related conviction of Reshat Shabani when it ruled that in the case of certain antidrug laws,[11] "it is presumed that Congress intended to adopt the common law definition of conspiracy, which does not make the doing of any act other than the act of conspiring a condition of liability."[12] Hence, according to the Court, "the criminal agreement itself," even in the absence of actions directed toward realizing the target crime, can be grounds for arrest and prosecution.

A Guilty Mind (*Mens Rea*)

Mens rea, the second general component of crime, is a term that literally means "guilty mind," referring to the defendant's specific mental state at the time the behavior in question occurred. The importance of *mens rea* as a component of crime cannot be overemphasized. It can be seen in the fact that some courts have held that "[a]ll crime exists primarily in the mind."[13] The extent to which a person can be held criminally responsible for his or her actions generally depends on the nature of the mental state under which he or she was laboring at the time of the offense.

mens rea
The state of mind that accompanies a criminal act. Also, a guilty mind.

Four levels, or types, of *mens rea* can be distinguished: (1) purposeful (or intentional), (2) knowing, (3) reckless, and (4) negligent. Purposeful or intentional action is that which is undertaken to achieve some goal. Sometimes the harm that results from intentional action may be unintended; however, this does not reduce criminal liability. The doctrine of *transferred intent*, for example, which operates in all U.S. jurisdictions, holds a person guilty of murder if he or she took aim and shot at an intended victim but missed, killing another person instead. The philosophical notion behind the concept of transferred intent is that the killer's intent to kill, which existed at the time of the crime, transferred from the intended victim to the person who was struck by the bullet and died.

Knowing behavior is action undertaken with awareness. A person who acts purposefully always acts knowingly, but a person may act in a knowingly criminal way but for a purpose other than criminal intent. For example, an airline captain who allows a flight attendant to transport cocaine aboard an airplane may do so to gain sexual favors from the attendant, but without the purpose of drug smuggling. Knowing behavior involves near certainty. In this scenario, if the airline captain allows the flight attendant to carry cocaine aboard the plane, it *will* be transported, and the pilot knows it. In another example, if an HIV-infected individual knowingly has unprotected sexual intercourse with another person, the partner *will* be exposed to the virus.

Reckless Behavior and Criminal Negligence

Reckless behavior is activity that increases the risk of harm. In contrast to knowing behavior, knowledge may be part of recklessness, but it exists more in the form of probability than certainty. As a practical example, reckless driving is a frequent charge in many jurisdictions; it is generally brought when a driver engages in risky activity that endangers others.

reckless behavior
An activity that increases the risk of harm.

Nevertheless, *mens rea* is said to be present when a person should have known better, even if the person did not directly intend the consequences of his or her action. A person who acts negligently and thereby endangers others may be found guilty of **criminal negligence** when harm occurs, even though no negative consequences were intended. For example, a parent who leaves a 12-month-old child alone in the tub can be prosecuted for negligent homicide if the child drowns.[14] It should be emphasized, however, that

criminal negligence
A behavior in which a person fails to reasonably perceive substantial and unjustifiable risks of dangerous consequences.

negligence in and of itself is not a crime. Negligent conduct can be evidence of crime only when it falls below some acceptable standard of care. That standard is applied today in criminal courts through the fictional creation of a *reasonable person.* The question to be asked in a given case is whether a reasonable person, in the same situation, would have known better and acted differently from the defendant. The reasonable person criterion provides a yardstick for juries faced with thorny issues of guilt or innocence.

motive
A person's reason for committing a crime.

It is important to note that *mens rea*, even in the sense of intent, is not the same thing as motive. A **motive** refers to a person's reason for committing a crime. While evidence of motive may be admissible during a criminal trial to help prove a crime, motive itself is not an essential element of a crime. As a result, we cannot say that a bad or immoral motive makes an act a crime.

Mens rea is a tricky concept. Not only is it philosophically and legally complex, but a person's state of mind during the commission of an offense can rarely be known directly unless the person confesses. Hence *mens rea* must generally be inferred from a person's actions and from all the circumstances surrounding those actions. Pure accident, however, which involves no recklessness or negligence, cannot serve as the basis for either criminal or civil liability. "Even a dog," the famous Supreme Court Justice Oliver Wendell Holmes once wrote, "distinguishes between being stumbled over and being kicked."[15]

Strict Liability

strict liability
A liability without fault or intention. Strict liability offenses do not require *mens rea*.

A special category of crimes called **strict liability** requires no culpable mental state and presents a significant exception to the principle that all crimes require a concurrence of *actus reus* and *mens rea.* Strict liability offenses, also called *absolute liability offenses*, make it a crime simply to *do* something, even if the offender has no intention of violating the law. Strict liability is philosophically based on the presumption that causing harm is in itself blameworthy, regardless of the actor's intent.

Routine traffic offenses are generally considered strict liability offenses. Driving 65 mph in a 55-mph zone is a violation of the law, even though the driver may be listening to music, thinking, or simply going with the flow of traffic, entirely unaware that his or her vehicle is exceeding the posted speed limit. Statutory rape is another example of strict liability.[16] This crime generally occurs between two consenting individuals; it requires only that the offender have sexual intercourse with a person under the age of legal consent. Statutes describing the crime routinely avoid any mention of a culpable mental state. In many jurisdictions, it matters little whether the "perpetrator" knew the exact age of the "victim" or whether the "victim" lied about his or her age or had given consent, since statutory rape laws are "an attempt to prevent the sexual exploitation of persons deemed legally incapable of giving consent."[17]

Concurrence

concurrence
The coexistence of (1) an act in violation of the law and (2) a culpable mental state.

The concurrence of an unlawful act and a culpable mental state provides the third basic component of crime. **Concurrence** requires that the act and the mental state occur together in order for a crime to take place. If one precedes the other, the requirements of the criminal law have not been met. A person may intend to kill a rival, for example. He drives to the intended victim's house with his gun, fantasizing about how he will commit the murder. Just as he nears the victim's home, the victim crosses the street on the way to the grocery store. If the two accidentally collide and the intended victim dies, there has been no concurrence of act and intent.

Other Features of Crime

5 List and describe the eight general features of crime.

Some scholars contend that the three features of crime that we have just outlined—*actus reus, mens rea*, and concurrence—are sufficient to constitute the essence of the legal concept of *crime.* Other scholars, however, see modern Western law as more complex. They argue that recognition of five additional principles is necessary to fully appreciate contemporary understandings of crime: (1) causation, (2) resulting harm, (3) the principle of legality, (4) the principle of punishment, and (5) necessary attendant circumstances. We will now discuss each of these additional features in turn.

Causation

Causation refers to the fact that the concurrence of a guilty mind and a criminal act may cause harm. While some statutes criminalize only conduct, others require that the offender *cause* a particular result before criminal liability can be incurred. Sometimes, however, a causal link is unclear. For example, let's consider a case of assault with a deadly weapon with intent to kill. A person shoots another, and the victim is seriously injured but is not immediately killed. The victim, who remains in the hospital, survives for more than a year. The victim's death occurs due to a blood clot that forms from lack of activity. In such a case, it is likely that defense attorneys will argue that the defendant did not cause the death; rather, the death occurred because of disease. If a jury agrees with the defense's claim, the shooter may go free or be found guilty of a lesser charge, such as assault.

To clarify the issue of causation, the American Law Institute suggests use of the term **legal cause** to emphasize the notion of a legally recognizable cause and to preclude any assumption that such a cause must be close in time and space to the result it produces. Legal causes can be distinguished from those causes that may have produced the result in question but do not provide the basis for a criminal prosecution because they are too complex, too indistinguishable from other causes, not knowable, or not provable in a court of law.

legal cause
A legally recognizable cause. A legal cause must be demonstrated in court in order to hold an individual criminally liable for causing harm.

Harm

A harm occurs in any crime, although not all harms are crimes. When a person is murdered or raped, harm can be clearly identified. Some crimes, however, can be said to be *victimless.* Perpetrators (and their attorneys) maintain that in committing such crimes, they harm no one but themselves; rather, they say, the crime may actually be pleasurable for those involved. Prostitution, illegal gambling, and drug use are commonly classified as "victimless." What these offenders fail to recognize, say legal theorists, is the social harm caused by their behavior. In areas afflicted with chronic prostitution, illegal gambling, and drug use, property values fall; family life disintegrates; other, more traditional crimes increase as money is sought to support the "victimless" activities; and law-abiding citizens abandon the area.

In a criminal prosecution, however, it is rarely necessary to prove harm as a separate element of a crime since it is subsumed under the notion of a guilty act. In the crime of murder, for example, the "killing of a human being" brings about a harm but is, properly speaking, an act. When committed with the requisite *mens rea*, it becomes a crime. A similar type of reasoning applies to the criminalization of *attempts* that cause no harm. A scenario commonly raised to illustrate this dilemma is one in which attackers throw rocks at a blind man, but because of bad aim, the rocks hit no one and the intended target remains unaware that anyone is trying to harm him. In such a case, should throwing rocks provide a basis for criminal liability? As one authority on the subject observes, "Criticism of the principle of harm has . . . been based on the view that the harm actually caused may be a matter of sheer accident and that the rational thing to do is to base the punishment on the *mens rea*, and the action, disregarding any actual harm or lack of harm or its degree."[18] This observation also shows why we have said that the essence of crime consists only of three things: (1) *actus reus*, (2) *mens rea*, and (3) concurrence of an illegal act and a culpable mental state.

Legality

The principle of legality highlights the fact that a behavior cannot be criminal if no law exists that defines it as such. For example, as long as you are of drinking age, it is all right to drink beer because there is no statute on the books prohibiting it. During Prohibition, of course, the situation was quite different. (In fact, some parts of the United States are still "dry," and the purchase or public consumption of alcohol can be a law violation regardless of age.) The principle of legality also includes the notion that ***ex post facto*** laws are not binding, which means that a law cannot be created tomorrow that will hold a person legally responsible for something he or she does today—laws are binding only from the date of their creation or from some future date at which they are specified as taking effect.[19]

ex post facto
Latin for "after the fact." The Constitution prohibits the enactment of *ex post facto* laws, which make acts committed before the laws in question were passed punishable as crimes.

Punishment

The principle of punishment holds that no crime can be said to occur where punishment has not been specified in the law. Larceny, for example, would not be a crime if the law simply said, "It is illegal to steal." Punishment for the crime must be specified so that if a person is found guilty of violating the law, sanctions can be lawfully imposed.

Necessary Attendant Circumstances

attendant circumstances
The facts surrounding an event.

Finally, statutes defining some crimes specify that certain additional elements must be present for a conviction to be obtained. Generally speaking, these **attendant circumstances** are the "facts surrounding an event";[20] they include such things as time and place. Attendant circumstances that are specified by law as necessary elements of an offense are sometimes called *necessary attendant circumstances*, indicating that the existence of such circumstances is necessary, along with the other elements included in the relevant statute, for a crime to have been committed. Florida law, for example, makes it a crime to "[k]nowingly commit any lewd or lascivious act in the presence of any child under the age of 16 years."[21] In this case, the behavior in question might not be a crime if committed in the presence of someone who is older than 16 years. Sometimes attendant circumstances increase the degree, or level of seriousness, of an offense.

Circumstances surrounding a crime can also be classified as aggravating or mitigating and may, by law, increase or lessen the penalty that can be imposed on a convicted offender. Aggravating and mitigating circumstances are not elements of an offense, however, since they are primarily relevant at the sentencing stage of a criminal prosecution.

Elements of a Specific Criminal Offense

element (of a crime)
In a specific crime, one of the essential features of that crime, as specified by law or statute.

Now that we have identified the principles that constitute the *general* notion of crime, we can examine individual statutes to see what particular statutory **elements (of a crime)** constitute a *specific* crime. Written laws specify exactly what conditions are necessary for a person to be charged in a given instance of criminal activity, and they do so for every offense. Hence elements of a crime are specific legal aspects of a criminal offense that the prosecution must prove to obtain a conviction. In almost every jurisdiction in the United States, for example, the crime of first-degree murder involves four quite distinct elements:

1. An unlawful killing
2. Of a human being
3. Intentionally
4. With planning (or "malice aforethought")

6 Explain what is meant by the elements of a specific criminal offense.

The elements of any specific crime are the statutory minimum without which that crime cannot be said to have occurred. Since statutes differ between jurisdictions, the specific elements of a particular crime may vary. To convict a defendant of a particular crime, prosecutors must prove to a judge or jury that all of the required statutory elements are present[22] and that the accused was responsible for producing them. If even one element of an offense cannot be established beyond a reasonable doubt, criminal liability will not have been demonstrated, and the defendant will be found not guilty.

The Example of Murder

Every statutory element of a crime serves a purpose. As mentioned, the crime of first-degree murder includes an *unlawful killing* as one of its required elements. Not all killings are unlawful. In war, for instance, human beings are killed. These killings are committed with planning and sometimes with "malice" and are certainly intentional, yet killing in war is not unlawful as long as the belligerents wage war according to international conventions.

The second element of first-degree murder specifies that the killing must be *of a human being*. People kill all the time. They kill animals for meat, they hunt, and they practice euthanasia on aged and injured pets. Even if the killing of an animal is planned and involves malice (perhaps a vendetta against a neighborhood dog that overturns trash cans), it does not constitute first-degree murder. Such a killing, however, may violate statutes pertaining to cruelty to animals.

The third element of first-degree murder, *intentionality*, is the basis for the defense of accident. An unintentional or nonpurposeful killing is not first-degree murder, although it may violate some other statute.

Finally, murder has not been committed unless *malice* is involved. There are different kinds of malice. Second-degree murder involves malice in the sense of hatred or spite. A more extreme form of malice is necessary for a finding of first-degree murder; sometimes the phrase used to describe this requirement is *malice aforethought.* This extreme kind of malice can be demonstrated by showing that planning was involved in the commission of the murder. Often, first-degree murder is described as "lying in wait," a practice that shows that thought and planning went into the illegal killing.

A charge of second-degree murder in most jurisdictions would necessitate proving that a voluntary (or intentional) killing of a human being had taken place—although without the degree of malice necessary for it to be classified as first-degree murder. A crime of passion is an example of second-degree murder. In a crime of passion, the malice felt by the perpetrator is hatred or spite, which is considered less severe than malice aforethought. Manslaughter, or third-degree murder, another type of homicide, can be defined simply as the unlawful killing of a human being. Not only is malice lacking in third-degree murder cases, but so is intention; in fact, the killer may not have intended that *any* harm come to the victim.

Manslaughter charges are often brought when a defendant acted in a negligent or reckless manner. The 2001 sentencing of 21-year-old Nathan Hall to 90 days in jail on charges of criminally negligent homicide following a fatal collision with another ski racer on Vail Mountain near Eagle, Colorado, provides such an example.[23] Hall had been tried on a more serious charge of reckless manslaughter, which carries a sentence of up to 16 years under Colorado law, but the jury convicted him of the lesser charge.

Manslaughter statutes, however, frequently necessitate some degree of negligence on the part of the killer. When a wanton disregard for human life is present—legally defined as "gross negligence"—some jurisdictions permit the offender to be charged with a more serious count of murder.

The *Corpus Delicti* of a Crime

corpus delicti
The facts that show that a crime has occurred. The term literally means "the body of the crime."

The term ***corpus delicti*** literally means "the body of the crime." One way to understand the concept of *corpus delicti* is to realize that a person cannot be tried for a crime unless it can first be shown that the offense has, in fact, occurred. In other words, to establish the *corpus delicti* of a crime, the state has to demonstrate that a criminal law has been violated and that someone violated it (Figure 4). This term is often confused with the statutory elements of a crime, and sometimes it is mistakenly thought to refer to the body of a murder victim or some other physical result of criminal activity. It actually means something quite different.

There are two aspects to the *corpus delicti* of an offense: (1) that a certain result has been produced and (2) that a person is criminally responsible for its production. For example, the crime of larceny requires proof that the property of another has been stolen—that is, unlawfully taken by someone whose intent it was to permanently deprive the owner of its possession.[24] Hence evidence offered to prove the *corpus delicti* in a trial for larceny is insufficient if it fails to prove that any property was stolen or if property found in a defendant's possession cannot be identified as having been stolen. "In an arson case, the *corpus delicti* consists of (1) a burned building or other property, and (2) some criminal agency which caused the burning. . . . In other words, the *corpus delicti* includes not only the fact of burning, but it must also appear that the burning was by the willful act of some person, and not as a result of a natural or accidental cause."[25]

We should note that the identity of the perpetrator is not an element of the *corpus delicti* of an offense. Hence the fact that a crime has occurred can be established without having any idea who committed it or even why it was committed. This principle was clearly enunciated in a Montana case when that state's supreme court held that "the identity of the

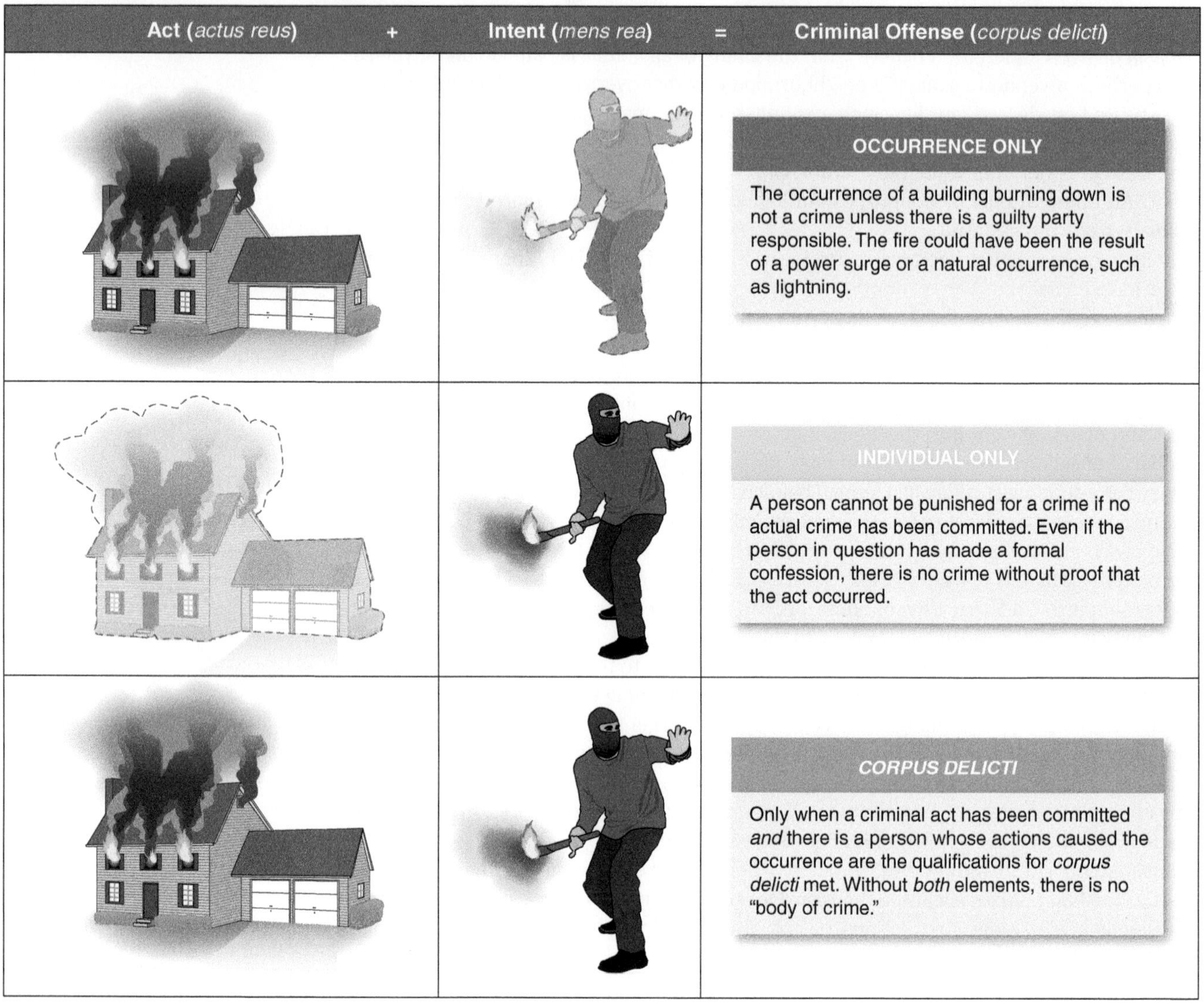

FIGURE 4
The Body of Crime

Source: Frank J. Schmalleger, Daniel E. Hall, and John J. Dolatowski, *Criminal Law Today,* 4th Ed. (Upper Saddle River: NJ 2010), pg. 61. Reprinted by permission of Pearson Education, Inc., Upper Saddle River, NJ.

defense (to a criminal charge)
The evidence and arguments offered by a defendant and his or her attorney to show why the defendant should not be held liable for a criminal charge.

alibi
A statement or contention by an individual charged with a crime that he or she was so distant when the crime was committed, or so engaged in other provable activities, that his or her participation in the commission of that crime was impossible.

justification
A legal defense in which the defendant admits to committing the act in question but claims it was necessary in order to avoid some greater evil.

perpetrator is not an element of the *corpus delicti*." In *State* v. *Kindle* (1924),[26] the court said, "We stated that '[i]n a prosecution for murder, proof of the *corpus delicti* does not necessarily carry with it the identity of the slain nor of the slayer.' . . . The essential elements of the *corpus delicti* are . . . establishing the death and the fact that the death was caused by a criminal agency, nothing more." *Black's Law Dictionary* puts it another way: "The *corpus delicti* [of a crime] is the fact of its having been actually committed."[27]

Types of Defenses to a Criminal Charge

7 Discuss the four broad categories of criminal defenses that our legal system recognizes.

When a person is charged with a crime, he or she typically offers some defense. A **defense (to a criminal charge)** consists of evidence and arguments offered by the defendant to show why he or she should not be held liable for a criminal charge. Our legal system generally recognizes four broad categories of defenses: (1) alibi, (2) justifications, (3) excuses, and (4) procedural defenses (Figure 5). An **alibi**, if shown to be valid, means that the defendant could not have committed the crime in question because he or she was somewhere else (and generally with someone else) at the time of the crime. When a defendant offers a **justification** as a defense, he or she admits committing the act in

Multiculturalism and Diversity
Islamic Law

Islamic law (or *Shari'ah* in Arabic, which means "path of God") has been of much interest in the United States since the September 11, 2001, terrorist attacks on the United States, the resulting destruction of the Taliban regime in Afghanistan, and the war in Iraq. It is important for American students of criminal justice to recognize that Islamic law refers to legal ideas based on the teachings of Islam and that it bears no intrinsic relationship to acts of terrorism committed by misguided zealots with Islamic backgrounds. Similarly, Islamic law is by no means the same thing as Jihad (Muslim holy war) or Islamic fundamentalism.

Various interpretations of Islam form the basis of laws in many countries, and the entire legal systems of some nations are based on Islamic principles. For example, Article 2 of Chapter 1 (titled "Basic Principles") of the Iraqi Constitution declares that "Islam is the official religion of the state and is a basic source of legislation." Subsection (a) reads: "No law can be passed that contradicts the undisputed rules of Islam." The Iraqi Constitution was approved by a wide margin in a 2005 national referendum. Islamic law also holds considerable sway in many other countries, including Syria, Iran, Pakistan, Saudi Arabia, Kuwait, the United Arab Emirates, Bahrain, Algeria, Jordan, Lebanon, Libya, Ethiopia, Tajikistan, Uzbekistan, and Turkey (which practices official separation of church and state).

Islamic law is based on four historical sources. In order of importance, these sources are (1) the Koran (also spelled *Quran* and *Qur'an*), or Holy Book of Islam, which Muslims believe is the word of God, or Allah; (2) the teachings of the prophet Muhammad; (3) a consensus of the clergy in cases where neither the Koran nor the prophet directly addresses an issue; and (4) reason or logic, which should be used when no solution can be found in the other three sources.[1]

The prophet Muhammad, whom the *Cambridge Encyclopedia of Islam* describes as a "prophet-lawyer,"[2] rose to fame in the city of Mecca (in what is now Saudi Arabia) as a religious reformer. Later, however, he traveled to Medina, where he became the ruler and lawgiver of a newly formed religious society. In his role as lawgiver, Muhammad enacted legislation whose aim was to teach people what to do and how to behave to achieve salvation. As a consequence, Islamic law today is a system of duties and rituals founded on legal and moral obligations, all of which are ultimately sanctioned by the authority of a religious leader (or leaders) who may issue commands (known as fatwas) that the faithful are bound to obey.

Contemporary Islamic law recognizes seven ***Hudud* crimes**—or crimes based on religious strictures. *Hudud* (sometimes spelled *Hodood* or *Huddud*) crimes are essentially violations of "natural law" as interpreted by Arab culture. These crimes are often described as crimes against God. Four *Hudud* crimes for which punishments are specified in the Koran are (1) war against Allah and His messengers, (2) theft, (3) adultery or fornication, and (4) false accusation of fornication or adultery. Three other *Hudud* offenses are mentioned by the Koran for which no punishment is specified: (1) "corruption on earth," (2) drinking of alcohol, and (3) highway robbery. The punishments for these crimes are determined by tradition.[3] "Corruption on earth" is a general category of religious offense, not well understood in the West, which includes activities such as embezzlement, revolution against lawful authority, fraud, and "weakening the society of God."

All crimes other than *Hudud* crimes fall into an offense category called *tazirat*. ***Tazir* crimes** are regarded as any actions not considered acceptable in a spiritual society. They include crimes against society and against individuals, but not against God. *Tazir* crimes may call for *quesas* (retribution) or *diya* (compensation or fines). Crimes requiring *quesas* are based on the Arabic principle of "an eye for an eye, a nose for a nose, a tooth for a tooth" and generally require physical punishments up to and including death. *Quesas* offenses may include murder, manslaughter, assault, and maiming. Learn more about Islamic law via **Web Extra 2**.

▲ Iraqi Shiite Muslims flagellating themselves during a procession in Karbala, Iraq, in 2006. Islamic law, which is based on the teachings of Islam, underpins the legal systems of many nations in the Middle East and elsewhere. How does Islamic law differ from the laws of most Western nations?
Hadi Mizban/AP Wide World Photos

[1]Parviz Saney, "Iran," in Elmer H. Johnson, ed., *International Handbook of Contemporary Developments in Criminology* (Westport, CT: Greenwood, 1983), p. 359.

[2]J. Schact, "Law and Justice," *Cambridge Encyclopedia of Islam*, Vol. 2, p. 539, from which most of the information in this paragraph comes.

[3]This paragraph owes much to Matthew Lippman, "Iran: A Question of Justice?" *Criminal Justice International* (1987), pp. 6–7.

question but claims that it was necessary to avoid some greater evil. A defendant who offers an **excuse** as a defense, on the other hand, claims that some personal condition or circumstance at the time of the act was such that he or she should not be held accountable under the criminal law. **Procedural defenses** make the claim that the defendant was in some significant way discriminated against in the justice process or that some important aspect of official procedure was not properly followed in the investigation or prosecution of the crime charged.

excuse
A legal defense in which the defendant claims that some personal condition or circumstance at the time of the act was such that he or she should not be held accountable under the criminal law.

FIGURE 5
Types of Defenses to a Criminal Charge

ALIBI: The defendant could not have committed the offense because he or she was somewhere else at the time of the crime.

EXCUSE: Some personal condition or circumstance at the time of the act was such that the actor should not be held accountable under the criminal law.

EXAMPLES: Duress, age, mistake, involuntary intoxication, unconsciousness, provocation, insanity, diminished capacity, and mental incompetence are examples of excuse defenses.

JUSTIFICATION: The defendant admits committing the act in question but claims that it was necessary to avoid some greater evil.

EXAMPLES: Self-defense, necessity, defense of others, consent, defense of home and property, and resisting unlawful arrest are examples of justification defenses.

PROCEDURAL DEFENSE: The defendant was in some significant way discriminated against in the justice process, or some important aspect of official procedure was not properly followed in the investigation or prosecution of the crime charged.

EXAMPLES: Entrapment, denial of a speedy trial, double jeopardy, prosecutorial misconduct, *collateral estoppel*, police fraud, and selective prosecution are examples of procedural defenses.

procedural defense
A defense that claims that the defendant was in some significant way discriminated against in the justice process or that some important aspect of official procedure was not properly followed in the investigation or prosecution of the crime charged.

Islamic law
A system of laws, operative in some Arab countries, based on the Muslim religion and especially the holy book of Islam, the Koran.

***Hudud* crime**
A serious violation of Islamic law that is regarded as an offense against God.

***Tazir* crime**
A minor violation of Islamic law that is regarded as an offense against society, not God.

Alibi

A reference book for criminal trial lawyers says, "Alibi is different from all of the other defenses . . . because . . . it is based upon the premise that the defendant is truly innocent."[28] The defense of alibi denies that the defendant committed the act in question. All of the other defenses we are about to discuss grant that the defendant committed the act but deny that he or she should be held criminally responsible. While justifications and excuses may produce findings of "not guilty," the defense of alibi claims outright innocence.

Alibi is best supported by witnesses and documentation. A person charged with a crime can use the defense of alibi to show that he or she was not present at the scene when the crime was alleged to have occurred. Hotel receipts, eyewitness identifications, and participation in social events have all been used to prove alibis.

Justifications

As defenses, justifications claim a kind of moral high ground. Justifications may be offered by people who find themselves forced to choose between "two evils." Generally speaking, conduct that a person believes is necessary to avoid harm to him- or herself or to another is justifiable if the harm he or she is trying to avoid is greater than the harm the offense seeks to avoid. For example, a firefighter might set a controlled fire to create a firebreak to head off a conflagration threatening a community; while intentionally setting a fire might constitute arson, destroying property to save a town by creating a firebreak may be justifiable behavior in the eyes of the community and in the eyes of the law. Included under the broad category of justifications are (1) self-defense, (2) defense of others, (3) defense of home and property, (4) necessity, (5) consent, and (6) resisting unlawful arrest.

Self-Defense

In May 2009, when Oklahoma City pharmacist Jerome Ersland was confronted by two holdup men, he allegedly pulled a gun and shot one of them in the head.[29] The second man ran away. Then, prosecutors say, Ersland went behind the counter, got another gun, and pumped five more bullets into the wounded robber as he lay on the floor, killing him. The scene was recorded by a security camera in the drugstore, which had been robbed before and is located in a crime-ridden part of the city. Following the incident, Ersland was charged with first-degree murder in a case that has stirred a furious debate over vigilante justice and self-defense. As this book goes to press, Ersland, 57, is free on $100,000 bail, posted by an anonymous donor. Not everyone thinks that Ersland is a hero, however. Anthony Douglas, president of the Oklahoma chapter of the NAACP, calls Ersland's actions "an execution-style murder" and praises the district attorney for bringing charges. Complicating the situation is the fact that Ersland is white, while the two robbery suspects were black. If convicted, Ersland could receive the death penalty.

Self-defense is probably the best known of the justifications. This defense strategy makes the claim that it was necessary for someone to inflict harm on another to ensure his or her own safety in the face of near-certain injury or death. A person who harms an attacker can generally use this defense. However, the courts have held that where a "path of retreat" exists for a person being attacked, it should be taken. In other words, the safest use of self-defense, legally speaking, is only when cornered, with no path of escape.

The amount of defensive force used must be proportional to the amount of force or the perceived degree of threat that one is seeking to defend against. **Reasonable force** is the degree of force that is appropriate in a given situation and that is not excessive. Reasonable force can also be thought of as the minimum degree of force necessary to protect oneself, one's property, a third party, or the property of another in the face of a substantial threat. Deadly force, the highest degree of force, is considered reasonable only when used to counter an immediate threat of great bodily harm or death. Deadly force cannot be used against nondeadly force.

Force, as the term is used within the context of self-defense, means physical force and does not extend to emotional, psychological, economic, psychic, or other forms of coercion. A person who turns the tables on a robber and assaults him during a robbery attempt, for example, may be able to claim self-defense, but a businessperson who physically assaults a financial rival to prevent a hostile takeover of her company will have no such recourse.

Self-defense has sometimes been claimed in killings of abusive spouses. A jury is likely to accept as justified a killing that occurs while the physical abuse is in progress, especially where a history of such abuse can be shown. On the other hand, wives who suffer repeated abuse but coldly plan the killing of their husbands have not fared well in court.

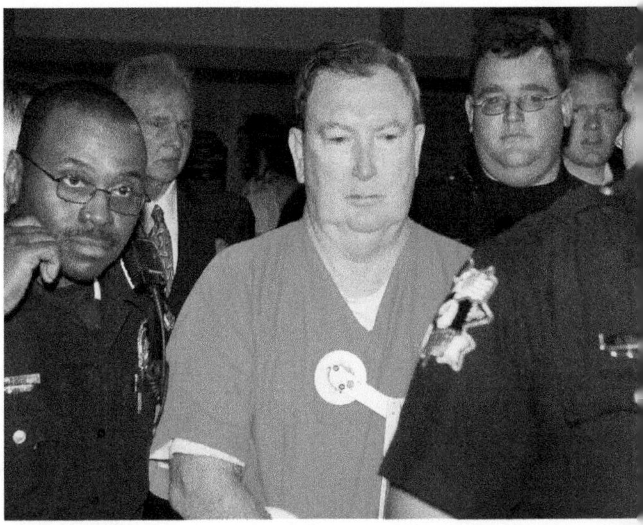

▲ Pharmacist Jerome Ersland being escorted out of a courtroom at the Oklahoma County Courthouse in Oklahoma City in 2009, following a bond hearing. Ersland was charged with first-degree murder, but his case stirred vigorous debate over vigilante justice and self-defense. Was Ersland justified in what he allegedly did?
*Paul B. Southerland/*The Oklahoman*/AP Wide World Photos*

self-defense
The protection of oneself or of one's property from unlawful injury or from the immediate risk of unlawful injury. Also, the justification that the person who committed an act that would otherwise constitute an offense reasonably believed that the act was necessary to protect self or property from immediate danger.

reasonable force
A degree of force that is appropriate in a given situation and is not excessive. Also, the minimum degree of force necessary to protect oneself, one's property, a third party, or the property of another in the face of a substantial threat.

alter ego rule
In some jurisdictions, a rule of law that holds that a person can only defend a third party under circumstances and only to the degree that the third party could legally act on his or her own behalf.

Defense of Others

The use of force to defend oneself has generally been extended to permit the use of reasonable force to defend others who are or who appear to be in imminent danger. The defense of others, sometimes called *defense of a third person*, is circumscribed in some jurisdictions by the **alter ego rule**. This rule holds that a person can only defend a third party under circumstances and only to the degree that the third party could act. In other words, a person who aids another whom he sees being attacked may become criminally liable if that person initiated the attack or if the assault is a lawful one—for example, an assault made by a law enforcement officer conducting a lawful arrest of a person who is resisting. A few jurisdictions, however, do not recognize the alter ego rule and allow a person to act in defense of another if the actor reasonably believes that his or her intervention is immediately necessary to protect the third person.

Defense of others cannot be claimed by an individual who joins an illegal fight merely to assist a friend or family member. Likewise, one who intentionally aids an offender in an assault, even though the tables have turned and the offender is losing the battle, cannot claim defense of others. Under the law, defense of a third person always requires that the defender be free from fault and that he or she act to aid an innocent person who is in the process of being victimized. The same restrictions that apply to self-defense also apply to the defense of a third party. Hence a defender may act only in the face of an immediate threat to another person, cannot use deadly force against nondeadly force, and must act only to the extent and use only the degree of force needed to repel the attack.

Defense of Home and Property

In most jurisdictions, the owner of property can justifiably use reasonable *nondeadly* force to prevent others from unlawfully taking or damaging it. As a general rule, the preservation of human life outweighs the protection of property, and the use of deadly force to protect property is not justified unless the perpetrator of the illegal act may intend to commit, or is in the act of committing, a violent act against another human being. A person who shoots and kills an unarmed trespasser, for example, could not claim "defense of property" to avoid criminal liability.[30] However, a person who shoots and kills an armed robber while being robbed can make such a claim.

The use of mechanical devices to protect property is a special area of law. Because deadly force is usually not permitted in defense of property, the setting of booby traps, such as spring-loaded shotguns, electrified gates, and explosive devices, is generally not permitted to protect property that is unattended and unoccupied. If an individual is injured as a result of a mechanical device intended to cause injury or death in the protection of property, criminal charges may be brought against the person who set the device.

On the other hand, acts that would otherwise be criminal may carry no criminal liability if undertaken to protect one's home. For purposes of the law, one's "home" is one's dwelling, whether owned, rented, or merely borrowed. Hotel rooms, rooms aboard vessels, and rented rooms in houses belonging to others are all considered, for purposes of the law, one's home. The retreat rule referred to earlier, which requires a person under attack to retreat when possible before resorting to deadly force, is subject to what some call the *castle exception*. The castle exception can be traced to the writings of the sixteenth-century English jurist Sir Edward Coke, who said, "A man's house is his castle—for where shall a man be safe if it be not in his house?"[31] The castle exception generally recognizes that a person has a fundamental right to be in his or her home and that the home is a final and inviolable place of retreat. That is, the home offers a place of retreat from which a person can be expected to retreat no farther. Hence it is not necessary for one to retreat from one's home in the face of an immediate threat, even where such retreat is possible, before resorting to deadly force in protection of the home. A number of court decisions have extended the castle exception to include one's place of business, such as a store or an office.

Necessity

Necessity, or the claim that some illegal action was needed to prevent an even greater harm, is a useful defense in cases that do not involve serious bodily harm. A famous but unsuccessful use of this defense occurred in *The Crown* v. *Dudly & Stephens* in the late nineteenth century.[32] This British case involved a shipwreck in which three sailors and a cabin boy were set adrift in a lifeboat. After a number of days at sea without food, two of the sailors decided to kill and eat the cabin boy. At their trial, they argued that it was necessary to do so, or none of them would have survived. The court, however, reasoned that the cabin boy was not a direct threat to the survival of the men and rejected this defense. Convicted of murder, they were sentenced to death, although they were spared the gallows by royal intervention. Although cannibalism is usually against the law, courts have sometimes recognized the necessity of consuming human flesh where survival was at issue. Those cases, however, involved only "victims" who had already died of natural causes.

> No State shall . . . deprive any person of life, liberty, or property, without due process of law.
>
> —Fourteenth Amendment to the U.S. Constitution

Consent

The defense of consent claims that whatever harm was done occurred only after the injured person gave his or her permission for the behavior in question. In the "Condom Rapist Case," for example, Joel Valdez was found guilty of rape in 1993 after a jury in Austin, Texas, rejected his claim that the act became consensual once he complied with his victim's request to use a condom. Valdez, who was drunk and armed with a knife at the time of the offense, claimed that his victim's request was a consent to sex. After that, he said, "we were making love."[33]

Resisting Unlawful Arrest

All jurisdictions make resisting arrest a crime. Resistance, however, may be justifiable, especially if the arresting officer uses excessive force. Some states have statutory provisions detailing the limits imposed on such resistance and the conditions under which it can be used. Such laws generally say that a person may use a reasonable amount of force, other than deadly force, to resist arrest or an unlawful search by a law enforcement officer if the officer uses or attempts to use greater force than necessary to make the arrest or search. Such laws are inapplicable in cases where the defendant is the first to resort to force. Deadly force to resist arrest is not justified unless the law enforcement officer resorts to deadly force when it is not called for.

Excuses

In contrast to a justification, an excuse does not claim that the conduct in question is justified by the situation or that it is moral. An excuse claims, rather, that the actor who engaged in the unlawful behavior was, at the time, not legally responsible for his or her actions and should not be held accountable under the law. For example, a person who assaults a police officer, thinking that the officer is really a disguised space alien who has come to abduct him, may be found "not guilty" of the charge of assault and battery by reason of insanity. Actions for which excuses are offered do not morally outweigh the wrong committed, but criminal liability may still be negated on the basis of some personal disability that the actor has or because of some special circumstances that characterize the situation. Excuses recognized by the law include (1) duress, (2) age, (3) mistake, (4) involuntary intoxication, (5) unconsciousness, (6) provocation, (7) insanity, (8) diminished capacity, and (9) mental incompetence.

Duress

The defense of duress depends on an understanding of the situation. *Duress* has been defined as "any unlawful threat or coercion used by a person to induce another to act (or to refrain from acting) in a manner he or she otherwise would not (or would)."[34] A person may act under duress if, for example, he or she steals an employer's payroll to meet a ransom demand for kidnappers holding the person's children. Should the person later be arrested for larceny or embezzlement, the person can claim that he or she felt compelled to commit the crime to help ensure the safety of the children. Duress is generally not a useful defense when the crime committed involves serious physical harm, since the harm committed may outweigh the coercive influence in the minds of jurors and judges. Duress is sometimes also called *coercion*.

Age

Age offers another kind of excuse to a criminal charge. The defense of "infancy"—as it is sometimes known in legal jargon—has its roots in the ancient belief that children cannot reason logically until around the age of seven. Early doctrine in the Christian church sanctioned that belief by declaring that rationality develops around that age. As a consequence, only older children could be held responsible for their crimes.

The defense of infancy today has been expanded to include young people well beyond the age of seven. Many states set 16 as the age at which a person becomes an adult for purposes of criminal prosecution; others use the age of 17, and still others 18. When a person younger than the age required for adult prosecution commits a "crime," it is termed a *juvenile offense*. He or she is not guilty of a criminal violation of the law by virtue of youth. In most jurisdictions, children below the age of seven cannot be charged even with juvenile offenses, no matter how serious their actions may appear to others.

Mistake

Two types of mistakes can serve as a defense. One is mistake of law, and the other is mistake of fact. Rarely is mistake of law held to be an acceptable defense. Most people realize that it is their responsibility to know the law as it applies to them. "Ignorance of the law is no excuse" is an old dictum still heard today. On occasion, however, cases do arise in which such a defense is accepted by authorities. For example, an elderly woman raised marijuana plants because they could be used to make a tea that relieved her arthritis pain. When her garden was discovered, she was not arrested but was advised as to how the law applied to her.

Mistake of fact is a much more useful form of the mistake defense. In 2000, for example, the statutory rape conviction of 39-year-old Charles Ballinger of Bradley County, Tennessee, was reversed by Tennessee's Court of Criminal Appeals at Knoxville on a mistake-of-fact claim.[35] Ballinger admitted that he had had sex with his 15-year-old neighbor, who was under the age of legal consent at the time of the act. In his defense, however, Ballinger claimed that he had had good reason to mistake the girl's age.

Involuntary Intoxication

The claim of involuntary intoxication may form the basis for another excuse defense. Both drugs and alcohol may produce intoxication. Voluntary intoxication is rarely a defense to a criminal charge because it is a self-induced condition. It is widely recognized in our legal tradition that an altered mental condition that is the product of voluntary activity cannot be used to exonerate guilty actions that follow from it. Some state statutes formalize this general principle of law and specifically state that voluntary intoxication cannot be offered as a defense against a charge of criminal behavior.[36]

Involuntary intoxication, however, is another matter. A person might be tricked into consuming an intoxicating substance. Secretly "spiked" punch, popular aphrodisiacs, or drug-laced desserts might be ingested unknowingly. Because the effects and taste of alcohol are so widely known in our society, the defense of involuntary intoxication due to alcohol consumption can be difficult to demonstrate.

▲ Andrea Pia Yates, the Texas mother who admitted to drowning her five young children in a bathtub in 2001, conferring with attorney George Parnham at her retrial in 2006. Convicted of capital murder in 2002, she was found not guilty by reason of insanity in a retrial ordered by a three-judge panel of the First Texas Court of Appeals. In a civil action that followed her acquittal, Yates was ordered committed to the maximum-security North Texas State Hospital in Vernon, Texas. What does *insanity* mean for purposes of the criminal law?
Brett Coomer-Pool/Getty Images–GINS/ Entertainment News & Sports

Unconsciousness

A very rarely used excuse is that of unconsciousness. An individual cannot be held responsible for anything he or she does while unconscious. Because unconscious people rarely do anything at all, this defense is almost never seen in the courts. However, cases of sleepwalking, epileptic seizure, and neurological dysfunction may result in injurious, although unintentional, actions by people so afflicted. Under such circumstances, a defense of unconsciousness might be argued with success.

Provocation

Provocation recognizes that a person can be emotionally enraged by another who intends to elicit just such a reaction. Should the person then strike out at the tormentor, some courts have held, he or she may not be guilty of criminality or may be guilty of a lesser degree of criminality than might otherwise be the case. The defense of provocation is commonly used in cases arising from barroom brawls in which a person's parentage was called into question, although most states don't look favorably on verbal provocation alone. This defense has also been used in some spectacular cases where wives have killed their husbands, or children their fathers, citing years of verbal and physical abuse. In these latter instances, perhaps because the degree of physical harm inflicted—the death of the husband or father—appears to be out of proportion to the abuse suffered by the wife or child, the courts have not readily accepted the defense of provocation. As a rule, the defense of provocation is generally more acceptable in minor offenses than in serious violations of the law.

Insanity

From the point of view of the criminal law, *insanity* is a legal concept, not a medical one. The legal definition of insanity often has very little to do with psychological or psychiatric understandings of mental illness; rather, it is a concept developed to enable the judicial system to assign guilt or innocence to particular defendants. As a consequence, medical conceptions of mental illness do not always fit well into the legal categories of mental illness created by courts and legislatures. The differences between psychiatric and legal conceptualizations of insanity often lead to disagreements among expert witnesses who, in criminal court, may provide conflicting testimony as to the sanity of a defendant.

The **insanity defense** is given a lot of play in the entertainment industry; movies and television shows regularly employ it because it makes for good drama. In practice, however, the defense of insanity is rarely raised. According to an eight-state study funded by the National Institute of Mental Health, the insanity defense was used in less than 1% of the cases that came before county-level courts.[37] The study showed that only 26% of all insanity pleas were argued successfully and that 90% of those who employed the defense had been previously diagnosed with a mental illness. As the American Bar Association says, "The best evidence suggests that the mental nonresponsibility defense is raised in less than one percent of all felony cases in the United States and is successful in about a fourth of these."[38] Even so, there are several rules that guide the legal definition of insanity.

insanity defense
A legal defense based on claims of mental illness or mental incapacity.

The M'Naghten Rule

The insanity defense, as we know it today, was nonexistent prior to the nineteenth century. Until then, insane people who committed crimes were punished in the same way as other law violators. It was Daniel M'Naghten (sometimes spelled McNaughten or M'Naughten), a woodworker from Glasgow, Scotland, who became the first person to be found not guilty of a crime by reason of insanity in 1844. M'Naghten had tried to assassinate Sir Robert Peel, the British prime minister. He mistook Edward Drummond, Peel's secretary, for Peel himself and killed Drummond instead. At his trial, defense attorneys argued that M'Naghten suffered from vague delusions centered on the idea that the Tories, a British political party, were persecuting him. Medical testimony at the trial supported the defense's assertion that he didn't know what he was doing at the time of the shooting. The jury accepted M'Naghten's claim, and the insanity defense was born. Later, the House of Lords defined the criteria necessary for a finding of insanity. The **M'Naghten rule**, as it is called today, holds that a person is not guilty of a crime if, at the time of the crime, the person either didn't know what he or she was doing or didn't know that it was wrong. The inability to distinguish right from wrong must be the result of some mental defect or disability.

M'Naghten rule
A rule for determining insanity that asks whether the defendant knew what he or she was doing or whether the defendant knew that what he or she was doing was wrong.

The M'Naghten rule is followed in many U.S. jurisdictions (Figure 6) today. In those states, the burden of proving insanity falls on the defendant. Just as defendants are assumed to be innocent, they are also assumed to be sane at the outset of any criminal trial. Learn more about the M'Naghten rule at **Web Extra 3**.

Irresistible Impulse

The M'Naghten rule worked well for a time. Eventually, however, some cases arose in which defendants clearly knew what they were doing, and they knew it was wrong. Even so, they argued in their defense that they couldn't stop doing what they knew was wrong. Such people are said to suffer from an *irresistible impulse*, and in a number of states today, they may be found not guilty by reason of that particular brand of insanity. Some states that do not use the irresistible-impulse test in determining insanity may still allow the successful demonstration of such an impulse to be considered in sentencing decisions.

The irresistible-impulse test has been criticized on a number of grounds. Primary among them is the belief that all of us suffer from compulsions. Most of us, however, learn to control them. If we give in to a compulsion, the critique goes, then why not just say it was unavoidable so as to escape any legal consequences?

The Durham Rule

Another rule for gauging insanity is called the *Durham rule.* Originally created in 1871 by a New Hampshire court, it was later adopted by Judge David Bazelon in 1954 as he decided the case of *Durham* v. *U.S.* for the court of appeals in the District of Columbia.[39] The Durham rule states that a person is not criminally responsible for his or her behavior if the person's illegal actions were the result of some mental disease or defect.

Courts that follow the Durham rule typically hear from an array of psychiatric specialists as to the mental state of the defendant. Their testimony is inevitably clouded by the need to

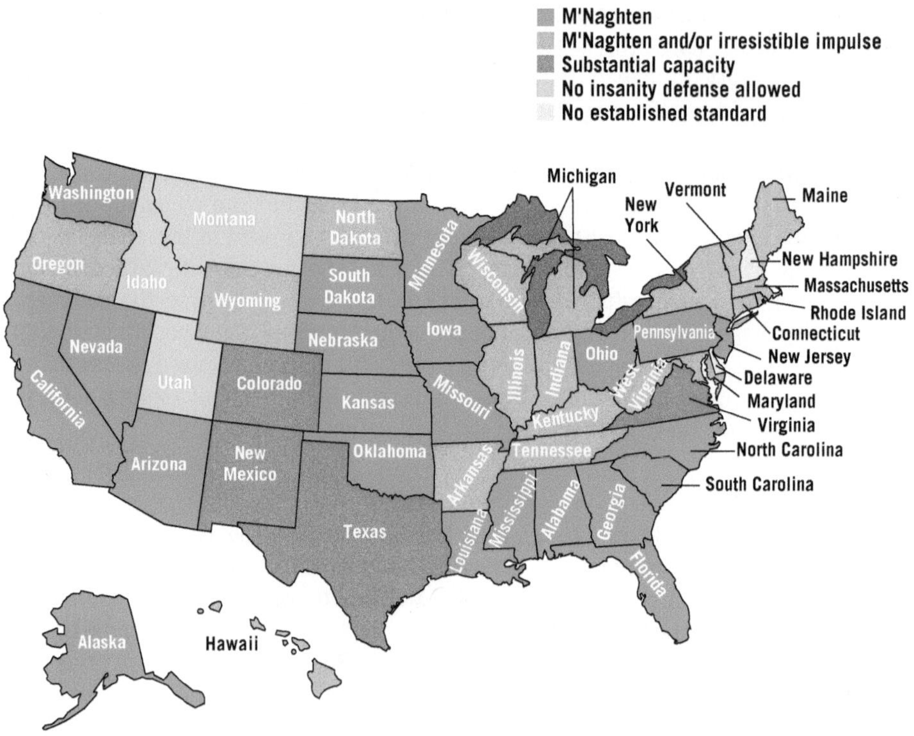

FIGURE 6
Standards for Insanity Determinations by Jurisdiction

Source: Adapted from David B. Rottman and Shauna M. Strickland, *State Court Organization, 2004* (Washington, DC: Bureau of Justice Statistics, 2006), pp. 199–202.

address the question of cause. A successful defense under the Durham rule necessitates that jurors be able to see the criminal activity in question as the *product* of the defendant's mental deficiencies. And yet many people who suffer from mental diseases or defects never commit crimes. In fact, low IQ, mental retardation, and lack of general mental capacity are not allowable excuses for criminal behavior. Because the Durham rule is especially vague, it provides fertile ground for conflicting claims.

The Substantial-Capacity Test

Nineteen states follow another guideline—the substantial-capacity test—as found in the Model Penal Code (MPC) of the American Law Institute (ALI).[40] Also called the *ALI rule* or the *MPC rule*, it suggests that insanity should be defined as the lack of a substantial capacity to control one's behavior. This test requires a judgment to the effect that the defendant either had or lacked "the mental capacity needed to understand the wrongfulness of his act or to conform his behavior to the requirements of the law."[41] The substantial-capacity test is a blending of the M'Naghten rule and the irresistible-impulse standard. "Substantial capacity" does not require total mental incompetence, nor does the rule require the behavior in question to live up to the criterion of total irresistibility. However, the problem of establishing just what constitutes "substantial mental capacity" has plagued this rule from its conception.

Equal Justice under Law

—Inscription above U.S. Supreme Court building entrance

The Brawner Rule

Judge Bazelon, apparently dissatisfied with the application of the Durham rule, created a new criterion for gauging insanity in the 1972 case of *U.S.* v. *Brawner*.[42] The Brawner rule, as it has come to be called, places responsibility for deciding insanity squarely with the jury. Bazelon suggested that the jury should be concerned with whether the defendant could justly be held responsible for the criminal act in the face of any claims of insanity. Under this proposal, juries are left with few rules to guide them other than their own sense of fairness.

The Insanity Defense and Social Reaction

The insanity defense originated as a way to recognize the social reality of mental disease. However, the history of this defense has been rife with difficulty and contradiction. First, psychiatric testimony is expensive, and expert witnesses are often at odds with one another. Another difficulty with this defense is society's acceptance of it. When "not guilty due to insanity" findings have been made, the public has not always been satisfied that justice has been served. Dissatisfaction with the jumble of rules defining legal insanity peaked in 1982 when John Hinckley was acquitted of trying to assassinate then-President Ronald Reagan. At his trial, Hinckley's lawyers claimed that a series of delusions brought about by a history of schizophrenia left him unable to control his behavior. Government prosecutors were unable to counter defense contentions of insanity. The resulting acquittal shocked the nation and resulted in calls for a review of the insanity defense.

One response has been to ban the insanity defense from use at trial. A ruling by the U.S. Supreme Court in support of a Montana law allows states to prohibit defendants from claiming that they were insane at the time they committed their crimes. In 1994, without comment, the high court let stand a Montana Supreme Court ruling that held that eliminating the insanity defense does not violate the U.S. Constitution. Currently, only three states—Montana, Idaho, and Utah—bar use of the insanity defense.[43]

The Guilty But Mentally Ill Verdict

Another response to public frustration with the insanity and responsibility issue is the **guilty but mentally ill (GBMI)** verdict, now possible in at least 11 states. (In a few states, the finding is "guilty but insane.") A GBMI verdict means that a person can be held responsible for a specific criminal act even though a degree of mental incompetence may be present in his or her personality. In most GBMI jurisdictions, a jury must return a finding of "guilty but mentally ill" if (1) every element necessary for a conviction has been proved beyond a reasonable doubt, (2) the defendant is found to have been *mentally ill* at the time the crime was committed, and (3) the defendant was *not* found to have been *legally insane* at the time the crime was committed. The difference between mental illness and legal insanity is a crucial one, since a defendant can be mentally ill by standards of the medical profession but sane for purposes of the law.

guilty but mentally ill (GBMI)
A verdict, equivalent to a finding of "guilty," that establishes that the defendant, although mentally ill, was in sufficient possession of his or her faculties to be morally blameworthy for his or her acts.

Upon return of a GBMI verdict, a judge may impose any sentence possible under the law for the crime in question. Mandated psychiatric treatment, however, is often part of the commitment order. Once cured, the offender is usually placed in the general prison population to serve any remaining sentence.

As some authors have observed, the GBMI finding has three purposes: "first, to protect society; second, to hold some offenders who were mentally ill accountable for their criminal acts; [and] third, to make treatment available to convicted offenders suffering from some form of mental illness."[44] The U.S. Supreme Court case of *Ford* v. *Wainwright* recognized an issue of a different sort.[45] The 1986 decision specified that prisoners who become insane while incarcerated cannot be executed. Hence, although insanity may not always be a successful defense to criminal prosecution, it can later become a block to the ultimate punishment.

The Defense of Temporary Insanity

Temporary insanity is another possible defense against a criminal charge. Widely used in the 1940s and 1950s, temporary insanity means that the offender claims to have been insane only at the time of the commission of the offense. If a jury agrees, the defendant goes free. The defendant is not guilty of the criminal action by virtue of having been insane at the time, yet he or she cannot be ordered to undergo psychiatric counseling or treatment because the insanity is no longer present. This type of plea has become less popular as legislatures have regulated the circumstances under which it can be made.

The Insanity Defense under Federal Law

Yet another response to the public's concern with the insanity defense and responsibility issue is the federal Insanity Defense Reform Act (IDRA). In 1984, Congress passed this act, which created major revisions in the federal insanity defense. Insanity under the law is now defined as a condition in which the defendant can be shown to have been suffering under a "severe mental disease or defect" and, as a result, "was unable to appreciate the nature and quality or the wrongfulness of his acts."[46] This definition of insanity comes close to that set forth in the old M'Naghten rule.

The act also places the burden of proving the insanity defense squarely on the defendant—a provision that has been challenged a number of times since the act was passed. The Supreme Court supported a similar requirement prior to the act's passage. In 1983, in the case of *Jones* v. *U.S.*,[47] the Court ruled that defendants can be required to prove their insanity when it becomes an issue in their defense. Shortly after the act became law, the Court held in *Ake* v. *Oklahoma* (1985)[48] that the government must ensure access to a competent psychiatrist whenever a defendant indicates that insanity will be an issue at trial.

The Consequences of an Insanity Ruling

The insanity defense today is not an easy way out of criminal prosecution, as some people assume. Once a verdict of "not guilty by reason of insanity" is returned, the judge may order the defendant to undergo psychiatric treatment until cured. Because psychiatrists are reluctant to declare any potential criminal "cured," such a sentence may result in more time spent in an institution than would have been spent in a prison. In *Foucha* v. *Louisiana* (1992),[49] however, the U.S. Supreme Court held that a defendant found not guilty by reason of insanity in a criminal trial could not thereafter be institutionalized indefinitely without a showing that he or she was either dangerous or mentally ill.

Diminished Capacity

diminished capacity
A defense based on claims of a mental condition that may be insufficient to exonerate the defendant of guilt but that may be relevant to specific mental elements of certain crimes or degrees of crime.

Diminished capacity, or *diminished responsibility*, is a defense available in some jurisdictions. In 2003, the U.S. Sentencing Commission issued a policy statement saying that diminished capacity may mean that "the defendant, although convicted, *has a significantly impaired ability* to (A) understand the wrongfulness of the behavior comprising the offense or to exercise the power of reason; or (B) control behavior that the defendant knows is wrongful."[50] Still, "the terms 'diminished responsibility' and 'diminished capacity' do not have a clearly accepted meaning in [many] courts."[51] Some defendants who offer diminished-capacity defenses do so in recognition of the fact that such claims may be based on a mental condition that would not qualify as mental disease or mental defect or be sufficient to support the defense of insanity but that might still lower criminal culpability. According to Peter Arenella, professor of law at UCLA, "the defense [of diminished capacity] was first recognized by Scottish common law courts to reduce the punishment of the 'partially insane' from murder to culpable homicide, a non-capital offense."[52]

The diminished-capacity defense is similar to the defense of insanity in that it depends on a showing that the defendant's mental state was impaired at the time of the crime. As a defense, diminished capacity is most useful when it can be shown that because of some defect of reason or mental shortcoming, the defendant's capacity to form the *mens rea* required by a specific crime was impaired. Unlike an insanity defense, however, which can result in a finding of "not guilty," a diminished-capacity defense is built on the recognition that "[m]ental condition, though insufficient to exonerate, may be relevant to specific mental elements of certain crimes or degrees of crime."[53] For example, a defendant might present evidence of mental abnormality in an effort to reduce first-degree murder to second-degree murder, or second-degree murder to manslaughter, when a killing occurs under extreme emotional disturbance. Similarly, in some jurisdictions, very low intelligence will, if proved, serve to reduce first-degree murder to manslaughter.[54]

As is the case with the insanity defense, some jurisdictions have entirely eliminated the diminished-capacity defense. The California Penal Code, for example, abolished the defense,[55] stating that "[a]s a matter of public policy there shall be no defense of diminished capacity, diminished responsibility, or irresistible impulse in a criminal action or juvenile adjudication hearing."[56]

Mental Incompetence

incompetent to stand trial
In criminal proceedings, a finding by a court that as a result of mental illness, defect, or disability, a defendant is incapable of understanding the nature of the charges and proceedings against him or her, of consulting with an attorney, and of aiding in his or her own defense.

In most states, the defendant must be capable of understanding the nature of the proceedings and must be able to assist in his or her own legal defense before being deemed competent to stand trial. Whereas insanity refers to an assessment of the offender's mental condition at the time the crime was committed, mental incompetence refers to his or her condition immediately before prosecution. Mental illness short of being found **incompetent to stand trial** can bar a defendant from self-representation. In 2008, in the case of *Indiana* v. *Edwards*, the U.S. Supreme Court held that even defendants found competent to stand trial can be prohibited from representing themselves before the court if they are too mentally disturbed to conduct trial proceedings by themselves.[57]

Procedural Defenses

Procedural defenses make the claim that the defendant was in some manner discriminated against in the justice process or that some important aspect of official procedure was not properly followed. As a result, those offering this defense say, the defendant should be released from any criminal liability. The procedural defenses we will discuss here are (1) entrapment, (2) double jeopardy, (3) *collateral estoppel*, (4) selective prosecution, (5) denial of a speedy trial, (6) prosecutorial misconduct, and (7) police fraud.

Entrapment

Entrapment is an improper or illegal inducement to crime by enforcement agents. Entrapment defenses argue that enforcement agents effectively created a crime where there would otherwise have been none. For entrapment to occur, the idea for the criminal activity must originate with official agents of the criminal justice system. Entrapment can also result when overzealous undercover police officers convince a defendant that the contemplated law-violating behavior is not a crime. To avoid claims of entrapment, officers must not engage in activity that would cause a person to commit a crime that he or she would not otherwise commit. Merely providing an opportunity for a willing offender to commit a crime, however, is not entrapment.

No person shall be . . . twice put in jeopardy of life or limb.
—Fifth Amendment to the U.S. Constitution

entrapment
An improper or illegal inducement to crime by agents of law enforcement. Also, a defense that may be raised when such inducements have occurred.

double jeopardy
A common law and constitutional prohibition against a second trial for the same offense.

Double Jeopardy

The Fifth Amendment to the U.S. Constitution makes it clear that no person may be tried twice for the same offense, which is known as **double jeopardy**. In other words, people who have been acquitted or found innocent may not again be "put in jeopardy of life or limb" for the same crime. The same is true of those who have been convicted: They cannot be tried again for the same offense. Cases that are dismissed for a lack of evidence also come under the double jeopardy rule and cannot result in a new trial. The U.S. Supreme Court has ruled that "the Double Jeopardy Clause protects against three distinct abuses: a second prosecution for the same offense after acquittal; a second prosecution for the same offense after conviction; and multiple punishments for the same offense."[58]

Double jeopardy does not apply in cases of trial error. A defendant whose conviction was set aside because of some error in proceedings at a lower court level (for example, inappropriate instructions to the jury by the trial court judge) can be retried on the same charges. Similarly, when a defendant's motion for a mistrial is successful or when members of the jury cannot agree on a verdict (resulting in a hung jury), a second trial may be held. Defendants, however, may be tried in both federal and state courts without necessarily violating the principle of double jeopardy.

Generally, because civil and criminal laws differ as to purpose, it is possible to try someone in civil court to collect damages for a possible violation of civil law, even if they were found "not guilty" in criminal court, without violating the principle of double jeopardy. For example, the 2005 civil trial of actor Robert Blake, following his acquittal at a criminal trial for murdering his wife, resulted in Blake's being ordered to pay $30 million to his wife's children.[59] In cases where civil penalties are "so punitive in form and effect as to render them criminal,"[60] however, a person sanctioned by a court in a civil case may not be tried in criminal court.

▲ Members of the New York City Police Department's Street Crimes Unit preparing for a day's work. Entrapment will likely not be an effective defense for muggers who attack these decoys. Why not?
Courtesy of the New York City Police Department

Collateral Estoppel

Collateral estoppel is similar to double jeopardy, but it applies to facts that have been determined by a "valid and final judgment."[61] Such facts cannot become the object of new litigation. For example, if a defendant has been acquitted of a murder charge by virtue of an alibi, it would not be permissible to try that person again for the murder of a second person killed along with the first.

> In all criminal prosecutions, the accused shall enjoy the right to a speedy and public trial, by an impartial jury.
>
> —Sixth Amendment to the U.S. Constitution

Selective Prosecution

The procedural defense of selective prosecution is based on the Fourteenth Amendment's guarantee of "equal protection of the laws." This defense may be available where two or more individuals are suspected of criminal involvement but not all are actively prosecuted. Selective prosecution based fairly on the strength of available evidence is not the object of this defense. However, when prosecution proceeds unfairly on the basis of some arbitrary and discriminatory attribute, such as race, sex, friendship, age, or religious preference, this defense may offer protection. In 1996, in a case that reaffirmed reasonable limits on claims of selective prosecution, the U.S. Supreme Court ruled that for a defendant to successfully "claim that he was singled out for prosecution on the basis of his race, he must make a . . . showing that the Government declined to prosecute similarly situated suspects of other races."[62]

Denial of a Speedy Trial

The Sixth Amendment to the Constitution guarantees a right to a speedy trial. The purpose of the guarantee is to prevent unconvicted and potentially innocent people from languishing in jail. The federal government[63] and most states have laws (generally referred to as *speedy trial acts*) that define the time limit necessary for a trial to be "speedy." They generally set a reasonable period, such as 90 or 120 days following arrest. Excluded from the total number of days are delays that result from requests by the defense to prepare the defendant's case. If the limit set by law is exceeded, the defendant must be set free, and no trial can occur.

Speedy trial claims became an issue in New Orleans after it was ravaged by Hurricane Katrina in August 2005. Nine months after the storm battered the city, Chief District Judge Calvin Johnson told reporters that his staff was continuing to find people who shouldn't be in jail and who were doing "Katrina time."[64] Most pre-Katrina arrestees discovered by Johnson's staff had been taken into custody for misdemeanors before the storm hit. The judge said that he released them when they were found. "We can't have people in jail indeterminately," he said.

Prosecutorial Misconduct

Another procedural defense is prosecutorial misconduct. Generally speaking, legal scholars use the term *prosecutorial misconduct* to describe actions undertaken by prosecutors that give the government an unfair advantage or that prejudice the rights of a defendant or a witness. Prosecutors are expected to uphold the highest ethical standards in the performance of their roles. When they knowingly permit false testimony, when they hide information that would clearly help the defense, or when they make unduly biased statements to the jury in closing arguments, the defense of prosecutorial misconduct may be available to the defendant.

Police Fraud

During the 1995 double-murder trial of O. J. Simpson, defense attorneys suggested that evidence against Simpson had been concocted and planted by police officers with a personal dislike of the defendant. In particular, defense attorneys pointed a finger at Los Angeles Police Detective Mark Fuhrman, suggesting that he had planted a bloody glove at the Simpson estate and had tampered with bloodstain evidence taken from Simpson's white

Ford Bronco. To support allegations that Fuhrman was motivated by racist leanings, defense attorneys subpoenaed tapes Fuhrman had made over a ten-year period with a North Carolina screenwriter who had been documenting life within the Los Angeles Police Department.

As one observer put it, however, the defense of police fraud builds on extreme paranoia about the government and police agencies. This type of defense, says political economist Francis Fukuyama, carries "to extremes a distrust of government and the belief that public authorities are in a vast conspiracy to violate the rights of individuals."[65] It can also be extremely unfair to innocent people, for a strategy of this sort subjects otherwise well-meaning public servants to intense public scrutiny, effectively shifting attention away from criminal defendants and onto the police officers—sometimes with disastrous personal results. The 43-year-old Fuhrman retired from police work before the Simpson trial concluded and has since written two books.

Summary

CRIMINAL LAW

- Laws are rules of conduct, usually found enacted in the form of statutes, that regulate relationships between people and also between parties. One of the primary functions of the law is to maintain public order. Laws also serve to regulate human interaction, enforce moral beliefs, define the economic environment of a society, enhance predictability, promote orderly social change, sustain individual rights, identify wrongdoers and redress wrongs, and mandate punishment and retribution. Because laws are made by those in power and are influenced by those with access to power brokers, they tend to reflect and support the interests of society's most powerful members.
- The rule of law, which is sometimes referred to as the *supremacy of law*, encompasses the principle that an orderly society must be governed by established principles and known codes that are applied uniformly and fairly to all of its members. It means that no one is above the law, and it mandates that even those who make or enforce the law must also abide by it. The rule of law is regarded as a vital underpinning in Western democracies, for without it disorder and chaos might prevail.
- This chapter identified various types of law, including criminal law, civil law, administrative law, case law, and procedural law. This chapter is concerned primarily with criminal law, which is that form of the law that defines and specifies punishments for offenses of a public nature or for wrongs committed against the state or against society.
- Violations of the criminal law can be of many different types and can vary in severity. Five categories of violations were discussed in this chapter: (1) felonies, (2) misdemeanors, (3) offenses, (4) treason and espionage, and (5) inchoate offenses.
- From the perspective of Western jurisprudence, all crimes can be said to share certain features. Taken together, these features make up the legal essence of the concept of crime. The essence of crime consists of three conjoined elements: (1) the criminal act, which in legal parlance is termed the *actus reus;* (2) a culpable mental state, or *mens rea;* and (3) a concurrence of the two. Hence the essence of criminal conduct consists of a concurrence of a criminal act with a culpable mental state. Five additional principles, added to these three, allow us to fully appreciate contemporary understandings of crime: (1) causation, (2) resulting harm, (3) legality, (4) punishment, and (5) necessary attendant circumstances.
- Written laws specify exactly what conditions are required for a person to be charged in a given instance of criminal activity. The elements of a crime are specific legal aspects of the criminal offense that the prosecution must prove in order to obtain a conviction. Guilt can be demonstrated, and criminal offenders convicted, only if all of the statutory elements of the particular crime can be proved in court.
- Our legal system recognizes four broad categories of defenses to a criminal charge: (1) alibi, (2) justifications, (3) excuses, and (4) procedural defenses. An alibi, if shown to be valid, means that the defendant could not have committed the crime in question because he or she was not present at the time of the crime. When a defendant offers a justification as a defense,

he or she admits committing the act in question but claims that it was necessary to avoid some greater evil. A defendant who offers an excuse as a defense claims that some personal condition or circumstance at the time of the act was such that he or she should not be held accountable under the criminal law. Procedural defenses make the claim that the defendant was in some significant way discriminated against in the justice process or that some important aspect of official procedure was not properly followed in the investigation or prosecution of the crime charged.

QUESTIONS FOR REVIEW

1. What is the purpose of law? What would a society without laws be like?
2. What is the rule of law? What is its importance in Western democracies? What does it mean to say that "nobody is above the law"?
3. What types of law does this chapter discuss? What purpose does each serve?
4. What are the five categories of criminal law violations? Describe each, and rank the categories in terms of seriousness.
5. List and describe the eight general features of crime. What are the "three conjoined elements" that comprise the legal essence of the concept of crime?
6. What is meant by the *corpus delicti* of a crime? How does the *corpus delicti* of a crime differ from the statutory elements that must be proved to convict a particular defendant of committing that crime?
7. What four broad categories of criminal defenses does our legal system recognize? Under what circumstances might each be employed?

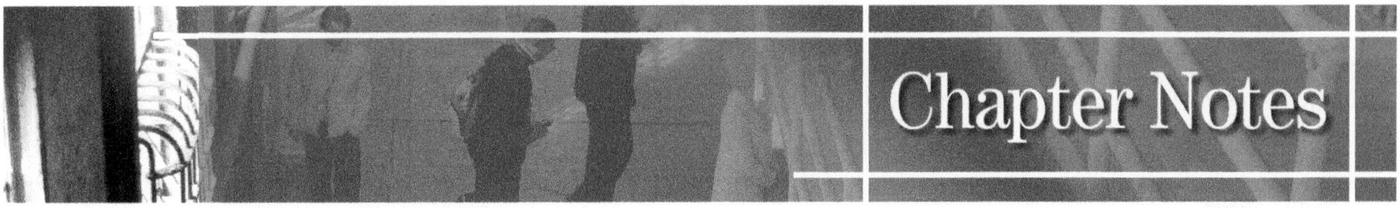

Chapter Notes

i. World of Quotes, http://www.worldofquotes.com/author/Raymond-Chandler/1/index.html (accessed January 10, 2010).
ii. 'Lectric Law Library, http://www.lectlaw.com/ref.html (accessed July 28, 2006).
iii. Daniel Oran, *Oran's Dictionary of the Law* (St. Paul, MN: West, 1983), p. 306.
iv. Henry Campbell Black, Joseph R. Nolan, and Jacqueline M. Nolan-Haley, *Black's Law Dictionary*, 6th ed. (St. Paul, MN: West, 1990), p. 24.

---

1. The details for this story come from Maureen Fan, "Iraqi Legal System in Transition: U.S. Occupiers Trying to Re-establish Order Even without Laws," *San Jose Mercury News*, June 7, 2003, http://www.bayarea.com/mld/mercurynews/news/world/6036097.htm (accessed June 8, 2008).
2. Ibid.
3. Henry Campbell Black, Joseph R. Nolan, and Jacqueline M. Nolan-Haley, *Black's Law Dictionary*, 6th ed. (St. Paul, MN: West, 1990), p. 884.
4. Ibid.
5. Susan Schmidt and James V. Grimaldi, "Ney Sentenced to 30 Months in Prison for Abramoff Deals," *Washington Post*, January 20, 2007.
6. John F. Kennedy, *Profiles in Courage* (New York: Harper and Row, 1956).
7. Fareed Zakaria, "The Enemy Within," *New York Times*, December 17, 2006, http://www.nytimes.com/2006/12/17/books/review/Zakaria.t.html (accessed August 28, 2008).
8. American Bar Association Section of International and Comparative Law, *The Rule of Law in the United States* (Chicago: American Bar Association, 1958).
9. Daniel Oran, *Oran's Dictionary of the Law* (St. Paul, MN: West, 1983), p. 306.
10. Black, Nolan, and Nolan-Haley, *Black's Law Dictionary*, p. 24.
11. Specifically, U.S. Code, Title 21, Section 846.
12. *U.S.* v. *Shabani*, 510 U.S. 1108 (1994).
13. *Gordon* v. *State*, 52 Ala. 3008, 23 Am. Rep. 575 (1875).
14. But not for a more serious degree of homicide, since leaving a young child alone in a tub of water, even if intentional, does not necessarily mean that the person who so acts intends the child to drown.
15. O. W. Holmes, *The Common Law*, Vol. 3 (Boston: Little, Brown, 1881).
16. There is disagreement among some jurists as to whether the crime of statutory rape is a strict liability offense. Some jurisdictions treat it as such and will not accept as a defense a reasonable mistake about the victim's age. Others, however, do accept such a mistake as a defense.
17. *State* v. *Stiffler*, 763 P.2d 308 (Idaho App. 1988).
18. John S. Baker, Jr., et al., *Hall's Criminal Law*, 5th ed. (Charlottesville, VA: Michie, 1993), p. 138.
19. The same is not true for procedures within the criminal justice system, which can be modified even after a person has been sentenced and, hence, become retroactive. See, for example, the U.S. Supreme Court case of *California Department of Corrections* v. *Morales*, 514 U.S. 499 (1995), in which the Court allowed changes in the length of time between parole hearings, even though those changes applied to offenders who had already been sentenced.
20. Black, Nolan, and Nolan-Haley, *Black's Law Dictionary*, p. 127.
21. The statute also says, "A mother's breastfeeding of her baby does not under any circumstance violate this section."
22. Common law crimes, of course, are not based on statutory elements.
23. *People* v. *Hall—Final Analysis*, SkiSafety.com, http://www.skisafety.com/amicuscases-hall2.html (accessed August 28, 2007).
24. See *Maughs* v. *Commonwealth*, 181 Va. 117, 120, 23 S.E.2d 784, 786 (1943).
25. *State* v. *Stephenson*, Opinion No. 24403 (South Carolina, 1996). See also *State* v. *Blocker*, 205 S.C. 303, 31 S.E.2d 908 (1944).
26. *State* v. *Kindle*, 71 Mont. 58, 64, 227 (1924).
27. Black, Nolan, and Nolan-Haley, *Black's Law Dictionary*, p. 343.
28. Patrick L. McCloskey and Ronald L. Schoenberg, *Criminal Law Deskbook* (New York: Matthew Bender, 1988), Section 20.03[13].
29. Details for this story come from Tim Talley, "Folk Hero or Killer: Druggist Who Killed Robber," Associated Press, May 30, 2009, http://abcnews.go.com/US/wireStory?id=7713776 (accessed May 31, 2009).
30. The exception, of course, is that of a trespasser who trespasses in order to commit a more serious crime.
31. Sir Edward Coke, 3 *Institute*, 162.
32. *The Crown* v. *Dudly & Stephens*, 14 Q.B.D. 273, 286, 15 Cox C. C. 624, 636 (1884).
33. "Jury Convicts Condom Rapist," *USA Today*, May 14, 1993.
34. Black, Nolan, and Nolan-Haley, *Black's Law Dictionary*, p. 504.
35. *State of Tennessee* v. *Charles Arnold Ballinger*, No. E2000-01339-CCA-R3-CD (Tenn. Crim. App. 01/09/2000).
36. See, for example, *Montana* v. *Egelhoff*, 116 S.Ct. 2013, 135 L.Ed.2d 361 (1996).
37. L. A. Callahan et al., "The Volume and Characteristics of Insanity Defense Pleas: An Eight-State Study," *Bulletin of the American Academy of Psychiatry and the Law*, Vol. 19, No. 4 (1991), pp. 331–338.
38. American Bar Association Standing Committee on Association Standards for Criminal Justice, *Proposed Criminal Justice Mental Health Standards* (Chicago: American Bar Association, 1984).
39. *Durham* v. *U.S.*, 214 F.2d 867, 875 (D.C. Cir. 1954).
40. American Law Institute, *Model Penal Code: Official Draft and Explanatory Notes* (Philadelphia: American Law Institute, 1985).
41. Ibid.
42. *U.S.* v. *Brawner*, 471 F.2d 969, 973 (D.C. Cir. 1972).
43. See Joan Biskupic, "Insanity Defense: Not a Right; In Montana Case, Justices Give States Option to Prohibit Claim," *Washington Post* wire service, March 29, 1994.
44. Ibid.
45. *Ford* v. *Wainwright*, 477 U.S. 399, 106 S.Ct. 2595, 91 L.Ed.2d 335 (1986).
46. U.S. Code, Title 18, Section 401.
47. *Jones* v. *U.S.*, U.S. Sup. Ct., 33 CrL. 3233 (1983).

48. *Ake* v. *Oklahoma*, 470 U.S. 68, 105 S.Ct. 1087, 84 L.Ed.2d 53 (1985).
49. *Foucha* v. *Louisiana*, 504 U.S. 71 (1992).
50. U.S. Sentencing Commission, "Supplement to the 2002 Federal Sentencing Guidelines: Section 5K2.13. Diminished Capacity (Policy Statement)," April 30, 2003, http://www.ussc.gov/2002suppb/5K2_13.htm (accessed May 8, 2008). Italics added.
51. *U.S.* v. *Pohlot*, 827 F.2d 889 (1987).
52. Peter Arenella, "The Diminished Capacity and Diminished Responsibility Defenses: Two Children of a Doomed Marriage," *Columbia Law Review*, Vol. 77 (1977), p. 830.
53. *U.S.* v. *Brawner*, 471 F.2d 969 (1972).
54. Black, Nolan, and Nolan-Haley, *Black's Law Dictionary*, p. 458.
55. California Penal Code, Section 25(a).
56. Ibid., Section 28(b).
57. *Indiana* v. *Edwards*, 554 U.S. 164 (2008).
58. *U.S.* v. *Halper*, 490 U.S. 435 (1989).
59. "Robert Blake Found Liable for Wife's Death," Associated Press, November 18, 2005.
60. See, for example, *Hudson* v. *U.S.*, 18 S.Ct. 488 (1997); and *U.S.* v. *Ursery*, 518 U.S. 267 (1996).
61. McCloskey and Schoenberg, *Criminal Law Deskbook*, Section 20.02[4].
62. *U.S.* v. *Armstrong*, 116 S.Ct. 1480, 134 L.Ed.2d 687 (1996).
63. Speedy Trial Act, U.S. Code, Title 18, Section 3161. Significant cases involving the Speedy Trial Act are those of *U.S.* v. *Carter*, 476 U.S. 1138, 106 S.Ct. 2241, 90 L.Ed.2d 688 (1986); and *Henderson* v. *U.S.*, 476 U.S. 321, 106 S.Ct. 1871, 90 L.Ed.2d 299 (1986).
64. Peter Whoriskey, "New Orleans Justice System Besieged," *Boston Globe*, April 17, 2006, http://www.boston.com/news/nation/articles/2006/04/17/new_orleans_justice_system_besieged (accessed May 10, 2007).
65. Francis Fukuyama, "Extreme Paranoia about Government Abounds," *USA Today*, August 24, 1995.

Policing: Purpose and Organization

Learning Objectives

After reading this chapter, you should be able to:

1. Explain the police mission in democratic societies.
2. List and describe the three major levels of public law enforcement in the United States today.
3. Discuss the various components of police administration, including management, chain of command, organization, and department structure.
4. Identify the various historical stages of development in American policing, and describe the characteristics of each stage.
5. Describe community policing, and explain how it differs from traditional forms of policing.
6. Explain evidence-based policing, and demonstrate the potential that it holds in the area of police management.
7. Explain police discretion, and identify some of the factors that influence a police officer's use of discretion.

he police in the United States are not separate from the people. They draw their authority from the will and nsent of the people, and they cruit their officers from them. he police are the instrument of the people to achieve and aintain order; their efforts are founded on principles of public service and ultimate responsibility to the public."

—National Advisory Commission on Criminal Justice Standards and Goals

B. O'Kane/Alamy

"The tragedies of September 11, 2001, have forever changed the roles of traditional law enforcement in this country."

—Major Cities Chiefs Association[1]

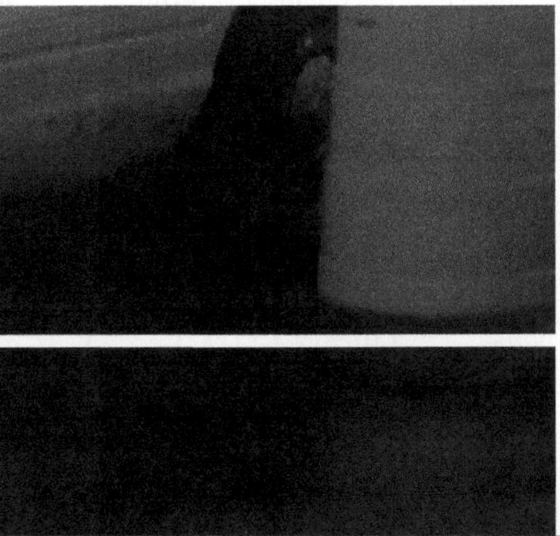

▲ Miami riot police advancing through burning trash to control demonstrators protesting a meeting of foreign delegates who were attempting to negotiate an international free-trade agreement in 2003. Order maintenance is an important part of the police mission. What other aspects of the police mission can you identify?
David Adame/AP Wide World Photos

Introduction

In mid-November 2003, thousands of demonstrators protesting the proposed creation of the Free Trade Area of the Americas (FTAA) clashed with hundreds of Miami police officers equipped with riot gear. The protesters—concerned that the creation of the 34-nation FTAA would send thousands of U.S. jobs overseas, exploit cheap labor, and waste natural resources—were targeting a meeting by foreign trade ministers.[2]

Although most demonstrators paraded peacefully and avoided confrontations, some pulled down crowd-control barriers with grappling hooks and scuffled with officers who were trying to maintain order. Before the melee ended, officers had to use batons, plastic shields, concussion grenades, pepper spray, and stun guns to regain control over the unruly protesters. Armored personnel carriers stood ready to move into "hot spots." "We're basically trying to maintain the peace downtown," said police spokesperson Jorge Pino, as demonstrators advanced on police lines.[3] By the time the event ended, 74 people had been arrested and 42 protesters were injured, including ten who had to be hospitalized. Three police officers were also hurt. As the Miami riots demonstrate, the maintenance of social order is an important part of police work today.

The Police Mission

1 Explain the police mission in democratic societies.

The basic purposes of policing in democratic societies are to (1) enforce the laws of the society of which the police are a part, (2) apprehend offenders who participate in crime, (3) prevent crime, (4) preserve domestic peace and tranquillity, and (5) provide the community with needed enforcement-related services. Simply put, as Sir Robert Peel, founder of the British system of policing, explained in 1822, "The basic mission for which the police exist is to reduce crime and disorder."[4] In the paragraphs that follow, we turn our attention to these five basic elements of the police mission.

Enforcing the Law

The police operate under an official public mandate that requires them to enforce the law. Collectively speaking, police agencies are the primary enforcers of federal, state, and local criminal laws. Not surprisingly, police officers see themselves as crime fighters, a view shared by the public and promoted by the popular media.

Although it is the job of the police to enforce the law, it is not their *only* job. Practically speaking, most officers spend the majority of their time answering nonemergency public service calls,[5] controlling traffic, or writing tickets. Most are not involved in intensive, ongoing crime-fighting activities. Research shows that only about 10% to 20% of all calls to the police involve situations that actually require a law enforcement response (that is, situations that might lead to arrest and eventual prosecution), a fact that is described in more detail later in this chapter.[6]

Even when the police are busy enforcing laws, they can't enforce them all. Police resources, including labor, vehicles, and investigative assets, are limited, causing officers to focus more on certain types of law violation than on others. Old laws prohibiting minor offenses that today hold little social significance, like spitting on the sidewalk or scaring horses with a noisy automobile, are typically relegated to the dustbin of statutory history. Even though they are still "on the books," few (if any) officers even think about enforcing such laws. A number of writers have observed that the police tend to tailor their enforcement efforts to meet the contemporary concerns of the populace they serve.[7] For example, if the local community is upset about "massage parlors" operating in certain neighborhoods, it is likely that the local police department will bring enforcement efforts to bear that might eventually lead to the relocation or closing of such businesses. Although the enforcement practices of police agencies are significantly influenced by community interests, individual officers take their cue on enforcement priorities from their departments, their peers, and their supervisors. Learn more about how police supervisory styles influence patrol officer behavior at **Library Extra 1**.

The police are expected not only to enforce the law but also to support it. This means that the personal actions of law enforcement personnel should be exemplary and should inspire others to respect and obey the law. Off-duty officers who are seen speeding down the highway or smoking marijuana at a party, for example, do a disservice to the police profession and engender disrespect for all agents of enforcement and for the law itself. Hence, in an important sense, we can say that respect for the law begins with the personal and public behavior of law enforcement officers.

Apprehending Offenders

Some offenders are apprehended during the investigation of a crime or even during its commission or immediately afterward. Fleeing Oklahoma City bomber Timothy McVeigh, for example, was stopped by an Oklahoma Highway Patrol officer on routine patrol only 90 minutes after the destruction of the Alfred P. Murrah Federal Building[8] for driving a car with no license plate. When the officer questioned McVeigh about a bulge in his jacket, McVeigh admitted that it was a gun. The officer then took McVeigh into custody for carrying a concealed weapon. Typically, McVeigh would then have made an immediate appearance before a judge and have been released on bail. As fate would have it, however, the judge assigned to see McVeigh was involved in a protracted divorce case. The longer jail stay proved to be McVeigh's undoing. As the investigation into the bombing progressed, profiler Clinton R. Van Zandt of the Federal Bureau of Investigation (FBI) Behavioral Science Unit concluded that the bomber was likely a native-born white male in his twenties who had been in the military and was probably a member of a fringe militia group—all of which were true of McVeigh.[9] Working together, the FBI and the Oklahoma State Police realized that McVeigh was a likely suspect and questioned him. While McVeigh's capture was the result of a bit of good luck, many offenders are only caught as the result of extensive police work involving a painstaking investigation.

crime prevention
The anticipation, recognition, and appraisal of a crime risk and the initiation of action to eliminate or reduce it.

Preventing Crime

Crime prevention is a proactive approach to the problem of crime; it is "the anticipation, recognition and appraisal of a crime risk and initiation of action to remove or reduce it."[10] In preventing crime, police agencies act before a crime happens, thus preventing victimization from occurring. Although the term *crime prevention* is relatively new, the idea is probably as old as human society. Securing valuables, limiting access to sensitive areas, and monitoring the activities of suspicious people are techniques that were in use long before the establishment of Western police forces in the 1800s.

▲ Chief Deputy Paula Townsend of the Watauga County (North Carolina) Sheriff's Department carrying 11-month-old Breanna Chambers to safety in 2005 after the capture of the child's parents. The parents, who were already wanted on charges related to methamphetamine manufacture, were charged with additional counts of child abduction, felonious restraint, and assault with a gun after they abducted Breanna and her two-year-old brother, James Paul Chambers, from a foster home. Today's police officers are expected to enforce the law while meeting the needs of the community. Do those goals conflict? If so, how?
Watauga Democrat/Marie Freeman/AP Wide World Photos

Techniques and Programs

Modern crime-prevention efforts aim not only to reduce crime and criminal opportunities and lower the potential rewards of criminal activity but also to lessen the public's fear of crime.[11] Law enforcement–led crime-prevention efforts include both techniques and programs. Crime-prevention *techniques* include access control (including barriers to entry and exit), surveillance (such as video surveillance), theft-deterrence devices (that is, locks, alarms, and tethers), security lighting, and visibility landscaping. Crime prevention through environmental design (CPTED) is a tool that can be used by crime-prevention specialists, including architects and public-safety consultants.

In contrast to techniques, crime-prevention *programs* are organized efforts that focus resources on reducing a specific form of criminal threat. The Philadelphia Police Department's Operation Identification, for example, is designed to discourage theft and to help recover stolen property.[12] The program seeks to educate citizens on the importance of identifying, marking, and listing their valuables to deter theft and to aid in their recovery. Through Operation Identification, the police department provides engraving pens, suggests ways of photographing and engraving valuables, and provides window decals and car bumper stickers that identify citizens as participants in the program. Other crime-prevention programs typically target school-based crime, gang activity, drug abuse, violence, domestic abuse, identity theft, vehicle theft, or neighborhood crimes such as burglary.

Today's crime-prevention programs depend on community involvement, an open flow of information, and public education about risks and possible preventive measures. For example,

Neighborhood Watch programs build on active observation by home owners and businesspeople on the lookout for anything unusual. Crime Stoppers International and Crime Stoppers USA are examples of privately sponsored programs that accept tips about criminal activity that they pass on to the appropriate law enforcement organization. Crime Stoppers International can be accessed at **Web Extra 1**, and the National Crime Prevention Council can be found at **Web Extra 2**.

Predicting Crime

CompStat
A crime-analysis and police-management process built on crime mapping that was developed by the New York City Police Department in the mid-1990s.

Law enforcement's ability to prevent crimes relies in part on the ability of police planners to predict when and where crimes will occur. Effective prediction means that limited police resources can be correctly assigned to the areas with the greatest need. One technique for predicting criminal activity is **CompStat**.[13] While CompStat may sound like a software program, it is actually a process of crime analysis and police management developed by the New York City Police Department in the mid-1990s to help police managers better assess their performance and foresee the potential for crime.[14] The CompStat process involves first collecting and analyzing the information received from 9-1-1 calls and officer reports.[15] This detailed and timely information is then mapped using special software developed for the purpose. The resulting map sequences, generated over time, reveal the time and place of crime patterns and identify hot spots of ongoing criminal activity. The maps also show the number of patrol officers active in an area, ongoing investigations, arrests made, and so on, thus helping commanders see which anticrime strategies are working.

CrimeStat, a Windows-based spatial statistics analysis software program for analyzing crime-incident locations, is a second technique for predicting criminal activity. It produces results similar to CompStat's.[16] Developed by Ned Levine and Associates with grants from the National Institute of Justice (NIJ), CrimeStat provides statistical tools for crime mapping and analysis—including identification of crime hot spots, spatial distribution of incidents, and distance analysis—that help crime analysts target offenses that might be related to one another. CrimeStat software is available online via **Web Extra 3**; **Web Extra 4** provides a link to chicagocrime.org, which overlays crime statistics on maps of the city.

Preserving the Peace

Enforcing the law, investigating crime and apprehending offenders, and preventing crime are all daunting tasks requiring the full attention of police departments. There are, after all, many laws and numerous offenders. Still, crimes are clearly defined by statute and are therefore limited in number. Peacekeeping, however, is a virtually limitless police activity involving not only activities that violate the law (and hence the community's peace) but many other activities as well. Law enforcement officers who supervise parades, public demonstrations, and picketing strikers, for example, typically attempt to ensure that the behavior of everyone involved remains civil so that it does not disrupt community life.

Robert H. Langworthy, who has written extensively about the police, says that keeping the peace is often left to individual officers.[17] Basically, he says, departments depend on patrol officers "to define the peace and decide how to support it." An officer is doing a good job when his or her beat is quiet, "meaning there are no complaints about loiterers or traffic flow, and commerce is supported."

quality-of-life offense
A minor violation of the law (sometimes called a *petty crime*) that demoralizes community residents and businesspeople. Quality-of-life offenses involve acts that create physical disorder (for example, excessive noise and vandalism) or that reflect social decay (for example, panhandling and prostitution).

Many police departments focus on quality-of-life offenses as a crime-reduction and peacekeeping strategy. **Quality-of-life offenses** are minor law violations (sometimes called *petty crimes*) that demoralize residents and businesspeople by creating disorder (for example, excessive noise, graffiti, abandoned cars, and vandalism) or by reflecting social decay (panhandling and aggressive begging, public urination, prostitution, roaming youth gangs, public consumption of alcohol, and street-level substance abuse).[18] Homelessness, while not necessarily a violation of the law (unless it involves some form of trespass),[19] is also typically addressed under quality-of-life programs through police interviews with the homeless, many of whom are relocated to shelters or hospitals or are arrested for some other offense. Many claim that reducing the number of quality-of-life offenses in a community can restore a sense of order, reduce the fear of crime, and lessen the number of serious crimes that occur. However, quality-of-life programs have been criticized by those who say that the police should not be taking a law enforcement approach to social and economic problems.[20]

A similar approach to keeping the peace can be found in the broken windows model of policing.[21] This thesis is based on the notion that physical decay, such as litter and abandoned buildings, can breed disorder in a community and can lead to crime by signaling that laws are not being enforced.[22] Such decay, the theory postulates, pushes law-abiding citizens to withdraw from the streets, which sends a signal that lawbreakers can operate freely.[23] The broken windows thesis suggests that by encouraging the repair of rundown buildings and controlling disorderly behavior in public spaces, police agencies can create an environment in which serious crime cannot easily flourish.[24]

Fidelity, bravery, and integrity.
—FBI motto

While desirable, public order has its own costs. Noted police author Charles R. Swanson says, "The degree to which any society achieves some amount of public order through police action depends in part upon the price that society is willing to pay to obtain it."[25] Swanson goes on to describe the price to be paid in terms of (1) police resources paid for by tax dollars and (2) "a reduction in the number, kinds, and extent of liberties" that are available to members of the public.

Providing Services

Writers for the NIJ observe that "any citizen from any city, suburb, or town across the United States can mobilize police resources by simply picking up the phone and placing a direct call to the police."[26] "Calling the cops" has been described as the cornerstone of policing in a democratic society. About 70% of the millions of daily calls to 9-1-1 systems across the country are directed to the police, although callers can also request emergency medical and fire services.

Calls received by 9-1-1 operators are prioritized and then relayed to patrol officers, specialized field units, or other emergency personnel. In 2001, for example, the Hastings (Minnesota) Police Department handled a total of 12,895 calls for service.[27] A breakdown of those calls shows that there were 1,837 calls related to serious crimes such as arson, assault, auto theft, burglary, larceny, rape, and robbery. The remaining 11,058 calls were nonemergency calls involving lost and found articles, minor motor vehicle accidents, barking dogs, suspicious persons, and parking and traffic violation reports. Numbers like these have led some cities to adopt nonemergency "Citizen Service System" call numbers in addition to 9-1-1. More than a dozen metropolitan areas, including Baltimore, Dallas, Detroit, Las Vegas, New York, and San Jose, now staff 3-1-1 nonemergency systems around the clock. Plans are afoot in some states to adopt the 3-1-1 system statewide.

American Policing Today: From the Federal to the Local Level

The organization of American law enforcement has been called the most complex in the world. Three major legislative and judicial jurisdictions exist in the United States—federal, state, and local—and each has created a variety of police agencies to enforce its laws. Unfortunately, little uniformity is seen among jurisdictions regarding the naming, function, or authority of enforcement agencies. The matter is complicated still more by the rapid growth of private security firms, which operate on a for-profit basis and provide services that have traditionally been regarded as law enforcement activities.

2 List and describe the three major levels of public law enforcement in the United States today.

Federal Agencies

Dozens of federal law enforcement agencies are distributed among 14 U.S. government departments and 28 nondepartmental entities (Table 1). In addition to the enforcement agencies listed in the table, many other federal government offices are involved in enforcement through inspection, regulation, and control activities. The Government Accounting Office (GAO) reports that nonmilitary federal agencies employ a total of 139,929 law enforcement officers, which it defines as individuals authorized to perform any of four specific functions: (1) conduct criminal investigations, (2) execute search warrants, (3) make arrests, or (4) carry firearms.[28] The Federal Bureau of Investigation, one of the best-known federal law enforcement agencies, is described in the paragraphs that follow.

Visit the home pages of many federal law enforcement agencies at **Web Extra 5**. Learn more about staffing levels of federal criminal justice agencies at **Library Extra 2**.

TABLE 1
American Policing: Federal Law Enforcement Agencies

Department of Agriculture
U.S. Forest Service

Department of Commerce
Bureau of Export Enforcement
National Marine Fisheries Administration

Department of Defense
Air Force Office of Special Investigations
Army Criminal Investigation Division
Defense Criminal Investigative Service
Naval Investigative Service

Department of Energy
National Nuclear Safety Administration
Office of Mission Operations
Office of Secure Transportation

Department of Health and Human Services
Food and Drug Administration (FDA), Office of Criminal Investigations

Department of Homeland Security (DHS)
Federal Law Enforcement Training Center (FLETC)
Federal Protective Service
Transportation Security Administration
U.S. Coast Guard
U.S. Customs and Border Protection (CBP), including U.S. Border Patrol
U.S. Immigration and Customs Enforcement (ICE)
U.S. Secret Service (SS)

Department of the Interior
Bureau of Indian Affairs
Bureau of Land Management
Fish and Wildlife Service
National Park Service
U.S. Park Police

Department of Justice
Bureau of Alcohol, Tobacco, Firearms and Explosives (ATF)
Bureau of Prisons (BOP)
Drug Enforcement Administration (DEA)
Federal Bureau of Investigation (FBI)
U.S. Marshals Service

Department of Labor
Office of Labor Racketeering

Department of State
Diplomatic Security Service

Department of Transportation
Federal Air Marshals Program

Department of the Treasury
Internal Revenue Service (IRS), Criminal Investigation Division
Treasury Inspector General for Tax Enforcement

Department of Veterans Affairs (VA)
Office of Security and Law Enforcement

U.S. Postal Service
Postal Inspection Service

Other Offices with Enforcement Personnel
Administrative Office of the U.S. Courts
Amtrak Police
Bureau of Engraving and Printing Police
Environmental Protection Agency (EPA), Criminal Investigations Division
Federal Reserve Board
Tennessee Valley Authority (TVA)
U.S. Capitol Police
U.S. Mint
U.S. Supreme Court Police
Washington, D.C., Metropolitan Police Department

Note: Virtually every cabinet-level federal agency has its own Office of Inspector General, which has enforcement authority.

Background of the FBI

> What we need to do better is be predictive. We have to be proactive. We have to develop the capability to anticipate attacks.
> —Robert S. Mueller, director of the FBI[i]

The FBI may be the most famous law enforcement agency in the country and in the world. The FBI has traditionally been held in high regard by many Americans, who think of it as an example of what a law enforcement organization should be and who believe that FBI agents are exemplary police officers. William Webster, former director of the FBI, reflected this sentiment when he said, "Over the years the American people have come to expect the most professional law enforcement from the FBI. Although we use the most modern forms of management and technology in the fight against crime, our strength is in our people—in the character of the men and women of the FBI. For that reason we seek only those who have demonstrated that they can perform as professional people who can, and will, carry on our tradition of fidelity, bravery, and integrity."[29]

The history of the FBI spans more than 100 years. It began in 1908 as the Bureau of Investigation. It was designed to serve as the investigative arm of the U.S. Department of Justice. The creation of the bureau was motivated, at least in part, by the inability of other

CJ News
FBI Retools Most Wanted List

Those grainy mug shots, once confined to post office lobbies, are coming to a billboard near you.

The FBI is retooling its Ten Most Wanted list into an increasingly multimedia international appeal for help as it tries to keep its signature program relevant in a crowded media landscape.

"We're trying to exploit every opportunity," FBI spokesman Chris Allen says. The strategy is "probably pretty surprising for a government agency."

Among the changes:

- Launching a billboard campaign. Earlier this month, the FBI began featuring top fugitives on billboards in 20 cities.
- Expanding the list's international reach. The FBI is building on its broadcast alliance with the popular *America's Most Wanted* TV show to solicit tips on similar programs in Hungary, Israel, the Netherlands, Great Britain, and Germany.
- Posting video. The FBI has video of the most recent sightings of some fugitives on its Top 10 website.

In the billboard deal with Clear Channel Outdoor Holdings Inc., which is donating the space, the FBI will get access to about 150 electronic billboards, Allen says.

In Los Angeles, images of Most Wanted suspect Emigdio Preciado, Jr., accused in the attempted murders of two sheriff's deputies, are on display throughout the city.

Marine Cpl. Cesar Laurean, a suspect in the murder of pregnant Lance Cpl. Maria Lauterbach, is not on the Top 10 list, but his image appears on some billboards.

As of December [2007], 489 fugitives had appeared on the list since it began in 1950. Of those, 458 have been located, at least 150 with citizen help, the FBI says. Agents hunt for an estimated 12,000 fugitives at a time.

Rex Tomb, a former chief of the FBI's investigative publicity unit, says the list reflects the evolving nature of crime. The bureau added Osama bin Laden after the 1998 U.S. embassy bombings in Africa. "In the 1950s, it was bank robbery," Tomb says. "Now, you see bin Laden up there."

The bureau . . . quietly removed accused cop killer Donald Eugene Webb from the Top 10, marking only the sixth time a fugitive was taken off before capture.

"That's pretty valuable real estate, and you have to make sure . . . there is going to be a benefit," Tomb says. "Sometimes it works. Sometimes it doesn't."

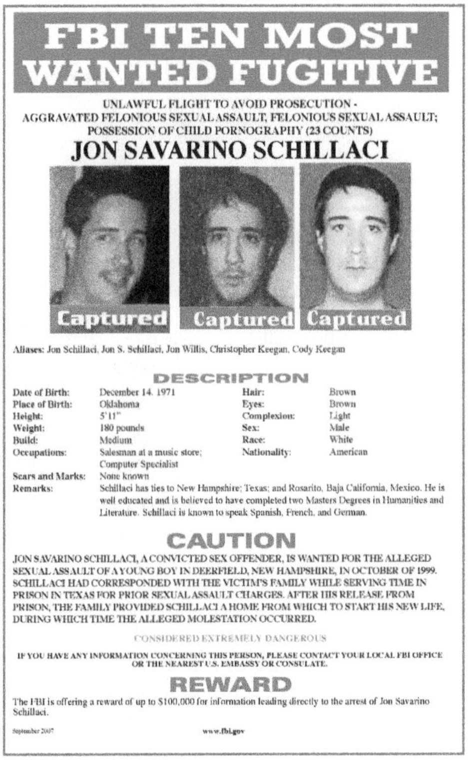

▲ An electronic Ten Most Wanted poster. How is the FBI changing the way it uses new types of media and other news outlets to publicize information about fugitives who are on the list?
Federal Bureau of Investigation

See the FBI's ten most wanted fugitives at http://www.fbi.gov/wanted.htm.

Source: Kevin Johnson, "FBI Retools Most Wanted List," *USA Today*, January 16, 2008. Reprinted with permission.

agencies to stem the rising tide of American political and business corruption.[30] Learn about the history of the FBI at **Web Extra 6**.

The official purpose of today's FBI is succinctly stated in the agency's mission statement: "The Mission of the FBI is to protect and defend the United States against terrorist and foreign intelligence threats, to uphold and enforce the criminal laws of the United States, and to provide leadership and criminal justice services to federal, state, municipal, and international agencies and partners."[31]

FBI headquarters are located in the J. Edgar Hoover Building on Pennsylvania Avenue in Washington, D.C. Special agents and support personnel who work at the agency's headquarters organize and coordinate FBI activities throughout the country and around the world. Headquarters staffers determine investigative priorities, oversee major cases, and manage the organization's resources, technology, and personnel.

The daily work of the FBI is done by nearly 13,000 special agents assigned to 56 field offices and 400 satellite offices (known as *resident agencies*). A special agent in charge oversees each field office, except for the three largest field offices in Washington, D.C., Los Angeles, and New York City, each of which is headed by an assistant director.

▲ FBI Director Robert S. Mueller III explaining his agency's shift in priorities following the 2001 terrorist attacks on the World Trade Center and the Pentagon. How did the agency's priorities change?
AP Wide World Photos

The FBI also operates legal attaché offices (called *Legats*) in a number of major cities around the world, including London and Paris. Such offices permit the international coordination of enforcement activities and facilitate the flow of law enforcement–related information between the FBI and police agencies in host countries. In 1995, a few years after the end of the cold war, the FBI opened a legal attaché office in Moscow. The Moscow office assists Russian police agencies in the growing battle against organized crime in that country and helps American officials track suspected Russian criminals operating in the United States. Also in 1995, an Eastern European version of the FBI Academy, known as the International Law Enforcement Academy (ILEA), opened in Budapest, Hungary. Its purpose is to train police administrators from all of Eastern Europe in the latest crime-fighting techniques.[32]

The FBI also operates the Combined DNA Index System (CODIS), a computerized forensic database of DNA profiles of offenders convicted of serious crimes (such as rape, other sexual assaults, murder, and certain crimes against children), as well as DNA profiles from unknown offenders.[33] CODIS, now a part of the National DNA Index System (NDIS), was formally authorized by the federal DNA Identification Act of 1994.[34] It is being enhanced daily through the work of federal, state, and local law enforcement agencies that take DNA samples from biological evidence gathered at crime scenes and from offenders themselves. CODIS can rapidly identify a perpetrator when it finds a match between an evidence sample and a stored profile. By 1998, every state had enacted legislation establishing a CODIS database and requiring that DNA from offenders convicted of certain serious crimes be entered into the system. By April 2010, the CODIS database contained more than 8.5 million DNA profiles.[35] Learn more about CODIS at **Web Extra 7**.

The FBI Laboratory Division, located in Quantico, Virginia, operates one of the largest and most comprehensive crime laboratories in the world. It provides services related to the scientific solution and prosecution of crimes throughout the country. It is also the only full-service federal forensic laboratory in the United States. Laboratory activities include crime-scene searches, special surveillance photography, latent-fingerprint examinations, forensic examinations of evidence (including DNA testing), court testimony by laboratory personnel, and other scientific and technical services. The FBI offers laboratory services, free of charge, to all law enforcement agencies in the United States. Learn more about the FBI's administrative divisions, including the activities of each, via **Web Extra 8**.

The FBI also runs a National Academy Program, which is part of its Training Division. The program offered its first class in 1935 and had 23 students. It was then known as the FBI National Police Training School. In 1940, the school moved from Washington, D.C., to the U.S. Marine Amphibious Base at Quantico, Virginia. In 1972, the facility expanded to 334 acres, and the FBI Academy, as we know it today, officially opened.[36] According to the most recent statistics available, the academy program has produced 37,990 graduates since it began operations. This includes 2,475 graduates from 151 foreign countries and 328 graduates from U.S. territories and possessions. More than 200 sessions have been offered since inception of the training program. Visit the FBI Academy on the Web at **Web Extra 9**.

Much of what is wrong with the police is the result of the absurd, fragmented, unworkable nonsystem of more than 17,000 local [police] departments.

—Patrick V. Murphy, former New York City police commissioner

The FBI and Counterterrorism

Soon after the attacks of September 11, 2001, the FBI reshaped its priorities to focus on preventing future terrorist attacks. To combat terrorism, the FBI's Counterterrorism Division collects, analyzes, and shares information and critical intelligence with various federal agencies and departments—including the Central Intelligence Agency (CIA), the National Security Agency (NSA), and the Department of Homeland Security (DHS)—and with law enforcement agencies throughout the country. An essential weapon in the FBI's battle against terrorism is the Joint Terrorism Task Force (JTTF).

In testimony before Congress in 2005, FBI Director Robert S. Mueller III identified three areas of special concern relative to the bureau's ongoing antiterrorism efforts. First, said Mueller, "is the threat from covert operatives who may be inside the U.S. who have the intention to facilitate or conduct an attack."[37] The very nature of trained covert operatives, said the director, is that they are difficult to detect. "I remain very concerned about what we are *not* seeing," said Mueller. Second, Mueller identified a concern "with the growing body of sensitive reporting that continues to show al-Qaeda's clear intention to obtain and ultimately use some form of chemical, biological, radiological, nuclear, or high-energy explosives (CBRNE) material in its attacks against America." Finally, said Mueller, "We remain concerned about the potential for al-Qaeda to . . . exploit radical American converts and other indigenous extremists."

TABLE 2
American Policing: State Law Enforcement Agencies

Alcohol law enforcement agencies	Port authorities	State police
Fish and wildlife agencies	State bureaus of investigation	State university police
Highway patrol	State park services	Weigh station operations

State Agencies

Most state police agencies were created in the late nineteenth or early twentieth century to meet specific needs. The Texas Rangers, created in 1835 before Texas attained statehood, functioned as a military organization responsible for patrolling the republic's borders. The apprehension of Mexican cattle rustlers was one of its main concerns.[38] Massachusetts, targeting vice control, was the second state to create a law enforcement agency. Today, a wide diversity of state policing agencies exists. Table 2 provides a list of typical state-sponsored law enforcement agencies.

▲ The new LAPD's $437 million headquarters building which opened in 2009. The 500,000-square-foot headquarters building is home to 2,300 LAPD officers and civilian employees. How do the roles of federal, state, and municipal law enforcement agencies differ?
Hans Gutknecht/Los Angeles Daily News/ZUMApress.com/Newscom

State law enforcement agencies are usually organized after one of two models. In the first, a centralized model, the tasks of major criminal investigations are combined with the patrol of state highways. Centralized state police agencies generally do the following:

- Assist local law enforcement departments in criminal investigations when asked to do so
- Operate a centralized identification bureau
- Maintain a centralized criminal records repository
- Patrol the state's highways
- Provide select training for municipal and county officers

The Pennsylvania Constabulary, known today as the Pennsylvania State Police, was the first modern force to combine these duties and has been called the "first modern state police agency."[39] Michigan, New Jersey, New York, Vermont, and Delaware are a few of the states that patterned their state-level enforcement activities after the Pennsylvania model.

The second state model, the decentralized model of police organization, characterizes operations in the southern United States but is found as well in the Midwest and in some western states. The model draws a clear distinction between traffic enforcement on state highways and other state-level law enforcement functions by creating at least two separate agencies. North Carolina, South Carolina, and Georgia are a few of the many states that employ both a highway patrol and a state bureau of investigation. The names of the respective agencies may vary, however, even though their functions are largely the same. In North Carolina, for example, the two major state-level law enforcement agencies are the North Carolina Highway Patrol and the State Bureau of Investigation. Georgia fields a highway patrol and the Georgia Bureau of Investigation, and South Carolina operates a highway patrol and the South Carolina Law Enforcement Division.

States that use the decentralized model usually have a number of other adjunct state-level law enforcement agencies. North Carolina, for example, has created a State Wildlife Commission with enforcement powers, a Board of Alcohol Beverage Control with additional agents, and a separate Enforcement and Theft Bureau for enforcement of certain motor vehicle and theft laws. Learn more about state-level law enforcement agencies by visiting **Web Extra 10**.

Local Agencies

Local police agencies, including city and county agencies, represent a third level of law enforcement activity in the United States. The term *local police* encompasses a wide variety of agencies. Municipal departments, rural sheriff's departments, and specialized groups like campus police and transit police can all be grouped under the "local" rubric. Large municipal departments are highly visible because of their vast size, huge budgets, and innovative programs. The nation's largest law enforcement agency, the New York City Police Department (NYPD), for example, has about 45,000 full-time employees, including about 37,800 full-time sworn officers.[40] Learn more about the NYPD via "Inside the Department" podcasts available at **Web Extra 11**.

Far greater in number, however, are small-town and county sheriff's departments. There are approximately 12,760 municipal police departments and 3,100 sheriff's departments in the United States.[41] Every incorporated municipality in the country has the authority to create its own police force. Some very small communities hire only one officer, who fills the roles of chief, investigator, and night watch—as well as everything in between. The majority of local agencies employ fewer than ten full-time officers, and about three in eight agencies (more than 7,000 in all) employ fewer than five full-time officers. These smaller agencies include 2,245 (or 12%) with just one full-time officer and 1,164 (or 6%) with only part-time officers.[42] A few communities contract with private security firms for police services, and still others have no active police force at all, depending instead on local sheriff's departments to deal with law violators.

City police chiefs are typically appointed by the mayor or selected by the city council. Their departments' jurisdictions are limited by convention to the geographic boundaries of their communities. **Sheriffs**, on the other hand, are elected public officials whose agencies are responsible for law enforcement throughout the counties in which they function. Sheriff's deputies mostly patrol the unincorporated areas of the county, or those that lie between municipalities. They do, however, have jurisdiction throughout the county, and in some areas they routinely work alongside municipal police to enforce laws within towns and cities.

sheriff
The elected chief officer of a county law enforcement agency. The sheriff is usually responsible for law enforcement in unincorporated areas and for the operation of the county jail.

Sheriff's departments are generally responsible for serving court papers, including civil summonses, and for maintaining security within state courtrooms. Sheriffs also run county jails and are responsible for more detainees awaiting trial than any other type of law enforcement department in the country. For example, the Los Angeles County Jail System, operated by the Custody Operations Division of the L.A. County Sheriff's Department (LASD), is the largest in the world.[43] In 2003, with eight separate facilities, the Custody Operations Division of the LASD had an average daily population of 18,423 inmates—considerably larger than the number of inmates held in many state prison systems.[44] More than 2,200 uniformed officers and 1,265 civilian employees work in the Custody Division of the LASD. That division alone operates with a yearly budget in excess of $200 million.[45]

Sheriff's departments remain strong across most of the country, although in parts of New England, deputies mostly function as court agents with limited law enforcement duties. One report found that most sheriff's departments are small, with more than half of them employing fewer than 25 sworn officers.[46] Only 12 departments employ more than 1,000 officers. Even so, southern and western sheriffs are still considered the chief law enforcement officers in their counties.

A list of conventional police agencies found at the local level is shown in Table 3. For information on selected local law enforcement agencies, view **Web Extra 12**. Visit **Library Extras 3** and **4** to learn more about staffing levels at local and state police agencies.

Fusion Centers

In March 2008, more than 900 federal, state, and local law enforcement and homeland security officials attended the National Fusion Center Conference in Washington, D.C.[47] **Fusion centers**, a new concept in policing, pool and analyze information from law enforcement

fusion center
A multiagency law enforcement facility designed to enhance cooperative efforts through a coordinated process for collecting, sharing, and analyzing information in order to develop actionable intelligence.

TABLE 3
American Policing: Local Law Enforcement Agencies

Campus police	Housing authority agencies	Sheriff's departments
City/county agencies	Marine patrol agencies	Transit police
Constables	Municipal police departments	Tribal police
Coroners or medical examiners		

agencies at all levels, looking for meaningful patterns and actionable intelligence. More than 70 fusion centers currently operate in 37 states, and they have received $380 million in federal funding over the last five years.[48] These centers are largely an outgrowth of one of the 9/11 Commission's criticisms that law enforcement agencies do not communicate with one another as they should.

Fusion centers vary greatly in size and in the equipment and personnel available to them. Some are small, consisting of little more than limited conference facilities, and have only a few participants. Others are large, high-technology offices that make use of the latest information and computer technologies and that house representatives from many different organizations. Some fusion centers are physically located within the offices of other agencies. The Kentucky Fusion Center, for example, is housed within the state's Department of Transportation building in the state's capitol. Others operate out of stand-alone facilities that are physically separated from parent agencies.

Similarly, although information sharing is their central purpose, the activities of fusion centers are not uniform. Some centers perform investigations, some make arrests, and some exist only to share information. A number of fusion centers, like the National Counterterrorism Center and the National Gang Intelligence Center, focus on clearly defined issues. Most of today's fusion centers do more than target terrorists, however. They work to collect information on a wide variety of offenders, gangs, immigrant smuggling operations, and other threats. Michael Mines, the FBI's deputy assistant director of intelligence, recognizes that actionable intelligence can come from seemingly unrelated areas. He notes that the nation's network of fusion centers is intended to "maximize the ability to detect, prevent, investigate, and respond to criminal and terrorist activity."[49]

▲ Texas Governor Rick Perry speaking to a group of Texas Rangers in Austin, Texas, in 2009. The Texas Rangers have long been held in high regard among state police agencies. How do police agencies in the United States relate to one another?
AP Photo/Harry Cabluck

Many fusion centers are still developing, and a number of problems remain. Obtaining security clearances for employees of local law enforcement agencies, for example, has sometimes been difficult or time-consuming. Even representatives of federal agencies like the DHS and the FBI sometimes refuse to accept one another's clearances. Nonetheless, a recent hearing before a House intelligence subcommittee shows that federal lawmakers are hopeful about the success of fusion centers and are willing to find the federal dollars needed to support them. As Representative Jane Harman, chairwoman of the Subcommittee on Intelligence, Information Sharing and Terrorism Risk Assessment, said recently, "Everyone recognizes that fusion centers hold tremendous promise."[50]

police management
The administrative activities of controlling, directing, and coordinating police personnel, resources, and activities in the service of crime prevention, the apprehension of criminals, the recovery of stolen property, and the performance of a variety of regulatory and helping services.

Police Administration

Police management entails administrative activities that control, direct, and coordinate police personnel, resources, and activities in the service of crime prevention, the apprehension of criminals, the recovery of stolen property, and the performance of a variety of regulatory and helping services.[51] Police managers include sworn law enforcement personnel with administrative authority, from the rank of sergeant to captain, chief, or sheriff, and civilian personnel, such as police commissioners, attorneys general, state secretaries of crime control, and public-safety directors.

3 Discuss the various components of police administration, including management, chain of command, organization, and department structure.

Police Organization and Structure

Almost all American law enforcement organizations are formally structured among divisions and along lines of authority. Roles within police agencies generally fall into one of two categories: line and staff. **Line operations** are field or supervisory activities directly related to daily police work; **staff operations** include support roles such as administration. In organizations that have line operations only, authority flows from the top down in a clear, unbroken line,[52] and no supporting elements (media relations, training, fiscal management divisions, and so on) exist. All line operations are directly involved in providing field services. Because almost all police agencies need support, only the smallest departments have only line operations.

line operations
In police organizations, the field activities or supervisory activities directly related to day-to-day police work.

staff operations
In police organizations, activities (such as administration and training) that provide support for line operations.

Most police organizations include both line and staff operations. In such organizations, line managers are largely unencumbered with staff operations, such as budgets, training, scientific analysis of evidence, legal advice, shift assignments, and personnel management. Support personnel handle these activities, freeing line personnel to focus on the day-to-day requirements of providing field services.

CJ News
Fusion Centers

In Arizona, after determining that the subjects of an international terrorism case were involved in local criminal activity, the FBI referred the case to local law enforcement. In New Mexico, several individuals linked to FBI investigations, including an MS-13 gang member, were identified. In Tennessee, the FBI and its partners developed a formal process for collecting, sharing, and analyzing suspicious activity reports, looking for trends and patterns.

These cooperative efforts—and many more like them—have been made possible through the work of intelligence fusion centers around the country. These centers, usually set up by states or major urban areas and run by state or local authorities, are often supported by federal law enforcement, including the FBI.

Fusion center personnel "fuse" intelligence from participating agencies to create a more comprehensive threat picture, locally and nationally. They don't just collect information. They integrate new data into existing information, evaluate it to determine its worth, analyze it for links and trends, and disseminate their findings to the agency in the best position to do something about it.

In March 2009, nearly 2,000 local, state, tribal, and federal representatives working in fusion centers across the country gathered in Kansas City, Missouri, to continue the process of standardizing fusion center operations. Their goal was to create a network of centers presenting a unified front against terrorism and other national security and criminal threats that put Americans at risk.

Speaking at the Kansas City conference, FBI Chief Intelligence Officer Don Van Duyn said that although the information process could be made "more seamless," the FBI is committed to expanding its "interconnectedness" to help combat threats from terrorist and criminal networks. He also said that during the past year the FBI has rolled out—to all of its 56 field offices—standardized intelligence operations structures, roles, and procedures in an effort to enhance its collaboration with its partners.

Although a few fusion centers were already in existence before 9/11, they really began to crop up after the attacks when local and federal officials recognized the need to quickly coordinate the sharing of information related to terrorism. Their number has been growing ever since. Today, there are some 50 state and 20 regional centers around the country. And some have expanded their focus to include public-safety matters and major criminal threats.

The FBI currently has 114 employees working in 38 fusion centers. About 36% are agents, 61% are intelligence analysts, and the rest are in positions such as language and financial analysts. Fourteen of these centers share space with an FBI Field Intelligence Group or Joint Terrorism Task Force.

▲ Inside the Miami-Dade Police Department's Fusion Center, which serves much of South Florida. The center's combined technologies enhance the power of instant collaboration and information sharing among analysts and investigators from various law enforcement agencies. Why did fusion centers develop?

Reprinted with permission from Microsoft Corporation

Elaine Cummins, the FBI's Chief Information Sharing Officer, says, "Participating in a national network of fusion centers definitely helps us share timely, relevant, and actionable intelligence with our partners—an increasingly important component to our unique national security and law enforcement mission."

Through fusion centers, state and local law enforcement agencies gain access to certain federal databases. They also get the benefit of big-picture terrorism and crime perspectives from their federal partners, along with grant funding, technical assistance, and training. Federal agencies like the FBI gain intelligence from the local level that may fuel terrorism or national security investigations elsewhere in the country or even overseas.

Source: Adapted from FBI, "Fusion Centers: Unifying Intelligence to Protect Americans," March 12, 2009, http://www.fbi.gov/page2/march04/fusion_031209.html (accessed September 3, 2010).

Fusion Centers versus Joint Terrorist Task Forces (JTTFs)

Fusion Centers	Joint Terrorism Task Forces
Run by state and local authorities	Sponsored by the FBI
Are state and locally focused	Are regionally and nationally focused
Deal with terrorism, criminal, and public-safety matters	Deal exclusively with terrorism matters
Produce actionable intelligence for dissemination to appropriate law enforcement agencies but do not generally conduct investigations	Conduct investigations

In a line and staff agency, divisions are likely to exist within both line operations and staff operations. For example, field services, a line operation, may be broken down into enforcement and investigation. Administrative services, a staff operation, may be divided into human resources management, training and education, materials supply, financial management, and facilities management. The line and staff structure easily accommodates functional areas of responsibility within line and staff divisions. The organizational chart detailing the line and staff structure of the Los Angeles County Sheriff's Department—the largest sheriff's department in the world[53]—is shown in Figure 1.

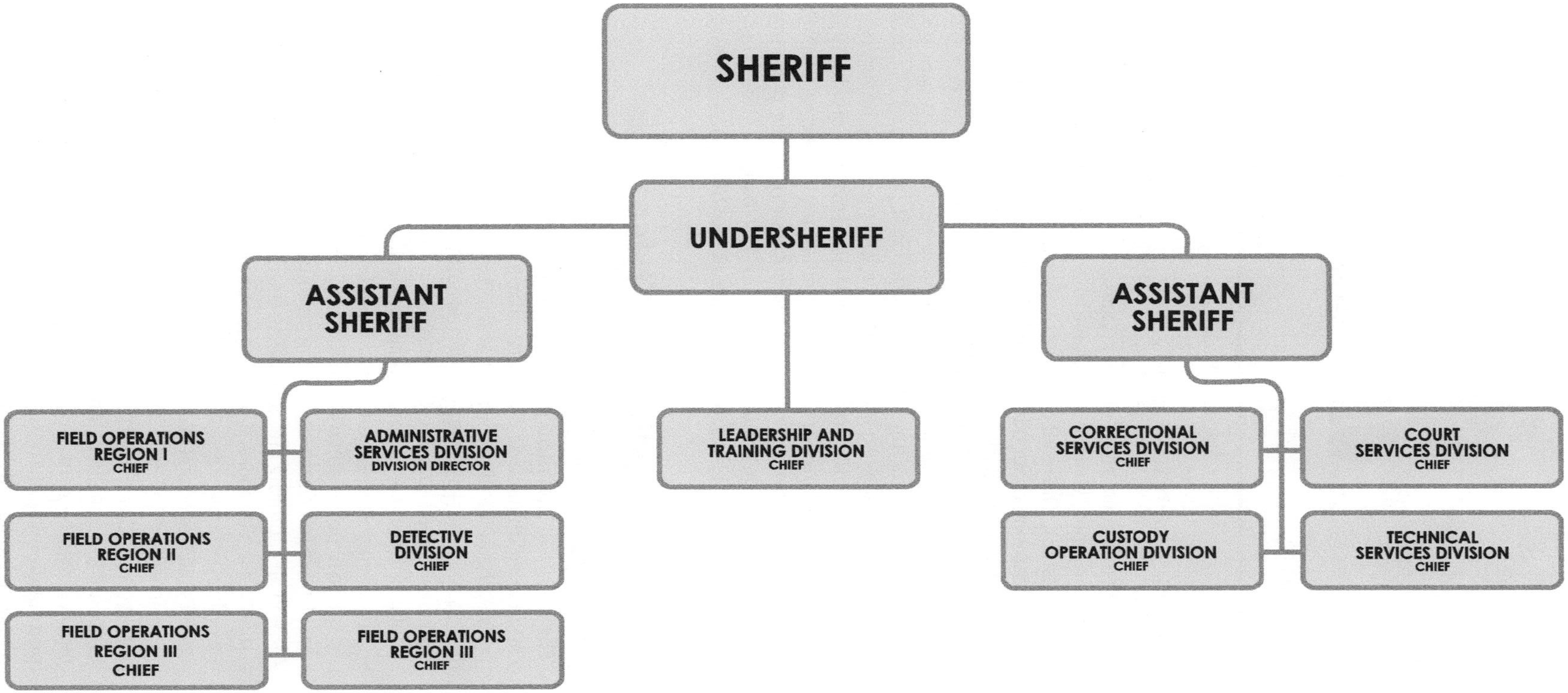

FIGURE 1
Organizational Chart of the Los Angeles County Sheriff's Department
Source: Courtesy of Los Angeles County Sheriff's Department.

FIGURE 2 Historical Eras in American Policing

POLITICAL ERA ▶

- Close ties between the police and political officials
- Police were organized in paramilitary style, focused on serving the politically powerful
- Politicians appointed/hired the police

1840s–1930

- Came about because of a need for social order and security in a dynamic and rapidly changing society

REFORM ERA ▶

- Police gained pride in their profession
- Law enforcement focused on "traditional" crime-fighting and the capture of criminals
- Crackdown on organized crime

1930–1970s

- Progressive policing policy led by August Vollmer and O. W. Wilson
- Came about because citizens called for reform and the removal of politics from policing

Chain of Command

chain of command
The unbroken line of authority that extends through all levels of an organization, from the highest to the lowest.

The organizational chart of any police agency shows a hierarchical **chain of command**, or the order of authority within the department. The chain of command clarifies who reports to whom. Usually, the chief of police or sheriff is at the top of the command chain (although his or her boss may be a police commissioner, city council, or mayor), followed by the subordinate leaders of each division.

Because police departments employ a quasi-military chain-of-command structure, the titles assigned to personnel (captain, lieutenant, sergeant) are similar to those used by the military. It is important for individual personnel to know who is in charge; hence unity of command is an important principle that must be firmly established within the department. When unity of command exists, every individual has only one supervisor to whom he or she answers and from whom, under normal circumstances, he or she takes orders. **Span of control** refers to the number of police personnel or the number of units supervised by a particular commander. For example, one sergeant may be in charge of five or six officers; they represent the sergeant's span of control.

span of control
The number of police personnel or the number of units supervised by a particular officer.

Policing Epochs and Styles

Policing Epochs

4 Identify the various historical stages of development in American policing, and describe the characteristics of each stage.

The history of American policing can be divided into four epochs,[54] each distinguishable by the relative dominance of a particular approach to police operations (Figure 2). The first period, the political era, was characterized by close ties between police and public officials. It began in the 1840s and ended around 1930. Throughout the period, American police agencies tended to serve the interests of powerful politicians and their cronies, providing public-order and order-maintenance services almost as an afterthought. The second period, the reform era, began around 1930 and lasted until the 1970s. It was characterized by pride in professional crime fighting. Police departments during this period focused most of their resources on solving "traditional" crimes, such as murder, rape, and burglary, and on capturing offenders. The third period, and the one that continues to characterize much of contemporary policing in America today, is the community policing era. This approach to policing stresses the service role of police officers and envisions a partnership between police agencies and their communities.

A fourth period, which we call the *new era*, has made its appearance only recently and is still evolving. Some say that the primary feature of this new law enforcement era is policing to secure the homeland, and they have dubbed it the *homeland security era*.[55] From their perspective, the homeland security era has grown out of national concerns with terrorism prevention born of the terrorist attacks of September 11, 2001. As police scholar Gene Stephens explains it, "The twenty-first century has put policing into a whole new milieu—one in which the causes of crime and disorder often lie outside the immediate community, demanding new and innovative approaches."[56] A decline in street crime, says Stephens, has

COMMUNITY ERA ▶

- Police departments work to identify and serve the needs of their communities
- Envisions a partnership between the police and the community

1970s–Today

- Police focus on quality-of-life offenses
- Broken windows model of policing
- Came about because of a realization that effective community partnerships can help prevent and solve crimes

THE NEW ERA

- Policing to secure the homeland; emphasis on terrorism prevention and intelligence-led policing
- Builds on partnership with the community to gather intelligence

2001–Today

- Creation of counterterrorism divisions and offices within police departments and the development of actionable intelligence
- Came about because of the terrorist attacks of September 11, 2001, and ongoing threats to the safety and security of Americans

Photo sources (from left): Image Asset Management Ltd./SuperStock, Inc.; SuperStock, Inc.; UpperCut Images/Superstock Royalty Free; and P-59 Photos/Alamy Images

been replaced by concern with new and more insidious types of offending, including terrorism and Internet-assisted crimes. These new kinds of crimes, while they threaten the integrity of local communities, often involve offenders thousands of miles away.

Others, however, see the new era as underpinned by an emphasis on intelligence-led policing (ILP), and they refer to it as the *ILP era*. Michael Downing, commander of the Counter-terrorism/Criminal Intelligence Bureau of the Los Angeles Police Department, says that ILP represents the next evolutionary stage in how police and sheriff's officers should approach their work. "The necessity to successfully shift into a [new] era, the intelligence-led policing era, with seamless precision has never been more important considering the great threat we face as a nation," says Downing.[57] The good news, some say, "is that ILP is not only an important strategic tool to thwart al-Qaeda and other groups but also a practical one geared toward crime control and quality of life issues."[58] The new era, whatever we choose to call it, is still emerging, but it clearly involves efforts to deal with threats to the homeland and to inform those efforts with situational awareness and shared intelligence.

> Crime is a community problem and stands today as one of the most serious challenges of our generation. Our citizens must . . . recognize their responsibilities in its suppression.
>
> —O. W. Wilson (1900–1972)

The influence of the first three historical phases survives today in what noted social commentator and Presidential Medal of Freedom recipient James Q. Wilson[59] calls "policing styles."[60] A style of policing describes how a particular agency sees its purpose and chooses the methods it uses to fulfill that purpose. Wilson's three policing styles—which he does not link to any particular historical era—are (1) the watchman (which is characteristic of the political era), (2) the legalistic (which is akin to the professional crime fighting of the reform era), and (3) the service (which is common today). These three styles characterize nearly all municipal law enforcement agencies now operating in the United States, although some departments are a mixture of two or more styles.

The Watchman Style of Policing

Police departments marked by the **watchman style** of policing are primarily concerned with achieving a goal that Wilson called "order maintenance." They see their job as controlling illegal and disruptive behaviors. The watchman style makes considerable use of discretion compared to the legalistic style. Order in watchman-style communities may be arrived at by using informal police intervention, including persuasion and threats, or even by "roughing up" a few disruptive people from time to time. Some authors have condemned this style of policing, suggesting that it is unfairly found in lower-class or lower-middle-class communities, especially where interpersonal relations include a fair amount of violence or physical abuse.

watchman style
A style of policing marked by a concern for order maintenance. Watchman policing is characteristic of lower-class communities where informal police intervention into the lives of residents is employed in the service of keeping the peace.

The watchman style was typified by the Los Angeles police officers who took part in the infamous beating of Rodney King in 1992. After the ensuing riots, the Independent Commission on the Los Angeles Police Department (the Christopher Commission) determined that the Los Angeles police "placed greater emphasis on crime control over crime prevention, a policy that distanced cops from the people they serve."[61]

Freedom or Safety? You Decide.
Liberty Is a Double-Edged Sword

This chapter builds on the following theme: For police action to be "just," it must recognize the rights of individuals while holding them accountable to the social obligations defined by law. It is important to realize that many democratically inspired legal restraints on the police stem from the Bill of Rights, which comprises the first ten amendments to the U.S. Constitution. Such restraints help ensure individual freedoms in our society and prevent the development of a "police state" in America.

In police work and elsewhere, the principles of individual liberty and social justice are cornerstones on which the American way of life rests. Ideally, the work of police agencies, as well as the American system of criminal justice, is to ensure justice while guarding liberty. The liberty-justice issue is the dual thread that holds together the tapestry of the justice system, from the simplest daily activities of police officers on the beat to the often complex and lengthy renderings of the U.S. Supreme Court.

For the criminal justice system as a whole, the question becomes this: How can individual liberties be maintained in the face of the need for official action, including arrest, interrogation, incarceration, and the like? The answer is far from simple, but it begins with the recognition that liberty is a double-edged sword, entailing obligations as well as rights.

YOU DECIDE

What does it mean to say "For police action to be 'just,' it must recognize the rights of individuals while holding them accountable to the social obligations defined by law"? How can police agencies accomplish this? What can individual officers do to help their agencies in this regard?

The Legalistic Style of Policing

legalistic style
A style of policing marked by a strict concern with enforcing the precise letter of the law. Legalistic departments may take a hands-off approach to disruptive or problematic behavior that does not violate the criminal law.

Departments operating under the **legalistic style** of policing enforce the letter of the law. For example, an officer who tickets a person going 71 mph in a 70-mph zone is likely a member of a department that adheres to the legalistic style of policing. Conversely, legalistic departments routinely avoid community disputes arising from violations of social norms that do not break the law. Police expert Gary Sykes calls this enforcement style "laissez-faire policing" in recognition of its hands-off approach to behaviors that are simply bothersome or inconsiderate of community principles.[62]

The Service Style of Policing

service style
A style of policing marked by a concern with helping rather than strict enforcement. Service-oriented police agencies are more likely to refer citizens to community resources, such as drug-treatment programs, than are other types of agencies.

In police departments using the **service style**, which strives to meet the needs of the community and serve its members, the police see themselves more as helpers than as soldiers in a "war on crime," and they work with social services and other agencies to provide counseling for minor offenders and to assist community groups in preventing crimes and solving problems. Prosecutors may support the service style of policing by agreeing not to prosecute law violators who seek psychiatric help or who voluntarily participate in programs like Alcoholics Anonymous, family counseling, or drug treatment. The service style is supported in part by citizens who seek to avoid the embarrassment that might result from a public airing of personal problems, thereby reducing the number of criminal complaints filed, especially in minor disputes. While the service style of policing may seem more appropriate to wealthy communities or small towns, it can also exist in cities whose police departments actively seek citizen involvement in identifying issues that the police can help address.

Police-Community Relations

5 Describe community policing, and explain how it differs from traditional forms of policing.

The 1960s were fraught with riots, unrest, and student activism as the war in Vietnam, civil rights concerns, and other social movements produced large demonstrations and marches. The police, generally inexperienced in crowd control, were all too often embroiled in tumultuous encounters—even pitched battles—with citizen groups that viewed the police as agents of "the establishment." To manage these new challenges, the legalistic style of policing, so common in America until then, began to yield to the newer service-oriented style of policing.

As social disorganization increased, police departments across the nation, seeking to understand and better cope with the problems they faced, created **police-community relations (PCR)** programs. PCR programs represented a movement away from an exclusive police emphasis on the apprehension of law violators and meant increasing the level of positive police-citizen interaction. At the height of the PCR movement, city police departments across the country opened storefront centers where citizens could air complaints and interact easily with police representatives. As police scholar Egon Bittner recognized in 1976, PCR programs need to reach to "the grassroots of discontent," where citizen dissatisfaction with the police exists,[63] if they are to be truly effective.

police-community relations (PCR)
An area of police activity that recognizes the need for the community and the police to work together effectively and is based on the notion that the police derive their legitimacy from the community they serve. Many police agencies began to explore PCR in the 1960s and 1970s.

In many contemporary PCR programs, public-relations officers are appointed to provide an array of services, such as Neighborhood Watch programs, drug-awareness workshops, identification projects (using police equipment and expertise to mark valuables for identification in the event of theft), and victims' assistance programs. Modern PCR programs, however, often fail to achieve their goal of increased community satisfaction with police services because they focus on servicing groups already well satisfied with the police. PCR initiatives that do reach disaffected community groups are difficult to manage and may even alienate participating officers from the communities they are assigned to serve. Thus, as Bittner noted, "while the first approach fails because it leaves out those groups to which the program is primarily directed, the second fails because it leaves out the police department."

> Every society gets the kind of criminal it deserves. What is equally true is that every community gets the kind of law enforcement it insists on.
> —Robert Kennedy, former U.S. attorney general[ii]

Team Policing

During the 1960s and 1970s, a number of communities experimented with the concept of **team policing**, which rapidly became an extension of the PCR movement. With team policing, officers were assigned semipermanently to particular neighborhoods, where they were expected to become familiar with the inhabitants and with their problems and concerns. Patrol officers were given considerable authority in processing complaints, from receipt through resolution. Crimes were investigated and solved at the local level, with specialists called in only if the resources needed to continue an investigation were not available locally. Some authors called team policing a "technique to deliver total police services to a neighborhood."[64] Others, however, dismissed it as "little more than an attempt to return to the style of policing that was prevalent in the United States over a century ago."[65]

team policing
The reorganization of conventional patrol strategies into "an integrated and versatile police team assigned to a fixed district."[iii]

Community Policing

Over the past quarter century, the role of the police in police-community relations has changed considerably. Originally, the PCR model was based on the fact that many police administrators saw police officers as enforcers of the law who were isolated from, and often in opposition to, the communities they policed. As a result, PCR programs were often a shallowly disguised effort to overcome public suspicion and community hostility.

Today, increasing numbers of law enforcement administrators embrace the role of service provider. Modern departments frequently help citizens solve a vast array of personal problems, many of which involve no lawbreaking activity. For example, officers regularly aid sick or distraught people, organize community crime-prevention efforts, resolve minor domestic disputes, regulate traffic, and educate children and teens about drug abuse. Because service calls far exceed calls directly related to law violations, most officers more often make referrals for interpersonal problems to agencies such as Alcoholics Anonymous, domestic-violence centers, and drug-rehabilitation programs rather than make arrests.

▲ Los Angeles bike patrol officers conferring with a supervisor. The community policing concept requires that officers become an integral part of the communities they serve. How can community policing help to both prevent and solve crimes?
Michael Newman/PhotoEdit Inc.

In contemporary America, some say, police departments function a lot like business corporations. According to Harvard University's Executive Session on Policing, three generic kinds of "corporate strategies" guide American policing: (1) strategic policing, (2) problem-solving policing, and (3) community policing.[66]

strategic policing
A type of policing that retains the traditional police goal of professional crime fighting but enlarges the enforcement target to include nontraditional kinds of criminals, such as serial offenders, gangs and criminal associations, drug-distribution networks, and sophisticated white-collar and computer criminals. Strategic policing generally makes use of innovative enforcement techniques, including intelligence operations, undercover stings, electronic surveillance, and sophisticated forensic methods.

problem-solving policing
A type of policing that assumes that many crimes are caused by existing social conditions within the community and that crimes can be controlled by uncovering and effectively addressing underlying social problems. Problem-solving policing makes use of community resources, such as counseling centers, welfare programs, and job-training facilities. It also attempts to involve citizens in crime prevention through education, negotiation, and conflict management.

community policing
"A philosophy that promotes organizational strategies, which support the systematic use of partnerships and problem-solving techniques, to proactively address the immediate conditions that give rise to public safety issues such as crime, social disorder, and fear of crime."[iv]

Strategic policing, something of a holdover from the reform era, "emphasizes an increased capacity to deal with crimes that are not well controlled by traditional methods."[67] Strategic policing retains the traditional police goal of professional crime fighting but enlarges the enforcement target to include nontraditional kinds of criminals, such as serial offenders, gangs and criminal associations, drug-distribution networks, and sophisticated white-collar and computer criminals. To meet its goals, strategic policing generally makes use of innovative enforcement techniques, including intelligence operations, undercover sting operations, electronic surveillance, and sophisticated forensic methods.

The other two strategies give greater recognition to Wilson's service style. **Problem-solving policing** (or problem-oriented policing) takes the view that many crimes are caused by existing social conditions in the communities. To control crime, problem-oriented police managers attempt to uncover and effectively address these underlying social problems. Problem-solving policing makes thorough use of community resources, such as counseling centers, welfare programs, and job-training facilities. It also attempts to involve citizens in crime prevention through education, negotiation, and conflict management. For example, police may ask residents of poorly maintained housing areas to clean up litter, install better lighting, and provide security devices for their houses and apartments in the belief that clean, well-lighted, secure areas are a deterrent to criminal activity.

The third and newest strategy, **community policing** (sometimes called community-oriented policing), goes a step beyond the other two. It has been described as a partnership between the police and the community, so that they can work together on solving problems of crime and disorder.[68] A more formal definition, offered by the Office of Community Oriented Policing Services (COPS) office says that community policing "is a philosophy that promotes organizational strategies, which support the systematic use of partnerships and problem-solving techniques, to proactively address the immediate conditions that give rise to public safety issues such as crime, social disorder, and fear of crime."[69]

The community policing concept evolved from the early works of police researchers George Kelling and Robert Trojanowicz. Their studies of foot-patrol programs in Newark, New Jersey,[70] and Flint, Michigan,[71] showed that "police could develop more positive attitudes toward community members and could promote positive attitudes toward police if they spent time on foot in their neighborhoods."[72] Trojanowicz's *Community Policing*, published in 1990,[73] may be the definitive work on this topic.

> A successful community policing program . . . requires officers to be well versed in cultural diversity and competent to perform tasks needed to accomplish their duties.
>
> —Samuel D. Pratcher, chief of police, Wilmington, Delaware

Community policing seeks to actively involve the community in the task of crime control by creating an effective working partnership between the community and the police.[74] Under the community policing ideal, community members and the police are expected to share responsibility for establishing and maintaining peaceful neighborhoods.[75] As a result, community policing permits members of the community to participate more fully than ever before in defining the police role. Police expert Jerome H. Skolnick says community policing is "grounded on the notion that, together, police and public are more effective and more humane coproducers of safety and public order than are the police alone."[76] According to Skolnick, community policing involves at least one of four elements: (1) community-based crime prevention, (2) reorientation of patrol activities to emphasize the importance of nonemergency services, (3) increased police accountability to the public, and (4) decentralization of command, including a greater use of civilians at all levels of police decision making.[77] As one writer explains it, "Community policing seeks to integrate what was traditionally seen as the different law enforcement, order maintenance and social service roles of the police. Central to the integration of these roles is a working partnership with the community in determining what neighborhood problems are to be addressed, and how."[78]

Community policing is a two-way street. It requires not only police awareness of community needs but also both involvement and crime-fighting action on the part of citizens themselves. As Detective Tracie Harrison of the Denver Police Department explains, "When the neighborhood takes stock in their community and they're serious they don't want crime, then you start to see crime go down. . . . They're basically fed up and know the police can't do it alone."[79]

Police departments throughout the country continue to join the community policing bandwagon. A recent report by the Bureau of Justice Statistics (BJS) showed that state and local law enforcement agencies across the United States had nearly 113,000 full-time sworn personnel regularly engaged in community policing activities.[80] BJS noted that only about 21,000 officers would have been so categorized in 1997. At the time of the report, 64% of local police departments serving 86% of all residents had full-time officers engaged in some form of community policing activity, compared to 34% of departments serving 62% of all residents in 1997.

The Chicago Police Department launched its comprehensive community policing program, called Chicago's Alternative Policing Strategy (CAPS), in 1993. The development of a strategic plan for "reinventing the Chicago Police Department," from which CAPS evolved, included significant contributions by Mayor Richard M. Daley, who noted that community policing "means doing more than responding to calls for service and solving crimes. It means transforming the Department to support a new, proactive approach to preventing crimes before they occur. It means forging new partnerships among residents, business owners, community leaders, the police, and City services to solve long-range community problems."[81] Read the mayor's original report, written in conjunction with the Chicago Police Department, at **Library Extra 5**. Today, CAPS functions on a department-wide basis throughout the city. Learn more about CAPS at **Web Extra 13**. A review of Chicago's experience with community policing is available at **Library Extra 6**.

Although community policing efforts began in metropolitan areas, the community engagement and problem-solving spirit of these programs has spread to rural regions. Sheriff's departments operating community policing programs sometimes refer to them as *neighborhood-oriented policing* in recognition of the decentralized nature of rural communities. A Bureau of Justice Assistance (BJA) report on neighborhood-oriented policing notes that "the stereotypical view is that police officers in rural areas naturally work more closely with the public than do officers in metropolitan areas."[82] This view, warns the BJA, may not be entirely accurate, and rural departments would do well "to recognize that considerable diversity exists among rural communities and rural law enforcement agencies." As in metropolitan areas, effective community policing requires the involvement of all members of the community in identifying and solving problems.

The emphasis on community policing continues to grow. Title I of the Violent Crime Control and Law Enforcement Act of 1994, known as the Public Safety Partnership and Community Policing Act of 1994, highlighted community policing's role in combating crime and funded (among other things) "increas[ing] the number of law enforcement officers involved in activities that are focused on interaction with members of the community on proactive crime control and prevention." The avowed purposes of the Community Policing Act were to (1) substantially increase the number of law enforcement officers interacting directly with the public (through a program known as Cops on the Beat); (2) provide additional and more effective training to law enforcement officers to enhance their problem solving, service, and other skills needed in interacting with community members; (3) encourage development and implementation of innovative programs to permit community members to assist local law enforcement agencies in the prevention of crime; and (4) encourage development of new technologies to assist local law enforcement agencies in reorienting their emphasis from reacting to crime to preventing crime.

In response to the 1994 law, the U.S. Department of Justice created the Office of Community Oriented Policing Services (COPS). The COPS Office administered the funds necessary to add 100,000 community policing officers to our nation's streets—the number originally targeted by law. In 1999, the U.S. Department of Justice and COPS reached an important milestone by funding the last of the 100,000 officers ahead of schedule and under budget. Although the Community Policing Act originally provided COPS funding only through 2000, Congress has continued to fund COPS, making another $500 million available for the hiring of an additional 50,000 officers.[83] In 2002, the COPS Office adopted the theme "Homeland Security through Community Policing," which emphasizes the local police officer's crucial role in gathering information on terrorist suspects—a topic that is discussed later in this chapter. The federal COPS Office can be found at **Web Extra 14**.

About the same time that the Violent Crime Control and Law Enforcement Act was passed, the Community Policing Consortium, based in Washington, D.C., began operations. Administered and funded by the BJA, the consortium provides a forum for training and information exchange in the area of community policing. Members of the consortium include the International Association of Chiefs of Police, the National Sheriff's Association, the Police Executive Research Forum, the Police Foundation, and the National Organization of Black Law Enforcement Executives. Visit the Community Policing Consortium via **Web Extra 15**.

Community Policing and Antiterrorism

Noted police scholar David L. Carter says that "a common concern expressed by police executives is that the shift toward increased counterterrorism responsibilities may require a shift of resources away from community policing."[84] That concern, he says, is misdirected because community policing provides a natural conduit for information gathering and the development of counterterrorism intelligence. Information gathered by state and local police departments can be funneled to federal agencies, especially the FBI, that have been charged with developing national security intelligence. Carter notes that the "increased social tension" resulting from the current concern with terrorism has led to a greater need "to maintain a close, interactive dialogue between law enforcement and the community."

The importance of community policing in the fight against terrorism was reflected in comments made by FBI Director Robert Mueller during the summer of 2004. While pointing to photographs of seven terrorist suspects believed to be in the United States, Mueller said: "We need the support of the American people . . . to cooperate when called upon, as agents will be reaching out to many across the nation to help gather information and intelligence . . . to be aware of your surroundings and report anything suspicious . . . to 'BOLO' [be on the lookout] for those pictured above. . . . Have you seen them in your communities? Have you heard that someone might be helping them to hide? Do you have any idea where they might be? If so, we need you to come forward."[85]

Citizens are coproducers of justice.
—Bureau of Justice Statistics, Princeton Project

Members of the U.S. Department of Justice's Global Intelligence Working Group (GIWG) also recognized the importance of community-oriented policing efforts when developing the national intelligence sharing plan. "Over the past decade," members noted, "thousands of community policing officers have been building close and productive relationships with the citizens they serve."[86] Community policing officers, they observed, "have immediate and unfettered access to local, neighborhood information as it develops. Citizens are aware of and seek out [community policing] officers to provide them with new information that may be useful to criminal interdiction or long-term problem solving. The positive nature of police/citizen relationships promotes a continuous and reliable transfer of information from one to the other. It is time to maximize the potential for community policing efforts to serve as a gateway of locally based information to prevent terrorism, and all other crimes."[87]

The Office for Domestic Preparedness (ODP) of the DHS notes that community policing can play the following roles in the intelligence process:[88]

- Provide materials to community policing contacts that may aid in the recognition of terrorism-related activities in order to make members of the community aware of suspicious actions, behaviors, and events
- Organize community meetings to emphasize prevention strategies, vigilance, and public awareness
- Ensure that members of the community are aware of the means of and processes for relaying information to police officers and police organizations
- Encourage crime prevention, proactive policing, and close working relationships between the police and the community

In any successful police-community interaction, information flows both ways. While community policing efforts seek information from the public about offenders, police departments can also communicate critical information to the public to aid in preventing crime and reducing fear.

Critique of Community Policing

As some authors have noted, "Community policing has become the dominant theme of contemporary police reform in America."[89] Yet problems have plagued the movement since its inception.[90] For one thing, the range, complexity, and evolving nature of community policing programs make their effectiveness difficult to measure.[91] Moreover, citizen satisfaction with police performance can be difficult to conceptualize and quantify. Most early studies examined citizens' attitudes developed through face-to-face interaction with individual police officers. They generally found a far higher level of dissatisfaction with the police among African Americans than among most other groups. Recent findings continue to show that the attitudes of African Americans toward the police remain poor. The wider reach of these studies, however, led evaluators to discover that this dissatisfaction may be rooted in overall quality of life and type of neighborhood.[92] On average, African Americans continue to experience a lower quality of life than most other U.S. citizens, and they often live in neighborhoods characterized by economic problems, drug trafficking, and street crime. Recent studies conclude that it is these conditions of life, rather than race, that are most predictive of citizen dissatisfaction with the police.

Those who study community policing have often been stymied by ambiguity surrounding the concept of community.[93] Sociologists, who sometimes define the word *community* as "any area in which members of a common culture share common interests,"[94] tend to deny that a community needs to be limited geographically. Police departments, on the other hand, tend to define communities "within jurisdictional, district or precinct lines, or within the confines of public or private housing developments."[95] Robert Trojanowicz cautioned police planners that "the impact of mass transit, mass communications and mass media [has] widened the rift between a sense of community based on geography and one [based] on interest."[96]

Researchers who follow the police definition of *community* recognize that there may be little consensus within and between members of a local community about community problems and appropriate solutions. Robert Bohm and colleagues at the University of Central Florida have found, for example, that while there may be some "consensus about social problems and their solutions . . . the consensus may not be community-wide." It may, in fact, exist only among "a relatively small group of 'active' stakeholders who differ significantly about the seriousness of most of the problems and the utility of some solutions."[97]

Finally, there is continuing evidence that not all police officers or managers are willing to accept nontraditional images of police work. One reason is that the goals of community policing often conflict with standard police performance criteria (such as arrests), leading to a perception among officers that community policing is inefficient at best and, at worst, a waste of time.[98] Similarly, many officers are loathe to take on new responsibilities as service providers whose role is more defined by community needs and less by strict interpretation of the law.

Thematic Question How might community policing alter the police subculture and the types of personalities that characterize it?

Some authors have warned that police subculture is so committed to a traditional view of police work, which is focused almost exclusively on crime fighting, that efforts to promote community policing can demoralize an entire department, rendering it ineffective at its basic tasks.[99] As the Christopher Commission found following the 1992 Rodney King riots, "Too many . . . patrol officers view citizens with resentment and hostility; too many treat the public with rudeness and disrespect."[100] Some analysts warn that only when the formal values espoused by today's innovative police administrators begin to match those of rank-and-file officers can any police agency begin to perform well in terms of the goals espoused by community policing reformers.[101]

Some public officials, too, are unwilling to accept community policing. Fifteen years ago, for example, New York City Mayor Rudolph W. Giuliani criticized the police department's Community Police Officer Program (CPOP), saying that it "has resulted in officers doing too much social work and making too few arrests."[102] Similarly, many citizens are not ready to accept a greater involvement of the police in their personal lives. Although the turbulent, protest-prone years of the 1960s and early 1970s are long gone, some groups remain suspicious of the police. No matter how inclusive community policing programs become, it is doubtful that the gap between the police and the public will ever be entirely bridged. The police role of restraining behavior that violates the law will always produce friction between police departments and some segments of the community. Learn more about measures of police effectiveness, including those related to community policing, at **Library Extra 7**, and read a COPS Office perspective on the future of community policing at **Library Extra 8**.

Evidence-Based Policing

Law Enforcement Assistance Administration (LEAA)
A now-defunct federal agency established under Title I of the Omnibus Crime Control and Safe Streets Act of 1969 to funnel federal funding to state and local law enforcement agencies.

6 Explain evidence-based policing, and demonstrate the potential that it holds in the area of police management.

In 1968, with the passage of the Omnibus Crime Control and Safe Streets Act, the U.S. Congress created the **Law Enforcement Assistance Administration (LEAA)**. LEAA was charged with combating crime through the expenditure of huge amounts of money in support of crime-prevention and crime-reduction programs. Some have compared the philosophy establishing LEAA to that which supported the American space program's goal of landing people on the moon: Put enough money into any problem, and it will be solved! Unfortunately, the crime problem was more difficult to address than the challenge of a moon landing; even after the expenditure of nearly $8 billion, LEAA had not come close to its goal. In 1982, LEAA expired when Congress refused it further funding.

scientific police management
The application of social sciences techniques to the study of police administration for the purpose of increasing effectiveness, reducing the frequency of citizen complaints, and enhancing the efficient use of available resources.

The legacy of LEAA is an important one for police managers, however. The research-rich years of 1969 to 1982, supported largely through LEAA funding, have left a plethora of scientific findings relevant to police administration and, more important, have established a tradition of program evaluation within police-management circles. This tradition, which is known as **scientific police management**, is a natural outgrowth of LEAA's insistence that every funded program contain a plan for its evaluation. *Scientific police management* refers to the application of social science techniques to the study of police administration for the purpose of increasing effectiveness, reducing the frequency of citizen complaints, and enhancing the efficient use of available resources. The heyday of scientific police management occurred in the 1970s, when federal monies were far more readily available to support such studies than they are today.

LEAA was not alone in funding police research during the 1970s. On July 1, 1970, the Ford Foundation announced the establishment of a Police Development Fund totaling $30 million, to be spent over the next five years to support major crime-fighting strategies of police departments. This funding led to the establishment of the Police Foundation, which continues to exist today with the mission of "foster[ing] improvement and innovation in American policing."[103] Police Foundation–sponsored studies during the past 20 years have added to the growing body of scientific knowledge about policing.

Today, federal support for criminal justice research and evaluation continues under the NIJ and the BJS, both part of the Office of Justice Programs (OJP). OJP, created by Congress in 1984, provides federal leadership in developing the nation's capacity to prevent and control crime. The National Criminal Justice Reference Service (NCJRS), a part of NIJ, assists researchers nationwide in locating information applicable to their research projects. "Custom searches" of the NCJRS computer database can be done online and can yield abundant information in most criminal justice subject areas. NIJ also publishes a series of informative periodic reports, such as the *NIJ Journal* and *NIJ Research in Review*, which serve to keep criminal justice practitioners and researchers informed about recent findings. View the NIJ online publication list at **Web Extra 16**.

The Kansas City Experiment

History

Kansas City experiment
The first large-scale scientific study of law enforcement practices. Sponsored by the Police Foundation, it focused on the practice of preventive patrol.

By far the most famous application of social research principles to police management was the **Kansas City experiment** regarding preventive patrol.[104] The results of the yearlong experiment were published in 1974. The study, sponsored by the Police Foundation, divided the southern part of Kansas City, Missouri, into 15 areas. Five of these "beats" were patrolled in the usual fashion. In another group of five beats, patrol activities were doubled. The final third of the beats received a novel treatment indeed: No patrols were assigned to them, and no uniformed officers entered that part of the city unless they were called. The program was kept secret, and citizens were unaware of the difference between the patrolled and unpatrolled parts of the city.

The results of the Kansas City experiment were surprising. Records of "preventable crimes" (those toward which the activities of patrol were oriented), such as burglary, robbery, auto theft, larceny, and vandalism, showed no significant differences in rate of occurrence among the three experimental beats. Similarly, citizens didn't seem to notice the change in patrol patterns in the two areas where patrol frequency was changed. Surveys conducted at the conclusion of the experiment showed no difference in citizens' fear of crime before and after the study. The 1974 study can be summed up in the words of the author of the final report: "The whole idea of riding around in cars to create a feeling of omnipresence just hasn't worked. . . . Good people with good intentions tried something that logically should have worked, but didn't."[105] This study has been credited with beginning the now-established tradition of scientific studies of policing.

▲ Members of the Kansas City (Missouri) Police Department being briefed on security measures for a planned city tour by President George W. Bush. Scientific police management was given early credence by studies of preventive patrol undertaken in Kansas City in 1974. What have scientific studies of the police since that time demonstrated?
Courtesy of the Media Office of the Kansas City Missouri Police Department

A second Kansas City study focused on "response time."[106] It found that even consistently fast police response to citizen reports of crime had little effect either on citizen satisfaction with the police or on the arrest of suspects. The study uncovered the fact that most reports made to the police came only after a considerable amount of time had passed. Hence the police were initially handicapped by the timing of the report, and even the fastest police response was not especially effective.

Effects

The Kansas City studies greatly affected managerial assumptions about the role of preventive patrol and traditional strategies for responding to citizen calls for assistance. As Joseph Lewis, then director of evaluation at the Police Foundation, said, "I think that now almost everyone would agree that almost anything you do is better than random patrol."[107]

While the Kansas City studies called into question some basic assumptions about patrol, it remains the backbone of police work. New patrol strategies for the effective utilization of human resources have led to various activities of **directed patrol**. One form of directed patrol varies the number of officers involved in patrolling according to the time of day or the frequency of reported crimes within an area. The idea is to put the most officers on the street where and when crime is most prevalent. Wilmington, Delaware, was one of the first cities to make use of split-force patrol, in which only a part of the patrol force performs routine patrol.[108] The remaining officers respond to calls for service, take reports, and conduct investigations.

directed patrol
A police-management strategy designed to increase the productivity of patrol officers through the scientific analysis and evaluation of patrol techniques.

In response to the Kansas City study on response time, some cities have prioritized calls for service,[109] ordering a quick police response only when crimes are in progress or when serious crimes have occurred. Less significant offenses, such as minor larcenies and certain citizen complaints, are handled by using the mail or by having citizens come to the police station to make a report.

Early policing studies, such as the Kansas City patrol experiment, were designed to identify and probe some of the basic assumptions that guided police work. The initial response to many such studies was "Why should we study that? Everybody knows the answer already!" As in the case of the Kansas City experiment, however, it soon became obvious that conventional wisdom was not always correct. Scientific studies of special significance to law enforcement are summarized in Table 4.

> You can't measure what a patrolman standing on a corner has prevented. There is no product at the end of a policeman's day.
> —Charles McCarthy[v]

Evidence-Based Policing Today

At the close of the twentieth century, noted police researcher Lawrence W. Sherman addressed an audience of criminal justice policymakers, scholars, and practitioners at the Police Foundation in Washington, D.C., and called for a new approach to American policing that would use research to guide and evaluate practice. "Police practices should be based on scientific evidence about what works best," Sherman told his audience. Sherman's lecture, titled "Evidence-Based Policing: Policing Based on Science, Not Anecdote,"[110]

TABLE 4
Selected Scientific Studies in Law Enforcement

Year	Study Name	Focus
2009	Evaluation of the Prince William County (Virginia) Police Department's Illegal Immigration Enforcement Policy (Interim Report)	The department's new policy of requiring immigration status checks under certain circumstances[a]
2007	Minneapolis Neighborhood Gunfire Detection System Evaluation	Police response time to gunfire within the city
2005	Effectiveness of Designated Driver Programs	Designated driver campaigns to reduce highway accidents
2002	Reducing Gun Violence (Indianapolis)	Targeted police patrols to reduce gun crime and violence
2001	Boston's Operation Ceasefire Evaluation	Citywide effort to reduce gun violence, especially gang-related homicides
1999	National Evaluation of Weed-and-Seed Programs	Weed-and-seed programs in eight states
1998	Community Policing in Action (Indianapolis)	Police and citizen cooperation and neighborhood security
1994	Kansas City Gun Experiment	Supplemental police patrol to reduce gun crime
1992	New York City Police Department's Cadet Corps Study	Level of education among officers, and hiring of minority officers
1992	Metro-Dade Spouse Abuse Experiment Replication (Florida)	Replication of a 1984 Minneapolis study
1990	Minneapolis "Hot Spot" Patrolling	Intensive patrol of problem areas
1987	Newport News (Virginia) Problem-Oriented Policing	Police solutions to community crime problems
1986	Crime Stoppers: A National Evaluation	Media crime-reduction programs
1986	Reducing Fear of Crime in Houston and Newark	Strategies for fear reduction among urban populations
1984	Minneapolis Domestic Violence Experiment	Effective police action in domestic-violence situations
1981	Newark Foot Patrol Experiment	Costs versus benefits of foot patrol
1977	Cincinnati Team Policing Experiment	Team versus traditional policing
1977	Patrol Staffing in San Diego	One- versus two-officer units
1976	Police Response Time (Kansas City)	Citizen satisfaction with police response
1976	Kansas City Peer Review Panel	Improvement in police behavior
1974	Kansas City Preventive Patrol Experiment	Effectiveness of police patrol

[a] A final report is scheduled for release after this book goes to press.

evidence-based policing (EBP)
The use of the best available research on the outcomes of police work to implement guidelines and evaluate agencies, units, and officers.[vi]

popularized the term **evidence-based policing (EBP)**. EBP, says Sherman, "is the use of best available research on the outcomes of police work to implement guidelines and evaluate agencies, units, and officers."[111] In other words, EBP uses research into everyday police procedures to evaluate current practices and to guide officers and police executives in future decision making. In any discussion of EBP, it is important to remember that the word *evidence* refers to scientific evidence, not criminal evidence.

"The basic premise of evidence-based practice," says Sherman, "is that we are all entitled to our own opinions, but not to our own facts."[112] Our own facts, or our beliefs about the way things should be done, says Sherman, often turn out to be wrong. During the civil rights movement of the 1960s and 1970s, for example, police executives in many areas took a heavy-handed approach in their attempts to control demonstrators. Images of tear gas filling the streets, high-pressure fire hoses being aimed at marchers, and police dogs biting fleeing demonstrators symbolize that era for many people. This heavy-handed approach had unintended consequences and served to inflame protesters. Situations that might have otherwise been contained with simple crowd-control tactics and the use of physical barriers became largely uncontrollable. Sherman reminds us that "the mythic power of subjective and unstructured wisdom holds back every field and keeps it from systematically discovering and implementing what works best in repeated tasks."

In 2008, the EBP movement gained additional traction when Sherman taught a course on the topic to police leaders from a number of countries at Cambridge University's Institute of Criminology. "There is a need for much more scientific guidance behind the way police are used," Sherman told representatives at Cambridge. "In Britain, the government has invested heavily in police resources, but we have not established how to obtain best value for money in deploying those resources. This is an opportunity for us to do that, working in a collaborative way with the police and tying together the education of police officers and the research base of criminology."[113]

▲ An officer writing a traffic ticket. Police officers wield a wide degree of discretion, and an individual officer's decision to enforce a particular law or to effect an arrest varies not just with the law's applicability to a particular set of circumstances but with the officer's subjective judgments about the nature of appropriate enforcement activity. What other factors influence police discretion? *David Young-Wolff/PhotoEdit Inc.*

The Institute of Criminology at Cambridge University identified the following questions as goals to be answered by evidence-based studies:[114]

- How can policing produce greater public safety without eroding civil liberties?
- How can more value for money be returned from investments in policing to cut the costs of crime?
- Can crime be better forecast for preventive policing by time and place?
- Can unsuccessful police methods be distinguished from cost-effective ones?
- Can better policing reduce the high costs of a growing prison population?
- Can evaluation tools used in evidence-based medicine be adopted by police?
- What are the possibilities for a police service based on cost-effectiveness?
- What are the prospects for developing the knowledge base for such evidence?

Today's EBP model has been called the single "most powerful force for change" in policing today.[115] Leading the movement toward EBP are organizations like the FBI's Futures Working Group, the Campbell Crime and Justice Group, and the Center for Evidence-Based Crime Policy at George Mason University. FBI Supervisory Special Agent Carl J. Jensen III, a member of the Futures Working Group, notes that in the future "successful law enforcement executives will have to be consumers and appliers of research." They won't need to be researchers themselves, Jensen notes, "but they must use research in their everyday work."[116] The Campbell Crime and Justice Group, which emphasizes the use of experimental studies in crime and justice policy making, can be accessed at **Web Extra 17**. The Center for Evidence-Based Crime Policy can be accessed at **Web Extra 18**. The center's Evidence-Based Policing Hall of Fame recognizes innovative law enforcement practitioners who have been central to the implementation of high-quality research programs. Visit the Hall of Fame at **Web Extra 19**.

Discretion and the Individual Officer

7 Explain police discretion, and identify some of the factors that influence a police officer's use of discretion.

Even as law enforcement agencies struggle to adapt to the threats posed by international terrorism, individual officers continue to retain considerable discretion in terms of their actions. **Police discretion** refers to the exercise of choice by law enforcement officers in the decision to investigate or apprehend, the disposition of suspects, the carrying out of official duties, and the application of sanctions. As one author has observed, "Police authority can be, at once, highly specific and exceedingly vague."[117] Decisions to stop and question someone, arrest a suspect, and perform many other police tasks are made solely by individual officers and must often be made quickly and in the absence of any close supervision. Kenneth Culp Davis, who pioneered the study

police discretion
The opportunity of law enforcement officers to exercise choice in their daily activities.

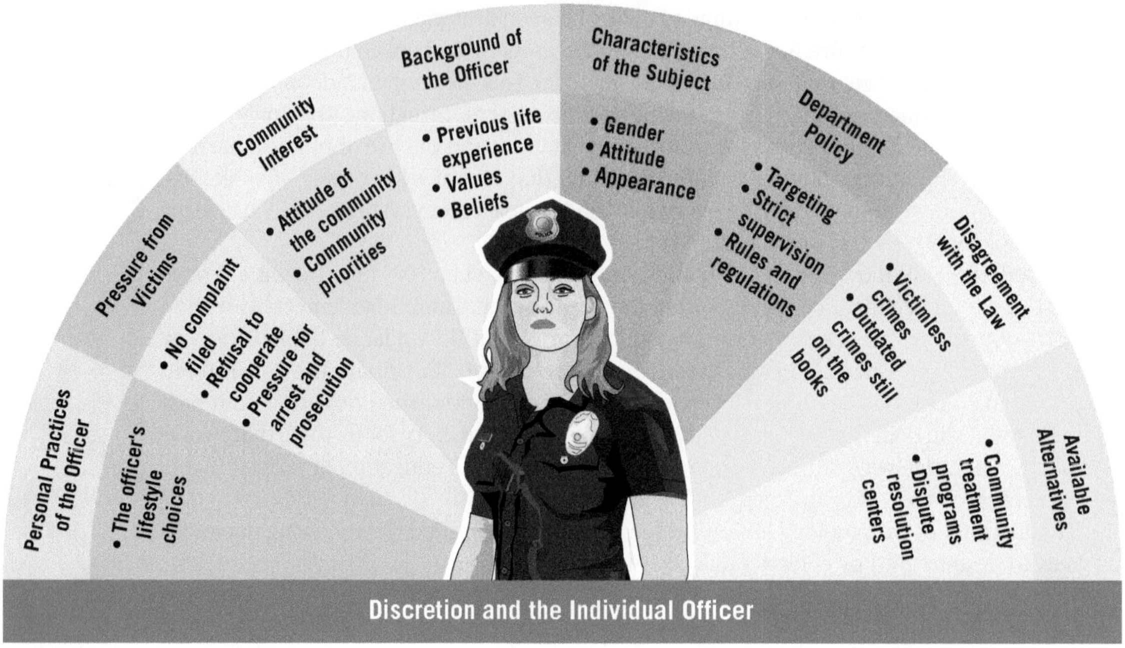

FIGURE 3
Discretion and the Individual Officer

of police discretion, says, "The police make policy about what law to enforce, how much to enforce it, against whom, and on what occasions."[118] To those who have contact with the police, the discretionary authority exercised by individual officers is of greater significance than all the department manuals and official policy statements combined.

Patrolling officers often decide against a strict enforcement of the law, preferring instead to handle situations informally. Infractions where minor law violations are committed, crimes committed out of the officer's presence where the victim refuses to file a complaint, and certain violations of the criminal law where the officer suspects that sufficient evidence to guarantee a conviction is lacking may all lead to discretionary action short of arrest. Although the widest exercise of discretion is more likely in routine situations involving relatively less serious violations of the law, serious and clear-cut criminal behavior may occasionally result in discretionary decisions not to make an arrest. Drunk driving, possession of controlled substances, and assault are but a few examples of crimes in which on-the-scene officers may decide warnings or referrals are more appropriate than arrest. Figure 3 illustrates a number of factors that studies of police discretion have found to influence the discretionary decisions of individual officers.

Summary

POLICING: PURPOSE AND ORGANIZATION

- The fundamental police mission in democratic societies includes five components: (1) enforcing the law (especially the criminal law), (2) apprehending offenders, (3) preventing crime, (4) preserving the peace, and (5) providing the community with needed enforcement-related services.
- Contemporary American policing presents a complex picture that is structured along federal, state, and local lines. Each federal agency empowered by Congress to enforce specific statutes has its own enforcement arm. In addition, tasks deemed especially significant by state legislatures, such as patrol of the highways, have resulted in the creation of specialized law enforcement agencies under state jurisdiction. For many of today's local law enforcement agencies,

created under county and municipal authority, patrol retains a central role—with investigation, interrogation, and numerous support roles rounding out an increasingly specialized profession.

- Police administration involves the activities of managing, controlling, directing, and coordinating police personnel, resources, and activities in the service of preventing crime, apprehending criminals, recovering stolen property, and performing regulatory and helping services. Virtually all American law enforcement organizations are formally structured among divisions and along lines of authority. Roles within police agencies usually fall into one of two categories: line and staff. Line operations are field or supervisory activities directly related to daily police work; staff operations include support roles such as administration.
- Four historical policing epochs are identified in this chapter: (1) the political era, (2) the reform era, (3) the community policing era, and (4) the new era. Some say that the primary feature of the new law enforcement era is policing to secure the homeland. Others see the new era as being underpinned by an emphasis on intelligence-led policing.
- Police-community relations programs represent a movement away from an exclusive police emphasis on the apprehension of law violators and signify an increasing level of positive police-citizen interaction. Community policing is built on the principle that police departments and the communities they serve should work together as partners in the fight against crime.
- Evidence-based policing consists of the use of best available research on the outcomes of police work to implement guidelines and evaluate agencies, units, and officers. EBP uses research into everyday police procedures to evaluate current practices and to guide officers and police executives in future decision making.
- *Police discretion* refers to the opportunity for police officers to exercise choice in their enforcement activities. Put another way, discretion is the exercise of choice by law enforcement officers in the decision to investigate or apprehend, the disposition of suspects, the carrying out of official duties, and the application of sanctions. The widest exercise of discretion can be found in routine situations involving relatively less serious violations of the law, but serious criminal behavior may also result in discretionary decisions not to make an arrest.

QUESTIONS FOR REVIEW

1. What are the basic purposes of policing in democratic societies? How are they consistent with one another? In what ways might they be inconsistent?
2. What are the three major levels of public law enforcement described in this chapter? Why do we have so many different types of enforcement agencies in the United States? What problems, if any, do you think are created by such a diversity of agencies?
3. What are the various features of police administration described in this chapter? What is a chain of command?
4. What were the stages of historical development in American policing? How did policing styles differ by historical era?
5. What is community policing? How does it differ from traditional policing? Does community policing offer a real opportunity to improve policing services in the United States? Why or why not?
6. What is evidence-based policing? What potential does it hold for managing police organizations in the future?
7. What is police discretion? How does the practice of discretion by today's officers affect their departments and the policing profession as a whole?

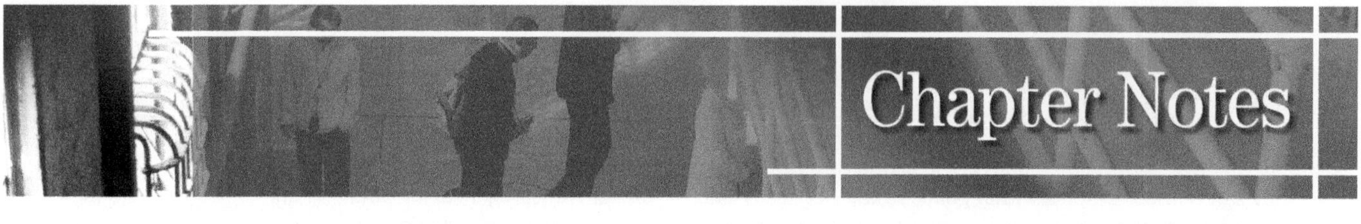

Chapter Notes

i. Quote of the Day, *New York Times*, May 30, 2002.
ii. Robert Kennedy, *The Pursuit of Justice*, part 3, "Eradicating Free Enterprise in Organized Crime" (New York: Harper and Row, 1964).
iii. Sam S. Souryal, *Police Administration and Management* (St. Paul, MN: West, 1977), p. 261.
iv. Office of Community Oriented Policing Services, *Community Policing Defined* (Washington, DC: U.S. Department of Justice, 2009), p. 3.
v. Cited in Anderson's Police Pages at http://andersonspolicepage.tripod.com/
vi. Lawrence W. Sherman, *Evidence-Based Policing* (Washington, DC: Police Foundation, 1998), p. 3.

---

1. Major Cities Chiefs Association, *Terrorism: The Impact on State and Local Law Enforcement*, Intelligence Commanders Conference Report, June 2002, http://www.neiassociates.org/mccintelligencereport.pdf (accessed September 30, 2009).
2. "Police, Protestors Clash Near Miami Trade Talks," CNN.com, November 20, 2003, http://www.cnn.com/2003/US/South/11/20/miami.protests (accessed June 3, 2009).
3. "Demonstrators, Police Clash during Free Trade Talks," *USA Today*, November 20, 2003, http://www.usatoday.com/news/nation/2003-11-20-miami-protests_x.htm (accessed June 3, 2009).
4. Andrew P. Sutor, *Police Operations: Tactical Approaches to Crimes in Progress* (St. Paul, MN: West, 1976), p. 68, citing Peel.
5. C. D. Hale, *Police Patrol: Operations and Management* (Englewood Cliffs, NJ: Prentice Hall, 1994).
6. Victor Kappeler et al., *The Mythology of Crime and Criminal Justice* (Prospect Heights, IL: Waveland Press, 1996).
7. Darl H. Champion and Michael K. Hooper, *Introduction to American Policing* (New York: McGraw-Hill, 2003), p. 133.
8. Details for this story come from Ted Ottley, "Bad Day Dawning," Court TV's Crime Library, http://www.crimelibrary.com/serial_killers/notorious/mcveigh/dawning_1.html (accessed June 22, 2008).
9. Ibid.
10. This definition has been attributed to the National Crime Prevention Institute (see http://www.lvmpd.com/community/crmtip25.htm).
11. See Steven P. Lab, *Crime Prevention at a Crossroads* (Cincinnati, OH: Anderson, 1997).
12. Visit the Philadelphia Police Department online at http://www.phillypolice.com.
13. The term *CompStat* is sometimes interpreted to mean computer statistics, comparative statistics, or computer comparative statistics, although it is generally accorded no specific meaning.
14. Learn more about CompStat from Vincent E. Henry, *The COMPSTAT Paradigm: Management Accountability in Policing, Business, and the Public Sector* (Flushing, NY: Looseleaf Law Publications, 2002).
15. Much of the information in this section comes from the Philadelphia Police Department, "The COMPSTAT Process," http://www.ppdonline.org/ppd_compstat.htm (accessed May 28, 2007).
16. See Ned Levine, *CrimeStat: A Spatial Statistics Program for the Analysis of Crime Incident Locations*, version 2.0 (Washington, DC: National Institute of Justice, May 2002).
17. Robert H. Langworthy and Lawrence P. Travis III, *Policing in America: A Balance of Forces*, 2nd ed. (Upper Saddle River, NJ: Prentice Hall, 1999), p. 194.
18. Adapted from Bronx County (New York) District Attorney's Office, "Quality of Life Offenses," December 24, 2002, http://www.bronxda.net/fighting_crime/quality_of_life_offenses.html (accessed June 20, 2003).
19. Other violations may be involved as well. On December 29, 2000, for example, Judge John S. Martin, Jr., of the Federal District Court in Manhattan, ruled that homeless people in New York City could be arrested for sleeping in cardboard boxes in public. Judge Martin held that a city Sanitation Department regulation barring people from abandoning cars or boxes on city streets could be applied to the homeless who were sleeping in boxes.
20. Norman Siegel, executive director of the New York Civil Liberties Union, as reported in "Quality of Life Offenses Targeted," *Western Queens Gazette*, November 22, 2000, http://www.qgazette.com/News/2000/1122/Editorial_pages/e01.html (accessed June 12, 2007).
21. The broken windows thesis was first suggested by George L. Kelling and James Q. Wilson in "Broken Windows: The Police and Neighborhood Safety," *Atlantic Monthly*, March 1982.
22. For a critique of the broken windows thesis, see Bernard E. Harcourt, *Illusion of Order: The False Promise of Broken Windows Policing* (Cambridge, MA: Harvard University Press, 2001).
23. Peter Schuler, "Law Professor Harcourt Challenges Popular Policing Method, Gun Violence Interventions," *Chicago Chronicle*, Vol. 22, No. 12 (March 20, 2003), http://chronicle.uchicago.edu/030320/harcourt.shtml (accessed August 28, 2008).
24. George L. Kelling, Catherine M. Coles, and James Q. Wilson, *Fixing Broken Windows: Restoring Order and Reducing Crime in Our Communities* (reprint, New York: Touchstone, 1998).
25. Charles R. Swanson, Leonard Territo, and Robert W. Taylor, *Police Administration: Structures, Processes, and Behavior*, 4th ed. (Upper Saddle River, NJ: Prentice Hall, 1998), p. 1.
26. Lorraine Mazerolle et al., *Managing Citizen Calls to the Police: An Assessment of Nonemergency Call Systems* (Washington, DC: National Institute of Justice, 2001), p. 1.
27. The Hastings (Minnesota) Police Department website at http://www.ci.hastings.mn.us/Police/deptnews.htm (accessed May 24, 2009).
28. Government Accounting Office, "Federal Law Enforcement: Survey of Federal Civilian Law Enforcement Functions and Authorities," December 2006 (highlights of GAO-07-121).
29. U.S. Department of Justice, *A Proud History, a Bright Future: Careers with the FBI*, pamphlet (Washington, DC: DOJ, October 1986), p. 1.
30. Much of the information in this section comes from U.S. Department of Justice, *The FBI: The First Seventy-Five Years* (Washington, DC: U.S. Government Printing Office, 1986).
31. Some of the information in this section is adapted from Federal Bureau of Investigation, "Facts and Figures 2003,"

http://www.fbi.gov/priorities/priorities.htm (accessed March 25, 2006).
32. Telephone conversation with FBI officials, April 21, 1995.
33. Information in this section comes from Christopher H. Asplen, "National Commission Explores Its Future," *NIJ Journal* (January 1999), pp. 17–24.
34. The DNA Identification Act is Section 210301 of the Violent Crime Control and Law Enforcement Act of 1994.
35. Federal Bureau of Investigation, "NDIS Statistics," http://www.fbi.gov/hq/lab/codis/clickmap.htm (accessed May 28, 2010).
36. Much of the information in this paragraph comes from the FBI Academy website at http://www.fbi.gov/hq/td/academy/academy.htm (accessed March 3, 2008).
37. Testimony of Robert S. Mueller III, director of the Federal Bureau of Investigation, before the Senate Committee on Intelligence, February 16, 2005.
38. Henry M. Wrobleski and Karen M. Hess, *Introduction to Law Enforcement and Criminal Justice*, 4th ed. (St. Paul, MN: West, 1993), p. 34.
39. Ibid., p. 35.
40. New York City Police Department website, http://www.nyc.gov/html/nypd (accessed June 21, 2009). *PoliceLink* reported a head count of 34,771 in early 2009 but said that the city had plans to hire an additional 1,600 officers. See "NYPD Cuts 2010 Academy, Affects 1,000 Recruits," *PoliceLink*, February 12, 2009, http://www.policelink.com/news/articles/94792-nypd-cuts-2010-academy-affects-1000-recruits (accessed May 9, 2010).
41. Brian A. Reaves, *Census of State and Local Law Enforcement Agencies, 2004* (Washington, DC: Bureau of Justice Statistics, 2007).
42. Ibid. See also Matthew J. Hickman and Brian A. Reaves, *Local Police Departments, 2003* (Washington, DC: Bureau of Justice Statistics, 2006).
43. Note, however, that New York City jails may have daily populations that, on a given day, exceed those of Los Angeles County.
44. Los Angeles County Sheriff's Department, "About LASD," http://www.lasd.org/aboutlasd/about.html (accessed June 25, 2008).
45. Police Assessment Resource Center, *The Los Angeles County Sheriff's Department—19th Semiannual Report* (Los Angeles: PARC, February 2005); and telephone communication with Deputy Ethan Marquez, L.A. County Sheriff's Department, Custodial Division, January 24, 2002.
46. Reaves, *Census of State and Local Law Enforcement Agencies, 2004.*
47. Office of the Director of National Intelligence, "Second National Fusion Center Conference Held to Foster Greater Collaboration," news release, March 20, 2008.
48. Estimates of the number of centers vary, and classifying a work group as a "fusion center" depends largely on the perspective assumed. A March 2008 press release by the federal Office of the Director of National Intelligence (see note 47) put the number of operational fusion centers at more than 50 in 46 states.
49. Michael C. Mines, "Statement before the House Committee on Homeland Security, Subcommittee on Intelligence, Information Sharing and Terrorism Risk Assessment," September 27, 2007.
50. "State and Local Fusion Centers Face Challenges as They Grow," *Criminal Justice Newsletter*, September 18, 2007, p. 1.
51. The elements of this definition draw on the now-classic work by O. W. Wilson, *Police Administration* (New York: McGraw-Hill, 1950), pp. 2–3.
52. Charles R. Swanson, Leonard Territo, and Robert W. Taylor, *Police Administration: Structures, Processes, and Behavior* (Upper Saddle River, NJ: Prentice Hall, 1998), p. 167.
53. Los Angeles County Sheriff's Department, "About LASD," http://www.lasd.org/aboutlasd/about.html (accessed June 25, 2010).
54. For more information on the first three categories, see Francis X. Hartmann, "Debating the Evolution of American Policing," *Perspectives on Policing*, No. 5 (Washington, DC: National Institute of Justice, 1988).
55. Willard M. Oliver, "The Homeland Security Juggernaut: TheEnd of the Community Policing Era," *Crime and Justice International*, Vol. 20, No. 79 (2004), pp. 4–10. See also Willard M. Oliver, "The Era of Homeland Security: September 11, 2001 to . . ." *Crime and Justice International*, Vol. 21, No. 85 (2005), pp. 9–17.
56. Gene Stephens, "Policing the Future: Law Enforcement's New Challenges," *The Futurist*, March/April 2005, pp. 51–57.
57. As cited in Bernie G. Thompson, *A Law Enforcement Assistance and Partnership Strategy* (Washington, DC: U.S. Congress, 2008), p. 5. Congressman Thompson is ranking member of the Democratic staff of the Committee on Homeland Security.
58. Ibid., p. 5.
59. To learn more about Wilson, see http://www.nndb.com/people/796/000167295 (accessed January 5, 2011).
60. James Q. Wilson, *Varieties of Police Behavior: The Management of Law and Order in Eight Communities* (Cambridge, MA: Harvard University Press, 1968).
61. Independent Commission on the Los Angeles Police Department, *Report of the Independent Commission on the Los Angeles Police Department* (Los Angeles: The Commission, 1991).
62. Gary W. Sykes, "Street Justice: A Moral Defense of Order Maintenance Policing," *Justice Quarterly*, Vol. 3, No. 4 (December 1986), p. 505.
63. Egon Bittner, "Community Relations," in Alvin W. Cohn and Emilio C. Viano, eds., *Police Community Relations: Images, Roles, Realities* (Philadelphia: J. B. Lippincott, 1976), pp. 77–82.
64. Paul B. Weston, *Police Organization and Management* (Pacific Palisades, CA: Goodyear, 1976), p. 159.
65. Hale, *Police Patrol.*
66. Mark H. Moore and Robert C. Trojanowicz, "Corporate Strategies for Policing," *Perspectives on Policing*, No. 6 (Washington, DC: National Institute of Justice, 1998).
67. Ibid., p. 6.
68. Community Policing Consortium, *Community Policing Is Alive and Well* (Washington, DC: Community Policing Consortium, 1995), p. 1.
69. Office of Community Oriented Policing Services, *Community Policing Defined* (Washington, DC: U.S. Department of Justice, 2009), p. 3.
70. George L. Kelling, *The Newark Foot Patrol Experiment* (Washington, DC: Police Foundation, 1981).
71. Robert C. Trojanowicz, "An Evaluation of a Neighborhood Foot Patrol Program," *Journal of Police Science and Administration*, Vol. 11 (1983), pp. 410–419.
72. Bureau of Justice Assistance, *Understanding Community Policing: A Framework for Action* (Washington, DC: Bureau of Justice Statistics, 1994), p. 10.
73. Robert C. Trojanowicz and Bonnie Bucqueroux, *Community Policing* (Cincinnati, OH: Anderson, 1990).
74. Moore and Trojanowicz, "Corporate Strategies for Policing," p. 8.

75. S. M. Hartnett and W. G. Skogan, "Community Policing: Chicago's Experience," *National Institute of Justice Journal* (April 1999), pp. 2–11.
76. Jerome H. Skolnick and David H. Bayley, *Community Policing: Issues and Practices around the World* (Washington, DC: National Institute of Justice, 1988).
77. Ibid.
78. William L. Goodbody, "What Do We Expect New-Age Cops to Do?" *Law Enforcement News* (April 30, 1995), pp. 14, 18.
79. Sam Vincent Meddis and Desda Moss, "Many 'Fed-Up' Communities Cornering Crime," *USA Today*, May 22, 1995, p. 8A.
80. Matthew J. Hickman and Brian A. Reaves, *Community Policing in Local Police Departments, 1997 and 1999*, Bureau of Justice Statistics Special Report (Washington, DC: U.S. Department of Justice, 2001).
81. Richard M. Daley and Matt L. Rodriguez, *Together We Can: A Strategic Plan for Reinventing the Chicago Police Department* (Chicago: Chicago Police Department, 1993), http://www.ci.chi.il.us/CommunityPolicing/Statistics/Reports/TWC.pdf (accessed March 5, 2007).
82. Bureau of Justice Assistance, *Neighborhood-Oriented Policing in Rural Communities: A Program Planning Guide* (Washington, DC: Bureau of Justice Statistics, 1994), p. 4.
83. See the COPS Office website at http://www.cops.usdoj.gov (accessed September 6, 2010).
84. David L. Carter, *Law Enforcement Intelligence: A Guide for State, Local, and Tribal Law Enforcement Agencies* (Washington, DC: U.S. Department of Justice, 2004), p. 39.
85. Federal Bureau of Investigation, "Protecting America from Terrorist Attacks," Press BOLO for US, May 26, 2004, http://www.fbi.gov/page2/may04/bolo052604.htm (accessed August 28, 2007).
86. Office of Justice Programs, *The National Criminal Intelligence Sharing Plan* (Washington, DC: U.S. Department of Justice, 2005), p. 4.
87. International Association of Chiefs of Police, *Recommendations from the IACP Intelligence Summit, Criminal Intelligence Sharing: A National Plan for Intelligence-Led Policing at the Local, State and Federal Levels* (Alexandria, VA: IACP, 2002), p. 2.
88. Office for Domestic Preparedness, *Guidelines for Homeland Security* (Washington, DC: U.S. Department of Homeland Security, 2003).
89. Jihong Zhao, Nicholas P. Lovrich, and Quint Thurman, "The Status of Community Policing in American Cities: Facilitators and Impediments Revisited," *Policing*, Vol. 22, No. 1 (1999), p. 74.
90. For a good critique and overview of community policing, see Geoffrey P. Alpert et al., *Community Policing: Contemporary Readings* (Prospect Heights, IL: Waveland Press, 1998).
91. Jack R. Greene, "Community Policing in America: Changing the Nature, Structure, and Function of the Police," in U.S. Department of Justice, *Criminal Justice 2000*, Vol. 3 (Washington, DC: DOJ, 2000), pp. 299–370.
92. Michael D. Reisig and Roger B. Parks, "Experience, Quality of Life, and Neighborhood Context: A Hierarchical Analysis of Satisfaction with Police," *Justice Quarterly*, Vol. 17, No. 3 (2000), p. 607.
93. Mark E. Correla, "The Conceptual Ambiguity of Community in Community Policing: Filtering the Muddy Waters," *Policing*, Vol. 23, No. 2 (2000), pp. 218–233.
94. Adapted from Donald R. Fessler, *Facilitating Community Change: A Basic Guide* (San Diego: San Diego State University, 1976), p. 7.
95. Daniel W. Flynn, *Defining the "Community" in Community Policing* (Washington, DC: Police Executive Research Forum, 1998).
96. Robert C. Trojanowicz and Mark H. Moore, *The Meaning of Community in Community Policing* (East Lansing: Michigan State University's National Neighborhood Foot Patrol Center, 1988).
97. Robert M. Bohm, K. Michael Reynolds, and Stephen T. Holms, "Perceptions of Neighborhood Problems and Their Solutions: Implications for Community Policing," *Policing*, Vol. 23, No. 4 (2000), p. 439.
98. Ibid., p. 442.
99. Malcolm K. Sparrow, "Implementing Community Policing," *Perspectives on Policing*, No. 9 (Washington, DC: National Institute of Justice, 1988).
100. "L.A. Police Chief: Treat People Like Customers," *USA Today*, March 29, 1993.
101. Robert Wasserman and Mark H. Moore, "Values in Policing," *Perspectives in Policing*, No. 8 (Washington, DC: National Institute of Justice, 1988), p. 7.
102. "New York City Mayor Sparks Debate on Community Policing," *Criminal Justice Newsletter*, Vol. 25, No. 2 (January 18, 1994), p. 1.
103. Thomas J. Deakin, "The Police Foundation: A Special Report," *FBI Law Enforcement Bulletin* (November 1986), p. 2.
104. George L. Kelling et al., *The Kansas City Patrol Experiment* (Washington, DC: Police Foundation, 1974).
105. George Kelling quoted in Kevin Krajick, "Does Patrol Prevent Crime?" *Police* (September 1978), pp. 11–13.
106. William Bieck and David Kessler, *Response Time Analysis* (Kansas City, MO: Board of Police Commissioners, 1977). See also J. Thomas McEwen et al., *Evaluation of the Differential Police Response Field Test: Executive Summary* (Alexandria, VA: Research Management Associates, 1984); and Lawrence Sherman, "Policing Communities: What Works?" in Michael Tonry and Norval Morris, eds., *Crime and Justice: An Annual Review of Research*, Vol. 8 (Chicago: University of Chicago Press, 1986), pp. 343–386.
107. Kevin Krajick, "Does Patrol Prevent Crime?" *Police Magazine* (September 1978): pp. 11–13.
108. Ibid.
109. Ibid.
110. "Evidence-Based Policing," Police Foundation press release, March 17, 1998, www.policefoundation.org/docs/evidence.html (accessed January 5, 2006).
111. Lawrence W. Sherman, *Evidence-Based Policing* (Washington, DC: Police Foundation, 1998), p. 3.
112. Much of the information in this section comes from Sherman, *Evidence-Based Policing*.
113. "World's Top Police Officers to Study at Cambridge University," University of Cambridge, News and Events, December 3, 2007, http://www.admin.cam.ac.uk/news/dp/2007120301 (accessed July 5, 2008).
114. University of Cambridge, "Evidence-Based Policing: Possibilities and Prospects," revised and final program announcement, June 30 2008.
115. Carl J. Jensen III, "Consuming and Applying Research: Evidence-Based Policing," *Police Chief*, Vol. 73, No. 2 (February 2006), http://policechiefmagazine.org/magazine/index.cfm?fuseaction=display_arch&article_id=815&issue_id=22006 (accessed May 17, 2007).
116. Ibid.
117. Howard Cohen, "Overstepping Police Authority," *Criminal Justice Ethics* (summer/fall 1987), pp. 52–60.
118. Kenneth Culp Davis, *Police Discretion* (St. Paul, MN: West, 1975).

Policing: Legal Aspects

Policing: Legal Aspects

Learning Objectives

After reading this chapter, you should be able to:

1. Identify legal restraints on police action, and list instances of the abuse of police power.
2. Explain how the Bill of Rights and democratically inspired legal restraints help protect personal freedoms in our society.
3. Describe the circumstances under which police officers may properly conduct searches or seize property.
4. Define *arrest*, and describe how popular depictions of the arrest process may not be consistent with legal understandings of the term.
5. Describe the intelligence function, including police interrogations, and explain the role of *Miranda* warnings.

> "No one is compelled to choose the profession of a police officer, but having chosen it, everyone is obliged to live up to the standard of its requirements."
>
> —Calvin Coolidge[1]

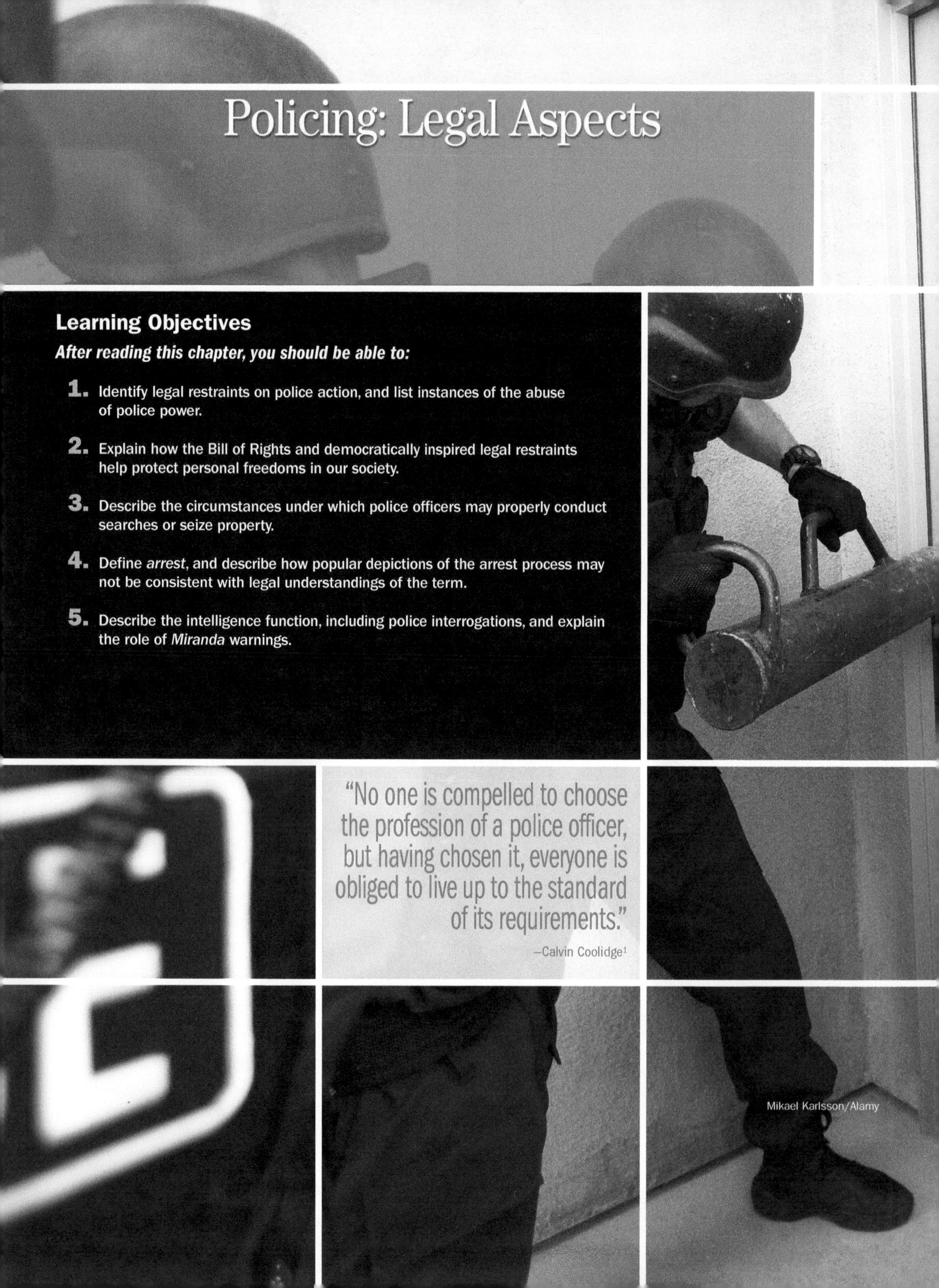

Mikael Karlsson/Alamy

Introduction

▲ Protesters at a rally in Queens, New York, demanding answers for the fatal police shooting of Sean Bell as he left a bachelor's party on the night before his wedding in 2006. Bell, who was unarmed, was killed by NYPD officers who fired 50 rounds at him and two friends after they drove Bell's car into a minivan carrying plainclothes officers who were investigating the club where the party took place. The officers were found "not guilty" in a 2008 trial. Might "contagious shooting" explain what happened that night?
Reuters/Mike Segar/Landov Media

Early on a cold November morning in 2006, 23-year-old Sean Bell left a bachelor party at New York City's Kalua Cabaret strip club with two of his friends and climbed into his gray Nissan Altima. Although Bell, who was to be married later that day, didn't know it, undercover New York City Police Department (NYPD) officers had been staking out the club in an investigation into suspected drug and gun dealing there. What happened next remains unclear, but after a chaotic confrontation between Bell's group and the police, followed by a crash involving a van carrying some of the NYPD officers and Bell's car, officers opened fire on the vehicle, firing 50 rounds before the shooting ended. Bell died at the scene, and his friends were seriously injured. The officers later said that they thought Bell and his companions were armed and that they might have been drug dealers. It was not clear if Bell ever knew that the men, dressed in plain clothes, were police officers; he may have thought that he was being robbed or carjacked. On March 17, 2007, a Queens, New York, grand jury indicted three of the detectives involved in the case, charging two with first- and second-degree manslaughter and a third with reckless endangerment.

Shortly after the indictments were handed down, demonstrators paraded through Queens demanding justice for Bell, who was African American, as were two of the three officers indicted in the shooting. New York City Mayor Michael R. Bloomberg urged residents to "respect the result of our justice system." He added, "It also needs to be said that being a police officer . . . is a very dangerous job. And although a trial will decide whether crimes were committed in this case, day in and day out the N.Y.P.D. does an incredible job under very difficult circumstances."[2] The mayor's words seemed prophetic when, on April 25, 2008, Judge Arthur J. Cooperman found the defendants not guilty of any crime. Describing the evidence, Judge Cooperman said that it was reasonable for the detectives to fear that someone in the crowd had been carrying a gun on the night that the shooting took place. He added that many of the prosecution's witnesses, including Bell's friends and the two wounded victims, were simply not believable.[3]

The Bell shooting was reminiscent of the death of West African immigrant Amadou Diallo, who was killed in a hail of 41 bullets in 1999 as he stood in a New York City doorway and apparently reached for his identification after being told to raise his hands. Diallo reportedly had a poor command of the English language and may not have understood police commands to stay still. Officers had apparently mistaken him for a suspect they were pursuing. Although the officers who shot Diallo were charged with second-degree murder, they were later acquitted.[4] Law enforcement experts said that what happened in both cases might be explained by "contagious shooting"—gunfire that spreads "in the adrenaline-pumping, split-second heat of the moment"[5] among officers who believe that they, or their colleagues, are facing a deadly threat.[6]

Not all questionable cases of police use of force involve shootings. Two months after Hurricane Katrina devastated New Orleans, members of the city's overworked police department became embroiled in a public relations nightmare when an Associated Press Television News (APTN) crew working in the French Quarter filmed two white officers beating an apparently dazed and unresisting 64-year-old African American retired elementary school teacher named Robert Davis. A third officer could be seen grabbing and shoving an APTN producer working with the news team. As the incident ended, Davis, whose family had property in the city, was arrested and charged with public intoxication, resisting arrest, battery on a police officer, and public intimidation. He later told reporters that he hadn't had an alcoholic drink in 25 years but that trouble began when he asked a mounted officer for directions.[7] New Orleans Police Superintendent Warren Riley was quick to condemn the officers' behavior. "The actions that were observed on this video are certainly unacceptable [to] this department," Riley said as he announced the firings of officers Lance Schilling and Robert Evangelist, as well as the suspension without pay of another officer, S. M. Smith. Soon afterward, the U.S. Department of Justice announced that it was opening a civil rights investigation into the incident.[8]

The Abuse of Police Power

The Rodney King Incident

1 Identify legal restraints on police action, and list instances of the abuse of police power.

National publicity surrounding the Davis beating was considerably less intense than that which centered on the 1991 videotaped beating of motorist Rodney King by Los Angeles Police Department (LAPD) officers. King, an unemployed 25-year-old African American, was stopped by LAPD officers for an alleged violation of motor vehicle laws. Police said King had been speeding and had refused to stop for a pursuing patrol car. Officers claimed to have clocked his 1988 Hyundai at 115 mph on the suburban Los Angeles Foothill Freeway—even though the car's manufacturer later said the vehicle was not capable of speeds over 100 mph.

Eventually King did stop, but then officers of the LAPD appeared to attack him, shocking him twice with electronic stun guns and striking him with nightsticks and fists. Kicked in the stomach, face, and back, he was left with 11 skull fractures, missing teeth, a crushed cheekbone, and a broken ankle. A witness told reporters that she heard King begging officers to stop the beating but that they "were all laughing, like they just had a party."[9] King eventually underwent surgery for brain injuries. Officers involved in the beating claimed that King, at 6 feet 3 inches and 225 pounds, appeared strung out on phencyclidine (PCP) and that he and his two companions made the officers feel threatened.[10]

The entire incident was captured on videotape by an amateur photographer with a night-sensitive video camera. The two-minute videotape was repeatedly broadcast over national television and was picked up by hundreds of local TV stations. The furor that erupted over the tape led to the ouster of LAPD Chief Daryl Gates and initiated a Justice Department review of law enforcement practices across the country.[11]

In 1992, a California jury found four police defendants not guilty—a verdict that resulted in days of rioting across Los Angeles. A year later, however, in the spring of 1993, two of the officers, Sergeant Stacey Koon and Officer Laurence Powell, were found guilty in federal court of denying King his constitutional right "not to be deprived of liberty without due process of law, including the right to be . . . free from the intentional use of unreasonable force."[12] Later that year, both were sentenced to two and a half years in prison, far less than might have been expected under federal sentencing guidelines. They were released from prison in December 1995, and a three-year court battle over whether federal sentencing guidelines were violated was resolved in the officers' favor in 1996. Officers Theodore Briseno and Timothy Wind were exonerated at the federal level.

In 1994, King settled a civil suit against the city of Los Angeles for a reported $3.8 million. Observers later concluded that King himself was not a model citizen. At the time of the beating, he was on parole after having served time in prison for robbery. Since then he has been arrested on a variety of other charges, including battery, assault, drug use, and indecent exposure.[13] Learn more about the Rodney King incident and its ramifications at **Web Extra 1**.

This chapter shows how no one is above the law—even the police. It describes the legal environment surrounding police activities, from search and seizure through arrest and the interrogation of suspects. As we shall see throughout, democratically inspired legal restraints on the police help ensure individual freedoms in our society and prevent the development of a police state in America. Like anything else, however, the rules by which the police are expected to operate are in constant flux, and their continuing development forms the meat of this chapter. For a police perspective on these issues, visit **Web Extra 2**.

A Changing Legal Climate

Bill of Rights
The popular name given to the first ten amendments to the U.S. Constitution, which are considered especially important in the processing of criminal defendants.

The Constitution of the United States is designed—especially in the **Bill of Rights**—to protect citizens against abuses of police power (Table 1). However, the legal environment surrounding the police in modern America is much more complex than it was just 45 years ago. Up until that time, the Bill of Rights was largely given only lip service in criminal justice proceedings around the country. In practice, law enforcement, especially on the state and local levels, revolved around tried-and-true methods of

TABLE 1
Constitutional Amendments of Special Significance to the American System of Justice

This Right Is Guaranteed	By This Amendment
The right against unreasonable searches and seizures	Fourth
The right against arrest without probable cause	Fourth
The right against self-incrimination	Fifth
The right against "double jeopardy"	Fifth
The right to due process of law	Fifth, Sixth, Fourteenth
The right to a speedy trial	Sixth
The right to a jury trial	Sixth
The right to know the charges	Sixth
The right to cross-examine witnesses	Sixth
The right to a lawyer	Sixth
The right to compel witnesses on one's behalf	Sixth
The right to reasonable bail	Eighth
The right against excessive fines	Eighth
The right against cruel and unusual punishments	Eighth
The applicability of constitutional rights to all citizens, regardless of state law or procedure	Fourteenth

search, arrest, and interrogation that sometimes left little room for recognition of individual rights. Police operations during that period were often far more informal than they are today, and investigating officers frequently assumed that they could come and go as they pleased, even to the extent of invading someone's home without a search warrant. Interrogations could quickly turn violent, and the infamous "rubber hose," which was reputed to leave few marks on the body, was probably more widely used during the questioning of suspects than many would like to believe. Similarly, "doing things by the book" could mean the use of thick telephone books for beating suspects, since the books spread out the force of blows and left few visible bruises. Although such abuses were not necessarily day-to-day practices in all police agencies and although they probably did not characterize more than a relatively small proportion of all officers, such conduct pointed to the need for greater control over police activities so that even the potential for abuse might be curtailed.

In the 1960s the U.S. Supreme Court, under the direction of Chief Justice Earl Warren (1891–1974), accelerated the process of guaranteeing individual rights in the face of criminal prosecution. Warren Court rulings bound the police to strict procedural requirements in the areas of investigation, arrest, and interrogation. Later rulings scrutinized trial court procedures and enforced humanitarian standards in sentencing and punishment. The Warren Court also seized on the Fourteenth Amendment and made it a basis for judicial mandates requiring that both state and federal criminal justice agencies adhere to the Court's interpretation of the Constitution. The apex of the individual-rights emphasis in Supreme Court decisions was reached in the 1966 case of *Miranda* v. *Arizona*,[14] which established the famous requirement of a police "rights advisement" of suspects. In wielding its brand of idealism, the Warren Court (which held sway from 1953 until 1969) accepted the fact that a few guilty people would go free so that the rights of the majority of Americans would be protected.

In the decades since the Warren Court, a new conservative Court philosophy has resulted in Supreme Court decisions that have brought about what some call a reversal of Warren-era advances in the area of individual rights. By creating exceptions to some of the Warren Court's rules and restraints and by allowing for the emergency questioning of suspects before they are read their rights, a changed Supreme Court has recognized the realities attending day-to-day police work and the need to ensure public safety.

There is more law at the end of the policeman's nightstick than in all the decisions of the Supreme Court.

—Alexander "Clubber" Williams, late-nineteenth-century New York police officer

Individual Rights

Checks and Balances

2 Explain how the Bill of Rights and democratically inspired legal restraints help protect personal freedoms in our society.

The Constitution of the United States provides for a system of checks and balances among the legislative, judicial, and executive (presidential) branches of government. One branch of government is always held accountable to the other branches. The system is designed to ensure that no one individual or agency can become powerful enough to usurp the rights and freedoms guaranteed under the Constitution. Without accountability, it is possible to imagine a police state in which the power of law enforcement is absolute and is related more to political considerations and personal vendettas than to objective considerations of guilt or innocence.

Under our system of government, courts become the arena for dispute resolution, not just between individuals but between citizens and the agencies of government. After handling by the justice system, people who feel they have not received the respect and dignity due them under the law can appeal to the courts for redress. Such appeals are usually based on procedural issues and are independent of more narrow considerations of guilt or innocence.

In this chapter, we focus on cases that are important for having clarified constitutional guarantees concerning individual liberties within the criminal justice arena. They involve issues that most of us have come to call *rights.* Rights are concerned with procedure, that is, with how police and other actors in the criminal justice system handle each part of the process of dealing with suspects. Rights violations have often become the basis for the dismissal of charges, the acquittal of defendants, or the release of convicted offenders after an appeal to a higher court.

Due Process Requirements

Due process is a requirement of the Fifth, Sixth, and Fourteenth Amendments to the U.S. Constitution. It mandates that justice system officials respect the rights of accused individuals throughout the criminal justice process. Most due process requirements of relevance to the police pertain to three major areas: (1) evidence and investigation (often called *search and seizure*), (2) arrest, and (3) interrogation. Each of these areas has been addressed by a plethora of landmark U.S. Supreme Court decisions. **Landmark cases** produce substantial changes both in the understanding of the requirements of due process and in the practical day-to-day operations of the justice system. Another way to think of landmark cases is that they help significantly in clarifying the "rules of the game"—the procedural guidelines that the police and the rest of the justice system must follow.

landmark case
A precedent-setting court decision that produces substantial changes both in the understanding of the requirements of due process and in the practical day-to-day operations of the justice system.

The three areas we will discuss have been well defined by decades of court precedent. Keep in mind, however, that judicial interpretations of the constitutional requirement of due process are constantly evolving. As new decisions are rendered and as the composition of the Court itself changes, major changes and additional refinements may occur.

[The police] are not perfect; we don't sign them up on some far-off planet and bring them into police service. They are products of society.
—Daryl Gates, former Los Angeles police chief

Search And Seizure

3 Describe the circumstances under which police officers may properly conduct searches or seize property.

The Fourth Amendment to the U.S. Constitution declares that people must be secure in their homes and in their persons against unreasonable searches and seizures. This amendment reads, "The right of the people to be secure in their persons, houses, papers, and effects, against unreasonable searches and seizures, shall not be violated, and no

Warrants shall issue, but upon probable cause, supported by Oath or affirmation, and particularly describing the place to be searched, and the persons or things to be seized." The Fourth Amendment, a part of the Bill of Rights, was adopted by Congress and became effective on December 15, 1791.

The language of the Fourth Amendment is familiar to all of us. "**Warrant**," "probable cause," and other phrases from the amendment are frequently cited in editorials, TV news shows, and daily conversations about **illegally seized evidence**. It is the interpretation of these phrases over time by the U.S. Supreme Court, however, that has given them the impact they have on the justice system today.

warrant
In criminal proceedings, a writ issued by a judicial officer directing a law enforcement officer to perform a specified act and affording the officer protection from damages if he or she performs it.

illegally seized evidence
Any evidence seized without regard to the principles of due process as described by the Bill of Rights. Most illegally seized evidence is the result of police searches conducted without a proper warrant or of improperly conducted interrogations.

The Exclusionary Rule

The first landmark case concerning search and seizure was that of *Weeks* v. *U.S.* (1914).[15] Freemont Weeks was suspected of using the U.S. mail to sell lottery tickets, a federal crime. Weeks was arrested, and federal agents went to his home to conduct a search. They had no search warrant, because at the time investigators did not routinely use warrants. They confiscated many incriminating items of evidence, as well as some of the suspect's personal possessions, including clothes, papers, books, and even candy.

Prior to trial, Weeks's attorney asked that the personal items be returned, claiming that they had been illegally seized under Fourth Amendment guarantees. A judge agreed and ordered the materials returned. On the basis of the evidence that was retained, however, Weeks was convicted in federal court and was sentenced to prison. He appealed his conviction through other courts, and his case eventually reached the U.S. Supreme Court. There, his lawyer reasoned that if some of his client's belongings had been illegally seized, then the remainder of them were also taken improperly. The Court agreed and overturned Weeks's earlier conviction.

The *Weeks* case forms the basis of what is now called the **exclusionary rule**, which holds that evidence illegally seized by the police cannot be used in a trial. The rule acts as a control over police behavior and specifically focuses on the failure of officers to obtain warrants authorizing them either to conduct searches or to effect arrests (especially where arrest may lead to the acquisition of incriminating statements or to the seizure of physical evidence).

exclusionary rule
The understanding, based on U.S. Supreme Court precedent, that incriminating information must be seized according to constitutional specifications of due process or it will not be allowed as evidence in a criminal trial.

The decision of the Supreme Court in the *Weeks* case was binding, at the time, only on federal officers because only federal agents were involved in the illegal seizure. Learn more about *Weeks* v. *U.S.* at **Library Extra 1**. See Figure 1 for more about the exclusionary rule and its development since *Weeks*.

Problems with Precedent

The *Weeks* case demonstrates the Supreme Court's power in enforcing what we have called the "rules of the game." It also lays bare the much more significant role that the Court plays in rule creation. Until the *Weeks* case was decided, federal law enforcement officers had little reason to think they were acting in violation of due process. Common practice had not required that they obtain a warrant before conducting searches. The rule that resulted from *Weeks* was new, and it would forever alter the enforcement activities of federal officers.

The *Weeks* case reveals that the present appeals system, focusing as it does on the "rules of the game," presents a ready-made channel for the guilty to go free. There is little doubt that Freemont Weeks had violated federal law; a jury had convicted him. Yet he escaped punishment because of the illegal behavior of the police—behavior that, until the Court ruled, had been widely regarded as legitimate. Even if the police knowingly violate the principles of due process, which they sometimes do, our sense of justice is compromised when the guilty go free. Famed Supreme Court Justice Benjamin Cardozo (1870–1938) once complained, "The criminal is to go free because the constable has blundered."

One solution to the problem would be to allow the Supreme Court to address theoretical questions involving issues of due process. Concerned supervisors and officials could ask how the Court would rule "if. . . ." As things now work, however, the Court can only address

FIGURE 1
The Exclusionary Rule

THE FOURTH AMENDMENT TO THE U.S. CONSTITUTION

The right of the people to be secure in their persons, houses, papers, and effects, against unreasonable searches and seizures, shall not be violated, and no Warrants shall issue, but upon probable cause, supported by Oath or affirmation, and particularly describing the place to be searched, and the persons or things to be seized.

Based upon the Fourth Amendment, **the Exclusionary Rule** holds that evidence of an offense that is collected or obtained by law enforcement officers in violation of a defendant's constitutional rights is inadmissible for use in a criminal prosecution in a court of law.

SIGNIFICANT CASES

***Weeks* v. *U.S.* (1914)**

Established the exclusionary rule at the federal level, holding that evidence that is illegally obtained cannot be used in a criminal trial; and that federal officers must have a valid warrant before conducting searches or seizing evidence. Prior to *Weeks*, common practice generally allowed all relevant evidence, no matter how it was obtained, to be used in court.

***Silverthorne Lumber Co.* v. *U.S.* (1920)**

Set forth the **Fruit of the Poisonous Tree Doctrine**, which says that just as illegally seized evidence cannot be used in a trial, neither can evidence that *derives* from an illegal search or seizure. Under this doctrine, complex cases developed after years of police investigative effort may be ruined if defense attorneys are able to demonstrate that the prosecution's case was originally based on a search or seizure that, at the time it occurred, violated due process.

***Mapp* v. *Ohio* (1961)**

Applied the exclusionary rule to criminal prosecutions at the state level. The Court held that the due process clause of the Fourteenth Amendment to the U.S. Constitution makes Fourth Amendment provisions applicable to state proceedings.

SUBSTANTIAL SOCIAL COSTS

***United States* v. *Leon* (1984)** and ***Hudson* v. *Michigan* (2006)**
Recognized that the exclusionary rule generates "substantial social costs," which may include letting the guilty go free and setting the dangerous at large.

EXCEPTIONS TO THE EXCLUSIONARY RULE

THE GOOD-FAITH EXCEPTION

***U.S.* v. *Leon* (1984)**
Allowed evidence that officers had seized in "reasonable good faith" to be used in court, even though the search was later ruled illegal.

***Illinois* v. *Krull* (1987)**
The good-faith exception applied to a warrantless search supported by state law even though the state statute was later found to violate the Fourth Amendment.

***Maryland* v. *Garrison* (1987)**
The use of evidence obtained by officers with a search warrant that was inaccurate in its specifics was allowed.

THE PLAIN-VIEW DOCTRINE

***Harris* v. *U.S.* (1968)**

Police officers have the opportunity to begin investigations or to confiscate evidence, without a warrant, based on what they find in plain view and open to public inspection.

CLERICAL ERRORS EXCEPTION

***Arizona* v. *Evans* (1995)**
A traffic stop that led to the seizure of marijuana was legal even though officers conducted the stop based on an arrest warrant that should have been deleted from the computer database to which they had access.

***Herring* v. *U.S.* (2009)**
When police mistakes leading to an unlawful search are the result of isolated negligence rather than systemic error or reckless disregard of constitutional requirements, the exclusionary rule does not apply.

EMERGENCY SEARCHES OF PROPERTY/EMERGENCY ENTRY

***Brigham City* v. *Stuart* (2006)**
Certain emergencies may justify a police officer's decision to search or enter premises without a warrant.

writ of *certiorari*
A writ issued from an appellate court for the purpose of obtaining from a lower court the record of its proceedings in a particular case. In some states, this writ is the mechanism for discretionary review. A request for review is made by petitioning for a writ of *certiorari*, and the granting of review is indicated by the issuance of the writ.

real cases and does so on a **writ of *certiorari***, in which the Court orders the record of a lower court case to be prepared for review.

The Fruit of the Poisonous Tree Doctrine

The Court continued to build on the rules concerning evidence with its decision in *Silverthorne Lumber Co.* v. *U.S.* (1920).[16] The case against the Silverthornes, owners of a lumberyard, was built on evidence that was illegally seized. Although the tainted evidence was itself not

> The public safety exception [to the exclusionary rule] was intended to protect the police, as well as the public, from danger.
> —*U.S.* v. *Brady* (1987)

used in court, its "fruits" (later evidence that derived from the illegal seizure) were and the Silverthornes were convicted. The Supreme Court overturned the decision, holding that any evidence that derives from a seizure that was in itself illegal cannot be used at trial. The *Silverthorne* case articulated a new principle of due process that today we call the **fruit of the poisonous tree doctrine**. This doctrine is potentially far reaching. Complex cases developed after years of police investigative effort may be ruined if defense attorneys are able to demonstrate that the prosecution's case was originally based on a search or seizure that violated due process. In such cases, it is likely that all evidence will be declared "tainted" and will become useless.

▲ An officer patting down a suspect. The legal environment surrounding the police helps ensure proper official conduct. In a stop like this, inappropriate behavior on the part of the officer can later become the basis for civil or criminal action against the officer and the police department. What might constitute inappropriate behavior?
John Boykin/PhotoEdit Inc.

fruit of the poisonous tree doctrine
A legal principle that excludes from introduction at trial any evidence later developed as a result of an illegal search or seizure.

The Warren Court (1953–1969)

Before the 1960s, the U.S. Supreme Court intruded only infrequently on the overall operation of the criminal justice system at the state and local levels. As one author has observed, however, the 1960s were a time of youthful idealism, and "without the distraction of a depression or world war, individual liberties were examined at all levels of society."[17] While the exclusionary rule became an overriding consideration in federal law enforcement from the time that it was first defined by the Supreme Court in the *Weeks* case in 1914, it was not until 1961 that the Court, under Chief Justice Earl Warren, decided a case that was to change the face of American law enforcement forever. That case, *Mapp* v. *Ohio* (1961),[18] made the exclusionary rule applicable to criminal prosecutions at the state level. Beginning with the now-famous *Mapp* case, the Warren Court charted a course that would guarantee nationwide recognition of individual rights, as it understood them, by agencies at all levels of the criminal justice system. Learn more about the case of *Mapp* v. *Ohio* at **Library Extra 2**.

Searches Incident to Arrest

Another important Warren-era case, that of *Chimel* v. *California* (1969),[19] involved both arrest and search activities by local law enforcement officers. Ted Chimel was convicted of the burglary of a coin shop based on evidence gathered at his home, where he was arrested. Officers, armed with an arrest warrant but not a search warrant, took Chimel into custody when they arrived at his residence and then searched his entire three-bedroom house, including the attic, a small workshop, and the garage. Although officers realized that the search might be challenged in court, they justified it by claiming that it was conducted not so much to uncover evidence but as part of the arrest process. Searches that are conducted incident to arrest, they argued, are necessary for the officers' protection and should not require a search warrant. Coins taken from the burglarized coin shop were found in various places in Chimel's residence, including the garage, and were presented as evidence against him at trial.

Chimel's appeal eventually reached the U.S. Supreme Court, which ruled that the search of Chimel's residence, although incident to arrest, became invalid when it went beyond the person arrested and the area subject to that person's "immediate control." The thrust of the Court's decision was that searches during arrest can be made to protect arresting officers but that without a search warrant, their scope must be strongly circumscribed. The legal implications of *Chimel* v. *California* are summarized in Table 2.

Since the early days of the exclusionary rule, other court decisions have highlighted the fact that "the Fourth Amendment protects people, not places."[20] In other words, although the commonly heard claim that "a person's home is his or her castle" has a great deal of validity within the context of constitutional law, people can have a reasonable expectation to privacy in "homes" of many descriptions. Apartments, duplex dwellings, motel rooms—even the cardboard boxes or makeshift tents of the homeless—can all become protected places under the Fourth Amendment. In *Minnesota* v. *Olson* (1990),[21] for example, the U.S. Supreme Court extended the protection against warrantless searches to overnight guests residing in the home of another. The capacity to claim the protection of the Fourth Amendment, said the Court, depends on whether the *person* who makes that claim has a legitimate expectation of privacy in the place searched.

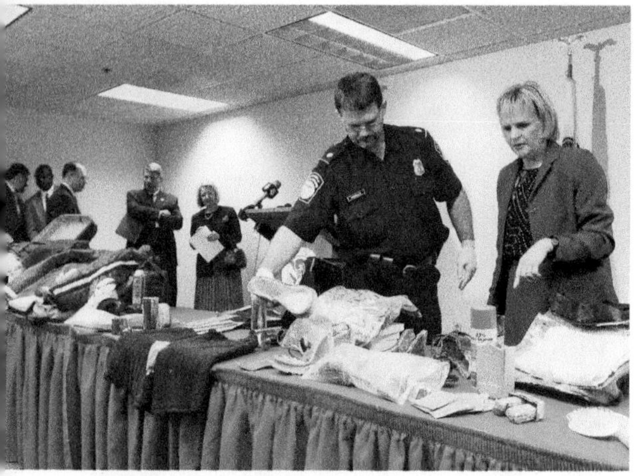

▲ Police officers examining suspected controlled substances after a raid. The exclusionary rule means that illegally gathered evidence cannot be used later in court, requiring that police officers pay close attention to how they gather and handle evidence. How did the exclusionary rule come into being?
Chris O'Meara/AP Wide World Photos

TABLE 2
Implications of *Chimel* v. *California* (1969)

What Arresting Officers May Search
The defendant
The physical area within easy reach of the defendant
Valid Reasons for Conducting a Search
To protect the arresting officers
To prevent evidence from being destroyed
To keep the defendant from escaping
When a Search Becomes Illegal
When it goes beyond the defendant and the area within the defendant's immediate control
When it is conducted for other than a valid reason

In 1998, in the case of *Minnesota* v. *Carter*,[22] the Court held that for a defendant to be entitled to Fourth Amendment protection, "he must demonstrate that he personally has an expectation of privacy in the place searched, and that his expectation is reasonable." The Court noted that "the extent to which the Amendment protects people may depend upon where those people are. While an overnight guest may have a legitimate expectation of privacy in someone else's home . . . one who is merely present with the consent of the householder may not." Hence an appliance repair person visiting a residence is unlikely to be accorded privacy protection while on the job.

In 2006, in the case of *Georgia* v. *Randolph*,[23] the Court ruled that police officers may not enter a home to conduct a warrrantless search if one resident gives permission but the other says no. The *Randolph* ruling was a narrow one and centered on the stated refusal by a physically present co-occupant to permit warrantless entry in the absence of evidence of physical abuse or other circumstances that might otherwise justify an immediate police entry.[24]

The Burger Court (1969–1986) and the Rehnquist Court (1986–2005)

During the 1980s and 1990s, the United States experienced a swing toward conservatism, giving rise to a renewed concern with protecting the interests—financial and otherwise—of those who live within the law. The Reagan–Bush years, and the popularity of the two presidents who many thought embodied "old-fashioned" values, reflected the tenor of a nation seeking a return to "simpler," less volatile times.

Throughout the late 1980s, the U.S. Supreme Court mirrored the nation's conservative tenor by distancing itself from some earlier decisions of the Warren Court. While the Warren Court embodied the individual-rights heyday in Court jurisprudence, Court decisions beginning in the 1970s were generally supportive of a "greater good era"—one in which the justices increasingly acknowledged the importance of social order and communal safety. Under Chief Justice Warren E. Burger, the new Court adhered to the principle that criminal defendants who claimed violations of their due process rights needed to bear most of the responsibility of showing that police went beyond the law in the performance of their duties. This tenet is still held by the Court today.

good-faith exception
An exception to the exclusionary rule. Law enforcement officers who conduct a search or who seize evidence on the basis of good faith (that is, when they believe they are operating according to the dictates of the law) and who later discover that a mistake was made (perhaps in the format of the application for a search warrant) may still use the seized evidence in court.

Good-Faith Exceptions to the Exclusionary Rule

The Burger Court, which held sway from 1969 until 1986, "chipped away" at the strict application of the exclusionary rule originally set forth in the *Weeks* and *Silverthorne* cases. In the 1984 case of *U.S.* v. *Leon*,[25] the Court recognized what has come to be called the **good-faith exception** to the exclusionary rule. In this case, the Court modified the exclusionary rule to allow evidence that officers had seized in "reasonable good faith" to be used in court, even though the search was later ruled illegal. The suspect, Alberto Leon, was placed under surveillance for drug trafficking following a tip from a confidential informant. Burbank (California) Police Department investigators applied for a search warrant based on information gleaned from the surveillance, believing they were in compliance with the Fourth Amendment requirement that "no Warrants shall issue, but upon probable cause."

Probable cause is a tricky but important concept. Its legal criteria are based on facts and circumstances that would cause a reasonable person to believe that a particular other person has committed a specific crime. Before a warrant can be issued, police officers must satisfactorily demonstrate probable cause in a written affidavit to a magistrate[26]—a low-level judge who ensures that the police establish the probable cause needed for warrants to be obtained. Upon a demonstration of probable cause, the magistrate will issue a warrant authorizing law enforcement officers to effect an arrest or conduct a search.

probable cause
A set of facts and circumstances that would induce a reasonably intelligent and prudent person to believe that a particular other person has committed a specific crime. Also, reasonable grounds to make or believe an accusation. Probable cause refers to the necessary level of belief that would allow for police seizures (arrests) of individuals and full searches of dwellings, vehicles, and possessions.

In *U.S.* v. *Leon*, a warrant was issued, and a search of Leon's three residences yielded a large amount of drugs and other evidence. Although Leon was convicted of drug trafficking, a later ruling in a federal district court resulted in the suppression of evidence against him on the basis that the original affidavit prepared by the police had not, in the opinion of the reviewing court, been sufficient to establish probable cause.

The federal government petitioned the U.S. Supreme Court to consider whether evidence gathered by officers acting in good faith as to the validity of a warrant should fairly be excluded at trial. The impending modification of the exclusionary rule was presaged in the first paragraph of the Court's written decision: "When law enforcement officers have acted in objective good faith or their transgressions have been minor, the magnitude of the benefit conferred on . . . guilty defendants offends basic concepts of the criminal justice system." Reflecting the renewed conservatism of the Burger Court, the justices found for the government and reinstated Leon's conviction.

In that same year, the Supreme Court case of *Massachusetts* v. *Sheppard* (1984)[27] further reinforced the concept of good faith. In the *Sheppard* case, officers executed a search warrant that failed to describe accurately the property to be seized. Although they were aware of the error, a magistrate had assured them that the warrant was valid. After the seizure was complete and a conviction had been obtained, the Massachusetts Supreme Judicial Court reversed the finding of the trial court. Upon appeal, the U.S. Supreme Court reiterated the good-faith exception and reinstated the original conviction.

The cases of *Leon* and *Sheppard* represented a clear reversal of the Warren Court's philosophy, and the trend continued with the 1987 case of *Illinois* v. *Krull*.[28] In *Krull*, the Court, now under the leadership of Chief Justice William H. Rehnquist, held that the good-faith exception applied to a warrantless search supported by state law even though the state statute was later found to violate the Fourth Amendment. Similarly, another 1987 Supreme Court case, *Maryland* v. *Garrison*,[29] supported the use of evidence obtained with a search warrant that was inaccurate in its specifics. In *Garrison*, officers had procured a warrant to search an apartment, believing it was the only dwelling on the building's third floor. After searching the entire floor, they discovered that it housed more than one apartment. Even so, evidence acquired in the search was held to be admissible based on the reasonable mistake of the officers.

The 1990 case of *Illinois* v. *Rodriguez*[30] further diminished the scope of the exclusionary rule. In *Rodriguez*, a badly beaten woman named Gail Fischer complained to police that she had been assaulted in a Chicago apartment. Fischer led police to the apartment—which she indicated she shared with the defendant—produced a key, and opened the door to the dwelling. Inside, investigators found the defendant, Edward Rodriguez, asleep on a bed, with drug paraphernalia and cocaine spread around him. Rodriguez was arrested and charged with assault and possession of a controlled substance.

Before a warrant can be issued, police officers must demonstrate probable cause.

Upon appeal, Rodriguez demonstrated that Fischer had not lived with him for at least a month and argued that she could no longer be said to have legal control over the apartment. Hence, the defense claimed, Fischer had no authority to provide investigators with access to the dwelling. According to arguments made by the defense, the evidence, which had been obtained without a warrant, had not been properly seized. The Supreme Court disagreed, ruling that "even if Fischer did not possess common authority over the premises, there was no Fourth Amendment violation if the police *reasonably believed* at the time of their entry that Fischer possessed the authority to consent."

The touchstone of the Fourth Amendment is reasonableness. The Fourth Amendment does not proscribe all state-initiated searches and seizures. It merely proscribes those which are unreasonable.
—*Florida v. Jimeno* (1991)

In 1995, in the case of *Arizona* v. *Evans*,[31] the U.S. Supreme Court created a "computer errors exception" to the exclusionary rule, holding that a traffic stop that led to the seizure of marijuana was legal even though officers conducted the stop based on an arrest warrant that should have been deleted from the computer database to which they had access. The arrest warrant reported to the officers by their computer had actually been quashed a few weeks earlier but, through the oversight of a court employee, had never been removed from the database.

In reaching its decision, the high court reasoned that police officers could not be held responsible for a clerical error made by a court worker and concluded that the arresting officers had acted in good faith based on the information available to them at the time of the arrest. In addition, the majority opinion said that "the rule excluding evidence obtained without a warrant was intended to deter police misconduct, not mistakes by court employees." In 2009, in the case of *Herring* v. *U.S.*,[32] the Court reinforced its ruling in *Evans*, holding that "when police mistakes leading to an unlawful search are the result of isolated negligence . . . rather than systemic error or reckless disregard of constitutional requirements, the exclusionary rule does not apply." A general listing of established exceptions to the exclusionary rule, along with other investigative powers created by court precedent, is provided in Table 3.

During Rehnquist's tenure as chief justice, the Court invoked a characteristically conservative approach to many important criminal justice issues—from limiting the exclusionary rule[33] and generally broadening police powers to sharply limiting the opportunities for state prisoners to bring appeals in federal courts.[34] Preventive detention, "no knock" police searches,[35] the death penalty,[36] and habitual offender statutes[37] (often known as *three-strikes laws*) all found decisive support under Chief Justice Rehnquist.[38] The particular cases in which the Court addressed these issues are discussed elsewhere in this text.

Following Rehnquist's death in 2005, John G. Roberts, Jr., became the nation's seventeenth chief justice. Roberts had previously served as a judge on the U.S. Court of Appeals for the District of Columbia Circuit.

The Plain-View Doctrine

plain view
A legal term describing the ready visibility of objects that might be seized as evidence during a search by police in the absence of a search warrant specifying the seizure of those objects. To lawfully seize evidence in plain view, officers must have a legal right to be in the viewing area and must have cause to believe that the evidence is somehow associated with criminal activity.

Police officers have the opportunity to begin investigations or to confiscate evidence, without a warrant, based on what they find in **plain view** and open to public inspection. The plain-view doctrine was succinctly stated in the U.S. Supreme Court case of *Harris* v. *U.S.* (1968),[39] in which a police officer inventorying an impounded vehicle discovered evidence of a robbery.[40] In the *Harris* case, the Court ruled that "objects falling in the plain view of an officer who has a right to be in the position to have that view are subject to seizure and may be introduced in evidence."[41]

The plain-view doctrine is applicable in common situations such as crimes in progress, fires, accidents, and other emergencies. A police officer responding to a call for assistance, for example, might enter a residence intending to provide aid to an injured person and find drugs or other contraband in plain view. If so, the officer would be within his or her legitimate authority to confiscate the materials and to effect an arrest if the owner can be identified.

The plain-view doctrine applies only to sightings by the police under legal circumstances—that is, in places where the police have a legitimate right to be and, typically, only if the sighting was coincidental. Similarly, the incriminating nature of the evidence seized must have been "immediately apparent" to the officers making the seizure.[42] If officers conspired to avoid the necessity for a search warrant by helping to create a plain-view situation through surveillance, duplicity, or other means, the doctrine likely would not apply.

The plain-view doctrine was restricted by later federal court decisions. In the 1982 case of *U.S.* v. *Irizarry*,[43] the First Circuit Court of Appeals held that officers could not move objects to gain a view of evidence otherwise hidden from view. In the Supreme Court case of *Arizona* v. *Hicks* (1987),[44] the requirement that evidence be in plain view, without requiring officers (who did not have a warrant but who had been invited into a residence) to move or dislodge objects, was reiterated.

TABLE 3
Selected Investigative Activities Supported by Court Precedent

This Police Power	Is Supported By
Arrest based on isolated clerical error or negligence	*Herring* v. *U.S.* (2009) *Arizona* v. *Evans* (1995)
Authority to enter and/or search an "open field" without a warrant	*U.S.* v. *Dunn* (1987) *Oliver* v. *U.S.* (1984) *Hester* v. *U.S.* (1924)
Authority to search incident to arrest and/or to conduct a protective sweep in conjunction with an in-home arrest	*Maryland* v. *Buie* (1990) *U.S.* v. *Edwards* (1974) *Chimel* v. *California* (1969)
Gathering of incriminating evidence during interrogation in noncustodial circumstances	*Yarborough* v. *Alvarado* (2004) *Thompson* v. *Keohane* (1996) *Stansbury* v. *California* (1994) *U.S.* v. *Mendenhall* (1980) *Beckwith* v. *U.S.* (1976)
Gathering of incriminating evidence during *Miranda*-less custodial interrogation	*Montejo* v. *Louisiana* (2009) *U.S.* v. *Patane* (2004)
Inevitable discovery of evidence	*Nix* v. *Williams* (1984)
"No knock" searches or quick entry	*Brigham City* v. *Stuart* (2006) *Hudson* v. *Michigan* (2006) *U.S.* v. *Barnes* (2003) *Richards* v. *Wisconsin* (1997) *Wilson* v. *Arkansas* (1995)
Prompt action in the face of threat to public or personal safety or destruction of evidence	*U.S.* v. *Banks* (2003) *Borchardt* v. *U.S.* (1987) *New York* v. *Quarles* (1984) *Warden* v. *Hayden* (1967)
Seizure of evidence in good faith, even in the face of some exclusionary rule violations	*Illinois* v. *Krull* (1987) *U.S.* v. *Leon* (1984)
Seizure of evidence in plain view	*Horton* v. *California* (1990) *Coolidge* v. *New Hampshire* (1971) *Harris* v. *U.S.* (1968)
Stop and frisk/request personal identification	*Arizona* v. *Johnson* (2009) *Hiibel* v. *Sixth Judicial District Court of Nevada* (2004) *Terry* v. *Ohio* (1968)
Use of police informants in jail cells	*Arizona* v. *Fulminante* (1991) *Illinois* v. *Perkins* (1990) *Kuhlmann* v. *Wilson* (1986)
Warrantless naked-eye aerial observation of open areas and/or greenhouses	*Florida* v. *Riley* (1989) *California* v. *Ciraolo* (1986)
Warrantless search incident to a lawful arrest	*U.S.* v. *Rabinowitz* (1950)
Warrantless seizure of abandoned materials and refuse	*California* v. *Greenwood* (1988)
Warrantless vehicle search where probable cause exists to believe that the vehicle contains contraband and/or that the occupants have been lawfully arrested	*Thornton* v. *U.S.* (2004) *Ornelas* v. *U.S.* (1996) *California* v. *Acevedo* (1991) *California* v. *Carney* (1985) *U.S.* v. *Ross* (1982) *New York* v. *Belton* (1981) *Carroll* v. *U.S.* (1925)

CJ Exhibit 1
Plain-View Requirements

Following the opinion of the U.S. Supreme Court in the case of *Horton* v. *California* (1990), items seized under the plain-view doctrine may be admissible as evidence in a court of law if *both* of the following conditions are met:

1. The officer who seized the evidence was in the viewing area lawfully.
2. The officer had probable cause to believe that the evidence was somehow associated with criminal activity.

Emergencies may justify a police officer's decision to search or enter premises without a warrant.

Most evidence seized under the plain-view doctrine is discovered "inadvertently"—that is, by accident.[45] However, in 1990, the U.S. Supreme Court ruled in the case of *Horton* v. *California*[46] that "even though inadvertence *is* a characteristic of most legitimate 'plain view' seizures, it is not a necessary condition."[47] In the *Horton* case, a warrant was issued authorizing the search of Terry Brice Horton's home for stolen jewelry. The affidavit, completed by the officer who requested the warrant, alluded to an Uzi submachine gun and a stun gun—weapons purportedly used in the jewelry robbery. It did not request that those weapons be listed on the search warrant. Officers searched the defendant's home but did not find the stolen jewelry. They did, however, seize a number of weapons, among them an Uzi, two stun guns, and a .38-caliber revolver. Horton was convicted of robbery in a trial in which the seized weapons were introduced into evidence. He appealed his conviction, claiming that officers had reason to believe that the weapons were in his home at the time of the search, so they were not seized inadvertently. His appeal was rejected by the Court. As a result of the *Horton* case, inadvertence is no longer considered a condition necessary to ensure the legitimacy of a seizure that results when evidence other than that listed in a search warrant is discovered. See CJ Exhibit 1 for more on evidence and the plain-view doctrine.

Emergency Searches of Property and Emergency Entry

Certain emergencies may justify a police officer's decision to search or enter premises without a warrant. In 2006, for example, in the case of *Brigham City* v. *Stuart*,[48] the Court recognized the need for emergency warrantless entries under certain circumstances when it ruled that police officers "may enter a home without a warrant when they have an objectively reasonable basis for believing that an occupant is seriously injured or imminently threatened with such injury." The case involved police entry into a private home to break up a fight.

According to the Legal Counsel Division of the Federal Bureau of Investigation (FBI), there are three threats that "provide justification for emergency warrantless action."[49] They are clear dangers (1) to life, (2) of escape, and (3) of the removal or destruction of evidence. Any one of these situations may create an exception to the Fourth Amendment's requirement of a search warrant.

emergency search
A search conducted by the police without a warrant, which is justified on the basis of some immediate and overriding need, such as public safety, the likely escape of a dangerous suspect, or the removal or destruction of evidence.

Emergency searches, or those conducted without a warrant when special needs arise, are legally termed *exigent circumstances searches*. When emergencies necessitate a quick search of premises, however, law enforcement officers are responsible for demonstrating that a dire situation existed that justified their actions. Failure to do so successfully in court will, of course, taint any seized evidence and make it unusable.

The U.S. Supreme Court first recognized the need for emergency searches in 1967 in the case of *Warden* v. *Hayden*.[50] In that case, the Court approved the warrantless search of a residence following reports that an armed robber had fled into the building. In *Mincey* v. *Arizona* (1978),[51] the Supreme Court held that "the Fourth Amendment does not require police officers to delay in the course of an investigation if to do so would gravely endanger their lives or the lives of others."[52]

A 1990 decision, rendered in the case of *Maryland* v. *Buie*,[53] extended the authority of police to search locations in a house where a potentially dangerous person could hide while an arrest warrant is being served. The *Buie* decision was meant primarily to protect investigators from potential danger and can apply even when officers lack a warrant, probable cause, or even reasonable suspicion.

In 1995, in the case of *Wilson* v. *Arkansas*,[54] the U.S. Supreme Court ruled that police officers generally must knock and announce their identity before entering a dwelling or other premises, even when armed with a search warrant. Under certain emergency circumstances, however, exceptions may be made, and officers may not need to knock or to identify themselves before entering.[55] In *Wilson*, the Court added that the Fourth Amendment requirement that searches be reasonable "should not be read to mandate a rigid rule of announcement that ignores countervailing law enforcement interests." Officers need not announce themselves, the Court said, when suspects may be in the process of destroying evidence, officers are pursuing a recently escaped arrestee, or officers' lives may be endangered by such an announcement. Because the *Wilson* case involved an appeal from a drug dealer who was apprehended by police officers who entered her unlocked house while she was flushing marijuana down a toilet, some said that it establishes a "drug-law exception" to the knock-and-announce requirement.

In 1997, in *Richards* v. *Wisconsin*,[56] the Supreme Court clarified its position on "no knock" exceptions, saying that individual courts have the duty in each case to "determine whether the facts and circumstances of the particular entry justified dispensing with the requirement." The Court went on to say that "[a] 'no knock' entry is justified when the police have a reasonable suspicion that knocking and announcing their presence, under the particular circumstances, would be dangerous or futile, or that it would inhibit the effective investigation of the crime." The Court noted, "This standard strikes the appropriate balance between the legitimate law enforcement concerns at issue in the execution of search warrants and the individual privacy interests affected by no knock entries."

▲ Latasha Smith, who was arrested for failing to appear in court for a previous misdemeanor violation. Although the concept of plain view is difficult to define, Smith provides a personal example of the concept. After Dallas narcotics officers searched the house behind her for crack cocaine, they turned their attention to Smith and discovered the outstanding charges. How would you explain the concept of plain view?
AP Wide World Photos

In 2001, in the case of *Illinois* v. *McArthur*,[57] the U.S. Supreme Court ruled that police officers with probable cause to believe that a home contains contraband or evidence of criminal activity may reasonably prevent a suspect found outside the home from reentering it while they apply for a search warrant. In 2003, in a case involving drug possession, the Court held that a 15- to 20-second wait after officers knocked, announced themselves, and requested entry was sufficient to satisfy Fourth Amendment requirements.[58]

In the 2006 case of *Hudson* v. *Michigan*,[59] the Court surprised many when it ruled that evidence found by police officers who enter a home to execute a warrant without first following the knock-and-announce requirement can be used at trial despite that constitutional violation. In the words of the Court, "The interests protected by the knock-and-announce rule include human life and limb (because an unannounced entry may provoke violence from a surprised resident), property (because citizens presumably would open the door upon an announcement, whereas a forcible entry may destroy it), and privacy and dignity of the sort that can be offended by a sudden entrance." But, said the Court, "the rule has never protected one's interest in preventing the government from seeing or taking evidence described in a warrant." The justices reasoned that the social costs of strictly adhering to the knock-and-announce rule are considerable and may include "the grave adverse consequence that excluding relevant incriminating evidence always entails—the risk of releasing dangerous criminals." In a ruling that some said signaled a new era of lessened restraints on the police, the Court's majority opinion said that since the interests violated by ignoring the knock-and-announce rule "have nothing to do with the seizure of the evidence, the exclusionary rule is inapplicable."

Anticipatory Warrants

Anticipatory warrants are search warrants issued on the basis of probable cause to believe that evidence of a crime, while not currently at the place described, will likely be there when the warrant is executed. Such warrants anticipate the presence of contraband or other evidence of criminal culpability but do not claim that the evidence is present at the time that the warrant is requested or issued.

anticipatory warrant
A search warrant issued on the basis of probable cause to believe that evidence of a crime, while not currently at the place described, will likely be there when the warrant is executed.

Anticipatory warrants are no different in principle from ordinary search warrants. They require an issuing magistrate to determine that it is probable that contraband, evidence of a crime, or a fugitive will be on the described premises when the warrant is executed.

Career Profile
Patrol Officer

Name: Timothy D. Radtke

Position: Patrol Officer, San Diego, California

Colleges attended: Winona State University (BS); University of Nevada, Las Vegas (MA)

Major: Criminal justice

Year hired: 2008

Please give a brief description of your job. Within a specified area of the city, I respond to radio calls for police service and perform self-initiated activities such as traffic stops and citizen contacts.

What appealed to you most about the position when you applied for it? While pursuing my degrees, I worked closely with two police departments. The officers there inspired me to commit my life to a cause greater than myself—protecting communities. I was eager to put the knowledge I obtained through my education to practical use, to work closely with the community and apply the community-oriented policing and problem-oriented policing strategies I learned during my academic studies.

How would you describe the interview process? The testing process was strenuous. There were eight different tests: written test, preinvestigation questionnaire, physical ability test, comprehensive background investigation, polygraph, appointing authority interview, psychological screening, and medical exam. The most challenging was the appointing authority interview, which was conducted by a lieutenant and a sergeant. They asked questions about my background and what I had done to prepare to serve as a police officer. I was asked to respond to a series of scenarios that police officers often encounter in the field. This process helped them determine whether I could quickly find a logical and appropriate response when presented with an unexpected or stressful situation.

What is a typical day like? Patrol officers begin with "lineup," in which they are briefed about recent crimes and events and assigned to the specific patrol beat they will work throughout their shift. Patrol officers must be prepared to handle the unexpected. One day they may respond to a domestic disturbance, the next help to establish a DUI checkpoint to deter drunk drivers, and the next be asked to locate warrant suspects.

What qualities/characteristics are most helpful for this job? A successful officer must know how to speak with people. The people they interact with daily often need immediate help or have difficulty controlling their emotions. An officer may be faced with an individual who is attempting suicide or an individual who is angry and showing signs of assaultive behavior, or [the officer may be] called upon to interview a child who has suffered abuse. The ability to speak tactfully and quickly build rapport with others is crucial.

What is a typical starting salary? Between $40,000 and $50,000.

What is the salary potential as you move up into higher-level jobs? An officer's salary will increase after graduating from the academy and when promoted within the department. Those with a BA or MA will also receive percentage increases in pay.

What career advice would you give someone in college beginning studies in criminal justice? Classroom instruction in college will help students understand the basics of police work and give them the skills to interpret and appropriately apply laws. It will also increase students' problem-solving and critical thinking skills, which are necessary for finding solutions to the complex problems officers encounter daily.

Source: Reprinted with permission of Timothy D. Radtke. Photo courtesy of Timothy D. Radtke. Logo courtesy University of Nevada at Las Vegas.

The constitutionality of anticipatory warrants was affirmed in 2006, in the U.S. Supreme Court case of *U.S.* v. *Grubbs*. In *Grubbs*,[60] an anticipatory search warrant had been issued for Grubbs's house based on a federal officer's affidavit stating that the warrant would not be executed until a parcel containing a videotape of child pornography—which Grubbs had ordered from an undercover postal inspector—was received at and physically taken into Grubbs's residence. After the package was delivered, the anticipatory search warrant was executed, the videotape seized, and Grubbs arrested.

Arrest

4 Define *arrest*, and describe how popular depictions of the arrest process may not be consistent with legal understandings of the term.

Officers seize not only property but people as well, a process referred to as *arrest*. Most people think of arrest in terms of what they see on popular TV crime shows: The suspect is chased, subdued, and "cuffed" after committing some loathsome act in view of the camera. Some arrests do occur that way. In reality, however, most arrests are far more mundane.

arrest
The act of taking an adult or juvenile into physical custody by authority of law for the purpose of charging the person with a criminal offense, a delinquent act, or a status offense, terminating with the recording of a specific offense. Technically, an arrest occurs whenever a law enforcement officer curtails a person's freedom to leave.

In technical terms, an **arrest** occurs whenever a law enforcement officer restricts a person's freedom to leave. The officer may not yell, "You're under arrest!" No *Miranda* warnings may be offered, and in fact, the suspect may not even consider himself or herself to be in custody. Arrests, and the decisions to enforce them, evolve as the situations between officers and suspects develop. A situation usually begins with polite conversation and a request by the officer for information. Only when the suspect tries to leave and tests the limits of the police response may the suspect discover that he or she is really in custody. In the 1980 case of *U.S.* v. *Mendenhall*,[61] Justice Potter Stewart set forth the "free to leave" test for determining whether a person has been arrested. Stewart wrote, "A person has been 'seized' within the meaning of the Fourth Amendment only if in view of all the circumstances surrounding the incident, a reasonable person would have believed that he was not free to leave." The "free to leave" test has been repeatedly adopted by the Court as the test for a seizure. In 1994, in the case of *Stansbury* v. *California*,[62] the Court once again used such a test in determining the point at which an arrest had been made. In *Stansbury*, where the focus was on the interrogation of a suspected child molester and murderer, the Court ruled, "In determining whether an individual was in custody, a court must examine all of the circumstances surrounding the interrogation, but the ultimate inquiry is simply whether there [was] a formal arrest or restraint on freedom of movement of the degree associated with a formal arrest."

Youth and inexperience do not automatically undermine a reasonable person's ability to assess when someone is free to leave. In the 2004 case of *Yarborough* v. *Alvarado*,[63] the U.S. Supreme Court found that a 17-year-old boy's two-hour interrogation in a police station without a *Miranda* advisement was not custodial, even though the boy confessed to his involvement in a murder and was later arrested. The boy, said the Court, had not actually been in police custody even though he was in a building used by the police for questioning, because actions taken by the interviewing officer indicated that the juvenile had been free to leave. Whether a person is actually free to leave, said the Court, can only be determined by examining the totality of the circumstances surrounding the interrogation.[64]

The 2005 U.S. Supreme Court case of *Muehler* v. *Mena*[65] made clear that an officer's authority to detain occupants of a dwelling incident to the execution of a valid search warrant is absolute and unqualified and does not require any justification beyond the warrant itself—even when the occupants are not suspected of any wrongdoing. In other words, officers who are conducting a lawful search under the authority of a warrant may detain individuals found occupying the premises being searched in order to prevent flights in the event incriminating evidence is found, to minimize the risk of harm to the officers, and simply to facilitate the search itself.[66]

> You can only protect your liberties in this world by protecting the other man's freedom.
>
> —Clarence Darrow (1857–1938)

Arrests that follow the questioning of a suspect are probably the most common type of arrest. When the decision to arrest is reached, the officer has come to the conclusion that a crime has been committed and that the suspect is probably the one who committed it. The presence of these elements constitutes the probable cause needed for an arrest. Probable cause is the minimum standard necessary for an arrest under any circumstances.

Arrests may also occur when an officer comes upon a crime in progress. Such situations often require apprehension of the offender to ensure the safety of the public. Most arrests made during crimes in progress, however, are for misdemeanors rather than felonies. In fact, many states do not allow arrest for a misdemeanor unless it is committed in the presence of an officer, since visible crimes in progress clearly provide the probable cause necessary for an arrest. In 2001, in a case that made headlines nationwide,[67] the U.S. Supreme Court upheld a warrantless arrest made by Lago Vista (Texas) Patrolman Bart Turek for a seat belt violation. In what many saw as an unreasonable exercise of discretion, Turek stopped and then arrested Gail Atwater, a young local woman whom he observed driving a pickup truck in which she and her two small children (ages three and five) were unbelted. Facts in the case showed that Turek verbally berated the woman after stopping her vehicle and that he handcuffed her, placed her in his squad car, and drove her to the local police station, where she was made to remove her shoes, jewelry, and eyeglasses and empty her pockets. Officers took her "mug shot" and placed her alone in a jail cell for about an hour, after which she was taken before a magistrate and released on $310 bond. Atwater was charged with a misdemeanor violation of Texas seat belt law. She later pleaded no contest and paid a $50 fine. Soon afterward, she and her husband filed a Section 1983 lawsuit against the officer, his department, and the police chief, alleging that the actions of the officer violated Atwater's Fourth Amendment right to be free from unreasonable seizures. The Court, however, concluded that "the Fourth Amendment does not forbid a warrantless arrest for a minor criminal offense, such as a misdemeanor seatbelt violation punishable only by a fine."

CJ News
Legal Issues Being Raised in Subway Searches

Even more than security experts and intelligence analysts, one group of employees has become central to the new program of bag searches in the transit networks of the New York region: lawyers.

The decision in July 2005 to have police officers inspect the belongings of thousands of subway riders has opened a thicket of legal and constitutional issues, involving criminal procedure, transit security and concerns about potential misuse of the new tactic.

Donna Lieberman, the executive director of the New York Civil Liberties Union, said the organization had begun work on a federal lawsuit, which could be filed soon. Such a challenge will most likely claim that the policy violates the Fourth Amendment's prohibition against "unreasonable searches and seizures.". . .

"It is by no means a foregone conclusion that these searches will be found reasonable under the Fourth Amendment," said Tracey Maclin, a law professor at Boston University. "The number of people involved, the nature and severity of the intrusions, and the uncertain duration of the searches all make this fundamentally very different from anything we have seen before."

▲ A police officer checking the bag of a subway rider at New York City's 42nd Street/Bryant Park station. Should random bag checks be permitted, or do they unfairly impinge on the rights of people wanting to ride the subway?
John Marshall Mantel/AP Wide World Photos

At least three United States Supreme Court cases will probably influence any judge assessing the searches.

In 1979, in *Delaware* v. *Prouse*, the court held that random traffic stops, left to the discretion of police officers, were unconstitutional. In 1990, in *Michigan* v. *Sitz*, the court upheld the legality of sobriety checkpoints in which a consistent proportion of drivers was stopped. The court ruled that such roadblocks were permitted as a way to prevent drunken driving. . . .

In 2000, in *Indianapolis* v. *Edmond*, it struck down the use of traffic checkpoints to stop drivers so that trained dogs could sniff the vehicles for narcotics. Unlike checkpoints to make sure that drivers were sober or had valid licenses and registrations, the court said, roadblocks for general law enforcement were unconstitutional.

David D. Cole, a law professor at Georgetown University, said the government was likely to succeed in demonstrating a special need for the current searches in New York.

A judge evaluating a legal challenge, he said, would probably look at three factors: whether the searches are truly random or use standardized criteria; whether riders were given advance notice or provided their consent to the searches; and the degree of intrusiveness. . . .

According to a two-page directive sent to all police commanders . . . the searches were begun "to increase deterrence and detection of potential terrorist activity and to give greater protection to the mass transit-riding public.". . .

The degree of intrusiveness could become a thorny issue. The directive provides that officers may open a package and "physically inspect and manipulate the contents to ensure it does not contain an explosive device." Leaving aside the issue of illegal drugs or weapons, some riders have already voiced misgivings about having the police examine sensitive possessions, like medications and personal hygiene products. . . .

"For a split second, I thought that because of my skin complexion, they picked me," said James Hamilton, 38, whose attaché case was searched at Herald Square. "I'm not sure if I had brown hair and blue eyes, that that would have happened.". . .

Charles Wilson, 35, a schoolteacher whose bag was searched at Fulton Street in Lower Manhattan, said, "This is not going to make things better between the police and people of color.". . .

A police spokesman, Paul J. Browne, said he strongly disagreed. "These inspections are being conducted in a constitutional manner and have been met with enthusiastic cooperation by the overwhelming majority of riders we've come into contact with," he said.

Source: Sewell Chan and Kareem Fahim, "Legal Issues Being Raised on Searches in Subways," *New York Times*, www.nytimes.com, © July 24, 2005,

Most jurisdictions allow arrest for a felony without a warrant when a crime is not in progress, as long as probable cause can be established; some, however, require a warrant. In those jurisdictions, arrest warrants are issued by magistrates when police officers can demonstrate probable cause. Magistrates will usually require that the officers seeking an arrest warrant submit a written affidavit outlining their reason for the arrest. In the case of *Payton* v. *New York* (1980),[68] the U.S. Supreme Court ruled that unless the suspect gives consent or an emergency exists, an arrest warrant is necessary if an arrest requires entry into a suspect's private residence.[69] In *Payton*, the justices held that "[a]bsent exigent circumstances," the "firm line at the entrance to the house . . . may not reasonably be crossed without a warrant." The Court reiterated its *Payton* holding in the 2002 case of *Kirk* v. *Louisiana*.[70] In *Kirk*, which involved an anonymous complaint about drug sales said to be taking place in the apartment of Kennedy Kirk, the justices reaffirmed their belief that "[t]he Fourth Amendment to the United States Constitution has drawn a firm line at the entrance to the home, and thus, the police need both probable cause to either arrest or search and exigent circumstances to justify a nonconsensual warrantless intrusion into private premises."

Searches Incident to Arrest

The U.S. Supreme Court has established a clear rule that police officers have the right to conduct a search of a person being arrested and to search the area under the arrestee's immediate control to protect themselves from attack. This is true even if the officer and the arrestee are of different sexes.

This "rule of the game" regarding **search incident to an arrest** became firmly established in cases involving personal searches, such as the 1973 case of *U.S.* v. *Robinson*.[71] In *Robinson*, the Court upheld an officer's right to conduct a search without a warrant for purposes of personal protection and to use the fruits of the search when it turns up contraband. In the words of the Court, "A custodial arrest of a suspect based upon probable cause is a reasonable intrusion under the Fourth Amendment; that intrusion being lawful, a search incident to the arrest requires no additional jurisdiction."[72]

search incident to an arrest
A warrantless search of an arrested individual conducted to ensure the safety of the arresting officer. Because individuals placed under arrest may be in possession of weapons, courts have recognized the need for arresting officers to protect themselves by conducting an immediate search of arrestees without obtaining a warrant.

The Court's decision in *Robinson* reinforced an earlier ruling in *Terry* v. *Ohio* (1968)[73] involving a seasoned officer who conducted a pat-down search of two men whom he suspected were casing a store, about to commit a robbery. The arresting officer was a 39-year veteran of police work who testified that the men "did not look right." When he approached them, he suspected they might be armed. Fearing for his life, he quickly spun the men around, put them up against a wall, patted down their clothing, and found a gun on one of the men. The man, Terry, was later convicted in Ohio courts of carrying a concealed weapon.

Terry's appeal was based on the argument that the suspicious officer had no probable cause to arrest him and therefore no cause to search him. The search, he argued, was illegal, and the evidence obtained should not have been used against him. The Supreme Court disagreed, saying, "In view of these facts, we cannot blind ourselves to the need for law enforcement officers to protect themselves and other prospective victims of violence in situations where they may lack probable cause for an arrest."

The *Terry* case set the standard for a brief stop and frisk based on reasonable suspicion. Attorneys refer to such brief encounters as *Terry-type stops*. **Reasonable suspicion** can be defined as a belief, based on a consideration of the facts at hand and on reasonable inferences drawn from those facts, that would induce an ordinarily prudent and cautious person under the same circumstances to conclude that criminal activity is taking place or that criminal activity has recently occurred. It is the level of suspicion needed to justify an officer in making further inquiry or in conducting further investigation. Reasonable suspicion, which is a *general* and reasonable belief that a crime is in progress or has occurred, should be differentiated from probable cause. Probable cause, as noted earlier, is a reasonable belief that a *particular* person has committed a *specific* crime. It is important to note that the *Terry* case, for all the authority it conferred on officers, also made it clear that officers must have reasonable grounds for any stop and frisk that they conduct. Read more about the case of *Terry* v. *Ohio* at **Library Extra 3**.

reasonable suspicion
The level of suspicion that would justify an officer in making further inquiry or in conducting further investigation. Reasonable suspicion may permit stopping a person for questioning or for a simple pat-down search. Also, a belief, based on a consideration of the facts at hand and on reasonable inferences drawn from those facts, that would induce an ordinarily prudent and cautious person under the same circumstances to conclude that criminal activity is taking place or that criminal activity has recently occurred. Reasonable suspicion is a *general* and reasonable belief that a crime is in progress or has occurred, whereas probable cause is a reasonable belief that a *particular* person has committed a *specific* crime.

In 1989, in the case of *U.S.* v. *Sokolow*,[74] the Supreme Court clarified the basis on which law enforcement officers, lacking probable cause to believe that a crime has occurred, may stop and briefly detain a person for investigative purposes. In *Sokolow*, the Court ruled that the legitimacy of such a stop must be evaluated according to a "totality of circumstances" criterion in which all aspects of the defendant's behavior, taken in concert, may provide the basis for a legitimate stop based on reasonable suspicion. In this case, the defendant, Andrew Sokolow, appeared suspicious to police because while traveling under an alias from Honolulu, he had paid $2,100 in $20 bills (from a large roll of money) for two airplane tickets after spending a surprisingly small amount of time in Miami. In addition, the defendant was

▲ Arresting officers patting down a drug suspect. The courts have generally held that to protect themselves and the public, officers have the authority to search suspects being arrested. What are the limits of such searches?
Craig Filipacchi

obviously nervous and checked no luggage. A warrantless airport investigation by Drug Enforcement Administration (DEA) agents uncovered more than 1,000 grams of cocaine in the defendant's belongings. In upholding Sokolow's conviction, the Court ruled that although no single type of behavior was proof of illegal activity, all his actions together created circumstances under which suspicion of illegal activity was justified.

In 2002, the Court reinforced the *Sokolow* decision in *U.S.* v. *Arvizu* when it ruled that the "balance between the public interest and the individual's right to personal security"[75] "tilts in favor of a standard less than probable cause in brief investigatory stops of persons or vehicles . . . if the officer's action is supported by reasonable suspicion to believe that criminal activity may be afoot."[76] In the words of the Court, "This process allows officers to draw on their own experiences and specialized training to make inferences from and deductions about the cumulative information available."[77]

In 1993, in the case of *Minnesota* v. *Dickerson*,[78] the U.S. Supreme Court placed new limits on an officer's ability to seize evidence discovered during a pat-down search conducted for protective reasons when the search itself was based merely on suspicion and failed to immediately reveal the presence of a weapon. In this case, the high court ruled that "if an officer lawfully pats down a suspect's outer clothing and feels an object whose contour or mass makes its identity immediately apparent, there has been no invasion of the suspect's privacy beyond that already authorized by the officer's search for weapons." However, in *Dickerson*, the justices ruled that "the officer never thought that the lump was a weapon, but did not immediately recognize it as cocaine." The lump was determined to be cocaine only after the officer "squeezed, slid, and otherwise manipulated the pocket's contents." Hence, the Court held, the officer's actions in this case did not qualify under what might be called a "plain feel" exception. In any case, said the Court, the search in *Dickerson* went far beyond what is permissible under *Terry*, where officer safety was the crucial issue. The Court summed up its ruling in *Dickerson* this way: "While *Terry* entitled [the officer] to place his hands on respondent's jacket and to feel the lump in the pocket, his continued exploration of the pocket after he concluded that it contained no weapon was unrelated to the sole justification for the search under *Terry*" and was therefore illegal.

Just as arrest must be based on probable cause, officers may not stop and question an unwilling citizen whom they have no reason to suspect of a crime. In the case of *Brown* v. *Texas* (1979),[79] two Texas law enforcement officers stopped the defendant and asked for identification. Ed Brown, they later testified, had not been acting suspiciously, nor did they think he might have a weapon. The stop was made simply because officers wanted to know who he was. Brown was arrested under a Texas statute that required a person to identify himself properly and accurately when asked to do so by peace officers. Eventually, his appeal reached the U.S. Supreme Court, which ruled that under the circumstances of the *Brown* case, a person "may not be punished for refusing to identify himself."

In the 2004 case of *Hiibel* v. *Sixth Judicial District Court of Nevada*,[80] however, the Court upheld Nevada's "stop and identify" law that requires a person to identify himself or herself to police if they encounter the person under circumstances that reasonably indicate that he or she "has committed, is committing or is about to commit a crime." The *Hiibel* case was an extension of the reasonable suspicion doctrine set forth earlier in *Terry*.

In *Smith* v. *Ohio* (1990),[81] the Court held that an individual has the right to protect his or her belongings from unwarranted police inspection. In *Smith*, the defendant was approached by two officers in plain clothes who observed that he was carrying a brown paper bag. The officers asked him to "come here a minute" and, when he kept walking, identified themselves as police officers. The defendant threw the bag onto the hood of his car and attempted to protect it from the officers' intrusion. Marijuana was found inside the bag, and the defendant was arrested. Since there was little reason to stop the suspect in this case and because control over the bag was not thought necessary for the officers' protection, the Court found that the Fourth Amendment protects both "the traveler who carries a toothbrush and a few articles of clothing in a paper bag" and "the sophisticated executive with the locked attaché case."

The following year, however, in what some Court observers saw as a turnabout, the Court ruled in *California* v. *Hodari D.* (1991)[82] that suspects who flee from the police and throw away evidence as they retreat may later be arrested based on the incriminating nature of the abandoned evidence. The significance of *Hodari* for future police action was highlighted by California prosecutors who pointed out that cases like *Hodari* occur "almost every day in this nation's urban areas."[83]

Police work is the only profession that gives you the test first, then the lesson.

—Anonymous

In 2000, the Court decided the case of William Wardlow.[84] Wardlow had fled upon seeing a caravan of police vehicles converge on an area of Chicago known for narcotics trafficking. Officers caught him, however, and conducted a pat-down search of his clothing for weapons, revealing a handgun. The officers arrested Wardlow on weapons charges, but his lawyer argued that police had acted illegally in stopping him since they did not have reasonable suspicion that he had committed an offense. The Illinois Supreme Court agreed with Wardlow's attorney, holding that "sudden flight in a high crime area does not create a reasonable suspicion justifying a *Terry* stop because flight may simply be an exercise of the right to 'go on one's way.' "[85] The case eventually reached the U.S. Supreme Court, which overturned the Illinois court, finding instead that the officers' actions did not violate the Fourth Amendment. In the words of the Court, "This case, involving a brief encounter between a citizen and a police officer on a public street, is governed by *Terry*, under which an officer who has a reasonable, articulable suspicion that criminal activity is afoot may conduct a brief, investigatory stop. While 'reasonable suspicion' is a less demanding standard than probable cause, there must be at least a minimal level of objective justification for the stop. An individual's presence in a 'high crime area,' standing alone, is not enough to support a reasonable, particularized suspicion of criminal activity, but a location's characteristics are relevant in determining whether the circumstances are sufficiently suspicious to warrant further investigation. . . . In this case, moreover, it was also Wardlow's unprovoked flight that aroused the officers' suspicions. Nervous, evasive behavior is another pertinent factor in determining reasonable suspicion . . . and headlong flight is the consummate act of evasion."[86]

Emergency Searches of Persons

It is easy to imagine emergency situations in which officers may have to search people based on quick decisions: a person who matches the description of an armed robber, a woman who is found unconscious on the floor, a man who has what appears to be blood on his shoes. Such searches can save lives by disarming fleeing felons or by uncovering a medical reason for an emergency situation. They may also prevent criminals from escaping or destroying evidence.

Emergency searches of persons, like those of premises, fall under the exigent circumstances exception to the warrant requirement of the Fourth Amendment. In the 1979 case of *Arkansas* v. *Sanders*,[87] the Supreme Court recognized the need for such searches "where the societal costs of obtaining a warrant, such as danger to law officers or the risk of loss or destruction of evidence, outweigh the reasons for prior recourse to a neutral magistrate."[88]

The 1987 case of *U.S.* v. *Borchardt*,[89] decided by the Fifth Circuit Court of Appeals, held that Ira Eugene Borchardt could be prosecuted for heroin uncovered during medical treatment, even though the defendant had objected to the treatment.

The Legal Counsel Division of the FBI provides the following guidelines for conducting emergency warrantless searches of individuals where the possible destruction of evidence is at issue.[90] (Keep in mind that there may be no probable cause to *arrest* the individual being searched.) All four conditions must apply:

1. There was probable cause at the time of the search to believe that there was evidence concealed on the person searched.
2. There was probable cause to believe an emergency threat of destruction of evidence existed at the time of the search.
3. The officer had no prior opportunity to obtain a warrant authorizing the search.
4. The action was no greater than necessary to eliminate the threat of destruction of evidence.

Vehicle Searches

Vehicles present a special law enforcement problem. They are highly mobile, and when a driver or an occupant is arrested, the need to search the vehicle may be immediate.

The first significant Supreme Court case involving an automobile was that of *Carroll* v. *U.S.*[91] in 1925. In the *Carroll* case, a divided Court ruled that a warrantless search of an automobile or other vehicle is valid if it is based on a reasonable belief that contraband is present. In 1964, however, in the case of *Preston* v. *U.S.*,[92] the limits of warrantless vehicle searches were defined. Preston was arrested for vagrancy and taken to jail. His vehicle was impounded, towed to the police garage, and later searched. Two revolvers were uncovered in the glove compartment, and more incriminating evidence was found in the trunk. Preston was convicted on weapons possession and other charges and eventually appealed to the U.S. Supreme Court. The Court held that the warrantless search of Preston's vehicle had occurred while the automobile was in secure custody and had therefore been illegal. Time and circumstances would have permitted acquisition of a warrant to conduct the search, the Court reasoned. Similarly, in 2009, the Court, in the case of *Arizona* v. *Gant*,[93] found that vehicle searches "incident to a recent occupant's arrest" cannot be authorized without a warrant if there is no possibility the arrestee could gain access to the vehicle at the time of the search."

When the search of a vehicle occurs after it has been impounded, however, that search may be legitimate if it is undertaken for routine and reasonable purposes. In the case of *South Dakota* v. *Opperman* (1976),[94] for example, the Court held that a warrantless search undertaken for purposes of inventorying and safekeeping the personal possessions of the car's owner was not illegal. The intent of the search, which had turned up marijuana, had not been to discover contraband but to secure the owner's belongings from possible theft. Again, in *Colorado* v. *Bertine* (1987),[95] the Court reinforced the idea that officers may open closed containers found in a vehicle while conducting a routine search for inventorying purposes. In the words of the Court, such searches are "now a well-defined exception in the warrant requirement." In 1990, however, in the precedent-setting case of *Florida* v. *Wells*,[96] the Court agreed with a lower court's suppression of marijuana evidence discovered in a locked suitcase in the trunk of a defendant's impounded vehicle. In *Wells*, the Court held that standardized criteria authorizing the search of a vehicle for inventorying purposes were necessary before such a discovery could be legitimate. Standardized criteria, said the Court, might take the form of department policies, written general orders, or established routines.

Generally speaking, where vehicles are concerned, an investigatory stop is permissible under the Fourth Amendment if supported by reasonable suspicion,[97] and a warrantless search of a stopped car is valid if it is based on probable cause.[98] Reasonable suspicion can expand into probable cause when the facts in a given situation so warrant. In the 1996 case of *Ornelas* v. *U.S.*,[99] for example, two experienced Milwaukee police officers stopped a car with California license plates that had been spotted in a motel parking lot known for drug trafficking after the Narcotics and Dangerous Drugs Information System (NADDIS) identified the car's owner as a known or suspected drug trafficker. One of the officers noticed a loose panel above an armrest in the vehicle's backseat and then searched the car. A package of cocaine was found beneath the panel, and the driver and a passenger were arrested. Following conviction, the defendants appealed to the U.S. Supreme Court, claiming that no probable cause to search the car existed at the time of the stop. The majority opinion, however, noted that in the view of the court that originally heard the case, "the model, age, and source-State origin of the car, and the fact that two men traveling together checked into a motel at 4 o'clock in the morning without reservations, formed a drug-courier profile and . . . this profile together with the [computer] reports gave rise to a reasonable suspicion of drug-trafficking activity. . . . [I]n the court's view, reasonable suspicion became probable cause when [the deputy] found the loose panel."[100] Probable cause permits a warrantless search of a vehicle because it is able to quickly leave a jurisdiction. This exception to the exclusionary rule is called the **fleeting-targets exception**.[101]

fleeting-targets exception
An exception to the exclusionary rule that permits law enforcement officers to search a motor vehicle based on probable cause but without a warrant. The fleeting-targets exception is predicated on the fact that vehicles can quickly leave the jurisdiction of a law enforcement agency.

Warrantless vehicle searches can extend to any area of the vehicle and may include sealed containers, the trunk, and the glove compartment if officers have probable cause to conduct a purposeful search or if officers have been given permission to search the vehicle. In the 1991

Freedom or Safety? You Decide.
Religion and Public Safety

In 2003, Florida Judge Janet Thorpe ruled that a Muslim woman could not wear a veil while being photographed for a state driver's license. The woman, Sultaana Freeman, claimed that her religious rights were violated when the state department of motor vehicles required that she reveal her face for the photograph. She offered to show her eyes, but not the rest of her face, to the camera.

Judge Thorpe said, however, that a "compelling interest in protecting the public from criminal activities and security threats" did not place an undue burden on Freeman's ability to practice her religion.

After the hearing, Freeman's husband, Abdul-Maalik Freeman, told reporters, "This is a religious principle; this is a principle that's imbedded in us as believers. So, she's not going to do that. We'll take the next step, and this is what we call the American way." Howard Marks, the Freemans' attorney, said that he would file an appeal in a higher court.

YOU DECIDE

Do the demands of public safety justify the kind of restriction on religious practice described here? Should photo IDs, such as driver's licenses, be replaced with other forms of identification (such as an individual's stored DNA profile) in order to accommodate the beliefs of individuals like the Freemans?

Reference: "Judge: No Veil in Driver's License Photo," Associated Press, June 6, 2003.

case of *Florida* v. *Jimeno*,[102] arresting officers stopped a motorist, who gave them permission to search his car. The defendant was later convicted on a drug charge when a bag on the floor of the car was found to contain cocaine. Upon appeal to the U.S. Supreme Court, however, he argued that the permission given to search his car did not extend to bags and other items within the car. In a decision that may have implications beyond vehicle searches, the Court held that "[a] criminal suspect's Fourth Amendment right to be free from unreasonable searches is not violated when, after he gives police permission to search his car, they open a closed container found within the car that might reasonably hold the object of the search. The amendment is satisfied when, under the circumstances, it is objectively reasonable for the police to believe that the scope of the suspect's consent permitted them to open the particular container."[103]

In *U.S.* v. *Ross* (1982),[104] the Court found that officers had not exceeded their authority in opening a bag in the defendant's trunk that was found to contain heroin. The search was held to be justifiable on the basis of information developed from a search of the passenger compartment. The Court said, "If probable cause justifies the search of a lawfully stopped vehicle, it justifies the search of every part of the vehicle and its contents that may conceal the object of the search."[105] Moreover, according to the 1996 U.S. Supreme Court decision in *Whren* v. *U.S.*,[106] officers may stop a vehicle being driven suspiciously and then search it once probable cause has developed, even if their primary assignment centers on duties other than traffic enforcement or "if a reasonable officer would not have stopped the motorist absent some additional law enforcement objective" (which in the case of *Whren* was drug enforcement).

Motorists[107] and their passengers may be ordered out of stopped vehicles in the interest of officer safety, and any evidence developed as a result of such a procedure may be used in court. In 1997, for example, in the case of *Maryland* v. *Wilson*,[108] the U.S. Supreme Court overturned a decision by a Maryland court that held that crack cocaine found during a traffic stop was seized illegally when it fell from the lap of a passenger ordered out of a stopped vehicle by a Maryland state trooper. The Maryland court reasoned that the police should not have authority to order seemingly innocent passengers out of vehicles—even vehicles that have been stopped for legitimate reasons. The Supreme Court cited concerns for officer safety in overturning the Maryland court's ruling and held that the activities of passengers are subject to police control. Similarly, in 2007, in the case of *Brendlin* v. *California*,[109] the Court ruled that passengers in stopped vehicles are necessarily detained as a result of the stop and that they should expect that, for safety reasons, officers will exercise "unquestioned police command" over them for the duration of the stop. However, any passenger in a stopped automobile may use his or her Fourth Amendment rights to challenge the stop's legality.

In 1998, however, the U.S. Supreme Court placed clear limits on warrantless vehicle searches. In the case of *Knowles* v. *Iowa*,[110] an Iowa policeman stopped Patrick Knowles for speeding, issued him a citation, but did not make a custodial arrest. The officer then conducted a full search of his car without Knowles's consent and without probable cause. Marijuana was found, and Knowles was arrested. At the time, Iowa state law gave officers authority to conduct full-blown automobile searches when issuing only a citation. The Supreme Court found, however, that while concern for officer safety during a routine traffic stop may justify the minimal intrusion of ordering a driver and passengers out of a car, it does not by itself justify what it called "the considerably greater intrusion attending a full field-type search." Hence while a search incident to arrest may be justifiable in the eyes of the Court, a search incident to citation clearly is not.

In the 1999 case of *Wyoming* v. *Houghton*,[111] the Court ruled that police officers with probable cause to search a car may inspect passengers' belongings found in the car that are capable of concealing the object of the search. *Thornton* v. *U.S.* (2004) established the authority of arresting officers to search a car without a warrant even if the driver had previously exited the vehicle.[112]

In 2005, in the case of *Illinois* v. *Caballes*,[113] the Court held that the use of a drug-sniffing dog during a routine and lawful traffic stop is permissible and may not even be a search within the meaning of the Fourth Amendment. In writing for the majority, Justice John Paul Stevens said that "the use of a well-trained narcotics-detection dog—one that does not expose noncontraband items that otherwise would remain hidden from public view—during a lawful traffic stop generally does not implicate legitimate privacy interests." Learn more about motor vehicle searches at **Library Extra 4**.

Roadblocks and Motor Vehicle Checkpoints

▲ A law enforcement officer searching a vehicle in San Diego, California. Warrantless vehicle searches, where the driver is suspected of a crime, have generally been justified by the fact that vehicles are highly mobile and can quickly leave police jurisdiction. Can passengers in the vehicle also be searched?
Mike Karlsson/Arresting Images Royalty Free

The Fourth and Fourteenth Amendments to the U.S. Constitution guarantee liberty and personal security to all people residing within the United States. Courts have generally held that police officers have no legitimate authority to detain or arrest people who are going about their business in a peaceful manner, unless there is probable cause to believe that a crime has been committed. In a number of instances, however, the U.S. Supreme Court has decided that community interests may necessitate a temporary suspension of personal liberty, even when probable cause is lacking. One such case is that of *Michigan Dept. of State Police* v. *Sitz* (1990),[114] which involved the legality of highway sobriety checkpoints, including those at which nonsuspicious drivers are subjected to scrutiny. In *Sitz*, the Court ruled that such stops are reasonable insofar as they are essential to the welfare of the community as a whole.

In a second case, *U.S.* v. *Martinez-Fuerte* (1976),[115] the Court upheld brief suspicionless seizures at a fixed international checkpoint designed to intercept illegal aliens. The Court noted that "to require that such stops always be based on reasonable suspicion would be impractical because the flow of traffic tends to be too heavy to allow the particularized study of a given car necessary to identify it as a possible carrier of illegal aliens. Such a requirement also would largely eliminate any deterrent to the conduct of well-disguised smuggling operations, even though smugglers are known to use these highways regularly."[116]

In fact, in 2004, in the case of *Illinois* v. *Lidster*,[117] the Court held that information-seeking highway roadblocks are permissible. The stop in *Lidster*, said the Court, was permissible because its intent was merely to solicit motorists' help in solving a crime. "The law," said the Court, "ordinarily permits police to seek the public's voluntary cooperation in a criminal investigation."

Watercraft and Motor Homes

The 1983 case of *U.S.* v. *Villamonte-Marquez*[118] widened the *Carroll* decision (discussed earlier) to include watercraft. In this case, the Court reasoned that a vehicle on the water can easily leave the jurisdiction of enforcement officials, just as a car or truck can.

In *California* v. *Carney* (1985),[119] the Court extended police authority to conduct warrantless searches of vehicles to include motor homes. Earlier arguments had been advanced that a motor home, because it is more like a permanent residence, should not be considered a vehicle for purposes of search and seizure. In a 6–3 decision, the Court rejected those arguments, reasoning that a vehicle's appointments and size do not alter its basic function of providing transportation.

Houseboats were brought under the automobile exception to the Fourth Amendment warrant requirement in the 1988 Tenth Circuit Court case of *U.S.* v. *Hill.*[120]

Suspicionless Searches

In two 1989 decisions, the U.S. Supreme Court ruled for the first time in its history that there may be instances when the need to ensure public safety provides a **compelling interest** that negates the rights of any individual to privacy, permitting **suspicionless searches**—those that occur when a person is not suspected of a crime. In the case of *National Treasury Employees Union* v. *Von Raab* (1989),[121] the Court, by a 5–4 vote, upheld a program of the U.S. Customs Service that required mandatory drug testing for all workers seeking promotions or job transfers involving drug interdiction and the carrying of firearms. The Court's majority opinion read, "We think the government's need to conduct the suspicionless searches required by the Customs program outweighs the privacy interest of employees engaged directly in drug interdiction, and of those who otherwise are required to carry firearms."

compelling interest
A legal concept that provides a basis for suspicionless searches when public safety is at issue. In two cases, the U.S. Supreme Court held that public safety may sometimes provide a sufficiently compelling interest to justify limiting an individual's right to privacy.

suspicionless search
A search conducted by law enforcement personnel without a warrant and without suspicion. Suspicionless searches are permissible only if based on an overriding concern for public safety.

The second case, *Skinner* v. *Railway Labor Executives' Association* (1989),[122] was decided on the same day. In *Skinner*, the justices voted 7 to 2 to permit the mandatory testing of railway crews for the presence of drugs or alcohol following serious train accidents. The *Skinner* case involved evidence of drugs in a 1987 train wreck outside of Baltimore, Maryland, in which 16 people were killed and hundreds were injured.

The 1991 Supreme Court case of *Florida* v. *Bostick*,[123] which permitted warrantless "sweeps" of intercity buses, moved the Court deeply into conservative territory. The *Bostick* case came to the attention of the Court as a result of the Broward County (Florida) Sheriff's Department's routine practice of boarding buses at scheduled stops and asking passengers for permission to search their bags. Terrance Bostick, a passenger on one of the buses, gave police permission to search his luggage, which was found to contain cocaine. Bostick was arrested and eventually pleaded guilty to charges of drug trafficking. The Florida Supreme Court, however, found merit in Bostick's appeal, which was based on a Fourth Amendment claim that the search of his luggage had been unreasonable. The Florida court held that "a reasonable passenger in [Bostick's] situation would not have felt free to leave the bus to avoid questioning by the police," and it overturned the conviction.

The reasonable person test presumes an innocent person.

The state appealed to the U.S. Supreme Court, which held that the Florida Supreme Court had erred in interpreting Bostick's *feelings* that he was not free to leave the bus. In the words of the Court, "Bostick was a passenger on a bus that was scheduled to depart. He would not have felt free to leave the bus even if the police had not been present. Bostick's movements were 'confined' in a sense, but this was the natural result of his decision to take the bus." In other words, Bostick was constrained not so much by police action as by his own feelings that he might miss the bus were he to get off. Following this line of reasoning, the Court concluded that warrantless, suspicionless "sweeps" of buses, "trains, planes, and city streets" are permissible as long as officers (1) ask individual passengers for permission before searching their possessions, (2) do not coerce passengers to consent to a search, and (3) do not convey the message that citizen compliance with the search request is mandatory. Passenger compliance with police searches must be voluntary for the searches to be legal.

In contrast to the tone of Court decisions more than two decades earlier, the justices did not require officers to inform passengers that they were free to leave or that they had the right to deny officers the opportunity to search (although Bostick himself was so advised by Florida officers). Any reasonable person, the Court ruled, should feel free to deny the police request. In the words of the Court, "The appropriate test is whether, taking into account all of the circumstances surrounding the encounter, a reasonable passenger would feel free to decline the officers' requests or otherwise terminate the encounter." The Court continued, "Rejected, however, is Bostick's argument that he must have been seized because no reasonable person would freely consent to a search of luggage containing drugs, since the 'reasonable person' test presumes an innocent person."

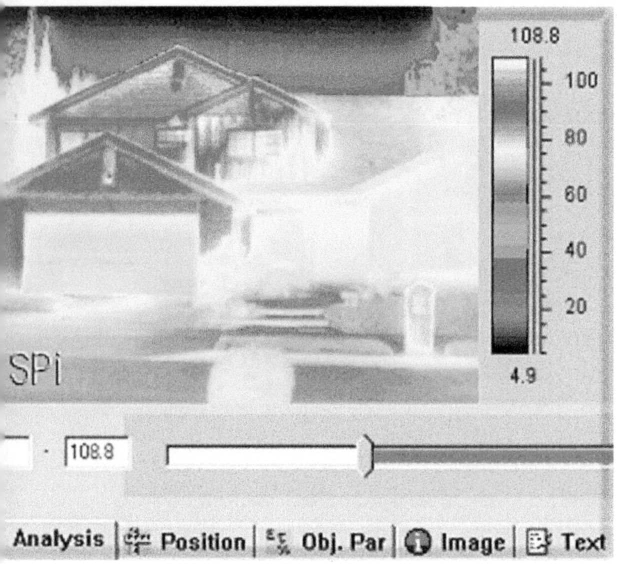

▲ A photo created by a thermal-imaging device. The photo shows "hot spots" in a suspected marijuana grower's home that might be produced by lights used to grow the plants indoors. In *Kyllo* v. *U.S.* (2001), the U.S. Supreme Court held that the police may not use such devices without a search warrant. What was the Court's rationale? *Image compliments of SPi, www.x20.org*

Critics of the decision saw it as creating new "gestapo-like" police powers in the face of which citizens on public transportation will feel compelled to comply with police searches. Dissenting Justices Harry Blackmun, John Paul Stevens, and Thurgood Marshall held that "the bus sweep at issue in this case violates the core values of the Fourth Amendment." The Court's majority, however, defended its ruling by writing, "[T]he Fourth Amendment proscribes unreasonable searches and seizures; it does not proscribe voluntary cooperation." In 2000, however, in the case of *Bond* v. *U.S.*,[124] the Court ruled that physical manipulation of a carry-on bag in the possession of a bus passenger without the owner's consent does violate the Fourth Amendment's proscription against unreasonable searches. In the case of *U.S.* v. *Drayton* (2002),[125] the U.S. Supreme Court reiterated its position that police officers are not required to advise bus passengers of their right to refuse to cooperate with officers conducting searches or to refuse to be searched.

In 2004, the U.S. Supreme Court made it clear that suspicionless searches of vehicles at our nation's borders are permitted, even when the searches are extensive. In the case of *U.S.* v. *Flores-Montano*,[126] customs officials disassembled the gas tank of a car belonging to a man entering the country from Mexico and found that it contained 37 kilograms of marijuana. Although the officers admitted that their actions were not motivated by any particular belief that the search would reveal contraband, the Court held that Congress has always granted "plenary authority to conduct routine searches and seizures at the border without probable cause or a warrant." The Court stated that "the Government's authority to conduct suspicionless inspections at the border includes the authority to remove, disassemble, and reassemble a vehicle's fuel tank."

High-Technology Searches

The burgeoning use of high technology to investigate crime and to uncover violations of the criminal law is forcing courts throughout the nation to evaluate the applicability of constitutional guarantees in light of high-tech searches and seizures. In 1996, the California appellate court decision in *People* v. *Deutsch*[127] presaged the kinds of issues that are being encountered as American law enforcement expands its use of cutting-edge technology. In *Deutsch*, judges faced the question of whether a warrantless scan of a private dwelling with a thermal-imaging device constitutes an unreasonable search within the meaning of the Fourth Amendment. Such devices (also called *forward-looking infrared [FLIR] systems*) measure radiant energy in the radiant heat portion of the electromagnetic spectrum[128] and display their readings as thermographs. The "heat picture" that a thermal imager produces can be used, as it was in the case of Dorian Deutsch, to reveal unusually warm areas or rooms that might be associated with the cultivation of drug-bearing plants, such as marijuana. Two hundred cannabis plants, which were being grown hydroponically under high-wattage lights in two walled-off portions of Deutsch's home, were seized following an exterior thermal scan of her home by a police officer who drove by at 1:30 in the morning. Because no entry of the house was anticipated during the search, the officer had acted without a search warrant. The California court ruled that the scan was an illegal search because "society accepts a reasonable expectation of privacy" surrounding "nondisclosed activities within the home."[129]

In the similar case of *Kyllo* v. *U.S.* (2001),[130] the U.S. Supreme Court reached much the same conclusion. Based on the results of a warrantless search conducted by officers using a thermal-imaging device, investigators applied for a search warrant of Kyllo's home. The subsequent search uncovered more than 100 marijuana plants that were being grown under bright lights. In overturning Kyllo's conviction on drug-manufacturing charges, the Court held (with regard to the original warrantless search with the thermal-imaging device), "Where, as here, the Government uses a device that is not in general public use, to explore details of a private home that would previously have been unknowable without physical intrusion, the surveillance is a Fourth Amendment 'search,' and is presumptively unreasonable without a warrant."[131] Learn more about the issues surrounding search and seizure at **Web Extra 3**.

The Intelligence Function

5 Describe the intelligence function, including police interrogations, and explain the role of *Miranda* warnings.

The need for information leads police investigators to question both suspects and informants and, even more often, potentially knowledgeable citizens who may have been witnesses or victims. Data gathering is a crucial form of intelligence; without it, enforcement agencies would be virtually powerless to plan and effect arrests.

The importance of gathering information in police work cannot be overstressed. Studies have found that the one factor most likely to lead to arrest in serious crimes is the presence of a witness who can provide information to the police. Undercover operations, Neighborhood Watch programs, Crime Stoppers groups, and organized detective work all contribute this vital information.

Informants

Information gathering is a complex process, and many ethical questions have been raised about the techniques police use to gather information. The use of paid informants, for example, is an area of concern to ethicists who believe that informants are often paid to get away with crimes. The police practice (endorsed by some prosecutors) of agreeing not to charge one offender out of a group if he or she will talk and testify against others is another concern.

The right of the people to be secure in their persons, houses, papers, and effects, against unreasonable searches and seizures, shall not be violated, and no Warrants shall issue, but upon probable cause, supported by Oath or affirmation, and particularly describing the place to be searched, and the persons or things to be seized.

—Fourth Amendment to the U.S. Constitution

As we have seen, probable cause is an important aspect of both police searches and legal arrests. The Fourth Amendment specifies that "no Warrants shall issue, but upon probable cause." As a consequence, the successful use of informants in supporting requests for a warrant depends on the demonstrable reliability of their information. The case of *Aguilar* v. *Texas* (1964)[132] clarified the use of informants and established a two-pronged test. The U.S. Supreme Court ruled that informant information could establish probable cause if both of the following criteria are met:

1. The source of the informant's information is made clear.
2. The police officer has a reasonable belief that the informant is reliable.

The two-pronged test of *Aguilar* v. *Texas* was intended to prevent the issuance of warrants on the basis of false or fabricated information. The case of *U.S.* v. *Harris* (1971)[133] provided an exception to the two-pronged *Aguilar* test. The *Harris* Court recognized the fact that when an informant provides information that is damaging to him or her, it is probably true. In *Harris*, an informant told police that he had purchased non-tax-paid whiskey from another person. Since the information also implicated the informant in a crime, it was held to be accurate, even though it could not meet the second prong of the *Aguilar* test. "Admissions of crime," said the Court, "carry their own indicia of credibility—sufficient at least to support a finding of probable cause to search."[134]

In 1983, in the case of *Illinois* v. *Gates*,[135] the Court adopted a totality-of-circumstances approach, which held that sufficient probable cause for issuing a warrant exists where an informant can be reasonably believed on the basis of everything that the police know. The *Gates* case involved an anonymous informant who provided incriminating information about another person through a letter to the police. Although the source of the information was not stated and the police were unable to say whether the informant was reliable, the overall sense of things, given what was already known to police, was that the information supplied was probably valid. In *Gates*, the Court held that probable cause exists when "there is a fair probability that contraband or evidence of a crime will be found in a particular place."

In the 1990 case of *Alabama* v. *White*, [136] the Supreme Court ruled that an anonymous tip, even in the absence of other corroborating information about a suspect, could form the basis for an investigatory stop if the informant accurately predicted the *future* behavior of the suspect. The Court reasoned that the ability to predict a suspect's behavior demonstrates

The mandatory recording of police interrogations offers overwhelming benefits at minimal cost.

a significant degree of familiarity with the suspect's affairs. In the words of the Court, "Because only a small number of people are generally privy to an individual's itinerary, it is reasonable for the police to believe that a person with access to such information is likely to also have access to reliable information about that individual's illegal activities."[137]

In 2000, in the case of *Florida* v. *J.L.*,[138] the Court held that an anonymous tip that a person is carrying a gun does not, without more, justify a police officer's stop and frisk of that person. Ruling that such a search is invalid under the Fourth Amendment, the Court rejected the suggestion of a firearm exception to the general stop-and-frisk rule.

The identity of informants may be kept secret only if sources have been explicitly assured of confidentiality by investigating officers or if a reasonably implied assurance of confidentiality has been made. In *U.S. Dept. of Justice* v. *Landano* (1993),[139] the U.S. Supreme Court required that an informant's identity be revealed through a request made under the federal Freedom of Information Act. In that case, the FBI had not specifically assured the informant of confidentiality, and the Court ruled that "the government is not entitled to a presumption that all sources supplying information to the FBI in the course of a criminal investigation are confidential sources."

Police Interrogation

In 2003, Illinois became the first state in the nation to require the electronic recording of police interrogations and confessions in homicide cases.[140] State lawmakers hoped that the use of recordings would reduce the incidence of false confessions as well as the likelihood of convictions based on such confessions. Under the law, police interrogators must create video- or audiotape recordings of any questioning involving suspects. The law prohibits the introduction in court of statements and confessions that have not been taped. Proponents of the law say that it will prevent police intimidation of murder suspects and will put an end to coerced confessions.

Some argue that the mandatory recording of police interrogations offers overwhelming benefits at minimal cost. "By creating an objective and reviewable record," says University of San Francisco Law School's Richard A. Leo, "electronic recording promotes truth-finding in the criminal process, relegates 'swearing contests' to the past, and saves scarce resources at multiple levels of the criminal justice system."[141] According to Leo, requiring that all interrogations be recorded will benefit police and prosecutors by increasing the accuracy of confessions and convictions and "will also reduce the number of police-induced false confessions and the wrongful convictions they cause."

Interrogation
The information-gathering activity of police officers that involves the direct questioning of suspects.

The U.S. Supreme Court has defined **interrogation** as any behaviors by the police "that the police should know are reasonably likely to elicit an incriminating response from the suspect."[142] Interrogation may involve activities that go well beyond mere verbal questioning, and the Court has held that interrogation may include "staged lineups, reverse lineups, positing guilt, minimizing the moral seriousness of crime, and casting blame on the victim or society." It is noteworthy that the Court has also held that "police words or actions normally attendant to arrest and custody do not constitute interrogation" unless they involve pointed or directed questions. An arresting officer may instruct a suspect on what to do and may chitchat with him or her without engaging in interrogation within the meaning of the law. Once police officers make inquiries intended to elicit information about the crime in question, however, interrogation has begun. The interrogation of suspects, like other areas of police activity, is subject to constitutional limits as interpreted by the courts. A series of landmark decisions by the U.S. Supreme Court has focused on police interrogation (Figure 2).

Physical Abuse

The first in a series of significant cases was that of *Brown* v. *Mississippi*,[143] decided in 1936. The *Brown* case began with the robbery of a white store owner in Mississippi in 1934. During the robbery, the victim was killed. A posse formed and went to the home of a local African American man rumored to have been one of the perpetrators. They dragged the suspect from his home, put a rope around his neck, and hoisted him into a tree. They repeated this process a number of times, hoping to get a confession from the man but failing to do so. The posse was headed by a deputy sheriff who then arrested other suspects in the case and laid

FIGURE 2
Police Interrogation

INTERROGATION

The U.S. Supreme Court has defined interrogation as any behaviors by the police "that the police should know are reasonably likely to elicit an incriminating response from the suspect." The Court also noted that "police words or actions normally attendant to arrest and custody do not constitute interrogation" unless they involve pointed or directed questions. The interrogation of suspects, like other areas of police activity, is subject to constitutional limits as interpreted by the courts, and a series of landmark decisions by the U.S Supreme Court has focused on police interrogations.

Physical Abuse:
The first in a series of significant cases was ***Brown* v. *Mississippi*.** In 1936 the court determined that physical abuse cannot be used to obtain a confession or elicit information from a suspect.

Inherent Coercion:
In the case of ***Ashcraft* v. *Tennessee*** (1944), the U.S. Supreme Court found that interrogation involving inherent coercion was not acceptable. Inherent coercion refers to any form of non-physical coercion, hostility, or pressure to try to force a confession from a suspect.

Psychological Manipulation:
Interrogation should not involve sophisticated trickery or manipulation. In the case of ***Arizona* v. *Fulminante*** (1991) the U.S. Supreme Court determined that it was not legal to allow an FBI informat posing as a fellow inmate to trick the suspect into a confession. Interrogators do not have to be scrupulously honest in confronting suspects, but there must be limits to the lengths that can be pursued in questioning a suspect.

Right to Lawyer at Interrogation:
Escobedo* v. *Illinois (1964) and ***Minnick* v. *Mississippi*** (1990).

them over chairs in the local jail and whipped them with belts and buckles until they "confessed." These confessions were used in the trial that followed, and all three defendants were convicted of murder. Their convictions were upheld by the Mississippi Supreme Court. In 1936, however, the case was reviewed by the U.S. Supreme Court, which overturned all of the convictions, saying that it was difficult to imagine techniques of interrogation more "revolting" to the sense of justice than those used in this case.

Inherent Coercion

Interrogation need not involve physical abuse for it to be contrary to constitutional principles. In the case of *Ashcraft* v. *Tennessee* (1944),[144] the U.S. Supreme Court found that interrogation involving **inherent coercion** was not acceptable. Ashcraft had been charged with the murder of his wife, Zelma. He was arrested on a Saturday night and interrogated by relays of skilled interrogators until Monday morning, when he purportedly made a statement implicating himself in the murder. During questioning, he had faced a blinding light but was not physically mistreated. Investigators later testified that when the suspect requested cigarettes, food, or water, they "kindly" provided them. The Court's ruling, which reversed Ashcraft's conviction, made it plain that the Fifth Amendment guarantee against self-incrimination prohibits any form of official coercion or pressure during interrogation.

inherent coercion
The tactics used by police interviewers that fall short of physical abuse but that nonetheless pressure suspects to divulge information.

A similar case, *Chambers* v. *Florida*, was decided in 1940.[145] In that case, four black men were arrested without warrants as suspects in the robbery and murder of an elderly white man. After several days of questioning in a hostile atmosphere, the men confessed to the murder. The confessions were used as the primary evidence against them at their trial, and all four were sentenced to die. Upon appeal, the U.S. Supreme Court held that "the very circumstances surrounding their confinement and their questioning, without any formal charges having been brought, were such as to fill petitioners with terror and frightful misgivings."[146] Learn more about *Chambers* v. *Florida* at **Library Extra 5**.

Psychological Manipulation

Not only must interrogation be free of coercion and hostility, but it also cannot involve sophisticated trickery designed to ferret out a confession. Interrogators do not necessarily have to be scrupulously honest in confronting suspects, and the expert opinions of medical and psychiatric practitioners may be sought in investigations. However, the use of professionals skilled in **psychological manipulation** to gain confessions was banned by the Court in the case of *Leyra* v. *Denno*[147] in 1954, during the heyday of psychiatric perspectives on criminal behavior.

psychological manipulation
The manipulative actions by police interviewers, designed to pressure suspects to divulge information, that are based on subtle forms of intimidation and control.

In 1991, in the case of *Arizona* v. *Fulminante*,[148] the U.S. Supreme Court threw an even more dampening blanket of uncertainty over the use of sophisticated techniques to gain a confession. Oreste Fulminante was an inmate in a federal prison when he was approached secretly by a fellow inmate who was an FBI informant. The informant told Fulminante that other inmates were plotting to kill him because of a rumor that he had killed a child. He offered to protect Fulminante if he was told the details of the crime. Fulminante then described his role in the murder of his 11-year-old stepdaughter. Fulminante was arrested for that murder, tried, and convicted.

On appeal to the U.S. Supreme Court, Fulminante's lawyers argued that his confession had been coerced because of the threat of violence communicated by the informant. The Court agreed that the confession had been coerced and ordered a new trial at which the confession could not be admitted into evidence. Simultaneously, however, the Court found that the admission of a coerced confession should be considered a harmless "trial error" that need not necessarily result in reversal of a conviction if other evidence still proves guilt. The decision was especially significant because it partially reversed the Court's earlier ruling, in *Chapman* v. *California* (1967),[149] where it was held that forced confessions were such a basic form of constitutional error that they automatically invalidated any conviction to which they related. At a second trial, where his confession was not entered into evidence, Fulminante was convicted again and sentenced to die. The Arizona Supreme Court overturned his conviction, however, ruling that testimony describing statements the victim had made about fearing for her life prior to her murder, and which had been entered into evidence, were hearsay and had prejudiced the jury.[150]

The Right to a Lawyer at Interrogation

In 1964, in the case of *Escobedo* v. *Illinois*,[151] the right to have legal counsel present during police interrogation was formally recognized. In 1981, the case of *Edwards* v. *Arizona*[152] established a "bright-line rule" (that is, it specified a criterion that cannot be violated) for investigators to use in interpreting a suspect's right to counsel. In *Edwards*, the U.S. Supreme Court reiterated its *Miranda* concern that once a suspect who is in custody and is being questioned has requested the assistance of counsel, all questioning must cease until an attorney is present. The 1986 case of *Michigan* v. *Jackson*[153] provided further support for *Edwards*. In *Jackson*, the Court forbade police from initiating the interrogation of criminal defendants who had invoked their right to counsel at an arraignment or similar proceeding. In 1990, the Court refined the rule in *Minnick* v. *Mississippi*,[154] when it held that after the suspect has had an opportunity to consult his or her lawyer, interrogation may *not* resume unless the lawyer is present. Similarly, according to *Arizona* v. *Roberson* (1988),[155] the police may not avoid the suspect's request for a lawyer by beginning a new line of questioning, even if it is about an unrelated offense.

In 1994, in the case of *Davis* v. *U.S.*,[156] the Court "put the burden on custodial suspects to make unequivocal invocations of the right to counsel." In the *Davis* case, a man being interrogated in the death of a sailor waived his *Miranda* rights but later said, "Maybe I should talk to a lawyer." Investigators asked the suspect clarifying questions, and he responded, "No, I don't want a lawyer." Upon conviction he appealed, claiming that interrogation should have ceased when he mentioned a lawyer. The Court, in affirming the conviction, stated that "it will often be good police practice for the interviewing officers to clarify whether or not [the suspect] actually wants an attorney."

In 2009, in something of an about-face, the U.S. Supreme Court held that "*Michigan* v. *Jackson* should be and now is overruled." In the case of *Montejo* v. *Louisiana*,[157]the Court found that strict interpretations of *Jackson* could lead to practical problems. Montejo had been charged with first-degree murder, and appointment of counsel was ordered at his arraignment. He did not, however, ask to see his attorney. Later that same day, the police read Montejo his *Miranda* rights, and he agreed to accompany them on a trip to locate the murder weapon. During the trip, he wrote an incriminating letter of apology to the victim's widow. Upon returning, he met with his court-appointed attorney for the first time. At trial, his letter was admitted over defense objection, and he was convicted and sentenced to death. In the words of the Court, "Both *Edwards* and *Jackson* are meant to prevent police from badgering defendants into changing their minds about the right to counsel once they have invoked it, but a defendant who never asked for counsel has not yet made up his mind." In effect, although an attorney had been appointed to represent Montejo, he had never actually invoked his right to counsel.

▲ Ernesto Miranda, shown here after a jury convicted him for a second time. Miranda was convicted on rape and kidnapping charges after arresting officers failed to advise him of his rights. His case led to the now-famous *Miranda* warnings. How do the *Miranda* warnings read?
AP Wide World Photos

Suspect Rights: The *Miranda* Decision

In the area of suspect rights, no case is as famous as that of *Miranda* v. *Arizona* (1966),[158] which established the well-known ***Miranda* warnings**. Many people regard *Miranda* as the centerpiece of the Warren Court due process rulings.

The case involved Ernesto Miranda, who was arrested in Phoenix, Arizona, and was accused of having kidnapped and raped a young woman. At police headquarters, he was identified by the victim. After being interrogated for two hours, Miranda signed a confession that formed the basis of his later conviction on the charges.

On appeal, the U.S. Supreme Court rendered what some regard as the most far-reaching opinion to have affected criminal justice in the last half century. The Court ruled that Miranda's conviction was unconstitutional because "[t]he entire aura and atmosphere of police interrogation without notification of rights and an offer of assistance of counsel [tend] to subjugate the individual to the will of his examiner."

The Court continued, saying that the suspect "must be warned prior to any questioning that he has the right to remain silent, that anything he says can be used against him in a court of law, that he has the right to the presence of an attorney, and that if he cannot afford an attorney one will be appointed for him prior to any questioning if he so desires. Opportunity to exercise these rights must be afforded to him throughout the interrogation. After such warnings have been given, and such opportunity afforded him, the individual may knowingly and intelligently waive these rights and agree to answer the questions or make a statement. But unless and until such warnings and waiver are demonstrated by the prosecution at the trial, no evidence obtained as a result of interrogation can be used against him."

Miranda warnings
The advisement of rights due criminal suspects by the police before questioning begins. *Miranda* warnings were first set forth by the U.S. Supreme Court in the 1966 case of *Miranda* v. *Arizona*.

To ensure that proper advice is given to suspects at the time of their arrest, the now-famous *Miranda* rights are read before any questioning begins. These rights, as they appear on a *Miranda* warning card commonly used by police agencies, are shown in CJ Exhibit 2.

Once suspects have been advised of their *Miranda* rights, they are commonly asked to sign a paper that lists each right in order to confirm that they were advised of their rights and that they understand each right. Questioning may then begin, but only if suspects waive the right not to talk or to have a lawyer present during interrogation.

In 1992, *Miranda* rights were effectively extended to illegal immigrants living in the United States. In a settlement of a class-action lawsuit reached in Los Angeles with the Immigration and Naturalization Service, U.S. District Court Judge William Byrne, Jr., approved the printing of millions of notices in several languages to be given to arrestees. The approximately 1.5 million illegal aliens arrested each year must be told they may (1) talk with a lawyer, (2) make a phone call, (3) request a list of available legal services, (4) seek a hearing before an immigration judge, (5) possibly obtain release on bond, and (6) contact a diplomatic officer representing their country. Notice of this type was "long overdue," said Roberto Martinez of the American Friends

CJ Exhibit 2
The *Miranda* Warnings

ADULT RIGHTS WARNING

Suspects 18 years old or older who are in custody must be advised of the following rights before any questioning begins:

1. You have the right to remain silent.
2. Anything you say can be used against you in a court of law.
3. You have the right to talk to a lawyer and to have a lawyer present while you are being questioned.
4. If you want a lawyer before or during questioning but cannot afford to hire a lawyer, one will be appointed to represent you at no cost before any questioning.
5. If you answer questions now without a lawyer here, you still have the right to stop answering questions at any time.

WAIVER OF RIGHTS

After reading and explaining the rights of a person in custody, an officer must also ask for a waiver of those rights before any questioning. The following waiver questions must be answered affirmatively, either by express answer or by clear implication. Silence alone is not a waiver.

1. Do you understand each of these rights I have explained to you? (Answer must be YES.)
2. Having these rights in mind, do you now wish to answer questions? (Answer must be YES.)
3. Do you now wish to answer questions without a lawyer present? (Answer must be YES.)

The following question must be asked of juveniles ages 14, 15, 16, and 17:

1. Do you now wish to answer questions without your parents, guardians, or custodians present? (Answer must be YES.)

Source: North Carolina Justice Academy. Reprinted with permission.

Service Committee's Mexico-U.S. border program. "Up to now, we've had total mistreatment of civil rights of undocumented people."[159]

When the *Miranda* decision was originally handed down, some hailed it as ensuring the protection of individual rights guaranteed under the Constitution. To guarantee those rights, they suggested, no better agency is available than the police themselves, since the police are present at the initial stages of the criminal justice process. Critics of *Miranda*, however, argued that the decision put police agencies in the uncomfortable and contradictory position not only of enforcing the law but also of having to offer defendants advice on how they might circumvent conviction and punishment. Under *Miranda*, the police partially assume the role of legal adviser to the accused.

In 1999, however, in the case of *U.S.* v. *Dickerson*,[160] the Fourth Circuit U.S. Court of Appeals upheld an almost-forgotten law that Congress had passed in 1968 with the intention of overturning *Miranda*. That law, Section 3501 of Chapter 223, Part II of Title 18 of the U.S. Code, says that "a confession . . . shall be admissible in evidence if it is voluntarily given." Upon appeal in 2000, the U.S. Supreme Court upheld its original *Miranda* ruling by a 7–2 vote and found that *Miranda* is a constitutional rule (that is, a fundamental right inherent in the U.S. Constitution) that cannot be dismissed by an act of Congress. "*Miranda* and its progeny," the majority wrote in *Dickerson* v. *U.S.*, will continue to "govern the admissibility of statements made during custodial interrogation in both state and federal courts."[161]

In 2004, in the case of *U.S.* v. *Patane*,[162] the U.S. Supreme Court continued to refine its original 1966 *Miranda* ruling. *Patane* surprised some Court watchers because in it the Court held that "a mere failure to give *Miranda* warnings does not, by itself, violate a suspect's constitutional rights or even the *Miranda* rule." The *Patane* case began with the arrest of a convicted felon after a federal agent told officers that the man owned a handgun illegally. At the time of arrest, the officers tried to advise the defendant of his rights, but he interrupted them, saying that he already knew his rights. The officers then asked him about the pistol, and he told them where it was. After the weapon was recovered, the defendant was charged with illegal possession of a firearm by a convicted felon.

At first glance, *Patane* appears to contradict the fruit of the poisonous tree doctrine that the Court established in the 1920 case of *Silverthorne Lumber Co.* v. *U.S.*[163] and that *Wong Sun* v. *U.S.* (1963)[164] made applicable to verbal evidence derived immediately from an illegal search and seizure. An understanding of *Patane*, however, requires recognition of the fact that the *Miranda* rule is based on the self-incrimination clause of the Fifth Amendment to the U.S. Constitution. According to the Court in *Patane*, "that Clause's core protection is a prohibition on compelling a criminal defendant to testify against himself at trial." It cannot be violated, the Court said, "by the introduction of nontestimonial evidence obtained as a result of voluntary statements." In other words, according to the Court, only (1) coerced statements and (2) those voluntary statements made by a defendant that might directly incriminate him or her at a later trial are precluded by a failure to read a suspect his or her *Miranda* rights. Such voluntary statements would, of course, include such things as an outright confession.

Significantly, however, oral statements must be distinguished, the Court said, from the "physical fruits of the suspect's unwarned but voluntary statements." In other words, if an unwarned suspect is questioned by police officers and tells the officers where they can find an illegal weapon or a weapon that has been used in a crime, the weapon can be recovered and later introduced as evidence at the suspect's trial. If the same unwarned suspect, however, tells police that he committed a murder, then his confession will not be allowed into evidence at trial. The line drawn by the Court is against the admissibility of *oral statements* made by an unwarned defendant, not the *nontestimonial physical evidence* resulting from continued police investigation of such statements. Under *Patane*, the oral statements themselves cannot be admitted, but the physical evidence derived from them can be. "Thus," wrote the justices in *Patane*, "admission of nontestimonial physical fruits (the pistol here) does not run the risk of admitting into trial an accused's coerced incriminating statements against himself."

▲ A suspect being read his *Miranda* rights immediately after arrest. Officers often read *Miranda* rights from a card to preclude the possibility of making a mistake. What might be the consequences of a mistake?
Michael Newman/PhotoEdit Inc.

Waiver of *Miranda* Rights by Suspects

Suspects in police custody may legally waive their *Miranda* rights through a voluntary "knowing and intelligent" waiver. A knowing waiver can only be made if a suspect has been advised of his or her rights and was in a condition to understand the advisement. A rights advisement made in English to a Spanish-speaking suspect, for example, cannot produce a knowing waiver. Likewise, an intelligent waiver of rights requires that the defendant be able to understand the consequences of not invoking the *Miranda* rights. In the case of *Moran* v. *Burbine* (1986),[165] the U.S. Supreme Court defined an intelligent and knowing waiver as one "made with a full awareness both of the nature of the right being abandoned and the consequences of the decision to abandon it." In *Colorado* v. *Spring* (1987),[166] the Court held that an intelligent and knowing waiver can be made even though a suspect has not been informed of all the alleged offenses about which he or she is about to be questioned.

Inevitable-Discovery Exception to *Miranda*

The case of Robert Anthony Williams provides a good example of the change in the U.S. Supreme Court philosophy, alluded to earlier in this chapter, from an individual-rights perspective toward a public-order perspective. The case epitomizes what some have called a "nibbling away" at the advances in defendant rights, which reached their apex in *Miranda*. The case began in 1969, at the close of the Warren Court era, when Williams was convicted of murdering a ten-year-old girl, Pamela Powers, around Christmastime. Although Williams had been advised of his rights, detectives searching for the girl's body were riding in a car with the defendant when one of them made what has since come to be known as the "Christian burial speech." The detective told Williams that since Christmas was almost upon them, it would be "the Christian thing to do" to see to it that Pamela could have a decent burial rather than having to lay in a field somewhere. Williams relented and led detectives to the body. However, because Williams had not been reminded of his right to have a lawyer present during his conversation with the detective, the Supreme Court in *Brewer* v. *Williams* (1977)[167] overturned Williams's conviction, saying that the detective's remarks were "a deliberate eliciting of incriminating evidence from an accused in the absence of his lawyer."

In 1977, Williams was retried for the murder, but his remarks in leading detectives to the body were not entered into evidence. The discovery of the body was itself used, however, prompting another appeal to the Supreme Court based on the argument that the body should not have been used as evidence since it was discovered due to the illegally gathered statements. This time, in *Nix* v. *Williams* (1984),[168] the Supreme Court affirmed Williams's

Suspects may legally waive their *Miranda* rights through a voluntary "knowing and intelligent" waiver.

second conviction, holding that the body would have been found anyway, since detectives were searching in the direction where it lay when Williams revealed its location. That ruling came during the heyday of the Burger Court and clearly demonstrates a tilt by the Court away from suspects' rights and an accommodation with the imperfect world of police procedure. The *Williams* case, as it was finally resolved, is said to have created the *inevitable-discovery exception* to the *Miranda* requirements. The inevitable-discovery exception means that evidence, even if it was otherwise gathered inappropriately, can be used in a court of law if it would have invariably turned up in the normal course of events.

Public-Safety Exception to *Miranda*

Also in 1984, the U.S. Supreme Court established what has come to be known as the *public-safety exception* to the *Miranda* rule. The case of *New York* v. *Quarles*[169] centered on a rape in which the victim told police her assailant had fled, with a gun, into a nearby A&P supermarket. Two police officers entered the store and apprehended the suspect. One officer immediately noticed that the man was wearing an empty shoulder holster and, apparently fearing that a child might find the discarded weapon, quickly asked, "Where's the gun?" Quarles was convicted of rape but appealed his conviction, requesting that the weapon be suppressed as evidence because officers had not advised him of his *Miranda* rights before asking him about it. The Supreme Court disagreed, stating that considerations of public safety were overriding and negated the need for rights advisement before limited questioning that focused on the need to prevent further harm.

The U.S. Supreme Court has also held that in cases when the police issue *Miranda* warnings, a later demonstration that a person may have been suffering from mental problems does not necessarily negate a confession. *Colorado* v. *Connelly* (1986)[170] involved a man who approached a Denver police officer and said he wanted to confess to the murder of a young girl. The officer immediately informed him of his *Miranda* rights, but the man waived them and continued to talk. When a detective arrived, the man was again advised of his rights and again waived them. After being taken to the local jail, the man began to hear "voices" and later claimed that it was these voices that had made him confess. At the trial, the defense moved to have the earlier confession negated on the basis that it was not voluntarily or freely given because of the defendant's mental condition. Upon appeal, the U.S. Supreme Court disagreed, saying that "no coercive government conduct occurred in this case." Hence "self-coercion," be it through the agency of a guilty conscience or faulty thought processes, does not appear to bar prosecution based on information revealed willingly by a suspect.

In another refinement of *Miranda*, the lawful ability of a police informant placed in a jail cell along with a defendant to gather information for later use at trial was upheld in the 1986 case of *Kuhlmann* v. *Wilson*.[171] The passive gathering of information was judged to be acceptable, provided that the informant did not make attempts to elicit information.

In the case of *Illinois* v. *Perkins* (1990),[172] the Court expanded its position to say that under appropriate circumstances, even the active questioning of a suspect by an undercover officer posing as a fellow inmate does not require *Miranda* warnings. In *Perkins*, the Court found that, lacking other forms of coercion, the fact that the suspect was not aware of the questioner's identity as a law enforcement officer ensured that his statements were freely given. In the words of the Court, "The essential ingredients of a 'police-dominated atmosphere' and compulsion are not present when an incarcerated person speaks freely to someone that he believes to be a fellow inmate."

In-court references to a defendant's silence following *Miranda* warnings are unconstitutional.

Miranda and the Meaning of Interrogation

Modern interpretations of the applicability of *Miranda* warnings turn on an understanding of interrogation. The *Miranda* decision, as originally rendered, specifically recognized the need for police investigators to make inquiries at crime scenes to determine facts or to establish identities. As long as the individual questioned is not yet in custody and as long as probable cause is lacking in the investigator's mind, such questioning can proceed without *Miranda* warnings. In such cases, interrogation, within the meaning of *Miranda*, has not yet begun.

The case of *Rock* v. *Zimmerman* (1982)[173] provides a different sort of example—one in which a suspect willingly made statements to the police before interrogation began.

The suspect had burned his own house and shot and killed a neighbor. When the fire department arrived, he began shooting again and killed the fire chief. Cornered later in a field, the defendant, gun in hand, spontaneously shouted at police, "How many people did I kill? How many people are dead?"[174] These spontaneous questions were held to be admissible evidence at the suspect's trial.

It is also important to recognize that the Supreme Court, in the *Miranda* decision, required that officers provide warnings only in those situations involving *both* arrest and custodial interrogation—what some call the ***Miranda* triggers**. In other words, it is generally permissible for officers to take a suspect into custody and listen without asking questions while he or she tells a story. Similarly, they may ask questions without providing a *Miranda* warning, even within the confines of a police station house, as long as the person questioned is not a suspect and is not under arrest.[175] Warnings are required only when officers begin to actively and deliberately elicit responses from a suspect whom they know has been indicted or who is in custody.

***Miranda* triggers**
The dual principles of custody and interrogation, both of which are necessary before an advisement of rights is required.

A third-party conversation recorded by the police after a suspect has invoked the *Miranda* right to remain silent may be used as evidence, according to a 1987 ruling in *Arizona* v. *Mauro*.[176] In *Mauro*, a man who willingly conversed with his wife in the presence of a police tape recorder, even after invoking his right to keep silent, was held to have effectively abandoned that right.

When a waiver is not made, however, in-court references to a defendant's silence following the issuing of *Miranda* warnings are unconstitutional. In the 1976 case of *Doyle* v. *Ohio*,[177] the U.S. Supreme Court definitively ruled that "a suspect's [post-*Miranda*] silence will not be used against him." Even so, according to the Court in *Brecht* v. *Abrahamson* (1993),[178] prosecution efforts to use such silence against a defendant may not invalidate a finding of guilt by a jury unless the "error had substantial and injurious effect or influence in determining the jury's verdict."[179]

The 2004 case of *Missouri* v. *Seibert*[180] addressed the legality of a two-step police interrogation technique in which suspects were questioned and—if they made incriminating statements—were then advised of their *Miranda* rights and questioned again. The justices found that such a technique could not meet constitutional muster, writing, "When the [*Miranda*] warnings are inserted in the midst of coordinated and continuing interrogation, they are likely to mislead and deprive a defendant of knowledge essential to his ability to understand the nature of his rights and the consequences of abandoning them. . . . And it would be unrealistic to treat two spates of integrated and proximately conducted questioning as independent interrogations . . . simply because *Miranda* warnings formally punctuate them in the middle."

Finally, in the 2010 case of *Florida* v. *Powell*, the U.S. Supreme Court held that although *Miranda* warnings are generally required prior to police interrogation, the wording of those warnings is not set in stone. The Court ruled that "in determining whether police warnings were satisfactory, reviewing courts are not required to examine them as if construing a will or defining the terms of an easement. The inquiry is simply whether the warnings reasonably convey to a suspect his rights as required by *Miranda*."[181]

Gathering of Special Kinds of Nontestimonial Evidence

The role of law enforcement is complicated by the fact that suspects are often privy to special evidence of a nontestimonial sort. Nontestimonial evidence is generally physical evidence, and most physical evidence is subject to normal procedures of search and seizure. A special category of nontestimonial evidence, however, includes very personal items that may be within or part of a person's body, such as ingested drugs, blood cells, foreign objects, medical implants, and human DNA. Also included in this category might be fingerprints and other kinds of biological residue. The gathering of such special kinds of nontestimonial evidence is a complex area rich in precedent. The Fourth Amendment guarantee that people be secure in their homes and in their persons has generally been interpreted by the courts to mean that the improper seizure of physical evidence of any kind is illegal and will result in exclusion of that evidence at trial. When very personal kinds of nontestimonial evidence are considered, however, the issue becomes more complicated.

The Right to Privacy

Two 1985 cases, *Hayes* v. *Florida*[182] and *Winston* v. *Lee*,[183] are examples of limits the courts have placed on the seizure of very personal forms of nontestimonial evidence. The *Hayes* case established the right of suspects to refuse to be fingerprinted when probable cause necessary to effect an arrest does not exist. *Winston* demonstrated the inviolability of the body against surgical and other substantially invasive techniques that might be ordered by authorities against a suspect's will.

In the *Winston* case, Rudolph Lee, Jr., was found a few blocks from the scene of a robbery with a gunshot wound in his chest. The robbery had involved an exchange of gunshots by a store owner and the robber, with the owner noting that the robber had apparently been hit by a bullet. At the hospital, the store owner identified Lee as the robber. The prosecution sought to have Lee submit to surgery to remove the bullet in his chest, arguing that the bullet would provide physical evidence linking him to the crime. Lee refused the surgery, and in *Winston* v. *Lee*, the U.S. Supreme Court ruled that Lee could not be ordered to undergo surgery because such a magnitude of intrusion into his body was unacceptable under the right to privacy guaranteed by the Fourth Amendment. The *Winston* case was based on precedent established in *Schmerber* v. *California* (1966).[184] The *Schmerber* case turned on the extraction against the defendant's will of a blood sample to be measured for alcohol content. In *Schmerber*, the Court ruled that warrants must be obtained for bodily intrusions unless fast action is necessary to prevent the destruction of evidence by natural physiological processes.

Body-Cavity Searches

In early 2005, officers of the Suffolk County (New York) Police Department arrested 36-year-old Terrance Haynes and charged him with marijuana possession.[185] After placing him in the back of a patrol car, Haynes appeared to choke and had difficulty breathing. Soon his breathing stopped, prompting officers to use the Heimlich maneuver, which dislodged a plastic bag from Haynes's windpipe. The bag contained 11 packets of cocaine. Although Haynes survived the ordeal, he faced up to 25 years in prison.

While some suspects might literally "cough up" evidence, some are more successful at hiding it *in* their bodies. Body-cavity searches are among the most problematic types of searches for police today. "Strip" searches of convicts in prison, including the search of body cavities, have generally been held to be permissible.

The 1985 Supreme Court case of *U.S.* v. *Montoya de Hernandez*[186] focused on the issue of "alimentary canal smuggling," in which the offender typically swallows condoms filled with cocaine or heroin and waits for nature to take its course to recover the substance. In the *Montoya* case, a woman known to be a "balloon swallower" arrived in the United States on a flight from Colombia. She was detained by customs officials and given a pat-down search by a female agent. The agent reported that the woman's abdomen was firm and suggested that X-rays be taken. The suspect refused and was given the choice of submitting to further tests or taking the next flight back to Colombia. No flight was immediately available, however, and the suspect was placed in a room for 16 hours, where she refused all food and drink. Finally, a court order for an X-ray was obtained. The procedure revealed "balloons," and the woman was detained another four days, during which time she passed numerous cocaine-filled plastic condoms. The Court ruled that the woman's confinement was not unreasonable, based as it was on the supportable suspicion that she was "body-packing" cocaine. Any discomfort she experienced, the Court ruled, "resulted solely from the method that she chose to smuggle illicit drugs."[187]

Electronic Eavesdropping

Modern technology makes possible increasingly complex forms of communication. One of the first and best known of the U.S. Supreme Court decisions involving electronic communications was the 1928 case of *Olmstead* v. *U.S.*[188] In *Olmstead*, bootleggers used their home telephones to discuss and transact business. Agents tapped the lines and based their investigation and ensuing arrests on conversations they overheard. The defendants were convicted and eventually appealed to the high court, arguing that the agents had in effect seized information illegally without a search warrant in violation of the defendants' Fourth Amendment right to be secure in their homes. The Court ruled, however, that telephone lines were not an extension of the defendants' home and therefore were not protected by the constitutional guarantee of security. Subsequent federal statutes (discussed shortly) have substantially modified the significance of *Olmstead*.

Recording devices carried on the body of an undercover agent or an informant were ruled to produce admissible evidence in *On Lee* v. *U.S.* (1952)[189] and *Lopez* v. *U.S.* (1963).[190] The 1967 case of *Berger* v. *New York*[191] permitted wiretaps and "bugs" in instances where state law provided for the use of such devices and where officers obtained a warrant based on probable cause.

Recording devices carried on the body of an undercover agent produce admissible evidence.

The Court appeared to undertake a significant change of direction in the area of electronic eavesdropping when it decided the case of *Katz* v. *U.S.* in 1967.[192] Federal agents had monitored a number of Katz's telephone calls from a public phone using a device separate from the phone lines and attached to the glass of the phone booth. The Court, in this case, stated that what a person makes an effort to keep private, even in a public place, requires a judicial decision, in the form of a warrant issued upon probable cause, to unveil. In the words of the Court, "The government's activities in electronically listening to and recording the petitioner's words violated the privacy upon which he justifiably relied while using the telephone booth and thus constituted a 'search and seizure' within the meaning of the Fourth Amendment."

In 1968, with the case of *Lee* v. *Florida*,[193] the Court applied the Federal Communications Act[194] to telephone conversations that may be the object of police investigation and held that evidence obtained without a warrant could not be used in state proceedings if it resulted from a wiretap. The only person who has the authority to permit eavesdropping, according to that act, is the sender of the message.

The Federal Communications Act, originally passed in 1934, does not specifically mention the potential interest of law enforcement agencies in monitoring communications. Title III of the Omnibus Crime Control and Safe Streets Act of 1968, however, mostly prohibits wiretaps but does allow officers to listen to electronic communications when (1) an officer is one of the parties involved in the communication, (2) one of the parties is not the officer but willingly decides to share the communication with the officer, or (3) officers obtain a warrant based on probable cause. In the 1971 case of *U.S.* v. *White*,[195] the Court held that law enforcement officers may intercept electronic information when one of the parties involved in the communication gives his or her consent, even without a warrant.

In 1984, the Supreme Court decided the case of *U.S.* v. *Karo*,[196] in which DEA agents had arrested James Karo for cocaine importation. Officers had placed a radio transmitter inside a 50-gallon drum of ether purchased by Karo for use in processing the cocaine. The transmitter was placed inside the drum with the consent of the seller of the ether but without a search warrant. The shipment of ether was followed to the Karo house, and Karo was arrested and convicted of cocaine-trafficking charges. Karo appealed to the U.S. Supreme Court, claiming that the radio beeper had violated his reasonable expectation of privacy inside his premises and that, without a warrant, the evidence it produced was tainted. The Court agreed and overturned his conviction.

Minimization Requirement for Electronic Surveillance

The Supreme Court established a minimization requirement pertinent to electronic surveillance in the 1978 case of *U.S.* v. *Scott*.[197] *Minimization* means that officers must make every reasonable effort to monitor only those conversations, through the use of phone taps, body bugs, and the like, that are specifically related to the criminal activity under investigation. As soon as it becomes obvious that a conversation is innocent, then the monitoring personnel are required to cease their invasion of privacy. Problems arise if the conversation occurs in a foreign language, if it is "coded," or if it is ambiguous. It has been suggested that investigators involved in electronic surveillance maintain logbooks of their activities that specifically show monitored conversations, as well as efforts made at minimization.[198]

The Electronic Communications Privacy Act of 1986

Passed by Congress in 1986, the **Electronic Communications Privacy Act (ECPA)**[199] brought major changes in the requirements law enforcement officers must meet to intercept wire communications (those involving the human voice). The ECPA deals specifically with

Electronic Communications Privacy Act (ECPA)
A law passed by Congress in 1986 establishing the due process requirements that law enforcement officers must meet in order to legally intercept wire communications.

> The PATRIOT Act has not diminished our liberty. It has defended our liberty and made America more secure.
>
> —George W. Bush, forty-third president of the United States

three areas of communication: (1) wiretaps and bugs, (2) pen registers that record the numbers dialed from a telephone, and (3) tracing devices that determine the number from which a call emanates. The act also addresses the procedures to be followed by officers in obtaining records relating to communications services, and it establishes requirements for gaining access to stored electronic communications and records of those communications. The ECPA basically requires that investigating officers must obtain wiretap-type court orders to eavesdrop on *ongoing communications.* The use of pen registers and recording devices, however, is specifically excluded by the law from court order requirements.[200]

A related measure, the Communications Assistance for Law Enforcement Act of 1994,[201] appropriated $500 million to modify the U.S. phone system to allow for continued wiretapping by law enforcement agencies. The law also specifies a standard-setting process for the redesign of existing equipment that would permit effective wiretapping in the face of coming technological advances. In the words of the FBI's Telecommunications Industry Liaison Unit, "This law requires telecommunications carriers, as defined in the Act, to ensure law enforcement's ability, pursuant to court order or other lawful authorization, to intercept communications notwithstanding advanced telecommunications technologies."[202] In 2009, 2,376 wiretap requests were approved by federal and state judges, and approximately 4.6 million conversations were intercepted by law enforcement agencies throughout the country.[203]

The Telecommunications Act of 1996

Title V of the Telecommunications Act of 1996[204] made it a federal offense for anyone engaged in interstate or international communications to knowingly use a telecommunications device "to create, solicit, or initiate the transmission of any comment, request, suggestion, proposal, image, or other communication which is obscene, lewd, lascivious, filthy, or indecent, with intent to annoy, abuse, threaten, or harass another person." The law also provided special penalties for anyone who "makes a telephone call . . . without disclosing his identity and with intent to annoy, abuse, threaten, or harass any person at the called number or who receives the communication" or who "makes or causes the telephone of another repeatedly or continuously to ring, with intent to harass any person at the called number; or makes repeated telephone calls" for the purpose of harassing a person at the called number.

A section of the law, known as the Communications Decency Act (CDA),[205] criminalized the transmission to minors of "patently offensive" obscene materials over the Internet or other computer telecommunications services. Portions of the CDA, however, were invalidated by the U.S. Supreme Court in the case of *Reno* v. *ACLU* (1997).[206]

The USA PATRIOT Act of 2001

USA PATRIOT Act
A federal law (Public Law 107–56) enacted in response to terrorist attacks on the World Trade Center and the Pentagon on September 11, 2001. The law, officially titled the Uniting and Strengthening America by Providing Appropriate Tools Required to Intercept and Obstruct Terrorism Act, substantially broadened the investigative authority of law enforcement agencies throughout America and is applicable to many crimes other than terrorism. The law was slightly revised and reauthorized by Congress in 2006.

The **USA PATRIOT Act** of 2001, which is also discussed in CJ Exhibit 3, made it easier for police investigators to intercept many forms of electronic communications. Under previous federal law, for example, investigators could not obtain a wiretap order to intercept *wire* communications for violations of the Computer Fraud and Abuse Act.[207] In several well-known investigations, however, hackers had stolen teleconferencing services from telephone companies and then used those services to plan and execute hacking attacks.

The act[208] added felony violations of the Computer Fraud and Abuse Act to Section 2516(1) of Title 18 of the U.S. Code—the portion of federal law that lists specific types of crimes for which investigators may obtain a wiretap order for wire communications.

The USA PATRIOT Act of 2001 also modified that portion of the ECPA that governs law enforcement access to stored electronic communications (such as e-mail) to include stored wire communications (such as voice mail). Before the modification, law enforcement officers needed to obtain a wiretap order (rather than a search warrant) to obtain unopened voice communications. Because today's e-mail messages may contain digitized voice "attachments," investigators were sometimes required to obtain both a search warrant and a wiretap order to learn the contents of a specific message. Under the act, the same rules now apply to both stored wire communications and stored electronic communications. Wiretap

CJ Exhibit 3
The USA PATRIOT Act of 2001 and the USA PATRIOT Improvement and Reauthorization Act of 2005

On October 26, 2001, President George W. Bush signed into law the USA PATRIOT Act, also known as the Uniting and Strengthening America by Providing Appropriate Tools Required to Intercept and Obstruct Terrorism Act. The law, which was drafted in response to the September 11, 2001, terrorist attacks on American targets, substantially increased the investigatory authority of federal, state, and local police agencies.

The act permits longer jail terms for certain suspects arrested without a warrant, broadens authority for **"sneak and peek" searches** (searches conducted without prior notice and in the absence of the suspect), and enhances the power of prosecutors. The law also increases the ability of federal authorities to tap phones (including wireless devices), share intelligence information, track Internet usage, crack down on money laundering, and protect U.S. borders. Many of the crime-fighting powers created under the legislation are not limited to acts of terrorism but apply to many different kinds of criminal offenses.

The 2001 law led individual-rights advocates to question whether the government unfairly expanded police powers at the expense of civil liberties. While many aspects of the USA PATRIOT Act have been criticized as potentially unconstitutional, Section 213, which authorizes delayed notice of the execution of a warrant, may be most vulnerable to court challenge. The American Civil Liberties Union (ACLU) maintains that under this section, law enforcement agents could enter a house, apartment, or office with a search warrant while the occupant is away, search through his or her property, and take photographs without having to tell the suspect about the search until later.[1] The ACLU also believes that this provision is illegal because the Fourth Amendment to the Constitution protects against unreasonable searches and seizures and requires the government to obtain a warrant and to give notice to the person whose property will be searched before conducting the search. The notice requirement enables the suspect to assert his or her Fourth Amendment rights.

In 2005, the U.S. Congress reauthorized most provisions of the USA PATRIOT Act, and on February 27, 2011, President Obama signed legislation providing for an extension of several terrorist surveillance provisions included in the USA PATRIOT Act and in the Intelligence Reform and Terrorism Prevention Act of 2004.

Read the entire USA PATRIOT Act of 2001 at **Library Extra 6**. Title 18 of the U.S. Code is available at **Library Extra 7**. The USA PATRIOT Improvement and Reauthorization Act of 2005 is available at **Library Extra 8**.

[1] Much of the information in this paragraph is taken from American Civil Liberties Union, "How the Anti-Terrorism Bill Expands Law Enforcement 'Sneak and Peek' Warrants," http://www.aclu.org/congress/1102301b.html (accessed February 12, 2005).

References: USA PATRIOT Improvement and Reauthorization Act of 2005 (Public Law 109–177); U.S. Department of Justice, Field Guidance on Authorities (Redacted) Enacted in the 2001 Anti-Terrorism Legislation (Washington, DC: DOJ, no date), http://www.epic.org/terrorism/DOJguidance.pdf (accessed August 28, 2009); USA PATRIOT Act, 2001 (Public Law 107–56); American Civil Liberties Union, "How the Anti-Terrorism Bill Expands Law Enforcement 'Sneak and Peek' Warrants," http://www.aclu.org/congress/1102301b.html (accessed August 28, 2009); American Civil Liberties Union, "How the Anti-Terrorism Bill Limits Judicial Oversight of Telephone and Internet Surveillance," http://www.aclu.org/congress/1102301g.html (accessed August 28, 2009); and the White House, "Bills Signed into Law by the President," February 27, 2010, http://www.whitehouse.gov/the-press-office/bills-signed-law-president (accessed September 16, 2010).

orders, which are often much more difficult to obtain than search warrants, are now only required to intercept real-time telephone conversations.

"sneak and peek" search
A search that occurs in the suspect's absence and without his or her prior knowledge. Also known as a *delayed-notification search.*

Before passage of the USA PATRIOT Act, federal law allowed investigators to use an administrative subpoena (that is, a subpoena authorized by a federal or state statute or by a federal or state grand jury or trial court) to compel Internet service providers to provide a limited class of information, such as a customer's name, address, length of service, and means of payment. Also under previous law, investigators could not subpoena certain records, including credit card numbers or details about other forms of payment for Internet service. Such information, however, can be highly relevant in determining a suspect's true identity because, in many cases, users register with Internet service providers using false names.

Previous federal law[209] was also technology specific, relating primarily to telephone communications. Local and long-distance telephone billing records, for example, could be subpoenaed but not billing information for Internet communications or records of Internet session times and durations. Similarly, previous law allowed the government to use a subpoena to obtain the customer's "telephone number or other subscriber number or identity" but did not define what that phrase meant in the context of Internet communications.

The USA PATRIOT Act amended portions of this federal law[210] to update and expand the types of records that law enforcement authorities may obtain with a subpoena. "Records of session times and durations," as well as "any temporarily assigned network address," may now be gathered. Such changes should make the process of identifying computer criminals and tracing their Internet communications faster and easier.

Finally, the USA PATRIOT Act facilitates the use of roving, or multipoint, wiretaps. Roving wiretaps, issued with court approval, target a specific individual and not a particular telephone number or communications device. Hence law enforcement agents armed with an order for a multipoint wiretap can follow the flow of communications engaged in by a person as he or she switches from one cellular phone to another or to a wired telephone.

In 2006, President George W. Bush signed the USA PATRIOT Improvement and Reauthorization Act of 2005[211] into law. The act, also referred to as PATRIOT II, made permanent 14 provisions of the original 2001 legislation that had been slated to expire and extended others for another four years (including the roving wiretap provision and a provision that allows authorities to seize business records). It also addressed some of the concerns of civil libertarians who had criticized the earlier law as too restrictive. Finally, the new law provided additional protections for mass transportation systems and seaports, closed some legal loopholes in laws aimed at preventing terrorist financing, and included a subsection called the Combat Methamphetamine Epidemic Act (CMEA). The CMEA contains significant provisions intended to strengthen federal, state, and local efforts designed at curtailing the spread of methamphetamine use.

On February 27, 2010, President Barack Obama signed into law legislation extending a number of provisions of the PATRIOT Act that would have otherwise expired. The president's signature gave new life to the roving wiretap and business records provisions of the act, as well as some others.[212]

Learn more about electronic surveillance and wiretapping in criminal cases via **Web Extra 4**, and read the complete 2006 USA PATRIOT Act reauthorization legislation at **Library Extra 9**.

Electronic and Latent Evidence

The Internet, computer networks, and automated data systems present many new opportunities for committing criminal activity.[213] Computers and other electronic devices are increasingly being used to commit, enable, or support crimes perpetrated against people, organizations, and property. Whether the crime involves attacks against computer systems or the information they contain or more traditional offenses such as murder, money laundering, trafficking, or fraud, the proper seizure of **electronic evidence** that is specifically described in a valid search warrant has become increasingly important.

electronic evidence
Information and data of investigative value that are stored in or transmitted by an electronic device.[i]

Electronic evidence is "information and data of investigative value that are stored in or transmitted by an electronic device."[214] Such evidence is often acquired when physical items, such as computers, removable disks, CDs, DVDs, SSDs, flash drives, smart phones, SIM cards, iPads, iPods, Blackberrys, and other electronic devices, are collected from a crime scene or are obtained from a suspect.

Electronic evidence has special characteristics: (1) It is latent; (2) it can be sent across national and state borders quickly and easily; (3) it is fragile and can easily be altered, damaged, compromised, or destroyed by improper handling or improper examination; (4) it may be time sensitive. Like DNA or fingerprints, electronic evidence is **latent evidence** because it is not readily visible to the human eye under normal conditions. Special equipment and software are required to "see" and evaluate electronic evidence. In the courtroom, expert testimony may be needed to explain the acquisition of electronic evidence and the examination process used to interpret it.

latent evidence
Evidence of relevance to a criminal investigation that is not readily seen by the unaided eye.

In 2002, in recognition of the special challenges posed by electronic evidence, the Computer Crime and Intellectual Property Section (CCIPS) of the Criminal Division of the U.S. Department of Justice released a how-to manual for law enforcement officers called *Searching and Seizing Computers and Obtaining Electronic Evidence in Criminal Investigations.*[215] The manual, which is a how-to in **digital criminal forensics**, can be accessed via **Library Extra 10**.

digital criminal forensics
The lawful seizure, acquisition, analysis, reporting, and safeguarding of data from digital devices that may contain information of evidentiary value to the trier of fact in criminal events.[ii]

About the same time, the Technical Working Group for Electronic Crime Scene Investigation (TWGECSI) released a much more detailed guide for law enforcement officers to use in gathering electronic evidence. The manual, *Electronic Crime Scene Investigation: A Guide for First Responders*,[216] grew out of a partnership formed in 1998 between the National Cybercrime Training Partnership, the Office of Law Enforcement Standards, and the National Institute of Justice. The working group was asked to identify, define, and establish basic criteria to assist federal and state agencies in handling electronic investigations and related prosecutions.

TWGECSI guidelines say that law enforcement must take special precautions when documenting, collecting, and preserving electronic evidence to maintain its integrity. The guidelines also note that the first law enforcement officer on the scene (commonly called the *first responder*) should take steps to ensure the safety of everyone at the scene and to protect the integrity of all evidence, both traditional and electronic. The entire TWGECSI guide, which includes many practical instructions for investigators working with electronic evidence, is available at **Library Extra 11**.

Once digital evidence has been gathered, it must be analyzed. Consequently, in 2004, the government-sponsored Technical Working Group for the Examination of Digital Evidence (TWGEDE) published *Forensic Examination of Digital Evidence: A Guide for Law Enforcement*.[217] Among the guide's recommendations are that digital evidence should be acquired in a manner that protects and preserves the integrity of the original evidence and that examination should only be conducted on a *copy* of the original evidence. The entire guide, which is nearly 100 pages long, can be accessed via **Library Extra 12**.

Warrantless searches bear special mention in any discussion of electronic evidence. In the 1999 case of *U.S.* v. *Carey*,[218] a federal appellate court held that the consent a defendant had given to police for his apartment to be searched did not extend to the search of his computer once it was taken to a police station. Similarly, in *U.S.* v. *Turner* (1999),[219] the First Circuit Court of Appeals held that the warrantless police search of a defendant's personal computer while in his apartment exceeded the scope of the defendant's consent.

Summary

POLICING: LEGAL ASPECTS

- Legal restraints on police action stem primarily from the U.S. Constitution's Bill of Rights, especially the Fourth, Fifth, and Sixth Amendments, which (along with the Fourteenth Amendment) require due process of law. Most due process requirements of relevance to police work concern three major areas: (1) evidence and investigation (often called *search* and *seizure*), (2) arrest, and (3) interrogation. Each of these areas has been addressed by a number of important U.S. Supreme Court decisions, and this chapter discusses those decisions and their significance for police work.
- The Bill of Rights was designed to protect citizens against abuses of police power. It does so by guaranteeing due process of law for everyone suspected of having committed a crime and by ensuring the availability of constitutional rights to all citizens, regardless of state or local law or procedure. Within the context of criminal case processing, due process requirements mandate that all justice system officials, not only the police, respect the rights of accused individuals throughout the criminal justice process.
- The Fourth Amendment to the Constitution declares that people must be secure in their homes and in their persons against unreasonable searches and seizures. Consequently, law enforcement officers are generally required to demonstrate probable cause in order to obtain a search warrant if they are to conduct searches and seize the property of criminal suspects legally. The Supreme Court has established that police officers, in order to protect themselves from attack, have the right to search a person being arrested and to search the area under the arrestee's immediate control.
- An arrest takes place whenever a law enforcement officer restricts a person's freedom to leave. Arrests may occur when an officer comes upon a crime in progress, but most jurisdictions also allow warrantless arrests for felonies when a crime is not in progress, as long as probable cause can later be demonstrated.
- Information that is useful for law enforcement purposes is called *intelligence*, and as this chapter has shown, intelligence gathering is vital to police work. The need for useful information often leads police investigators to question suspects, informants, and potentially knowledgeable citizens. When suspects who are in custody become subject to interrogation, they must be advised of their *Miranda* rights before questioning begins. The *Miranda* warnings, which were mandated by the Supreme Court in the 1966 case of *Miranda* v. *Arizona*, are listed in this chapter. They ensure that suspects know their rights—including the right to remain silent—in the face of police interrogation.

QUESTIONS FOR REVIEW

1. Name some of the legal restraints on police action, and list some types of behavior that might be considered abuse of police authority.
2. How do the Bill of Rights and democratically inspired legal restraints on the police help ensure personal freedoms in our society?
3. Describe the legal standards for assessing searches and seizures conducted by law enforcement agents.
4. What is arrest, and when does it occur? How do legal understandings of the term differ from popular depictions of the arrest process?
5. What is the role of interrogation in intelligence gathering? List each of the *Miranda* warnings. Which recent U.S. Supreme Court cases have affected *Miranda* warning requirements?

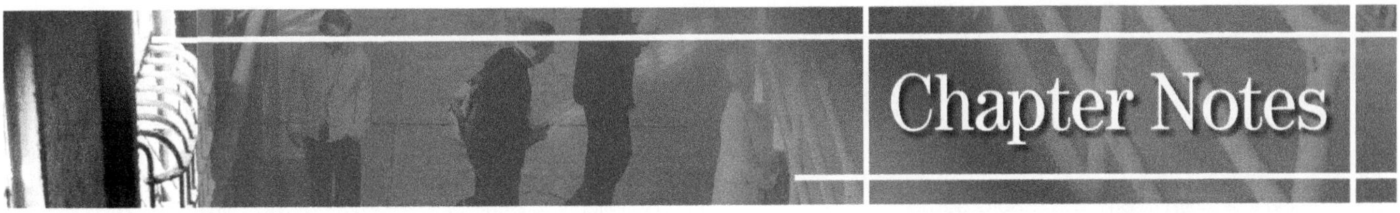

Chapter Notes

i. Adapted from Technical Working Group for Electronic Crime Scene Investigation, *Electronic Crime Scene Investigation: A Guide for First Responders* (Washington, DC: National Institute of Justice, 2001), p. 2.

ii. Adapted from Larry R. Leibrock, "Overview and Impact on 21st Century Legal Practice: Digital Forensics and Electronic Discovery," no date, http://www.courtroom21.net/FDIC.pps (accessed July 5, 2008).

---

1. Remarks of Governor Calvin Coolidge at the Worcester Police Outing, Worcester, Massachusetts (October 2, 1920).
2. Ellen Barry and Colin Moynihan, "Three Detectives Plead Not Guilty in 50-Shot Killing," *New York Times*, March 20, 2007, http://www.nytimes.com/2007/03/20/nyregion/20cops.html (accessed August 28, 2008).
3. Michael Wilson, "3 Detectives Acquitted in Bell Shooting," *New York Times*, April 26, 2008, www.nytimes.com/2008/04/26/nyregion/26BELL.html?ref=nyregion (accessed August 28, 2008).
4. Cara Buckley, "Diallo Verdict May Have Made Prosecutors Cautious," *New York Times*, March 20, 2007, http://www.nytimes.com/2007/03/20/nyregion/20charges.html?fta=y (accessed August 28, 2008).
5. Marcus Baram, "How Common Is Contagious Shooting?" ABC News, November 17, 2006, http://abcnews.go.com/Politics/story?id=2681947&page=1 (accessed May 21, 2007).
6. Michael Wilson, "50 Shots Fired, and the Experts Offer a Theory," *New York Times*, November 27, 2006, http://www.nytimes.com/2006/11/27/nyregion/27fire.html (accessed August 28, 2008).
7. "Victim of Police Beating Says He Was Sober," Associated Press, October 10, 2005, http://www.msnbc.msn.com/id/9645260 (accessed July 10, 2007).
8. "New Investigation May Postpone Police Trial in Video-Tape," KATC-TV, http://www.katc.com/Global/story.asp?S=4345819&nav=EyAz (accessed March 19, 2008).
9. "Police Brutality!" *Time*, March 25, 1991, p. 18.
10. "Police Charged in Beating Case Say They Feared for Their Lives," *Boston Globe*, May 22, 1991.
11. "Police Brutality!" pp. 16–19.
12. "Cries of Relief," *Time*, April 26, 1993, p. 18.
13. "Rodney King Slams SUV into House, Breaks Pelvis," CNN.com, April 16, 2003, http://www.cnn.com/2003/US/West/04/15/rodney.king.ap/index.html (accessed April 18, 2006).
14. *Miranda* v. *Arizona*, 384 U.S. 436 (1966).
15. *Weeks* v. *U.S.*, 232 U.S. 383 (1914).
16. *Silverthorne Lumber Co.* v. *U.S.*, 251 U.S. 385 (1920).
17. Clemmens Bartollas, *American Criminal Justice* (New York: Macmillan, 1988), p. 186.
18. *Mapp* v. *Ohio*, 367 U.S. 643 (1961).
19. *Chimel* v. *California*, 395 U.S. 752 (1969).
20. *Katz* v. *U.S.*, 389 U.S. 347, 88 S.Ct. 507 (1967).
21. *Minnesota* v. *Olson*, 110 S.Ct. 1684 (1990).
22. *Minnesota* v. *Carter*, 525 U.S. 83 (1998).
23. *Georgia* v. *Randolph*, 547 U.S. 103 (2006).
24. The ruling left open the possibility that any evidence relating to criminal activity undertaken by the consenting party might be admissible in court. In the words of the Court, refusal by a co-occupant "renders entry and search unreasonable and invalid as to him."
25. *U.S.* v. *Leon*, 468 U.S. 897, 104 S.Ct. 3405, 82 L.Ed.2d 677, 52 U.S.L.W. 5155 (1984).
26. Judicial titles vary among jurisdictions. Many lower-level state judicial officers are called *magistrates*. Federal magistrates, however, generally have a significantly higher level of judicial authority.
27. *Massachusetts* v. *Sheppard*, 104 S.Ct. 3424 (1984).
28. *Illinois* v. *Krull*, 107 S.Ct. 1160 (1987).
29. *Maryland* v. *Garrison*, 107 S.Ct. 1013 (1987).
30. *Illinois* v. *Rodriguez*, 110 S.Ct. 2793 (1990).
31. *Arizona* v. *Evans*, 115 S.Ct. 1185, 131 L.Ed.2d 34 (1995).
32. *Herring* v. *U.S.*, 555 U.S. ___ (2009).
33. See *California* v. *Acevedo*, 500 U.S. 565 (1991); *Ornelas* v. *U.S.*, 517 U.S. 690 (1996); and others.
34. See *Edwards* v. *Balisok*, 520 U.S. 641 (1997); *Booth* v. *Churner*, 532 U.S. 731 (2001); and *Porter* v. *Nussle*, 534 U.S. 516 (2002).
35. See *Wilson* v. *Arkansas*, 115 S.Ct. 1914 (1995); and *Richards* v. *Wisconsin*, 117 S.Ct. 1416 (1997).
36. See *McCleskey* v. *Kemp*, 481 U.S. 279, 107 S.Ct. 1756, 95 L.Ed.2d 262 (1987); *McCleskey* v. *Zant*, 499 U.S. 467, 493–494 (1991); *Coleman* v. *Thompson*, 501 U.S. 722 (1991); *Schlup* v. *Delo*, 115 S.Ct. 851, 130 L.Ed.2d 808 (1995); *Felker* v. *Turpin, Warden*, 117 S.Ct. 30, 135 L.Ed.2d 1123 (1996); *Boyde* v. *California*, 494 U.S. 370 (1990); and others.
37. See *Ewing* v. *California*, 538 U.S. 11 (2003); and *Lockyer* v. *Andrade*, 538 U.S. 63 (2003).
38. Richard Lacayo and Viveca Novak, "How Rehnquist Changed America," *Time*, June 30, 2003, pp. 20–25.
39. *Harris* v. *U.S.*, 390 U.S. 234 (1968).
40. The legality of plain-view seizures was also confirmed in earlier cases, including *Ker* v. *California*, 374 U.S. 23, 42–43 (1963); *U.S.* v. *Lee*, 274 U.S. 559 (1927); *U.S.* v. *Lefkowitz*, 285 U.S. 452, 465 (1932); and *Hester* v. *U.S.*, 265 U.S. 57 (1924).
41. As cited in Kimberly A. Kingston, "Look But Don't Touch: The Plain View Doctrine," *FBI Law Enforcement Bulletin* (December 1987), p. 18.
42. *Horton* v. *California*, 110 S.Ct. 2301, 47 CrL. 2135 (1990).
43. *U.S.* v. *Irizarry*, 673 F.2d 554, 556–67 (1st Cir. 1982).
44. *Arizona* v. *Hicks*, 107 S.Ct. 1149 (1987).
45. Inadvertence, as a requirement of legitimate plain-view seizures, was first cited in the U.S. Supreme Court case of *Coolidge* v. *New Hampshire*, 403 U.S. 443, 91 S.Ct. 2022 (1971).
46. *Horton* v. *California*, 110 S.Ct. 2301, 47 CrL. 2135 (1990).
47. Ibid.
48. *Brigham City* v. *Stuart*, 547 U.S. 398 (2006).
49. John Gales Sauls, "Emergency Searches of Premises," Part 1, *FBI Law Enforcement Bulletin* (March 1987), p. 23.
50. *Warden* v. *Hayden*, 387 U.S. 294 (1967).
51. *Mincey* v. *Arizona*, 437 U.S. 385, 392 (1978).
52. Sauls, "Emergency Searches of Premises," p. 25.
53. *Maryland* v. *Buie*, 110 S.Ct. 1093 (1990).

54. *Wilson* v. *Arkansas*, 115 S.Ct. 1914 (1995).
55. For additional information, see Michael J. Bulzomi, "Knock and Announce: A Fourth Amendment Standard," *FBI Law Enforcement Bulletin* (May 1997), pp. 27–31.
56. *Richards* v. *Wisconsin*, 117 S.Ct. 1416 (1997), syllabus.
57. *Illinois* v. *McArthur*, 531 U.S. 326 (2001).
58. *U.S.* v. *Banks*, 124 S.Ct. 521 (December 2, 2003).
59. *Hudson* v. *Michigan*, 547 U.S. 586 (2006).
60. *U.S.* v. *Grubbs*, 547 U.S. 90 (2006).
61. *U.S.* v. *Mendenhall*, 446 U.S. 544 (1980).
62. *Stansbury* v. *California*, 114 S.Ct. 1526, 1529, 128 L.Ed.2d 293 (1994).
63. *Yarborough* v. *Alvarado*, 541 U.S. 652 (2004).
64. *Thompson* v. *Keohane*, 516 U.S. 99, 112 (1996).
65. *Muehler* v. *Mena*, 125 S.Ct. 1465 (2005).
66. See *Michigan* v. *Summers*, 452 U.S. 692 (1981).
67. *Atwater* v. *Lago Vista*, 532 U.S. 318 (2001).
68. *Payton* v. *New York*, 445 U.S. 573 (1980).
69. In 1981, in the case of *U.S.* v. *Steagald* (451 U.S. 204), the Court ruled that a search warrant is also necessary when the planned arrest involves entry into a third party's premises.
70. *Kirk* v. *Louisiana*, 536 U.S. 635 (2002).
71. *U.S.* v. *Robinson*, 414 U.S. 218 (1973).
72. Ibid.
73. *Terry* v. *Ohio*, 392 U.S. 1 (1968).
74. *U.S.* v. *Sokolow*, 109 S.Ct. 1581 (1989).
75. The Court was quoting from *U.S.* v. *Brignoni-Ponce*, 422 U.S. 873, 878 (1975).
76. *U.S.* v. *Arvizu*, 534 U.S. 266 (2002).
77. Ibid.
78. *Minnesota* v. *Dickerson*, 113 S.Ct. 2130, 124 L.Ed.2d 334 (1993).
79. *Brown* v. *Texas*, 443 U.S. 47 (1979).
80. *Hiibel* v. *Sixth Judicial District Court of Nevada*, 542 U.S. 177 (2004).
81. *Smith* v. *Ohio*, 110 S.Ct. 1288 (1990).
82. *California* v. *Hodari D.*, 111 S.Ct. 1547 (1991).
83. *Criminal Justice Newsletter*, May 1, 1991, p. 2.
84. *Illinois* v. *Wardlow*, 528 U.S. 119 (2000).
85. Ibid., syllabus, http://supct.law.cornell.edu/supct/html/98-1036.ZS.html (accessed April 1, 2008).
86. Ibid.
87. *Arkansas* v. *Sanders*, 442 U.S. 753 (1979).
88. Ibid.
89. *U.S.* v. *Borchardt*, 809 F.2d 1115 (5th Cir. 1987).
90. *FBI Law Enforcement Bulletin* (January 1988), p. 28.
91. *Carroll* v. *U.S.*, 267 U.S. 132 (1925).
92. *Preston* v. *U.S.*, 376 U.S. 364 (1964).
93. *Arizona* v. *Gant*, U.S. Supreme Court, No. 07-542 (decided April 21, 2009).
94. *South Dakota* v. *Opperman*, 428 U.S. 364 (1976).
95. *Colorado* v. *Bertine*, 479 U.S. 367, 107 S.Ct. 741 (1987).
96. *Florida* v. *Wells*, 110 S.Ct. 1632 (1990).
97. *Terry* v. *Ohio*, 392 U.S. 1 (1968).
98. *California* v. *Acevedo*, 500 U.S. 565 (1991).
99. *Ornelas* v. *U.S.*, 517 U.S. 690, 696 (1996).
100. Ibid.
101. The phrase is usually attributed to the 1991 U.S. Supreme Court case of *California* v. *Acevedo* (500 U.S. 565 [1991]). See Devallis Rutledge, "Taking an Inventory," *Police*, November 1995, pp. 8–9.
102. *Florida* v. *Jimeno*, 111 S.Ct. 1801 (1991).
103. Ibid., syllabus, http://laws.findlaw.com/us/500/248.html (accessed March 2, 2008).
104. *U.S.* v. *Ross*, 456 U.S. 798 (1982).
105. Ibid.
106. *Whren* v. *U.S.*, 517 U.S. 806 (1996).
107. See *Pennsylvania* v. *Mimms*, 434 U.S. 106 (1977).
108. *Maryland* v. *Wilson*, 117 S.Ct. 882 (1997).
109. *Brendlin* v. *California*, 551 U.S. (2007).
110. *Knowles* v. *Iowa*, 525 U.S. 113 (1998).
111. *Wyoming* v. *Houghton*, 526 U.S. 295 (1999).
112. *Thornton* v. *U.S.*, 541 U.S. 615 (2004).
113. *Illinois* v. *Caballes*, 543 U.S. 405 (2005).
114. *Michigan Dept. of State Police* v. *Sitz*, 110 S.Ct. 2481 (1990).
115. *U.S.* v. *Martinez-Fuerte*, 428 U.S. 543 (1976).
116. Ibid., syllabus.
117. *Illinois* v. *Lidster*, 540 U.S. 419 (2004).
118. *U.S.* v. *Villamonte-Marquez*, 462 U.S. 579 (1983).
119. *California* v. *Carney*, 471 U.S. 386, 105 S.Ct. 2066, 85 L.Ed.2d 406, 53 U.S.L.W. 4521 (1985).
120. *U.S.* v. *Hill*, 855 F.2d 664 (10th Cir. 1988).
121. *National Treasury Employees Union* v. *Von Raab*, 489 U.S. 656 (1989).
122. *Skinner* v. *Railway Labor Executives' Association*, 489 U.S. 602 (1989).
123. *Florida* v. *Bostick*, 111 S.Ct. 2382 (1991).
124. *Bond* v. *U.S.*, 529 U.S. 334 (2000).
125. *U.S.* v. *Drayton*, 122 S.Ct. 2105 (2002).
126. *U.S.* v. *Flores-Montano*, 541 U.S. 149 (2004).
127. *People* v. *Deutsch*, 96 C.D.O.S. 2827 (1996).
128. The thermal imager differs from infrared devices (such as night-vision goggles) in that infrared devices amplify the infrared spectrum of light, whereas thermal imagers register solely the portion of the infrared spectrum that we call *heat*.
129. *People* v. *Deutsch*, 96 C.D.O.S. 2827 (1996).
130. *Kyllo* v. *U.S.*, 533 U.S. 27 (2001).
131. Ibid.
132. *Aguilar* v. *Texas*, 378 U.S. 108 (1964).
133. *U.S.* v. *Harris*, 403 U.S. 573 (1971).
134. Ibid., at 584.
135. *Illinois* v. *Gates*, 426 U.S. 213 (1983).
136. *Alabama* v. *White*, 110 S.Ct. 2412 (1990).
137. Ibid., at 2417.
138. *Florida* v. *J.L.*, 529 U.S. 266 (2000).
139. *U.S. Dept. of Justice* v. *Landano*, 113 S.Ct. 2014, 124 L.Ed.2d 84 (1993).
140. Richard Willing, "Third Law First to Order Taping Murder Confessions," *USA Today*, July 18, 2003.
141. Richard A. Leo and Kimberly D. Richman, "Mandate the Electronic Recording of Police Interrogations," *Crime and Public Policy*, Vol. 6 (June 2008), http://ssrn.com/abstract=1141335 (accessed September 8, 2010).
142. *South Dakota* v. *Neville*, 103 S.Ct. 916 (1983).
143. *Brown* v. *Mississippi*, 297 U.S. 278 (1936).
144. *Ashcraft* v. *Tennessee*, 322 U.S. 143 (1944).
145. *Chambers* v. *Florida*, 309 U.S. 227 (1940).
146. Ibid.
147. *Leyra* v. *Denno*, 347 U.S. 556 (1954).
148. *Arizona* v. *Fulminante*, 111 S.Ct. 1246 (1991).
149. *Chapman* v. *California*, 386 U.S. 18 (1967).
150. *State* v. *Fulminante*, No. CR-95-0160-AP (1999).
151. *Escobedo* v. *Illinois*, 378 U.S. 478 (1964).
152. *Edwards* v. *Arizona*, 451 U.S. 477, 101 S.Ct. 1880, 68 L.Ed.2d 378 (1981).
153. *Michigan* v. *Jackson*, 475 U.S. 625 (1986).
154. *Minnick* v. *Mississippi*, 498 U.S. 146 (1990).
155. *Arizona* v. *Roberson*, 486 U.S. 675, 108 S.Ct. 2093 (1988).
156. *Davis* v. *U.S.*, 114 S.Ct. 2350 (1994).
157. *Montejo* v. *Louisiana*, 556 U.S. ___ (2009).
158. *Miranda* v. *Arizona*, 384 U.S. 436 (1966).
159. "Immigrants Get Civil Rights," *USA Today*, June 11, 1992.
160. *U.S.* v. *Dickerson*, 166 F.3d 667 (1999).
161. *Dickerson* v. *U.S.*, 530 U.S. 428 (2000).
162. *U.S.* v. *Patane*, 542 U.S. 630 (2004).

163. *Silverthorne Lumber Co.* v. *U.S.*, 251 U.S. 385 (1920).
164. *Wong Sun* v. *U.S.*, 371 U.S. 471 (1963).
165. *Moran* v. *Burbine*, 475 U.S. 412, 421 (1986).
166. *Colorado* v. *Spring*, 479 U.S. 564, 107 S.Ct. 851 (1987).
167. *Brewer* v. *Williams*, 430 U.S. 387 (1977).
168. *Nix* v. *Williams*, 104 S.Ct. 2501 (1984).
169. *New York* v. *Quarles*, 104 S.Ct. 2626, 81 L.Ed.2d 550 (1984).
170. *Colorado* v. *Connelly*, 107 S.Ct. 515, 93 L.Ed.2d 473 (1986).
171. *Kuhlmann* v. *Wilson*, 477 U.S. 436 (1986).
172. *Illinois* v. *Perkins*, 495 U.S. 292 (1990).
173. *Rock* v. *Zimmerman*, 543 F.Supp. 179 (M.D. Pa. 1982).
174. Ibid.
175. See *Oregon* v. *Mathiason*, 429 U.S. 492, 97 S.Ct. 711 (1977).
176. *Arizona* v. *Mauro*, 107 S.Ct. 1931, 95 L.Ed.2d 458 (1987).
177. *Doyle* v. *Ohio*, 426 U.S. 610 (1976).
178. *Brecht* v. *Abrahamson*, 113 S.Ct. 1710, 123 L.Ed.2d 353 (1993).
179. Citing *Kotteakos* v. *U.S.*, 328 U.S. 750 (1946).
180. *Missouri* v. *Seibert*, 542 U.S. 600 (2004).
181. *Florida* v. *Powell*, U.S. Supreme Court, No. 08-1175 (decided February 23, 2010).
182. *Hayes* v. *Florida*, 470 U.S. 811, 105 S.Ct. 1643 (1985).
183. *Winston* v. *Lee*, 470 U.S. 753, 105 S.Ct. 1611 (1985).
184. *Schmerber* v. *California*, 384 U.S. 757 (1966).
185. "Man Coughs Up Cocaine While in Custody," *Police Magazine*, March 4, 2005, http://www.policemag.com/t_newspick .cfm?rank574703 (accessed January 4, 2007).
186. *U.S.* v. *Montoya de Hernandez*, 473 U.S. 531, 105 S.Ct. 3304 (1985).
187. Ibid.
188. *Olmstead* v. *U.S.*, 277 U.S. 438 (1928).
189. *On Lee* v. *U.S.*, 343 U.S. 747 (1952).
190. *Lopez* v. *U.S.*, 373 U.S. 427 (1963).
191. *Berger* v. *New York*, 388 U.S. 41 (1967).
192. *Katz* v. *U.S.*, 389 U.S. 347 (1967).
193. *Lee* v. *Florida*, 392 U.S. 378 (1968).
194. Federal Communications Act of 1934, 47 U.S.C. Section 151.
195. *U.S.* v. *White*, 401 U.S. 745 (1971).
196. *U.S.* v. *Karo*, 468 U.S. 705 (1984).
197. *U.S.* v. *Scott*, 436 U.S. 128 (1978).
198. For more information, see *FBI Law Enforcement Bulletin* (June 1987), p. 25.
199. Electronic Communications Privacy Act of 1986, Public Law 99–508.
200. For more information on the ECPA, see Robert A. Fiatal, "The Electronic Communications Privacy Act: Addressing Today's Technology," *FBI Law Enforcement Bulletin* (April 1988), pp. 24–30.
201. Communications Assistance for Law Enforcement Act of 1994, Public Law 103–414.
202. Federal Bureau of Investigation, "Notice: Implementation of the Communications Assistance for Law Enforcement Act," February 23, 1995.
203. Administrative Office of the United States Courts, *2009 Wiretap Report*, http://www.uscourts.gov/Statistics/ WiretapReports/WiretapReport2009.aspx (accessed July 20, 2010).
204. Telecommunications Act of 1996, Public Law 104, 110 Stat. 56.
205. Title 47, U.S.C.A., Section 223(a)(1)(B)(ii) (Supp. 1997).
206. *Reno* v. *ACLU*, 117 S.Ct. 2329 (1997).
207. 18 U.S.C. Section 1030.
208. Section 202.
209. 18 U.S.C. Section 2703(c).
210. Ibid.
211. Public Law 109–177.
212. Stephanie Woodrow, "Obama Signs Reauthorization of Three Patriot Act Provisions," February 27, 2010, http://www.mainjustice.com/2010/02/27/ obama-signs-patriot-act-reauthorization (accessed May 20, 2010).
213. Adapted from Technical Working Group for Electronic Crime Scene Investigation, *Electronic Crime Scene Investigation: A Guide for First Responders* (Washington, DC: National Institute of Justice, 2001), from which much of the information in this section is taken.
214. Ibid., p. 2.
215. Computer Crime and Intellectual Property Section, U.S. Department of Justice, *Searching and Seizing Computers and Obtaining Electronic Evidence in Criminal Investigations* (Washington, DC: U.S. Department of Justice, 2002), http:// www.usdoj.gov/criminal/cybercrime/s&smanual2002 .htm (accessed August 4, 2007).
216. Technical Working Group, *Electronic Crime Scene Investigation*, p. 2.
217. Technical Working Group for the Examination of Digital Evidence, *Forensic Examination of Digital Evidence: A Guide for Law Enforcement* (Washington, DC: National Institute of Justice, 2004).
218. *U.S.* v. *Carey*, 172 F.3d 1268 (10th Cir. 1999).
219. *U.S.* v. *Turner*, 169 F.3d 84 (1st Cir. 1999).

Policing: Issues and Challenges

Learning Objectives

After reading this chapter, you should be able to:

1. Describe the police working personality, relating it to police subculture.
2. List and describe different types of police corruption, and discuss possible methods for building police integrity.
3. Explain the dangers of police work, and discuss what can be done to reduce those dangers.
4. Describe the changed role of American police in the post-9/11 environment.
5. Describe the civil liability issues associated with policing, and identify common sources of civil suits against the police.
6. Describe racial profiling and biased policing, and explain why they have become significant issues in policing today.
7. Describe the situations in which police officers are most likely to use force, and provide some guidelines for determining when too much force has been used.
8. Demonstrate why professionalism and ethics are important in policing today.
9. Identify some of the issues related to ethnic and gender diversity in policing, and suggest ways of addressing them.
10. Describe the nature and extent of private protective services in the United States today, and discuss what role you think they will play in the future.

"The continuous threat of terrorism has thrust domestic preparedness obligations to the very top of the law enforcement agenda."

—Colonel Joel Leson, director, IACP Center for Police Leadership[1]

Chris Polydoroff/Associated Press

▲ New York City Police Department officers embrace as the ball drops during a Times Square New Year's Eve party, ushering in a new year. The police working personality has been characterized as authoritarian, suspicious, and conservative. How does the police working personality develop?
Gregory Bull/AP Wide World Photos

Introduction

Today's police officers and administrators face many complex issues. Some concerns, such as corruption, on-the-job dangers, and the use of deadly force, derive from the very nature of police work. Others, like racial profiling and exposure to civil liability, have arisen due to common practices, characteristic police values, public expectations, legislative action, and ongoing societal change. One of the most significant challenges facing American law enforcement today is policing a multicultural society. All of these issues are discussed in the pages that follow. We begin, however, with the police recruit socialization process. It is vital to understand this process because the values and expectations learned through it not only contribute to the nature of many important police issues but also determine how the police view and respond to those issues.

Police Personality and Culture

1 Describe the police working personality, relating it to police subculture.

police subculture
A particular set of values, beliefs, and acceptable forms of behavior characteristic of American police with which the police profession strives to imbue new recruits. Socialization into the police subculture commences with recruit training and continues thereafter.

New police officers learn what is considered appropriate police behavior by working with seasoned veterans. Through conversations with other officers in the locker room, in a squad car, or over a cup of coffee, a new recruit is introduced to the value-laden subculture of police work. **Police subculture** can be understood as "the set of informal values which characterize the police force as a distinct community with a common identity."[2] This process of informal socialization plays a much bigger role than formal police academy training in determining how rookies come to see police work. Through it, new officers gain a shared view of the world that can best be described as "streetwise." Streetwise cops know what official department policy is, but they also know the most efficient way to get a job done. By the time rookie officers become streetwise, they know which of the various informal means of accomplishing the job are acceptable to other officers. The police subculture creates few real mavericks, but it also produces few officers who view their jobs exclusively in terms of public mandates and official dictums.

police working personality
All aspects of the traditional values and patterns of behavior evidenced by police officers who have been effectively socialized into the police subculture. Characteristics of the police personality often extend to the personal lives of law enforcement personnel.

In the 1960s, renowned criminologist Jerome Skolnick described what he called the **police working personality**.[3] Skolnick's description of the police personality was consistent with William Westley's classic study of the Gary (Indiana) Police Department, in which he found a police subculture with its own "customs, laws, and morality,"[4] and with Arthur Niederhoffer's observation that cynicism was pervasive among officers in New York City.[5] More recent authors have claimed that the "big curtain of secrecy" surrounding much of police work shields knowledge of the nature of the police personality from outsiders.[6] Taken in concert, these writers offer the picture of the police working personality shown in Table 1.

Some characteristics of the police working personality are essential for survival and effectiveness. For example, because officers are often exposed to highly emotional and potentially threatening confrontations with belligerent people, they must develop efficient authoritarian strategies for gaining control over others. Similarly, a suspicious nature makes for a good police officer, especially during interrogations and investigations.

TABLE 1
The Police Personality

Authoritarian	Cynical	Secret	Efficient
Honorable			
Insecure	Loyal	Individualistic	Dogmatic
Suspicious	Hostile	Conservative	Prejudiced

However, other characteristics of the police working personality are not as advantageous. For example, many officers are cynical, and some can be hostile toward members of the public who do not share their conservative values. These traits result from regular interaction with suspects, most of whom deny any wrongdoing even when they are clearly guilty in the eyes of the police. Eventually, personal traits that result from typical police work become firmly ingrained, setting the cornerstone of the police working personality.

There are at least two sources of the police personality. On the one hand, it may be that components of the police personality already exist in some individuals and draw them toward police work.[7] Supporting this view are studies that indicate that police officers who come from conservative backgrounds view themselves as defenders of middle-class morality.[8] On the other hand, some aspects of the police personality can be attributed to the socialization into the police subculture that rookie officers experience when they are inducted into police ranks.

Researchers have reported similar elements in police subculture throughout the United States.[9] They have concluded that like all cultures, police subculture is a relatively stable collection of beliefs and values that is unlikely to change from within. Police subculture may, however, be changed through external pressures, such as new hiring practices, investigations into police corruption or misuse of authority, and commission reports that create pressure for police reform.[10] Learn more about police subculture and police behavior at **Web Extra 1**.

Corruption and Integrity

2 List and describe different types of police corruption, and discuss possible methods for building police integrity.

Good cops always seem to be able to identify causes of problems and to come up with the least troublesome ways of solving them.
—Jerome Skolnick

Although most law enforcement officers perform their duties responsibly and with honor, some do not. In 2006, for example, Border Patrol Agent Oscar Antonio Ortiz pleaded guilty to charges of conspiracy to smuggle aliens into the United States, making a false claim to U.S. citizenship, making a false statement in the acquisition of a firearm, and being an illegal alien in possession of a firearm.[11] Ortiz, a Mexican citizen who was born in Tijuana, secured a job with the Border Patrol in 2001 by using a fake birth certificate that listed Chicago as his place of birth. Court documents show that he conspired with at least one other Border Patrol agent to smuggle more than 100 Mexican nationals into the United States. Officials revealed that intercepted phone calls between Ortiz and another agent spoke of payments of up to $2,000 per person smuggled into the United States. The recorded calls also discussed rates that human traffickers working with the agents should be charged to secure the agents' cooperation.[12] On July 28, 2006, a federal district court judge sentenced Ortiz to serve 60 months in prison. He will likely be deported after his sentence is complete.

The kind of corruption seen in Ortiz's case pales alongside that of two retired New York City police detectives who were convicted in 2006 of giving confidential information to mob leaders and of misusing their authority as law enforcement officers to kidnap and kill rival gangsters.[13] Federal prosecutors successfully portrayed retired police investigator Louis Eppolito, 56, and his former partner, Stephen Caracappa, 63, as assassins working for the Lucchese crime family. The two are suspected of killing at least eight men in one of the city's most spectacular police corruption scandals ever. Their convictions, on 70 counts of racketeering, came 20 years after their first victim was gunned down in a New York City parking garage. Caracappa, who may have been the trigger man in most of the killings, was known for helping to create the New York Police Department (NYPD) Organized Crime Homicide Unit and was described as "a gatekeeper of information about Mafia killings investigated by police." Although the jurors remained anonymous throughout the trial for protection from possible retaliation, one of them, a building safety official from Long Island, told reporters after the trial that he was shocked at the detectives for having broken their oath to uphold the law. "When you're given an oath, and an oath as precious as being a police officer, and a duty to protect and serve people, that is the highest oath ever," said the juror. "It's like, 'How dare you violate that oath?' . . . When you violate [that] oath, you lose the respect of the people you're sworn to protect."[14] In 2010, in an interesting footnote to the Eppolito case, the NYPD agreed to pay $9.9 million in an out-of-court settlement to 62-year-old Barry Gibbs, whom Eppolito had framed for murder in 1988.[15] Gibbs spent 18 years in prison before the injustice was discovered.

Multiculturalism and Diversity
Policing a Multicultural Society

Members of some social groups have backgrounds, values, and perspectives that, while not directly supportive of law-breaking, contrast sharply with those of many police officials. Robert M. Shusta, a well-known writer on multicultural law enforcement, says that police officers "need to recognize the fact of poor police–minority relations historically, including *unequal* treatment under the law."[1] Moreover, says Shusta, "many officers and citizens are defensive with each other because their contact is tinged with negative historical 'baggage.'"

In other words, even though discrimination in the enforcement of the criminal law may not be commonplace today, it *was* in the past—and perceptions built on past experience are often difficult to change. Moreover, if the function of law enforcement is to "protect and serve" law-abiding citizens from all backgrounds, then it becomes vital for officers to understand and respect differences in habits, customs, beliefs, patterns of thought, and traditions.[2] As Shusta says, "the acts of approaching, communicating, questioning, assisting, and establishing trust with members of different groups require special knowledge and skills that have nothing to do with the fact that 'the law is the law' and must be enforced equally. Acquiring sensitivity, knowledge, and skills leads to [an increased appreciation for the position of others] that will contribute to improved communications with members of all groups."[3]

How can police officers acquire greater sensitivity to the issues involved in policing a diverse multicultural society? Some researchers suggest that law enforcement officers of *all* backgrounds begin by exploring their own prejudices. Prejudices, which are judgments or opinions formed before facts are known and which usually involve negative or unfavorable thoughts about groups of people, can lead to discrimination. Most people, including police officers, are able to reduce their tendency to discriminate against those who are different by exploring and uprooting their own personal prejudices.

One technique for identifying prejudices is cultural awareness training. As practiced in some police departments today, cultural awareness training explores the impact of culture on human behavior—and especially law-breaking behavior. Cultural awareness training generally involves four stages:[4]

- *Clarifying the relationship between cultural awareness and police professionalism.* As Shusta explains it, "The more professional a police officer is, the more sophisticated he or she is in responding to people of all backgrounds and the more successful he or she is in cross-cultural contact."[5]
- *Recognizing personal prejudices.* In the second stage of cultural awareness training, participating officers are asked to recognize and identify their own personal prejudices and biases. Once prejudices have been identified, trainers strive to show how they can affect daily behavior.
- *Acquiring sensitivity to police-community relations.* In this stage of training, participating officers learn about historical and existing community perceptions of the police. Training can often be enhanced through the use of carefully chosen and well-qualified guest speakers or participants from minority communities.
- *Developing interpersonal relations skills.* The goal of this last stage of training is to assist with the development of the positive verbal and nonverbal communications skills necessary for successful interaction with community members. Many trainers believe that basic skills training will result in the continuing development of such skills because officers will quickly begin to see the benefits (in terms of lessened interpersonal conflict) of effective interpersonal skills.

[1]Robert M. Shusta et al., *Multicultural Law Enforcement: Strategies for Peacekeeping in a Diverse Society*, 2nd ed. (Upper Saddle River, NJ: Prentice Hall, 2002), p. 4.
[2]Ibid., p. 16.
[3]Ibid., p. 4.
[4]Ibid., pp. 104–106.
[5]Ibid., p. 4.

police corruption
The abuse of police authority for personal or organizational gain.[i]

Police corruption has been a problem in American society since the early days of policing. It is probably an ancient and natural tendency of human beings to attempt to placate or win over those in positions of authority over them. This tendency is complicated in today's materialistic society by greed and by the personal and financial benefits to be derived from evading the law. The temptations toward illegality offered to police range from a free cup of coffee from a restaurant owner to huge monetary bribes arranged by drug dealers to guarantee that the police will look the other way as an important shipment of contraband arrives. As noted criminologist Carl B. Klockars says, policing, by its very nature, "is an occupation that is rife with opportunities for misconduct. Policing is a highly discretionary, coercive activity that routinely takes place in private settings, out of the sight of supervisors, and in the presence of witnesses who are often regarded as unreliable."[16]

The effects of police corruption can be far-reaching. As Michael Palmiotto of Wichita State University notes, "Not only does misconduct committed by an officer personally affect that officer, it also affects the community, the police department that employs the officer and every police department and police officer in America. Frequently, negative police actions caused by inappropriate police behavior reach every corner of the nation, and at times, the world."[17]

Exactly what constitutes corruption is not always clear. Ethicists say that police corruption ranges from minor offenses to serious violations of the law. In recognition of what some have called corruption's "slippery slope,"[18] most police departments now explicitly prohibit even the acceptance of minor gratuities, like a free cup of coffee. The slippery slope perspective holds that even a small thank-you accepted from a member of the public can lead to a more ready acceptance of larger bribes. An officer who begins to accept, and then expect, gratuities may soon find that his or her practice of policing becomes influenced by such gifts and that larger ones soon follow. At that point, the officer may easily slide to the bottom of the moral slope, which was made slippery by previous small concessions.

Thomas Barker and David Carter, who have studied police corruption in depth, make the distinction between "occupational deviance," which is motivated by the desire for personal benefit, and "abuse of authority, which occurs most often to further the organizational goals of law enforcement, including arrest, ticketing, and the successful conviction of suspects."[19]

FBI Special Agent Frank Perry, former chief of the bureau's ethics unit, distinguishes between police deviance and police corruption. Police deviance, according to Perry, consists of "unprofessional on- and off-duty misconduct, isolated instances of misuse of position, improper relationships with informants or criminals, sexual harassment, disparaging racial or sexual comments, embellished/falsified reporting, time and attendance abuse, insubordination, nepotism, cronyism, and noncriminal unauthorized disclosure of information."[20] Deviance, says Perry, is a precursor to individual and organizational corruption. It may eventually lead to outright corruption unless police supervisors and internal affairs units are alert to the warning signs and actively intervene to prevent corruption from developing.

Nearly all men can stand adversity, but if you want to test a man's character, give him power.

—Abraham Lincoln, sixteenth president of the United States[ii]

Figure 1 sorts examples of police corruption by their level of seriousness, though not everyone would agree with this ranking. In fact, a survey of 6,982 New York City police officers found that 65% did not classify excessive force, which we define later in this chapter,

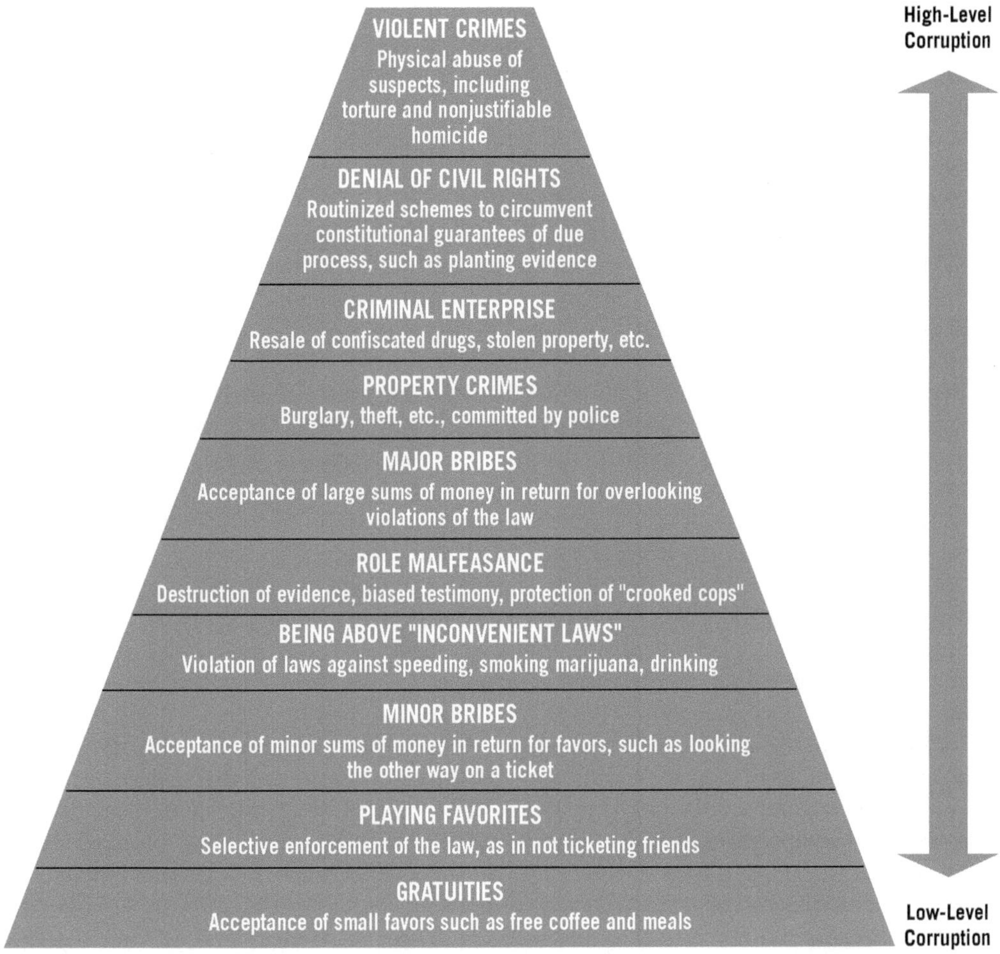

FIGURE 1
Types and Examples of Police Corruption

as a corrupt behavior.[21] Likewise, 71% of responding officers said that accepting a free meal is not a corrupt practice, and another 15% said that the personal use of illegal drugs by law enforcement officers should not be considered corruption.

Knapp Commission
A committee that investigated police corruption in New York City in the early 1970s.

In the early 1970s, Frank Serpico made headlines as he testified before the **Knapp Commission** on police corruption in New York City.[22] Serpico, an undercover operative within the police department, revealed a complex web of corruption in which money and services routinely changed hands in "protection rackets" created by unethical officers. The authors of the Knapp Commission report distinguished between two types of corrupt officers, which they termed "grass eaters" and "meat eaters."[23] "Grass eating," the most common form of police corruption, was described as illegitimate activity that occurs from time to time in the normal course of police work. It involves mostly small bribes or relatively minor services offered by citizens seeking to avoid arrest and prosecution. "Meat eating" is a much more serious form of corruption, involving the active seeking of illicit moneymaking opportunities by officers. Meat eaters solicit bribes through threat or intimidation, whereas grass eaters make the simpler mistake of not refusing bribes that are offered.

If you ever get lost, you can go find a policeman. The policeman will help you because he is your friend.
—A second-grade teacher

In 1993, during 11 days of corruption hearings reminiscent of the Knapp Commission era, a parade of crooked New York police officers testified before a commission headed by Milton Mollen, a former judge and deputy mayor of New York. Among the many revelations, officers spoke of dealing drugs, stealing confiscated drug funds, stifling investigations, and beating innocent people. Officer Michael Dowd, for example, told the commission that he had run a cocaine ring out of his station house in Brooklyn and had bought three homes on Long Island and a Corvette with the money he made. Most shocking of all, however, were allegations that high-level police officials attempted to hide embarrassing incidents in a "phantom file" and that many officials may have condoned unprofessional and even criminal practices by the officers under their command. Honest officers, including internal affairs investigators, described how their efforts to end corruption among their fellows had been defused and resisted by higher authorities.

Repercussions from the Mollen Commission hearings continue to be felt. In 2004, for example, a New York State judge ruled that the city of New York must pay special disability benefits to former police officer Jeffrey W. Baird, who served as an informer for the commission. Baird helped uncover corruption while working as an internal affairs officer but suffered from post-traumatic stress disorder after fellow officers threatened him, vandalized his work area, and sent obscene materials to his home.[24]

Another example of police corruption centered on the Los Angeles Police Department (LAPD) Rampart Division's antigang unit known as CRASH (Community Resources against Street Hoodlums).[25] The scandal began in mid-2000 when many of the CRASH unit's officers became embroiled in accusations claiming that they were operating like members of a criminal organization to threaten and frame hundreds of people through beatings, by planting evidence, and by committing perjury. They and other officers were alleged to be running a drug ring while eliminating competition from civilian dealers by framing them and seeing them sent to prison.[26] Seven shootings and at least two killings were among the illegal activities allegedly committed by officers. The scandal came to light after LAPD Officer Rafael Perez was caught stealing $1 million worth of cocaine from an evidence room. In exchange for an offer of leniency, Perez turned informant and cooperated with prosecutors. Perez, who was also accused of murder by a former girlfriend, provided investigators with details about ongoing corruption in the Rampart area.[27] As events unfolded, LAPD Chief Bernard Parks was accused by prosecutors of withholding critical information needed to build a case against the accused officers. The prosecutors claimed that "on several occasions, the LAPD . . . actually hindered the progress of the investigation."[28] Parks was replaced as chief by William J. Bratton in 2002.

By 2005, more than 100 falsely obtained convictions had been thrown out, and 20 LAPD officers had left active duty.[29] Another seven officers were convicted of conspiring to frame innocent people, but a judge overturned three of the convictions on procedural grounds. The remaining four officers received sentences of up to five years in prison.[30] The Los Angeles City Attorney agreed to pay a total of $70.2 million to settle approximately 214 lawsuits stemming from the corruption scandal. At the time of the settlement, the *Los Angeles Times* complained that much of the money, averaging $400,000 per settlement, went to "drug dealers, gang members and other criminals who said they had been framed, shot, beaten or otherwise mistreated by police."[31] The largest settlement, $15 million, went to former gang member Javier Francisco Ovando, who had been paralyzed by a police shooting. In responding to critics, Cindy Miscikowski, chairwoman of the Los Angeles City Council's Public Safety Committee, pointed out that "regardless of who the plaintiffs were, there was evidence of wrongdoing. That's what we had to recognize. . . . Civil rights are civil rights, and they apply to everyone across the board."[32]

The LAPD is now operating under a consent decree, a legally binding agreement with the U.S. Department of Justice (DOJ) that calls for major reforms. The decree requires the department to install a computer system to track complaints and disciplinary actions against LAPD officers; to collect data on the racial makeup of citizens stopped for traffic violations; and to create a special unit within the department to investigate shootings and beatings by police officers to determine whether excessive force was used.[33] Rafael Perez, sentenced to five years in prison, warned young officers as he was sentenced that "whoever chases monsters must see that he not become a monster himself."[34] Learn more about the Rampart scandal at **Web Extra 2**.

▲ The Los Angeles Police Department's Rampart station office, where a corruption scandal occurred in 2000 and 2001. A number of officers assigned to the Rampart Division were investigated on charges ranging from falsifying evidence to the theft and sale of illegal drugs. In what some have called "the biggest police scandal case in Los Angeles history," many criminal cases had to be dismissed. What other forms can police corruption take?
David McNew/Liaison/Getty Images, Inc.

Money—The Root of Police Evil?

Years ago, criminologist Edwin Sutherland applied the concept of *differential association* to the study of deviant behavior.[35] Sutherland suggested that the frequent, continued association of one person with another makes the associates similar. Of course, Sutherland was talking about criminals, not police officers. Consider, however, the dilemma of average officers: Their job entails issuing traffic citations to citizens who try to talk their way out of a ticket, dealing with prostitutes who feel hassled by police, and arresting drug users who think it should be their right to do what they want as long as "it doesn't hurt anyone." Officers regularly encounter personal hostility and experience consistent and often quite vocal rejection of society's formalized norms. And they receive relatively low pay, which indicates to them that their work is not really valued. By looking at the combination of these factors, it is easy to understand how officers often develop a jaded attitude toward the society they are sworn to protect.

Police officers' low pay may be a critical ingredient of the corruption mix. Salaries paid to police officers in this country have been notoriously low when compared to those of other professions involving personal dedication, extensive training, high stress, and risk of bodily harm. As police professionalism increases, many police administrators hope that salaries will rise. No matter how much police pay grows, however, it will never be able to compete with the staggering amounts of money to be made through dealing in contraband.

Working hand in hand with monetary pressures toward corruption is the moral dilemma produced by unenforceable laws that provide the basis for criminal profit. During the Prohibition era, the Wickersham Commission warned of the potential for official corruption inherent in the legislative taboos on alcohol. The immense demand for drink called into question the wisdom of the law while simultaneously providing vast resources designed to circumvent it. Today's drug scene bears some similarities to the Prohibition era. As long as many people are willing to make large financial and other sacrifices to feed the drug trade, the pressures on the police to embrace corruption will remain substantial.

Building Police Integrity

The difficulties of controlling corruption can be traced to several factors, including the reluctance of police officers to report corrupt activities by their fellow officers, the reluctance of police administrators to acknowledge the existence of corruption in their agencies, the benefits of corrupt transactions to the parties involved, and the lack of victims willing to report corruption. High moral standards, however, embedded in the principles of the police profession and effectively communicated to individual officers through formal training and peer-group socialization can raise the level of integrity in any department. There are, of course, many officers of great personal integrity who hold to the highest of professional ideals. There

Ethics and Professionalism
The Law Enforcement Oath of Honor

On my honor, I will never
Betray my badge, my integrity,
My character or the public trust.
I will always have the courage to hold
Myself and others accountable
for our actions.
I will always uphold the Constitution,
My community, and the agency I serve.

Honor means that one's word is given as a guarantee.
Betray is defined as breaking faith with the public trust.
Badge is the symbol of your office.
Integrity is being the same person in both private and public life.
Character means the qualities that distinguish an individual.
Public trust is a charge of duty imposed in faith toward those you serve.
Courage is having the strength to withstand unethical pressure, fear or danger.
Accountability means that you are answerable and responsible to your oath of office.
Community is the jurisdiction and citizens served.

THINKING ABOUT ETHICS

1. ***How is the Law Enforcement Oath of Honor similar to the Law Enforcement Code of Ethics, which is also found in this chapter? How does it differ?***
2. ***How do the two support one another?***

Source: Adopted at the 107th International Association of Chiefs of Police Annual Conference, November 15, 2000. Reprinted with permission.

is evidence that law enforcement training programs are becoming increasingly concerned with instruction designed to reinforce the high ideals many recruits bring to police work. As one Federal Bureau of Investigation (FBI) article explains it, "Ethics training must become an integral part of academy and in-service training for new and experienced officers alike."[36]

Ethics training is part of a "reframing" strategy that emphasizes integrity to target police corruption. In 2001, the DOJ released a document titled *Principles for Promoting Police Integrity.*[37] The foreword to that document states, "For community policing to be successful, and crime reduction efforts to be effective, citizens must have trust in the police. All of us must work together to address the problems of excessive use of force and racial profiling, and—equally important—the perceptions of many minority residents that law enforcement treats them unfairly, if we are to build the confidence in law enforcement necessary for continued progress. Our goal must be professional law enforcement that gives all citizens of our country the feeling that they are being treated fairly, equally and with respect." The report covered such topics as the use of force; complaints and misconduct investigations; accountability and effective management; training; nondiscriminatory policing; and recruitment, hiring, and retention. Read the full report, which provides examples of promising police practices and policies in support of increased integrity, at **Library Extra 1**.

In 2000, the International Association of Chiefs of Police (IACP), in an effort to reinforce the importance of ethical standards in policing, adopted the Law Enforcement Oath of Honor, shown in an "Ethics and Professionalism" box in this chapter. The IACP suggests that the Law Enforcement Oath of Honor should be seen by individual officers as a statement of commitment to ethical behavior. It is meant to reinforce the principles embodied in the Law Enforcement Code of Ethics, which is printed in another "Ethics and Professionalism" box in this chapter.

In December 2005, the National Institute of Justice weighed in on the issue of police integrity with a Research for Practice report titled *Enhancing Police Integrity.*[38] The report noted that "an agency's culture of integrity, as defined by clearly understood and implemented policies and rules, may be more important in shaping the ethics of police officers than hiring the 'right' people."[39] Report authors also noted that officers tend to evaluate the seriousness of various types of misconduct by observing and assessing their department's response in detecting and disciplining it. If unwritten policies conflict with written policies, the authors observed, then the resulting confusion undermines an agency's overall integrity-enhancing efforts. *Enhancing Police Integrity* is available online at **Library Extra 2**.

internal affairs
The branch of a police organization tasked with investigating charges of wrongdoing involving members of the department.

Most large law enforcement agencies have their own division of **internal affairs**, which is empowered to investigate charges of wrongdoing made against officers. Where necessary, state police agencies may be called on to examine reported incidents. Federal agencies,

> There is more to being a professional than just looking like one.
> —Rob Edwards

including the FBI and the Drug Enforcement Administration (DEA), involve themselves when corruption goes far enough to violate federal statutes. The DOJ, through various investigative offices, has the authority to examine possible violations of civil rights that may result from the misuse of police authority. The DOJ is often supported in these endeavors by the American Civil Liberties Union (ACLU), the National Association for the Advancement of Colored People (NAACP), and other watchdog groups.

▲ Federal Way Police Officer G. Castro with flowers given to him by a motorist passing the Lakewood police station. Four Lakewood officers were killed by a gunman at a Parkland coffee shop in November 2009. How might the dangers associated with police work be reduced?
*AP Photo/*The New Tribune, *Dean J. Koepfler*

Drug Testing of Police Employees

The widespread potential for police corruption created by illicit drugs has led to focused efforts to combat drug use by officers. Drug-testing programs in local police departments are an example of such efforts. The IACP has developed a Model Drug Testing Policy for police managers. The policy, designed to meet the needs of local departments, suggests routinely testing all applicants and recruits as well as all employees who are assigned to special "high-risk" areas, such as narcotics and vice.[40]

Today, many police departments require all officers to submit to routine drug testing, and in 2008, the NYPD began randomly testing its officers for anabolic steroid abuse. The department began the testing after several police officers were linked to the investigation of a Brooklyn pharmacy suspected of illegally selling millions of dollars of steroids and human growth hormone.[41]

The courts have supported drug testing based on a reasonable suspicion that drug abuse has been or is occurring,[42] although random testing of officers was banned by a 1986 New York State Supreme Court.[43] Citing overriding public interests, a 1989 decision by the U.S. Supreme Court upheld the testing of U.S. Customs personnel applying for transfer into positions involving drug-law enforcement or requiring a firearm.[44] Many legal issues surrounding employee drug testing remain to be resolved in court, however.

Complicating this issue is the fact that drug and alcohol addictions are "handicaps" protected by the Federal Rehabilitation Act of 1973. As such, federal law enforcement employees, as well as those working for agencies with federal contracts, are entitled to counseling and treatment before action can be taken toward termination.

Employee drug testing in police departments, as in many other agencies, is a sensitive subject. Some claim that existing tests for drug use are inaccurate, yielding a significant number of "false positives." Repeated testing and high threshold levels for narcotic substances in the blood may eliminate many of these concerns. Less easy to address, however, is the belief that drug testing intrudes on the personal rights and professional dignity of individual employees. Learn more about employee drug-testing policies in police departments at **Web Extra 3**, and discover more about corruption and the continuing drive toward police integrity with **Library Extras 3** and **4**.

The Dangers of Police Work

> 3 Explain the dangers of police work, and discuss what can be done to reduce those dangers.

On October 15, 1991, the National Law Enforcement Officers' Memorial was unveiled in Washington, D.C. The memorial contained the names of 12,561 law enforcement officers killed in the line of duty, including U.S. Marshals Service Officer Robert Forsyth, who in 1794 became the nation's first law enforcement officer to be killed. More than 6,000 names have been added since opening day.[45] At the memorial, an interactive video system provides visitors with brief biographies and photographs of officers who have died. Tour the memorial by visiting **Web Extra 4**.

As the memorial suggests, police work is, by its very nature, dangerous. Although many officers never once fire their weapons in the line of duty, we also know that some officers

CJ News

Police DNA Collection Sparks Questions

When a 60-year-old man spat on the sidewalk, his DNA became as public as if he had been advertising it across his chest.

Police officers secretly following Leon Chatt . . . collected the saliva—loaded with Chatt's unique genetic makeup—to compare with DNA evidence from the scene of an old murder they believed he'd committed.

[Later,] Chatt was charged in one of Buffalo's oldest unsolved cases, the 1974 rape and stabbing of . . . Barbara Lloyd.

While secretly collecting a suspect's DNA may be an unorthodox approach to solving crimes, prosecutors say it crosses no legal boundaries—that when someone leaves their DNA in a public place via . . . saliva, for example, they give up any expectation of privacy. . . .

"If we felt it wasn't proper and we didn't have a strong legal foundation, we wouldn't have done it," Erie County [New York] District Attorney Frank Clark said. . . .

DNA, which is unique to every person, has become a cold case squad's best friend. Investigators can re-examine things like hair, blood, semen . . . from decades-old crime scenes and cross-reference the DNA with ever expanding databases kept by law enforcement.

"It's one of the greatest tools that law enforcement has today," said Dennis Richards, the Buffalo Police Department's chief of detectives. . . .

But it is the so-called "abandoned" DNA like that collected from . . . Chatt . . . that concerns people like Elizabeth Joh. The University of California law professor believes it is time legislators consider regulating such collections. . . .

"If we look at this kind of evidence as abandoned, then it really permits the police to collect DNA from anyone—not just cold case issues—from anyone at any time and really for no good reason or any reason at all," Joh said. . . .

Asked whether there should be boundaries on such collections, Richards said, "That's one for the lawyers to argue in a court of law." . . .

Prosecutors tend to view abandoned DNA as akin to trash . . . Joh said.

She pointed to the case of *California* v. *Greenwood*, in which the U.S. Supreme Court ruled in 1988 that police did not need a warrant to search a suspected drug dealer's trash because he should have had no expectation of privacy when he placed it on the curb. . . .

But Joh argued comparing DNA and trash is a poor analogy.

"Obviously, we might want to discard that cigarette, but do we really mean to give up all kinds of privacy claims in the genetic material that might lie therein?" she asked. . . .

Richards, meanwhile, pointed out that while abandoned DNA can confirm a suspect's identity, it also works to the benefit of someone who is innocent.

"DNA rules people in, but it also rules people out," he said.

Barbara Lloyd was killed as her [children] slept. The now-grown children recently persuaded police to take another look at the killing. . . .

▲ Karin Strom, who was strangled in her home almost 30 years ago, allegedly by Utah resident Edward Owens, 56. Owens surrendered to police in 2007 after tests determined that it was his skin that had been scraped from under Strom's fingernails after her murder and had been saved in an evidence locker. Owens was charged with first-degree felony murder in Strom's death. His arrest, like others discussed in this box, has raised questions about how DNA samples can best be collected from criminal suspects. Should "public" DNA be readily available to investigators?
Woods Cross Police Department

"We were very fortunate that at that time there was a detective in the evidence collection unit who was able to secure evidence from the scene which was later used for comparison," Richards said. . . .

Joh suggests proceeding with caution. "My hope is there will be much greater awareness of what this means, not just for these particular cases, but for everyone," she said. "Is DNA sampling going to be ordinary and uncontroversial for the general population, in which case abandoned DNA may not be so alarming, or does it raise a whole host of privacy questions?"

Source: Carolyn Thompson, "Police DNA Collection Sparks Questions," The Associated Press, March 17, 2007. Used with permission of The Associated Press.

meet death while performing their jobs. On-the-job police deaths occur from stress, training accidents, and auto crashes; however, it is violent death at the hands of criminal offenders that police officers and their families fear most.

Violence in the Line of Duty

When officers are shot and killed, it is most often by a lone suspect armed with a single weapon. In 2009, 127 American law enforcement officers were killed in the line of duty.[46] Figure 2 shows the number of officers killed in different types of incidents in 2009. In 2001, the attacks on the World Trade Center resulted in the greatest ever single-incident loss of life of on-duty law enforcement officers when 72 police officers perished.[47]

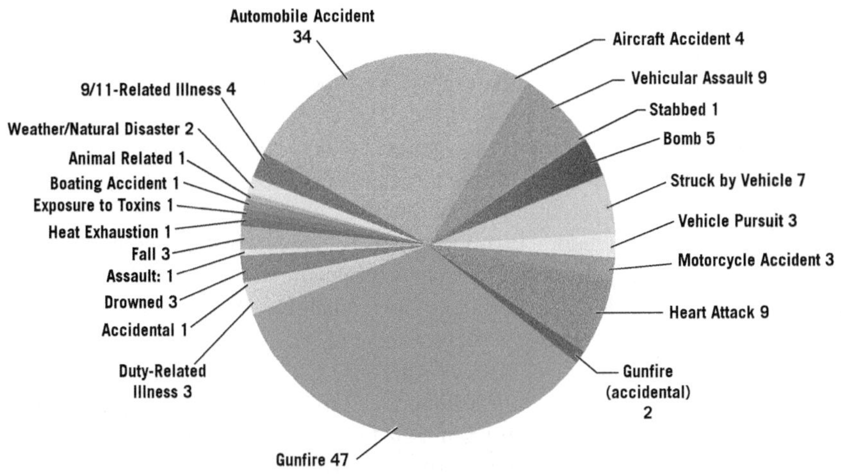

FIGURE 2
U.S. Law Enforcement Officers Killed in the Line of Duty, 2009

Source: Based on data from the Officer Down Memorial Page website, http://www.odmp.org.

A study by the FBI found that slain officers appeared to be good-natured and conservative in the use of physical force, "as compared to other law enforcement officers in similar situations. They were also perceived as being well-liked by the community and the department, friendly to everyone, laid back, and easy going."[48] Finally, the study, which was published before the September 11, 2001, terrorist attacks, also found that most officers who were killed failed to wear protective vests.

For statistics on police killings to have meaning beyond the personal tragedy they entail, it is necessary to place them within a larger framework. There are approximately 730,000 state and local police employees in this country[49] and another 88,000 federal agents.[50] Such numbers demonstrate that the rate of violent death among law enforcement officers in the line of duty is small indeed—and it appears to be declining.

> Unlike the soldier fighting a war on foreign soil, police officers, who provide for our safety at home, have never been given the honor that was their due.
>
> —Hubert Williams, president, Police Foundation[iii]

A significant recent decline in police deaths from all causes prompted Craig Floyd, chairman of the National Law Enforcement Officers Memorial Fund, to attribute the drop to an enhanced focus on officer safety by police departments and officers' unions. "Clearly, there is a heightened awareness [of the need for safety] among officers, trainers, union leaders and chiefs," Floyd said.[51] Others attribute the decline in law enforcement deaths to a renewed push for the use of body armor; an increased availability of less-lethal weapons; a broader use of mandatory handcuffing, even at traffic stops; widespread and better analysis of police dashboard videos to critique officer behavior; and better arming of police officers.

Risk of Disease and Infected Evidence

Dangers other than violence also threaten enforcement officers. The increase in serious diseases that can be transmitted by blood and other body fluids, the possible planned release of active **biological weapons** such as anthrax or smallpox, and the fact that crime and accident scenes are inherently dangerous combine to make *caution* a necessary watchword among investigators and first responders. Routine criminal and accident investigations hold the potential for infection through minor cuts and abrasions resulting from contact with the broken glass and torn metal of a wrecked vehicle, the sharp edges of knives found at the scene of an assault or murder, or drug implements such as razor blades and hypodermic needles secreted in vehicles, homes, and pockets. Such minor injuries, previously shrugged off by many police personnel, have become a focal point for warnings about the dangers of AIDS, hepatitis B, tuberculosis, and other diseases spread through contact with infected blood.

biological weapon
A biological agent used to threaten human life (for example, anthrax, smallpox, or any infectious disease).[iv]

Infection can also occur from the use of breath alcohol instruments on infected persons, the handling of evidence of all types, seemingly innocuous implements such as staples, the emergency delivery of babies in squad cars, and the attack (especially bites) by infected individuals who are being questioned or who are in custody. Understandably, officers are concerned about how to handle the threat of AIDS and other bloodborne diseases. However, as a publication of the NYPD reminds its officers, "Police officers have a professional responsibility to render assistance to those who are in need of our services. We cannot refuse to help. Persons with infectious diseases must be treated with the care and dignity we show all citizens."[52]

Of equal concern is the threat of biological agents. Although crime scenes and sites known to harbor (or that are suspected of harboring) dangerous active biological agents require a response by teams equipped with special protective equipment, all law enforcement officers should take reasonable precautions against exposure to the wide variety of infectious agents known to exist at even routine crime scenes. Emergency management agencies generally recommend a number of precautions to defend against exposure to infectious substances, as shown in Table 2.

To better combat the threat of infectious diseases among public-safety employees and health-care professionals, the federal Bloodborne Pathogens Act of 1991[53] requires that police officers receive proper training in how to prevent contamination by bloodborne infectious agents. The act also requires that police officers undergo an annual refresher course on the topic.

Police departments will face an increasing number of legal challenges in the years to come in cases involving infectious diseases such as AIDS and in cases involving the release of biological agents. Predictable areas of concern include (1) the need to educate officers and other police employees about AIDS, anthrax, and other serious infectious diseases; (2) the responsibility of police departments to prevent the spread of AIDS and other infectious diseases in police lockups; and (3) the necessity of effective and nondiscriminatory enforcement activities and lifesaving measures by police officers in environments contaminated with active biological agents. With regard to nondiscriminatory activities, the National Institute of Justice (NIJ) has suggested that legal claims in support of an officer's refusal to render assistance to people with AIDS would probably not be effective in court.[54] The reason is twofold: The officer has a basic duty to render assistance to individuals in need of it, and the possibility of AIDS transmission by casual contact has been scientifically established as extremely remote.

A final issue of growing concern involves activities by police officers infected with the AIDS virus. Few statistics are currently available on the number of officers with AIDS, but public reaction to those officers may become a problem that police managers will need to address.

TABLE 2
Biological Incident Law Enforcement Concerns

Concern	Precaution and Response
Suspicious material	Responding officers should not handle or come in close physical contact with suspicious material. If it is necessary to handle the material to evaluate it, officers should wear surgical gloves and masks and wash their hands thoroughly with soap and water after handling it.
Human bites	The biter usually receives the victim's blood. Viral transmission through saliva is highly unlikely. If bitten by anyone, milk the wound to make it bleed, wash the area thoroughly, and seek medical attention.
Spitting	Viral transmission through saliva is highly unlikely.
Urine/feces	Virus has been isolated in only very low concentrations in urine and not at all in feces.
	No cases of AIDS or AIDS virus infection associated with either urine or feces have been reported.
Cuts/puncture wounds	Use caution when handling sharp objects and searching areas hidden from view. Needle-stick studies show risk of infection is very low.
CPR/first aid	To eliminate the already minimal risk associated with CPR, use masks/airways.
	Avoid blood-to-blood contact by keeping open wounds covered and wearing gloves when in contact with bleeding wounds.
Body removal	Observe crime-scene rules; do not touch anything. Those who must come in contact with blood or other body fluids should wear gloves.
Casual contact	No cases of AIDS or AIDS virus infection have been attributed to casual contact.
Any contact with blood or body fluids	Wear gloves if contact with blood or body fluids is considered likely. If contact occurs, wash thoroughly with soap and water; clean up spills with one part water to nine parts household bleach.
Contact with dried blood	No cases of infection have been traced to exposure to dried blood. The drying process itself appears to inactivate the virus. Despite low risk, however, caution dictates wearing gloves, a mask, and protective shoe coverings if exposure to dried blood particles is likely (for example, crime-scene investigation).

References: Michigan Department of Community Health, *Anthrax (Bacillus anthracis) Information for Health Care Providers*, http://www.michigan.gov/documents/Healthcare_provider_FAQ-anthrax_08-2004_104327_7.pdf (accessed June 12, 2010); Massachusetts Administrative Office of the Trial Court, *Personnel Policies and Procedures Manual*, Section 24.000 ("Statement of Policy and Procedures on AIDS"), http://www.state.ma.us/courts/admin/hr/section24.html (accessed January 25, 2009); and "Collecting and Handling Evidence Infected with Human Disease-Causing Organisms," *FBI Law Enforcement Bulletin*, July 1987.

Stress and Fatigue among Police Officers

In the week after Hurricane Katrina, two New Orleans police officers used their service weapons to take their own lives. One was Sergeant Paul Accardo, the department's spokesperson; the other was patrolman Lawrence Celestine, an officer described by Deputy Police Chief W. J. Riley as "an outstanding cop."[55] Feelings of powerlessness, personal loss, and an inability to help those in need all seriously heightened the level of stress felt by officers in New Orleans following the 2005 hurricane. "The most stressing part is seeing the citizens we serve every day being treated like refugees," said Riley. "There were cops walking through the crowd at the convention center and people were coming up to beg for food. Not being able to help is a difficult thing. People were calling our names because we knew them and to not be able to help, man, that's stressful."[56]

Long-term stress may be the most insidious of all threats facing law enforcement personnel.

Traumatic events, like hurricanes, terrorist attacks, and violent confrontations, are instantly stressful, but long-term stress, whose debilitating effects accumulate over years, may be the most insidious and least visible of all threats facing law enforcement personnel today. While some degree of stress can be a positive motivator, serious stress over long periods of time is generally regarded as destructive, even life-threatening.

Stress is a natural component of police work (Figure 3).[57] The American Institute of Stress, based in Yonkers, New York, ranks policing among the top ten stress-producing jobs in the country.[58] Danger, frustration, paperwork, the daily demands of the job, and a lack of understanding from family members and friends contribute to the negative stress that officers experience. The Bureau of Justice Statistics points out the following:

> [E]xposure to violence, suffering, and death is inherent to the profession of the law enforcement officer. There are other sources of stress as well. Officers who deal with offenders on a daily basis may perceive the public's opinion of police performance to be unfavorable; they often are required to work mandatory, rotating shifts; and they may not have enough time to spend with their families. Police officers also face unusual, often highly disturbing, situations, such as dealing with a child homicide victim or the survivors of vehicle crashes.[59]

Some stressors in police work are particularly destructive. One is frustration brought on by the inability to be effective, regardless of the amount of personal effort expended. The crux of police work involves making arrests based on thorough investigations that lead to convictions and the removal of individuals who are damaging to the social fabric of the community—all under the umbrella of criminal law. Unfortunately, reality is often far from

FIGURE 3
Stress and Fatigue among Police Officers

Career Profile
Police Officer

Name: Robert D. Smith, Jr.

Position: Police Officer, Dearborn, Michigan

Colleges attended: Monroe County Community College, University of Michigan-Dearborn, Toledo College of Law, Oakland County Police Academy

Major: Finance, law

Year hired: 2009

Please give a brief description of your job. I am in the police academy, training to be a police officer.

What appealed to you most about the position when you applied for it? My goal is to make a difference in my community. Knowing that each day I go to work I can make a positive difference in people's lives is very rewarding.

How would you describe the interview process? The process lasted over a year, involved many steps, and required patience. The competition for the few available positions was great.

What is a typical day like? Generally I start out with physical training, followed by defensive tactic training and class study. We do a lot of role playing to enact real-life scenarios, which helps us prepare for the streets.

What qualities/characteristics are most helpful for this job? One must desire to help people and be willing to put one's life in dangerous situations. The position requires absolute integrity and courage. Criminals can sense weakness; an officer must show absolute confidence at all times. Officers must have patience and a high tolerance for stress.

What is a typical starting salary? Salaries vary depending on department size and city size. Larger departments *usually* pay better than departments with 10 or fewer officers. Salaries can range from $30,000 to over $65,000, not counting overtime and holiday pay. The benefits are outstanding, and most departments offer a pension.

What is the salary potential as you move up into higher-level jobs? Large departments have more opportunity for growth and offer many different areas, such as the detective bureau, SWAT team, evidence technicians, etc. Education can also help you attain a higher-level job. For example, many large-department police chiefs have a Juris Doctor degree. The higher-rank positions can range from $70,000 up to six figures.

What career advice would you give someone in college beginning their studies in criminal justice? Evaluate your career goals. Early research and networking can help you clarify which field to pursue. Seek out internships or cadet positions with local police departments. Work hard on getting high grades and internship experience, which will be essential in landing prime positions.

Source: Reprinted with permission of Robert D. Smith, Jr. Photo courtesy of Robert D. Smith, Jr. Logo courtesy Monroe County Community College.

the ideal: Arrests may not lead to convictions; evidence available to the officer may not be allowed in court; the sentences imposed may seem too light to the arresting officer. The feelings of powerlessness and frustration that come from seeing repeat offenders back on the streets and from witnessing numerous injustices worked on seemingly innocent victims may greatly stress police officers and cause them to question the purpose of their professional lives. It may also lead to desperate attempts to find relief. As one researcher observes, "The suicide rate of police officers is more than twice that of the general population."[60]

Stress is not unique to the police profession, but because of the "macho" attitude that has traditionally been associated with police work, denial of the stress is more prevalent among police officers than in other occupational groups. Certain types of individuals are probably more susceptible to the negative effects of stress than are others. The type A personality, popularized 30 years ago, is more likely to perceive life in terms of pressure and performance, whereas type B people are more laid back and less likely to suffer from the negative effects of stress. Police ranks, drawn as they are from the general population, are filled with both stress-sensitive and stress-resistant personalities.

Stress Reduction

It is natural to want to reduce stress.[61] Humor helps, even if it's somewhat cynical. Health-care professionals, for example, are noted for their ability to joke even though they are caring for patients who are seriously ill or even dying. At times, police officers use humor similarly to defuse their reactions to dark or threatening situations. Keeping an emotional distance from stressful events is another way of coping with them, although such distance is not always easy to maintain. Police officers who have had to deal with serious cases of child abuse often report that they experienced emotional turmoil as a consequence.

Exercise, meditation, deep breathing, biofeedback, self-hypnosis, guided imaging, induced relaxation, subliminal conditioning, music, prayer, and diet have all been cited as useful techniques for stress reduction. Devices to measure stress levels are available in the form of handheld heart-rate monitors, blood pressure devices, "biodots" (which change color according to the amount of blood flow in the extremities), and psychological inventories.

One theory regarding stress among police officers holds that the amount of stress an officer experiences is directly related to his or her reactions to potentially stressful situations.[62] Officers who can filter out extraneous stimuli and who can distinguish between truly threatening situations and those that are benign are much less likely to report job-related stressors than officers lacking these abilities. Because stress-filtering abilities are often closely linked to innate personality characteristics, some researchers suggest careful psychological screening of police applicants to better identify those who have a natural ability to cope with situations that others might perceive as stressful.[63]

▲ A Washington, D.C., Metro Transit police officer searching a train after subway bombings in London prompted increased security in 2005. How has the threat of terrorism altered the police role in America?
Reuters/Larry Downing/Landov Media

A police officer's family members often report feelings of stress that are directly related to the officer's work. As a result, some departments have developed innovative programs to allay family stress. The Collier County (Florida) Spousal Academy, for example, is a family support program that offers training to spouses and other domestic partners of deputies and recruits who are enrolled in the department's training academy. The ten-hour program deals directly with issues that are likely to produce stress and informs participants of department and community resources that are available to help them. Peer-support programs for spouses and life partners and for the adolescent children of officers are also beginning to operate nationwide. **Library Extra 5** provides a comprehensive overview of issues related to police officer stress.

Officer Fatigue

Like stress, fatigue can affect a police officer's performance. As criminologist Bryan Vila points out, "Tired, urban street cops are a national icon. Weary from overtime assignments, shift work, night school, endless hours spent waiting to testify, and the emotional and physical demands of the job, not to mention trying to patch together a family and social life during irregular islands of off-duty time, they fend off fatigue with coffee and hard-bitten humor."[64] Vila found levels of police officer fatigue to be six times as high as those of shift workers in industrial and mining jobs.[65] As Vila notes, few departments set work-hour standards, and fatigue associated with the pattern and length of work hours may be expected to contribute to police accidents, injuries, and misconduct.

To address the problem, Vila recommends that police departments "review the policies, procedures, and practices that affect shift scheduling and rotation, overtime moonlighting, the number of consecutive work hours allowed, and the way in which the department deals with overly tired employees."[66] Vila also suggests controlling the work hours of police officers, "just as we control the working hours of many other occupational groups."[67]

Terrorism's Impact on Policing

The terrorist attacks of September 11, 2001, have had a significant impact on policing in the United States. While the core mission of American police departments has not changed, law enforcement agencies at all levels now devote an increased amount of time and other resources to preparing for possible terrorist attacks and to gathering the intelligence necessary to thwart them.

4 Describe the changed role of American police in the post-9/11 environment.

In today's post-9/11 world, local police departments play an especially important role in responding to the challenges of terrorism. They must help prevent attacks and respond when attacks occur—offering critical evacuation, emergency medical, and security functions to help stabilize communities following an incident. A recent survey of 250 police chiefs by the Police Executive Research Forum (PERF) found that the chiefs strongly believe that their departments can make valuable contributions to terrorism prevention by using community policing networks to exchange information with citizens and to gather intelligence.[68] Read the results of the PERF survey online at **Library Extra 6**.

The Council on Foreign Relations, headquartered in New York City and Washington, D.C., agrees with PERF that American police departments can no longer assume that federal counterterrorism efforts alone will be sufficient to protect the communities they serve. Consequently, says the council, many police departments have responded to the terrorist threat by strengthening liaisons with federal, state, and local agencies (including fire departments and other police departments); by refining their training and emergency response plans; by creating antiterrorism divisions; and in a number of other ways.[69]

> It is very important that our first line of defense against terrorism—the seven hundred thousand officers on the street—be given adequate training and background information on terrorism, the methods and techniques of the terrorists, and the likelihood of an imminent attack.
>
> —Major Cities Chiefs Association[V]

The extent of local departments' engagement in preventive activities depends substantially on budgetary considerations and is strongly influenced by the assessed likelihood of attack. For example, the NYPD, which has firsthand experience in responding to terrorist attacks (23 of its officers were killed when the World Trade Center towers collapsed), has created a special bureau headed by a deputy police commissioner responsible for counterterrorism training, prevention, and investigation.[70] About 1,000 officers have been reassigned to antiterrorism duties, and the department is training its entire 38,000-member force in how to respond to biological, radiological, and chemical attacks.[71] The NYPD has assigned detectives to work abroad with law enforcement agencies in Canada, Israel, Southeast Asia, and the Middle East to track terrorists who might target New York City,[72] and it now employs officers with a command of the Pashto, Farsi, and Urdu languages of the Middle East to monitor foreign television, radio, and Internet communications. The department has also invested heavily in new hazardous materials protective suits, gas masks, and portable radiation detectors.

In November 2004, in an effort to provide the law enforcement community and policymakers with guidance on critical issues related to antiterrorism planning and critical incident response, the IACP announced its Taking Command Initiative. The IACP described the initiative as "an aggressive project to assess the current state of homeland security efforts in the United States and to develop and implement the actions necessary to protect our communities from the specter of both crime and terrorism."[73] Initial deliberations under the initiative led the IACP to conclude that "the current homeland security strategy is handicapped by a fundamental flaw: It was developed without sufficiently seeking or incorporating the advice, expertise, or consent of public safety organizations at the state, tribal, or local level."[74] Building on that premise, the IACP identified a number of key principles that it says must form the basis of any effective national homeland security strategy.[75] Learn more at **Web Extra 5** about the ongoing Taking Command Initiative as its leaders work to "transform the concept of a locally designed, nationally coordinated homeland security strategy into a reality."

Finally, in 2005, the IACP coordinated publication of a Post-9/11 Policing Project resource titled *Assessing and Managing the Terrorism Threat.* The Post-9/11 Policing Project is a collaborative effort of the IACP, the National Sheriffs' Association (NSA), the National Organization of Black Law Enforcement Executives (NOBLE), the Major Cities Chiefs Association (MCCA), and the Police Foundation. Download the publication at **Library Extra 7**.

The FBI's Joint Terrorism Task Forces

As the IACP recognizes, workable antiterrorism programs at the local level require effective sharing of critical information between agencies. FBI-sponsored Joint Terrorism Task Forces (JTTFs) facilitate this by bringing together federal and local law enforcement personnel to focus on specific threats. The FBI currently has established or authorized JTTFs in each of its

56 field offices. In addition to the JTTFs, the FBI has created Regional Terrorism Task Forces (RTTFs) to share information with local enforcement agencies. Through the RTTFs, FBI special agents assigned to terrorism prevention and investigation meet twice a year with their federal, state, and local counterparts for common training, discussion of investigations, and intelligence sharing. The FBI says that "the design of this non-traditional terrorism task force provides the necessary mechanism and structure to direct counterterrorism resources toward localized terrorism problems within the United States."[76] Six RTTFs are currently in operation: Inland Northwest, South Central, Southeastern, Northeast Border, Deep South, and Southwest.

Given the changes that have taken place in American law enforcement since the terrorist attacks of September 11, 2001, some say that traditional distinctions between crime, terrorism, and war are fading and that, at least in some instances, military action and civil law enforcement are becoming integrated. The critical question for law enforcement administrators in the near future may be one of discerning the role that law enforcement is to play in the emerging global context.

Intelligence-Led Policing and Antiterrorism

In 2005, the DOJ embraced the concept of **intelligence-led policing (ILP)** as an important technique to be employed by American law enforcement agencies in the battle against terrorism.[77] Intelligence is information that has been analyzed and integrated into a useful perspective. The information used in the development of effective intelligence is typically gathered from many sources, such as newspapers, surveillance, covert operations, financial records, electronic eavesdropping, interviews, the Internet, and interrogations. Law enforcement intelligence, or **criminal intelligence**, is the result of a "process that evaluates information collected from diverse sources, integrates the relevant information into a cohesive package, and produces a conclusion or estimate about a criminal phenomenon by using the scientific approach to problem solving."[78] Although criminal investigation is typically part of the intelligence-gathering process, the intelligence function of a police department is more exploratory and more broadly focused than a single criminal investigation.[79]

intelligence-led policing (ILP)
The collection and analysis of information to produce an intelligence end product designed to inform police decision making at both the tactical and strategic levels.[vi]

criminal intelligence
The information compiled, analyzed, and/or disseminated in an effort to anticipate, prevent, or monitor criminal activity.[vii]

ILP (also known as *intelligence-driven policing*) is the use of criminal intelligence to guide policing. A detailed description of ILP and its applicability to American law enforcement agencies is provided in the FBI publication *The Law Enforcement Intelligence Function* by David L. Carter of Michigan State University's School of Criminal Justice. The document is available at **Library Extra 8**.

According to Carter, criminal intelligence "is a synergistic product intended to provide meaningful and trustworthy direction to law enforcement decision makers about complex criminality, criminal enterprises, criminal extremists, and terrorists."[80] Carter goes on to point out that law enforcement intelligence consists of two types: tactical and strategic. Tactical intelligence "includes gaining or developing information related to threats of terrorism or crime and using this information to apprehend offenders, harden targets, and use strategies that will eliminate or mitigate the threat." Strategic intelligence, in contrast, provides information to decision makers about the changing nature of threats for the purpose of "developing response strategies and reallocating resources" to accomplish effective prevention.

Not every agency (especially small ones) has the staff or resources needed to create a dedicated intelligence unit. Even without an intelligence unit, however, a law enforcement organization should have the ability to effectively utilize the information and intelligence products that are developed and disseminated by organizations at all levels of government. In other words, even though a police agency may not have the resources necessary to analyze all of the information it acquires, it should still be able to mount an effective response to credible threat information that it receives. Learn more about the law enforcement intelligence function and ILP at **Library Extra 9**.

Information Sharing and Antiterrorism

The need to effectively share criminal intelligence across jurisdictions and between law enforcement agencies nationwide became apparent with the tragic events of September 11, 2001. Consequently, governments at all levels are today working toward the creation of a fully integrated criminal justice information system. According to a recent task force report, a fully

> The need for improving homeland security requires a joint effort of all levels of law enforcement, including local, state and federal agencies.
> —Major Cities Chiefs Association[viii]

integrated system would be "a network of public safety, justice and homeland security computer systems which provides to each agency the information it needs, at the time it is needed, in the form that it is needed, regardless of the source and regardless of the physical location at which it is stored."[81] The information that is provided would be complete, accurate, and formatted in whatever way is most useful for the agency's tasks. In a fully integrated criminal justice information system, information would be made available at the practitioner's workstation, whether that workstation is a patrol car, desk, laptop, or judge's bench. Within such a system, each agency would share information not only with other agencies in its own jurisdiction but with multiple justice agencies at the federal, state, and local levels. In such an idealized justice information system, accurate information would also be available to nonjustice agencies with statutory authority and a legal obligation to check criminal histories before licensure, employment, weapons purchase, and so on.

One widely used information-sharing system is Law Enforcement Online (LEO). LEO, an intranet intended exclusively for use by the law enforcement community, is a national interactive computer communications system and information service. A user-friendly system, it can be accessed by any approved employee of a duly constituted local, state, or federal law enforcement agency or by an approved member of an authorized law enforcement special-interest group. LEO provides a state-of-the-art communications mechanism to link all levels of law enforcement throughout the United States. The system includes password-accessed e-mail, Internet chat rooms, an electronic library, an online calendar, special-interest topical focus areas, and self-paced distance-learning modules.[82]

NLETS
An acronym referring to the International Justice and Public Safety Information Sharing Network, an important law enforcement information-sharing resource.

Another important law enforcement information-sharing resource is the International Justice and Public Safety Information Sharing Network, which uses the acronym **NLETS**. NLETS members include all 50 states, most federal agencies and territories, and the Royal Canadian Mounted Police (RCMP). NLETS, which has been in operation for nearly 40 years, was formerly called the National Law Enforcement Telecommunications System. It has recently been enhanced to facilitate a variety of encrypted digital communications. It now links 30,000 agencies and more than half a million access devices in the United States and Canada, and it facilitates nearly 41 million transmissions each month. Information available through NLETS includes state criminal histories, homeland alert messages, immigration databases, driver's records and vehicle registrations, aircraft registrations, AMBER Alerts, weather advisories, and hazardous materials (HAZMAT) notifications and regulations. You can reach NLETS on the Web at **Web Extra 6**.

The National Criminal Intelligence Sharing Plan

Although information-sharing efforts continue to evolve, most experts agree that a fully integrated, nationwide criminal justice information system does not yet exist.[83] Efforts to create one began with the 2003 National Criminal Intelligence Sharing Plan (NCISP). The NCISP was developed under the auspices of the DOJ's Global Justice Information Sharing Initiative and was authored by its Global Intelligence Working Group (GIWG).[84] Federal, local, state, and tribal law enforcement representatives all had a voice in the development of the plan. The NCISP provides specific steps that law enforcement agencies can take to participate in the sharing of critical law enforcement and terrorism prevention information.

Authors of the plan note that not every agency has the staff or resources needed to create a formal intelligence unit. Even without a dedicated intelligence unit, however, the plan says that every law enforcement organization must have the ability to effectively consume the intelligence available from a wide range of organizations at all levels of government.[85] The NCISP is available in its entirety at **Library Extra 10**.

Police Civil Liability

> **5** Describe the civil liability issues associated with policing, and identify common sources of civil suits against the police.

In 1996, 51-year-old Richard Kelley filed suit in federal court against the Massachusetts State Police and the Weymouth (Massachusetts) Police Department.[86] The suit resulted from an incident during which, Kelley alleged, state troopers and Weymouth police officers treated him as a drunk rather than recognizing that he had just suffered a stroke while driving. According to Kelley, following a minor traffic accident caused by the stroke, officers pulled him from his car, handcuffed him, dragged him along the ground, and ignored his pleas for help—forcing him to stay at a state police barracks for seven hours before taking him for medical treatment. Drunk-driving charges against Kelley were dropped after medical tests failed to reveal the presence of any intoxicating substances in his body.

Suits of **civil liability** brought against law enforcement personnel are of two types: state and federal. Suits brought in state courts have generally been the more common form of civil litigation involving police officers. In recent years, however, an increasing number of suits have been brought in federal courts on the claim that the civil rights of the plaintiff, as guaranteed by federal law, were denied.

civil liability
The potential responsibility for payment of damages or other court-ordered enforcement as a result of a ruling in a lawsuit. Civil liability is not the same as criminal liability, which means "open to punishment for a crime."[ix]

Common Sources of Civil Suits

Police officers may become involved in a variety of situations that could result in civil suits against the officers, their superiors, and their departments. Major sources of police civil liability are listed in Table 3. Charles R. Swanson, an expert in police procedure, says that the most common sources of lawsuits against the police are "assault, battery, false imprisonment, and malicious prosecution."[87]

Of all complaints brought against the police, assault charges are the best known, being subject to high media visibility. Less visible (but not uncommon) are civil suits charging the police with false arrest or false imprisonment. In the 1986 case of *Malley* v. *Briggs*,[88] the U.S. Supreme Court held that a police officer who effects an arrest or conducts a search on the basis of an improperly issued warrant may be liable for monetary damages when a reasonably well-trained officer, under the same circumstances, "would have known that his affidavit failed to establish probable cause and that he should not have applied for the warrant." Significantly, the Court ruled that an officer "cannot excuse his own default by pointing to the greater incompetence of the magistrate."[89] The officer, rather than the judge who issued the warrant, is ultimately responsible for establishing the basis for pursuing the arrest or search.

When an officer makes an arrest without just cause or simply impedes an individual's right to leave the scene without good reason, he or she may be liable for the charge of false arrest. Officers who "throw their weight around" are especially subject to this type of suit, grounded as it is in the abuse of police authority. Because employers may be sued for the negligent or malicious actions of their employees, many police departments are being named as codefendants in lawsuits today.

Civil suits are also brought against officers whose actions are deemed negligent. High-speed vehicle pursuits are especially dangerous because of the potential for injury to innocent bystanders. In the case of *Biscoe* v. *Arlington County* (1984),[90] for example, Alvin Biscoe was awarded $5 million after he lost both legs as a consequence of a high-speed chase while he was waiting to cross the street. Biscoe, an innocent bystander, was struck by a police car that went out of control. The officer driving the car had violated department policies prohibiting high-speed chases, and the court found that he had not been properly trained.

Departments may protect themselves to some degree through training combined with regulations limiting the authority of their personnel. One year after the *Biscoe* case was decided, for example, a Louisiana police officer, who had an accident while driving 75 mph in a 40-mph zone, was found to be negligent and was held liable for damages.[91] However, the department was not held liable

TABLE 3
Major Sources of Police Civil Liability

Failure to protect property in police custody
Negligence in the care of suspects in police custody
Failure to render proper emergency medical assistance
Failure to prevent a foreseeable crime
Failure to aid private citizens
Lack of due regard for the safety of others
False arrest
False imprisonment
Inappropriate use of deadly force
Unnecessary assault or battery
Malicious prosecution
Violation of constitutional rights
Pattern of unfair and inequitable treatment
Racial profiling

because it had a policy limiting emergency driving to no more than 20 mph over the posted speed limit and because officers were trained in that policy.

The FBI states that "a traffic accident constitutes the most common terminating event in an urban pursuit."[92] Some cities are actively replacing high-speed vehicle pursuits with surveillance technologies employing unmanned aerial vehicles (UAVs). Although helicopters have long been used in this capacity, the advent of UAV technology promises to make the tracking of fleeing suspects much quicker and far safer for all involved.

Law enforcement supervisors may be the object of lawsuits by virtue of the fact that they are responsible for the actions of their officers. If it can be shown that supervisors were negligent in hiring (as when someone with a history of alcoholism, mental problems, sexual deviance, or drug abuse is employed) or if supervisors failed in their responsibility to properly train officers before arming and deploying them, they may be found liable for damages.

In the 1989 case of the *City of Canton, Ohio* v. *Harris*,[93] the U.S. Supreme Court ruled that a "failure to train" can become the basis for legal liability on the part of a municipality where the "failure to train amounts to deliberate indifference to the rights of persons with whom the police come in contact."[94] In that case, Geraldine Harris was arrested and taken to the Canton, Ohio, police station. While at the station, she slumped to the floor several times. Officers left her on the floor and did not call for medical assistance. Upon release, Harris's family took her to a local hospital, where she was found to be suffering from several emotional ailments. Harris was hospitalized for a week and received follow-up outpatient treatment for the next year.

In the 1997 case of *Board of the County Commissioners of Bryan County, Oklahoma* v. *Brown*, however, the Supreme Court ruled that to establish liability, plaintiffs must show that "the municipal action in question was not simply negligent, but was taken with 'deliberate indifference' as to its known or obvious consequences."[95]

Federal Lawsuits

1983 lawsuit
A civil suit brought under Title 42, Section 1983, of the U.S. Code against anyone who denies others their constitutional right to life, liberty, or property without due process of law.

Civil suits alleging police misconduct that are filed in federal courts are often called **1983 lawsuits** because they are based on Section 1983 of Title 42 of the U.S. Code—an act passed by Congress in 1871 to ensure the civil rights of men and women of all races. That act requires due process of law before any person can be deprived of life, liberty, or property and specifically provides redress for the denial of these constitutional rights by officials acting under color of state law. It reads as follows:

> Every person who, under color of any statute, ordinance, regulation, custom, or usage, of any State or Territory, subjects, or causes to be subjected, any citizen of the United States or other person within the jurisdiction thereof to the deprivation of any rights, privileges, or immunities secured by the Constitution and laws, shall be liable to the party injured in an action at law, suit in equity, or other proper proceeding for redress.[96]

A 1983 suit may be brought, for example, against officers who shoot suspects under questionable circumstances, thereby denying them, without due process, their right to life. Similarly, an officer who makes an arrest based on accusations that he or she knows to be untrue may be subject to a 1983 lawsuit.

***Bivens* action**
A civil suit, based on the case of *Bivens* v. *Six Unknown Federal Agents*, brought against federal government officials for denying the constitutional rights of others.

Another type of liability action, this one directed specifically at federal officials or enforcement agents, is called a ***Bivens* action**. The case of *Bivens* v. *Six Unknown Federal Agents* (1971)[97] established a path for legal action against agents enforcing federal laws, which is similar to that found in a 1983 suit. *Bivens* actions may be addressed against individuals but not against the United States or its agencies.[98] Federal officers have generally been granted a court-created qualified immunity and have been protected from suits where they were found to have acted in the belief that their action was consistent with federal law.[99]

> Everyone is a prisoner of his own experiences. No one can eliminate prejudices—just recognize them.
> —Edward R. Murrow (1908–1965)

In the past, the doctrine of sovereign immunity barred legal actions against state and local governments. Sovereign immunity was a legal theory that held that a governing body could not be sued because it made the law and therefore could not be bound by it. Immunity is a much more complex issue today. Some states have officially abandoned any pretext of immunity through legislative action. New York State, for example, has declared that public agencies are equally as liable as private agencies for violations of constitutional rights. Other states, like California, have enacted statutory provisions that define and limit governmental liability.[100] A number of state immunity statutes have been struck down by court decisions. In general, states are moving in the direction of setting dollar limits on liability and adopting federal immunity principles to protect individual officers, including "good-faith" and "reasonable belief" rules.

▲ Major Juanita Walker-Kirkland of the Miami Police Department, *left*, listening to Manjit Singh, *right*, chairman of Sikh Mediawatch and Task Force during a Building Cultural Competency training program in June 2003. The training program was sponsored by the U.S. Department of Justice in hopes of improving community relations between law enforcement officials and diverse cultural and religious groups. Why are such programs important?
Yesikka Vivancos/AP Wide World Photos

At the federal level, the concept of sovereign immunity is embodied in the Federal Tort Claims Act (FTCA),[101] which grants broad immunity to federal government agencies engaged in discretionary activities. When a federal employee is sued for a wrongful or negligent act, the Federal Employees Liability Reform and Tort Compensation Act of 1988, commonly known as the Westfall Act, empowers the attorney general to certify that the employee was acting within the scope of his or her office or employment at the time of the incident. Upon certification, the employee is dismissed from the action, and the United States is substituted as defendant; the case then falls under the governance of the FTCA.

The U.S. Supreme Court has supported a type of "qualified immunity" for individual officers (as opposed to the agencies for which they work) that "shields law enforcement officers from constitutional lawsuits if reasonable officers believe their actions to be lawful in light of clearly established law and the information the officers possess." The Supreme Court has also described qualified immunity as a defense "which shields public officials from actions for damages unless their conduct was unreasonable in light of clearly established law."[102] The Court said that "the qualified immunity doctrine's central objective is to protect public officials from undue interference with their duties and from potentially disabling threats of liability."[103] In the context of a warrantless arrest, the Court said in *Hunter* v. *Bryant* (1991),[104] "even law enforcement officials who reasonably but mistakenly conclude that probable cause is present are entitled to immunity."[105]

The doctrine of qualified immunity, as it exists today, rests largely on the 2001 U.S. Supreme Court decision of *Saucier* v. *Katz*,[106] in which the Court established a two-pronged test for assessing constitutional violations by government agents.[107] First, the court hearing the case must decide whether the facts, taken in the light most favorable to the party asserting the injury, show that the defendant's conduct violated a constitutional right. Second, the court must then decide whether that right was clearly established. For a right to be clearly established, the Court ruled, "it would be clear to a reasonable [defendant] that his conduct was unlawful in the situation he confronted." In summary, qualified immunity protects law enforcement agents from being sued for damages unless they violate clearly established law that a reasonable official in the agents' position would have known.

The *Saucier* decision has recently faced substantial legal challenges, leading the Court to rule in 2009 that "the rigid *Saucier* procedure" has serious shortcomings. The Court noted that "*stare decisis* does not prevent this Court from determining whether the *Saucier* procedure should be modified or abandoned." The 2009 ruling, *Pearson et al.* v. *Callahan*,[108] is available online at **Library Extra 11**.

In 2007, in the case of *Scott* v. *Harris*, the Supreme Court sided with an officer who had rammed a speeding car driven by a teenager, sending it down an embankment and leaving the driver a quadriplegic.[109] The justices reasoned that the driver "intentionally placed himself and the public in danger by unlawfully engaging in reckless, high-speed flight" and noted that those who might have been harmed had the officer not forced him off the road "were entirely innocent." The Court concluded that it was reasonable for the officer, Deputy Timothy Scott, to take the action that he did and rejected the "argument that safety could have been assured if the police simply ceased their pursuit." In essence, the Court found that "a police officer's attempt to terminate a dangerous high-speed car chase that threatens the lives of innocent bystanders does not violate the Fourth Amendment, even when it places the fleeing motorist at risk of serious injury or death."

Criminal charges can be brought against officers who overstep legal boundaries or who act in violation of set standards. In 2001, for example, in the case of *Idaho* v. *Horiuchi*,[110] the Ninth U.S. Circuit Court of Appeals ruled that federal law enforcement officers are not immune from state prosecution where their actions violate state law "either through malice or excessive zeal." The case involved FBI sharpshooter Lon Horiuchi, who was charged with negligent manslaughter by prosecutors in Boundary County, Idaho, following the 1992 incident at Ruby Ridge. Learn more about the Ruby Ridge incident at **Library Extra 12**.

Today, most police departments at both state and federal levels carry liability insurance to protect themselves against the severe financial damage that can result from the loss of a large civil suit. Some officers also acquire private policies that provide coverage in the event they are named as individuals in a civil suit. Both types of insurance policies generally cover legal fees up to a certain amount, regardless of the outcome of the case. Police departments that face civil prosecution because of the actions of an officer may find that legal and financial liability extends to supervisors, city managers, and the community itself. Where insurance coverage does not exist or is inadequate, city coffers may be nearly drained to meet the damages awarded.[111]

One study of a large sample of police chiefs throughout Texas found that most believed that lawsuits or the threat of civil litigation against the police makes it harder for individual officers to do their jobs. Most of the chiefs espoused the idea that adequate training, better screening of applicants, close supervision of officers, and "treating people fairly" all reduced the likelihood of lawsuits.[112]

racial profiling
"Any police-initiated action that relies on the race, ethnicity, or national origin rather than [1] on the behavior of an individual, or [2] on information that leads the police to a particular individual who has been identified as being, or having been, engaged in criminal activity."[x]

Racial Profiling and Biased Policing

Racial Profiling

▲ An elderly woman showing her displeasure with Transportation Security Administration requirements. Some people fear that the use of profiling techniques could lead to unfair discrimination against members of certain racial and ethnic groups. Others suggest that the careful use of profiling can provide an important advantage in an age of scarce resources. Which perspective appeals to you?
Henry Ray Abrams/AP Wide World Photos

Racial profiling has been defined as any police action initiated on the basis of the race, ethnicity, or national origin of a suspect rather than on the behavior of that individual or on information that identifies the individual as being, or having been, engaged in criminal activity.[113]

6 Describe racial profiling and biased policing, and explain why they have become significant issues in policing today.

Profiling was originally intended to help catch drug couriers attempting to enter the country. The U.S. Customs Service and the DEA developed a number of "personal indicators" that seemed, from the agency's day-to-day enforcement experiences, to be associated with increased likelihood of law violation. Among the indicators were these: speaking Spanish, entering the United States on flights originating in particular Central and South American countries, being an 18- to 32-year-old male, having purchased tickets with cash, and having a short planned stay (often of only a day or two) in the United States. Federal agents frequently used these criteria in deciding which airline passengers to search and which bags to inspect.

The alleged use by police of racial profiling may take a number of forms. Minority accounts of disparate treatment at the hands of police officers include being stopped for being "in the wrong car" (for example, driving an expensive, late-model BMW); being stopped and questioned for being in the wrong neighborhood (that is, driving through a traditionally white residential neighborhood); and being harassed at the hands of police officers for petty traffic violations (such as having underinflated tires, or having an illegible license plate).[114]

Racial profiling has been derisively referred to as "driving while black" or "driving while brown," although it may also apply to situations other than those involving traffic violations. Racial profiling came to the attention of the public in the late 1990s when police in New Jersey and Maryland were accused of unfair treatment of African American motorists and admitted that race was a factor in traffic stops.

It is practically an article of faith among young, black males that they are more likely than whites to be stopped, frisked, spread-eagled, and arrested by the police, often on the flimsiest of charges.

—Hutchinson Report, July 2001

In 2003, in response to widespread public outcry over the use of racial profiling, the DOJ banned its practice in all federal law enforcement agencies except in cases that involve the possible identification of terrorist suspects.[115] According to the DOJ, "The guidance provides that in making routine law enforcement decisions—such as deciding which motorists to stop for traffic infractions—consideration of the driver's race or ethnicity is absolutely forbidden."[116]

Those who defend the use of racial profiling by the police argue that it is not a bigoted practice when based on facts (such as when a police department decides to increase patrols in a particular area because of exceptionally high crime rates) or when significant criminal potential exists among even a few members of a group. An example of the latter is the widespread public suspicions that focused on Arab Americans (and other Arabs living in the United States or traveling through the country) following the terrorist attacks of September 11, 2001. As soon as it was publicly announced that the hijackers had been of Middle Eastern origin, some flight crews demanded that Arab-looking passengers be removed from their airplanes before takeoff, and passengers refused to fly with people who looked like Arabs.[117]

None of this is to say, of course, that race or ethnicity somehow inherently causes crime (or that it somehow causes poverty or increases the risk of victimization). If anything, race and ethnicity may simply display a significant correlation with certain types of crime, as they do with certain kinds of victimization. Although the *real* causes of criminality may be socialization into criminal subcultures, economically deprived neighborhoods, lack of salable job skills, and intergenerational poverty, and not race per se, to some law enforcement agencies race provides one more indicator of the likelihood of criminality. David Cole, a professor at Georgetown University's Law Center, for example, notes that in the minds of many police officials, "racial and ethnic disparities reflect not discrimination [or bigotry] but higher rates of offenses among minorities."[118]

Freedom or Safety? You Decide.

Was the LAPD's Community Mapping Project a Form of Religious Profiling?

In 2007, the Los Angeles Police Department announced that it would terminate plans to have its counterterrorism unit identify isolated social enclaves within the city. Weeks earlier Deputy Chief Michael P. Downing, who heads the department's counterterrorism bureau, issued a press release detailing how the LAPD intended to work with the University of Southern California's Center for Risk and Economic Analysis of Terrorism Events to determine which areas of the city were socially isolated and susceptible to "violent, ideologically based extremism."

The plan had been originally touted as a mapping project "intended to study the language, culture, history, socioeconomic conditions, and country of origin of various communities and neighborhoods" and as an effort to "help groups integrate into broader society by offering access to government and social services."

Although the plan did not specifically target Muslim neighborhoods, Islamic leaders felt that it was a thinly disguised form of racial and religious profiling and that it was aimed squarely at them and at members of their communities. Islamic leaders protested the plan, saying that any mapping based on faith and ethnicity is inappropriate for police departments, which should be concerned instead with crime mapping. "Police should not be in the business of analyzing political views, and religious views," said Hussam Ayloush, a member of the Los Angeles chapter of the Council on American-Islamic Relations.

Estimates hold that about half a million Muslims live in California's Los Angeles, Riverside, and Orange counties.

YOU DECIDE

Is Hussam Ayloush right in saying that police departments should concern themselves with crime mapping and not with other forms of mapping in the cities they serve? Why or why not? Was the LAPD's proposed community mapping project really a form of religious and ethnic profiling? If so, should such profiling be permitted? Why or why not?

References: Peter Prengaman, "LAPD Shelves Muslim Mapping Plan," Associated Press, November 15, 2007 and Mimi Hall, "LAPD Plan Draws Ire from Muslims," *USA Today*, November 9–11, 2007.

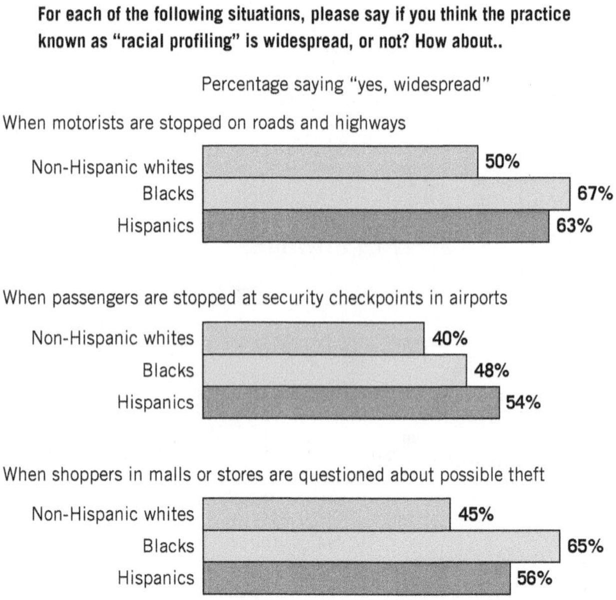

FIGURE 4
Racial Profiling and Biased Policing, Perceptions by Race

Source: From The Gallup Poll, http://www.gallup.com. Reprinted with permission of The Gallup Organization.

"Nationwide," says Cole, "blacks are 13 times more likely to be sent to state prisons for drug convictions than are whites, so it would seem rational for police to assume that all other things being equal, a black driver is more likely than a white driver to be carrying drugs." Statistics like this, of course, may further enhance police focus on minorities and may result in even more arrests, thereby reinforcing the beliefs on which racial profiling by enforcement agents is based. Such observations led esteemed sociologist Amitai Etzioni to declare in 2001 that racial profiling is not necessarily racist.[119] Moreover, warned Etzioni, an end to racial profiling "would penalize those African-American communities with high incidences of violent crime" because they would lose the levels of policing that they need to remain relatively secure.

Regardless of arguments offered in support of racial profiling as an enforcement tool, the practice has been widely condemned as being contrary to basic ethical principles. National public opinion polls conducted by the Gallup Poll Organization show that more than 80% of respondents are morally opposed to the practice of racial profiling by the police, although beliefs about the use of racial profiling vary widely by race (Figure 4).[120] From a more pragmatic viewpoint, however, racial profiling is unacceptable because it weakens the public's confidence in the police, thereby decreasing police-citizen trust and cooperation.[121] A number of states have enacted legislation banning the use of racial profiling by law enforcement agencies (Figure 5). Learn more about racial profiling and police management via **Library Extra 13**.

> We must strive to eliminate any racial, ethnic, or cultural bias that may exist among our ranks.
>
> —Sherman Block, former Los Angeles County sheriff

Racially Biased Policing

In 2001, PERF released a detailed report titled *Racially Biased Policing: A Principled Response*.[122] PERF researchers surveyed more than 1,000 police executives, analyzed material from over 250 law enforcement agencies, and sought input from law enforcement agency personnel, community activists, and civil rights leaders about racial bias in policing. Researchers concluded that "the vast majority of law enforcement officers—of all ranks, nationwide—are dedicated men and women committed to serving all citizens

FIGURE 5
States That Have Banned Racial Profiling

Source: Amnesty International USA, *Threat and Humiliation: Racial Profiling, Domestic Security, and Human Rights in the United States* (New York: Amnesty International USA Publications, 2004), p. 6. http://www.amnestyusa.org. © Amnesty International USA. Reprinted with permission.

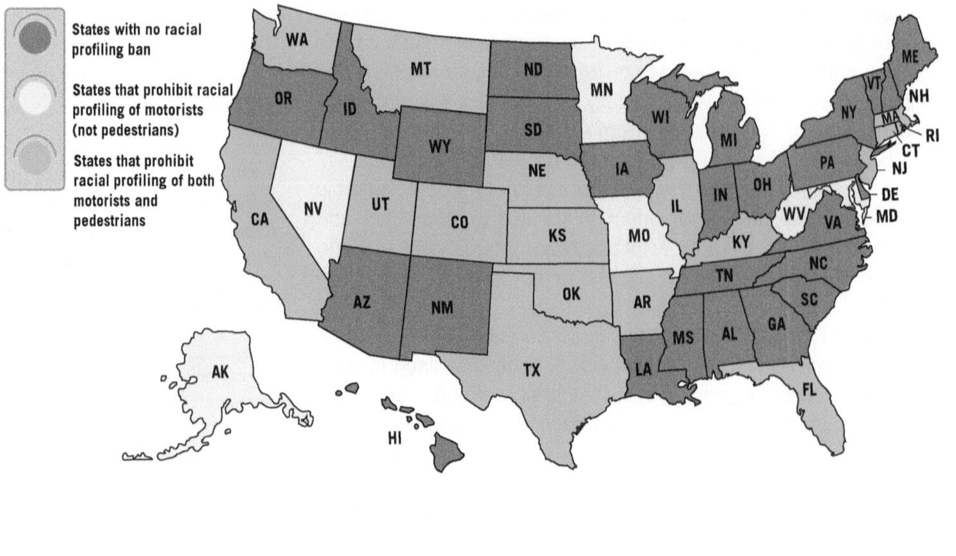

with fairness and dignity." [123] Most police officers, said the report, share an intolerance for racially biased policing. The report's authors noted that some police behaviors may be misinterpreted as biased when, in fact, the officers are just doing their job. "The good officer continually scans the environment for anomalies to normalcy—for conditions, people and behavior that are unusual for that environment," they said. "In learning and practicing their craft, officers quickly develop a sense for what is normal and expected, and conversely, for what is not."[124] Hence for officers of any race to take special notice of unknown young white males who unexpectedly appear in a traditionally African American neighborhood, for example, might be nothing other than routine police procedure. Such an observation, however, is not in itself sufficient for an investigatory stop but might be used in conjunction with other trustworthy and relevant information already in the officers' possession—such as the officers' prior knowledge that young white men have been routinely visiting a particular apartment complex in the neighborhood to purchase drugs—to justify such a stop.

The PERF report provides many specific recommendations to help police departments be free of bias. One recommendation, for example, says that "supervisors should monitor activity reports for evidence of improper practices and patterns. They should conduct spot-checks and regular sampling of in-car videotapes, radio transmissions, and in-car computer and central communications records to determine if both formal and informal communications are professional and free from racial bias and other disrespect."[125] Read the entire PERF report at **Library Extra 14**.

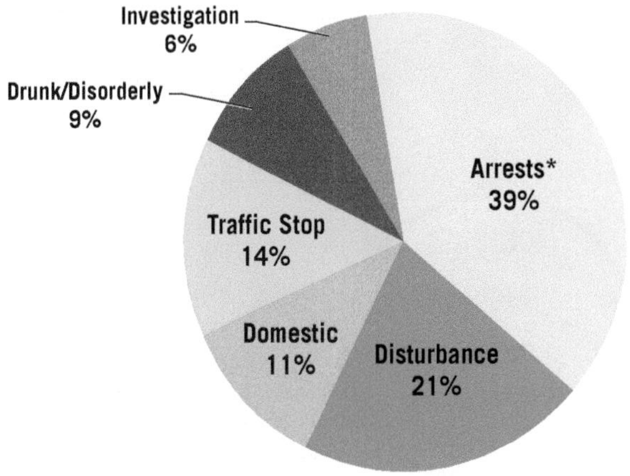

*Includes serving arrest warrants, making field arrests, and effecting other arrests.

FIGURE 6
Police Use of Force by Type of Encounter

Source: International Association of Chiefs of Police, *Police Use of Force in America, 2001* (Alexandria, VA: IACP, 2001), p. iii. Reprinted with permission.

Police Use Of Force

Police use of force is defined as the use of physical restraint by a police officer when dealing with a member of the public.[126] Law enforcement officers are authorized to use the amount of force that is reasonable and necessary given the circumstances. Most officers are trained in the use of force and typically encounter numerous situations during their careers when the use of force is appropriate—for example, when making some arrests, restraining unruly combatants, or controlling a disruptive demonstration. Force may involve hitting; holding or restraining; pushing; choking; threatening with a flashlight, baton, or chemical or pepper spray; restraining with a police dog; or threatening with a gun. Some definitions of police use of force also include handcuffing.

7 Describe the situations in which police officers are most likely to use force, and provide some guidelines for determining when too much force has been used.

police use of force
The use of physical restraint by a police officer when dealing with a member of the public.[xi]

The NIJ estimates that more than 43.5 million people nationwide have face-to-face contact with the police over a typical 12-month period (nearly 18 million as a result of traffic stops) and that approximately 1.6%, or about 700,000 of these people, become subject to the use of force or the threat of force.[127] When handcuffing is included in the definition of force, the number of people subjected to force increases to 1.2 million, or slightly more than 2.5% of those having contact with the police. Other studies show that police use weaponless tactics in approximately 80% of use-of-force incidents and that half of all use-of-force incidents involve merely grabbing or holding the suspect.[128]

Studies show that police use force in fewer than 20% of adult custodial arrests. Even in instances where force is used, the police primarily use weaponless tactics. Female officers have been found less likely to use physical force and firearms and are more likely to use chemical weapons (mostly pepper spray) than their male counterparts. Figure 6 shows the types of encounters in which the use of force is most likely to be employed.

A more complex issue is the use of excessive force. The IACP defines **excessive force** as "the application of an amount and/or frequency of force greater than that required to

excessive force
The application of an amount or frequency of force greater than that required to compel compliance from a willing or unwilling subject.[xii]

compel compliance from a willing or unwilling subject."[129] When excessive force is employed, the activities of the police often come under public scrutiny and receive attention from the media and legislators. Police officers' use of excessive force can also result in lawsuits by members of the public who feel that they have been treated unfairly. Whether the use of excessive force is aberrant behavior on the part of an individual officer or is a practice of an entire law enforcement agency, both the law and public opinion generally condemn it.

Nothing's so sacred as honor.
—Inscription on Wyatt Earp's headstone

Kenneth Adams, an expert in the use of force by police, notes that there is an important difference between the terms *excessive force*, such as shoving or pushing when simply grabbing a suspect would be adequate, and the *excessive use of force*, which refers to the phenomenon of force being used unacceptably, often on a department-wide basis. The second term, says Adams, "deals with relative comparisons among police agencies, and there are no established criteria for judgment."[130] *Use of excessive force* and the *excessive use of force* may be distinguished from the *illegal use of force*, which refers to situations in which the use of force by police violates a law or statute.[131]

In a study reported in 2001, Geoffrey Alpert and Roger Dunham found that the "force factor"—the level of force used by the police relative to the suspect's level of resistance—is a key element to consider in attempting to reduce injuries to both the police and suspects.[132] The force factor is calculated by measuring both the suspect's level of resistance and the officer's level of force on an equivalent scale and by then subtracting the level of resistance from the level of police force used. Results from the study indicate that, on average, the level of force that officers use is closely related to the type of training that their departments emphasize.

problem police officer
A law enforcement officer who exhibits problem behavior, as indicated by high rates of citizen complaints and use-of-force incidents and by other evidence.[xiii]

Excessive force can also be symptomatic of **problem police officers**. Problem police officers are those who exhibit problem behavior, as indicated by high rates of citizen complaints and use-of-force incidents and by other evidence.[133] The Christopher Commission, which studied the structure and operation of the LAPD in the wake of the Rodney King beating, found a number of repeat offenders on the LAPD force.[134] According to the commission, approximately 1,800 LAPD officers were alleged to have used excessive force or improper tactics between 1986 and 1990. Of these officers, more than 1,400 had only one or two allegations against them, another 183 officers had four or more allegations, 44 had six or more, 16 had eight or more, and one had 16 such allegations. The commission also found that, generally speaking, the 44 officers with six complaints or more had received positive performance evaluations that failed to record "sustained" complaints or to discuss their significance.

Recent studies have found that problem police officers do not differ significantly in race or ethnicity from other officers, although they tend to be male and have disciplinary records that are more serious than those of other officers. Some departments are developing early-warning systems to allow police managers to identify potentially problematic officers and to reduce problem police officer behavior. Learn more about the police use of force, as well as force used against the police, from **Library Extras 15** and **16**.

Deadly Force

deadly force
The force likely to cause death or great bodily harm. Also, "the intentional use of a firearm or other instrument resulting in a high probability of death."[xiv]

Generally speaking, **deadly force** is likely to cause death or great bodily harm. The FBI defines *deadly force* as "the intentional use of a firearm or other instrument resulting in a high probability of death."[135] According to a report released by the Bureau of Justice Statistics in 2001, nearly 400 felons each year die in justifiable homicides by police.[136]

The use of deadly force by law enforcement officers, especially when it is *not* considered justifiable (as in the *Horiuchi* case mentioned earlier in this chapter), is one area of potential civil liability that has received considerable attention in recent years. Historically, the fleeing-felon rule applied to most U.S. jurisdictions. It held that officers could use deadly force to prevent the escape of a suspected felon even when that person represented no immediate threat to the officer or to the public.

The 1985 U.S. Supreme Court case of *Tennessee* v. *Garner*[137] specified the conditions under which deadly force could be used in the apprehension of suspected felons. Edward Garner, a 15-year-old suspected burglar, was shot to death by Memphis police after he refused their order to halt and attempted to climb over a chain-link fence. In an action initiated by Garner's father, who claimed that his son's constitutional rights had been violated, the Court held that the use of deadly force by the police to prevent the escape of a fleeing felon could be justified only where the suspect could reasonably be thought to represent a significant threat of serious injury or death to the public or to the officer and where deadly force is necessary to effect the arrest. In reaching its decision, the Court declared that "[t]he use of deadly force to prevent the escape of all felony suspects, whatever the circumstances, is constitutionally unreasonable."

Cincinnati Police Officer Princess Davis talking with community member Gil Steinberger following a police-sponsored showing of a movie for senior citizens. The event was part of police efforts to improve police-community relations in the city following the November 30, 2003, beating death of 41-year-old Nathaniel Jones. Jones, a 350-pound black man who had ingested PCP and cocaine, lunged at two white officers and knocked one of them down before other officers beat him in an effort to subdue him. His family, charging that excessive force had been used, filed a wrongful death lawsuit against the city in federal court. How can police agencies win the support of the communities they serve?
Al Behrman/AP Wide World Photos

In 1989, in the case of *Graham* v. *Connor*,[138] the Court established the standard of "objective reasonableness" under which an officer's use of deadly force could be assessed in terms of "reasonableness at the moment." In other words, whether deadly force has been used appropriately should be judged, the Court said, from the perspective of a reasonable officer on the scene and not with the benefit of "20/20 hindsight." The justices wrote, "The calculus of reasonableness must embody allowance for the fact that police officers are often forced to make split-second judgments—in circumstances that are tense, uncertain, and rapidly evolving—about the amount of force that is necessary in a particular situation."

In 1995, following investigations into the actions of federal agents at the deadly siege of the Branch Davidian compound at Waco, Texas, and the tragic deaths associated with a 1992 FBI assault on antigovernment separatists in Ruby Ridge, Idaho, the federal government announced that it was adopting an "imminent danger" standard for the use of deadly force by federal agents. The imminent danger standard restricts the use of deadly force to those situations in which the lives of agents or others are in danger. As the new standard was announced, federal agencies were criticized for having taken so long to adopt it. The federal deadly force policy, as adopted by the FBI, contains the following elements:[139]

- *Defense of life.* Agents may use deadly force only when necessary, that is, only when they have probable cause to believe that the subject poses an imminent danger of serious physical injury or death to the agents or to others.
- *Fleeing subject.* Deadly force may be used to prevent the escape of a fleeing subject if there is probable cause to believe that the subject has committed a felony involving the infliction or threatened infliction of serious physical injury or death and that the subject's escape would pose an imminent danger of serious physical injury or death to the agents or to others.
- *Verbal warning.* If feasible, and if doing so would not increase the danger to the agents or to others, a verbal warning to submit to the authority of the agents should be given before the use of deadly force.
- *Warning shot.* Agents may not fire warning shots.
- *Vehicle.* Agents may not fire weapons solely to disable moving vehicles. Weapons may be fired at the driver or other occupant of a moving motor vehicle only when the agents have probable cause to believe that the subject poses an imminent danger of serious physical injury or death to the agents or to others and when the use of deadly force does not create a danger to the public that outweighs the likely benefits of its use.

Studies of killings by the police have often focused on claims of discrimination—that black and minority suspects are more likely to be shot than whites—but research has not provided solid support for such claims. While individuals shot by police are more likely to be minorities, an early study by James Fyfe found that police officers will generally respond with deadly force when mortally threatened and that minorities are considerably more likely to use weapons in assaults on officers than are whites.[140] Complicating the picture further, Fyfe's study showed that minority officers are involved in the shootings of suspects more often than other officers, a finding that may be due to the assignment of minority officers to inner-city and ghetto areas.

▲ Demonstrators in Harris County, Texas, protesting the police use of Tasers. This less-lethal weapon, manufactured by Taser International, incapacitates potential attackers by delivering an electrical shock to the person's nervous system. The technology is intended to reduce injury rates to both suspects and officers. Why do some people oppose its use?
Ben DeSoto/AP/AP Wide World Photos

However, a later study by Fyfe, which analyzed police shootings in Memphis, Tennessee, found that black property offenders were twice as likely as whites to be shot by police.[141]

Although relatively few police officers ever fire their weapons at suspects during the course of their careers, those who do may find themselves embroiled in a web of social, legal, and personal complications. It is estimated that in an average year, 600 suspects are killed by public police in America, while another 1,200 are shot and wounded, and 1,800 are shot at and missed.[142] The personal side of police shootings is well summarized in the title of an article that appeared in *Police Magazine*. The article, "I've Killed That Man Ten Thousand Times," demonstrates how police officers who have to use their weapons may be haunted by years of depression and despair.[143] Not long ago, according to author Anne Cohen, all departments did to help an officer who had shot someone was to "give him enough bullets to reload his gun." The stress and trauma that result from police shootings are only now being realized, and many departments have yet to develop mechanisms for adequately dealing with them.[144]

Police officers have particular difficulty dealing with instances of "suicide by cop," in which individuals bent on dying engage in behavior that causes responding officers to resort to deadly force. On March 10, 2005, for example, John T. Garczynski, Jr., a father of two preteen boys, died in a hail of 26 police bullets fired by officers who had surrounded his vehicle in a Boca Raton, Florida, condominium parking lot.[145] Garczynski, a Florida Power and Light Company employee, had been separated from his wife months earlier and appeared to have been despondent over financial problems and the breakup of his marriage. The night before his death, Garczynski met his wife at a bowling alley and handed her a packet containing a suicide note, a typed obituary, and a eulogy to be read at his funeral. After he left, Garczynski's wife called police, and officers used the help of a cell phone company to locate Garczynski. As deputies surrounded Garczynski's 2003 Ford Explorer, he attempted to start the vehicle. One of the officers yelled "Freeze!" and then shouted "Let me see your hands!" It was at that point, deputies said, that Garczynski pointed a gun at them and they fired.

Rebecca Stincelli, author of the book *Suicide by Cop: Victims from Both Sides of the Badge*,[146] says an incident like that involving Garczynski can be devastating for police officers. "In the past, people have used rope, a gun, gas, jumped off a building. A police officer is just another method," said Stincelli. "They say it's nothing personal. [But] they are wrong. It's very personal" for the officers involved.[147] The FBI says, "Suicide-by-cop incidents are painful and damaging experiences for the surviving families, the communities, and all law enforcement professionals."[148]

A study of fatal shootings by Los Angeles police officers found that an astonishingly large number—over 10%—could be classified as "suicide by cop."[149] Recently, researchers have identified three main "suicide by cop" categories: direct confrontations, in which suicidal subjects instigate attacks on police officers for the purpose of dying; disturbed interventions, in which potentially suicidal subjects take advantage of police intervention in their suicide attempt in order to die; and criminal interventions, in which criminal suspects prefer death to capture and arrest.[150]

Less-Lethal Weapons

Recent media reports tell of weapons being developed for the military that incapacitate rather than kill. Among them are flash guns (more formally known as optical systems incapacitators), which use powerful strobe lights to trigger "flicker illness"; sonic weapons, which employ intense inaudible sounds to cause pain; and focused microwave beams, which can produce extreme physical pain at close range. Such weapons, which employ less-lethal technologies, are being contemplated for use by military planners seeking to separate enemy fighters from civilian populations.[151] They might also be used by civilian law enforcement agencies in border enforcement or during riots or in other crowd-control situations where physical force is needed but where permanent injury must be avoided.

Less-lethal weapons also offer what may be a problem-specific solution to potential incidents of "suicide by cop," as well as a generic solution to at least some charges of use of excessive force. **Less-lethal weapons** are those that are designed to disable, capture, or immobilize a suspect rather than kill him or her. Efforts to provide law enforcement officers

less-lethal weapon
A weapon that is designed to disable, capture, or immobilize—but not kill—a suspect. Occasional deaths do result from the use of such weapons, however.

with less-lethal weapons began in 1987.[152] Stun guns, Tasers (also known as conducted energy devices), rubber bullets, beanbag projectiles, and pepper spray are examples of such weapons that are currently in use. More exotic types of less-lethal weapons, however, are on the horizon. These include snare nets that are fired from shotguns, disabling sticky foam that can be sprayed from a distance, microwave beams that heat the tissue of people exposed to them until they desist in their illegal or threatening behavior or lose consciousness, and high-tech guns that fire bolts of electromagnetic energy at a target, causing painful sensory overload and violent muscle spasms. The NIJ states, "The goal is to give line officers effective and safe alternatives to lethal force."[153]

As their name implies, however, less-lethal weapons are not always safe. On October 21, 2004, for example, 21-year-old Emerson College student Victoria Snelgrove died hours after being hit in the eye with a plastic pepper spray–filled projectile that police officers fired at a rowdy crowd celebrating a Red Sox victory. Witnesses said that officers fired the projectile into the crowd after a reveler near Fenway Park threw a bottle at a mounted Boston police officer.[154]

Professionalism and Ethics

Police administrators have responded in a variety of ways to issues of corruption, danger, and liability. Among the most significant responses have been calls for increased **police professionalism** at all levels of policing. A profession is an organized undertaking characterized by a body of specialized knowledge acquired through extensive education,[155] and by a well-considered set of internal standards and ethical guidelines that hold members of the profession accountable to one another and to society. Associations of like-minded practitioners generally serve to create and disseminate standards for the profession as a whole.

> The ability of the police to fulfill their sacred trust will improve as a lucid sense of ethical standards is developed.
>
> —Patrick V. Murphy, former New York City police commissioner

police professionalism
The increasing formalization of police work and the accompanying rise in public acceptance of the police.

8 Demonstrate why professionalism and ethics are important in policing today.

Contemporary policing has many of the attributes of a profession. Specialized knowledge in policing includes a close familiarity with criminal law, laws of procedure, constitutional guarantees, and relevant Supreme Court decisions; a working knowledge of weapons and hand-to-hand tactics, driving skills, and vehicle maintenance; a knowledge of radio communications; report-writing abilities; interviewing and interrogation techniques; and media and human relations skills. Other specialized knowledge may include equipment operation (such as vehicular radar, the Breathalyzer, and the polygraph), special weapons skills, conflict resolution, and hostage negotiation. Supervisory personnel require an even wider range of skills, including general and personnel administrative skills, management techniques, and strategies for optimum utilization of human and physical resources.

Police work is guided by an ethical code that was originally developed in 1956 by the Peace Officer's Research Association of California (PORAC) in conjunction with Dr. Douglas M. Kelley of Berkeley's School of Criminology.[156] The current version of the Law Enforcement Code of Ethics is reproduced in an "Ethics and Professionalism" box in this chapter. Ethics training has been integrated into most basic law enforcement training programs, and calls for expanded training in **police ethics** are being heard from many corners. A comprehensive resource for enhancing awareness of law enforcement ethics, called the "Ethics Toolkit," is available from the IACP and the federal office of Community Oriented Policing Services (COPS) at **Web Extra 7**.

police ethics
The special responsibility to adhere to moral duty and obligation that is inherent in police work.

Many professional associations support police work. One such organization, the Arlington, Virginia–based IACP, has done much to raise professional standards in policing and continually strives for improvements in law enforcement nationwide. In like manner, the Fraternal Order of Police (FOP) is one of the best-known organizations of public-service workers in the United States. The FOP is the world's largest organization of sworn law enforcement officers, with more than 318,000 members in more than 2,100 lodges.

Ethics and Professionalism
The Law Enforcement Code of Ethics

As a Law Enforcement Officer, my fundamental duty is to serve mankind; to safeguard lives and property; to protect the innocent against deception, the weak against oppression or intimidation, and the peaceful against violence or disorder; and to respect the Constitutional rights of all men to liberty, equality, and justice.

I will keep my private life unsullied as an example to all; maintain courageous calm in the face of danger, scorn, or ridicule; develop self-restraint; and be constantly mindful of the welfare of others. Honest in thought and deed in both my personal and official life, I will be exemplary in obeying the laws of the land and the regulations of my department. Whatever I see or hear of a confidential nature or that is confided to me in my official capacity will be kept secret unless revelation is necessary in the performance of my duty.

I will never act officiously or permit personal feelings, prejudices, animosities, or friendships to influence my decisions. With no compromise for crime and with relentless prosecution of criminals, I will enforce the law courteously and appropriately without fear or favor, malice or ill will, never employing unnecessary force or violence, and never accepting gratuities.

I recognize the badge of my office as a symbol of public faith, and I accept it as a public trust to be held so long as I am true to the ethics of the police service. I will constantly strive to achieve these objectives and ideals, dedicating myself before God to my chosen profession . . . law enforcement.

THINKING ABOUT ETHICS

1. ***Why does the Law Enforcement Code of Ethics ask law enforcement officers "to respect the Constitutional rights of all men to liberty, equality, and justice"? Does such respect further the goals of law enforcement? Why or why not?***
2. ***Why is it important for law enforcement officers to keep their private lives "unsullied as an example to all"? What are the potential consequences of not doing so?***

Source: International Association of Chiefs of Police. Reprinted with permission.

Accreditation is another avenue toward police professionalism. The Commission on Accreditation for Law Enforcement Agencies (CALEA) was formed in 1979. Police departments seeking accreditation through the commission must meet hundreds of standards in areas as diverse as day-to-day operations, administration, review of incidents involving the use of a weapon by officers, and evaluation and promotion of personnel. As of September 15, 2010, nearly 600 (3.4%) of the nation's 17,784 law enforcement agencies were accredited,[157] while a number of others were undergoing the accreditation process. However, many accredited agencies are among the nation's largest; as a result, 25% of full-time law enforcement officers in the United States at the state and local levels are members of CALEA-accredited programs.[158] Although accreditation makes possible the identification of high-quality police departments, it is often not valued by agency leaders because it offers few incentives. Accreditation does not guarantee a department any rewards beyond that of peer recognition. Visit CALEA online at **Web Extra 8**.

Education and Training

Peace Officer Standards and Training (POST) program The official program of a state or legislative jurisdiction that sets standards for the training of law enforcement officers. All states set such standards, although not all use the term *POST*.

Basic law enforcement training requirements were begun in the 1950s by the state of New York and through a voluntary **Peace Officer Standards and Training (POST) program** in California. (Additional information on California's POST standards can be accessed via **Web Extra 9**.) Today, every jurisdiction mandates POST-like requirements, although they vary considerably from region to region. Modern police education generally involves training in subject areas as diverse as self-defense, human relations, firearms and weapons, communications, legal aspects of policing, patrol, criminal investigations, administration, report writing, ethics, computers and information systems, and cultural diversity. According to a 2009 Bureau of Justice Statistics report, the median number of hours of training required of new officers is 881 in state police agencies, 965 in county departments, 883 in municipal agencies, and 719 in sheriff's departments.[159]

Federal law enforcement agents receive schooling at the Federal Law Enforcement Training Center (FLETC) in Glynco, Georgia. The center provides training for about 60 federal law enforcement agencies, excluding the FBI and the DEA, which have their own training academies in Quantico, Virginia. The center also offers advanced training to state and local police organizations through the National Center for State and Local Law Enforcement Training, located on the FLETC campus. Specialized schools, such as

Northwestern University's Traffic Institute, have also been credited with raising the level of police practice from purely operational concerns to a more professional level.

In 1987, in a move to further professionalize police training, the American Society for Law Enforcement Trainers was formed at the Ohio Peace Officer Training Academy. Today, the organization is known as the American Society for Law Enforcement Training (ASLET). Based in Frederick, Maryland, ASLET works to ensure quality in peace officer training and confers the title Certified Law Enforcement Trainer (CLET) on police training professionals who meet its high standards. ASLET also works with the Police Training Network to provide an ongoing and comprehensive calendar of law enforcement training activities nationwide.

A more recent innovation in law enforcement training is the Police Training Officer (PTO) program, whose development was funded by the COPS office starting in 1999.[160] The PTO program was designed by the Reno (Nevada) Police Department, in conjunction with PERF, as an alternative model for police field training. In fact, it represents the first new postacademy field training program for law enforcement agencies in more than 30 years. PTO uses contemporary methods of adult education and a version of problem-based learning specifically adapted to the police environment. It incorporates community policing and problem-solving principles and, according to the COPS office, fosters "the foundation for life-long learning that prepares new officers for the complexities of policing today and in the future."[161] Learn more about PTO at **Library Extra 17**.

As the concern for quality policing builds, increasing emphasis is also being placed on the formal education of police officers. As early as 1931, the National Commission on Law Observance and Enforcement (the Wickersham Commission) highlighted the importance of a well-educated police force by calling for "educationally sound" officers.[162] In 1967, the President's Commission on Law Enforcement and Administration of Justice voiced the belief that "the ultimate aim of all police departments should be that all personnel with general enforcement powers have baccalaureate degrees."[163] At the time, the average educational level of police officers in the United States was 12.4 years—slightly beyond a high school degree. In 1973, the National Advisory Commission on Criminal Justice Standards and Goals made the following specific recommendation: "Every police agency should, no later than 1982, require as a condition of initial employment the completion of at least four years of education . . . at an accredited college or university."[164]

A good cop stays a rookie at heart, excited by every shift.
—A Nashville, Tennessee, policeman

However, recommendations do not always translate into practice. One report found that one in three state agencies have a college requirement for new officers, with 12% requiring a two-year degree and 2%, a four-year degree. About one in four municipal and county police departments have a college requirement, with about one in 10 requiring a degree.[165] One in seven sheriff's offices have a college requirement, including 6% that require a minimum of a two-year degree for new hires.[166] A 2002 report on police departments in large cities found that the percentage of departments requiring new officers to have at least some college rose from 19% in 1990 to 37% in 2000, and the percentage requiring a two-year or four-year degree grew from 6% to 14% over the same period.[167] A Dallas Police Department policy requiring a minimum of 45 semester hours of successful college-level study for new recruits[168] was upheld in 1985 by the Fifth U.S. Circuit Court of Appeals in the case of *Davis v. Dallas*.[169]

An early survey of police departments by PERF stressed the need for educated police officers, citing the following benefits that accrue to police agencies from the hiring of educated officers:[170] (1) better written reports, (2) enhanced communications with the public, (3) more effective job performance, (4) fewer citizen complaints, (5) greater initiative, (6) wiser use of discretion, (7) heightened sensitivity to racial and ethnic issues, and (8) fewer disciplinary problems. However, there are drawbacks to having more educated police forces: Educated officers are more likely to leave police work and to question orders, and they request reassignment more frequently than other officers.

Most federal agencies require college degrees for entry-level positions. Among them are the FBI, the DEA, the Bureau of Alcohol, Tobacco, Firearms and Explosives, the Secret Service, the Bureau of Customs and Border Protection, and the Bureau of Immigration and Customs Enforcement.

Recruitment and Selection

All professions need informed, dedicated, and competent personnel. When the National Advisory Commission on Criminal Justice Standards and Goals issued its 1973 report on the police, it bemoaned the fact that "many college students are unaware of the varied, interesting, and challenging assignments and career opportunities that exist within the police service."[171] Today, police organizations actively recruit new officers from two- and four-year colleges and universities, technical institutions, and professional organizations. The national commission report stressed the setting of high standards for police recruits and recommended a strong emphasis on minority recruitment, an elimination of residence requirements (which required officers to live in the area they were hired to serve) for new officers, a decentralized application and testing procedure, and various recruiting incentives.

A Bureau of Justice Statistics study published in 2006 found that local police departments use a variety of applicant-screening methods.[172] Nearly all use personal interviews, and a large majority use basic skills tests, physical agility measurements, medical exams, drug tests, psychological evaluations, and background investigations into the personal character of applicants. Among departments serving 25,000 or more residents, about eight in ten use physical agility tests and written aptitude tests, more than half check credit records, and about half use personality inventories and polygraph exams. After training, successful applicants are typically placed on probation for one year. The probationary period in police work has been called the "first true job-related test . . . in the selection procedure,"[173] providing the opportunity for supervisors to gauge the new officer's response to real-life situations.

Effective policing, however, may depend more on innate personal qualities than on educational attainment or credit history. One of the first people to attempt to describe the personal attributes necessary in a successful police officer, famed 1930s' police administrator August Vollmer, said that the public expects police officers to have "the wisdom of Solomon, the courage of David, the strength of Samson, the patience of Job, the leadership of Moses, the kindness of the Good Samaritan, the strategic training of Alexander, the faith of Daniel, the diplomacy of Lincoln, the tolerance of the Carpenter of Nazareth, and finally, an intimate knowledge of every branch of the natural, biological, and social sciences."[174] More practically, O. W. Wilson, the well-known police administrator of the 1940s and 1950s, once enumerated some "desirable personal qualities of patrol officers":[175] (1) initiative; (2) responsibility; (3) the ability to deal alone with emergencies; (4) the capacity to communicate effectively with people from diverse social, cultural, and ethnic backgrounds; (5) the ability to learn a variety of tasks quickly; (6) the attitude and ability necessary to adapt to technological changes; (7) the desire to help people in need; (8) an understanding of others; (9) emotional maturity; and (10) sufficient physical strength and endurance.

▲ Former Birmingham (Alabama) Chief of Police Annetta Nunn. Nunn's tenure as chief from 2003 to 2007 exemplifies expanded opportunities in policing for women and minorities. Nunn, an African American who holds a bachelor's degree in criminal justice from the University of Alabama, was four years old in 1963, when thousands of civil rights demonstrators in Birmingham were beaten and arrested on orders of Police Chief Eugene "Bull" Connor. How do communities benefit from police agencies that are socially and culturally diverse?
Birmingham Police Department

High-quality police recruits, an emphasis on training with an eye toward ethical aspects of police performance, and higher levels of education are beginning to raise police pay, which has traditionally been low. The acceptance of police work as a true profession should contribute to significantly higher rates of pay in coming years.

Ethnic and Gender Diversity in Policing

9 Identify some of the issues related to ethnic and gender diversity in policing, and suggest ways of addressing them.

In 2003, Annetta W. Nunn took the reins of the Birmingham (Alabama) Police Department. For many, Nunn, a 44-year-old African American mother and Baptist choir singer, symbolized the changes that had taken place in American policing during the past few decades. The new chief sat in a chair once occupied by Eugene "Bull" Connor, the arch segregationist and a national symbol of the South's fight against integration who jailed thousands of civil rights demonstrators during the 1960s. A 23-year veteran of the department, Nunn headed a force of 838 men and women. She left the department in 2008 to become an advocate for a domestic-violence education program in municipal courts.

A 1968 survey of police supervisors by the National Advisory Commission on Civil Disorders[176] found a marked disparity between the number of black and white officers in leadership positions. One of every 26 black police officers had been promoted to the rank of sergeant, while the ratio among whites was 1 in 12. Only one of every 114 black officers had become a

Multiculturalism and Diversity
Investigating Crime in a Multicultural Setting

In the mid-1990s, the Washington, D.C.–based National Crime Prevention Council (NCPC) published an important guide for American law enforcement officers who work with multicultural groups. The principles it contains can be applied equally to most foreign-born individuals living in the United States and are especially important to patrol officers and criminal investigators.

The NCPC guide points out that it is important for well-intentioned newcomers to this country to learn that the law enforcement system in the United States is not a national police force but a series of local, state, and federal agencies that take seriously their obligation to "serve and protect" law-abiding residents. Newcomers need to know that police officers can teach them how to protect themselves and their families from crime. Many immigrants, especially political refugees, come from countries in which the criminal justice system is based on tyranny, repression, and fear.

The NCPC suggests that law enforcement officers and other members of the criminal justice system can help ease this transition by working not only to communicate with immigrants but also to understand them and the complexities of their native cultures. The mere absence of conflict in a neighborhood does not mean that residents of different cultures have found harmony and a cooperative working relationship, says the NCPC. True multicultural integration occurs when various cultures reach a comfortable day-to-day interaction marked by respect, interest, and caring.

Communities in which immigrants and law enforcement have established close positive ties benefit considerably, according to the NCPC. Immigrants gain greater access to police and other services, such as youth programs, victims' assistance, parenting classes, medical assistance programs, business networking, and neighborhood groups. Crime decreases in communities where law enforcement officers help immigrants learn to protect themselves against crime.

For police officers working in communities in which "language is a serious barrier between cultures," the NCPC suggests the following pointers for communicating more effectively:

- Be patient when speaking with someone who does not clearly understand your language. Speak slowly and distinctly. Be willing to repeat words or phrases if necessary. Remember that shouting never helps a nonnative speaker understand better.
- Be careful with your choice of words, selecting those that are clear, straightforward, and simple to understand. Avoid colloquialisms and slang.
- Allow extra time for investigation when the people involved have not mastered English.

▲ NYPD officers responding to a call for service in New York City's Chinatown. American society is composed of a wide variety of racial and ethnic heritages, diverse religions, incongruous values, disparate traditions, and distinct languages. How does multiculturalism impact American policing?
*Ting-Li Wang/*The New York Times

- Be sure that anyone who serves as an interpreter is fully qualified and has had experience. Interpreting under pressure is a difficult task; lack of training can lead to mistakes.
- Be candid about your ability to speak or understand a language. Trying to "fake it" just leads to confusion, misunderstanding, and misspent time.
- Never assume that someone is less intelligent just because he or she doesn't speak English well.

Visit the NCPC at **Web Extra 10**.

Reference: Adapted from National Crime Prevention Council, *Building and Crossing Bridges: Refugees and Law Enforcement Working Together* (Washington, DC: NCPC, 1994).

lieutenant, while among whites the ratio was one in 26. At the level of captain, the disparity was even greater: One out of every 235 black officers had achieved the rank of captain, while one of every 53 whites had climbed to that rank.

Today, many departments, through dedicated recruitment efforts, have dramatically increased their complement of officers from underrepresented groups. The Metropolitan Detroit Police Department, for example, now has a force that is more than 30% black. Nationwide, racial and ethnic minorities comprised 23.6% of full-time sworn police personnel in 2003—up from 17.0% in 1990[177]—and getting closer to the percentage of racial and ethnic minorities in our nation's population, which the U.S. Census Bureau reports is approximately 32%.[178] From 1990 to 2003, the number of African American local police officers increased by 14,800 (or 37%), and the number of Hispanic officers increased by 22,300 (or 98%). Moreover, a 2006 study of 123 African American police executives in the United States found that they were generally well accepted by their peers, well integrated into their leadership roles, and well adjusted socially.[179]

Although ethnic minorities are now employed in policing in significant numbers, women are still significantly underrepresented. The 2001 Status of Women in Policing Survey, conducted

▲ Lieutenant Gail Marsh of the Redmond (Washington) Police Department. Women in uniform are a common sight throughout our nation's cities and towns. What special benefits can women bring to policing?
Therese Frare/Black Star

by the National Center for Women and Policing (NCWP), found that women fill only 12.7% of all sworn law enforcement positions nationwide.[180] On the other hand, the NCWP notes that women account for 46.5% of employed people over the age of 16 nationwide, meaning that they are "strikingly under-represented within the field of sworn law enforcement."[181] A 2010 Bureau of Justice Statistics (BJS) study of women in law enforcement found the following:[182]

- Of 62 federal law enforcement agencies responding to the study, there were about 90,000 sworn officers, of whom approximately 18,200 (20%) were women.
- Women accounted for approximately 18% of total sworn law enforcement officers in large local police departments—those with 2,000 or more personnel. Women, however, held only six percent of full-time sworn positions in small local police departments—those with between one and ten full-time sworn officers.
- Female officers comprised about 13% of total sworn officers in large sheriff's departments; but they held only four percent of sworn positions in small sheriff's offices.

It is unclear just how many women actually *want* to work in policing. Nonetheless, many police departments continue to make substantial efforts to recruit and retain women because they understand the benefits of having more women among the ranks of sworn officers. Benefits stem from the fact that female police officers tend to use less physical force than male officers and are less likely to be accused of using excessive force; female officers are better at defusing and de-escalating potentially violent confrontations with citizens; female officers often possess better communication skills than their male counterparts; and they are better able to facilitate the cooperation and trust required to implement a community policing model. Moreover, the NCWP says that "female officers often respond more effectively to incidents of violence against women—crimes that represent one of the largest categories of calls to police departments. Increasing the representation of women on the force is also likely to address another costly problem for police administrators—the pervasive problem of sex discrimination and sexual harassment—by changing the climate of modern law enforcement agencies."[183] Finally, "because women frequently have different life experiences than men, they approach policing with a different perspective, and the very presence of women in the field will often bring about changes in policies and procedures that benefit both male and female officers."[184] For additional information on how police departments can recruit and retain female officers, see **Library Extra 18**.

Women as Effective Police Officers

A 2007 review of the status of women in policing found that "women police officers are no longer viewed as a unique presence in law enforcement and their ability to perform the job is less likely to be measured against traditional standards, though indoctrination in law enforcement continues to stress masculinity over ability."[185] One research report on female police officers in Massachusetts found that female officers (1) are "extremely devoted to their work," (2) "see themselves as women first, and then police officers," and (3) are more satisfied when working in nonuniformed capacities.[186] The researcher identified two groups of female officers: (1) those who felt themselves to be well integrated into their departments and were confident in their jobs and (2) those who experienced strain and on-the-job isolation. The officers' children were cited as a significant influence on what their self-perceptions were and on the way in which they viewed their jobs. The demands that attend child rearing in contemporary society were found to be a major factor contributing to the resignation of female officers. The study also found that the longer female officers stayed on the job, the greater the stress and frustration they tended to experience, primarily as a consequence of the uncooperative attitudes of male officers. Some of the female officers interviewed identified networking as a potential solution to the stresses encountered by female

> Police agencies that understand and value diverse communities create structures and systems that reach outward, enjoining and empowering police officers and citizens to collaborate in problem solving on issues of crime and disorder.
> —Police Executive Research Forum[xv]

officers but also said that when women get together to solve problems, they are seen as "crybabies" rather than professionals. Said one of the women in the study, "We've lost a lot of good women who never should have left the job. If we had helped each other, maybe they wouldn't have left."[187] For more information on working in policing, visit **Web Extra 11**.

Some studies have found that female officers are often underutilized and that many departments are hesitant to assign women to patrol and to other potentially dangerous field activities.[188] As a consequence, some women in police work experience frustration and a lack of satisfaction with their jobs. An analysis of the genderization of the criminal justice workplace by Susan Ehrlich Martin and Nancy C. Jurik, for example, points out that gender inequality is part of a historical pattern of entrenched forms of gender interaction relating to the division of labor, power, and culture.[189] According to Martin and Jurik, women working in the justice system are viewed in terms of such historically developed filters, causing them to be judged and treated according to normative standards developed for men rather than for women. As a consequence, formal and informal social controls continue to disenfranchise women who wish to work in the system and make it difficult to recognize the specific contributions that they make as women.

Private Protective Services

Growth of Private Protective Services

Public police are employed by the government and enforce public laws. Private security personnel work for corporate employers and secure private interests. Private security has been defined as "those self-employed individuals and privately funded business entities and organizations providing security-related services to specific clientele for a fee, for the individual or entity that retains or employs them, or for themselves, in order to protect their

10 Describe the nature and extent of private protective services in the United States today, and discuss what role you think they will play in the future.

Freedom or Safety? You Decide.
Do Sex-Offender Websites Spur Vigilantism?

In 2006, officials in Maine decided to temporarily shut down the state's sex-offender website after two convicted sex offenders whose identifying information was listed in the online registry were shot and killed. The site provides names, addresses, ages, and offender histories for more than 2,200 nonincarcerated registered sex offenders residing in Maine.

One of the offenders who died, 57-year-old Joseph Gray, was shot five times through a window after being awakened by barking dogs at three o'clock in the morning while sleeping on his living room couch. Gray had been convicted in Massachusetts in 1992 of indecent assault and battery on a child and child rape and had been sentenced to four to six years in prison. Five hours later, William Elliott, age 24, a registered sex offender living in Corinth, Maine, was shot and killed as he answered the door to his ramshackle trailer. In 2002, Elliott had pleaded guilty to two misdemeanor counts of sexual abuse of a minor. The charges stemmed from an intimate relationship he had with a girl two weeks shy of her 16th birthday. He was 19 years old at the time of the offense.

On the night of the killings, Canadian Stephen Marshall, a 20-year-old dishwasher from Nova Scotia and the only suspect in the killings, died when he shot himself in the head with a .45-caliber handgun as police stopped and boarded a bus he was riding to Boston. Marshall had been visiting his father in Houlton, Maine, a town near the Canadian border, where the two had planned to go target shooting. Maine Department of Public Safety officials had quickly zeroed in on Marshall after they determined that he had logged on to the state's sex-offender registry and obtained information on the victims and 32 other men shortly before the killings. Investigators found a small-caliber pistol and a laptop computer in his backpack.

Charles Onley, a research associate at the Center for Sex Offender Management, a U.S. Department of Justice project, told reporters following the Maine killings that critics had previously warned that online offender registries could be used to facilitate vigilante-type killings. The only other known case of vigilantism linked to a sex-offender website occurred in August 2005, when Washington State resident Michael Mullen killed two sex offenders in Bellingham, Washington, after locating them through the city's online sex-offender registry. At the time, Don Pierce, executive director of the Washington Association of Sheriffs and Police Chiefs, said that "the value [of sex-offender registries] to the community far outweighs the risks."

YOU DECIDE

Should society's interest in knowing the identities and residential locations of released sex offenders supersede the concerns for personal safety that those offenders may have? Do you agree with Don Pierce that the value of sex-offender registries far outweighs their risks? Why or why not?

References: Lisa Wangsness and Kathleen Burge, "Police Investigate Alleged Gunman's Motives in Killings," *Boston Globe*, April 18, 2006; and Emily Bazar, "Suspected Shooter Found Sex Offenders' Homes on Website," *USA Today*, April 18, 2006.

persons, private property, or interests from various hazards."[190] The growth in the size of private security in recent years has been phenomenal. In 2002, for example, $212.7 million was spent for security arrangements at the Olympic winter games in Salt Lake City, Utah—leading to the employment of more than 40,000 private security personnel in association with the event.[191]

Law enforcement can ill afford to continue its traditional policy of isolating and even ignoring the activities of private security.

—National Institute of Justice, *Crime and Protection in America*

A report released by the NIJ in 2001, titled *The New Structure of Policing*,[192] found that "policing is being transformed and restructured in the modern world" in ways that were unanticipated only a few decades ago. Much of the change is due to the development of **private protective services** as an important adjunct to public law enforcement activities in the United States and throughout much of the rest of the world. The NIJ report says that "the key to [understanding] the transformation is that policing, meaning the activity of making societies safe, is no longer carried out exclusively by governments" and that the distinction between private and public police has begun to blur. According to NIJ, "[G]radually, almost imperceptibly, policing has been 'multilateralized,'" meaning that "a host of nongovernmental agencies have undertaken to provide security services." As a result, the NIJ report says that "policing has entered a new era, an era characterized by a transformation in the governance of security." The report concludes:

private protective services
The independent or proprietary commercial organizations that provide protective services to employers on a contractual basis.

- In most countries, certainly in the democratic world, private police outnumber public police.
- In these same countries, people spend more time in their daily lives in places where visible crime prevention and control are provided by nongovernmental groups than by governmental police agencies.
- The reconstruction of policing is occurring worldwide despite differences in wealth and economic systems.

View the NIJ report in its entirety at **Library Extra 19**.

According to the *Hallcrest Report II*, another widely disseminated document describing the private security industry, more people are employed in private security than in all local, state, and federal police agencies combined.[193] Nearly 2 million people are estimated to be working in private security today, whereas slightly less than half that number are engaged in public law enforcement activities.[194] According to the *Hallcrest Report II*, employment in the field of private security is anticipated to continue to expand by around 4% per year, while public police agencies are expected to grow by only 2.8% per year for the foreseeable future. Still faster growth is predicted in private security industry revenues, which are expected to increase about 7% per year, a growth rate almost three times greater than that projected for the gross national product (GNP). Table 4 lists the ten largest private security agencies in business today and some of the services they offer.

TABLE 4
Private Security Agencies

Largest Private Security Agencies in the United States		
Advance Security, Inc.	Globe Security	Security Bureau, Inc.
Allied Security, Inc.	Guardsmark, Inc.	Wackenhut Corp.
American Protective Services	Pinkerton's, Inc.	Wells Fargo Guard Services
Burns International Security Services		
Private Security Services		
Airline security	Computer/information security	Nuclear facility security
Automated teller machine (ATM) services	Executive protection	Railroad detectives
Bank guards	Hospital security	School security
Company guards	Loss prevention	Store/mall security

Source: Adapted from William C. Cunningham, John J. Strauchs, and Clifford W. Van Meter, *The Hallcrest Report II: Private Security Trends, 1970–2000* (McLean, VA: Hallcrest Systems, 1990). Reprinted with permission.

Private agencies provide tailored policing funded by the guarded organization rather than through the expenditure of public monies. Experts estimate that the money spent on private security in this country exceeds the combined budgets of all law enforcement agencies—local, state, and federal.[195] Contributing to this vast expenditure is the federal government, which is itself a major employer of private security personnel, contracting for services that range from guards to highly specialized electronic snooping and computerized countermeasures at military installations and embassies throughout the world.

Major reasons for the quick growth of the American proprietary security sector include (1) an increase in crimes in the workplace; (2) an increase in fear (real or perceived) of crime and terrorism; (3) the fiscal crises of the states, which have limited public protection; and (4) an increased public and business awareness and use of more cost-effective private security products and services.[196]

▲ A private security officer conferring with a sworn public law enforcement officer. How can cooperation among private security companies and public law enforcement agencies help solve and prevent crimes?
Michael Newman/PhotoEdit Inc.

Integration of Public and Private Security

As the private security field grows, its relationship to public law enforcement continues to evolve. Some people feel that "today, a distinction between public and private policing is increasingly meaningless."[197] As a result, the focus has largely shifted from an analysis of competition between the sectors to the recognition that each form of policing can help the other. One government-sponsored report recommends that the resources of proprietary and contract security should be brought to bear in cooperative, community-based crime-prevention and security-awareness programs. Doing so, says the report, would maximize the cooperative crime-fighting potential of existing private and public security resources.[198]

Summary

POLICING: ISSUES AND CHALLENGES

- The police personality is created through informal pressures on officers by a powerful police subculture that communicates values that support law enforcement interests. This chapter described the police personality as (among other things) authoritarian, conservative, honorable, loyal, cynical, dogmatic, hostile, prejudiced, secret, and suspicious.
- Various types of police corruption were described in this chapter. One type, "grass eating," includes officers who accept small bribes and free services by those wishing to avoid legal problems. "Meat eating" includes much more serious forms of corruption, such as officers who actively seek illegal moneymaking opportunities through the exercise of their law enforcement duties. Ethics training was mentioned as part of a reframing strategy that emphasizes integrity in an effort to target police corruption. Also discussed was an NIJ report that focused on enhancing policing integrity. The report noted that a police department's "culture of integrity" might be more important "in shaping the ethics of police officers than hiring the 'right' people."
- The dangers of police work are many and varied. They consist of violent victimization, disease, exposure to biological or chemical toxins, stressful encounters with suspects and victims, and on-the-job fatigue. Stress-management programs, combined with department policies designed to reduce exposure to dangerous situations and agency practices that support officers' needs, can help combat the dangers and difficulties that police officers face in their day-to-day work.
- Policing in America was forever changed by the events of September 11, 2001. Local law enforcement agencies, many of which previously saw community protection and peacekeeping as their primary roles, are being called upon to protect against potential terrorist threats with international roots. The contemporary emphasis on terrorism prevention, alongside the

need for a rapid response to threats of terrorism, has led to what some see as a new era of policing to secure the homeland. Homeland security policing builds upon the established framework of community policing for the purpose of gathering intelligence to prevent terrorism. Consequently, the notion of intelligence-led policing has become significant and provides a glimpse at one of the features that may characterize American policing in the future.

- Civil liability issues are very important in policing. They arise because officers and their agencies sometimes inappropriately use power to curtail the civil and due process rights of criminal suspects. Both police departments and individual police officers can be targeted by civil lawsuits. Federal suits based on claims that officers acted with disregard for an individual's right to due process are called *1983 lawsuits* because they are based on Section 1983 of Title 42 of the U.S. Code. Another type of civil suit that can be brought specifically against federal agents is a *Bivens* action. Although the doctrine of sovereign immunity barred legal action against state and local governments in the past, recent court cases and legislative activity have restricted the opportunity for law enforcement agencies and their officers to exercise claims of immunity.
- Racial profiling, or racially biased policing, is any police action initiated on the basis of the race, ethnicity, or national origin of a suspect rather than on the behavior of that individual or on information that identifies the individual as being or having been engaged in criminal activity. Racial profiling is a bigoted practice unworthy of the law enforcement professional. It has been widely condemned as being contrary to basic ethical principles, and it weakens the public's confidence in the police, thereby decreasing police-citizen trust and cooperation. This chapter pointed out, however, that racial or ethnic indicators associated with particular suspects or suspect groups may have a place in legitimate law enforcement strategies if they accurately relate to suspects who are being sought for criminal law violations.
- Law enforcement officers are authorized to use the amount of force that is reasonable and necessary in a particular situation. Many officers have encounters where the use of force is appropriate. Nonetheless, studies show that the police use force in fewer than 20% of adult custodial arrests. Even in instances where force is used, police officers primarily use weaponless tactics. Excessive force is the application of an amount or frequency of force greater than that required to compel compliance from a willing or unwilling subject.
- Police professionalism requires that today's law enforcement officers adhere to ethical codes and standards established by the profession. Police professionalism places important limits on the discretionary activities of individual enforcement personnel and helps officers and the departments they work for gain the respect and regard of the public they police.
- This chapter points out that ethnic minorities are now employed in policing in numbers that approach their representation in the general population. Women, however, are still significantly underrepresented. Questions can be raised about the degree of minority participation in the command structure of law enforcement agencies, about the desire of significant numbers of women to work in policing, and about the respect accorded to women and members of other underrepresented groups in law enforcement by their fellow officers.
- Private policing, represented by the recent tremendous growth of for-hire security agencies, adds another important dimension to American policing. While public police are employed by the government and enforce public laws, private security personnel work for corporate or private employers and secure private interests. Private security personnel outnumber public law enforcement officers in the United States by nearly three to one, and private agencies provide tailored protective services funded by the guarded organization rather than by taxpayers. Recognizing the important services that private security personnel provide, many municipal police departments have begun concerted efforts to involve security organizations in their crime-detection and crime-prevention efforts.

QUESTIONS FOR REVIEW

1. What is the police working personality? What are its central features? How does it develop? How does it relate to police subculture?
2. What are the different types of police corruption? What themes run through the findings of the Knapp Commission and the Wickersham Commission? What innovative steps might police departments take to reduce or eliminate corruption among their officers?
3. What are the dangers of police work? What can be done to reduce those dangers?

4. How has the threat of terrorist attack affected American policing today? Are American police agencies prepared to prevent and respond to terrorism? Explain.
5. What are some of the civil liability issues associated with policing? How can civil liability be reduced?
6. What is racial profiling? Why has it become a significant issue in policing today?
7. In what kinds of situations are police officers most likely to use force? When has too much force been used?
8. Is police work a profession? Explain. What are the advantages of viewing policing as a profession? How can police professionalism be enhanced?
9. What ethnic and gender differences characterize policing today? What is the social significance of this diversity?
10. What are the nature and extent of private protective services in the United States today? What role do you think private protective services will play in the future? How can the quality of these services be ensured?

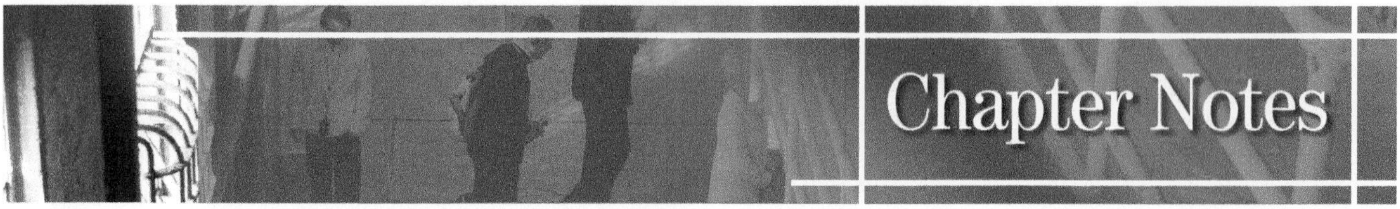

Chapter Notes

i. Carl B. Klockars et al., "The Measurement of Police Integrity," National Institute of Justice Research in Brief (Washington, DC: NIJ, 2000), p. 1.

ii. Karyn S. Hunttings, *Quotation World*, http://s-2000.com/quoteworld/character.html (accessed March 20, 2007).

iii. Police Foundation, *Annual Report, 1991* (Washington, DC: Police Foundation, 1992).

iv. Technical Working Group on Crime Scene Investigation, *Crime Scene Investigation: A Guide for Law Enforcement* (Washington, DC: National Institute of Justice, 2000), p. 12.

v. Major Cities Chiefs Association, *Terrorism: The Impact on State and Local Law Enforcement*, Intelligence Commanders Conference Report (June 2002), http://www.neiassociates.org/mccintelligencereport.pdf (accessed September 30, 2008).

vi. Angus Smith, ed., *Intelligence-Led Policing* (Richmond, VA: International Association of Law Enforcement Intelligence Analysts, 1997), p. 1.

vii. Office of Justice Programs, *The National Criminal Intelligence Sharing Plan* (Washington, DC: U.S. Department of Justice, 2005), p. 27.

viii. Major Cities Chiefs Association, *Terrorism.*

ix. Adapted from Gerald Hill and Kathleen Hill, *The Real Life Dictionary of the Law*, http://www.law.com (accessed June 11, 2008)

x. Deborah Ramirez, Jack McDevitt, and Amy Farrell, *A Resource Guide on Racial Profiling Data Collection Systems: Promising Practices and Lessons Learned* (Washington, DC: U.S. Department of Justice, 2000), p. 3.

xi. National Institute of Justice, *Use of Force by Police: Overview of National and Local Data* (Washington, DC: NIJ, 1999).

xii. International Association of Chiefs of Police, *Police Use of Force in America, 2001* (Alexandria, VA: IACP, 2001), p. 1.

xiii. Samuel Walker, Geoffrey P. Albert, and Dennis J. Kenney, *Responding to the Problem Police Officer: A National Study of Early Warning Systems* (Washington, DC: National Institute of Justice, 2000).

xiv. Sam W. Lathrop, "Reviewing Use of Force: A Systematic Approach," *FBI Law Enforcement Bulletin* (October 2000), p. 18.

xv. Lorie Fridell et al., *Racially Biased Policing: A Principled Response* (Washington, DC: Police Executive Research Forum, 2001), p. 41.

---

1. Joel Leson, *Assessing and Managing the Terrorism Threat* (Washington, DC: U.S. Department of Justice, 2005).
2. Janine Rauch and Etienne Marasis, "Contextualizing the Waddington Report," http://www.wits.ac.za/csvr/papers/papwadd.html (accessed January 5, 2009).
3. Jerome H. Skolnick, *Justice without Trial: Law Enforcement in a Democratic Society* (New York: John Wiley, 1966).
4. William A. Westley, *Violence and the Police: A Sociological Study of Law, Custom, and Morality* (Cambridge, MA: MIT Press, 1970); and William A. Westley, "Violence and the Police," *American Journal of Sociology*, Vol. 49 (1953), pp. 34–41.
5. Arthur Niederhoffer, *Behind the Shield: The Police in Urban Society* (Garden City, NY: Anchor, 1967).
6. Thomas Barker and David L. Carter, *Police Deviance* (Cincinnati, OH: Anderson, 1986). See also Christopher P. Wilson, *Cop Knowledge: Police Power and Cultural Narrative in Twentieth-Century America* (Chicago: University of Chicago Press, 2000).
7. Richard Bennett and Theodore Greenstein, "The Police Personality: A Test of the Predispositional Model," *Journal of Police Science and Administration*, Vol. 3 (1975), pp. 439–445.
8. James Teevan and Bernard Dolnick, "The Values of the Police: A Reconsideration and Interpretation," *Journal of Police Science and Administration* (1973), pp. 366–369.
9. Bennett and Greenstein, "The Police Personality," pp. 439–445.
10. Ibid.
11. Office of the U.S. Attorney for the Southern District of California press release, July 28, 2006.
12. NBC News San Diego, "Border Patrol Agent Faces Immigrant-Smuggling Charges," August 5, 2005, http://www.nbcsandiego.com/news/4816916/detail.html (accessed July 4, 2009).
13. Alan Feuer, "2 Ex-Detectives Guilty in Killings," *New York Times*, April 7, 2006, http://www.nytimes.com/2006/04/07/nyregion/07cops.html (accessed April 7, 2009).
14. Andy Newman, "A Juror's Question That Went Unanswered: 'How Dare You Violate That Oath?'" *New York Times*, April 7, 2006, http://www.nytimes.com/2006/04/07/nyregion/07scene.html (accessed April 7, 2009).
15. Jason Fisher, "$10 M for Victim of Mob Cop," *New York Post*, June 4, 2010, http://www.nypost.com/p/news/local/brooklyn/for_victim_of_mob_cop_fb4Ki0Ap3vDubZc41qC6OO (accessed June 5, 2010).
16. Carl B. Klockars et al., "The Measurement of Police Integrity," *National Institute of Justice Research in Brief* (Washington, DC: NIJ, 2000), p. 1.
17. Michael J. Palmiotto, ed., *Police Misconduct: A Reader for the Twenty-First Century* (Upper Saddle River, NJ: Prentice Hall, 2001), preface.
18. Tim Prenzler and Peta Mackay, "Police Gratuities: What the Public Thinks," *Criminal Justice Ethics* (winter/spring 1995), pp. 15–25.
19. Thomas Barker and David L. Carter, *Police Deviance* (Cincinnati, OH: Anderson, 1986). For a detailed overview of the issues involved in police corruption, see Victor E. Kappeler, Richard D. Sluder, and Geoffrey P. Alpert, *Forces of Deviance: Understanding the Dark Side of Policing*, 2nd ed. (Prospect Heights, IL: Waveland Press, 1998); Dean J. Champion, *Police Misconduct in America: A Reference Handbook* (Santa Barbara, CA: ABC-CLIO, 2002); and Kim Michelle Lersch, ed., *Policing and Misconduct* (Upper Saddle River, NJ: Prentice Hall, 2002).
20. Frank L. Perry, "Repairing Broken Windows: Preventing Corruption within Our Ranks," *FBI Law Enforcement Bulletin* (February 2001), pp. 23–26.
21. "Nationline: NYC Cops—Excess Force Not Corruption," *USA Today*, June 16, 1995.
22. *Knapp Commission Report on Police Corruption* (New York: George Braziller, 1973).
23. Ibid.
24. Sabrina Tavernise, "Victory for Officer Who Aided Corruption Inquiry," *New York Times*, April 3, 2004.

25. See Erwin Chemerinsky, *An Independent Analysis of the Los Angeles Police Department's Board of Inquiry Report on the Rampart Scandal*, September 11, 2000, http://www.usc.edu/dept/law/faculty/chemerinsky/rampartfinalrep.html (accessed January 10, 2002).
26. Linda Deutsch, "Appeals Court Intercedes in LAPD Corruption Trial," Associated Press, October 12, 2000, http://www.newstimes.com/archive2000/oct12/nah.htm (accessed January 20, 2002).
27. "Three LAPD Officers Convicted," *USA Today* Online, November 15, 2000 (accessed July 16, 2001).
28. "Prosecutors: LAPD Hindering Police Corruption Trial," Associated Press, October 6, 2000, http://www.newstimes.com/archive2000/oct06/nac.htm (accessed February 2, 2008).
29. Scott Glover and Matt Lait, "LAPD Settling Abuse Scandal," *Los Angeles Times*, March 31, 2005.
30. "Three LAPD Officers Convicted" and "This Week's Corrupt Cop Story," http://www.stopthedrugwar.org/chronicle/266/copcorruption.shtml (accessed October 2, 2003).
31. Glover and Lait, "LAPD Settling Abuse Scandal."
32. Ibid.
33. Tina Daunt and Jim Newton, "Council OKs Police Reform Pact with Justice Department," *Los Angeles Times* Online, November 3, 2000 (accessed May 20, 2006).
34. Scott Glover and Matt Lait, "A Tearful Perez Gets Five Years," *Los Angeles Times* Online, February 26, 2000 (accessed August 28, 2001).
35. Edwin H. Sutherland and Donald Cressey, *Principles of Criminology*, 8th ed. (Philadelphia: J. B. Lippincott, 1970).
36. Tim R. Jones, Compton Owens, and Melissa A. Smith, "Police Ethics Training: A Three-Tiered Approach," *FBI Law Enforcement Bulletin* (June 1995), pp. 22–26.
37. U.S. Department of Justice, *Principles for Promoting Police Integrity: Examples of Promising Police Practices* (Washington, DC: DOJ, 2001).
38. National Institute of Justice, *Enhancing Police Integrity* (Washington, DC: U.S. Department of Justice, 2005).
39. Ibid., p ii.
40. International Association of Chiefs of Police, *Employee Drug Testing* (St. Paul, MN: IACP, 1999).
41. Tom Hays, "NYPD to Start Random Steroid Testing," Associated Press, April 9, 2008, http://www.wtopnews.com/?sid=1383781&nid=104 (accessed July 24, 2008).
42. *Maurice Turner* v. *Fraternal Order of Police*, 500 A.2d 1005 (D.C. 1985).
43. *Philip Caruso, President of P.B.A.* v. *Benjamin Ward, Police Commissioner*, New York State Supreme Court, Pat. 37, Index no. 12632-86, 1986.
44. *National Treasury Employees Union* v. *Von Raab*, 489 U.S. 656, 659 (1989).
45. National Law Enforcement Officers' Memorial Fund, "Facts and Figures," http://www.nleomf.org/facts (accessed Octdober 1, 2010).
46. Officer Down Memorial Page, http://odmp.org/year.php?year=2009 (accessed June 15, 2010).
47. Officer Down Memorial Page, http://www.odmp.org/yeardisp.php?year52001 (accessed January 16, 2001).
48. Anthony J. Pinizzotto and Edward F. Davis, "Cop Killers and Their Victims," *FBI Law Enforcement Bulletin* (December 1992), p. 10.
49. Bureau of Labor Statistics, *Occupational Outlook Handbook, 2000–01 Edition* (Washington, DC: BLS, 2000); and Brian A. Reaves and Matthew J. Hickman, *Law Enforcement Management and Administrative Statistics, 2000: Data for Individual State and Local Agencies with 100 or More Officers* (Washington, DC: Bureau of Justice Statistics, 2004). Note that the LEMAS report only includes data from approximately 700 state and local law enforcement agencies that employ 100 or more full-time sworn personnel and that assign 50 or more of these officers to respond to calls for service. LEMAS reports finding 402,000 full-time sworn personnel among those departments in its 2000 survey. BLS data are more comprehensive and include part-time personnel.
50. Brian A. Reaves and Timothy C. Hart, *Federal Law Enforcement Officers, 2000* (Washington, DC: Bureau of Justice Statistics, 2001).
51. Kevin Johnson, "Better Defense Tactics Helping to Curb Police Deaths," *USA Today*, April 22, 2008, p. 3A.
52. *AIDS and Our Workplace*, New York City Police Department pamphlet, November 1987.
53. See Occupational Safety and Health Administration, OSHA Bloodborne Pathogens Act of 1991 (29 CFR 1910.1030).
54. *National Institute of Justice Reports*, No. 206 (November/December 1987).
55. "Suicides, Resignations Hit New Orleans' Thin Blue Line," *USA Today*, September 4, 2005, http://www.usatoday.com/news/nation/2005-09-04-neworleanspolicesuicides_x.htm (accessed April 2, 2006).
56. Ibid.
57. See "On-the-Job Stress in Policing: Reducing It, Preventing It," *National Institute of Justice Journal* (January 2000), pp. 18–24.
58. "Stress on the Job," *Newsweek*, April 25, 1988, p. 43.
59. "On-the-Job Stress in Policing," p. 19.
60. Kevin Barrett, "Police Suicide: Is Anyone Listening?" *Journal of Safe Management of Disruptive and Assaultive Behavior* (spring 1997), pp. 6–9.
61. For an excellent review of coping strategies among police officers, see Robin N. Haarr and Merry Morash, "Gender, Race, and Strategies of Coping with Occupational Stress in Policing," *Justice Quarterly*, Vol. 16, No. 2 (June 1999), pp. 303–336.
62. Mark H. Anshel, "A Conceptual Model and Implications for Coping with Stressful Events in Police Work," *Criminal Justice and Behavior*, Vol. 27, No. 3 (2000), p. 375.
63. Ibid.
64. Bryan Vila, "Tired Cops: Probable Connections between Fatigue and the Performance, Health, and Safety of Patrol Officers," *American Journal of Police*, Vol. 15, No. 2 (1996), pp. 51–92.
65. Bryan Vila et al., *Evaluating the Effects of Fatigue on Police Patrol Officers: Final Report* (Washington, DC: National Institute of Justice, 2000).
66. Bryan Vila and Dennis Jay Kenney, "Tired Cops: The Prevalence and Potential Consequences of Police Fatigue," *National Institute of Justice Journal*, No. 248 (2002), p. 19.
67. Bryan Vila and Erik Y. Taiji, "Fatigue and Police Officer Performance," paper presented at the annual meeting of the American Society of Criminology, Chicago, 1996.
68. Police Executive Research Forum, *Local Law Enforcement's Role in Preventing and Responding to Terrorism* (Washington, DC: PERF, October 2, 2001), http://www.policeforum.org/terrorismfinal.doc (accessed June 1, 2003).
69. Council on Foreign Relations, "Terrorism Questions and Answers: Police Departments," http://www.terrorismanswers.com/security/police.html (accessed April 19, 2005).
70. Ibid.
71. Michael Weissenstein, "NYPD Shifts Focus to Terrorism, Long Considered the Turf of Federal Agents," Associated Press, March 21, 2003, http://www.nj.com/newsflash/national/index.ssf?/cgi-free/getstory_ssf.cgi?a0801_BC_

NYPD-Counterterror&&news&newsflash-national (accessed May 25, 2003).
72. Ibid.
73. International Association of Chiefs of Police, *From Hometown Security to Homeland Security: IACP's Principles for a Locally Designed and Nationally Coordinated Homeland Security Strategy* (Alexandria, VA: IACP, 2005).
74. Ibid.
75. Joseph G. Estey, "President's Message: Taking Command Initiative—An Update" (Washington, DC: International Association of Chiefs of Police, 2005), http://www.theiacp.org/documents/index.cfm?fuseaction5document&document_id5697 (accessed July 25, 2009).
76. Robert J. Jordan (FBI), Congressional Statement on Information Sharing before the U.S. Senate Committee on the Judiciary, Subcommittee on Administrative Oversight and the Courts, Washington, DC, April 17, 2002, http://www.fbi.gov/congress/congress02/jordan041702.htm (accessed April 19, 2006).
77. The concept of intelligence-led policing appears to have been first fully articulated in Angus Smith, ed., *Intelligence-Led Policing* (Richmond, VA: International Association of Law Enforcement Intelligence Analysts, 1997).
78. David L. Carter, *Law Enforcement Intelligence: A Guide for State, Local, and Tribal Law Enforcement Agencies* (Washington, DC: U.S. Department of Justice, 2004), p. 7.
79. Much of the information and some of the wording in this section are taken from Carter, *Law Enforcement Intelligence*.
80. David L. Carter, "The Law Enforcement Intelligence Function," *FBI Law Enforcement Bulletin*, Vol. 74, No. 6 (June 2005), pp. 1–10.
81. Governor's Commission on Criminal Justice Innovation, *Final Report* (Boston: Governor's Commission, 2004), p. 57, from which much of the wording in the rest of this paragraph is taken.
82. Federal Bureau of Investigation, Law Enforcement online, http://www.fbi.gov/hq/cjisd/leo.htm (accessed September 1, 2006).
83. Bernard H. Levin, "Sharing Information: Some Open Secrets and a Glimpse at the Future," *Police Futurist*, Vol. 14, No. 1 (winter 2006), pp. 8–9.
84. The plan was an outgrowth of the IACP Criminal Intelligence Sharing Summit held in Alexandria, Virginia, in March 2002. Results of the summit are documented in International Association of Chiefs of Police, *Recommendations from the IACP Intelligence Summit, Criminal Intelligence Sharing*.
85. Office of Justice Programs, *The National Criminal Intelligence Sharing Plan* (Washington, DC: U.S. Department of Justice, 2003).
86. "Stroke Victim Sues State over Arrest," Associated Press, April 24, 1996.
87. Charles R. Swanson, Leonard Territo, and Robert W. Taylor, *Police Administration: Structures, Processes, and Behavior*, 2nd ed. (New York: Macmillan, 1988).
88. *Malley* v. *Briggs*, 475 U.S. 335, 106 S.Ct. 1092 (1986).
89. Ibid., at 4246.
90. *Biscoe* v. *Arlington County*, 238 U.S. App. D.C. 206, 738 F.2d 1352, 1362 (1984). See also 738 F.2d 1352 (D.C. Cir. 1984), *cert. denied*; 469 U.S. 1159; and 105 S.Ct. 909, 83 L.E.2d 923 (1985).
91. *Kaplan* v. *Lloyd's Insurance Co.*, 479 So.2d 961 (La. App. 1985).
92. John Hill, "High-Speed Police Pursuits: Dangers, Dynamics, and Risk Reduction," *FBI Law Enforcement Bulletin* (July 2002), pp. 14–18.
93. *City of Canton, Ohio* v. *Harris*, 489 U.S. 378 (1989).
94. Ibid., at 1204.
95. *Board of the County Commissioners of Bryan County, Oklahoma* v. *Brown*, 520 U.S. 397 (1997).
96. U.S. Code, Title 42, Section 1983.
97. *Bivens* v. *Six Unknown Federal Agents*, 403 U.S. 388 (1971).
98. See *F.D.I.C.* v. *Meyer*, 510 U.S. 471 (1994), in which the U.S. Supreme Court reiterated its ruling under *Bivens*, stating that only government employees and not government agencies can be sued.
99. *Wyler* v. *U.S.*, 725 F.2d 157 (2d Cir. 1983).
100. California Government Code, Section 818.
101. Federal Tort Claims Act, 28 U.S.C. 1346(b), 2671–2680.
102. *Elder* v. *Holloway*, 114 S.Ct. 1019, 127 L.Ed.2d 344 (1994).
103. Ibid.
104. *Hunter* v. *Bryant*, 112 S.Ct. 534 (1991).
105. William U. McCormack, "Supreme Court Cases: 1991–1992 Term," *FBI Law Enforcement Bulletin* (November 1992), p. 30.
106. *Saucier* v. *Katz*, 533 U.S. 194 (2001).
107. See also *Brosseau* v. *Haugen*, 543 U.S. 194 (2004).
108. *Pearson et al.* v. *Callahan*, 555 U.S. ___ (2009).
109. *Scott* v. *Harris*, 550 U.S. 372 (2007).
110. *Idaho* v. *Horiuchi*, 253 F.3d 359 (9th Cir. 2001).
111. For more information on police liability, see Daniel L. Schofield, "Legal Issues of Pursuit Driving," *FBI Law Enforcement Bulletin* (May 1988), pp. 23–29.
112. Michael S. Vaughn, Tab W. Cooper, and Rolando V. del Carmen, "Assessing Legal Liabilities in Law Enforcement: Police Chiefs' Views," *Crime and Delinquency*, Vol. 47, No. 1 (2001), p. 3.
113. Adapted from Deborah Ramirez, Jack McDevitt, and Amy Farrell, *A Resource Guide on Racial Profiling Data Collection Systems: Promising Practices and Lessons Learned* (Washington, DC: U.S. Department of Justice, 2000), p. 3.
114. David Harris, *Driving While Black: Racial Profiling on Our Nation's Highways* (Washington, DC: American Civil Liberties Union, 1999).
115. "Justice Department Bars Race Profiling, with Exception for Terrorism," *Criminal Justice Newsletter* (July 15, 2003), pp. 6–7.
116. "Justice Department Issues Policy Guidance to Ban Racial Profiling," U.S. Department of Justice press release (No. 355), June 17, 2003.
117. Blaine Harden and Somini Sengupta, "Some Passengers Singled Out for Exclusion by Flight Crew," *New York Times*, September 22, 2001.
118. David Cole and John Lambreth, "The Fallacy of Racial Profiling," *New York Times* Online, May 13, 2001, http://college1.nytimes.com/buests/articles/2001/05/13/846196.xml (accessed August 28, 2004).
119. Amitai Etzioni, "Another Side of Racial Profiling," *USA Today*, May 21, 2001.
120. Gallup Poll Organization, "Racial Profiling Seen as Pervasive, Unjust," July 20, 2004, http://www.gallup.com/poll/12406/Racial-Profiling-Seen-Pervasive-Unjust.aspx (accessed August 1, 2010).
121. Ramirez, McDevitt, and Farrell, *A Resource Guide on Racial Profiling Data Collection Systems*, p. 3.
122. Police Executive Research Forum, *Racially Biased Policing: A Principled Response* (Washington, DC: PERF, 2001).
123. Ibid., foreword.
124. Ibid., p. 39.
125. Ibid., p. 47.
126. Some of the material in this section is adapted or derived from National Institute of Justice, *Use of Force by Police: Overview of National and Local Data* (Washington, DC: NIJ, 1999).

127. Matthew R. Durose, Erica L. Smith, and Patrick A. Langan, *Contacts between Police and the Public, 2005* (Washington, DC: Bureau of Justice Statistics, 2007).
128. Joel H. Garner and Christopher D. Maxwell, "Measuring the Amount of Force Used by and against the Police in Six Jurisdictions," in National Institute of Justice, *Use of Force by Police*, p. 41.
129. International Association of Chiefs of Police, *Police Use of Force in America, 2001* (Alexandria, VA: IACP, 2001), p. 1.
130. Kenneth Adams, "What We Know about Police Use of Force," in National Institute of Justice, *Use of Force by Police,* p. 4.
131. International Association of Chiefs of Police, *Police Use of Force in America, 2001.*
132. Geoffrey P. Alpert and Roger G. Dunham, *The Force Factor: Measuring Police Use of Force Relative to Suspect Resistance—A Final Report* (Washington, DC: National Institute of Justice, 2001).
133. Samuel Walker, Geoffrey P. Alpert, and Dennis J. Kenney, *Responding to the Problem Police Officer: A National Study of Early Warning Systems* (Washington, DC: National Institute of Justice, 2000).
134. See Human Rights Watch, "The Christopher Commission Report," from which some of the wording in the paragraph is adapted, http://www.hrw.org/reports98/police/uspo73.htm (accessed March 30, 2002).
135. Sam W. Lathrop, "Reviewing Use of Force: A Systematic Approach," *FBI Law Enforcement Bulletin* (October 2000), p. 18.
136. Jodi M. Brown and Patrick A. Langan, *Policing and Homicide, 1976–98: Justifiable Homicide by Police, Police Officers Murdered by Felons* (Washington, DC: Bureau of Justice Statistics, 2001), p. iii.
137. *Tennessee* v. *Garner*, 471 U.S. 1 (1985).
138. *Graham* v. *Connor*, 490 U.S. 386, 396–397 (1989).
139. John C. Hall, "FBI Training on the New Federal Deadly Force Policy," *FBI Law Enforcement Bulletin* (April 1996), pp. 25–32.
140. James Fyfe, *Shots Fired: An Examination of New York City Police Firearms Discharges* (Ann Arbor, MI: University Microfilms, 1978).
141. James Fyfe, "Blind Justice? Police Shootings in Memphis," paper presented at the annual meeting of the Academy of Criminal Justice Sciences, Philadelphia, March 1981.
142. It is estimated that American police shoot at approximately 3,600 people every year. See William Geller, *Deadly Force* study guide, Crime File Series (Washington, DC: National Institute of Justice, n.d.).
143. Anne Cohen, "I've Killed That Man Ten Thousand Times," *Police Magazine* (July 1980).
144. For more information, see Joe Auten, "When Police Shoot," *North Carolina Criminal Justice Today*, Vol. 4, No. 4 (summer 1986), pp. 9–14.
145. Details for this story come from Stephanie Slater, "Suicidal Man Killed by Police Fusillade," *Palm Beach Post*, March 11, 2005, p. 1A.
146. Rebecca Stincelli, *Suicide by Cop: Victims from Both Sides of the Badge* (Folsom, CA: Interviews and Interrogations Institute, 2004).
147. Slater, "Suicidal Man Killed by Police Fusillade."
148. Anthony J. Pinizzotto, Edward F. Davis, and Charles E. Miller III, "Suicide by Cop: Defining a Devastating Dilemma," *FBI Law Enforcement Bulletin*, Vol. 74, No. 2 (February 2005), p. 15.
149. "Ten Percent of Police Shootings Found to Be 'Suicide by Cop,'" *Criminal Justice Newsletter* (September 1, 1998), pp. 1–2.
150. Robert J. Homant and Daniel B. Kennedy, "Suicide by Police: A Proposed Typology of Law Enforcement Officer–Assisted Suicide," *Policing: An International Journal of Police Strategies and Management*, Vol. 23, No. 3 (2000), pp. 339–355.
151. David Hambling, "Flash Gun," *Science News*, May 10–16, 2008, pp. 38–40.
152. David W. Hayeslip and Alan Preszler, "NIJ Initiative on Less-Than-Lethal Weapons," *NIJ Research in Brief* (Washington, DC: National Institute of Justice, 1993).
153. Ibid.
154. Thomas Farragher and David Abel, "Postgame Police Projectile Kills an Emerson Student," *Boston Globe*, October 22, 2004, http://www.boston.com/sports/baseball/redsox/articles/2004/10/22/postgame_police_projectile_kills_an_emerson_student (accessed July 25, 2005).
155. Michael Siegfried, "Notes on the Professionalization of Private Security," *Justice Professional* (spring 1989).
156. See Edward A. Farris, "Five Decades of American Policing, 1932–1982: The Path to Professionalism," *Police Chief* (November 1982), p. 34.
157. InsideDiscoverPolicing.org, "Inside CALEA Accreditation," http://blog.discoverpolicing.org/uncategorized/inside-calea-accreditation (accessed October 15, 2010). Agency estimates are from Reaves and Hickman, *Census of State and Local Law Enforcement Agencies, 2000.*
158. *CALEA Update*, No. 81 (February 2003), http://www.calea.org/newweb/newsletter/No81/81index.htm (accessed May 21, 2003).
159. Brian A. Reaves, *State and Local Law Enforcement Training Academies, 2006* (Washington, DC: Bureau of Justice Statistics, 2009), p. 6.
160. Information in this paragraph comes from "PTO Program," COPS Office, U.S. Department of Justice (no date), http://www.cops.usdoj.gov/print.asp?Item=461 (accessed June 3, 2007).
161. Ibid.
162. National Commission on Law Observance and Enforcement, *Report on Police* (Washington, DC: U.S. Government Printing Office, 1931).
163. President's Commission on Law Enforcement and Administration of Justice, *The Challenge of Crime in a Free Society* (Washington, DC: U.S. Government Printing Office, 1967).
164. National Advisory Commission on Criminal Justice Standards and Goals, *Report on the Police* (Washington, DC: U.S. Government Printing Office, 1973).
165. Reaves and Hickman, *Law Enforcement Management and Administrative Statistics, 2000.*
166. Ibid.
167. Brian A. Reaves and Matthew J. Hickman, *Police Departments in Large Cities, 1990–2000* (Washington, DC: Bureau of Justice Statistics, 2002), p. 1.
168. "Dallas PD College Rule Gets Final OK," *Law Enforcement News* (July 7, 1986), pp. 1, 13.
169. *Davis* v. *Dallas*, 777 F.2d 205 (5th Cir. 1985).
170. David L. Carter, Allen D. Sapp, and Darrel W. Stephens, *The State of Police Education: Policy Direction for the Twenty-First Century* (Washington, DC: Police Executive Research Forum, 1989), pp. xxii–xxiii.
171. National Advisory Commission on Criminal Justice Standards and Goals, *Report on the Police*, p. 238.
172. Matthew J. Hickman and Brian A. Reaves, *Local Police Departments, 2003* (Washington, DC: Bureau of Justice Statistics, 2006), p. 5.
173. Matthew J. Hickman and Brian A. Reaves, *Local Police Departments, 2000* (Washington, DC: Bureau of Justice Statistics, 2003), p. 270.
174. August Vollmer, *The Police and Modern Society* (Berkeley: University of California Press, 1936), p. 222.
175. O. W. Wilson and Roy Clinton McLaren, *Police Administration*, 4th ed. (New York: McGraw-Hill, 1977), p. 259.

176. *Report of the National Advisory Commission on Civil Disorders* (New York: E. P. Dutton, 1968), p. 332.
177. Hickman and Reaves, *Local Police Departments, 2003.*
178. U.S. Census Bureau, *National Population Estimates: Characteristics*, http://www.census.gov/popest/national/asrh/NC-EST2005-srh.html.
179. R. Alan Thompson, "Black Skin—Brass Shields: Assessing the Presumed Marginalization of Black Law Enforcement Executives," *American Journal of Criminal Justice*, Vol. 30, No. 2 (2006), pp. 163–175.
180. National Center for Women and Policing, *Equality Denied: The Status of Women in Policing, 2001* (Los Angeles: NCWP, 2002), p. 1.
181. Ibid.
182. Lynn Langston, *Women in Law Enforcement, 1987–2008* (Washington, DC: Bureau of Justice Statistics, June 2010).
183. National Center for Women and Policing, *Recruiting and Retaining Women: A Self-Assessment Guide for Law Enforcement* (Los Angeles: NCWP, 2001), p. 22.
184. Ibid.
185. Mary Dodge, "Women in Policing: Time to Forget the Differences and Focus on the Future," *Criminal Justice Research Reports* (July/August 2007), p. 82.
186. C. Lee Bennett, "Interviews with Female Police Officers in Western Massachusetts," paper presented at the annual meeting of the Academy of Criminal Justice Sciences, Nashville, TN, March 1991.
187. Ibid., p. 9.
188. Carole G. Garrison, Nancy K. Grant, and Kenneth L. J. McCormick, "Utilization of Police Women," unpublished manuscript.
189. Susan Ehrlich Martin and Nancy C. Jurik, *Doing Justice, Doing Gender: Women in Law and Criminal Justice Occupations* (Thousand Oaks, CA: Sage, 1996).
190. *Private Security: Report of the Task Force on Private Security* (Washington, DC: U.S. Government Printing Office, 1976), p. 4.
191. "Olympic Committee to Review Salt Lake Security in Wake of Terror Attacks," Associated Press, September 17, 2001.
192. David H. Bayley and Clifford D. Shearing, *The New Structure of Policing: Description, Conceptualization, and Research Agenda* (Washington, DC: National Institute of Justice, 2001).
193. William C. Cunningham, John J. Strauchs, and Clifford W. Van Meter, *The Hallcrest Report II: Private Security Trends, 1970–2000* (McLean, VA: Hallcrest Systems, 1990).
194. Includes full-time employees working for local police, sheriff's departments, special police, and state police. See Brian A. Reaves and Andrew L. Goldberg, *Census of State and Local Law Enforcement Agencies, 1996* (Washington, DC: Bureau of Justice Statistics, 1998); Reaves and Hickman, *Law Enforcement Management and Administrative Statistics, 2000*; Bureau of Labor Statistics, *Occupational Outlook Handbook, 2000–01 Edition*; and Bureau of Labor Statistics Occupational Outlook Handbook, http://www.bls.gov/oco/ocos159.htm#outlook (accessed May 20, 2010).
195. See http://www.spyandsecuritystore.com/conex.html (accessed June 5, 2010).
196. Cunningham, Strauchs, and Van Meter, *The Hallcrest Report II*, p. 236.
197. Bayley and Shearing, *The New Structure of Policing*, p. 15.
198. National Institute of Justice, *Crime and Protection in America: A Study of Private Security and Law Enforcement Resources and Relationships—Executive Summary* (Washington, DC: U.S. Department of Justice, 1985), pp. 59–72.

The Courts

The Courts

Learning Objectives

After reading this chapter, you should be able to:

1. Describe the development of the American court system.
2. Outline the structure of a typical state court system, and describe the jurisdiction of various types of state and local courts.
3. Identify the three levels of the federal judiciary, and enumerate some of the differences between the state and federal court systems.
4. Explain the typical steps taken during pretrial activities, and list the key factors considered by judicial officers in assessing the risks associated with pretrial release.

IndexStock/SuperStock

> "The criminal court is the central, crucial institution in the criminal justice system. It is the part of the system that is the most venerable, the most formally organized, and the most elaborately circumscribed by law and tradition. It is the institution around which the rest of the system has developed."
>
> —The President's Commission on Law Enforcement and Administration of Justice[1]

Introduction

▲ FBI and ATF agents investigating damage to the Edward J. Schwartz federal courthouse in San Diego, California, following a bombing that targeted the facility in 2008. What role do the courts play in the American criminal justice system?
Federal Bureau of Investigation/AP Wide World Photos

On May 4, 2008, a nail-filled pipe bomb exploded at the entrance to the Edward J. Schwartz Federal Courthouse in San Diego, California. The explosion shattered the building's glass door, damaged the lobby, and punched a hole in a window across the street. Although no one was injured, the FBI's Joint Terrorism Task Force in San Diego conducted a vigorous investigation. Three months later, two women and a man were charged with conspiring to bomb the federal courthouse and with another bombing that had taken place 10 days earlier. A 17-count indictment filed against the trio alleges the use of a weapon of mass destruction and shows that at least one of the alleged conspirators had filed over 100 lawsuits in the courthouse that was attacked. He had been sanctioned by a judge for frivolous filings, with the judge noting that "the lawsuits had been a lucrative cottage industry."[2]

Incidents like the San Diego bombing highlight the critical role that our nation's courts and the personnel who staff them play in the American system of justice. Without courts to decide guilt or innocence and to impose sentence on those convicted of crimes, the activities of law enforcement officials would become meaningless.

There are many different kinds of courts in the United States, but courts at all levels dispense justice daily and work to ensure that all official actors in the justice system carry out their duties in recognition of the rule of law. At many points in this textbook and in three specific chapters, we take a close look at court precedents that have defined the legality of enforcement efforts and correctional action. To provide a picture of how courts work, this chapter will describe the American court system at both the state and federal levels.

History and Structure of the American Court System

Two types of courts function within the American criminal justice system: state courts and federal courts. Figure 1 outlines the structure of today's **federal court system**, and Figure 2 diagrams a typical **state court system**. This dual-court system is the result of

federal court system
The three-tiered structure of federal courts, comprising U.S. district courts, U.S. courts of appeals, and the U.S. Supreme Court.

state court system
A state judicial structure. Most states generally have at least three court levels: trial courts, appellate courts, and a state supreme court.

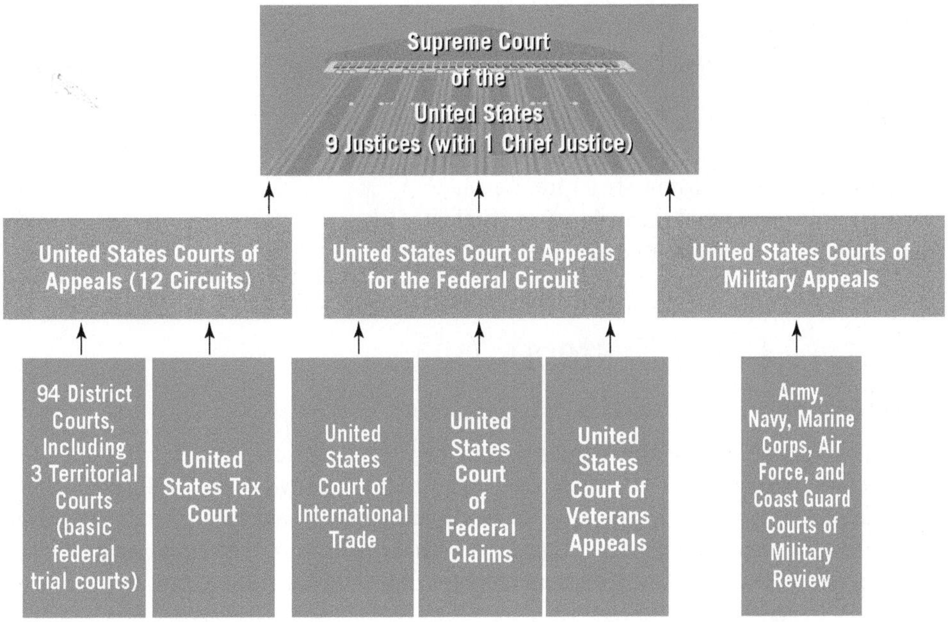

FIGURE 1
The Structure of the Federal Courts

FIGURE 2
A Typical State Court System

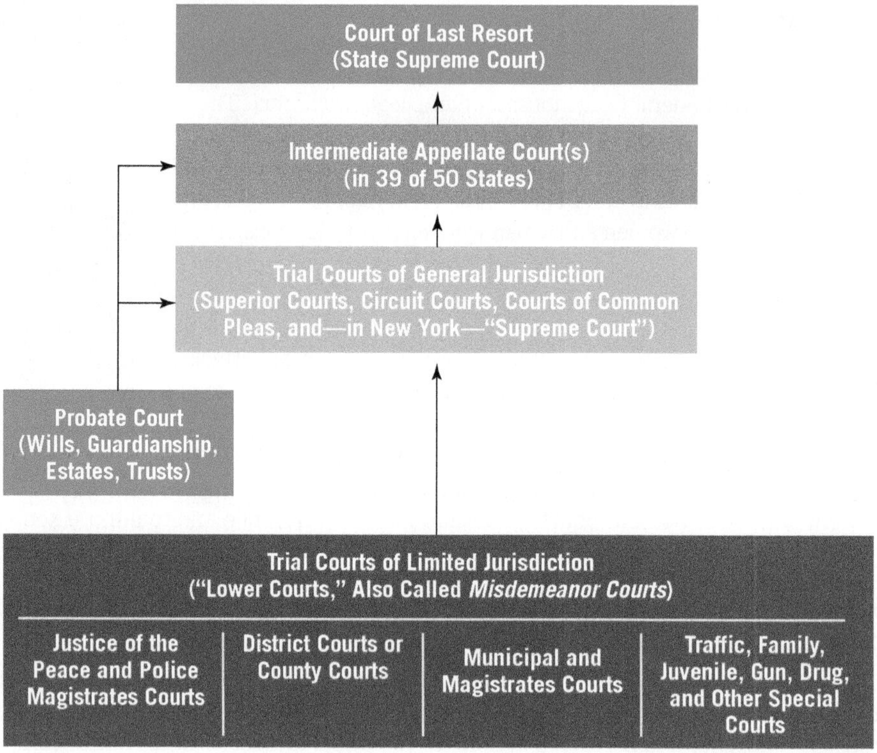

general agreement among the nation's founders about the need for individual states to retain significant legislative authority and judicial autonomy separate from federal control. Under this concept, the United States developed as a relatively loose federation of semi-independent provinces. New states joining the union were assured of limited federal intervention into local affairs. State legislatures were free to create laws, and state court systems were needed to hear cases alleging violations of those laws.

In the last 200 years, states' rights have gradually waned relative to the power of the federal government, but the dual-court system still exists. Even today, state courts do not hear cases involving alleged violations of federal law, nor do federal courts get involved in deciding issues of state law unless there is a conflict between local or state statutes and federal constitutional guarantees. When such conflicts arise, claimed violations of federal due process guarantees—especially those found in the Bill of Rights—can provide the basis for appeals made to federal courts by offenders convicted in state court systems. Learn more about the dual-court system in America at **Library Extra 1**.

This chapter describes both state and federal court systems in terms of their historical development, **jurisdiction**, and current structure. Because it is within state courts that the majority of criminal cases originate, we turn our attention first to them.

1 Describe the development of the American court system.

jurisdiction
The territory, subject matter, or people over which a court or other justice agency may exercise lawful authority, as determined by statute or constitution.

The State Court System

The Development of State Courts

Each of the original American colonies had its own court system for resolving disputes, both civil and criminal. In 1629, the Massachusetts Bay Colony created a General Court, composed of the governor, his deputy, 18 assistants, and 118 elected officials. The General Court was a combined legislature and court that made laws, held trials, and imposed sentences.[3] By 1776, all of the American colonies had established fully functioning court systems.

Following the American Revolution, state court systems were anything but uniform. Initially, most states made no distinction between **original jurisdiction** (the lawful authority of a court to hear cases that arise within a specified geographic area or that involve particular kinds of law violations) and **appellate jurisdiction** (the lawful authority of a court to review a decision made by a lower court). Many, in fact, had no provisions for appeal; Delaware, for example, did not allow appeals in criminal cases until 1897. States that did permit appeals often lacked any established appellate courts and sometimes used state legislatures for that purpose.

original jurisdiction
The lawful authority of a court to hear or to act on a case from its beginning and to pass judgment on the law and the facts. The authority may be over a specific geographic area or over particular types of cases.

appellate jurisdiction
The lawful authority of a court to review a decision made by a lower court.

By the late nineteenth century, a dramatic increase in population, growing urbanization, the settlement of the West, and other far-reaching changes in the American way of life led to a tremendous increase in civil litigation and criminal arrests. Legislatures tried to keep pace with the rising tide of cases. They created a multiplicity of courts at the trial, appellate, and supreme court levels, calling them by a diversity of names and assigning them functions that sometimes bore little resemblance to those of similarly named courts in neighboring states. City courts, which were limited in their jurisdiction by community boundaries, arose to handle the special problems of urban life, such as disorderly conduct, property disputes, and enforcement of restrictive and regulatory ordinances. Other tribunals, such as juvenile courts, developed to handle special kinds of problems or special clients. Some, like magistrate's or small-claims courts, handled only minor law violations and petty disputes; still others, like traffic courts, were very narrow in focus. The result was a patchwork quilt of hearing bodies, some only vaguely resembling modern notions of a trial court.

State court systems developed by following one of several models. One was the New York State Field Code of 1848, which was eventually copied by most other states. The Field Code clarified jurisdictional claims and specified matters of court procedure, but it was later amended so extensively that its usefulness as a model dissolved. Another court system model was provided by the federal Judiciary Act of 1789 and later by the federal Reorganization Act of 1801. States that followed the federal model developed a three-tiered structure of (1) trial courts of limited jurisdiction, (2) trial courts of general jurisdiction, and (3) appellate courts.

2 Outline the structure of a typical state court system, and describe the jurisdiction of various types of state and local courts.

State Court Systems Today

The three-tiered federal model was far from perfect, however. Within the structure it provided, many local and specialized courts proliferated. Traffic courts, magistrate's courts, municipal courts, recorder's courts, probate courts, and courts held by justices of the peace were but a few that functioned at the lower levels. A movement toward simplification of state court structures, led primarily by the American Bar Association and the American Judicature Society, began in the early twentieth century. Proponents of state court reform sought to unify redundant courts that held overlapping jurisdictions. Most reformers suggested a uniform model for states everywhere that would build on (1) a centralized court structure composed of a clear hierarchy of trial and appellate courts, (2) the consolidation of numerous lower-level courts with overlapping jurisdictions, and (3) a centralized state court authority that would be responsible for budgeting, financing, and managing all courts within a state.

▲ Junior high school children posing in the pillory in Williamsburg, Virginia. Just as criminal punishments have changed throughout the centuries, so too have criminal courts, which today provide a civilized forum for exploring conflicting claims about guilt and innocence. How might our courts continue to evolve?
Jeff Greenberg/PhotoEdit Inc.

The court reform movement continues today. Although reformers have made substantial progress in many states, there are still many differences between and among state court systems. Reform states, which early on embraced the reform movement, are now characterized by streamlined judicial systems consisting of precisely conceived trial courts of limited and general jurisdiction, supplemented by one or two appellate court levels. Nonreform, or traditional, states retain judicial systems that are a conglomeration of multilevel and sometimes redundant courts with poorly defined jurisdictions. Even in nonreform states, however, most criminal courts can be classified within the three-tiered structure of two trial court echelons and an appellate tier.

▲ A criminal trial in progress. Why are courts sometimes called "the fulcrum of the criminal justice system"?
Ron Chapple/Taxi/Getty Images, Inc.–Taxi

State Trial Courts

Trial courts are where criminal cases begin. The trial court conducts arraignments, sets bail, takes pleas, and conducts trials. (We will discuss these separate functions in more depth later in this chapter and in the next.) If the defendant is found guilty (or pleads guilty), the trial court imposes sentence. Trial courts of limited (or special) jurisdiction are also called *lower courts*. Lower courts are authorized to hear only less serious criminal cases, usually involving misdemeanors, or to hear special types of cases such as traffic violations, family disputes, and small claims. Courts of limited jurisdiction, which are depicted in TV shows like *Judge Judy* and *Joe Brown*, rarely hold jury trials, depending instead on the hearing judge to make determinations of both fact and law. At the lower-court level, a detailed record of the proceedings is not maintained, and case files only include information on the charge, the plea, the finding of the court, and the sentence. All but six of the states make use of trial courts of limited jurisdiction.[4] These lower courts are much less formal than courts of general jurisdiction.

Trial courts of general jurisdiction—variously called *high courts*, *circuit courts*, or *superior courts*—are authorized to hear any criminal case. In many states, they also provide the first appellate level for courts of limited jurisdiction. In most cases, superior courts offer defendants whose cases originated in lower courts the chance for a new trial instead of a review of the record of the earlier hearing. When a new trial is held, it is referred to as a **trial *de novo***.

trial *de novo*
Literally, "new trial." The term is applied to cases that are retried on appeal, as opposed to those that are simply reviewed on the record.

Trial courts of general jurisdiction operate within a fact-finding framework called the *adversarial process*. That process pits the interests of the state, represented by prosecutors, against the professional skills and abilities of defense attorneys. The adversarial process is not a free-for-all; rather, it is constrained by procedural rules specified in law and sustained through tradition. Take a virtual tour of California trial courts at **Web Extra 1.**

State Appellate Courts

Most states today have an appellate division, consisting of an intermediate appellate court (often called the *court of appeals*) and a high-level appellate court (generally termed the *state supreme court*). High-level appellate courts are referred to as **courts of last resort**, indicating that no other appellate route remains to a defendant within the state court system once the high court rules on a case. All states have supreme courts, although only 39 have intermediate appellate courts.[5]

court of last resort
The court authorized by law to hear the final appeal on a matter.

appeal
The request that a court with appellate jurisdiction review the judgment, decision, or order of a lower court and set it aside (reverse it) or modify it.

An **appeal** by a convicted defendant asks that a higher court review the actions of a lower court. Once they accept an appeal, courts within the appellate division do not conduct a new trial; instead, they review the case on the record. In other words, appellate courts examine the written transcript of lower-court hearings to ensure that those proceedings were carried out in a fair manner and in accordance with proper procedure and state law. They may also allow attorneys for both sides to make brief oral arguments and will generally consider other briefs or information filed by the appellant (the party initiating the appeal) or the appellee (the side opposed to the appeal). State statutes generally require that sentences of life imprisonment or death be automatically reviewed by the state supreme court.

Most convictions are affirmed on appeal. Occasionally, however, an appellate court will determine that the trial court erred in allowing certain kinds of evidence to be heard, that it failed to interpret properly the significance of a relevant statute, or that some other impropriety occurred. When that happens, the verdict of the trial court will be reversed, and the case may be sent back for a new trial, or *remanded*. When a conviction is overturned by an appellate court because of constitutional issues or when a statute is determined to be invalid, the state usually has recourse to the state supreme court; when an issue of federal law is involved, as when a state court has ruled a federal law unconstitutional, it goes to the U.S. Supreme Court.

Defendants who are not satisfied with the resolution of their case within the state court system may attempt an appeal to the U.S. Supreme Court. For such an appeal to have any chance of being heard, it must be based on claimed violations of the defendant's rights, as guaranteed under federal law or the U.S. Constitution. Under certain circumstances, federal district courts may also provide a path of relief for state defendants who can show that their federal constitutional rights were violated. However, in the 1992 case of *Keeney* v. *Tamayo-Reyes*,[6] the U.S. Supreme Court ruled that a "respondent is entitled to a federal evidentiary hearing [only] if he can show cause for his failure to develop the facts in the state-court proceedings and actual prejudice resulting from that failure, or if he can show that a fundamental miscarriage of justice would result from failure to hold such a hearing." Justice Byron White, writing for the Court, said, "It is hardly a good use of scarce judicial resources to duplicate fact-finding in federal court merely because a petitioner has negligently failed to take advantage of opportunities in state court proceedings."

Likewise, in *Herrera* v. *Collins* (1993),[7] the Court ruled that new evidence of innocence is no reason for a federal court to order a new state trial if constitutional grounds are lacking. The *Keeney* and *Herrera* decisions have severely limited access by state defendants to federal courts. See **Library Extra 2** for additional information on challenging state court criminal convictions within the federal court system.

State Court Administration

To function efficiently, courts require uninterrupted funding, adequate staffing, trained support personnel, well-managed case flow, and coordination between levels and among jurisdictions. To oversee these and other aspects of judicial management, every state today has its own mechanism for court administration. Most make use of **state court administrators** who manage these operational functions.

state court administrator
A coordinator who assists with case-flow management, operating funds budgeting, and court docket administration.

State court administrators can receive assistance from the National Center for State Courts (NCSC) in Williamsburg, Virginia. The NCSC, founded in 1971 at the behest of Chief Justice Warren E. Burger, is an independent, nonprofit organization dedicated to the improvement of the American court system. You can visit the NCSC at **Web Extra 2.**

At the federal level, the court system is administered by the Administrative Office of the United States Courts (AOUSC), located in Washington, D.C. The AOUSC, created by Congress in 1939, prepares the budget and legislative agenda for federal courts. It also performs audits of court accounts, manages funds for the operation of federal courts, compiles and publishes statistics on the volume and type of business conducted by the courts, and recommends plans and strategies to efficiently manage court business. You can visit the AOUSC at **Web Extra 3**.

Dispute-Resolution Centers and Community Courts

Often, it is possible to resolve minor disputes (in which minor criminal offenses might otherwise be charged) without a formal court hearing. Some communities have **dispute-resolution centers** that hear victims' claims of minor wrongs they have suffered, such as being subject to the passing of bad checks, trespassing, shoplifting, or petty theft. Such centers function today in more than 200 locations throughout the country.[8] Frequently staffed by volunteer mediators, such programs work to resolve disagreements without assigning blame. Dispute-resolution programs began in the early 1970s, with the earliest being the Community Assistance Project in Chester, Pennsylvania; the Columbus, Ohio, Night Prosecutor Program; and the Arbitration as an Alternative Program in Rochester, New York. Following the lead of these programs, the U.S. Department of Justice helped promote the development of three experimental Neighborhood Justice Centers in Los Angeles, Kansas City, and Atlanta. Each center accepted both minor civil and criminal cases.

dispute-resolution center
An informal hearing place designed to mediate interpersonal disputes without resorting to the more formal arrangements of a criminal trial court.

Mediation centers are often closely integrated with the formal criminal justice process and may substantially reduce the caseload of lower-level courts. Some centers are, in fact, run by the courts and work only with court-ordered referrals; others are semiautonomous but may be dependent on courts for endorsement of their decisions; and still others function with complete autonomy. Rarely, however, do dispute-resolution programs entirely supplant the formal criminal justice mechanism, and defendants who appear before a

▲ Graduates of the Oakland County (Michigan) Community Dispute Resolution training program. Staffed largely by volunteers, dispute-resolution programs facilitate cooperative solutions to relatively low-level disputes in which minor criminal offenses might otherwise be charged. How do dispute-resolution programs and centers help relieve some of the pressures facing our criminal courts?
Photo courtesy of Oakland Mediation Center, Bloomfield Hills, Michigan

community mediator may later be charged with a crime. Community mediation programs have become a central feature of today's restorative-justice movement.

Recently, the community justice movement has led to the creation of innovative low-level courts in certain parts of the country. Unlike dispute-resolution centers, **community courts** are always official components of the formal justice system and can hand down sentences, including fines and jail time, without further judicial review. Community courts typically begin as grassroots movements undertaken by community residents and local organizations seeking to build confidence in the way offenders are handled for less serious offenses. Community courts generally sentence convicted offenders to work within the community, "where neighbors can see what they are doing."[9] Like dispute-resolution centers, community courts, which are sometimes called *problem-solving courts*, focus on quality-of-life crimes that erode a neighborhood's morale, emphasize problem solving rather than punishment, and build on restorative principles like community service and restitution.

community court
A low-level court that focuses on quality-of-life crimes that erode a neighborhood's morale, that emphasizes problem solving rather than punishment, and that builds on restorative principles such as community service and restitution.

Both mediation centers and community courts have been criticized because they typically work only with minor offenders, thereby denying the opportunity for mediation to victims and offenders in more serious cases. They have also come under criticism because defendants may see them as just another form of criminal sanction rather than as a true alternative to processing by the criminal justice system.[10] Dispute-resolution centers, in particular, have been criticized for doing little more than providing a forum for shouting matches between the parties involved. Learn more about dispute-resolution centers and community courts at **Library Extra 3** and **Web Extras 4** and **5.**

The judicial Power of the United States shall be vested in one supreme Court, and in such inferior Courts as the Congress may from time to time ordain and establish.
—Article III of the U.S. Constitution

The Federal Court System

Whereas state courts evolved from early colonial arrangements, federal courts were created by the U.S. Constitution. Article III, Section 1, of the Constitution provides for the establishment of "one supreme Court, and . . . such inferior Courts as the Congress may from time to time ordain and establish." Article III, Section 2, specifies that such courts are to have jurisdiction over cases arising under the Constitution, federal laws, and treaties. Federal courts are also to settle disputes between states and to have jurisdiction in cases where one of the parties is a state.

Today's federal court system represents the culmination of a series of congressional mandates that have expanded the federal judicial infrastructure so that it can continue to carry out the duties envisioned by the Constitution. Notable federal statutes that have contributed to the present structure of the federal court system include the Judiciary Act of 1789, the Judiciary Act of 1925, and the Magistrate's Act of 1968.

3 Identify the three levels of the federal judiciary, and enumerate some of the differences between the state and federal court systems.

As a result of constitutional mandates, congressional action, and other historical developments, today's federal judiciary consists of three levels: (1) U.S. district courts, (2) U.S. courts of appeal, and (3) the U.S. Supreme Court. Each is described in turn in the following sections.

U.S. District Courts

The U.S. district courts are the trial courts of the federal court system.[11] Within limits set by Congress and the Constitution, the district courts have jurisdiction to hear nearly all categories of federal cases, including both civil and criminal matters. There are

94 federal judicial districts, including at least one district in each state (some states, like New York and California, have as many as four), the District of Columbia, and Puerto Rico. Each district includes a U.S. bankruptcy court as a unit of the district court. Three territories of the United States—the Virgin Islands, Guam, and the Northern Mariana Islands—have district courts that hear federal cases, including bankruptcy cases. There are two special trial courts that have nationwide jurisdiction over certain types of cases. The Court of International Trade addresses cases involving international trade and customs issues. The U.S. Court of Federal Claims has jurisdiction over most claims for money damages against the United States, disputes over federal contracts, unlawful "takings" of private property by the federal government, and a variety of other claims against the United States.

Federal district courts have original jurisdiction over all cases involving alleged violations of federal statutes. A district may itself be divided into divisions and may have several places where the court hears cases. District courts were first authorized by Congress through the Judiciary Act of 1789, which allocated one federal court to each state. Because of population increases over the years, new courts have been added in a number of states.

Nearly 650 district court judges staff federal district courts. Because some courts are much busier than others, the number of district court judges varies from a low of two in some jurisdictions to a high of 27 in others. District court judges are appointed by the president and confirmed by the Senate, and they serve for life. An additional 369 full-time and 110 part-time magistrate judges (referred to as *U.S. magistrates* before 1990) serve the district court system and assist the federal judges. Magistrate judges have the power to conduct arraignments and may set bail, issue warrants, and try minor offenders.

U.S. district courts handle tens of thousands of cases per year. During 2008, for example, 70,898 criminal cases[12] and 267,257 civil cases[13] were filed in U.S. district courts. Drug prosecutions, especially in courts located close to the U.S.–Mexico border, have led to considerable growth in the number of cases filed. Federal drug prosecutions in states abutting the Mexican border—California, Arizona, New Mexico, and Texas—more than doubled (from 2,864 to 6,116) between 1994 and 2000, and immigration prosecutions increased more than sevenfold (from 1,056 to 7,613).[14] During the last 20 years, the number of cases handled by the entire federal district court system has grown exponentially. The hiring of new judges and the creation of new courtroom facilities have not kept pace with the increase in caseload, and questions persist as to the quality of justice that overworked judges can deliver.

One of the most pressing issues facing district court judges is the fact that their pay, which at $174,000 in mid-2010[15] placed them in the top 1% of income-earning Americans, is small compared to what most could earn in private practice. Since 1993, the salaries of federal judges have remained relatively stagnant,[16] leading many judges to leave the bench.[17] In 2006, Chief Justice John Roberts called Congress's failure to raise judges' pay "a direct threat to judicial independence."[18] Because of low pay, said Roberts, "judges effectively serve for a term dictated by their financial position rather than for life." Learn more about the federal courts at **Library Extra 4.**

U.S. Courts of Appeal

The 94 judicial districts are organized into 12 regional circuits, each of which has a U.S. court of appeals.[19] A court of appeals hears appeals from the district courts located within its circuit, as well as appeals from decisions of federal administrative agencies.

The U.S. Court of Appeals for the Federal Circuit and the 12 regional courts of appeal are often referred to as *circuit courts.* Early in the nation's history, the judges of the first courts of appeal visited each of the courts in one region in a particular sequence, traveling by horseback and riding the "circuit." Today, the regional courts of appeal review matters from the district courts of their geographic regions, from the U.S. Tax Court, and from certain federal administrative agencies. A disappointed party in a district court often has the opportunity to have the case reviewed in the court of appeals for the circuit. Each of the First through Eleventh Circuits includes three or more states, as illustrated in Figure 3.

FIGURE 3
Geographic Boundaries of the U.S. Courts of Appeal and U.S. District Courts

Each court of appeals consists of six or more judges, depending on the caseload of the court. Circuit court judges are appointed for life by the president (with the advice and consent of the Senate). The judge who has served on the court the longest and who is under 65 years of age is designated as the chief judge. The chief judge performs administrative duties in addition to hearing cases and serves for a maximum term of seven years. There are 167 judges on the 12 regional courts of appeal.

The U.S. Court of Appeals for the District of Columbia, which is often called the Twelfth Circuit, hears cases arising in the District of Columbia and has appellate jurisdiction assigned by Congress in legislation concerning many departments of the federal government. The U.S. Court of Appeals for the Federal Circuit (in effect, the Thirteenth Circuit) was created in 1982 by the merging of the U.S. Court of Claims and the U.S. Court of Customs and Patent Appeals. The court hears appeals in cases from the U.S. Court of Federal Claims, the U.S. Court of International Trade, the U.S. Court of Veterans Appeals, the International Trade Commission, the Board of Contract Appeals, the Patent and Trademark Office, and the Merit Systems Protection Board. The court also hears appeals from certain decisions involving the secretaries of the Department of Agriculture and the Department of Commerce and cases from district courts involving patents and minor claims against the federal government.

Oyez, oyez, oyez! All persons having business before the honorable, the Supreme Court of the United States, are admonished to draw near and give their attention, for the court is now sitting. God save the United States and this honorable Court.

—Marshal's cry at the opening of public sessions of the U.S. Supreme Court

Almost all appeals from federal district courts go to the court of appeals serving the circuit in which the case was first heard. Federal appellate courts have appellate jurisdiction over the decisions of district courts within their circuits. Criminal appeals from federal district courts are usually heard by panels of three judges sitting on a court of appeals rather than by all the judges of each circuit. A defendant's request for appeal, when granted, has been interpreted to mean the opportunity for one appeal; hence the U.S. Supreme Court need not necessarily hear the appeals of defendants who are dissatisfied with the decision of a federal appeals court.

Federal appellate courts operate under the Federal Rules of Appellate Procedure, although each has also created its own separate Local Rules. Local Rules may mean that one circuit, such as the Second, will depend heavily on oral arguments, while others may prefer written summary depositions. Appeals generally fall into one of three categories: (1) frivolous appeals, which have little substance, raise no significant new issues, and are generally disposed of quickly; (2) ritualistic appeals, which are brought primarily because of the demands of litigants, even though the probability of reversal is negligible; and (3) nonconsensual appeals, which entail major questions of law and policy and on which there is considerable professional disagreement among the courts and within the legal profession.[20] The probability of reversal is, of course, highest in the case of nonconsensual appeals.

In 2007, the Judicial Conference of the United States, the primary policy-making arm of the federal courts, urged Congress to create 67 new federal judgeships in appellate and district courts.[21] The conference cited a need for nine permanent and three temporary court of appeals judgeships as well as 44 permanent and 11 temporary district judgeships. As of late-2010 Congress had yet to act on the recommendation. Learn more about criminal appeals in federal courts at **Library Extra 5**.

▲ Protesters in front of the U.S. Supreme Court in 2004. Highlighting its importance as our nation's premier legal institution, the Court became the backdrop for a rally against the USA PATRIOT Act. Protesters claimed that the act unfairly denies foreign terror suspects the right to a quick and impartial hearing. How does the Court serve to balance individual rights and freedoms with the need for public safety and social order?
© William Philpott/Reuters/Corbis

The U.S. Supreme Court

At the apex of the federal court system stands the U.S. Supreme Court. The Supreme Court is located in Washington, D.C., across the street from the U.S. Capitol. The Court consists of nine justices. Eight are associate justices, and the ninth presides over the Court as the chief justice of the United States (Table 1). Supreme Court justices are nominated by the president, are confirmed by the Senate, and serve for life. Lengthy terms of service are a tradition among justices. One of the earliest chief justices, John Marshall, served the Court for 34 years, from 1801 to 1835. The same was true of Justice Stephen J. Field, who sat on the bench between 1863 and 1897. Justice Hugo Black passed the 34-year milestone, serving an additional month before retiring in 1971. Justice William O. Douglas set a record for longevity on the bench, retiring in 1975 after 36 years and six months of service. You can view the biographies of today's Supreme Court justices via **Web Extra 6**.

The Supreme Court of the United States wields immense power. The Court's greatest authority lies in its capacity for **judicial review** of lower-court decisions and state and federal statutes. By exercising its power of judicial review, the Court decides what laws and lower-court decisions are in keeping with the intent of the U.S. Constitution. The power of judicial review is not explicit in the Constitution but was anticipated by its framers. In the *Federalist Papers*, which urged adoption of the Constitution, Alexander Hamilton wrote that through the practice of judicial review, the Court would ensure that "the will of the whole people," as grounded in the Constitution, would be supreme over the "will of the legislature," which might be subject to temporary whims.[22] It was not

judicial review
The power of a court to review actions and decisions made by other agencies of government.

TABLE 1
Justices of the U.S. Supreme Court (as of January 2010)

Justice	Start of Duty	Views
Chief Justice		
John G. Roberts, Jr.	September 2005	Conservative
Associate Justices		
Antonin Scalia	September 1986	Very conservative
Anthony Kennedy	February 1988	Conservative
Clarence Thomas	October 1991	Conservative
Ruth Bader Ginsburg	August 1993	Moderate to liberal
Stephen G. Breyer	August 1994	Moderate
Samuel A. Alito, Jr.	January 2006	Conservative
Sonia M. Sotomayor	August 2009	Moderate to liberal
Elena Kagan	August 2010	Liberal

▲ U.S. Supreme Court Justice Sonia Sotomayor (center) being applauded by President Barack Obama and Vice President Joe Biden at her 2009 nomination to the Court. Do you think that a justice's personal values and beliefs might influence his or her decisions on important matters that come before the court, or do such decisions always result from the impersonal application of relevant law?
Saul Loeb/Agence France Presse/Getty Images

until 1803, however, that the Court forcefully asserted its power of judicial review. In an opinion written for *Marbury* v. *Madison* (1803),[23] Chief Justice John Marshall established the Court's authority as final interpreter of the U.S. Constitution, declaring, "It is emphatically the province of the judicial department to say what the law is."

The Supreme Court Today

The Supreme Court reviews the decisions of lower courts and may accept cases both from U.S. courts of appeal and from state supreme courts. It has limited original jurisdiction and does not conduct trials except for disputes between states and for some cases of attorney disbarment. For a case to be heard, at least four justices must vote in favor of a hearing. When the Court agrees to hear a case, it will issue a writ of *certiorari* to a lower court, ordering it to send the records of the case forward for review. Once having granted *certiorari*, the justices can revoke the decision. In such cases, a writ is dismissed by ruling it improvidently granted.

The U.S. Supreme Court may review any decision appealed to it that it decides is worthy of review. In fact, however, the Court elects to review only cases that involve a substantial federal question. Of approximately 5,000 requests for review received by the Court yearly, only about 200 are actually heard.

A term of the Supreme Court begins, by statute, on the first Monday in October and lasts until early July. The term is divided among sittings, when cases will be heard, and periods of time for the writing and delivering of opinions. Between 22 and 24 cases are heard at each sitting, with each side allotted 30 minutes for arguments before the justices. Intervening recesses allow justices time to study arguments and supporting documentation and to work on their opinions.

Decisions rendered by the Supreme Court are rarely unanimous. Instead, the opinion that a majority of the Court's justices agree on becomes the judgment of the Court. Justices who agree with the Court's judgment write concurring opinions if they agree for a different

▲ Justices of the U.S. Supreme Court gather for a group portrait in Washington, DC, on Friday, Oct. 8, 2010. Seated from left are: Associate Justices Clarence Thomas, Antonin Scalia, Chief Justice John Roberts, Associate Justices Anthony M. Kennedy, and Ruth Bader Ginsburg. Standing, from left are: Associate Justices Sonia Sotomayor, Stephen Breyer, Samuel Alito Jr., and Elena Kagan.
Pablo Martinez Monsivais/AP Wide World Photos

reason than the majority opinion or if they feel that they have some new light to shed on a legal issue involved in the case. Justices who do not agree with the decision of the Court write dissenting opinions, and those dissenting opinions may offer new possibilities for successful appeals at a later date. Visit the U.S. Supreme Court at **Web Extra 7**, and learn more about the federal judiciary at **Library Extra 6**.

Pretrial Activities

The next chapter discusses the steps in a criminal trial and describes the many roles assumed by courtroom participants, including judges, prosecutors, defense attorneys, victims, and defendants. A number of court-related activities, however, routinely take place *before* trial can begin (Figure 4). Although these activities (as well as the names given to them) vary among jurisdictions, they are described generally in the pages that follow.

4 Explain the typical steps taken during pretrial activities, and list the key factors considered by judicial officers in assessing the risks associated with pretrial release.

FIGURE 4 Pretrial Activities

First Appearance

An appearance before a magistrate or lower-court judge for the purpose of:

1. hearing the charges against the defendant
2. rights advisement
3. being given the opportunity to retain a lawyer or to have one appointed
4. possibly being given the opportunity for bail

First appearance must be held within 48 hours after arrest (*McNabb* v. *U.S.* [1943]).

Probable Cause first appearance may involve a probable cause hearing; especially when arrests are made without a warrant. A judicial officer will review police documents and reports to ensure that probable cause supports the arrest.

Pretrial Release If the crime is very serious, or if the defendant is a flight risk, he or she will be held in jail until trial. This is called pretrial detention. The majority of defendants, however, are given the opportunity for release.

Early Intervention Programs These programs supervise defendants and monitor their compliance with release conditions and ensure that they appear for future court hearings. They also gather and present information about defendants and potential dispositional options.

Bail bonds The usual practice is for a defendant to seek bail through a professional bail bondsman. The bondsman will charge a fee (usually 10% to 15% of the bail amount) that the defendant pays up front. The bail bondsman is then responsible for the defendant showing up in court. In many states bail bondsmen are empowered to hunt down and bring back defendants who fail to appear.

Bail is the most common release mechanism. Bail serves two purposes, it helps ensure reapperance of the accused, and it prevents unconvicted persons from suffering imprisonment.

Alternatives to bail

Release on Recognizance (ROR)
Property Bonds
Deposit Bail
Conditional Release
Third-Party Custody
Unsecured Bonds
Signature Bonds

The Grand Jury

Involves the hearing of evidence presented by a district attorney or prosecutor to a group of jurors to determine whether there is sufficient evidence to bring the accused person to trial. An indictment by the grand jury is referred to the trial court and forms the basis for further prosecution.

Arraignment and the Plea

An arraignment is the first appearance of the defendant before the trial court. It offers the defendant an opportunity to enter a plea.

The First Appearance

first appearance
An appearance before a magistrate during which the legality of the defendant's arrest is initially assessed and the defendant is informed of the charges on which he or she is being held. At this stage in the criminal justice process, bail may be set or pretrial release arranged. Also called *initial appearance*.

bail
The money or property pledged to the court or actually deposited with the court to effect the release of a person from legal custody.

Following arrest, most defendants do not come into contact with an officer of the court until their **first appearance** before a magistrate or a lower-court judge.[24] A first appearance, sometimes called an *initial appearance* or *magistrate's review*, occurs when defendants are brought before a judge (1) to be given formal notice of the charges against them, (2) to be advised of their rights, (3) to be given the opportunity to retain a lawyer or to have one appointed to represent them, and (4) to possibly be afforded the opportunity for **bail**.

According to the procedural rules of all jurisdictions, defendants who have been taken into custody must be offered an in-court appearance before a magistrate "without unnecessary delay." The 1943 U.S. Supreme Court case of *McNabb* v. *U.S.*[25] established that any unreasonable delay in an initial court appearance would make confessions inadmissible if interrogating officers obtained them during the delay. Based on the *McNabb* decision, 48 hours following arrest became the standard maximum time by which a first appearance should be held.

The first appearance may also involve a probable cause hearing, although such hearings may be held separately because they do not require the defendant's presence. (In some jurisdictions, the probable cause hearing may be combined with the preliminary hearing.) Probable cause hearings are necessary when arrests are made without a warrant because such arrests do not require a prior judicial determination of probable cause. During a probable cause hearing, also called a *probable cause determination*, a judicial officer will review police documents and reports to ensure that probable cause supported the arrest. The review of the arrest proceeds in a relatively informal fashion, with the judge seeking to decide whether, at the time of apprehension, the arresting officer had reason to believe both (1) that a crime had been or was being committed and (2) that the defendant was the person who committed it. Most of the evidence presented to the judge comes either from the arresting officer or from the victim. If probable cause is not found to exist, the suspect is released. As with a first appearance, a probable cause hearing should take place within 48 hours.

In 1991, in a class-action suit entitled *County of Riverside* v. *McLaughlin*,[26] the U.S. Supreme Court imposed a promptness requirement on probable cause determinations for in-custody arrestees. The Court held that "a jurisdiction that provides judicial determinations of probable cause within 48 hours of arrest will, as a general matter, comply with the promptness requirement." The Court specified, however, that weekends and holidays could not be excluded from the 48-hour requirement (as they had been in Riverside County, California) and that, depending on the specifics of the case, delays of fewer than two days may still be unreasonable.

During a first appearance, the suspect is not given an opportunity to present evidence, although the U.S. Supreme Court has held that defendants are entitled to representation by counsel at their first appearance,[27] and that an indigent person is entitled to have an attorney appointed for him at his initial appearance.[28] Following a reading of the charges and advisement of rights, counsel may be appointed to represent indigent defendants and proceedings may be adjourned until counsel can be obtained. In cases where a suspect is unruly, intoxicated, or uncooperative, a judicial review may occur without the suspect being present.

Some states waive a first appearance and proceed directly to arraignment (discussed later), especially when the defendant has been arrested on a warrant. In states that move directly to arraignment, the procedures undertaken to obtain a warrant are regarded as sufficient to demonstrate a basis for detention before arraignment.

Pretrial Release

pretrial release
The release of an accused person from custody, for all or part of the time before or during prosecution, upon his or her promise to appear in court when required.

A significant aspect of the first appearance hearing is the consideration of **pretrial release**. Defendants charged with very serious crimes, as well as those thought likely to escape or to injure others, are usually held in jail until trial. Such a practice is called *pretrial detention*. The majority of defendants, however, are afforded the opportunity for release. Many jurisdictions make use of pretrial services programs, which may also be called *early intervention programs*.[29] Such programs, which are typically funded by the states or by individual counties,

Multiculturalism and Diversity
The International Criminal Court

On April 12, 2000, the International Criminal Court (ICC) was created under the auspices of the United Nations. The ICC is a permanent criminal court for trying individuals (not countries) who commit the most serious crimes of concern to the international community, such as genocide, war crimes, and crimes against humanity (including the wholesale murder of civilians, torture, and mass rape). The goal of the ICC is to be a global judicial institution with international jurisdiction complementing national legal systems around the world. Support for the ICC was developed through the United Nations. More than 70 countries approved the court's creation by ratifying the Rome Statute of the International Criminal Court. The ICC's first prosecutor, Luis Moreno Ocampo of Argentina, was elected in April 2003, and was still serving in that capacity in late-2010.[1]

The ICC initiative began after World War II with unsuccessful efforts to establish an international tribunal to try individuals accused of war crimes.[2] In lieu of such a court, military tribunals were held in Nuremberg, Germany, and Tokyo, Japan, to try defendants accused of war crimes. Although the 1948 Genocide Convention called for an international criminal court, efforts to establish a permanent court were delayed for decades by the cold war and by the refusal of some national governments to accept the court's proposed international legal jurisdiction.

In December 1948, the UN General Assembly adopted the Universal Declaration of Human Rights and the Convention on the Prevention and Punishment of the Crime of Genocide. It also called for criminals to be tried "by such international penal tribunals as may have jurisdiction." A number of member states soon asked the United Nations International Law Commission (ILC) to study the possibility of establishing an international criminal court.

Development of the ICC was delayed by the cold war that took place between the world's superpowers, which were not willing to subject their military personnel or commanders to international criminal jurisdiction in the event of a "hot" war. In 1981, however, the UN General Assembly asked the ILC to consider creating an international Code of Crimes.

The 1992 war in Bosnia-Herzegovina, which involved clear violations of the Genocide and Geneva Conventions, heightened world interest in the establishment of a permanent ICC. A few years later, 160 countries participated in a UN conference, held in Rome, to establish a criminal court.[3] At the end of that conference, member states voted overwhelmingly in favor of the Rome Statute calling for the establishment of the ICC.

In 2005, in one of the ICC's first official actions, a panel of judges decided to allow independent Dutch investigators to carry out forensic tests in the Democratic Republic of Congo (DRC) as part of an ongoing investigation into the deaths of thousands of people in genocidal violence throughout central Africa.[4] Learn more about these efforts and other activities of the ICC by visiting the International Criminal Court at **Web Extra 7–8.** You can watch video streams of court hearings when the court is in session at **Web Extra 7–9** (some archived streams are also available).

▲ Former UN Secretary-General Kofi Annan speaking at opening ceremonies that marked the signing of the Treaty on Establishment of the International Criminal Court in Rome, Italy, in 1998. What is the jurisdiction of the ICC?
UN/DPI/E. Schneider

[1]See the Coalition for an International Criminal Court, "Building the Court," http://www.iccnow.org/buildingthecourt.html (accessed July 10, 2010).

[2]Much of the information and some of the wording in this box are adapted from "The International Criminal Court Home Page," http://www.icc-cpi.int/menus/icc (accessed October 1, 2010); and the ICC "Timeline," http://www.iccnow.org/html/timeline.htm (accessed April 12, 2010).

[3]The conference was officially known as the Conference of Plenipotentiaries on the Establishment of an International Criminal Court. *Plenipotentiary* is another word for "diplomat."

[4]"Decision of Pre-Trial Chamber I on the Prosecutor's Request under Article 56 of the Rome Statute," ICC press release, April 26, 2005, http://www.icc-cpi.int/press/pressreleases/105.html (accessed May 20, 2008).

perform two critical functions: (1) They gather and present information about newly arrested defendants and about available release options for use by judicial officers in deciding what (if any) conditions are to be set for defendants' release before trial, and (2) they supervise defendants released from custody during the pretrial period by monitoring their compliance with release conditions and by helping to ensure that they appear for scheduled court events. Learn more about pretrial services at **Library Extra 7**.

The initial pretrial release/detention decision is usually made by a judicial officer or by a specially appointed hearing officer after considering the background information provided by the pretrial services program, along with the representations made by the prosecutor and the defense attorney. In making this decision, judicial officers are concerned about two types of risk: (1) the risk of flight or nonappearance for scheduled court appearances and (2) the risk to public safety.

▲ Bounty hunter Duane "Dog" Chapman, owner of Bounty Hunter International and self-proclaimed "greatest bounty hunter in the world." Bounty hunters collect fees from bail bondsmen, who otherwise stand to forfeit the money they posted for clients who do not appear in court. Chapman, an ex-con born-again Christian, makes a living pursuing felons who fail to appear for their court dates after posting bail through a bondsman. He has over 6,000 captures to his credit. Read more about him at http://www.dogthebountyhunter.com. Would you consider work as a bounty hunter?
Jim Ruymen/CORBIS–NY

Bail

Bail is the most common release/detention decision-making mechanism in American courts. Bail serves two purposes: (1) It helps ensure reappearance of the accused, and (2) it prevents unconvicted persons from suffering imprisonment unnecessarily.

Bail involves the posting of a bond as a pledge that the accused will return for further hearings. **Bail bonds** usually involve cash deposits but may be based on property or other valuables. A fully secured bond requires the defendant to post the full amount of bail set by the court. The usual practice, however, is for a defendant to seek privately secured bail through the services of a professional bail bondsman. The bondsman will assess a percentage (usually 10% to 15%) of the required bond as a fee, which the defendant will have to pay up front. Those who "skip bail" by hiding or fleeing will sometimes find that the court has ordered them to forfeit their bail. Forfeiture hearings must be held before a bond can be taken, and most courts will not order bail forfeited unless it appears that the defendant intends to avoid prosecution permanently. Bail forfeiture will often be reversed if the defendant later appears willingly to stand trial.

In many states, bondsmen are empowered to hunt down and bring back defendants who have fled. In some jurisdictions, bondsmen hold virtually unlimited powers and have been permitted by courts to pursue, arrest, and forcibly extradite their charges from foreign jurisdictions without concern for the due process considerations or statutory limitations that apply to law enforcement officers.[30] Recently, however, a number of states have enacted laws that eliminate for-profit bail bond businesses, replacing them instead with state-operated pretrial services agencies. Visit the Professional Bail Agents of the United States at **Web Extra 10** to learn more about the job of bail bondsman and to view the group's code of ethics.

bail bond
A document guaranteeing the appearance of a defendant in court as required and recording the pledge of money or property to be paid to the court if he or she does not appear. The bail bond is signed by the person to be released and by anyone else acting in his or her behalf.

Alternatives to Bail

The Eighth Amendment to the U.S. Constitution does not guarantee the opportunity for bail but does state that "[e]xcessive bail shall not be required." Some studies, however, have found that many defendants who are offered the opportunity for bail are unable to raise the money. Years ago, a report by the National Advisory Commission on Criminal Justice Standards and Goals found that as many as 93% of felony defendants in some jurisdictions were unable to make bail.[31]

To extend the opportunity for pretrial release to a greater proportion of nondangerous arrestees, a number of states and the federal government now make available various alternatives to the cash bond system. Alternatives include (1) release on recognizance, (2) property bond, (3) deposit bail, (4) conditional release, (5) third-party custody, (6) unsecured bond, and (7) signature bond.

Release on Recognizance (ROR)

release on recognizance (ROR)
The pretrial release of a criminal defendant on his or her written promise to appear in court as required. No cash or property bond is required.

Release on recognizance (ROR) involves no cash bond, requiring as a guarantee only that the defendant agree in writing to return for further hearings as specified by the court. As an alternative to a cash bond, ROR was tested during the 1960s in a social experiment called the Manhattan Bail Project.[32] In the experiment, not all defendants were eligible for release on their own recognizance; those arrested for serious crimes, including murder, rape, and robbery, and defendants with extensive prior criminal records were excluded from participating in the project. The rest of the defendants were scored and categorized according to a number of "ideal" criteria used as indicators of both dangerousness and likelihood of pretrial flight. Criteria included (1) no previous convictions, (2) residential stability, and (3) good employment record. Those likely to flee were not released.

Studies of the bail project revealed that it released four times as many defendants before trial as had been freed under the traditional cash bond system.[33] Even more surprising was the finding that only 1% of those released fled from prosecution—the same percentage as for those set free on cash bonds.[34] Later studies, however, were unclear as to the effectiveness of ROR, with some finding a no-show rate as high as 12%.[35]

Property Bonds

Property bonds substitute other items of value in place of cash. Land, houses, automobiles, stocks, and so on may be consigned to the court as collateral against pretrial flight.

property bond
The setting of bail in the form of land, houses, stocks, or other tangible property. In the event that the defendant absconds before trial, the bond becomes the property of the court.

Deposit Bail

Deposit bail, an alternative form of cash bond available in some jurisdictions, places the court in the role of the bondsman, allowing the defendant to post a percentage of the full bail with the court. Unlike private bail bondsmen, court-run deposit bail programs usually return the amount of the deposit except for a small administrative fee (perhaps 1%). If the defendant fails to appear for court, the entire amount of court-ordered bail is forfeited.

Conditional Release

Conditional release imposes a set of requirements on the defendant that might include participation in a drug-treatment program; staying away from specified others, such as potential witnesses; and attendance at a regular job. *Release under supervision* is similar to conditional release but adds the stipulation that defendants report to an officer of the court or to a police officer at designated times.

See CJ Exhibit 1 for a discussion of the different people and systems involved in making pretrial release decisions.

We are under a Constitution, but the Constitution is what the judges say it is, and the judiciary is the safeguard of our liberty and of our property under the Constitution.

—Charles Evans Hughes, eleventh chief justice of the United States

Third-Party Custody

Third-party custody is a bail bond alternative that assigns custody of the defendant to an individual or agency that promises to ensure his or her later appearance in court.[36] Some pretrial release programs allow attorneys to assume responsibility for their clients in this fashion. If a defendant fails to appear, the attorney's privilege to participate in the program may be ended.

Unsecured Bonds

Unsecured bonds are based on a court-determined dollar amount of bail. Like a credit contract, this bail alternative requires no monetary deposit with the court. The defendant agrees in writing that failure to appear will result in forfeiture of the entire amount of the bond, which might then be taken in seizures of land, personal property, bank accounts, and so on.

Signature Bonds

Signature bonds allow release based on the defendant's written promise to appear. Signature bonds involve no particular assessment of the defendant's dangerousness or likelihood of later appearance in court. They are used only in cases of minor offenses, such as traffic-law violations and some petty drug-law violations. Signature bonds may be issued by the arresting officer acting on behalf of the court.

Pretrial Release and Public Safety

Pretrial release is common practice. Approximately 57% of all state-level felony defendants[37] and 66% of all federal felony defendants[38] are released before trial (Figure 5). At the state level, 43% of all defendants are detained until the court disposes of their case. Murder defendants (88%) are the most likely to be detained. A majority of defendants charged with motor vehicle theft (61%), robbery (58%), or burglary (54%) are also detained until case disposition. Defendants on parole (83%) were the most likely to be detained.

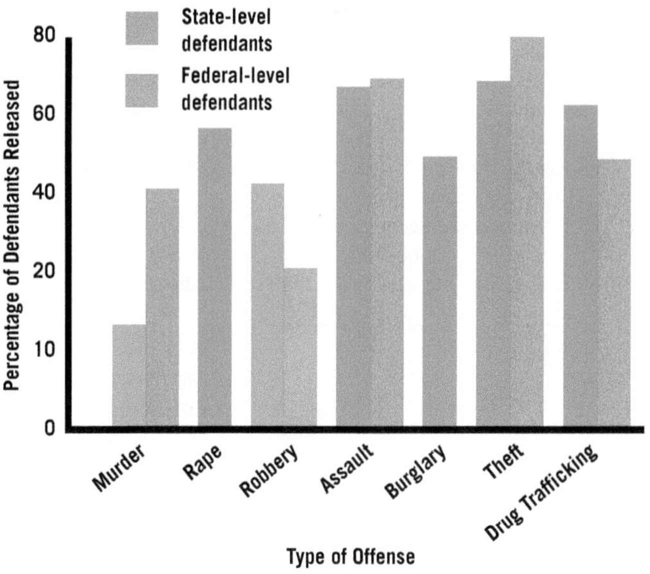

FIGURE 5
Proportion of State and Federal Felony Defendants Released before Trial

Note: Federal pretrial release statistics are not available for the crimes of rape and burglary.
Sources: Tracey Kyckelhahn and Thomas H. Cohen, *Felony Defendants in Large Urban Counties, 2004* (Washington, DC: Bureau of Justice Statistics, 2008); and Thomas H. Cohen and Brian A. Reaves, *Pretrial Release of Felony Defendants in State Courts* (Washington, DC: Bureau of Justice Statistics, 2007).

CJ Exhibit 1
Nonjudicial Pretrial Release Decisions

In most American jurisdictions, judicial officers decide whether an arrested person will be detained or released. Some jurisdictions, however, allow others to make that decision. Some observers argue that the critical issue is not whether the decision maker is a judge but whether there are clear and appropriate criteria for making the decision, whether the decision maker has adequate information, and whether he or she has been well trained in pretrial release/detention decision making. Nonjudicial decision makers and release/detention mechanisms include the following:

- *Police officers and desk appearance tickets.* Desk appearance tickets, or citations, are summonses given to defendants at the police station, usually for petty offenses or misdemeanor charges. The tickets can greatly reduce the use of pretrial detention and can save the court system a great deal of time by avoiding initial pretrial release or bail hearings in minor cases. However, because they are typically based only on the current charge (and sometimes on a computer search to check for outstanding warrants), high-risk defendants could be released without supervision or monitoring. As computerized access to more criminal history information becomes available, enabling rapid identification of individuals with prior records who pose a risk to the community, desk appearance tickets may be more widely used.
- *Jail administrators.* In many jurisdictions, jail officials have the authority to release (or to refuse to book into jail) arrestees who meet certain criteria. In some localities, jail officials exercise this authority pursuant to a court order that specifies priorities with respect to the categories of defendants who can be admitted to the jail and those who are to be released when the jail population exceeds a court-imposed ceiling. The "automatic release" approach helps minimize jail crowding, but it does so at the risk of releasing some defendants who pose a high risk of becoming fugitives or committing criminal acts. To help minimize these risks, some sheriffs and jail administrators have developed their own pretrial services or "release on recognizance" units with staff who conduct risk assessments based on interviews with arrestees, information from references, and criminal history checks.
- *Bail schedules.* These predetermined schedules set levels of bail (from release on recognizance to amounts of surety bond) based solely on the offense charged. Depending on local practices, release pursuant to a bail schedule may take place at a police station, at the local jail, or at court. This practice saves time for judicial officers and allows the rapid release of defendants who can afford to post the bail amount. However, release determinations based solely on the current charge are of dubious value because there is no proven relationship between a particular charge and the risk of flight or subsequent crime. Release pursuant to a bail schedule depends simply on the defendant's ability to post the amount of the bond; moreover, when a defendant is released by posting bond, there is generally no procedure for supervision to minimize the risks of nonappearance and subsequent crime.
- *Bail bondsmen.* When a judicial officer sets the amount of bond that a defendant must produce to be released or when bond is set mechanically on the basis of a bail schedule, the real decision makers are often the surety bail bondsmen. If no bondsman will offer bond, the defendant without other sources of money remains in jail. The defendant's ability to pay a bondsman the 10% fee (and sometimes to post collateral) bears no relationship to his or her risk of flight or danger to the community.
- *Pretrial services agencies.* In some jurisdictions, pretrial services agencies have authority to release certain categories of defendants. The authority is usually limited to relatively minor cases, although agencies in a few jurisdictions can release some categories of felony defendants. Because the pretrial services agency can obtain information about the defendant's prior record, community ties, and other pending charges, its decision to release or detain is based on more extensive information and criteria than when the decision is based on a bail schedule. However, because these programs lack the independence of judicial officers, they can be targets of political and public pressure.

Source: Adapted from Barry Mahoney et al., *Pretrial Services Programs: Responsibilities and Potential* (Washington, DC: National Institute of Justice, 2001).

A growing movement, arguing that defendants released before trial may be dangerous to themselves or to others, seeks to reduce the number of defendants released under any conditions. Advocates of this conservative policy cite a number of studies documenting crimes committed by defendants released on bond. One study found that 16% of defendants released before trial were rearrested, and of those, 30% were arrested more than once.[39] Another study determined that as many as 41% of those released before trial for serious crimes, such as rape and robbery, were rearrested before their trial date.[40] Not surprisingly, such studies generally find that the longer the time spent out on bail before trial, the greater the likelihood of misconduct.

danger law
A law intended to prevent the pretrial release of criminal defendants judged to represent a danger to others in the community.

In response to findings like these, some states have enacted **danger laws**, which limit the right to bail to certain kinds of offenders.[41] Other states, including Arizona, California, Colorado, Florida, and Illinois, have approved constitutional amendments restricting the use of bail.[42] Most such provisions exclude defendants charged with certain crimes from being eligible for bail and mandate that other defendants being considered for bail meet stringent conditions. Some states combine these strictures with tough release conditions designed to keep close control over defendants before trial.

▲ A grand jury in action. Grand jury proceedings are generally very informal, as this picture shows. What is the grand jury's job?
David Young-Wolff/Getty Images, Inc./Riser

The 1984 federal Bail Reform Act allows federal judges to assess the danger of an accused to the community and to deny bail to defendants who are thought to be dangerous. In the words of the act, a suspect held in pretrial custody on federal criminal charges must be detained if "after a hearing . . . he is found to pose a risk of flight and a danger to others or the community and if no condition of release can give reasonable assurances against these contingencies."[43] Defendants seeking bail must demonstrate a high likelihood of later court appearance. The act also requires that a defendant have a speedy first appearance and that a detention hearing be held in conjunction with the initial appearance if he or she is to be detained.

In the 1990 case of *U.S.* v. *Montalvo-Murillo*,[44] however, a defendant who was not provided with a detention hearing at the time of his first appearance and was subsequently released by an appeals court was found to have no "right" to freedom because of this "minor" statutory violation. The Supreme Court held that "unless it has a substantial influence on the outcome of the proceedings . . . failure to comply with the Act's prompt hearing provision does not require release of a person who should otherwise be detained" because "[a]utomatic release contravenes the statutory purpose of providing fair bail procedures while protecting the public's safety and assuring a defendant's appearance at trial."[45]

> I have tried to minimize what I feel is one of the less desirable aspects of the job . . . that judges can become isolated from the people whose lives their decisions affect.
>
> —Stephen Breyer, U.S. Supreme Court justice

Court challenges to the constitutionality of pretrial detention legislation have not met with much success. The U.S. Supreme Court case of *U.S.* v. *Hazzard* (1984),[46] decided only a few months after enactment of federal bail reform, held that Congress was justified in providing for denial of bail to offenders who represent a danger to the community. Later cases have supported the presumption of flight, which federal law presupposes for certain types of defendants.[47]

The Grand Jury

The federal government and about half of the states use grand juries as part of the pretrial process. **Grand juries** comprise private citizens (often 23 in number) who hear evidence presented by the prosecution. Grand juries serve primarily as filters to eliminate from further processing any cases for which there is not sufficient evidence.

grand jury
A group of jurors who have been selected according to law and have been sworn to hear the evidence and to determine whether there is sufficient evidence to bring the accused person to trial, to investigate criminal activity generally, or to investigate the conduct of a public agency or official.

In early times, grand juries served a far different purpose. The grand jury system began in England in 1166 as a way of identifying law violators. Lacking a law enforcement agency with investigative authority, the government looked to the grand jury as a source of information on criminal activity in the community. Even today, grand juries in most jurisdictions may initiate prosecution independently of the prosecutor, although they rarely do.

Grand jury hearings are held in secret, and the defendant is generally not afforded the opportunity to appear before the grand jury.[48] Similarly, the defense has no opportunity to cross-examine prosecution witnesses. Grand juries have the power to subpoena witnesses and to mandate a review of books, records, and other documents crucial to their investigation.

After hearing the evidence, the grand jury votes on the **indictment** (a formal listing of proposed charges) presented to it by the prosecution. If the majority of grand jury members agree to forward the indictment to the trial court, it becomes a "true bill" on which further prosecution will turn.

indictment
A formal written accusation submitted to the court by a grand jury, alleging that a specified person has committed a specified offense, usually a felony.

The Preliminary Hearing

preliminary hearing
A proceeding before a judicial officer in which three matters must be decided: (1) whether a crime was committed, (2) whether the crime occurred within the territorial jurisdiction of the court, and (3) whether there are reasonable grounds to believe that the defendant committed the crime.

information
A formal written accusation submitted to a court by a prosecutor, alleging that a specified person has committed a specified offense.

States that do not use grand juries rely instead on a **preliminary hearing** "for charging defendants in a fashion that is less cumbersome and arguably more protective of the innocent."[49] In these jurisdictions, the prosecutor files an accusatory document called an **information**, or complaint, against the accused. A preliminary hearing is then held to determine whether there is probable cause to hold the defendant for trial. A few states, notably Georgia and Tennessee, use both the grand jury mechanism and a preliminary hearing as a "double check against the possibility of unwarranted prosecution."[50]

Although the preliminary hearing is not nearly as elaborate as a criminal trial, it has many of the same characteristics. The defendant is taken before a lower-court judge, who summarizes the charges and reviews the rights to which all criminal defendants are entitled. The prosecution may present witnesses and offers evidence in support of the complaint. The defendant is afforded the right to testify and may also call witnesses.

competent to stand trial
A finding by a court, when the defendant's sanity at the time of trial is at issue, that the defendant has sufficient present ability to consult with his or her attorney with a reasonable degree of rational understanding and that the defendant has a rational as well as factual understanding of the proceedings against him or her.

The primary purpose of the preliminary hearing is to give the defendant an opportunity to challenge the legal basis for his or her detention. At this point, defendants who appear to be or claim to be mentally incompetent may be ordered to undergo further evaluation to determine whether they are competent to stand trial. Being **competent to stand trial** may become an issue when a defendant appears to be incapable of understanding the proceedings or is unable to assist in his or her own defense due to mental disease or defect.

In 2003, the U.S. Supreme Court placed strict limits on the government's power to forcibly medicate some mentally ill defendants to make them competent to stand trial.[51] In the case of *Sell* v. *U.S.*,[52] the Court ruled that the use of antipsychotic drugs on a nonviolent offender who does not represent a danger while institutionalized must be in the defendant's best medical interest and be "substantially unlikely" to cause side effects that might compromise the fairness of the trial.

Barring a finding of mental incompetence, all that is required for the wheels of justice to grind forward is a demonstration "sufficient to justify a prudent man's belief that the suspect has committed or was committing an offense" within the jurisdiction of the court.[53] If the magistrate finds enough evidence to justify a trial, the defendant is bound over to the grand jury. In states that do not require grand jury review, the defendant is sent directly to the trial court. If the complaint against the defendant cannot be substantiated during the preliminary hearing, he or she is released. A release is not a bar to further prosecution, however, and the defendant may be rearrested if further evidence comes to light.

Arraignment and the Plea

arraignment
Strictly, the hearing before a court having jurisdiction in a criminal case in which the identity of the defendant is established, the defendant is informed of the charge and of his or her rights, and the defendant is required to enter a plea. Also, in some usages, any appearance in criminal court before trial.

plea
In criminal proceedings, the defendant's formal answer in court to the charge contained in a complaint, information, or indictment that he or she is guilty of the offense charged, is not guilty of the offense charged, or does not contest the charge.

nolo contendere
A plea of "no contest." A no-contest plea is used when the defendant does not wish to contest conviction. Because the plea does not admit guilt, however, it cannot provide the basis for later civil suits that might follow a criminal conviction.

Arraignment

Once an indictment has been returned or an information has been filed, the accused will be formally arraigned. **Arraignment** is "the first appearance of the defendant before the court that has the authority to conduct a trial."[54] Arraignment is generally a brief process with two purposes: (1) to once again inform the defendant of the specific charges against him or her and (2) to allow the defendant to enter a **plea**. The Federal Rules of Criminal Procedure allow for one of three types of pleas to be entered: guilty, not guilty, and *nolo contendere*. A ***nolo contendere*** (no-contest) plea is much the same as a guilty plea. A defendant who pleads "no contest" is immediately convicted and may be sentenced just as though he or she had pleaded guilty. A no-contest plea, however, is not an admission of guilt and provides one major advantage to defendants: It may not be used later as a basis for civil proceedings that seek monetary or other damages against the defendant.

Some defendants refuse to enter any plea and are said to "stand mute." Standing mute is a defense strategy that is rarely employed. Defendants who choose this alternative simply do not answer the request for a plea; however, for procedural purposes, a defendant who stands mute is considered to have entered a plea of not guilty.

Plea Bargaining

Guilty pleas often are not as straightforward as they might seem and are typically arrived at only after complex negotiations. **Plea bargaining** is a process of negotiation that usually involves the defendant, the prosecutor, and the defense counsel and is founded on the mutual interests of all involved. Defense attorneys and their clients will agree to a plea of guilty when they are unsure of their ability to win acquittal at trial. Prosecutors may be willing to bargain because the evidence they have against the defendant is weaker than they would like it to be. Plea bargaining offers prosecutors the additional advantage of a quick conviction without the need to commit the time and resources necessary for trial. Benefits to the accused include the possibility of reduced or combined charges, reduced defense costs, and a shorter sentence than might otherwise be anticipated.

plea bargaining
The process of negotiating an agreement among the defendant, the prosecutor, and the court as to an appropriate plea and associated sentence in a given case. Plea bargaining circumvents the trial process and dramatically reduces the time required for the resolution of a criminal case.

The U.S. Supreme Court has held that a guilty plea constitutes conviction.[55] To validate the conviction, negotiated pleas require judicial consent. Judges often accept pleas that are the result of a bargaining process because such pleas reduce the court's workload. Although few judges are willing to guarantee a sentence before a plea is entered, most prosecutors and criminal trial lawyers know what sentences to expect from typical pleas.

Bargained pleas are commonplace. Some surveys have found that 90% of all criminal cases prepared for trial are eventually resolved through a negotiated plea.[56] In a study of 37 big-city prosecutors, the Bureau of Justice Statistics found that for every 100 adults arrested on a felony charge, half were eventually convicted of either a felony or a misdemeanor.[57] Of all convictions, fully 94% were the result of a plea; only 6% of convictions were the result of a criminal trial. After a guilty plea has been entered, it may be withdrawn with the consent of the court.

Some Supreme Court decisions, however, have enhanced the prosecutor's authority in the bargaining process by declaring that defendants cannot capriciously withdraw negotiated pleas.[58] Other rulings have supported discretionary actions by prosecutors in which sentencing recommendations were retracted even after bargains had been struck.[59] Some lower-court cases have upheld the government's authority to withdraw from a negotiated plea when the defendant fails to live up to certain conditions.[60] Conditions may include requiring the defendant to provide information on other criminals, on criminal cartels, or on activities of smugglers.

Although it is generally agreed that bargained pleas should relate in some way to the original charges, this is not always the case. Entered pleas may be chosen for the punishments likely to be associated with them rather than for their accuracy in describing the criminal offenses in which the defendants were involved.[61] This is especially true when the defendant wants to minimize the socially stigmatizing impact of the offense. For example, a charge of indecent liberties, in which the defendant is accused of sexual misconduct, may be pleaded out as assault. Such a plea, which takes advantage of the fact that indecent liberties can be considered a form of sexual assault, would effectively disguise the true nature of the offense.

Even though the Supreme Court has endorsed plea bargaining, the public sometimes views it suspiciously. Law-and-order advocates, who generally favor harsh punishments and long jail terms, claim that plea bargaining results in unjustifiably light sentences. As a consequence, prosecutors who regularly engage in the practice rarely advertise it. Plea bargaining can be a powerful prosecutorial tool, but this power carries with it the potential for misuse. Because they circumvent the trial process, plea bargains can be abused by prosecutors and defense attorneys who are more interested in the speedy resolution of cases than they are in seeing justice done. Carried to the extreme, plea bargaining may result in defendants being convicted of crimes they did not commit. Although it is rare, innocent defendants (especially those with prior criminal records) who think a jury will convict them—for whatever reason—may plead guilty to reduced charges to avoid a trial. In an effort to protect defendants against hastily arranged pleas, the Federal Rules of Criminal Procedure require judges to (1) inform the defendant of the various rights he or she is surrendering by pleading guilty, (2) determine that the plea is voluntary, (3) disclose any plea agreements, and (4) make sufficient inquiry to ensure there is a factual basis for the plea.[62]

There is no such thing as justice—in or out of court.
—Clarence Darrow (1857-1938)

Bargained pleas can take many forms and can be quite inventive. The case of Jeffrey Morse illustrates an unusual attempt at a bargained plea. In 1998, Morse, a convicted sex offender, petitioned courts in Illinois for permission to leave jail before sentencing for sexual assaults on two young girls so that he could undergo surgical castration. A judge agreed, and he was surgically castrated in a 45-minute outpatient procedure. Morse's mother noted that the surgery was done in an effort to avoid a long prison sentence. "He will cut whatever bodily part he has to [to] be able to reduce his sentence," she said.[63] Two months later, however, Kane County Judge Donald C. Hudson refused to show leniency for Morse. The judge sentenced Morse to 26 years in prison, saying that he wouldn't "place a seal of approval on trading body parts for a lesser sentence."[64]

Summary

THE COURTS

- In the United States, there are two judicial systems. One consists of state and local courts established under the authority of state and local governments. The other is the federal court system, created by Congress under the authority of the U.S. Constitution. This dual-court system historically results from general agreement among the nation's founders about the need for individual states to retain significant legislative authority and judicial autonomy separate from federal control.
- In most states, criminal courts can be classified within a three-tiered structure of two trial court echelons and an appellate level. There are many differences between and among state court systems, however. So-called reform states are characterized by relatively streamlined judicial systems consisting of trial courts of limited and general jurisdiction, supplemented by one or two appellate court levels. Nonreform, or traditional, states tend to retain judicial systems that are a conglomeration of multilevel and sometimes redundant courts with poorly defined jurisdictions. Regardless of their organizational style, state courts have virtually unlimited power to decide nearly every type of case, subject only to limitations imposed by the U.S. Constitution, their own state constitutions, and state law.
- Today's federal judiciary consists of three levels: (1) U.S. district courts, (2) U.S. courts of appeal, and (3) the U.S. Supreme Court. Federal courts, located principally in larger cities, decide only those cases over which the Constitution gives them authority. The highest federal court, the U.S. Supreme Court, is located in Washington, D.C., and hears cases only on appeal from lower courts.
- Pretrial activities involve the first appearance, the grand jury hearing (in some states), the preliminary hearing, the arraignment, and the plea, all of which are described in this chapter. Before trial, one of the most important decisions facing the courts is that of pretrial release. In considering whether a criminal defendant should be released prior to trial, courts must balance the rights of the unconvicted defendant against the potential for future harm that person may represent.

QUESTIONS FOR REVIEW

1. How did the American court system develop? What are some of the unique features of American court history? What is the dual-court system? Why do we have a dual-court system in America?
2. How is a typical state court system structured? What different types of courts might exist at the state level, and what kinds of jurisdiction might they have?
3. What are the three levels characteristic of the federal judiciary? What are some of the differences between the state and federal court systems in America?
4. What steps are typically taken before the start of a criminal trial?

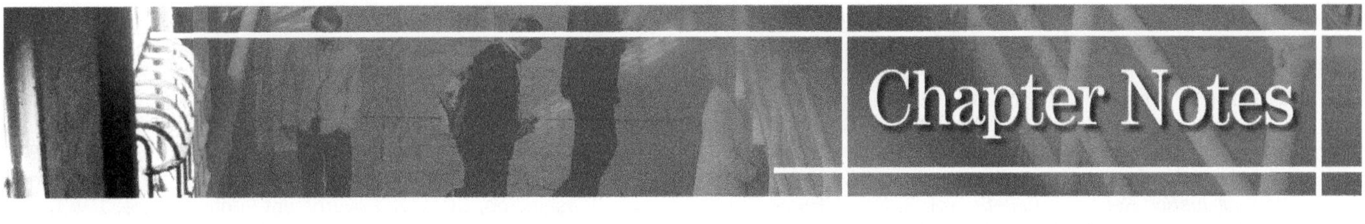

Chapter Notes

1. *The Challenge of Crime in a Free Society: Report of The President's Commission on Law Enforcement and the Administration of Justice* (Washington, DC: USGPO, 1967), p. 125.
2. John Mattes, "Motives for Bombing Downtown Federal Courthouse?" August 8, 2008, http://www.sandiego6.com/content/unit6/story/Motives-for-Bombing-Downtown-Federal-Courthouse/ZGo7RgwzaUagS6XDW7cypQ.cspx (accessed July 1, 2010).
3. Law Enforcement Assistance Administration, *Two Hundred Years of American Criminal Justice* (Washington, DC: U.S. Government Printing Office, 1976), p. 31.
4. David B. Rottman, Carol R. Flango, and R. Shedine Lockley, *State Court Organization, 1993* (Washington, DC: Bureau of Justice Statistics, 1995), p. 11.
5. In 1957, only 13 states had permanent intermediate appellate courts. Now, all but 12 states have these courts, and North Dakota is operating one on a temporary basis to assist in handling the rising appellate caseload in that state. See Rottman, Flango, and Lockley, *State Court Organization, 1993*, p. 5.
6. *Keeney* v. *Tamayo-Reyes*, 504 U.S. 1 (1992).
7. *Herrera* v. *Collins*, 113 S.Ct. 853, 122 L.Ed.2d 203 (1993).
8. Martin Wright, *Justice for Victims and Offenders* (Bristol, PA: Open University Press, 1991), p. 56.
9. "Bridging the Gap between Communities and Courts," http://www.communityjustice.org (accessed November 22, 2010).
10. Wright, *Justice for Victims and Offenders*, pp. 104 and 106.
11. Most of the information and some of the wording in this section come from Administrative Office of the U.S. Courts, "Understanding the Federal Courts," http://www.uscourts.gov/UFC99.pdf (accessed April 2, 2010).
12. Administrative Office of the U.S. Courts, "U.S. District Courts: Criminal Cases and Defendants Filed, Terminated, Pending," http://www.uscourts.gov/uscourts/Statistics/JudicialFactsAndFigures/2008/Table501.pdf (accessed August 4, 2010).
13. Administrative Office of the U.S. Courts, "U.S. District Courts: Civil Cases Filed, Terminated, Pending," http://www.uscourts.gov/uscourts/Statistics/JudicialFactsAndFigures/2008/Table401.pdf (accessed August 4, 2010).
14. Administrative Office of the U.S. Courts, "Federal Judicial Pay Increase Fact Sheet," http://www.uscourts.gov/JudgesAndJudgeships/JudicialCompensation/JudicialPayIncreaseFact.aspx (accessed August 4, 2010).
15. Administrative Office of the U.S. Courts, "Comparison of Average Salaries of Deans and Senior Professors of Top Law Schools with U.S. District Court Judges," http://www.uscourts.gov/judicialcompensation/payfactsheet.html, no date (accessed July 30, 2010).
16. See American Bar Association, *Federal Judicial Pay Erosion: A Report on the Need for Reform* (Chicago: ABA, 2001).
17. Although the Ethics Reform Act of 1989 was supposed to allow for a cost-of-living increase in federal judicial salaries, Congress blocked the automatic increases from 1995 to 1999 because they also applied to the salaries of members of Congress and were seen as politically unpalatable.
18. Justice John Roberts, "2005 Year-End Report on the Federal Judiciary," *The Third Branch*, Vol. 38, No. 1 (January 2006), http://www.uscourts.gov/ttb/jan06ttb/yearend/index.html (accessed March 30, 2008).
19. Much of the information and some of the wording in this section come from Administrative Office of the U.S. Courts, "About the Federal Courts," www.uscourts.gov/about.html (accessed October 4, 2010).
20. Stephen L. Wasby, *The Supreme Court in the Federal Judicial System*, 3rd ed. (Chicago: Nelson-Hall, 1988), p. 58.
21. Administrative Office of the U.S. Courts, "Federal Judiciary Says New Judgeships Needed," March 13, 2007, http://www.uscourts.gov/Press_Releases/judconf031307.html (accessed September 5, 2008).
22. *The Supreme Court of the United States* (Washington, DC: U.S. Government Printing Office, n.d.). p. 4.
23. *Marbury* v. *Madison*, 1 Cranch 137 (1803).
24. *Arraignment* is also a term used to describe an initial appearance, although we will reserve use of that word to describe a later court appearance following the defendant's indictment by a grand jury or the filing of an information by the prosecutor.
25. *McNabb* v. *U.S.*, 318 U.S. 332 (1943).
26. *County of Riverside* v. *McLaughlin*, 111 S.Ct. 1661 (1991).
27. *White* v. *Maryland*, 373 U.S. 59 (1963).
28. *Rothgery* v. *Gillespie County, Texas*, 554 U.S. _ (2008).
29. Much of the information in this section comes from Barry Mahoney et al., *Pretrial Services Programs: Responsibilities and Potential* (Washington, DC: National Institute of Justice, 2001).
30. *Taylor* v. *Taintor*, 83 U.S. 66 (1873).
31. National Advisory Commission on Criminal Justice Standards and Goals, *The Courts* (Washington, DC: U.S. Government Printing Office, 1973), p. 37.
32. C. Ares, A. Rankin, and H. Sturz, "The Manhattan Bail Project: An Interim Report on the Use of Pretrial Parole," *New York University Law Review*, Vol. 38 (January 1963), pp. 68–95.
33. H. Zeisel, "Bail Revisited," *American Bar Foundation Research Journal*, Vol. 4 (1979), pp. 769–789.
34. Ibid.
35. "Twelve Percent of Those Freed on Low Bail Fail to Appear," *New York Times*, December 2, 1983.
36. Bureau of Justice Statistics, *Report to the Nation on Crime and Justice*, 2nd ed. (Washington, DC: U.S. Department of Justice, 1988), p. 76.
37. Tracey Kyckelhahn and Thomas H. Cohen, *Felony Defendants in Large Urban Counties, 2004* (Washington, DC: Bureau of Justice Statistics, 2008), p. 2, http://www.ojp.gov/bjs/pub/pdf/fdluc04.pdf (accessed June 4, 2010). See also Thomas H. Cohen and Brian A. Reaves, *Pretrial Release of Felony Defendants in State Courts* (Washington, DC: Bureau of Justice Statistics, 2007).
38. Thomas H. Cohen and Brian A. Reaves, *Pretrial Release of Felony Defendants in State Courts* (Washington, DC: Bureau of Justice Statistics, 2007).
39. Donald E. Pryor and Walter F. Smith, "Significant Research Findings Concerning Pretrial Release," *Pretrial Issues*, Vol. 4, No. 1 (Washington, DC: Pretrial Services Resource Center,

February 1982). See also the Pretrial Justice Institute on the Web at http://www.pretrial.org/Pages.
40. BJS, *Report to the Nation on Crime and Justice*, p. 77.
41. According to Joseph B. Vaughn and Victor E. Kappeler, the first such legislation was the 1970 District of Columbia Court Reform and Criminal Procedure Act. See Vaughn and Kappeler, "The Denial of Bail: Pre-trial Preventive Detention," *Criminal Justice Research Bulletin*, Vol. 3, No. 6 (Huntsville, TX: Sam Houston State University, 1987), p. 1.
42. Ibid.
43. Bail Reform Act of 1984, 18 U.S.C. 3142(e).
44. *U.S.* v. *Montalvo-Murillo*, 495 U.S. 711 (1990).
45. Ibid., syllabus.
46. *U.S.* v. *Hazzard*, 35 CrL. 2217 (1984).
47. See, for example, *U.S.* v. *Motamedi*, 37 CrL. 2394, CA 9 (1985).
48. A few states now have laws that permit the defendant to appear before the grand jury.
49. John M. Scheb and John M. Scheb II, *American Criminal Law* (St. Paul, MN: West, 1996), p. 31.
50. Ibid.
51. The information in this paragraph is adapted from Linda Greenhouse, "Supreme Court Limits Forced Medication of Some for Trial," *New York Times*, June 16, 2003, http://www.nytimes.com/2003/06/17/politics/17DRUG.html (accessed June 17, 2003).
52. *Sell* v. *U.S.*, 123 S.Ct. 2174 (2003).
53. Federal Rules of Criminal Procedure, Rule 5.1(a).
54. Scheb and Scheb, *American Criminal Law*, p. 32.
55. *Kercheval* v. *U.S.*, 274 U.S. 220, 223, 47 S.Ct. 582, 583 (1927); *Boykin* v. *Alabama*, 395 U.S. 238 (1969); and *Dickerson* v. *New Banner Institute, Inc.*, 460 U.S. 103 (1983).
56. Bureau of Justice Statistics, *The Prosecution of Felony Arrests* (Washington, DC: U.S. Government Printing Office, 1983).
57. Barbara Boland et al., *The Prosecution of Felony Arrests, 1987* (Washington, DC: U.S. Government Printing Office, May 1990).
58. *Santobello* v. *New York*, 404 U.S. 257 (1971).
59. *Mabry* v. *Johnson*, 467 U.S. 504 (1984).
60. *U.S.* v. *Baldacchino*, 762 F.2d 170 (1st Cir. 1985); *U.S.* v. *Reardon*, 787 F.2d 512 (10th Cir. 1986); and *U.S.* v. *Donahey*, 529 F.2d 831 (11th Cir. 1976).
61. For a classic discussion of such considerations, see David Sudnow, "Normal Crimes: Sociological Features of the Penal Code in a Public Defender Office," *Social Problems*, Vol. 123, No. 3 (winter 1965), p. 255.
62. Federal Rules of Criminal Procedure, No. 11.
63. "A Desperate Act," *Prime Time Live*, ABCNews.com, January 28, 1998, http://archive.abcnews.go.com/onair/PTL/html-files/transcripts/ptl0128c.html (accessed July 21, 2001).
64. Dan Rozek, "Castration Doesn't Gain Leniency for Pedophile," *Chicago Sun-Times*, March 4, 1998.

The Courtroom Work Group and the Criminal Trial

Learning Objectives

After reading this chapter, you should be able to:

1. Identify and explain the roles of professional members of the courtroom work group.
2. Identify and explain the roles of nonprofessional or nonjudicial courtroom participants.
3. Describe the nature and purpose of the criminal trial.
4. Identify the various stages of a criminal trial.

"... in the jury room, ... you learn that justice doesn't merely happen (neatly, reliably, like a crystal taking shape in a distant vacuum); justice is, rather, done, made, manufactured. Made by imperfect, wrangling, venal and virtuous human beings, using whatever means are at their disposal."

—D. Graham Burnett, jury foreman[1]

Stan Rohrer/Alamy

Introduction

> The American criminal justice system is theater to the world.
> —Alan Dershowitz, Harvard University

On January 25, 2010, 23-year-old Casey Anthony pleaded guilty in an Orange County (Florida) courtroom to 13 charges involving check fraud, including one count of grand theft, four counts of check forgery, and other charges of fraudulent use of personal identification. The plea cleared the way for Anthony's attorneys to devote more of their efforts to defending her on first-degree murder charges in the death of her two-year-old daughter, Caylee Marie Anthony, who was reported missing on June 15, 2008, by her grandmother—a month after her mother later said she had disappeared.[2] According to prosecutors and law enforcement officials, Casey told a string of lies about her daughter's disappearance, and in October 2008, with Caylee still missing, she was charged with first-degree murder. Prosecutors also charged Casey with aggravated child abuse, aggravated manslaughter, and providing false information to law enforcement officers. Two months after the charges were brought, a utility worker found Caylee's remains among cloth laundry and plastic trash bags near her home. Glittery pink letters that spelled out the phrase "Big Trouble Comes Small" were found with the remains and appear to have been on the shirt that Caylee was wearing at the time of her death. Casey Anthony's trial is set to begin as this book goes to press. Keep up with the latest in the case at **Web Extra 1**.

The Courtroom Work Group: Professional Courtroom Actors

To the public eye, criminal trials frequently appear to be well-managed events even though they may entail quite a bit of drama. Like plays on a stage, trials involve many participants, each of whom has a different role to fill. Unlike such plays, however, they are real-life events, and the impact that a trial's outcome has on people's lives can be far-reaching.

trial
In criminal proceedings, the examination in court of the issues of fact and relevant law in a case for the purpose of convicting or acquitting the defendant.

courtroom work group
The professional courtroom actors, including judges, prosecuting attorneys, defense attorneys, public defenders, and others who earn a living serving the court.

Participants in a criminal **trial** can be divided into two categories: professionals and outsiders (Figure 1). The professionals are the official courtroom actors. They are well versed in criminal trial practice and set the stage for and conduct the business of the court. Judges, prosecuting attorneys, defense attorneys, public defenders, and others who earn a living serving the court fall into this category. Professional courtroom actors are also called the **courtroom work group**. Some writers have pointed out that aside from statutory requirements and ethical considerations, courtroom interaction among professionals involves an implicit recognition of informal rules of civility, cooperation, and shared goals.[3] Hence even within the adversarial framework of a criminal trial, the courtroom work group is dedicated to bringing the procedure to a successful close.[4]

In contrast, outsiders—those trial participants who are only temporarily involved with the court—are generally unfamiliar with courtroom organization and trial procedure. Jurors and

Two-year-old Caylee Marie Anthony (left), who was reported missing a month after she disappeared. Suspicion soon fell on her mother, Casey (right), who was charged with a number of crimes, including first-degree murder. Caylee's remains were later discovered near her home. Why was the mother charged with such a serious crime even before her daughter's body was found? *Orlando Sentinel*/MCT/NewsCom.com and Red Huber/*Orlando Sentinel*/MCT/NewsCom.com

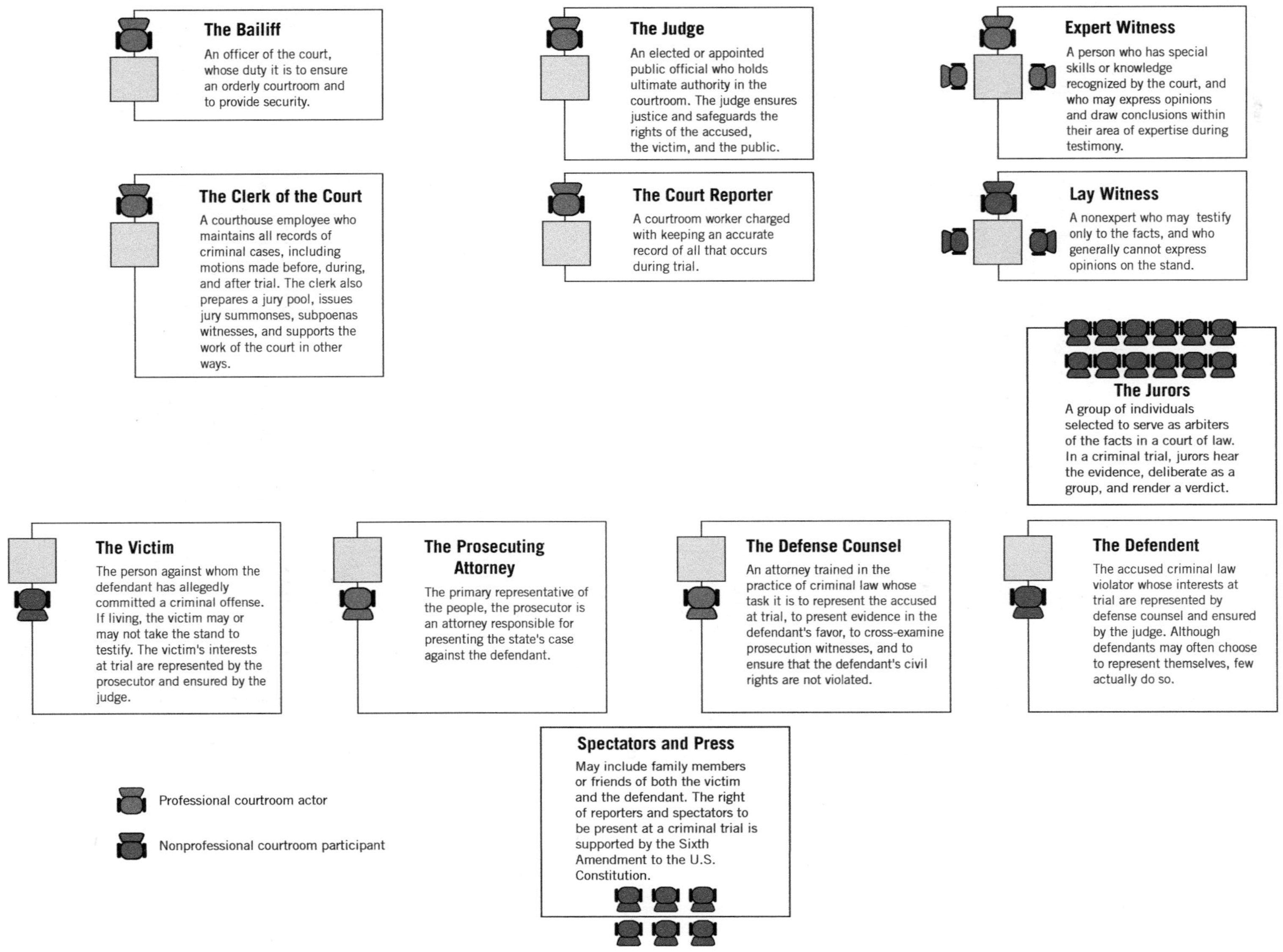

FIGURE 1 Participants in a Criminal Trial

1 Identify and explain the roles of professional members of the courtroom work group.

witnesses are outsiders; defendants and victims are also outsiders, even though they may have a greater personal investment in the outcome of the trial than anyone else.

This chapter examines trial court activities, building on the pretrial process. To place the trial process within its human context, however, the various roles of the many participants in a criminal trial are discussed first. Learn more about professional and nonprofessional courtroom participants at **Web Extra 2**.

The Judge

The Role of the Judge

judge
An elected or appointed public official who presides over a court of law and who is authorized to hear and sometimes to decide cases and to conduct trials.

The trial **judge** has the primary duty of ensuring justice. The American Bar Association (ABA) *Standards for Criminal Justice* describes the duties of the trial judge as follows: "The trial judge has the responsibility for safeguarding both the rights of the accused and the interests of the public in the administration of criminal justice. . . . The purpose of a criminal trial is to determine whether the prosecution has established the guilt of the accused as required by law, and the trial judge should not allow the proceedings to be used for any other purpose."[5]

In the courtroom, the judge holds ultimate authority, ruling on matters of law, weighing objections from both sides, deciding on the admissibility of evidence, and disciplining anyone who challenges the order of the court. In most jurisdictions, judges also sentence offenders after a verdict has been returned; in some states, judges decide guilt or innocence for defendants who waive a jury trial.

Most state jurisdictions have a chief judge who, besides serving on the bench as a trial judge, must also manage the court system. Management includes hiring staff, scheduling sessions of court, ensuring the adequate training of subordinate judges, and coordinating activities with other courtroom actors. Chief judges usually assume their position by virtue of seniority and rarely have any formal training in management. Hence the managerial effectiveness of a chief judge is often a matter of personality and dedication more than anything else.

Judicial Selection

Judges at the federal level are nominated by the president of the United States and take their place on the bench only after confirmation by the Senate. At the state level, things work somewhat differently. Depending on the jurisdiction, state judgeships are won through either popular election or political (usually gubernatorial) appointment. The processes involved in judicial selection at the state level are set by law.

Both judicial election and appointment have been criticized because each system allows politics to enter the judicial arena—although in somewhat different ways. Under the election system, judicial candidates must receive the endorsement of their parties, generate contributions, and manage an effective campaign. Under the appointment system, judicial hopefuls must be in favor with incumbent politicians to receive appointments. Because partisan politics plays a role in both systems, critics have claimed that sitting judges can rarely be as neutral as they should be. They carry to the bench with them campaign promises, personal indebtedness, and possible political agendas.

> To hear patiently, to weigh deliberately and dispassionately, and to decide impartially; these are the chief duties of a judge.
> —Albert Pike (1809–1891)

To counter some of these problems, a number of states have adopted the Missouri Plan (or the Missouri Bar Plan) for judicial selection,[6] which combines elements of both election and appointment. It requires candidates for judicial vacancies to undergo screening by a nonpartisan state judicial nominating committee. Candidates selected by the committee are reviewed by an arm of the governor's office, which selects a final list of names for appointment. Incumbent judges must face the electorate after a specified term in office. They then run unopposed in nonpartisan elections in which only their records may be considered. Voters have the choice of allowing a judge to continue in office or asking that another be appointed to take his or her place. Because the Missouri Plan provides for periodic public review of judicial performance, it is also called the *merit plan of judicial selection*.

Judicial Qualifications

A few decades ago, many states did not require any special training, education, or other qualifications for judges. Anyone (even someone without a law degree) who won election or was appointed could assume a judgeship. Today, however, almost all states require that judges in general jurisdiction and appellate courts hold a law degree, be a licensed attorney, and be a member of their state bar association. Many states also require newly elected judges to attend state-sponsored training sessions dealing with such subjects as courtroom procedure, evidence, dispute resolution, judicial writing, administrative record keeping, and ethics.

While most states provide instruction to meet the needs of trial judges, other organizations also provide specialized training. The National Judicial College (NJC), located on the campus of the University of Nevada at Reno, is one such institution. NJC was established in 1963 by the Joint Committee for the Effective Administration of Justice, chaired by Justice Tom C. Clark of the U.S. Supreme Court.[7] More than 3,000 judges enroll annually in courses offered by NJC, and many courses are offered online. NJC, in collaboration with the National Council of Juvenile and Family Court Judges and the University of Nevada at Reno, offers the nation's only advanced judicial degree programs, leading to a master's degree and a doctorate in judicial studies.[8] Visit the NJC at **Web Extra 3**.

In some parts of the United States, lower-court judges, such as justices of the peace, local magistrates, and "district" court judges, may still be elected without educational and other professional requirements. Today, in 43 states, some 1,300 nonlawyer judges are serving in mostly rural courts of limited jurisdiction.[9] In New York, for example, of the 3,300 judges in the state's unified court system, approximately 65% are part-time town or village justices, and approximately 80% of town and village justices are not lawyers.[10] The majority of cases that come before New York lay judges involve alleged traffic violations, although the cases may also include misdemeanors, small-claims actions, and some civil cases (of up to $3,000).

Even though some have defended lay judges as being closer to the citizenry in their understanding of justice,[11] in most jurisdictions the number of lay judges is declining. States that continue to use lay judges in lower courts do require that candidates for judgeships not have criminal records, and most states require that they attend special training sessions if elected.

The Prosecuting Attorney

The **prosecutor**—also called the *solicitor, district attorney, state's attorney, county attorney*, or *commonwealth attorney*—is responsible for presenting the state's case against the defendant. Technically speaking, the prosecuting attorney is the primary representative of the people by virtue of the belief that violations of the criminal law are an affront to the public. Except for federal prosecutors (called *U.S. attorneys*) and solicitors in five states, prosecutors are elected and generally serve four-year terms, with the possibility of continuing reelection.[12] Widespread criminal conspiracies, whether they involve government officials or private citizens, may require the services of a special prosecutor whose office can spend the time and resources needed for efficient prosecution.[13]

prosecutor
An attorney whose official duty is to conduct criminal proceedings on behalf of the state or the people against those accused of having committed criminal offenses.

Because the job of prosecutor entails too many duties for one person to handle, most prosecutors supervise a staff of assistant district attorneys who do most in-court work. Assistants are trained attorneys, licensed to practice law in the state where they work. They are usually hired directly by the chief prosecutor. Approximately 2,300 chief prosecutors, assisted by 24,000 deputy attorneys, serve the nation's counties and cities.[14]

Another prosecutorial role has traditionally been that of quasi-legal adviser to local police departments. Because prosecutors are sensitive to the kinds of information needed for conviction, they may help guide police investigations and will exhort detectives to identify credible witnesses, uncover additional evidence, and the like. This role is limited, however. Police departments are independent of the administrative authority of the prosecutor, and cooperation between them, although based on the common goal of conviction, is purely voluntary.

Once a trial begins, the job of the prosecutor is to vigorously present the state's case against the defendant. Prosecutors introduce evidence against the accused, steer the testimony of witnesses "for the people," and argue in favor of conviction. Because defendants are presumed innocent until proven guilty, the burden of demonstrating guilt beyond a reasonable doubt rests with the prosecutor.

▲ A reporter shouting questions at Durham County (North Carolina) District Attorney Mike Nifong (right) after a community forum to discuss rape allegations that had been made against three members of the Duke University lacrosse team in 2006. Nifong would not abandon his quest to prosecute the men even when the accuser was discredited and DNA evidence seemed to show definitively that the men were innocent. He was disbarred following a 2007 ethics hearing by the North Carolina State Bar Association. How did Nifong's actions demonstrate the power wielded by local prosecutors throughout the United States?
Gerry Broome/AP Wide World Photos

Prosecutorial Discretion

In May 2007, North Carolina Attorney General Roy A. Cooper dismissed rape charges that had been brought against three former members of the Duke University lacrosse team, saying that the players were innocent of all charges. Those charges had been brought by Durham County Prosecutor Michael B. Nifong after an exotic dancer who had performed at a house party in 2006 told police that she had been raped, sodomized, strangled, and beaten by the partygoers. Contradictions in the accuser's statements, however, along with a lack of DNA and other evidence, convinced Cooper that the attack had never occurred. Cooper told CBS's *60 Minutes* that Nifong should have seen the contradictions himself. Calling Nifong "a rogue prosecutor," Cooper said that "when you have a prosecutor who takes advantage of his enormous power and overreaches like this, then yes, it's offensive."[15] Cooper added that other prosecutors "were offended by a prosecutor who didn't take the time to make sure that he had all of the facts straight before leveling charges." A day later, Nifong apologized to the students, saying "to the extent that I made judgments that ultimately proved to be incorrect, I apologize to the three students that were wrongly accused." He added, "I also understand that when someone has been wrongly accused, the harm caused by the accusations might not be immediately undone merely by dismissing them. It is my sincere desire that the actions of Attorney General Cooper will serve to remedy any remaining injury that has resulted from these cases."[16] Calls for further action against Nifong led to his being disbarred in 2007 following an ethics hearing by the North Carolina Bar Association. He was later found guilty of criminal contempt of court and spent one day in jail.

prosecutorial discretion
The decision-making power of prosecutors, based on the wide range of choices available to them, in the handling of criminal defendants, the scheduling of cases for trial, the acceptance of negotiated pleas, and so on. The most important form of prosecutorial discretion lies in the power to charge, or not to charge, a person with an offense.

The "Duke rape case," as it came to be known in the media, highlights the fact that American prosecutors occupy a unique position in the nation's criminal justice system by virtue of the considerable **prosecutorial discretion** they exercise. As U.S. Supreme Court Justice Robert H. Jackson noted in 1940, "The prosecutor has more control over life, liberty, and reputation than any other person in America."[17] Before a case comes to trial, the prosecutor may decide to accept a plea bargain, divert the suspect to a public or private social services agency, ask the suspect to seek counseling, or dismiss the case entirely for lack of evidence or for a variety of other reasons. Studies have found that the prosecution dismisses from one-third to one-half of all felony cases before trial or before a plea bargain is made.[18] Prosecutors also play a significant role before grand juries because states that use the grand jury system depend on prosecutors to bring evidence before the grand jury and to be effective in seeing indictments returned against suspects.

In preparation for trial, the prosecutor decides what charges are to be brought against the defendant, examines the strength of the incriminating evidence, and decides which witnesses to call. Two important U.S. Supreme Court decisions have held that it is the duty of prosecutors to, in effect, assist the defense in building its case by making available any evidence in their possession. In the first case, *Brady* v. *Maryland* (1963),[19] the Court held that the prosecution is required to disclose to the defense evidence that directly relates to claims of either guilt or innocence. The second and more recent case is that of *U.S.* v. *Bagley*,[20] decided in 1985. In *Bagley*, the Court ruled that the prosecution must disclose any evidence that the defense requests. The Court reasoned that to withhold evidence, even when it does not relate directly to issues of guilt or innocence, may mislead the defense into thinking that such evidence does not exist.

exculpatory evidence
Any information having a tendency to clear a person of guilt or blame.

In 2004, in a decision predicated upon *Brady*, the U.S. Supreme Court intervened to stop the execution of 45-year-old Texan Delma Banks ten minutes before it was scheduled to begin. The Court found that prosecutors had withheld vital **exculpatory evidence**, or information that might have cleared Banks of blame, during his trial for the 1980 shooting death of a 16-year-old boy. The Court said that "a rule declaring 'prosecutor may hide, defendant must seek,' is not tenable in a system constitutionally bound to accord defendants due process."[21] Banks had spent 24 years on death row.

One special decision that the prosecutor makes concerns the filing of separate or multiple charges. The decision to try a defendant simultaneously on multiple charges allows for the presentation of a considerable amount of evidence and permits an in-court demonstration of a complete sequence of criminal events. This strategy has an additional practical advantage: It saves time and money by substituting one trial for what might otherwise be a number of trials if each charge were to be brought separately before the court. From the prosecutor's point of view, however, trying the charges one at a time carries the advantage of allowing for another trial on a new charge if a "not guilty" verdict is returned.

The activities of the prosecutor do not end with a finding of guilt or innocence. Following conviction, prosecutors are usually allowed to make sentencing recommendations to the judge. They can be expected to argue that aggravating factors, prior criminal record, or especially heinous qualities of the offense in question call for strict punishment. When a convicted defendant appeals, prosecutors may need to defend their own actions and to argue, in briefs filed with appellate courts, that the conviction was properly obtained. Most jurisdictions also allow prosecutors to make recommendations when defendants they have convicted are being considered for parole or for early release from prison.

Until relatively recently, it had generally been held that prosecutors enjoyed much the same kind of immunity against liability in the exercise of their official duties that judges do. The 1976 U.S. Supreme Court case of *Imbler* v. *Pachtman*[22] provided the basis for such thinking with its ruling that "state prosecutors are absolutely immune from liability . . . for their conduct in initiating a prosecution and in presenting the State's case." However, in the 1991 case of *Burns* v. *Reed*,[23] the Court held that "[a] state prosecuting attorney is absolutely immune from liability for damages . . . for participating in a probable cause hearing, but not for giving legal advice to the police." The *Burns* case involved Cathy Burns of Muncie, Indiana, who allegedly shot her sleeping sons while laboring under a multiple personality disorder. To explore the possibility of multiple personality further, the police asked the prosecuting attorney if it would be appropriate for them to hypnotize the defendant. The prosecutor agreed that hypnosis would be a permissible avenue for investigation, and the suspect confessed to the murders while hypnotized. She later alleged in her complaint to the Supreme Court "that [the prosecuting attorney] knew or should have known that hypnotically induced testimony was inadmissible" at trial.[24]

The Abuse of Discretion

Because prosecutors have so much discretion in their decision making, there is considerable potential for abuse. Many types of discretionary decisions are always inappropriate: accepting guilty pleas to drastically reduced charges in exchange for personal considerations, deciding not to prosecute friends or political cronies, and overzealously prosecuting a case to seek heightened visibility to support political ambitions.

Administrative decisions such as case scheduling, which can wreak havoc with the personal lives of defendants and the professional lives of defense attorneys, can also be used by prosecutors to harass defendants into pleading guilty. Some forms of abuse may be unconscious. At least one study suggests that some prosecutors have an inherent tendency toward leniency where female defendants are concerned and tend to discriminate against minorities when deciding whether to prosecute.[25]

Although the electorate is the final authority to which prosecutors must answer, gross misconduct by prosecutors may be addressed by the state supreme court or by the state attorney general's office. Short of addressing *criminal* misconduct, however, most of the options available to the court and to the attorney general are limited.

The Prosecutor's Professional Responsibility

As members of the legal profession, prosecutors are expected to abide by various standards of professional responsibility, such as those found in the ABA *Model Rules of Professional Conduct*. Most state bar associations have adopted their own versions of the ABA rules and expect their members to respect those standards. Serious violations of the rules may result in a prosecutor's being disbarred from the practice of law. Official ABA commentary on Rule 3.8, Special Responsibilities of the Prosecutor, says that "a prosecutor has the responsibility of a minister of justice and not simply that of an advocate; the prosecutor's duty is to seek justice, not merely to convict. This responsibility carries with it specific obligations to see that the defendant is accorded procedural justice and that guilt is decided upon the basis of sufficient evidence."[26] Hence prosecutors are barred by the standards of the legal profession from advocating any fact or position that they know is untrue.

Prosecutors have a voice in influencing public policy affecting the safety of America's communities through the National District Attorneys Association (NDAA). Visit the NDAA at **Web Extra 4**.

From the moment you walk into the courtroom, you are the defendant's only friend.

—Michael E. Tigar, Austin defense attorney

The Defense Counsel

defense counsel
A licensed trial lawyer, hired or appointed to conduct the legal defense of a person accused of a crime and to represent him or her before a court of law.

The **defense counsel** is a trained lawyer who may specialize in the practice of criminal law. The defense counsel's task is to represent the accused as soon as possible after arrest and to ensure that the defendant's civil rights are not violated during processing by the criminal justice system. Other duties of the defense counsel include testing the strength of the prosecution's case, taking part in plea negotiations, and preparing an adequate defense to be used at trial. In the preparation of a defense, criminal lawyers may enlist private detectives, experts, witnesses to the crime, and character witnesses. Some lawyers perform aspects of the role of private detective or investigator themselves. Defense attorneys also review relevant court precedents to identify the best defense strategy.

Defense preparation often entails conversations between lawyer and defendant. Such discussions are recognized as privileged communications protected under the umbrella of attorney-client confidentiality; in other words, lawyers cannot be compelled to reveal information that their clients have confided to them.[27]

If the defendant is found guilty, the defense attorney will be involved in arguments at sentencing, may be asked to file an appeal, and will probably counsel the defendant and the defendant's family about any civil matters (payment of debts, release from contractual obligations, and so on) that must be arranged after sentence is imposed. Hence the work of the defense attorney encompasses many roles, including attorney, negotiator, investigator, confidant, family and personal counselor, social worker, and even bill collector.

Three major categories of defense attorneys assist criminal defendants in the United States: (1) private attorneys, usually referred to as *criminal lawyers* or *retained counsel*; (2) court-appointed counsel; and (3) public defenders.

Private Attorneys

Private attorneys either have their own legal practices or work for law firms in which they are partners or employees. As those who have had to hire a defense attorney know, the fees of private attorneys can be high. Most privately retained criminal lawyers charge in the range of $100 to $200 per hour, and included in their bill is the time it takes to prepare for a case as well as time spent in the courtroom. High-powered criminal defense attorneys who have a reputation for successfully defending their clients can be far more expensive: Fees charged by famous criminal defense attorneys can run into the hundreds of thousands of dollars—and sometimes exceed $1 million—for handling just one case!

Few law students actually choose to specialize in criminal law, even though the job of a criminal lawyer may appear glamorous. Those who do specialize often begin their careers immediately following law school, while others seek to gain experience working as assistant district attorneys or assistant public defenders for a number of years before going into private practice. Visit the National Association of Criminal Defense Lawyers (NACDL) at **Web Extra 5** and the Association of Federal Defense Attorneys (AFDA) at **Web Extra 6** to learn more about the practice of criminal law.

Court-Appointed Counsel

The Sixth Amendment to the U.S. Constitution guarantees criminal defendants the effective assistance of counsel. A series of U.S. Supreme Court decisions has established that defendants who are unable to pay for private criminal defense attorneys will receive adequate representation at all stages of criminal justice processing. In *Powell* v. *Alabama* (1932),[28] the Court held that the Fourteenth Amendment requires state courts to appoint counsel for defendants in capital cases who are unable to afford their own. In 1938, in *Johnson* v. *Zerbst*,[29] the Court overturned the conviction of an indigent federal inmate, holding that his Sixth Amendment due process right to counsel had been violated. The Court declared, "If the accused . . . is not represented by counsel and has not competently and intelligently waived his constitutional right, the Sixth Amendment stands as a jurisdictional bar to a valid conviction and sentence depriving him of his life or his liberty." The decision established the right of indigent defendants to receive the assistance of appointed counsel in all criminal proceedings in federal courts. The 1963 case of *Gideon* v. *Wainwright*[30] extended the right to appointed counsel to all indigent defendants charged with a felony in state courts. In *Argersinger* v. *Hamlin* (1972),[31] the Court required adequate legal representation for anyone facing a potential sentence of imprisonment. Juveniles charged with delinquent acts were granted the right to appointed counsel in the case of *In re Gault* (1967).[32] In *Alabama* v. *Shelton* (2002),[33] a closely divided Court expanded the Sixth Amendment right to counsel, ruling that defendants in state courts who are facing relatively minor charges must be provided with an attorney at government expense even when they face only the slightest chance of incarceration.

States have responded to the federal mandate for indigent defense in a number of ways. Most now use one of three systems to deliver legal services to criminal defendants who are unable to afford their own: (1) assigned counsel, (2) public defenders, and (3) contractual arrangements. Most such systems are administered at the county level, although funding arrangements may involve state, county, and municipal monies, as well as federal grants and court fees.

Assigned Counsel

Assigned counsel, also known as court-appointed defense attorneys, are usually drawn from a roster of all practicing criminal attorneys within the jurisdiction of the trial court. Their fees are paid at a rate set by the state or local government. These fees are typically low, however, and may affect the amount of effort an assigned attorney puts into a case. In 2010, for example, New York's court-appointed attorneys were paid only $60 per hour for representing misdemeanants and $75 per hour for in-court representation of charged felons. Out-of-court preparation time was reimbursed at around $25 per hour—a rate of pay that is ten to 20 times less than what attorneys normally earn.[34]

Public Defenders

A **public defender** is a state-employed lawyer defending indigent defendants. A public defender program relies on full-time salaried staff, including defense attorneys, defense investigators, and office personnel. Defense investigators gather information in support of the defense effort and may interview friends, family members, and employers of the accused, with an eye toward effective defense.

public defender
An attorney employed by a government agency or subagency, or by a private organization under contract to a government body, for the purpose of providing defense services to indigents, or an attorney who has volunteered such service.

Two 2010 Bureau of Justice Statistics (BJS) reports found that a public defender system is the primary method used to provide indigent counsel for criminal defendants in the United States.[35] According to BJS, approximately 1,000 public defender offices in 49 states and the District of Columbia received nearly 5.6 million cases and employed over 15,000 litigating attorneys in 2007. County-based public defender offices, a system used by 28 states, received more than 4 million indigent defense cases in 2007, accounting for nearly three-quarters of the public defender cases received nationwide. Those offices employed about 10,700 litigating attorneys. Additionally, state-based public defender programs, used in the other 22 states, employed 4,300 litigating attorneys to handle the 1.5 million indigent defense cases that they received in 2007.

The BJS survey found that the majority of both state- and county-based public defender offices employed substantially fewer than the needed number of support staff, such as paralegals, investigators, indigency screeners, and clerical staff. Surveyors determined that the median entry-level salary for assistant public defenders ranged from $42,000 to $45,000 in county-based public defender offices and from $46,000 to $58,000 in state-based programs.

Critics charge that public defenders, because they are government employees, are not sufficiently independent from prosecutors and judges. For the same reason, clients may be suspicious of public defenders, viewing them as state functionaries. Finally, the huge caseloads typical of public defenders' offices create pressure toward an excessive use of plea bargaining.

Career Profile
Attorney and Instructor of Criminal Justice

Name: Maria A. Daniel

Position: Assistant Professor of Justice, Community College of Philadelphia

Community College of Philadelphia

Colleges attended: Spelman College (BS, Computer Science), Rutgers University School of Law (JD)

What criminal justice-related jobs have you held and when? 2000–2005: Assistant defender (public defender) for the Defender Association of Philadelphia, Pennsylvania (criminal defense). 1999–2000: Staff attorney at Mattleman, Weinroth and Miller in Cherry Hill, New Jersey (general practice, family, civil, prepaid legal services). 1998–1999: Law clerk for the Honorable Genece E. Brinkley, Court of Common Pleas in the Commonwealth of Pennsylvania (criminal and civil rotations)

What position did you like most? Assistant defender for the Defender Association of Philadelphia.

What qualities or characteristics most helped you succeed in the field? Passionate advocacy, meticulous preparation, keen knowledge of the law, persuasive writing skills, thinking outside of the box, personal character, determination, and professionalism.

What are the typical salary ranges students can expect entering these fields? $45,000 to $65,000.

What advice would you give students early in their college career to help them find a rewarding job in criminal justice? Discover what area you are passionate about. Locate criminal justice professionals who are in that particular area. Interview them and shadow them for a day. Volunteer your services or otherwise obtain an opportunity to get firsthand experience in this field. Secure a mentor who can guide your educational and career choices. Observe a criminal trial. See how your field of choice affects the criminal trial process.

Source: Reprinted with permission of Maria A. Daniel, Esquire, attorney and professor of criminal justice. Photo courtesy of Maria A. Daniel. Logo courtesy of Community College of Philadelphia.

Contractual Arrangements

Through a third type of indigent defense, contract attorney programs, county and state officials arrange with local criminal lawyers to provide for indigent defense on a contractual basis. Individual attorneys, local bar associations, and multipartner law firms may all be tapped to provide services. Contract defense programs are the least widely used form of indigent defense at present, although their popularity is growing.

Problems with Indigent Defense

Critics of the current system of indigent defense point out that the system is woefully underfunded. Findings from the most recent National Survey of Indigent Defense Systems were published in 2001.[36] In 2000, the report of the National Symposium on Indigent Defense proclaimed, "Indigent defense today, in terms of funding, caseloads, and quality, is in a chronic state of crisis."[37] Some question the quality of services available through public defender systems due to the fact that entry-level public defenders are paid poorly in comparison to what new attorneys entering private law firms might earn.

As a consequence of limited funding, many public defender offices employ what critics call a "plead 'em and speed 'em through" strategy, often involving a heavy use of plea bargaining and initial meetings with clients in courtrooms as trials are about to begin. Mary Broderick of the National Legal Aid and Defender Association says, "We aren't being given the same weapons. . . . It's like trying to deal with smart bombs when all you've got is a couple of cap pistols."[38] Proposed enhancements to indigent defense systems are offered by the National Legal Aid and Defender Association (NLADA). You can visit the NLADA at **Web Extra 7**.

The full text of presentations and speeches made at the 2010 National Symposium on Indigent Defense is available at **Library Extra 1**; a BJS overview of the National Survey of Indigent Defense Systems can be found at **Library Extra 2**. **Library Extra 3** provides an overview of state-funded indigent defense services, and **Library Extra 4** provides the full text of a recent American Bar Association review of the state of indigent defense in America.

Although state indigent defense services are sometimes woefully underfunded, the same is not true of the federal system. The defense of indigent Oklahoma City bomber Timothy McVeigh, for example, cost taxpayers an estimated $13.8 million—which doesn't include the cost of his appeal or execution. McVeigh's expenses included $6.7 million for attorneys,

$2 million for investigators, $3 million for expert witnesses, and approximately $1.4 million for office rent and secretarial assistance.[39]

In 2000, the BJS reported data on publicly financed counsel nationwide in two research reports that appear to conflict with the conclusions reached by the National Survey of Indigent Defense Systems.[40] BJS statisticians found that court-appointed defense attorneys represent 66% of federal felony defendants, as well as 82% of felony defendants in the nation's 75 most populous counties. The study also found that conviction rates for indigent defendants and those with their own lawyers were about the same in both federal and state courts. About 90% of the federal defendants and 75% of defendants in the most populous counties were found guilty regardless of the type of attorney they had. However, the study showed that those found guilty and represented by publicly financed attorneys were incarcerated at a higher rate than those defendants who paid for their own legal representation—88% compared to 77% in federal courts and 71% compared to 54% in the most populous counties. On average, however, prison sentences for defendants with publicly financed attorneys were shorter than were those with hired counsel. In federal district court, convicted defendants who had publicly financed attorneys were sentenced to less than five years on average and those with private attorneys to just over five years. In large counties, those with publicly financed attorneys were sentenced to an average of two and a half years, while those with private attorneys were sentenced to three years.

Of course, defendants need not accept any assigned counsel. Defendants may waive their right to an attorney and undertake their own defense—a right held to be inherent in the Sixth Amendment to the U.S. Constitution by the U.S. Supreme Court in the 1975 case of *Faretta* v. *California*.[41] Self-representation is uncommon, however, and only 1% of federal inmates and 3% of state inmates report having represented themselves.[42] Some famous instances of self-representation can be found in the 1995 trial of Long Island Rail Road commuter train shooter Colin Ferguson, the 1999 trial of Dr. Jack Kevorkian, and the 2002 federal competency hearings of Zacarias Moussaoui.

Defendants who are not pleased with the lawyer appointed to defend them are in a somewhat different situation. They may request, through the court, that a new lawyer be assigned to represent them, as Timothy McVeigh did following his conviction and death sentence in the Oklahoma City bombing case. However, unless there is clear reason for reassignment, such as an obvious personality conflict between defendant and attorney, few judges are likely to honor a request of this sort. Short of obvious difficulties, most judges will trust in the professionalism of appointed counsel.

State-supported indigent defense systems may also be called on to provide representation for clients upon appeal. An attorney who is appointed to represent an indigent defendant on appeal, however, may conclude that an appeal would be frivolous. If so, he or she may request that the appellate court allow him or her to withdraw from the case or that the court dispose of the case without requiring the attorney to file a brief arguing the merits of the appeal. In 1967, in the case of *Anders* v. *California*,[43] the U.S. Supreme Court found that to protect a defendant's constitutional right to appellate counsel, appellate courts must safeguard against the risk of accepting an attorney's negative assessment of a case where an appeal is not actually frivolous. The Court also found California's existing procedure for evaluating such requests to be inadequate, and the justices set forth an acceptable procedure. In 1979, in the case of *People* v. *Wende*,[44] the state of California adopted a new standardized procedure that, although not the same as that put forth in *Anders*, was designed to protect the right of a criminal defendant to appeal.

The *Wende* standard was put to the test in the 2000 case of *Smith* v. *Robbins*.[45] In that case, the U.S. Supreme Court held that the *Anders* procedure is only one method of satisfying the Constitution's requirements for indigent criminal appeals and that the states are free to adopt different procedures as long as those procedures adequately safeguard a defendant's right to appellate counsel.

Finally, in 2001, in the case of *Texas* v. *Cobb*,[46] the Court ruled that the Sixth Amendment right to counsel is "offense specific." It applies only to the offense with which a defendant is charged and not to other offenses, even if they are factually related to the charged offense.

▲ Defense attorney Lynne Stewart, who was sentenced to prison in 2006 for smuggling messages from her jailed client, the radical Egyptian sheik Omar Abdel-Rahman (also known as "the Blind Sheik"), to his terrorist followers outside of prison. Our adversarial system requires that attorneys sometimes defend unpopular clients, but the defense role is carefully prescribed by ethical and procedural standards. How did Stewart's actions violate those standards?

Stephen Chernin/AP Wide World Photos

CJ News
Public Defenders Reject New Cases

Public defenders are being hit so hard by budget cuts and growing caseloads that offices in several states are refusing to take on more cases because they say defendants' rights are being hurt. Other jurisdictions say they may follow suit.

The U.S. Supreme Court has ruled that poor people charged with a crime have a right to a lawyer. In most states, taxpayers fund a public defender's office that handles cases of people who cannot afford a private attorney. The American Bar Association cites studies saying a public defender can competently handle 150 to 200 cases a year.

The growing caseloads could force states to spend more money on public defenders, delay trials or lead to overturned convictions because of inadequate counsel.

"Many public defenders are feeling the squeeze at this point," says Maureen Dimino of the National Association of Criminal Defense Lawyers. She has heard from public defenders in more than a half-dozen states who are considering challenging their growing caseloads in court.

Miami-Dade County Public Defender Bennett Brummer sued Florida in June after the Legislature cut his budget 9%. He said his lawyers, who each handle an average of 436 cases a year, could not take any new clients charged with felonies without being in danger of committing malpractice.

A Miami judge ruled . . . that . . . Brummer can send his least serious felony cases to the state, which will have to provide attorneys or pay for private lawyers for poor defendants.

The ruling, which affects thousands of felonies, "will have statewide and some nationwide impact," Brummer says. "Many defenders would like to take meaningful steps to alleviate their caseloads."

Attorneys for the Miami-Dade County State Attorney's Office are appealing, saying Brummer is exaggerating the caseload. The public defenders are compromising victims' rights by withdrawing, spokesman Ed Griffith says. If a defendant does not get a trial within a set amount of time, a judge is obligated to set the defendant free "to the detriment of all the citizens," he says.

Other state public defender's offices taking action:

- Kentucky's former public advocate Ernie Lewis, who retired last month, has asked a judge to declare his office underfunded so it can refuse misdemeanor cases.

▲ Arthur J. Jones (*right*), who quit his job as a public defender in Miami because of low pay and a huge workload. Jones was afraid that his huge client load could lead to mistakes. How might an effective public defender system be funded?
*Oscar Hidalgo/*The New York Times*/Redux Pictures*

  Lewis says his attorneys' caseloads could top 500 each this year because budget cuts forced him to keep nearly 100 positions open. "It's very clear to me that our caseload would be unethical," he says.
- The Missouri public defender's office last month notified courts in two jurisdictions that public defenders will reject new cases there. In Ava and Jefferson City, public defenders exceeded the maximum caseload per attorney set by a new state rule. The public defender's office is negotiating the least disruptive way to lessen the caseloads.

  "Our lawyers have an ethical responsibility to not take on more cases than they can handle," says Cathy Kelly, deputy director for the Missouri State Public Defenders System. "We just feel like we have reached the point where we have to say no."

Source: Donna Leinwand, "Public Defenders Reject New Cases," *USA Today*, September 10, 2008. Reprinted with permission.

The Ethics of Defense

The job of defense counsel, as we have already mentioned, is to prepare and offer a vigorous defense on behalf of the accused at trial and to appeal cases with merit. A proper defense at trial often involves the presentation of evidence and the examination of witnesses, both of which require careful thought and planning. Good attorneys may become emotionally committed to the outcomes of trials in which they are involved. Some lawyers, however, cross the line when they lose their professional objectivity and embrace the wider cause of their clients. That's what happened to Lynne Stewart, who was convicted in 2005 of smuggling messages from her jailed client, the radical Egyptian sheik Omar Abdel-Rahman ("the Blind Sheik"), to his terrorist followers outside of prison.[47] Abdel-Rahman is serving life behind bars for his role in an unsuccessful 1993 plot to bomb New York City landmarks. Stewart, a 1960s-era radical, has often chosen to represent the most contemptible clients, believing that justice requires that everyone receive a vigorous defense. She was arrested, however, after she issued a public statement on behalf of the sheik expressing her client's withdrawal of support for a cease-fire involving his supporters in Egypt. Stewart had known in advance that making the statement violated an order to restrict the sheik's communications, but she later testified that she

Ethics and Professionalism

The American Bar Association's *Model Rules of Professional Conduct*

To help attorneys understand what is expected of them, the ABA has provided significant guidance in the areas of legal ethics and professional responsibility. The ABA has developed professional standards intended to serve as models for state bar associations and to guide legislative bodies focused on ensuring ethical behavior among attorneys.

The ABA's first major foray into the area of ethical guidelines resulted in the adoption of its original *Canons of Professional Ethics* on August 27, 1908. In 1913, in an effort to keep the association informed about state and local bar activities concerning professional ethics, the ABA established its Standing Committee on Professional Ethics. The name of the group was changed to the Committee on Ethics and Professional Responsibility in 1971, and the committee continues to function under that name today.

In 1969, the ABA formally adopted the committee's *Model Code of Professional Responsibility*. Eventually, the majority of state and federal jurisdictions adopted their own versions of the Model Code.

In 1977, the ABA Commission on Evaluation of Professional Standards was created and charged with rethinking the ethical problems of the legal profession. During the next six years, the commission drafted the *Model Rules of Professional Conduct*, which the ABA adopted on August 2, 1983. The *Model Rules* effectively supplanted the *Model Code of Professional Responsibility*, and today most state and federal jurisdictions have adapted the *Model Rules* to their own particular circumstances.

The *Model Rules* have been periodically amended—most significantly in 2002—but continue to provide the touchstone ethical standards of the American legal profession today. Visit the ABA on the Internet at **Web Extra 8**, and learn about its Center for Professional Responsibility at **Web Extra 9**.

THINKING ABOUT ETHICS

1. ***Should a defense attorney represent a client whom he or she knows to be guilty?***
2. ***Would it be unethical for an attorney to refuse to represent such a client? Why or why not?***

Reference: American Bar Association, *Model Rules of Professional Conduct—Preface* http://www.abanet.org/cpr/mrpc/preface.html (accessed July 10, 2010).

believed that violence is sometimes necessary to achieve justice. Other evidence showed that she had facilitated forbidden communications between Rahman and a translator by using prearranged cues such as tapping on a table, shaking a water bottle, and uttering key phrases like "chocolate" and "heart attack" during prison visits. In 2006 she was sentenced to serve 28 months in prison. She entered prison in 2009 after exhausting the appeals process.

The nature of the adversarial process, fed by the emotions of the participants combined with the often privileged and extensive knowledge that defense attorneys have about their cases, is enough to tempt the professional ethics of some counselors. Because the defense counsel may often know more about the guilt or innocence of the defendant than anyone else prior to trial, the defense role is carefully prescribed by ethical and procedural considerations. Attorneys violate both law and the standards of their profession if they knowingly misrepresent themselves or their clients. As Michael Ratner, president of the Center for Constitutional Rights, put it when commenting on the Stewart case, "Lawyers need to be advocates, but they don't need to be accomplices."[48]

> Society asks much of the criminal court. The court is expected to meet society's demand that serious offenders be convicted and punished, and at the same time it is expected to insure that the innocent and unfortunate are not oppressed.
>
> —President's Commission on Law Enforcement and Administration of Justice[i]

To help attorneys understand what is expected of them and what the appropriate limits of a vigorous defense might be, the ABA provides significant guidance in the areas of legal ethics and professional responsibility, as the Ethics and Professionalism box in this section explains. Even so, some attorney-client interactions remain especially tricky. Defense attorneys, for example, are under no obligation to reveal information obtained from a client without the client's permission. However, all states permit defense lawyers to violate a client's confidentiality without fear of reprisal if they reasonably believe that doing so could prevent serious injury or death to another person. In 2004, with passage of a new evidence law broadening the state's evidence code, California joined the other 49 states in freeing attorneys to violate client confidentiality in such cases. California law makes disclosure discretionary, not mandatory. Kevin Mohr, a professor at Western State University College of Law in Fullerton, California, noted that the new law provides the first exception to the attorney-client privilege in California in more than 130 years. "A lawyer can now take action and intervene and prevent [a] criminal act from occurring," said Mohr.[49]

Somewhat earlier, the 1986 U.S. Supreme Court case of *Nix* v. *Whiteside*[50] clarified the duty of lawyers to reveal known instances of client perjury. In that case, the Court held that a lawyer's duty to a client "is limited to legitimate, lawful conduct compatible with the very nature of a trial as a search for truth. . . . Counsel is precluded from taking steps or in any way assisting the client in presenting false evidence or otherwise violating the law."[51]

The Bailiff

bailiff
The court officer whose duties are to keep order in the courtroom, to secure witnesses, and to maintain physical custody of the jury.

The **bailiff**, another member of the professional courtroom work group, is usually an armed law enforcement officer. The job of the bailiff, also called a *court officer*, is to ensure order in the courtroom, to announce the judge's entry into the courtroom, to call witnesses, and to prevent the escape of the accused (if the accused has not been released on bond). The bailiff also supervises the jury when it is sequestered and controls public and media access to jury members. Bailiffs in federal courtrooms are deputy U.S. marshals.

The Trial Court Administrator

Many states now employ trial court administrators whose job is to facilitate the smooth functioning of courts in particular judicial districts or areas. A major impetus toward the hiring of local trial court administrators came from the 1967 President's Commission on Law Enforcement and Administration of Justice. Examining state courts, the report found "a system that treats defendants who are charged with minor offenses with less dignity and consideration than it treats those who are charged with serious crimes."[52] A few years later, the National Advisory Commission on Criminal Justice Standards and Goals recommended that all courts with five or more judges create the position of trial court administrator.[53]

Court administrators provide uniform court management, assuming many of the duties previously performed by chief judges, prosecutors, and court clerks. Where trial court administrators operate, the ultimate authority for running the court still rests with the chief judge. Administrators, however, are able to relieve the judge of many routine and repetitive tasks, such as record keeping, scheduling, case-flow analysis, personnel administration, space utilization, facilities planning, and budget management. They may also take the minutes at meetings of judges and their committees.

Juror management is another area in which trial court administrators are becoming increasingly involved. Juror utilization studies can identify problems such as the overselection of citizens for the jury pool and the reasons for excessive requests to be excused from jury service. They can also suggest ways to reduce the time jurors waste waiting to be called or impaneled.

Effective trial court administrators are able to track lengthy cases and identify bottlenecks in court processing. They then suggest strategies to make the administration of justice more efficient for courtroom professionals and more humane for lay participants.

The Court Reporter

The role of the court reporter (also called the *court stenographer* or *court recorder*) is to create a record of all that occurs during a trial. Accurate records are very important in criminal trial courts because appeals may be based entirely on what went on in the courtroom. Especially significant are all verbal comments made in the courtroom, including testimonies, objections, judge's rulings, judge's instructions to the jury, arguments made by lawyers, and results of conferences between the lawyers and the judge. Occasionally, the judge will rule that a statement should be "stricken from the record" because it is inappropriate or unfounded. The official trial record, often taken on a stenotype machine or an audio recorder, may later be transcribed in manuscript form and will become the basis for any appellate review of the trial.

Today's court reporters often employ computer-aided transcription (CAT) software, which translates typed stenographic shorthand into complete and readable transcripts. Court reporters may be members of the National Court Reporters Association, the United States Court Reporters Association, or the Association of Legal Administrators—all of which support the activities of these professionals. You can visit the National Court Reporters Association at **Web Extra 10**.

The Clerk of Court

The duties of the clerk of court (sometimes also known as the *county clerk*) extend beyond the courtroom. The clerk maintains all records of criminal cases, including all pleas and motions made both before and after the actual trial. The clerk also prepares a jury pool, issues jury summonses, and subpoenas witnesses for both the prosecution and the defense. During the trial, the clerk (or an assistant) marks physical evidence for identification as instructed by the judge and maintains custody of that evidence. The clerk also swears in witnesses and performs other functions as the judge directs. Some states allow the clerk limited judicial duties, such as the power to issue warrants, to handle certain matters relating to individuals declared mentally incompetent,[54] and to serve as a judge of probate to oversee wills and the administration of estates.

▲ An expert witness testifying in court. Expert witnesses may express opinions and draw conclusions in their area of expertise; they need not limit their testimony to facts alone. Why are expert witnesses permitted such leeway?
Corbis RF

Expert Witnesses

Most of the courtroom "insiders" we've talked about so far either are employees of the state or have ongoing professional relationships with the court (as in the case of defense counsel). Expert witnesses, however, may not have that kind of status, although some do. **Expert witnesses** are recognized as having specialized skills and knowledge in an established profession or technical area. They must demonstrate their expertise through education, work experience, publications, and awards. Their testimony at trial provides an effective way of introducing scientific evidence in such areas as medicine, psychology, ballistics, crime-scene analysis, and photography. Unlike lay witnesses, they are allowed to express opinions and to draw conclusions, but only within their particular area of expertise. Expert witnesses, like the other courtroom actors described in this chapter, are generally paid professionals and (like all other witnesses) are subject to cross-examination.

expert witness
A person who has special knowledge and skills recognized by the court as relevant to the determination of guilt or innocence. Unlike lay witnesses, expert witnesses may express opinions or draw conclusions in their testimony.

One difficulty with expert testimony is that it can be confusing to the jury. Sometimes the trouble is due to the nature of the subject matter and sometimes to disagreements between the experts themselves. Often, however, it arises from the strict interpretation given to expert testimony by procedural requirements. The difference between medical and legal definitions of insanity, for example, points to a divergence in both history and purpose between the law and medical science. Courts that attempt to apply criteria like the M'Naghten rule in deciding claims of "insanity" are often faced with the testimony of psychiatric experts who refuse even to recognize the word. Such experts may prefer, instead, to speak in terms of *psychosis* and *neurosis*, words that have no place in legal jargon. Because of the uncertainties they create, legal requirements may pit experts against one another and may confound the jury.

Even so, most authorities agree that expert testimony is usually viewed by jurors as more trustworthy than other forms of evidence. In a study of scientific evidence, one prosecutor commented that if he had to choose between presenting a fingerprint or an eyewitness at trial, he would always go with the fingerprint.[55] As a consequence of the effectiveness of scientific evidence, the National Institute of Justice recommends that "prosecutors consider the potential utility of such information in all cases where such evidence is available."[56]

Outsiders: Nonprofessional Courtroom Participants

Defendants, victims, jurors, and most witnesses are usually unwilling or inadvertent participants in criminal trials. Although they are outsiders who lack the status of paid professional participants, these are precisely the people who provide the grist for the judicial mill. The press, a willing player in many criminal trials, makes up another group of outsiders. Let's look now at each of these courtroom actors.

2 Identify and explain the roles of nonprofessional or nonjudicial courtroom participants.

Lay Witnesses

lay witness
An eyewitness, character witness, or other person called on to testify who is not considered an expert. Lay witnesses must testify to facts only and may not draw conclusions or express opinions.

Nonexpert witnesses, also known as **lay witnesses**, may be called to testify by either the prosecution or the defense. Lay witnesses may be eyewitnesses who saw the crime being committed or who came upon the crime scene shortly after the crime had occurred. Another

▲ A lay witness being sworn in before testifying in a criminal trial. Nonexpert witnesses must generally limit their testimony to facts about which they have direct knowledge. Why are such limits imposed?
© Royalty-Free/CORBIS

type of lay witness is the character witness, who frequently provides information about the personality, family life, business acumen, and so on of the defendant in an effort to show that this is not the kind of person who would commit the crime with which he or she is charged. Of course, the victim may also be a witness, providing detailed and sometimes lengthy testimony about the defendant and the crime.

A written document called a **subpoena** officially notifies witnesses that they are to appear in court to testify. Subpoenas are generally served by an officer of the court or by a police officer, though they are sometimes mailed. Both sides in a criminal case may subpoena witnesses and might ask that individuals called to testify bring with them books, papers, photographs, videotapes, or other forms of physical evidence. Witnesses who fail to appear when summoned may face contempt-of-court charges.

subpoena
A written order issued by a judicial officer or grand jury requiring an individual to appear in court and to give testimony or to bring material to be used as evidence. Some subpoenas mandate that books, papers, and other items be surrendered to the court.

The job of a witness is to provide accurate testimony concerning only those things of which he or she has direct knowledge. Normally, witnesses are not allowed to repeat things that others have told them unless they must do so to account for certain actions of their own. Since few witnesses are familiar with courtroom procedure, the task of testifying is fraught with uncertainty and can be traumatizing.

Everyone who testifies in a criminal trial must do so under oath, in which some reference to God is made, or after affirmation,[57] which is a pledge to tell the truth used by those who find either a reference or swearing to God objectionable.

All witnesses are subject to cross-examination. Lay witnesses may be surprised to find that cross-examination can force them to defend their personal and moral integrity. A cross-examiner may question a witness about past vicious, criminal, or immoral acts, even when such matters have never been the subject of a criminal proceeding.[58] As long as the intent of such questions is to demonstrate to the jury that the witness is not credible, the judge will normally permit them.

Witnesses have traditionally been shortchanged by the judicial process. Subpoenaed to attend court, they have often suffered from frequent and unannounced changes in trial dates. A witness who promptly responds to a summons to appear may find that legal maneuvering has resulted in unanticipated delays. Strategic changes by either side may make the testimony of some witnesses entirely unnecessary, and people who have prepared themselves for the psychological rigors of testifying often experience an emotional letdown.

To compensate witnesses for their time and to make up for lost income, many states pay witnesses for each day that they spend in court. Payments range from $5 to $30 per day,[59] although some states pay nothing at all (federal courts pay $40 per day). In a 2004 Chicago murder case in which Oprah Winfrey served as a juror, for example, all jurors, including Winfrey (a billionaire), were paid $17.20 a day for their services.[60] The 1991 U.S. Supreme Court case of *Demarest* v. *Manspeaker et al.*[61] held that federal prisoners subpoenaed to testify are entitled to witness fees just as other witnesses would be.

In an effort to make the job of witnesses less onerous, 39 states and the federal government have laws or guidelines requiring that witnesses be notified of scheduling changes and cancellations in criminal proceedings.[62] In 1982, Congress passed the Victim and Witness Protection Act, which required the U.S. attorney general to develop guidelines to assist victims and witnesses in meeting the demands placed on them by the justice system. A number of **victims' assistance programs** (also called *victim/witness assistance programs*) have also taken up a call for the rights of witnesses and are working to make the courtroom experience more manageable.

victims' assistance program
An organized program that offers services to victims of crime in the areas of crisis intervention and follow-up counseling and that helps victims secure their rights under the law.

Jurors

The Cook County (Chicago) jury on which television diva Oprah Winfrey served convicted a man of first-degree murder in 2004. "It was an eye-opener for all of us," Winfrey said after the three-day trial ended. "It was not an easy decision to make."[63]

Article III of the U.S. Constitution requires that "[t]he trial of all crimes . . . shall be by jury." **Jurors** are citizens selected for jury duty in a court of law. States have the authority to determine the number of jurors in criminal trial juries. Most states use juries composed of 12 people and one or two alternates designated to fill in for jurors who are unable to continue due to accident, illness, or personal emergency. Some states allow for juries smaller than 12 jurors, and juries with as few as six members have survived Supreme Court scrutiny.[64]

juror
A member of a trial or grand jury who has been selected for jury duty and is required to serve as an arbiter of the facts in a court of law. Jurors are expected to render verdicts of "guilty" or "not guilty" as to the charges brought against the accused, although they may sometimes fail to do so (as in the case of a hung jury).

The highest act of citizenship is jury service.
—Abraham Lincoln, sixteenth president of the United States

Jury duty is regarded as a responsibility of citizenship. Other than juveniles and people in certain occupations, such as police personnel, physicians, members of the armed services on active duty, and emergency services workers, those who are called for jury duty must serve unless they can convince a judge that they should be excused for overriding reasons. Noncitizens, convicted felons, and citizens who have served on a jury within the past two years are excluded from jury service in most jurisdictions.

The names of prospective jurors are often gathered from the tax register, motor vehicle records, or voter registration rolls of a county or municipality. Minimum qualifications for jury service include adulthood, basic command of spoken English, citizenship, "ordinary intelligence," and local residency. Jurors are also expected to possess their "natural faculties," meaning that they should be able to hear, speak, see, move, and so forth. Some jurisdictions have recently allowed people with physical disabilities to serve as jurors, although the nature of the evidence to be presented in a case may preclude people with certain kinds of disabilities from serving.

Ideally, the jury should be a microcosm of society, reflecting the values, rationality, and common sense of the average person. The U.S. Supreme Court has held that criminal defendants have a right to have their cases heard before a jury of their peers.[65] Peer juries are those composed of a representative cross section of the community in which the alleged crime occurred and where the trial is to be held. The idea of a peer jury stems from the Magna Carta's original guarantee of jury trials for "freemen." Freemen in England during the thirteenth century, however, were more likely to be of similar mind than is a cross section of Americans today. Hence, although the duty of the jury is to deliberate on the evidence and, ultimately, to determine guilt or innocence, social dynamics may play just as great a role in jury verdicts as do the facts of a case.

In a 1945 case, *Thiel* v. *Southern Pacific Co.*,[66] the Supreme Court clarified the concept of a "jury of one's peers" by noting that while it is not necessary for every jury to contain representatives of every conceivable racial, ethnic, religious, gender, and economic group in the community, court officials may not systematically and intentionally exclude any juror solely because of his or her social characteristics. Learn what it's like to serve on a jury in a criminal trial at **Web Extra 11**.

The Victim

Not all crimes have clearly identifiable victims. Some, such as murder, do not have victims who survive. Where there is an identifiable surviving victim, however, he or she is often one of the most forgotten people in the courtroom. Although the victim may have been profoundly affected by the crime itself and is often emotionally committed to the proceedings and trial outcome, he or she may not even be permitted to participate directly in the trial process. Although a powerful movement to recognize the interests of victims is in full swing in this country, it is still not unusual for crime victims to be totally unaware of the final outcome of a case that intimately concerns them.[67]

Hundreds of years ago, the situation surrounding victims was far different. During the early Middle Ages in much of Europe, victims or their survivors routinely played a central role in trial proceedings and in sentencing decisions. They testified, examined witnesses, challenged defense contentions, and pleaded with the judge or jury for justice, honor, and often revenge. Sometimes they were even expected to carry out the sentence of the court, by flogging the offender or by releasing the trapdoor used for hangings. This "golden age" of the victim ended with the consolidation of power into the hands of monarchs, who declared that vengeance was theirs alone.

Today, victims (like witnesses) experience many of the following hardships as they participate in the criminal court process:

- Uncertainty as to their role in the criminal justice process
- General lack of knowledge about the criminal justice system, courtroom procedure, and legal issues
- Trial delays resulting in frequent travel, missed work, and wasted time
- Fear of the defendant or of retaliation from the defendant's associates
- Trauma of testifying and of cross-examination

The trial process itself can make for a bitter experience. If victims take the stand, defense attorneys may test their memory, challenge their veracity, or even suggest that they were somehow responsible for their own victimization. After enduring cross-examination, some victims report feeling as though they—and not the offender—were portrayed as the criminal to the jury. The difficulties encountered by victims have been compared to a second victimization at the hands of the criminal justice system.

The Defendant

Generally, defendants must be present at their trials. The Federal Rules of Criminal Procedure, like state rules, require a defendant's presence at every stage of a trial, except that a defendant who is initially present may be voluntarily absent after the trial has commenced.[68] In *Crosby* v. *U.S.* (1993),[69] the U.S. Supreme Court held that a defendant may not be tried in absentia, even if he or she was present at the beginning of a trial, if his or her absence is due to escape or failure to appear. In a related issue in *Zafiro* v. *U.S.* (1993),[70] the justices held that, at least in federal courts, defendants charged with similar or related offenses may be tried together, even when their defenses differ substantially.

The majority of criminal defendants are poor, uneducated, and often alienated from the philosophy that undergirds the American justice system. Many are relatively powerless and are at the mercy of judicial mechanisms. However, experienced defendants, notably those who are career offenders, may be well versed in courtroom demeanor. As we discussed earlier, defendants in criminal trials may even choose to represent themselves, though such a choice may not be in their best interests.

Even without self-representation, every defendant who chooses to do so can substantially influence events in the courtroom. Defendants exercise choice in (1) selecting and retaining counsel, (2) planning a defense strategy with their attorney, (3) deciding what information to provide to (or withhold from) the defense team, (4) deciding what plea to enter, (5) deciding whether to testify personally, and (6) determining whether to file an appeal if convicted.

Nevertheless, even the most active defendants suffer from a number of disadvantages. One is the tendency of others to assume that anyone on trial must be guilty. Although a person is "innocent until proven guilty," the very fact that he or she is accused of an offense casts a shadow of suspicion that may foster biases in the minds of jurors and other courtroom actors. Another disadvantage lies in the often-substantial social and cultural differences that separate the offender from the professional courtroom staff. While lawyers and judges tend to identify with upper-middle-class values and lifestyles, few offenders do. The consequences of such a gap between defendant and courtroom staff may be insidious and far-reaching.

Spectators and the Press

Spectators and the press are often overlooked because they do not have an official role in courtroom proceedings. Both spectators and media representatives may be present in large numbers at any trial. Spectators include members of the families of both victim and defendant, friends of either side, and curious onlookers—some of whom are avocational court watchers. Journalists, TV reporters, and other members of the press are apt to be present at spectacular trials (those involving an especially gruesome crime or a famous personality) and at those involving a great deal of community interest. The right of reporters and spectators to be present at a criminal trial is supported by the Sixth Amendment's requirement of a public trial.

Press reports at all stages of a criminal investigation and trial often create problems for the justice system. Significant pretrial publicity about a case may make it difficult to find jurors who have not already formed an opinion as to the guilt or innocence of the defendant. News reports from the courtroom may influence or confuse nonsequestered jurors who hear them, especially when the reports contain information brought to the bench but not heard by the jury.

In the 1976 case of *Nebraska Press Association* v. *Stuart*,[71] the U.S. Supreme Court ruled that trial court judges could not legitimately issue gag orders preventing the pretrial publication of information about a criminal case as long as the defendant's right to a fair trial and an impartial jury could be ensured by traditional means.[72] These means include (1) **change of venue**, whereby the trial is moved to another jurisdiction less likely to have been exposed to the publicity; (2) trial postponement, which would allow for memories to fade and emotions to cool; and (3) jury selection and screening to eliminate biased people from the jury pool. In 1986, the Court extended press access to preliminary hearings, which it said are "sufficiently like a trial to require public access."[73] In 1993, in the case of *Caribbean International News Corporation* v. *Puerto Rico*,[74] the Court effectively applied that requirement to territories under U.S. control. Today, members of the press and their video, television, and still cameras are allowed into most state courtrooms.

change of venue
The movement of a trial or lawsuit from one jurisdiction to another or from one location to another within the same jurisdiction. A change of venue may be made in a criminal case to ensure that the defendant receives a fair trial.

The U.S. Supreme Court has been far less favorably disposed to television coverage than have state courts. In 1981, a Florida defendant appealed his burglary conviction to the Supreme Court,[75] arguing that the presence of television cameras at his trial had turned the court into a circus for attorneys and made the proceedings more a sideshow than a trial. The Supreme Court, recognizing that television cameras have an untoward effect on many people, found in favor of the defendant. In the words of the Court, "Trial courts must be especially vigilant to guard against any impairment of the defendant's right to a verdict based solely upon the evidence and the relevant law."

Cameras of all kinds have been prohibited in all federal district criminal proceedings since 1946 by Rule 53 of the Federal Rules of Criminal Procedure.[76] In 1972, the Judicial Conference of the United States adopted a policy opposing broadcast of civil proceedings in district courts, and that policy was incorporated into the Code of Conduct for United States Judges. Nonetheless, some district courts have local rules that allow photographs and filming during selected proceedings.

A three-year pilot project that allowed television cameras into six U.S. district courts and two appeals courts closed on December 31, 1994, when the Judicial Conference voted to end the project. Conference members expressed concerns that cameras were a distracting influence and were having a "negative impact on jurors [and] witnesses"[77] by exposing them to possible harm by revealing their identities. Still, some federal appellate courts have created their own policy on the use of cameras and broadcast equipment in the courtroom. The official policy of the U.S. Court of Appeals for the Ninth Circuit, for example, permits cameras and media broadcasts that meet certain rules. The policy stipulates, "Three business days advance notice is required from the media of a request to be present to broadcast, televise, record electronically, or take photographs at a particular session. Such requests must be submitted to the Clerk of Court." The policy adds, "The presiding judge of the panel may limit or terminate media coverage, or direct the removal of camera coverage personnel when necessary to protect the rights of the parties or to assure the orderly conduct of the proceedings."[78]

Today's new personal technologies, however, which include cellular telephones with digital camera capabilities, streaming Web-based video, and miniaturized recording devices, all threaten courtroom privacy. For more information on technology trends that might affect the use of cameras in courtrooms, see **Library Extra 5**.

The Criminal Trial

From arrest through sentencing, the criminal justice process is carefully choreographed. Arresting officers must follow proper procedure in the gathering of evidence and in the arrest and questioning of suspects. Magistrates, prosecutors, jailers, and prison officials are all subject to their own strictures. Nowhere, however, is the criminal justice process more closely circumscribed than it is at the criminal trial.

Procedure

rules of evidence
The court rules that govern the admissibility of evidence at criminal hearings and trials.

The procedure in a modern courtroom is highly formalized. **Rules of evidence**, which govern the admissibility of evidence, and other procedural guidelines determine the course of a criminal hearing and trial. Rules of evidence are partially based on tradition, but all U.S. jurisdictions have formalized rules of evidence in written form. Criminal trials at the federal level generally adhere to the requirements of the Federal Rules of Evidence.

Trials are also circumscribed by informal rules and professional expectations. An important component of law school education is the teaching of rules that structure and define appropriate courtroom demeanor. In addition to statutory rules, law students are thoroughly exposed to the ethical standards of their profession, as found in ABA standards and other writings.

Nature and Purpose

3 Describe the nature and purpose of the criminal trial.

In the remainder of this chapter, we will describe the chronology of a criminal trial and will comment on some of the widely accepted rules of criminal procedure. Before we begin the description, however, it is good to keep two points in mind. One is that the primary purpose of any criminal trial is the determination of the defendant's guilt or innocence. In this regard, it is important to recognize the crucial distinction that scholars make between factual guilt and legal guilt. The term *factual guilt* refers to the issue of whether the defendant is actually responsible for the crime of which he or she stands accused. If the defendant did it, then he or she is, in fact, guilty. *Legal guilt* is not as clear a term and is established only when the prosecutor presents evidence that is sufficient to convince the judge (when a jury trial has been waived and the judge determines the verdict) or the jury that the defendant is guilty as charged. The distinction between factual guilt and legal guilt is crucial because it points to the fact that the burden of proof rests with the prosecution. It indicates the possibility that guilty defendants may, nonetheless, be found "not guilty."

adversarial system
The two-sided structure under which American criminal trial courts operate that pits the prosecution against the defense. In theory, justice is done when the more effective adversary is able to convince the judge or jury that his or her perspective on the case is the correct one.

The second point to remember is that criminal trials under our system of justice are built around an **adversarial system** (prosecution versus defense) and that central to this system is the advocacy model. Participating in the adversarial system are advocates for the state (the prosecutor or the district attorney) and for the defendant (the defense counsel, the public defender, and so on). The philosophy behind the adversarial system is that the greatest number of just resolutions in criminal trials will occur when both sides are allowed to argue their cases effectively and vociferously before a fair and impartial jury. The system requires that advocates for both sides do their utmost, within the boundaries set by law and professional ethics, to protect and advance the interests of their clients (that is, the defendant and the state). The advocacy model makes clear that it is not the job of the defense attorney or the prosecution to determine the guilt of any defendant. Even defense attorneys who are convinced that their client is guilty are still exhorted to offer the best possible defense and to counsel their client as effectively as possible.

The adversarial system has been criticized by some thinkers who point to fundamental differences between law and science in the way the search for truth is conducted.[79] While proponents of traditional legal procedure accept the belief that truth can best be uncovered through an adversarial process, scientists adhere to a painstaking process of research and replication to acquire knowledge. Most of us would agree that scientific advances in recent years may have made factual issues less difficult to ascertain. For example, some of the new scientific techniques in evidence analysis, such as DNA fingerprinting, can now unequivocally link suspects to criminal activity or even show that offenders once thought guilty are actually innocent. Gary Dotson of Illinois became the first person exonerated through the use of such evidence in 1989. Since then, at least 328 convictions have been overturned using DNA evidence. (Read about Dotson's case in "The Rape That Wasn't" at **Library Extra 6.**) According to Samuel R. Gross and colleagues at the University of Michigan Law School, who published a comprehensive study of exonerations in 2004, those 328 people "had spent more than 3,400 years in prison for crimes for which they should never have been convicted."[80] Exonerations tend to occur more frequently in cases where DNA evidence is relatively easy to acquire, such as rape and murder. False conviction rates for other crimes, like robbery, are much more difficult to assess using DNA. Hence Gross states that "the clearest and most important lesson from the recent spike in rape exonerations is that false convictions that come to light are the tip of an iceberg."

The beauty of the jury is their morality. Tap into it.

—Tony Serra, San Francisco defense attorney

Whether scientific findings should continue to serve a subservient role to the adversarial process itself is a question now being raised. The ultimate answer will probably be determined by the results that the two processes are able to produce. If the adversarial model results in the acquittal of too many demonstrably guilty people because of legal "technicalities" or if the scientific approach identifies too many suspects inaccurately, either could be restricted.

4 Identify the various stages of a criminal trial.

Stages in a Criminal Trial

We turn now to a discussion of the steps in a criminal trial. As Figure 2 shows, trial chronology consists of eight stages:

1. Trial initiation
2. Jury selection
3. Opening statements
4. Presentation of evidence
5. Closing arguments
6. Judge's charge to the jury
7. Jury deliberations
8. Verdict

Jury deliberations and the verdict are discussed jointly. If the defendant is found guilty, a sentence is imposed by the judge at the conclusion of the trial. Sentencing is discussed in the next chapter.

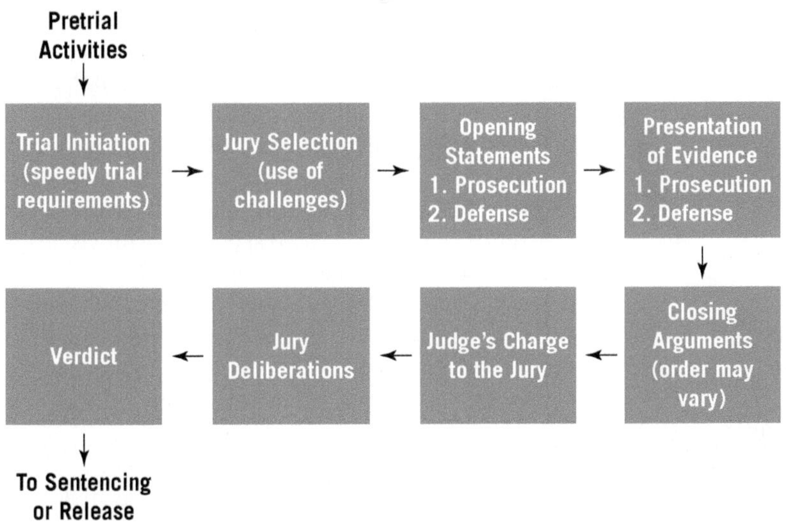

FIGURE 2 Stages in a Criminal Trial

▲ James Thomas, who was charged with murder in 1996 and freed in April 2005, after spending eight and a half years in a Louisiana jail waiting for his case to go to trial. A Louisiana state appeals court ruled that the state had taken too long to try him. Why does our system of justice require speedy trials?
Bill Feig/AP Wide World Photos

Trial Initiation

In 2005, a Louisiana state appeals court threw out murder charges against James Thomas and ordered him released. Thomas, an impoverished day laborer, had been arrested in 1996 and spent eight and a half years in jail waiting for a trial that never came. The ruling by the appeals court was widely seen as an indictment of Louisiana's understaffed and underfunded public defender system, members of which had simply been too busy to work on Thomas's case. A private attorney managed to get Thomas set free after his mother scraped together $500 to pay his fee.

The U.S. Constitution contains a speedy trial provision in its Sixth Amendment, which guarantees that "[i]n all criminal prosecutions, the accused shall enjoy the right to a speedy and public trial." Clogged court calendars, limited judicial resources, and general inefficiency, however, often combine to produce what appears to many to be unreasonable delays in trial initiation. The attention of the U.S. Supreme Court was brought to bear on trial delays in three precedent-setting cases: *Klopfer* v. *North Carolina* (1967),[81] *Barker* v. *Wingo* (1972),[82] and *Strunk* v. *U.S.* (1973).[83] The *Klopfer* case involved a Duke University professor and focused on civil disobedience in a protest against segregated facilities. In ruling on Klopfer's long-delayed trial, the Court asserted that the right to a speedy trial is a fundamental guarantee of the Constitution. In the *Barker* case, the Court held that Sixth Amendment guarantees to a quick trial could be illegally violated even in cases where the accused did not explicitly object to delays. In *Strunk*, it found that the denial of a speedy trial should result in the dismissal of all charges.

In 1974, against the advice of the Justice Department, the U.S. Congress passed the federal **Speedy Trial Act**.[84] The act allows for the dismissal of federal criminal charges in cases where the prosecution does not seek an indictment or information within 30 days of arrest (a 30-day extension is granted when the grand jury is not in session) or where a trial does not begin within 70 working days after indictment or initial appearance for defendants who plead not guilty. If a defendant is not available for trial or if witnesses cannot be called within the 70-day limit, the period may be extended up to 180 days. Delays brought about by the defendant, through requests for a continuance or because of escape, are not counted in the specified time periods.

Speedy Trial Act
A 1974 federal law requiring that proceedings against a defendant in a criminal case begin within a specified period of time, such as 70 working days after indictment. Some states also have speedy trial requirements.

In an important 1988 decision, *U.S.* v. *Taylor*,[85] the U.S. Supreme Court applied the requirements of the Speedy Trial Act to the case of a drug defendant who had escaped following arrest. The Court made it clear that trial delays that derive from the willful actions of the defendant do not apply to the 70-day period. The Court also held that trial delays, even when they result from government action, do not necessarily provide grounds for dismissal if they occur "without prejudice." Delays without prejudice are those that are due to circumstances beyond the control of criminal justice agencies.

In *Fex* v. *Michigan* (1993),[86] the U.S. Supreme Court ruled that "common sense compel[s] the conclusion that the 180-day period does not commence until the prisoner's disposition request has actually been delivered to the court and prosecutor of the jurisdiction that lodged the detainer against him." However, in a 1992 case, *Doggett* v. *U.S.*,[87] the Court held that a delay of eight and a half years violated speedy trial provisions because it resulted from government negligence.

In 2006, the Court refused to hear an appeal by suspected dirty bomb conspirator Jose Padilla, letting stand a lower court's decision that said the president could order a U.S. citizen who was arrested in this country for suspected terrorist ties to be held indefinitely without charges and without going to trial.[88]

> In all criminal prosecutions, the accused shall enjoy the right to a speedy and public trial, by an impartial jury . . . , and to be informed of the nature and cause of the accusation; to be confronted with the witnesses against him; to have compulsory process for obtaining witnesses in his favor; and to have the Assistance of Counsel for his defence.
>
> —Sixth Amendment to the U.S. Constitution

The federal Speedy Trial Act is applicable only to federal courts. However, the *Klopfer* case effectively made constitutional guarantees of a speedy trial applicable to state courts. In keeping with the trend toward reduced delays, many states have since enacted their own speedy trial legislation. Most state legislation sets a limit of 90 or 120 days as a reasonable period of time for a trial to commence.

Jury Selection

Challenges in Jury Selection

The Sixth Amendment guarantees the right to an impartial jury. An impartial jury is not necessarily an ignorant one. In other words, potential jurors will not always be excused from service on a jury if they have some knowledge of the case before them.[89] However, candidates who have already formed an opinion as to the guilt or innocence of the defendant are likely to be excused.

Some prospective jurors *try* to get excused, whereas others who would like to serve are excused because they are not judged to be suitable. Prosecution and defense attorneys use challenges to ensure the impartiality of the jury being impaneled. Three types of challenges are recognized in criminal courts: (1) challenges to the array, (2) challenges for cause, and (3) **peremptory challenges**.

peremptory challenge
The right to challenge a potential juror without disclosing the reason for the challenge. Prosecutors and defense attorneys routinely use peremptory challenges to eliminate from juries individuals who, although they express no obvious bias, are thought to be capable of swaying the jury in an undesirable direction.

Challenges to the array signify the belief, generally by the defense attorney, that the pool from which potential jurors are to be selected is not representative of the community or is biased in some significant way. A challenge to the array is argued before the hearing judge before jury selection begins.

During **jury selection**, both prosecution and defense attorneys question potential jurors in a process known as *voir dire* examination. Jurors are expected to be unbiased and free of preconceived notions of guilt or innocence. Challenges for cause, which may arise during *voir dire* examination, make the claim that an individual juror cannot be fair or impartial. One special issue of juror objectivity has concerned the U.S. Supreme Court: whether jurors with philosophical opposition to the death penalty should be excluded from juries whose decisions might result in the imposition of capital punishment. In the case of *Witherspoon* v. *Illinois* (1968),[90] the Court ruled that a juror opposed to the death penalty could be excluded from such juries if it were shown that (1) the juror would automatically vote against conviction without regard to the evidence or (2) the juror's philosophical orientation would prevent an objective consideration of the evidence. The *Witherspoon* case left unresolved a number of issues, among them the concern that it is difficult to demonstrate how a juror would automatically vote, a fact that might not even be known to the juror before trial begins.

jury selection
The process whereby, according to law and precedent, members of a particular trial jury are chosen.

Another area of concern that the Supreme Court has addressed involves the possibility that jurors could be influenced by pretrial news stories. In 1991, for example, the Court decided the case of *Mu'Min* v. *Virginia*.[91] Dawud Majud Mu'Min was a Virginia inmate who was serving time for first-degree murder. While accompanying a work detail outside the prison, he committed another murder. At the ensuing trial, eight of the 12 jurors who were seated admitted that they had heard or read something about the case, although none indicated that he or she had formed an opinion in advance as to Mu'Min's guilt or innocence. Following his conviction, Mu'Min appealed to the Supreme Court, claiming that his right to a fair trial had been denied due to pretrial publicity. The Court disagreed and upheld his conviction, citing the jurors' claims that they were not biased.

The third kind of challenge, the peremptory challenge, allows attorneys to remove potential jurors without having to give a reason. Peremptory challenges, used by both the prosecution and the defense, are limited in number: Federal courts allow each side up to 20 peremptory challenges in capital cases and as few as three in minor criminal cases.[92] States vary as to the number of peremptory challenges they permit.

A developing field that seeks to take advantage of peremptory challenges is **scientific jury selection**, which uses correlational techniques from the social sciences to gauge the likelihood that a potential juror will vote for conviction or acquittal. It makes predictions based on the economic, ethnic, and other personal and social characteristics of each member of the juror pool. Such techniques generally remove potential jurors who have any knowledge or opinions about the case to be tried. Also removed are people who have been trained in the law or in criminal justice. Anyone working for a criminal justice agency or anyone who has a family member working for such an agency or for a defense attorney will likely be dismissed through

scientific jury selection
The use of correlational techniques from the social sciences to gauge the likelihood that potential jurors will vote for conviction or for acquittal.

peremptory challenges on the chance that they may be biased in favor of one side or the other. Additionally, scientific jury selection techniques may result in the dismissal of highly educated or professionally successful individuals to eliminate the possibility of such individuals exercising undue control over jury deliberations.

Critics of the jury selection process charge that the end result is a jury composed of people who are uneducated, uninformed, and generally inexperienced at making any type of well-considered decision. Some jurors may not understand the charges against the defendant or comprehend what is required for a finding of guilt or innocence. Likewise, some may not even possess the attention span needed to hear all the testimony that will be offered in a case. As a consequence, critics say, decisions rendered by such a jury may be based more on emotion than on findings of fact.

Another emerging technique is the use of what is called a *shadow jury* to assess the impact of a defense attorney's arguments. Shadow jurors are hired court observers who sit in the courtroom and listen to what both sides in a criminal trial have to say. They hear evidence as it is presented and listen as witnesses are examined and cross-examined. Unlike professional legal experts, shadow jurors are laypeople who are expected to give defense attorneys a feel for what the "real" jurors are thinking and feeling as a case progresses, allowing for ongoing modifications in defense strategy.[93]

After the wrangling over jury selection has run its course, the jury is sworn in and alternate jurors are selected (alternates may be called to replace jurors taken ill or dismissed from the jury because they don't conform to the requirements of jury service once trial has begun). At this point, the judge will decide whether the jury is to be sequestered during the trial. Members of **sequestered juries** are not permitted to have contact with the public and are often housed in a motel or hotel until completion of the trial. Anyone who attempts to contact a sequestered jury or to influence members of a nonsequestered jury may be held accountable for jury tampering. Following jury selection, the stage is set for opening arguments[94] to begin.

sequestered jury
A jury that is isolated from the public during the course of a trial and throughout the deliberation process.

Jury Selection and Race

Race alone cannot provide the basis for jury selection, and juries may not be intentionally selected for racial imbalance. As long ago as 1880, the U.S. Supreme Court held that "a statute barring blacks from service on grand or petit juries denied equal protection of the laws to a black man convicted of murder by an all-white jury."[95] Even so, peremptory challenges continued to tend toward racial imbalance. In 1965, for example, a black defendant in Alabama was convicted of rape by an all-white jury (the local prosecutor had used his peremptory challenges to exclude blacks from the jury). The case eventually reached the Supreme Court, where the conviction was upheld.[96] At that time, the Court refused to limit the practice of peremptory challenges, reasoning that to do so would place them under the same judicial scrutiny as challenges for cause.

However, in the 1986 case of *Batson* v. *Kentucky*,[97] following what many claimed was widespread abuse of peremptory challenges by prosecution and defense alike, the Supreme Court was forced to overrule its earlier decision. Batson, an African American man, had been convicted of second-degree burglary and other offenses by an all-white jury. The prosecutor had used his peremptory challenges to remove all African Americans from jury service at the trial. The Court agreed that the use of peremptory challenges for purposeful discrimination constitutes a violation of the defendant's right to an impartial jury.

The *Batson* decision laid out the requirements that defendants must prove when seeking to establish the discriminatory use of peremptory challenges. They include the need to prove that the defendant is a member of a recognized racial group that has been intentionally excluded from the jury and the need to raise a reasonable suspicion that the prosecutor used peremptory challenges in a discriminatory manner. Justice Thurgood Marshall, writing a concurring opinion in *Batson*, presaged what was to come: "The inherent potential of peremptory challenges to destroy the jury process," he wrote, "by permitting the exclusion of jurors on racial grounds should ideally lead the Court to ban them entirely from the criminal justice system."

A few years later, in *Ford* v. *Georgia* (1991),[98] the Court moved much closer to Justice Marshall's position when it remanded a case for a new trial because the prosecutor had misused peremptory challenges. The prosecutor had used nine of the ten peremptory challenges available under Georgia law to eliminate prospective black jurors. In *Ford*, the Court did not find that the right of the defendant to an impartial jury had been breached, but it did determine that the civil rights of the jurors themselves had been violated under the Fourteenth Amendment due to a pattern of discrimination based on race. In another 1991 case, *Powers* v. *Ohio*,[99] the Court found in favor of a white defendant who claimed that his constitutional rights had been violated by the intentional exclusion of blacks from his jury through the use of peremptory challenges.

In the 1992 case of *Georgia* v. *McCollum*,[100] the Court barred defendants and their attorneys from using peremptory challenges to exclude potential jurors on the basis of race. In *McCollum*, Justice Harry Blackmun, writing for the majority, said, "Be it at the hands of the state or defense, if a court allows jurors to be excluded because of group bias, it is a willing participant in a scheme that could only undermine the very foundation of our system of justice—our citizens' confidence in it."

> The jury is such a cornerstone of justice and the democratic process, [but] the jury process needs to be brought into the 21st century.
>
> —Robert Grey, president, American Bar Association[ii]

Soon thereafter, peremptory challenges based on gender were similarly restricted (*J.E.B.* v. *Alabama*, 1994[101]), although at the time of this writing the Court has refused to ban peremptory challenges that exclude jurors because of religious or sexual orientation.[102] In the 1998 case of *Campbell* v. *Louisiana*,[103] the Court held that a white criminal defendant can raise equal protection and due process objections to discrimination against blacks in the selection of grand jurors. The Supreme Court reasoned that "regardless of skin color, an accused suffers a significant 'injury in fact' when the grand jury's composition is tainted by racial discrimination." The Court also said, "The integrity of the body's decisions depends on the integrity of the process used to select the grand jurors."

Finally, in the 2003 case of *Miller-El* v. *Cockrell*,[104] the Court found that a convicted capital defendant's constitutional rights had been violated by Dallas County (Texas) prosecutors who engaged in intentional efforts to remove eligible African Americans from the pool of potential jurors. Ten out of 11 eligible African Americans had been excluded through the use of peremptory strikes. The decision was reaffirmed in the 2005 U.S. Supreme Court case of *Miller-El* v. *Dretke*[105] and again in the 2008 case of *Snyder* v. *Louisiana*.[106] The Court's decision in *Snyder* v. *Louisiana*, which provides a good summary of its position on the use of peremptory strikes to eliminate black prospective jurors, is available at **Library Extra 7**.

Opening Statements

The presentation of information to the jury begins with **opening statements** made by the prosecution and the defense. The purposes of opening statements are to advise the jury of what the attorneys intend to prove and to describe how such proof will be offered. Evidence is not offered during opening statements. Eventually, however, the jury will have to weigh the evidence presented during the trial and decide which side made the more effective arguments. When a defendant has little evidence to present, the main job of the defense attorney will be to dispute the veracity of the prosecution's version of the facts. Under such circumstances, defense attorneys may choose not to present any evidence or testimony at all, focusing instead on the burden-of-proof requirement facing the prosecution. Such plans will generally be made clear during opening statements. At this time, the defense attorney is also likely to stress the human qualities of the defendant and to remind jurors of the awesome significance of their task.

opening statement
The initial statement of the prosecution or the defense, made in a court of law to a judge, or to a judge and jury, describing the facts that he or she intends to present during trial to prove the case.

Lawyers for both sides are bound by a good-faith ethical requirement in their opening statements. Attorneys may mention only the evidence that they believe actually can and will be presented as the trial progresses. Allusions to evidence that an attorney has no intention of offering are regarded as unprofessional and have been defined by the U.S. Supreme Court as "professional misconduct."[107] When material alluded to in an opening statement cannot, for whatever reason, later be presented in court, opposing counsel gains an opportunity to discredit the other side.

Presentation of Evidence

The crux of the criminal trial is the presentation of evidence. First, the state is given the opportunity to present evidence intended to prove the defendant's guilt. After prosecutors have rested their case, the defense is afforded the opportunity to provide evidence favorable to the defendant.

Types of Evidence

evidence
Anything useful to a judge or jury in deciding the facts of a case. Evidence may take the form of witness testimony, written documents, videotapes, magnetic media, photographs, physical objects, and so on.

direct evidence
The evidence that, if believed, directly proves a fact. Eyewitness testimony and videotaped documentation account for the majority of all direct evidence heard in the criminal courtroom.

circumstantial evidence
The evidence that requires interpretation or that requires a judge or jury to reach a conclusion based on what the evidence indicates. From the close proximity of the defendant to a smoking gun, for example, the jury might conclude that he or she pulled the trigger.

real evidence
Evidence that consists of physical material or traces of physical activity.

Evidence can be either direct or circumstantial. **Direct evidence**, if believed, proves a fact without requiring the judge or jury to draw inferences. For example, direct evidence may be the information contained in a photograph or videotape. It may be testimonial evidence provided by a witness on the stand. A straightforward statement by a witness—such as "I saw him do it!"—is a form of direct evidence.

Circumstantial evidence is indirect and requires the judge or jury to make inferences and to draw conclusions. At a murder trial, for example, a person who heard gunshots and moments later saw someone run by with a smoking gun in hand might testify to those facts. Even without an eyewitness to the actual homicide, the jury might later conclude that the person seen with the gun was the one who pulled the trigger and committed the crime. Contrary to popular belief, circumstantial evidence is sufficient to produce a verdict and conviction in a criminal trial. In fact, some prosecuting attorneys prefer to work entirely with circumstantial evidence, weaving a tapestry of the criminal act in their arguments to the jury.

Real evidence, which may be either direct or circumstantial, consists of physical material or traces of physical activity. Weapons, tire tracks, ransom notes, and fingerprints all fall into the category of real evidence. Real (or physical) evidence is introduced in the trial by means of *exhibits*, which are objects or displays that may be shown to members of the jury once they are formally accepted as evidence by the judge (see CJ Exhibit 1). Documentary evidence, which is one type of real evidence, includes writings such as business records, journals, written confessions, and letters. Documentary evidence can extend beyond paper and ink to include data on magnetic and optical storage devices used in computer operations and video and voice recordings.

Evaluation of Evidence

One of the most significant decisions a trial court judge makes is deciding which evidence can be presented to the jury. In making that decision, judges will examine the relevance of the evidence to the case at hand (relevant evidence has a bearing on the facts at issue). For example, a decade or two ago, it was not unusual for a woman's sexual history to be brought out in rape trials. Under what are called *rape shield statutes*, most states today will not allow this practice, recognizing that these details often have no bearing on the case. Rape shield statutes have been strengthened by U.S. Supreme Court decisions, including the 1991 case of *Michigan* v. *Lucas*.[108]

probative value
The degree to which a particular item of evidence is useful in, and relevant to, proving something important in a trial.

In evaluating evidence, judges must also weigh the **probative value** of an item of evidence (its usefulness and relevance) against its potential inflammatory or prejudicial qualities. Even useful evidence may unduly bias a jury if it is exceptionally gruesome or is presented in such a way as to imply guilt. For example, gory photographs, especially color photographs, may be withheld from the jury's eyes. In one recent case, a new trial was ordered when photos of the crime scene were projected on a wall over the head of the defendant as he sat in the courtroom, and an appellate court found that presentation to have prejudiced the jury.

Sometimes evidence is found to have only limited admissibility, which means that the evidence can be used for a specific purpose but that it might not be accurate in other details. Photographs, for example, may be admitted as evidence for the narrow purpose of showing spatial relationships between objects under discussion, even if the photographs were taken under conditions that did not exist when the offense was committed (such as daylight).

When judges allow the use of evidence that may have been illegally or unconstitutionally gathered, grounds may be created for a later appeal if the trial concludes with a "guilty" verdict. Even when evidence is improperly introduced at trial, however, a number of Supreme Court decisions[109] have held that there may be no grounds for an effective appeal unless such introduction "had substantial and injurious effect or influence in determining the jury's verdict."[110] Called the *harmless error rule*, this standard places the burden on the prosecution to show that the jury's decision would most likely have been the same even in the absence of the inappropriate evidence. The rule is not applicable when a defendant's constitutional guarantees are violated by "structural defects in the constitution of the trial mechanism" itself[111]—such as when a judge gives constitutionally improper instructions to a jury. (We'll discuss those instructions later in this chapter.)

CJ Exhibit 1
Pretrial and Post-Trial Motions

A *motion* is "an oral or written request made to a court at any time before, during, or after court proceedings, asking the court to make a specified finding, decision, or order."[1] Written motions are called *petitions*. This exhibit lists the most common motions made by both sides in a criminal case before and after trial.

MOTION FOR DISCOVERY

A motion for discovery, filed by the defense, asks the court to allow the defendant's lawyers to view the evidence that the prosecution intends to present at trial. Physical evidence, lists of witnesses, documents, photographs, and so on, which the prosecution plans to introduce in court, are usually made available to the defense as a result of a motion for discovery.

MOTION TO SUPPRESS EVIDENCE

The defense may file a motion to suppress evidence if it learns, in the preliminary hearing or through pretrial discovery, of evidence that it believes to have been unlawfully acquired.

MOTION TO DISMISS CHARGES

A variety of circumstances may result in the filing of a motion to dismiss charges. They include (1) an opinion, by defense counsel, that the indictment or information is not sound; (2) a violation of speedy trial legislation; (3) a plea bargain with the defendant, which may require testimony against codefendants; (4) the death of an important witness or the destruction or disappearance of necessary evidence; (5) the confession, by a supposed victim, that the facts in the case were fabricated; and (6) the success of a motion to suppress evidence that effectively eliminates the prosecution's case.

MOTION FOR CONTINUANCE

The motion for continuance seeks a delay in the start of the trial. Defense motions of this type are often based on an inability to locate important witnesses, the illness of the defendant, or a change in defense counsel immediately before trial.

MOTION FOR CHANGE OF VENUE

In well-known cases, pretrial publicity may lessen the opportunity for a case to be tried before an unbiased jury. A motion for change of venue asks that the trial be moved to some other area where prejudice against the defendant is less likely to exist.

MOTION FOR SEVERANCE OF OFFENSES

Defendants charged with a number of crimes may ask to be tried separately on all or some of the charges through use of a motion for severance of offenses. Although consolidating charges for trial saves time and money, some defendants believe that it is more likely to make them appear guilty.

MOTION FOR SEVERANCE OF DEFENDANTS

The motion for severance of defendants asks the court to try the accused separately from any codefendants. These motions are likely to be filed when the defendant believes that the jury may be prejudiced against him or her by evidence applicable only to other defendants.

MOTION TO DETERMINE PRESENT SANITY

A lack of "present sanity," even though it may be no defense against the criminal charge, can delay trial because a person cannot be tried, sentenced, or punished while insane. If a defendant is insane at the time a trial is to begin, a motion to determine present sanity may halt the proceedings until treatment can be arranged.

MOTION FOR A BILL OF PARTICULARS

The motion for a bill of particulars asks the court to order the prosecutor to provide detailed information about the charges that the defendant will be facing in court. Defendants charged with a number of offenses, or with a number of counts of the same offense, may make such a motion. They may, for example, seek to learn which alleged instances of an offense will become the basis for prosecution or which specific items of contraband allegedly found in their possession are held to violate the law.

MOTION FOR A MISTRIAL

A mistrial may be declared at any time, and a motion for a mistrial may be made by either side. Mistrials are likely to be declared in cases in which highly prejudicial comments are made by either attorney. Defense motions for a mistrial do not provide grounds for a later claim of double jeopardy.

MOTION FOR ARREST OF JUDGMENT

After the verdict of the jury has been announced but before the sentencing, the defendant may make a motion for arrest of judgment. With this motion, the defendant asserts that some legally acceptable reason exists as to why sentencing should not occur. Defendants who are seriously ill, who are hospitalized, or who have gone insane before judgment has been imposed may file such a motion.

MOTION FOR A NEW TRIAL

After a jury has returned a guilty verdict, the court may entertain a motion for a new trial from the defense. Acceptance of such a motion is usually based on the discovery of new evidence that is of significant benefit to the defense and that will set aside the conviction.

[1]U.S. Department of Justice, *Dictionary of Criminal Justice Data Terminology*, 2nd ed. (Washington, DC: U.S. Government Printing Office, 1982).

Testimony of Witnesses

Testimony given by witnesses is generally the chief means by which evidence is introduced at trial. Witnesses may include victims, police officers, the defendant, specialists in recognized fields, and others with useful information to provide. Some of these witnesses may have been present during the commission of the offense, while most will have had only a later opportunity to investigate the situation or to analyze evidence.

testimony
The oral evidence offered by a sworn witness on the witness stand during a criminal trial.

> A jury consists of 12 persons chosen to decide who has the better lawyer.
> —Robert Frost (1874–1963)

Before a witness will be allowed to testify to any fact, the questioning attorney must establish the person's competence. Competence to testify requires that witnesses have personal knowledge of the information they will discuss and that they understand their duty to tell the truth.

One of the defense attorney's most critical decisions is whether to put the defendant on the stand. Defendants have a Fifth Amendment right to remain silent and to refuse to testify. In the precedent-setting case of *Griffin* v. *California* (1965),[112] the U.S. Supreme Court declared that if a defendant refuses to testify, prosecutors and judges are enjoined from even commenting on this fact, although a judge should instruct the jury that such a failure cannot be held to indicate guilt. In 2001, in the case of *Ohio* v. *Reiner*,[113] the U.S. Supreme Court extended Fifth Amendment protections to *witnesses* who deny any and all guilt in association with a crime for which another person is being prosecuted.

Direct examination of a witness takes place when a witness is first called to the stand. If the prosecutor calls the witness, the witness is referred to as a *witness for the prosecution.* When the direct examiner is a defense attorney, the witness is called a *witness for the defense.*

The direct examiner may ask questions that require a "yes" or "no" answer or may ask narrative questions that allow the witness to tell a story in his or her own words. During direct examination, courts generally prohibit the use of leading questions, that is, those that suggest answers to the witness.[114]

Cross-examination refers to the examination of a witness by someone other than the direct examiner. Anyone who offers testimony in a criminal court has the duty to submit to cross-examination.[115] The purpose of cross-examination is to test the credibility and the memory of the witness.

Most states and the federal government restrict the scope of cross-examination to material covered during direct examination. Questions about other matters, even though they may relate to the case before the court, are not allowed. A small number of states allow the cross-examiner to raise any issue as long as the court deems it relevant. Leading questions, generally disallowed in direct examination, are regarded as the mainstay of cross-examination. Such questions allow for a concise restatement of testimony that has already been offered and serve to focus efficiently on potential problems that the cross-examiner seeks to address.

perjury
The intentional making of a false statement as part of the testimony by a sworn witness in a judicial proceeding on a matter relevant to the case at hand.

Some witnesses commit **perjury**—that is, they make statements that they know to be untrue. Reasons for perjured testimony vary, but most witnesses who lie on the stand probably do so in an effort to help friends accused of crimes. Witnesses who perjure themselves are subject to impeachment, in which either the defense or the prosecution demonstrates that a witness has intentionally offered false testimony. For example, previous statements made by the witness may be shown to be at odds with more recent declarations. When it can be demonstrated that a witness has offered inaccurate or false testimony, the witness has been effectively impeached. Perjury is a serious offense in its own right, and dishonest witnesses may face fines or jail time.

At the conclusion of the cross-examination, the direct examiner may again question the witness. This procedure is called *redirect examination* and may be followed by a recross-examination and so on, until both sides are satisfied that they have exhausted fruitful lines of questioning.

Children as Witnesses

An area of special concern involves the use of children as witnesses in a criminal trial, especially when the children are also victims. Currently, in an effort to avoid what may be traumatizing direct confrontations between child witnesses and the accused, 37 states allow the use of videotaped testimony in criminal courtrooms, and 32 permit the use of closed-circuit television, which allows the child to testify out of the presence of the defendant. In 1988, however, in the case of *Coy* v. *Iowa*,[116] the U.S. Supreme Court ruled that a courtroom screen, used to shield child witnesses from visual confrontation with a defendant in a child sex-abuse case, had violated the Confrontation Clause of the Constitution (found in the Sixth Amendment).

On the other hand, in the 1990 case of *Maryland* v. *Craig*,[117] the Court upheld the use of closed-circuit television to shield children who testify in criminal courts. The Court's decision was partially based on the realization that "a significant majority of States have enacted statutes to protect child witnesses from the trauma of giving testimony in child-abuse cases . . . [which] attests to the widespread belief in the importance of such a policy."

Although a face-to-face confrontation with a child victim may not be necessary in the courtroom, until 1992 the Supreme Court had been reluctant to allow into evidence descriptions of abuse and other statements made by children, even to child-care professionals, when those statements were made outside the courtroom. In *Idaho* v. *Wright* (1990),[118] the Court reasoned that such "statements [are] fraught with the dangers of unreliability which the Confrontation Clause is designed to highlight and obviate."

However, in *White* v. *Illinois* (1992),[119] the Court reversed its stance, ruling that in-court testimony given by a medical provider and the child's babysitter, which repeated what the child had said to them concerning White's sexually abusive behavior, was permissible.

The Hearsay Rule

Hearsay is anything not based on the personal knowledge of a witness. A witness may say, for example, "John told me that Fred did it!" Such a witness becomes a hearsay declarant, and following a likely objection by counsel, the trial judge will have to decide whether the witness's statement will be allowed to stand as evidence. In most cases, the judge will instruct the jury to disregard the witness's comment, thereby enforcing the **hearsay rule**, which prohibits the use of "secondhand evidence." The hearsay rule is based on the Sixth Amendment's Confrontation Clause, which gives a criminal defendant the right to confront his or her accusers. In today's courts, that generally means that the defendant has a right to cross-examine witnesses against him or her.

hearsay
Something that is not based on the personal knowledge of a witness. Witnesses who testify about something they have heard, for example, are offering hearsay by repeating information about a matter of which they have no direct knowledge.

hearsay rule
The long-standing precedent that hearsay cannot be used in American courtrooms. Rather than accepting testimony based on hearsay, the court will ask that the person who was the original source of the hearsay information be brought in to be questioned and cross-examined. Exceptions to the hearsay rule may occur when the person with direct knowledge is dead or is otherwise unable to testify.

Exceptions to the hearsay rule have been established by both precedent and tradition. One exception is the dying declaration, which is a statement made by a person who is about to die. When heard by a second party, it may usually be repeated in court, provided that certain conditions have been met. A dying declaration is generally a valid exception to the hearsay rule when it is made by someone who knows that he or she is about to die and when the statement made relates to the cause and circumstances of the impending death.

Spontaneous statements, also called *excited utterances*, provide another exception to the hearsay rule. A statement is considered spontaneous when it is made in the heat of excitement before the person has had time to make it up. For example, a defendant who is just regaining consciousness following a crime may make an utterance that could later be repeated in court by those who heard it.

Out-of-court statements, especially if they were recorded during a time when a person was experiencing great excitement or while a person was under considerable stress, may also become exceptions to the hearsay rule. Many states, for example, permit juries to hear 9-1-1 tape recordings or to read police transcripts of victim interviews without requiring that the people who made them appear in court. In two cases, however, the U.S. Supreme Court barred admission of tape-recorded 9-1-1 calls when the people making them were alive and in good health but not available for cross-examination. In *Crawford* v. *Washington*,[120] a 2004 case, the Court disallowed a woman's tape-recorded eyewitness account of a fight in which her husband stabbed another man, holding that the Constitution bars admission of testimonial statements of a witness who did not appear at trial unless he or she was unable to testify and the defendant had a prior opportunity for cross-examination. In *Davis* v. *Washington*,[121] decided in 2006, the Court held that a 9-1-1 call made by a woman who said that her former boyfriend was beating her had been improperly introduced as testimonial evidence. The woman had been subpoenaed but failed to appear in court. The key word in both cases is *testimonial*, and the Court indicated that "statements are nontestimonial when made in the course of police interrogation under circumstances objectively indicating that the primary purpose of interrogation is to enable police assistance to meet an ongoing emergency."[122]

The use of other out-of-court statements, such as writings or routine video or audio recordings, usually requires the witness to testify that the statements or depictions were accurate at the time they were made. Witnesses who so testify may be subject to cross-examination by the defendant's attorney. Nonetheless, this "past recollection recorded" exception to the hearsay rule is especially useful in drawn-out court proceedings that occur long after the crime. Under such circumstances, witnesses may no longer remember the details of an event. Their earlier statements to authorities, however, can be introduced into evidence as past recollection recorded.

▲ An attorney making a closing argument to the jury. What other features of the adversarial system can you identify?
Tim Pannell/Corbis RF

Closing Arguments

At the conclusion of a criminal trial, both sides have the opportunity for a final narrative presentation to the jury in the form of a **closing argument**. This summation provides a review and analysis of the evidence. Its purpose is to persuade the jury to draw a conclusion favorable to the presenter. Testimony can be quoted, exhibits referred to, and attention drawn to inconsistencies in the evidence presented by the other side.

States vary as to the order of closing arguments. Nearly all allow the defense attorney to speak to the jury before the prosecution makes its final points. A few permit the prosecutor the first opportunity for summation. Some jurisdictions and the Federal Rules of Criminal Procedure[123] authorize a defense rebuttal (a rebuttal is a response to the closing argument of the other side).

Some specific issues may need to be addressed during summation. If, for example, the defendant has not taken the stand during the trial, the defense attorney's closing argument will inevitably stress that this failure to testify cannot be regarded as indicating guilt. Where the prosecution's case rests entirely on circumstantial evidence, the defense can be expected to stress the lack of any direct proof, and the prosecutor is likely to argue that circumstantial evidence can be stronger than direct evidence, since it is not as easily affected by human error or false testimony.

closing argument
An oral summation of a case presented to a judge, or to a judge and jury, by the prosecution or by the defense in a criminal trial.

Judge's Charge to the Jury

After closing arguments, the judge charges the jury to "retire and select one of your number as a foreman . . . and deliberate upon the evidence which has been presented until you have reached a verdict." The words of the charge vary somewhat between jurisdictions and among judges, but all judges will remind members of the jury of their duty to consider objectively only the evidence that has been presented and of the need for impartiality. Most judges also remind jury members of the statutory elements of the alleged offense, of the burden of proof that rests on the prosecution, and of the need for the prosecution to have proved the defendant's guilt beyond a reasonable doubt before the jury can return a guilty verdict.

In their charge, many judges also provide a summary of the evidence presented, usually from notes they have taken during the trial, as a means of refreshing the jurors' memories of events. About half of all the states allow judges the freedom to express their own views as to the credibility of witnesses and the significance of evidence. The other states only permit judges to summarize the evidence in an objective and impartial manner.

Recently, as the CJ News box in this section shows, the plethora of digital communications devices now available has made it difficult for courts to control jurors' access to out-of-court information. Read a set of jury instructions designed to alleviate this problem at **Library Extra 8**.

Following the charge, the jury is removed from the courtroom and is permitted to begin its deliberations. In the absence of the jury, defense attorneys may choose to challenge portions of the judge's charge. If they feel that some oversight has occurred in the original charge, they may ask the judge to provide the jury with additional instructions or information. Such objections, if denied by the judge, often become the basis for an appeal when a conviction is returned.

Jury Deliberations and the Verdict

Deliberations Process

In cases in which the evidence is either very clear or very weak, jury deliberations may be brief, lasting only a matter of hours or even minutes. Some juries, however, deliberate days or sometimes weeks, carefully weighing all the nuances of the evidence they have seen and heard. Many jurisdictions require that juries reach a unanimous **verdict** (decision), although the U.S. Supreme Court has ruled that unanimous verdicts are not required in noncapital cases.[124] Even so, some juries are unable to agree on any verdict. When a jury is deadlocked,

verdict
The decision of the jury in a jury trial or of a judicial officer in a nonjury trial.

CJ News
Social Networking among Jurors Is Trying Judges' Patience

Al Schuler, one of 12 jurors weighing the fate of a 23-year-old charged with killing a homeless man in Maryland, was confused by the word "lividity" and what role it might have played in explaining the circumstances of the victim's beating death.

So, . . . [h]e looked up the definition on Wikipedia, the online encyclopedia. "It was just a definition, like going to the dictionary," Schuler said. "It was very innocent."

A Maryland appeals court didn't think so. In throwing out the defendant's first-degree murder conviction and ordering a new trial, the court ruled that Schuler's inquiry violated [the] judge's order prohibiting jurors from researching the case.

Schuler's query is just the latest example of how modern technology and an information-saturated culture are testing centuries-old notions of how juries and judges mete out justice. . . .

Judges and legal experts are particularly concerned about how technology and culture are affecting jurors and a defendant's right to a fair trial. The Internet has provided easy and instant access to newspaper archives, criminal records, detailed maps, legal opinions and social-networking sites, such as Facebook. . . .

Judges have long instructed jurors to avoid reading newspaper stories about trials and to not discuss the case with one another, aside from their deliberations. They also warn them not to conduct their own investigations. The rules are designed to ensure that jurors contemplate only the evidence admitted at trial and at the appropriate time. . . .

Today, technology has wiped out those barriers, and people have become increasingly reliant on the Internet for information. . . .

In recent years, a half-dozen cases have popped into public view because the misconduct was egregious enough that judges were forced to decide whether to grant new trials.

. . . [F]or example, a federal judge denied requests by defense attorneys to throw out the conviction of a former Pennsylvania state senator because a juror had posted updates to Twitter and Facebook during the trial. . . .

[A] New York appeals court upheld the second-degree murder conviction of a 30-year-old man despite a juror's Internet research into whether the victim's gunshot wound was inflicted at close range. In both instances, the judges found the tweeting and research did not harm the defendants' right to a fair trial.

But that isn't always the case. . . .

A New Jersey appeals court in July overturned the aggravated manslaughter convictions of three cousins because a juror had done Internet research about the victim, the defendants and the amount of prison time they faced and had told her colleagues about it. The men will get a new trial.

In Baltimore, defense attorneys for Baltimore Mayor Sheila Dixon, who was convicted of embezzling about $500 in retail gift cards, accused five jurors of improperly becoming friends and chatting about the case on Facebook. . . .

▲ Jurors listening to testimony in a criminal trial. How might jurors' unauthorized use of modern technology influence their deliberations?
Corbis RF

The counselors wanted Circuit Judge Dennis M. Sweeney to throw out the conviction and hold a new trial.

The issue nearly forced Sweeney to question jurors about their conduct, but Dixon and prosecutors reached a surprise plea deal that ended her appeals.

Jurors would probably have faced a less-than-sympathetic audience with Sweeney, who is considered one of the state's leading authorities on jury issues. . . .

"Modern jurors, so used to instant access, may not fully appreciate the need to divest themselves of the trappings of information-gathering and communication that otherwise dominate their lives," the judge lamented in Baltimore's *Daily Record.*

Sweeney urged judges to order jurors to specifically avoid discussing their cases on Facebook, MySpace and Twitter—a warning he repeated during Dixon's trial.

It appears that such admonishments were not enough for the "Facebook Friends."

Source: Del Quentin Wilber, "Social Networking among Jurors Is Trying Judges' Patience," *The Washington Post*, www.washingtonpost.com, © January 9, 2010 The Washington Post. All rights reserved. Used by permission and protected by the Copyright Laws of the United States. The printing, copying, redistribution, or retransmission of the Material without express written permission is prohibited.

it is said to be a *hung jury*. When a unanimous decision is required, juries may be deadlocked by the strong opposition of only one member to a verdict agreed on by all the others.

In some states, judges are allowed to add a boost to nearly hung juries by recharging them under a set of instructions that the Supreme Court put forth in the 1896 case of *Allen* v. *U.S.*[125] The *Allen* charge, as it is known in those jurisdictions, urges the jury to vigorous deliberations and suggests to obstinate jurors that their objections may be ill-founded if they make no impression on the other jurors.

Problems with the Jury System

> In Suits at common law . . . the right of trial by jury shall be preserved, and no fact tried by a jury, shall be otherwise re-examined in any Court of the United States, than according to the rules of the common law.
>
> —Seventh Amendment to the U.S. Constitution

Judge Harold J. Rothwax, a well-known critic of today's jury system, tells the tale of a rather startling case over which he presided in 1991. The case involved a murder defendant, a handsome young man who had been fired by a New York company that serviced automated teller machines (ATMs). After being fired, the defendant intentionally caused a machine in a remote area to malfunction. When two former colleagues arrived to fix it, he robbed them, stole the money inside the ATM, and shot both men repeatedly. One of the men survived long enough to identify his former coworker as the shooter. The man was arrested, and a trial ensued. After three weeks of hearing the case, the jury deadlocked. Judge Rothwax later learned that the jury had voted 11 to one to convict the defendant, but the one holdout just couldn't believe that "someone so good-looking could . . . commit such a crime."[126]

Many routine cases as well as some highly publicized cases, like the murder trial of O. J. Simpson which the whole world watched, have called into question the ability of the American jury system to do its job—that is, to sort through the evidence and to accurately determine the defendant's guilt or innocence. In a televised 1995 trial, Simpson was acquitted of the charge that he murdered his ex-wife, Nicole Brown, and her friend Ronald Goldman outside Brown's home in 1994. Many people believed that strong evidence tied Simpson to the crimes, and the criminal trial left many people feeling unsatisfied with the criminal justice system and with the criminal trial process. Later, a civil jury ordered Simpson to pay $33.5 million to the Goldman family and to Nicole Brown's estate.

Because jurors are drawn from all walks of life, many cannot be expected to understand modern legal complexities and to appreciate all the nuances of trial court practice. It is likely that even the best-intentioned jurors cannot understand and rarely observe some jury instructions.[127] In highly charged cases, emotions are often difficult to separate from fact, and during deliberations, some juries are dominated by one or two members with forceful personalities. Jurors may also suffer from inattention or may be unable to understand fully the testimony of expert witnesses or the significance of technical evidence.

Jurors may be less than effective in cases where they fear personal retaliation. In the state-level trial of the police officers accused in the infamous Rodney King beating, for example, jurors reported being afraid for their lives due to the riots in Los Angeles that broke out after their "not guilty" verdict was announced. Some slept with weapons by their side, and others sent their children away to safe locations.[128] Because of the potential for harm that jurors faced in the 1993 federal trial of the same officers, U.S. District Judge John G. Davies ruled that the names of the jurors be forever kept secret. Members of the press called the secrecy order "an unprecedented infringement of the public's right of access to the justice system."[129] Similarly, in the 1993 trial of three black men charged with the beating of white truck driver Reginald Denny during the Los Angeles riots, the judge ordered that the identities of the jurors not be released.

Opponents of the jury system have argued that it should be replaced by a panel of judges who would both render a verdict and impose sentence. Regardless of how well considered such a suggestion may be, such a change could not occur without modification of the Constitution's Sixth Amendment right to trial by jury.

An alternative suggestion for improving the process of trial by jury has been the call for professional jurors. Professional jurors would be paid by the government—like judges, prosecutors, and public defenders—and would be expected to have the expertise to sit on any jury. Professional jurors would be trained to listen objectively and would be taught the kinds of decision-making skills necessary to function effectively within an adversarial context. They would hear one case after another, perhaps moving between jurisdictions in cases of highly publicized crimes.

Multiculturalism and Diversity
The Bilingual Courtroom

One of the central multicultural issues facing the criminal justice system today is the need for clear communication with recent immigrants and subcultural groups that have not been fully acculturated. Many such groups hold to traditions and values that differ from those held by the majority of Americans. Such differences influence the interpretation of things seen and heard. Even more basic, however, are language differences that might prevent effective communication with criminal justice system personnel.

Techniques that law enforcement officers can use in overcoming language differences. This box focuses on the use of courtroom interpreters to facilitate effective and accurate communication. The role of the courtroom interpreter is to present neutral verbatim, or word-for-word, translations. Interpreters must provide true, accurate, and complete interpretations of the exact statements made by non-English-speaking defendants, victims, and witnesses—whether on the stand, in writing, or in court-related conferences. The Court Interpreters and Translators Association also requires, through its code of professional ethics, that translators remember their "absolute responsibility to keep all oral and written information gained completely confidential."

Although most court interpreters are actually present in the courtroom at the time of trial, telephone interpreting provides an alternative way for courts to reduce problems associated with the lack of access to qualified interpreters. Today, state court administrative offices in Florida, Idaho, New Jersey, and Washington State sponsor programs through which qualified interpreters in metropolitan counties are made available to courts in rural counties by telephone.

The federal Court Interpreters Act of 1978[1] specifically provides for the use of interpreters in federal courts if needed by a witness or defendant who speaks "only or primarily a language other than English" or suffers from a substantial hearing impairment. It applies to both criminal and civil trials and hearings. The act does not require that an interpreter be appointed when a person has a speech impairment that is not accompanied by a hearing impairment. A court is not prohibited, however, from providing assistance to that person if it will aid in the efficient administration of justice.

Because it is a federal law, the Court Interpreters Act does not apply to state courts. Nonetheless, most states have enacted similar legislation. A few states are starting to introduce high-standard testing for court interpreters, although most states currently conduct little or no interpreter screening. The federal government and states with high standards for court interpreters generally require interpreter certification. To become certified, an interpreter must pass an oral examination, such as the federal court interpreter's examination or an examination administered by a state court or by a recognized international agency such as the United Nations.

There is growing recognition among professional court interpreters of the need for standardized interstate testing and certification programs. To meet that need, the National Center for State Courts created the Consortium for State Court Interpreter Certification. The consortium works to pool state resources for developing and administering court interpreter testing and training programs. The consortium's founding states were Minnesota, New Jersey, Oregon, and Washington, although many other states have since joined.

Because certified interpreters are not always available, even by telephone, most states have created a special category of "language-skilled interpreters." To qualify as a language-skilled interpreter, a person must demonstrate to the court's satisfaction his or her ability to interpret court proceedings from English to a designated language and from that language to English. Many states require sign language interpreters to hold a Legal Specialist Certificate, or its equivalent, from the Registry of Interpreters for the Deaf, showing that they are certified in American Sign Language. Learn more about language interpretation in the courts from the National Association of Judiciary Interpreters and Translators via **Web Extra 12.**

[1]28 U.S.C. section 1827.

References: National Association of Judiciary Interpreters and Translators website, http://www.najit.org; Madelynn Herman and Anne Endress Skove, "State Court Rules for Language Interpreters," memorandum number IS 99.1242, National Center for State Courts, Knowledge Management Office, September 8, 1999; Madelynn Herman and Dot Bryant, "Language Interpreting in the Courts," National Center for State Courts, http://www.ncsc.dni.us/KMO/Projects/Trends/99-00/articles/CtInterpreters.htm; and National Crime Prevention Council, *Building and Crossing Bridges: Refugees and Law Enforcement Working Together* (Washington, DC: NCPC, 1994).

Summary

THE COURTROOM WORK GROUP AND THE CRIMINAL TRAIL

- The courtroom work group comprises professional courtroom personnel, including the judge, the prosecuting attorney, the defense counsel, the bailiff, the trial court administrator, the court reporter, the clerk of court, and expert witnesses. The courtroom work group is guided by statutory requirements and ethical considerations, and its members are generally dedicated to bringing the criminal trial and other courtroom procedures to a successful close.
- Also present in the courtroom during a criminal trial are "outsiders"—nonprofessional courtroom participants like lay witnesses, jurors, the victim, the defendant, and spectators and members of the press. Nonprofessional or nonjudicial courtroom personnel may be unwilling or inadvertent participants in a criminal trial.

- The criminal trial involves an adversarial process that pits the prosecution against the defense. Trials are peer-based fact-finding processes intended to protect the rights of the accused while disputed issues of guilt or innocence are resolved. The primary purpose of a criminal trial is to determine whether the defendant violated the criminal law of the jurisdiction in which the court has authority.
- A criminal trial has eight stages: trial initiation, jury selection, opening statements, presentation of evidence, closing arguments, judge's charge to the jury, jury deliberations, and verdict. Each is described in detail in this chapter. At least a few experts have suggested the training and use of a cadre of professional jurors, versed in the law and in trial practice, who could insulate themselves from media portrayals of famous defendants and who would resolve questions of guilt or innocence more on the basis of reason than emotion.

QUESTIONS FOR REVIEW

1. Who are the professional members of the courtroom work group, and what are their roles?
2. Who are the nonprofessional courtroom participants, and what are their roles?
3. What is the purpose of a criminal trial? What is the difference between factual guilt and legal guilt? What do we mean by the term *adversarial system*?
4. What are the various stages of a criminal trial? Describe each one.

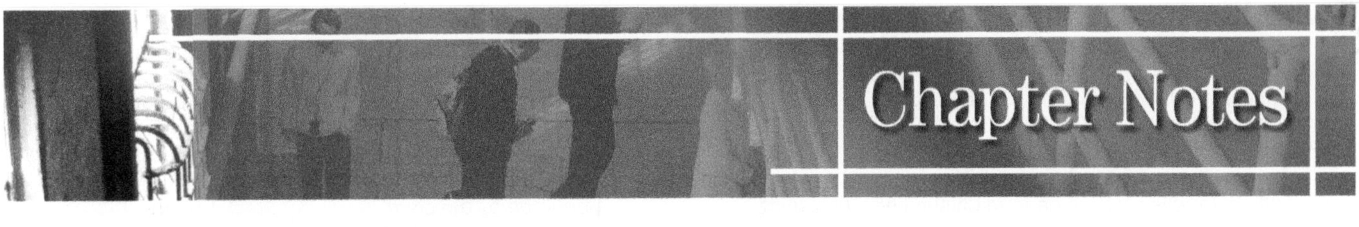

Chapter Notes

i. President's Commission on Law Enforcement and Administration of Justice, *The Challenge of Crime in a Free Society* (Washington, DC: U.S. Government Printing Office, 1967), p. 125.

ii. Quoted in Richard Willing, "Courts Try to Make Jury Duty Less of a Choice," *USA Today*, March 17, 2005.

---

1. D. Graham Burnett, "Anatomy of a Verdict: The View from a Juror's Chair," *New York Times Magazine*, August 26, 2001.
2. Many of the details for this story come from CBS News. See, for example, Mike Ballou, "Caylee Anthony Autopsy Reveals Grim Details But Sheds Little Light on Mystery," June 22, 2009, http://www.cbsnews.com/8301-504083_162-5103384-504083.html (accessed May 20, 2010).
3. See, for example, Jeffrey T. Ulmer, *Social Worlds of Sentencing: Court Communities under Sentencing Guidelines* (Ithaca: State University of New York Press, 1997); and Roy B. Flemming, Peter F. Nardulli, and James Eisenstein, *The Craft of Justice: Politics and Work in Criminal Court Communities* (Philadelphia: University of Pennsylvania Press, 1993).
4. See, for example, Edward J. Clynch and David W. Neubauer, "Trial Courts as Organizations," *Law and Policy Quarterly*, Vol. 3 (1981), pp. 69–94.
5. American Bar Association, *ABA Standards for Criminal Justice: Special Functions of the Trial Judge*, 3rd ed. (Chicago: ABA, 2000).
6. In 1940, Missouri became the first state to adopt a plan for the "merit selection" of judges based on periodic public review.
7. National Judicial College, "About the NJC," http://www.judges.org/about (accessed May 2, 2010).
8. See National Judicial College, *National Impact, 2006*, http://www.judges.org/downloads/general_information/national_impact06 (accessed May 22, 2006).
9. "Nonlawyer Judges and the Professionalization of Justice: Should an Endangered Species Be Preserved?" *Journal of Contemporary Criminal Justice*, No. 17 (February 2001), pp. 19–36; see also Doris Marie Provine, *Judging Credentials: Nonlawyer Judges and the Politics of Professionalism* (Chicago: University of Chicago Press, 1986).
10. Town and village justices in New York State serve part-time and may or may not be lawyers; judges of all other courts must be lawyers, whether or not they serve full-time. From New York State Commission on Judicial Conduct, *2001 Annual Report*, http://www.scjc.state.ny.us/annual.html (accessed March 10, 2006).
11. Ibid.
12. Bureau of Justice Statistics, *Report to the Nation on Crime and Justice: The Data* (Washington, DC: U.S. Department of Justice, 1983).
13. For a discussion of the resource limitations that district attorneys face in combating corporate crime, see Michael L. Benson et al., "District Attorneys and Corporate Crime: Surveying the Prosecutorial Gatekeepers," *Criminology*, Vol. 26, No. 3 (August 1988), pp. 505–517.
14. Carol J. DeFrances and Greg W. Steadman, *Prosecutors in State Courts, 1996* (Washington, DC: Bureau of Justice Statistics, 1998).
15. "Duke Case DA's Apology Not Accepted," USA *Today*, May 13, 2007.
16. Duff Wilson, "Prosecutor Apologizes to Former Duke Players," *New York Times*, April 12, 2007.
17. Kenneth Culp Davis, *Discretionary Justice* (Baton Rouge: Louisiana State University Press, 1969), p. 190.
18. Barbara Borland, *The Prosecution of Felony Arrests* (Washington, DC: Bureau of Justice Statistics, 1983).
19. *Brady* v. *Maryland*, 373 U.S. 83 (1963).
20. *U.S.* v. *Bagley*, 473 U.S. 667 (1985).
21. *Banks* v. *Dretke*, 124 S.Ct. 1256, 1280 (2004).
22. *Imbler* v. *Pachtman*, 424 U.S. 409 (1976).
23. *Burns* v. *Reed*, 500 U.S. 478 (1991).
24. Ibid., complaint, p. 29.
25. Cassia Spohn, John Gruhl, and Susan Welch, "The Impact of the Ethnicity and Gender of Defendants on the Decision to Reject or Dismiss Felony Charges," *Criminology*, Vol. 25, No. 1 (1987), pp. 175–191.
26. American Bar Association Center for Professional Responsibility, *Model Rules of Professional Conduct* (Chicago: ABA, 2003), p. 87.
27. The same is true under federal law, and in almost all of the states, of communications between defendants and members of the clergy, psychiatrists and psychologists, medical doctors, and licensed social workers in the course of psychotherapy. See, for example, *Jaffee* v. *Redmond*, 116 S.Ct. 1923 (1996).
28. *Powell* v. *Alabama*, 287 U.S. 45 (1932).
29. *Johnson* v. *Zerbst*, 304 U.S. 458 (1938).
30. *Gideon* v. *Wainwright*, 372 U.S. 335 (1963).
31. *Argersinger* v. *Hamlin*, 407 U.S. 25 (1972).
32. *In re Gault*, 387 U.S. 1 (1967).
33. *Alabama* v. *Shelton*, 535 U.S. 654 (2002).
34. New York State Supreme Court, Appellate Division, Assigned Counsel Plan (18B), http://www.nycourts.gov/courts/ad1/Committees&Programs/18B/index.shtml (accessed June 5, 2010).
35. Donald Farole, Jr., and Lynn Langton, *State Public Defender Programs, 2007* (Washington, DC: BJS, 2010); and Donald Farole, Jr., and Lynn Langton, *County-Based and Local Public Defender Offices, 2007* (Washington, DC: BJS, 2010).
36. Carol J. DeFrances, *State-Funded Indigent Defense Services, 1999* (Washington, DC: National Institute of Justice, 2001), from which the information in this paragraph is derived.
37. National Symposium on Indigent Defense, *Improving Criminal Justice Systems through Expanded Strategies and Innovative Collaborations* (Washington, DC: Office of Justice Programs, 2000).
38. Ibid.
39. "Nationline: McVeigh's Defense Cost Taxpayers $13.8 Million," *USA Today*, July 3, 2001.
40. Caroline Wolf Harlow, *Defense Counsel in Criminal Cases* (Washington, DC: Bureau of Justice Statistics, 2000); and Carol J. DeFrances and Marika F. X. Litras, *Indigent Defense Service in Large Counties, 1999* (Washington, DC: Bureau of Justice Statistics, 2000).
41. *Faretta* v. *California*, 422 U.S. 806 (1975).

42. S. K. Smith and C. J. DeFrances, *Indigent Defense* (Washington, DC: Bureau of Justice Statistics, 1996), pp. 2–3.
43. *Anders* v. *California*, 386 U.S. 738 (1967).
44. *People* v. *Wende*, 25 Cal.3d 436, 600 P.2d 1071 (1979).
45. *Smith* v. *Robbins*, 528 U.S. 259 (2000).
46. *Texas* v. *Cobb*, 532 U.S. 162 (2001).
47. Details for this story come from Chisun Lee, "Punishing Mmes. Stewart: The Parallel Universes of Martha and Lynne," *Village Voice*, February 15, 2005, http://www.refuseandresist.org/article-print.php?aid51757 (accessed January 5, 2006).
48. "Lawyer Convicted of Terrorist Support," *USA Today*, February 11, 2005.
49. Mike McKee, "California State Bar to Allow Lawyers to Break Confidentiality," *The Recorder*, May 17, 2004, http://www.law.com/jsp/article.jsp?id51084316038367 (accessed August 25, 2005).
50. *Nix* v. *Whiteside*, 475 U.S. 157 (1986).
51. Ibid.
52. President's Commission on Law Enforcement and Administration of Justice, *The Challenge of Crime in a Free Society* (Washington, DC: U.S. Government Printing Office, 1967), p. 129.
53. National Advisory Commission on Criminal Justice Standards and Goals, *Courts* (Washington, DC: U.S. Government Printing Office, 1973), Standard 9.3.
54. See, for example, Joan G. Brannon, *The Judicial System in North Carolina* (Raleigh, NC: Administrative Office of the United States Courts, 1984), p. 14.
55. Joseph L. Peterson, "Use of Forensic Evidence by the Police and Courts," *Research in Brief* (Washington, DC: National Institute of Justice, 1987), p. 3.
56. Ibid., p. 6.
57. *California* v. *Green*, 399 U.S. 149 (1970).
58. Patrick L. McCloskey and Ronald L. Schoenberg, *Criminal Law Deskbook* (New York: Matthew Bender, 1988), Section 17, p. 123.
59. Bureau of Justice Statistics, *Report to the Nation on Crime and Justice*, 2nd ed. (Washington, DC: BJS, 1988), p. 82.
60. Anna Johnson, "Jury with Oprah Winfrey Convicts Man of Murder," Associated Press, August 19, 2004.
61. *Demarest* v. *Manspeaker et al.*, 498 U.S. 184, 111 S.Ct. 599, 112 L.Ed.2d 608 (1991).
62. Bureau of Justice Statistics, *Report to the Nation on Crime and Justice.*
63. Johnson, "Jury with Oprah Winfrey Convicts Man of Murder."
64. *Williams* v. *Florida*, 399 U.S. 78, 90 S.Ct. 1893, 26 L.Ed.2d 446 (1970).
65. *Smith* v. *Texas*, 311 U.S. 128 (1940). That right does not apply when the defendants are facing the possibility of a prison sentence less than six months in length or even when the potential aggregate sentence for multiple petty offenses exceeds six months (see *Lewis* v. *U.S.*, 518 U.S. 322 [1996]).
66. *Thiel* v. *Southern Pacific Co.*, 328 U.S. 217 (1945).
67. The author was himself the victim of a felony some years ago. His car was stolen in Columbus, Ohio, and recovered a year later in Cleveland. He was informed that the person who had taken it was in custody, but he never heard what happened to him, nor could he learn where or whether a trial was to be held.
68. Federal Rules of Criminal Procedure, Rule 43.
69. *Crosby* v. *U.S.*, 113 S.Ct. 748, 122 L.Ed.2d 25 (1993).
70. *Zafiro* v. *U.S.*, 113 S.Ct. 933, 122 L.Ed.2d 317 (1993).
71. *Nebraska Press Association* v. *Stuart*, 427 U.S. 539 (1976).
72. However, it is generally accepted that trial judges may issue limited gag orders aimed at trial participants.
73. *Press Enterprise Company* v. *Superior Court of California, Riverside County*, 478 U.S. 1 (1986).
74. *Caribbean International News Corporation* v. *Puerto Rico*, 508 U.S. 147 (1993).
75. *Chandler* v. *Florida*, 499 U.S. 560 (1981).
76. Rule 53 of the Federal Rules of Criminal Procedure reads, "The taking of photographs in the court room during the progress of judicial proceedings or radio broadcasting of judicial proceedings from the court room shall not be permitted by the court."
77. Harry F. Rosenthal, "Courts-TV," Associated Press, September 21, 1994. See also "Judicial Conference Rejects Cameras in Federal Courts," *Criminal Justice Newsletter*, September 15, 1994, p. 6.
78. U.S. Court of Appeals for the Ninth Circuit, http://www.ce9.uscourts.gov/web/OCELibra.nsf/504ca249c786e20f85256284006da7ab/ba060a3e537d2866882569760067ac8e?OpenDocument (accessed September 16, 2005).
79. Marc G. Gertz and Edmond J. True, "Social Scientists in the Courtroom: The Frustrations of Two Expert Witnesses," in Susette M. Talarico, ed., *Courts and Criminal Justice: Emerging Issues* (Beverly Hills, CA: Sage, 1985), pp. 81–91.
80. Samuel R. Gross et al., *Exonerations in the United States, 1989 through 2003*, April 4, 2004, http://www.mindfully.org/Reform/2004/Prison-Exonerations-Gross19apr04.htm (accessed May 24, 2007).
81. *Klopfer* v. *North Carolina*, 386 U.S. 213 (1967).
82. *Barker* v. *Wingo*, 407 U.S. 514 (1972).
83. *Strunk* v. *U.S.*, 412 U.S. 434 (1973).
84. Speedy Trial Act, 18 U.S.C. 3161 (1974); Public Law 93–619.
85. *U.S.* v. *Taylor*, 487 U.S. 326, 108 S.Ct. 2413, 101 L.Ed.2d 297 (1988).
86. *Fex* v. *Michigan*, 113 S.Ct. 1085, 122 L.Ed.2d 406 (1993).
87. *Doggett* v. *U.S.*, 112 S.Ct. 2686 (1992).
88. *Padilla* v. *Hanft*, No. 05-533, *cert. denied.*
89. See, for example, the U.S. Supreme Court's decision in the case of *Murphy* v. *Florida*, 410 U.S. 525 (1973).
90. *Witherspoon* v. *Illinois*, 391 U.S. 510 (1968).
91. *Mu'Min* v. *Virginia*, 500 U.S. 415 (1991).
92. Federal Rules of Criminal Procedure, Rule 24(6).
93. Learn more about shadow juries from Molly McDonough, "Me and My Shadow: Shadow Juries Are Helping Litigators Shape Their Cases during Trial," *National Law Journal* (May 17, 2001).
94. Although the words *argument* and *statement* are sometimes used interchangeably to refer to opening remarks, defense attorneys are enjoined from drawing conclusions or "arguing" to the jury at this stage in the trial. Their task, as described in the section that follows, is simply to explain to the jury how the defense will be conducted.
95. Supreme Court majority opinion in *Powers* v. *Ohio*, 499 U.S. 400 (1991), citing *Strauder* v. *West Virginia*, 100 U.S. 303 (1880).
96. *Swain* v. *Alabama*, 380 U.S. 202 (1965).
97. *Batson* v. *Kentucky*, 476 U.S. 79, 106 S.Ct. 1712 (1986).
98. *Ford* v. *Georgia*, 498 U.S. 411 (1991), footnote 2.
99. *Powers* v. *Ohio*, 499 U.S. 400 (1991).
100. *Georgia* v. *McCollum*, 505 U.S. 42 (1992).
101. *J. E. B.* v. *Alabama*, 114 S.Ct. 1419 (1994).
102. See, for example, *Davis* v. *Minnesota*, 511 U.S. 1115 (1994).
103. *Campbell* v. *Louisiana*, 523 U.S. 392 (1998).
104. *Miller-El* v. *Cockrell*, 537 U.S. 322 (2003).
105. *Miller-El* v. *Dretke*, 545 U.S. 231 (2005).
106. *Snyder* v. *Louisiana*, 552 U.S. ___ (2008).
107. *U.S.* v. *Dinitz*, 424 U.S. 600, 612 (1976).
108. *Michigan* v. *Lucas*, 500 U.S. 145 (1991).
109. *Kotteakos* v. *U.S.*, 328 U.S. 750 (1946); *Brecht* v. *Abrahamson*, 113 S.Ct. 1710, 123 L.Ed.2d 353 (1993); and *Arizona* v. *Fulminante*, 111 S.Ct. 1246 (1991).

110. The Court, citing *Kotteakos* v. *U.S.*, 328 U.S. 750 (1946), in *Brecht* v. *Abrahamson*, 113 S.Ct. 1710, 123 L.Ed.2d 353 (1993).
111. *Sullivan* v. *Louisiana*, 113 S.Ct. 2078, 124 L.Ed.2d 182 (1993).
112. *Griffin* v. *California*, 380 U.S. 609 (1965).
113. *Ohio* v. *Reiner*, 123 S.Ct. 1252, 532 U.S. 17 (2001).
114. Leading questions may, in fact, be permitted for certain purposes, including refreshing a witness's memory, impeaching a hostile witness, introducing undisputed material, and helping a witness with impaired faculties.
115. *In re Oliver*, 333 U.S. 257 (1948).
116. *Coy* v. *Iowa*, 487 U.S. 1012, 108 S.Ct. 2798 (1988).
117. *Maryland* v. *Craig*, 497 U.S. 836, 845–847 (1990).
118. *Idaho* v. *Wright*, 497 U.S. 805 (1990).
119. *White* v. *Illinois*, 112 S.Ct. 736 (1992).
120. *Crawford* v. *Washington*, 541 U.S. 36 (2004).
121. *Davis* v. *Washington*, 547 U.S. 813 (2006). See also *Hammon* v. *Indiana*, 547 U.S. 813 (2006).
122. *Davis* v. *Washington*, syllabus.
123. Federal Rules of Criminal Procedure, Rule 29.1.
124. See *Johnson* v. *Louisiana*, 406 U.S. 356 (1972); and *Apodaca* v. *Oregon*, 406 U.S. 404 (1972).
125. *Allen* v. *U.S.*, 164 U.S. 492 (1896).
126. Judge Harold J. Rothwax, *Guilty: The Collapse of Criminal Justice* (New York: Random House, 1996).
127. Amiram Elwork, Bruce D. Sales, and James Alfini, *Making Jury Instructions Understandable* (Charlottesville, VA: Michie, 1982).
128. "King Jury Lives in Fear from Unpopular Verdict," *Fayetteville (N.C.) Observer-Times*, May 10, 1992.
129. "Los Angeles Trials Spark Debate over Anonymous Juries," *Criminal Justice Newsletter* (February 16, 1993), pp. 3–4.

Appendix Bill of Rights

Bill of Rights The first ten amendments to the U.S. Constitution are known as the *Bill of Rights.* These amendments, ratified in 1791, have special relevance to criminal justice and are reproduced here.

Amendment I Congress shall make no law respecting an establishment of religion, or prohibiting the free exercise thereof; or abridging the freedom of speech, or of the press; or the right of the people peaceably to assemble, and to petition the Government for a redress of grievances.

Amendment II A well regulated Militia, being necessary to the security of a free State, the right of the people to keep and bear Arms, shall not be infringed.

Amendment III No Soldier shall, in time of peace be quartered in any house, without the consent of the Owner, nor in time of war, but in a manner to be prescribed by law.

Amendment IV The right of the people to be secure in their persons, houses, papers, and effects, against unreasonable searches and seizures, shall not be violated, and no Warrants shall issue, but upon probable cause, supported by Oath or affirmation, and particularly describing the place to be searched, and the persons or things to be seized.

Amendment V No person shall be held to answer for a capital, or otherwise infamous crime, unless on a presentment or indictment of a Grand Jury, except in cases arising in the land or naval forces, or in the Militia, when in actual service in time of War or public danger; nor shall any person be subject for the same offence to be twice put in jeopardy of life or limb; nor shall be compelled in any criminal case to be a witness against himself, nor be deprived of life, liberty, or property, without due process of law; nor shall private property be taken for public use, without just compensation.

Amendment VI In all criminal prosecutions, the accused shall enjoy the right to a speedy and public trial, by an impartial jury of the State and district wherein the crime shall have been committed, which district shall have been previously ascertained by law, and to be informed of the nature and cause of the accusation; to be confronted with the witnesses against him; to have compulsory process for obtaining witnesses in his favor, and to have the Assistance of Counsel for his defence.

Amendment VII In Suits at common law, where the value in controversy shall exceed twenty dollars, the right of trial by jury shall be preserved, and no fact tried by a jury, shall be otherwise re-examined in any Court of the United States, than according to the rules of the common law.

Amendment VIII Excessive bail shall not be required, nor excessive fines imposed, nor cruel and unusual punishments inflicted.

Amendment IX The enumeration in the Constitution, of certain rights, shall not be construed to deny or disparage others retained by the people.

Amendment X The powers not delegated to the United States by the Constitution, nor prohibited by it to the States, are reserved to the States respectively, or to the people.

From Appendix A of *Criminal Justice: A Brief Introduction*, Ninth Edition, Frank Schmalleger.

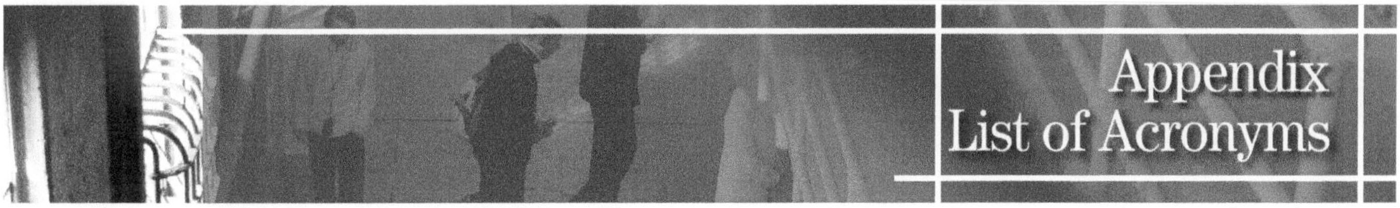

Appendix List of Acronyms

List of Acronyms

ABA	American Bar Association
ACA	American Correctional Association
ACJS	Academy of Criminal Justice Sciences
ACLU	American Civil Liberties Union
ADAM	Arrestee Drug Abuse Monitoring
ADMAX	administrative maximum
AEDPA	Antiterrorism and Effective Death Penalty Act (1996)
AFDA	Association of Federal Defense Attorneys
AFIS	automated fingerprint identification system
AIDS	acquired immunodeficiency syndrome
AJA	American Jail Association
ALI	American Law Institute
AMBER	America's Missing: Broadcast Emergency Response
AOUSC	Administrative Office of the United States Courts
APPA	American Probation and Parole Association
ASC	American Society of Criminology
ASIS	American Society for Industrial Security
ASLET	American Society for Law Enforcement Training
ATF	Bureau of Alcohol, Tobacco, Firearms and Explosives
BJA	Bureau of Justice Assistance
BJS	Bureau of Justice Statistics
BOP	Bureau of Prisons
CALEA	Commission on Accreditation for Law Enforcement Agencies
CAPS	Chicago's Alternative Policing Strategy
CAT	computer-aided transcription
CCA	Corrections Corporation of America
CDA	Communications Decency Act (1996)
CFAA	Computer Fraud and Abuse Act (1986)
CIA	Central Intelligence Agency
CID	Criminal Investigative Division
CJIS	Criminal Justice Information Services (FBI)
CLET	Certified Law Enforcement Trainer
CODIS	Combined DNA Index System (FBI)
COPS	Community Oriented Policing Services
CPOP	Community Police Officer Program (New York City)
CPTED	crime prevention through environmental design
CRIPA	Civil Rights of Institutionalized Persons Act (1980)
CRIPP	Courts Regimented Intensive Probation Program
CSA	Controlled Substances Act (1970)
CSC	Correctional Services Corporation
DEA	Drug Enforcement Administration
DHS	Department of Homeland Security
DNA	deoxyribonucleic acid
DOJ	U.S. Department of Justice
DPIC	Death Penalty Information Center
DUI	driving under the influence (of alcohol or drugs)
DWI	driving while intoxicated
ECPA	Electronic Communications Privacy Act (1986)
FBI	Federal Bureau of Investigation
FCC	federal correctional complex
FCI	federal correctional institution
FLETC	Federal Law Enforcement Training Center
FLIR	forward-looking infrared
FOP	Fraternal Order of Police
FPC	federal prison camp
FTCA	Federal Tort Claims Act (1946)
GBMI	guilty but mentally ill
HIV	human immunodeficiency virus
IACP	International Association of Chiefs of Police
ICC	International Criminal Court
ICE	Immigration and Customs Enforcement
IDRA	Insanity Defense Reform Act (1984)
ILC	International Law Commission (United Nations)
ILEA	International Law Enforcement Academy (FBI)
INTERPOL	International Criminal Police Organization
IPS	intensive probation supervision
JJDP	Juvenile Justice and Delinquency Prevention Act (1974)
JTTF	Joint Terrorism Task Force
LAPD	Los Angeles Police Department
LEAA	Law Enforcement Assistance Administration
LEMAS	Law Enforcement Management and Administrative Statistics
MCFP	medical center for federal prisoners
MDC	metropolitan detention center
MPC	Model Penal Code
NAACP	National Association for the Advancement of Colored People
NACDL	National Association of Criminal Defense Lawyers
NCAVC	National Center for the Analysis of Violent Crime
NCCD	National Council on Crime and Delinquency
NCIC	National Crime Information Center (FBI)
NCISP	National Criminal Intelligence Sharing Plan
NCJRS	National Criminal Justice Reference Service
NCPC	National Crime Prevention Council
NCSC	National Center for State Courts
NCVS	National Crime Victimization Survey
NCWP	National Center for Women and Policing

From Appendix B of *Criminal Justice: A Brief Introduction*, Ninth Edition, Frank Schmalleger.

NDAA	National District Attorneys Association
NDIS	National DNA Index System (FBI)
NIBRS	National Incident-Based Reporting System (FBI)
NIJ	National Institute of Justice
NJC	National Judicial College
NLADA	National Legal Aid and Defender Association
NOBLE	National Organization of Black Law Enforcement Executives
NVAWS	National Violence against Women Survey
NVC	National Victims Center
NVCAP	National Victims' Constitutional Amendment Project
NW3C	National White Collar Crime Center
NYGC	National Youth Gang Center
NYPD	New York Police Department
OJJDP	Office of Juvenile Justice and Delinquency Prevention
OJP	Office of Justice Programs
ONDCP	Office of National Drug Control Policy
PCR	police-community relations
PDS	podular/direct supervision
PERF	Police Executive Research Forum
PINS	persons in need of supervision
PLRA	Prison Litigation Reform Act (1996)
POST	Peace Officer Standards and Training
PROTECT Act	Prosecutorial Remedies and Other Tools to End the Exploitation of Children Today Act (2003)
RICO	Racketeer Influenced and Corrupt Organizations (statute)
RISE	Reintegrative Shaming Experiments (Australian Institute of Criminology)
RJC	Real Justice Conferencing (Pennsylvania)
ROR	release on recognizance
RTTF	Regional Terrorism Task Force
SAMHSA	Substance Abuse and Mental Health Services Administration
SBI	State Bureau of Investigation
SCU	Street Crimes Unit (New York City)
SEARCH	National Consortium for Justice Information and Statistics
SIIA	Software and Information Industry Association
STG	security threat group
SVORI	Serious Violent Offender Reentry Initiative
SWAT	special weapons and tactics
TFJJR	Task Force on Juvenile Justice Reform
TIPS	Terrorist Information and Prevention System
TWGEDE	Technical Working Group for the Examination of Digital Evidence
UCR	Uniform Crime Reports (FBI)
USA PATRIOT Act	Uniting and Strengthening America by Providing Appropriate Tools Required to Intercept and Obstruct Terrorism Act (2001)
U.S.C.	United States Code
USP	United States penitentiary
USSC	United States Sentencing Commission
VAWA	Violence against Women Act (1994)
VCAN	Victims' Constitutional Amendment Network
VICAP	Violent Criminal Apprehension Program (FBI)
VOCA	Victims of Crime Act (1984)
VWPA	Victim and Witness Protection Act (1982)

Index

Page references followed by "f" indicate illustrated figures or photographs; followed by "t" indicates a table.

Q

R